Contemporary Human Resource Management

Text and Cases

Edited by

Tom Redman and Adrian Wilkinson

FINANCIAL TIMES
Prentice Hall

An imprint of **Pearson Education**

Harlow, England · London · New York · Reading, Massachusetts · San Francisco
Toronto · Don Mills, Ontario · Sydney · Tokyo · Singapore · Hong Kong · Seoul
Taipei · Cape Town · Madrid · Mexico City · Amsterdam · Munich · Paris · Milan

Pearson Education Limited
Edinburgh Gate
Harlow
Essex CM20 2JE
England

and Associated Companies throughout the world

Visit us on the World Wide Web at:
http://www.pearsoneduc.com

———————————

First published 2001

ISBN 0 201 59613 X

British Library Cataloguing-in-Publication Data
A catalogue record for this book is available from the British Library

Library of Congress Cataloging-in-Publication Data
Contemporary human resource management : text and classes / edited by Tom Redman
and Adrian Wilkinson.
    p.cm
  Includes bibliographical references and index.
  ISBN 0-201-59613-X
    1. Personnel management. 2. Personnel management--Study and teaching. 3. Personnel
management--Case studies. I. Redman, Tom, 1952- II. Wilkinson, Adrian, 1963-

HF5549.15 .C66 2001
658.3--dc21   00-067772

10 9 8 7 6 5 4 3
06 05 04 03 02

Typeset by 30 in Sabon 10/12.5pt.
Printed in Great Britain by Henry Ling Ltd., at the Dorset Press, Dorchester, Dorset

To Edwina, Rachel and Rosie
Jackie, Erin and Aidan

Contents

14 New management techniques in small and medium-sized enterprises 432

Tony Dundon, Irena Grugulis and Adrian Wilkinson

List of case studies

List of boxes

List of contributors

Editors

Tom Redman is Senior Lecturer in Human Resource Management at University of Durham Business School. He is the editor of *Personnel Review* and his books include *Managing Managers* (1993) and *Managing through TQM: Theory and Practice* (1998). He is a Fellow of the Chartered Institute of Personnel and Development.

Adrian Wilkinson is Professor of Human Resource Management at Loughborough University Business School. His books include *Making Quality Critical* (1995), *Core Personnel and Development* (1996), *Managing Quality and Human Resource* (1997) and *Managing through TQM: Theory and Practice* (1998). He is a Fellow of the Chartered Institute of Personnel and Development.

Other contributors

Peter Ackers, Reader in Employment Relations, Loughborough University Business School.

Stephen Ackroyd, Professor of Organisational Behaviour, University of Lancaster.

Nick Bacon, Senior Lecturer in Human Resource Management, Nottingham Business School.

Paul Biddis, was a researcher at Manchester School of Management, University of Manchester Institute of Science and Technology.

Cathy Cassell, Senior Lecturer in Organisational Behaviour, Sheffield University Management School.

Laurie Cohen, Lecturer in Organisational Behaviour, Loughborough University Business School.

Graeme Currie, Lecturer in Human Resource Management, University of Nottingham, Business School.

Nicola Denham Lincoln, Consultant, Sheppard Moscow Ltd.

Tony Dundon, Lecturer in Human Resource Management, Department of Management, National University of Ireland, Galway.

John Gennard, Professor of Human Resource Management, Department of

Human Resource Management, University of Strathclyde.

Stephen Gibb, Lecturer in Human Resource Management, Department of Human Resource Management, University of Strathclyde.

Irena Grugulis, Lecturer in Employment Studies, Manchester School of Management, University of Manchester Institute of Science and Technology.

Fanny Ka-Ching Yan, was a researcher and university associate at Hong Kong Polytechnic.

Phil Lewis, Principal Lecturer in Human Resource Management, Cheltenham and Gloucester College of Higher Education.

David Megginson, Professor of Human Resource Development, Sheffield Hallam University.

Kevin Morrell, Research student, Loughborough University Business School.

Sue Newell, Professor of Innovation and Organisational Analysis, Nottingham Trent University.

Stephen Procter, Alcan Professor of Management, School of Management, University of Newcastle.

Doug Renwick, Lecturer in Human Resource Management, University of Sheffield Management School.

Ian Roberts, Lecturer in Sociology, University of Durham.

Viv Shackleton, Senior Lecturer in Work Psychology, Aston University Business School.

Ed Snape, Professor, Department of Management, Hong Kong Polytechnic

David Thompson, Associate Professor, Department of Management, Hong Kong Polytechnic.

Cheryl Travers, Lecturer in Organisational Behaviour, Loughborough University Business School.

Acknowledgements

As with any book, the list of acknowledgements is extensive. But these are the most important. Thanks to our editors Richard Beaumont, Anna Herbert, Scott Dustan and Catherine Newman for their patience and encouragement. Rebecca White was responsible for putting the manuscript together and co-ordinating communication of contributors and we are grateful to her for the work she has done. As usual, family and friends make the major contribution and Tom and Adrian are grateful to their families for support while the book was being written.

The publisher's are grateful to the following for permision to reproduce copyright material:

Extract from a case study adapted from *Critical Perspectives on Accounting*, Vol 2, No 4, pp.385–413, by permission of the publisher Academic Press, London (Robert and Wilkinson, 1991). Extract from *IEBM Handbook of Human Resource Management* published by Thomson Business Press, March 1998. Extract from 'Employment relations in SMEs', *Employee Relations*, Vol 21, No 3, p.207 (Wilkinson, 1999); extract from 'Empowerment: Theory and Practice' *Personnel Review*, Vol 27, No 1 (Wilkinson, 1998) both published by MCB University Press. The extract from *Human Resources Management Journal*, Vol 10, is reproduced with the kind permission of Personnel Publications Ltd (Redman et al., 2000). Figure 4.1, 'Types of Employer Control', from *Small Business and Society*, published by ITBP (Goss, 1991).

Part 1

Fundamentals of human resource management

Chapter 1

In search of human resource management

Tom Redman and Adrian Wilkinson

Introduction

This book is about human resource management (HRM) and is concerned with the way in which organisations manage their people. In this introductory chapter we discuss our own approach to the study of HRM and the rationale underpinning the ordering and presentation of material in the book. Our aim is to chart some of the broad terrain of a rapidly developing field of study in order to prepare the reader for the more finely grained treatment of specific HRM topics to be found in the individual chapters. In particular we examine the recent rise of HRM, the effects of the changing context of work on HRM, what it involves, the strategic nature of HRM practice, its impact on organisational performance and the changing role of the HRM function. The chapter concludes with a consideration of our views on the audience at which the book is targeted and some thoughts on how it may best be used.

The development of HRM

The last 20 years or so have seen the rise of what has been called the Human Resource Management new orthodoxy (Guest, 1991). In the mid-1980s in the UK, and earlier in the USA, the term 'HRM' became fashionable and gradually started to replace others such as 'personnel management' (PM) and 'industrial relations' (IR). The practitioners of people management are no longer personnel officers and trainers but are HR mangers and human resource developers (and, importantly, line managers – see below). The 1990s saw the launch of new journals and the flourishing of university courses in HRM. The then Institute of Personnel

Management, the main professional body for personnel practitioners, relaunched its journal *People Management*, but subtitled it 'The magazine for Human Resource professionals'. The millennium has now witnessed the professional body receiving a Royal Charter to become the Chartered Institute of Personnel and Development. The HRM bandwagon is well and truly rolling.

Early contributions on the implications of the rise of HRM were concerned to define it and to compare it with the more traditional British approach to personnel management (e.g. Fowler, 1987; Guest, 1987; Miller, 1987). HRM was in turn both heralded as 'a new era of humane people-oriented employment management' (Keenoy, 1990: 375) and derided as a 'blunt instrument to bully workers' (Monks, 1998). There has been considerable ambiguity in the use of the term, with various commentators using 'HRM' as simply a more modern label for traditional personnel management, as a 're-conceptualising and re-organising of personnel roles', or as a new and distinctive approach, attempting to develop and utilise the potential of human resources to the full in pursuit of the organisation's strategic objectives. It is the promise that is held by this latter view that has most excited practitioners and attracted the attention of management academics.

There has been a long debate over whether HRM is no more than a relabelling of personnel management, the 'old wine in new bottles' critique, or something more fundamental (Legge, 1989; Gennard and Kelly, 1997). Traditionally, personnel management is often characterised as having little focus on broader business links and being overly concentrated on the activities of personnel professionals and a range of operational techniques. Thus, personnel management was seen as a low-level record keeping and 'people maintenance' function. The HRM stereotype, in contrast, is characterised as being much more concerned with business strategy, and linkages with HR strategy, taking the view that HR is a, if not *the* most important organisational resource. Thus there has been much talk of an HRM 'revolution'. However, although evolution is less exciting than revolution, Torrington and Hall's (1998) view that HRM is merely the next stage in the development of personnel management is persuasive. Torrington (1993), a staunch defender of 'good' personnel management, has also suggested that much of what is now labelled 'HRM' may be seen much more simply as long-standing good people management practice, whilst what was less effective has been relegated to remain, rather unfairly it seems, with the 'personnel management' brand.

To a large extent the rise of HRM reflects the changing concerns of management more generally. In the 1970s, following the Donovan (1968) report, senior management tended to concentrate on formalisation of relations with unions, and national issues such as incomes policies put personnel into a position of entrenchment. In the 1980s, with a changing balance of power in the workplace following from reforming Conservative governments with an ideological distaste for trade unions, management concerns turned to efficiency and productivity, which many felt were best dealt with at line management level.

Even the more 'upbeat' HRM work such as that of Storey (1992) indicates that changes in the arena of HRM did not come from initiatives designed directly to do this. Change was driven by broader organisational initiatives and personnel specialists have not been seen as the key drivers of change. Similarly, Wood's (1999) work on high commitment practices suggests that innovations in HRM tend to accompany changes in production concepts and that innovations on humanistic grounds are unrealistic. Thus in part HRM can be seen as a consequence of managing in 'uncharted territory', with new rules governing the employment relationship (Beardwell, 1998). Furthermore, the changing nature of the context of work clearly has had a significant effect on the development of HRM. The next section briefly sketches some of the main developments in this area.

The changing context of work

Things are happening in employment that are neither a cause nor an effect of HRM but which could have some impact on it. These include the intensification of work, the choices of work location provided by technology and the divisive nature of a society in which many are idle and impoverished while many others are seriously over-worked.

(Guest, 1998b: 51)

In the main, developments in HRM, as we argue above, have been driven by large-scale organisational changes as employers adjust to a much more competitive global economic environment. To meet some of the challenges posed by intense competition organisations have been downsized, delayered and decentralised. Organisations are now less hierarchical in nature, have adopted more flexible forms, and have been subjected to continuing waves of organisational change programmes such as total quality management, business process re-engineering, performance management, lean production, learning organisation and a seemingly relentless series of culture change initiatives. The type of staff employed and the way they are organised has also undergone considerable change in the new organisational form. Employees are often now more likely to be female, work part-time, away from the workplace (e.g. teleworking and the so-called 'hot desking'), and be subcontractors, consultants, temps and interims, etc. The boundaries between work and home are now much more blurred (Cully et al., 1999).

Such pressures have not been restricted to the private sector and we have seen the rise of the so-called 'new public management', with its emphasis on economy and efficiency (Rocha, 1994). The public sector has undergone many similar changes, with new organisational forms emerging in the wake of 'marketisation', compulsory competitive tendering and most recently 'Best Value'. For example, the civil service has experienced downsizing, delayering, market testing, and citizen's charters as well as the creation of next step agencies. The NHS has seen the advent of trusts, the creation of an internal market via the separation of purchasers from providers of healthcare, and the introduction of performance league tables and patient's charters. Healthcare provision has changed from being a citizen's right to a customer service. The traditional NHS culture has moved from one based on professionalism to one imbued with the rhetoric of the market, with hospitals and clinics 'franchised' by the Department of Health to sell health-care services (see Dent, 1995).

Some of these changes are seen as facilitating more discretion for staff while at the same time retaining control of performance. Here the relevance of HRM comes to the fore; new forms of work and organisation demand new HRM strategies and practices. The new work context also brings new HRM challenges; not the least of these derives from the impact of such changes on the stresses and strains involved in working under such conditions. Here the growing literature on stress at work paints a rather disconcerting picture of organisational life in the new workplace. Typical of this work is the report by the ESRC Centre of Business Research at Cambridge University for the Rowntree Foundation, which found a rise in stress and anxiety, with a significant increase in job insecurity, especially for professional workers. Over 60 per cent of employees felt the pace of work has increased in the last five years. Job insecurity was linked to poor health. Workplaces were seen as lacking in trust, with only 26 per cent of workers saying they believed management and employees were on the same side, and, when asked if management could be expected to look after their best interests, 40 per cent said only a little or not at all.

Whilst HRM practices (e.g. employee assistance programmes, workplace counselling schemes, etc), are used in some organisations to provide a more supportive environment and there is evidence that these appear to have some potential to ease but not cure the impact of workplace stress, the general picture is rather bleak. Indeed, HRM practices may have added considerably to the stresses of modern work-life, with the increased use of such practices as performance management systems, contingent pay, and flexibilisation. For example, in relation to flexibility, one of the key dimensions of Guest's (1987) conceptualisation of HRM, a recent Citizens' Advice Bureau report finds numerous accounts of worker exploitation, with unilateral changes in contracts and forced reductions in hours and pay. The 1990s also witnessed the growth of 'zero hours contracts', particularly in retailing, whereby employers do not guarantee that any work will be offered but, should they require labour, the employee is expected to be available. Thus the number of employment complaints more than doubled between 1983–4 and 1992–3 (NACAB, 1997). The impact of organisational change on employees has been so considerable that commentators now argue there is a need to radically reconstruct the nature of the 'psychological contract' between employer and employee. The search is now on for new deals for new times (Herriot and Pemberton, 1995).

Thus HRM is clearly not a simple panacea, and may even contribute directly to some of the above problems, but it is relatively safe to speculate that it looks likely to play an increasingly important role in the workplaces of the future. However, in this discussion we must also be careful not to overstate the case for HRM. There is a danger that accounts of change in organisations are always portrayed as major paradigm-shifting events when the reality is rather different. The rhetoric of organisational change often relies too heavily on hype from unrepresentative examples (Thompson and O'Connel Davidson, 1995). Managers, it seems, often perceive themselves to be in the midst of massive organisational change. Eccles and Nohira's (1992) historical account of post-Second World War management traces how it has been the norm rather than the exception for practitioners and writers to view their organisational environment as turbulent and characterised by transformative change. Thus issues of continuity are in many respects overlooked in the brave new world of HRM (Noon and Blyton, 1998). As we note above, poor people management practice is not just a product of old management systems, such as that attributed to personnel management by HRM advocates. It may be that many commentators have been rather blinded by the glossy nature of the new HRM vision, but we would suggest that talk of the end of traditional career jobs and the demise of trade unions and the like is rather too premature. History generally has a fairly cruel way of treating such rash predictions.

In particular, the rose-tinted managerial accounts of HRM in practice have recently been tempered somewhat by a literature examining HRM 'from below'. Surprisingly, the voice of the worker in evaluating HRM's achievements has been rather silent. Where workers' views are mentioned, for example in Storey's work, the impression is one of scepticism that they would gain benefits. Workers' response to HRM initiatives have generally been limited in early studies to anecdotal evidence and some limited case study work (Mabey et al., 1998; Collinson et al., 1997; Scott, 1994; Wickens, 1987), with broader survey-based work taking some time to emerge (Guest and Conway, 1999).

Thus there is a danger, apparent in much of the prescriptive literature in HRM (Armstrong, 1987; Hendry et al., 1988; Williams et al., 1989), of focusing almost exclusively on the initiatives of management and thereby seeing employees as essentially passive beings, whose attitudes and behaviour are there to be moulded by HR strategy in the pursuit of competitive advantage. The feasibility of a 'top-down' approach to the management of organisational culture has already been challenged by a number of authors. Employees too may respond to changes in the competitive environment, and this suggests that the effective implementation of HRM may be more than simply a matter of management will. However, there is some evidence that the employee experience of HRM is not always negative and exploitative. According to Guest (1999: 23):

> it appears that workers like their experience of HRM. The more HR practices they are currently experiencing in their employment, the more satisfied they seem to be and the better their psychological contract.

Indeed, recent work by Guest and Conway (1999) found that management practices are more important than union membership in determining whether staff feel fairly treated. Interestingly, they argue that union leaders should overcome their natural scepticism and pressure management to adopt progressive HRM practices. Clearly more research is needed in this area.

What then is HRM?

In order to address this question we examine some of the key works on HRM theory. Storey's (1992) study of HRM identifies 27 points of difference between HRM and PM (see Table 1.1) and divides this into four broad categories: beliefs and assumptions, strategic qualities, the critical role of managers and key levers. Sisson (1990) sees HRM in terms of four aspects of employment practice: an integration of HR policies with business planning; a shift in responsibility for HR issues from personnel specialists to line managers; a shift from the collectivism of management – trade union relations to the individualism of management–employee relations and, finally, an emphasis on commitment.

Guest (1987) theorises HRM as having four key dimensions: commitment, flexibility, quality and integration. Commitment is sought in the sense that employees are expected to identify closely with the interests of the organisation, and to go beyond mere compliance to management by internalising the goals of the organisation and behaving accordingly. Flexibility involves the ability and willingness of staff to adapt to change, within the context of flexible organisation structures. The quality of staff and management is also seen to be important in achieving high levels of performance. Finally, integration refers to the matching of human resource strategies to the needs of the business strategy, and requires that the various elements of human resource management are themselves consistent and mutually supportive. Integration also implies that line managers should be fully involved in the management of their staff. Such a transformation would involve the pursuit of each of the four goals, with the adoption of a more long-term, strategic perspective, and the treatment of staff as a resource to be utilised to the full, rather than simply as a cost to be minimised (Guest, 1987).

Legge (1989) finds more common ground between the ideal types of personnel management and HRM than other commentators but also identifies three significant differences in the HRM literature. HRM concentrates on managers rather than on what managers do with shopfloor staff; it emphasises the key role of line managers rather than personnel managers and the responsibility of top management for managing culture. All these approaches in adopting stereotypical conceptualisations, however, thus tend to exaggerate the difference between HRM and PM in practice. Indeed, it could be said that HRM is depicted as aspirational whereas PM is what actually happens in practice in many organisations, so like is not being really compared with like.

A strong central theme of HRM in these accounts is that of linking the people management practice to business strategy and we now examine this in the next section of this chapter.

Table 1. The 27-item checklist

Dimension	Personnel and IR	HRM
Belief and assumptions		
1. Contract	Careful delineation of written contracts	Aim to go 'beyond contract'
2. Rules	Importance of devising clear rules/mutuality	'Can do' outlook: impatience with 'rule'
3. Guide to management action	Procedures/consistency control	'Business need'/flexibility/commitment
4. Behaviour referent	Norms/custom and practice	Values/mission
5. Managerial task vis-à-vis labour	Monitoring	Nurturing
6. Nature of relations	Pluralist	Unitarist
7. Conflict	Institutionalised	De-emphasised
Strategic aspects		
8. Key relations	Labour–management	Business–customer
9. Initiatives	Piecemeal	Integrated
10. Corporate plan	Marginal to	Central to
11. Speed of decisions	Slow	Fast
Line management		
12. Management role	Transactional	Transformational leadership
13. Key managers	Personnel/IR specialists	General/business/line managers
14. Communication	Indirect	Direct
15. Standardisation	High (e.g. 'parity' an issue)	Low (e.g. 'parity' not seen as relevant)
16. Prized management skills	Negotiation	Facilitation
Key levers		
17. Selection	Separate, marginal task	Integrated, key task
18. Pay	Job evaluation: multiple, fixed grades	Performance-related: few if any grades
19. Conditions	Separately negotiated	Harmonisation
20. Labour-management	Collective bargaining contracts	Towards individual contracts
21. Thrust of relations with stewards	Regularised through facilities and training	Marginalised (with the exception of some bargaining for change models)
22. Job categories and grades	Many	Few
23. Communication	Restricted flow/indirect	Increased flow/direct
24. Job design	Division of labour	Teamwork
25. Conflict handling	Reach temporary truces	Manage climate and culture
26. Training and development	Controlled access to courses	Learning companies
27. Foci of attention for interventions	Personnel procedures	Wide-ranging cultural, structural and personnel strategies

Source: Storey 1992

Strategy and HRM

More recently the study of HRM has adopted a cross-functional approach and expanded its breadth of analysis beyond the staple concerns of selection, training, reward, etc. In particular, one stream of research, strategic human resource management (SHRM) has emerged as being highly influential in this respect. In essence, SHRM theory posits that an organisation's human resource assets are potentially the sole source of sustainable competitive advantage. Much of the work in this area draws from the resource-based theory (RBT) of the firm (Barney, 1991, 1995). Here RBT suggests that competitive advantage depends ultimately on an organisation having superior, valuable, rare, non-substitutable resources at its disposal and that such resources are not easily imitated by others. The nonimitable nature of resources is a key aspect, otherwise competitors would be able to replicate them and the advantage would rapidly disappear. The subtleties of the human resource value creation process, however, are extremely difficult for competitors to imitate. The ambiguities and complexities associated with even the 'strongest' of organisational cultures, and how HRM practices are related to culture, are considerable and cannot be easily teased out by would-be imitators. Equally, any competitive advantage located in a codified and explicit set of HRM practices is also much less likely to be nonimitable than one based on the complex interaction of HRM policies and an organisation's 'social architecture' (Mueller, 1996). By social architecture Mueller is referring to skill formation activities, co-operative behaviour and the tacit knowledge organisations possess. Thus the value creation process arising from HRM competencies does appear to meet the criteria set out by RBT and consequently a growing body of empirical and theoretical work has emerged on SHRM (see Boxall, 1996; Boxall and Purcell, 2000 for reviews of this literature). However, our knowledge base of SHRM is still rather limited, not least by its somewhat fragmented nature and there is, as yet, little consensus in the empirical findings. In the discussion below we review some of the more influential debates and findings of SHRM research.

A classic early work by Kochan *et al.* examined the nature of 'strategic choice' in HRM and provides an example whereby changes in the competitive environment lead to business decisions which *'reverberate through the organisation and its industrial system'* (1983: 13). Whilst such a response is clearly connected with business changes, Miller (1987) is undoubtedly right to question whether, in such circumstances, 'strategy' is an appropriate term. The strategic management of human resources must be more than a mere knock-on effect: most business decisions will have some effects on the management of people, but such effects are not necessarily strategic decisions. For Miller operational linkages between the business strategy and the policy towards employees are the key, or in his words, the 'fit of HRM with the strategic thrust of the organisation'. This is clearly an important point but Miller's definition of SHRM:

> those decisions and actions which concern the management of employees at all levels in the business and which are directed towards creating and sustaining competitive advantage
>
> (Miller, 1987: 352)

while important in demanding that human resources be a corporate level concern, has a significant weakness because of its concentration on linkages to the neglect of content.

If we return to the work of Porter (1985), from which Miller borrows, we find that competitive advantage can be achieved *either* through cost leadership or differentiation. Thus Miller's definition of SHRM would cover firms adopting either of these two approaches, as long as there was a 'fit' of HRM with the business policy followed. Yet these two approaches are likely to embody very different strategies for the management of human resources: one being based on seeing employees as a commodity, with the emphasis on cost control, while the other may emphasise differentiation in terms of quality, with employees as a resource to be developed.

A more useful approach might be to characterise SHRM as entailing strategic integration and a 'positive' approach to the management of employees, with an emphasis on staff as a resource rather than a cost. Thus strategic integration is a necessary but not sufficient component of HRM. The emphasis on staff as a resource would be likely to embody policies designed to achieve the goals Guest (see above) has identified as being important, namely flexibility, quality and commitment, although Guest himself appears to regard integration as an outcome rather than a process. However, we would argue that an emphasis on staff as a resource without strategic integration is not SHRM either. For instance, the many customer care programmes owe much to the fact that other companies are doing them, rather than relating to the business strategy of the organisation concerned. Thus in circumstances whereby HRM programmes become ends in themselves it is hard to credit them with being strategic. Equally, it clearly fails one of the tests of resource-based theory, namely that of being nonimitable. In contrast, an 'accounting' view of labour management may well be strategic in that it may be related to competitive advantage through cost leadership and, as such, strategically integrated, but this is not what SHRM is supposed to be about (see Storey, 1992; Guest, 1987). Hence the latter approach sees the importance of staff in a 'negative' sense of not hindering existing business strategy as opposed to actively contributing towards it. Of course, many companies would fit neither category in that the management of staff may not be considered a strategic issue at all, and neither integrated into the strategic planning process nor considered as a resource (see Table 1.2). Thus there is generally much academic criticism of failure of SHRM in practice but we must ask whether our expectations are rather too high of what SHRM can deliver.

Table 1.2

	Strategic	Non-strategic
People as resource	HRM	PM
People as cost	Not HRM?	Traditional management

One recurrent theme in the SHRM literature is that organisations need to 'match' their human resource strategies to their business strategies, so that the former contribute towards the successful implementation of the latter (Miller, 1987; Lengnick-Hall and Lengnick-Hall, 1988; Schuler and Jackson, 1989; Boxall, 1992). A growing number of sectoral and company-level studies have shown how organisations facing change in their competitive environment have responded with new business strategies, which in turn have required a transformation in the organisation's approach to the management of staff (see, for example, Hendry and Pettigrew, 1992; Hendry *et al.*, 1988; McKinlay and Starkey, 1992; Snape *et al.*, 1993; Boxhall and Steenveld, 1999).

This approach, the so-called *'matching model'* by Boxall (1992), argues for a fit, or match, between business strategy and a human resource strategy, which fosters the required employee attitudes and behaviour. In this sense, human resource strategy flows from the initial choice of business strategy (Purcell, 1989). Furthermore, to the extent that changes in the corporate environment evoke a particular business strategy response, human resource strategies can also be seen as being strongly influenced by environmental change (Hendry *et al.*, 1988). As Sparrow and Hilltrop (1994: 628) argue, 'HRM strategies are all about making business strategies work.' A closely related body of work has recently called for a *configurational* approach to SHRM. Here it is argued that it is the pattern of HRM practices that supports the achievement of organisational goals and that, in line with the contingency approach, fit with strategy is vital to explaining the HR-performance nexus. The configurational approach takes the best fit view a step further in that it argues there are a number of specific ideal types that provide both horizontal fit, between HR practices, and vertical fit, between HR practices and business strategy (Ferris *et al.*, 1999). The configuration of practices which provides the tightest fits is then seen as being ideal for the particular strategy. Although this work is still in its infancy there has been some recent theorising on the nature of the 'ideal types' of configurations for customer-, operations-, product-, etc. led organisations (Sheppeck and Militello, 2000).

However, there is an issue as to how far human resource strategies can simply be 'matched' with the requirements of a changing business strategy. As Boxall (1992: 68) notes, much of the 'matching' literature has implicitly assumed that employee attitudes and behaviour can be moulded by management strategy in the pursuit of strategic fit. Human resource outcomes cannot be taken for granted, though, and whatever the merits of the view that personnel managers must increasingly see themselves as 'business managers' (Tyson, 1987; 1995), it is important to recognise that personnel management and industrial relations are about more than simply selecting the appropriate fit with a given business strategy. Thus the best-fit approach can be criticised for failing to acknowledge the importance of social norms and legal rules in the search for alignment. Indeed, the notion of fit is rather static and an inappropriate metaphor in a fast-changing and chaotic corporate world.

A commonly expressed view is that since the purpose of businesses is to produce profit, not good HRM, and to the extent that such practices are essentially
facilitative and not a stand-alone activity but must flow from corporate strategy, it
is inevitable that they are indeed second- or third-order (see the work of Purcell
here). However, the discussion on much of this debate has been rather unhelpful
because of the assumption that it is only first-order strategies that are really
'strategic', and other concerns relate essentially to operational considerations and
are hence non-strategic. This is potentially misleading as it assumes strategies are
of one kind (partly stemming from the view that strategy relates to product market
issues) and other matters are either strategic or non-strategic, whereas in fact it
may be better to think of degrees of strategy. It is clear, for instance, that HR is
downstream from the overall corporate mission, be it a return on assets or profits
through business decisions. The common argument posed above is undoubtedly
correct: businesses are not formed to create good HR practice. Nevertheless, this is
rather unhelpful in examining the significance of the relationship with business
issues. What is being called for is that such matters should be considered within
the overall business strategy of the organisation rather than separate from it. In
other words, HR should not merely be affected in a knock-on manner, but be
located much further up in the business strategy process.

What appears to be demanded is integration at two levels: firstly at the level of
implementation, where it is argued that much of the success of policy implementation depends on the effective management of human resources. Secondly, it is
argued that this is not in itself adequate, that human resources should actually be
considered further up the planning process, so that rather than just flowing from
the business strategy, it should be part of it, in that the human resource dimension
may constrain the type of business strategy adopted or provide opportunities. It is
no good making a business decision (strategic) to relocate if the organisation finds
it cannot recruit the workforce in the area. The existing skills of the workforce may
well constrain business growth, etc. Either or both of these approaches would be
consistent with SHRM. In other words, the first approach suggests that the human
resource strategy should be consistent with business strategy and implementation
should take account of human resource factors. The second approach demands
rather more: that human resource factors be considered not just in the implementation of policy but actually influence which business strategy is adopted.

Performance and HRM: it's the people, stupid!

For years, HR professionals have yearned for evidence to show that people were
really the most important asset a company had, and that good HR practice delivered in terms of organisational performance. By the mid-1990s their prayers
appeared to have been answered in that a growing number of studies appeared to
demonstrate just that. For example, in research undertaken on behalf of the

Institute of Personnel and Development in the UK the Sheffield effectiveness programme (based on 100 SMEs in manufacturing) concluded that people management is not only critical to business performance but is also much more important than an emphasis on quality, technology, competitive strategy or R&D in terms of influence on the bottom line. Effective people management was found to account for 19 per cent of the variation in profitability and 18 per cent of the variation in productivity, whilst in comparison R & D accounts for 8 per cent and the others barely 1 per cent (quality, technology and competitive strategy). Thus according to Patterson *et al.* (1998) this finding in one sense validates the oft-quoted claims of CEOs that people are the most important asset but is also paradoxical in that HRM is the most neglected aspect of business:

> Overall, the results of this study clearly indicate the importance of people management practices in influencing company performance. The results are unique, since no similar study has been conducted, comparing the influence of different types of managerial practices upon performance. If managers wish to influence the performance of their companies, the results show that the most important area to emphasise is the management of people. This is ironic, given that our research has also demonstrated that emphasis on HRM practices is one of the most neglected areas of managerial practice within organisations.
>
> (Patterson *et al.*, 1998: 21)

There are various terms used in these studies, for example, 'high performance management', 'high commitment management', 'best practice HRM', 'high involvement management', but a common message: the adoption of HRM practices pays in terms of where it matters most, the bottom line. It is worth noting that it is primarily in the USA that the case for the new approach has been demonstrated. The main studies have been American and, according to Huselid (1995), demonstrate that progressive HRM practices produce a significant magnitude of return. A 1 per cent standard deviation increase in such practices is associated with a 7.05 per cent decrease in labour turnover and, on a per employee basis, $27,044 more in sales and $18,641 and $3,814 more in market value and profits respectively. Other American studies (Arthur, 1994; MacDuffie, 1995) appear to generally support this and an exhaustive review by Ichniowski *et al.* (1996) concluded that a 'collage of evidence suggests that innovative workplace practices can increase performance, primarily through the use of systems of related practices that enhance worker participation, make work design less rigid and decentralise managerial tasks'. They also note that individual work practices have no effect on economic performance but 'the adoption of a *coherent and integrated system* of innovative practices, including extensive recruiting and careful selection, flexible job definitions and problem solving teams, gainsharing-type compensation plans, employment security and extensive labour–management communication, substantially improve productivity and quality outcomes'. Similarly Pfeffer (1994: 27) emphasises that 'these are interrelated practices that seem to characterise companies that are effective in achieving competitive success through how they manage people'. Wood (1995: 52) argues that his list of 'high commitment practices' should be used together since 'it is through the combined effects of such practices that management can most hope to elicit high levels of commitment'. The general argument is that piecemeal take-up of HR practices means that many managements miss out on the benefits to be gained from a more integrated approach (Marchington and Wilkinson, 2000: 94–7). Thus such collections of reinforcing HR practices have begun to be referred to as a 'bundle', and the task of HR managers is to identify and implement such HR systems.

However, this appears to be rather more easily prescribed than achieved. Many authors produce lists of HR practices which should be included in these bundles, but there is little consistency yet and we still await a definitive prescription of the best 'bundle'. As Wood and de Menezes (1998) point out, reviewing these studies indicates that there is a somewhat 'pick and mix' approach to the HRM bundle. Storey (1992: 35) identified aspects such as integrated selection systems, performance-related pay, harmonisation, individual contracts, teamworking and learning companies. Pfeffer (1994: 30–59) provides a list of 16, which includes employment security, selectivity in recruitment, incentive pay, employee ownership, participation and empowerment, teamworking, training and skill development, wage compression and promotion from within. These are held together under an overarching philosophy with a long-term commitment and a willingness to engage in consistent measurement of whether or not high standards are being achieved. Delaney et al. (1989) identified ten practices, Hueslid (1995) 13, Wood (1999) 17 whilst Delery and Doty (1996) appear quite miserly in comparison in only identifying seven strategic practices. All this must seem at the very least confusing to the practitioner but, more than this, there appear to be some quite contradictory notions in the various lists. For example, on the one hand formal grievance systems appear in some bundles as an indicator of best practice, but are associated in others with trade unionism and thus seen as part of the bureaucratic 'personnel management' approach.

Aside from the inconsistencies in the HRM bundle, the best practice and universalistic approach has received considerable criticism. Purcell, for example, is critical of the claim for a universal application:

> The claim that the bundle of best practice HRM is universally applicable leads us into a utopian cul-de-sac and ignores the powerful and highly significant changes in work, employment and society visible inside organisations and in the wider community. The search for bundles of high commitment work practices is important, but so too is the search for understanding of the circumstances of where and when it is applied, why some organisations do and others do not adopt HRM, and how some firms seem to have more appropriate HR systems for their current and future needs than others. It is only one of many ways in which employees are managed, all of which must come within the bounds of HRM.
>
> (Purcell, 1999: 36)

Whitfield and Poole (1997: 757) point out there are unresolved issues of causality, problems with the narrow base of the work undertaken (largely manufacturing), concerns that much of the data is self-reported by management, as well as doubts about measures of performance which are used. Even if the data does indicate a causal link, we lack understanding of the processes involved and the mechanisms by which practices translate into desired outcomes. Equally problematic is the implicit assumption that a particular bundle of practices is feasible for all organisations. Some organisational structures and cultures will present major difficulties in implementing certain HRM practices, for example, high involvement practices in highly bureaucratic and formal organisations will be particularly problematic. The notion of a reinforcing bundle of practices cannot be fully convincing either, given the variation in the bundles noted above. It cannot yet be dismissed that the different HR practices have a differential impact on firm performance. The best practice approach thus appears somewhat of a black box and many questions remain as yet unanswered. Why is there a linkage? What is it about having these practices which delivers performance? What is the process by which these outcomes have occurred? It is unlikely that, say, the very act of introducing practices X, Y and Z will deliver benefits directly. Much will depend on the context of their introduction, the way they are implemented, the support provided, etc. – but what are the critical factors?

The changing role of HRM

Despite the growing recognition of the importance of effective people management for organisational success, there are still a number of concerns about the future for HRM. Superficially, the HRM function seems to be in good health. The CIPD now claims over 100,000 members (CIPD National Conference, Harrogate, 2000) and WERS data found that the proportion of workplaces with personnel specialists, defined as managers whose job titles contain 'personnel', 'HR' or 'industrial', 'employee' or 'staff relations' and who spent at least a quarter of their time on such matters, rose by a third during the 1990s. In 1998 20 per cent of workplaces employed a personnel specialist, up from 14 per cent in 1984 (Cully *et al.*, 1999). However, deeper worries about the effectiveness of the HR function linger on.

According to Peter Drucker, there has been a tendency in the past for the HR department to be seen as something of a 'trash can' function, a repository for all those tasks which do not fit neatly anywhere else:

> Personnel administration . . . is largely a collection of incidental techniques without much internal cohesion. As personnel administration conceives the job of managing worker and work, it is partly a file-clerk's job, partly a housekeeping job, partly a social worker's job and partly fire-fighting to head off union trouble or to settle it . . . the things the personnel administrator is typically responsible for . . . are necessary chores. I doubt though that they should be put together in one department for they are a hodge-podge . . . They are neither one function by kinship of skills required to carry out the

activities, nor are they one function by being linked together in the work process, by forming a distinct stage in the work of the managers or in the process of the business.

(Drucker, 1961: 269–70; quoted in Legge, 1995: 6)

Table 1.3 lists some of the key functions that HR departments now provide. In part Drucker's critique that the HR function lacks coherence has been moderated by some recent organisational changes. In particular, the practice of outsourcing during the 1980s and 1990s saw many of the more peripheral HR responsibilities, such as catering arrangements and security, subcontracted to specialist firms. Equally, the practice of decentralising HR responsibility from corporate central departments to business unit level departments and further still to line management has seen much 'streamlining' of HR responsibilities. However, perhaps more worrying for the HR function is that these trends have also seen some traditional core personnel areas, such as recruitment, training, and employee welfare management, also outsourced to HR consultants. In some accounts these trends have been seen as part of a 'crisis' as HR struggled for legitimacy and status in cost-conscious times and the function has been described as being 'under siege from external consultants' (Clark and Clark, 1991). In Torrington's view this 'crisis' is nothing new and its recent intensity may owe rather more to critical academics than actual reality in the profession:

> There is a crisis of confidence among personnel specialists, as there always has been. Their results are almost impossible to measure and their successes and failures are largely the successes and failures of other people. Furthermore, they operate in a field – how people behave – in which everyone else is an expert with a personal point of view from which they will not depart. The difficulty for personnel people is that they know how intractable some of the people problems really are. They are not helped by the persistent disparagement of HRM academics, who go to considerable lengths to explain how badly their job is done.
>
> (Torrington, 1998: 36)

Others have interpreted the increasing use of consultants as reflecting a sign that HR is now seen as being much more important and thus merits additional investment. Management consultants are argued to be an important conduit along which new and more sophisticated HR practices flow between organisations. Nevertheless, some recent trends suggest that a 'crisis' interpretation may be more in tune with the facts. In particular, the reduction of the HR domains appears to have been taken one step further and there is now a considerable debate on the benefits of outsourcing the entire HR function. In part such changes have been driven by further cost pressures in a period of corporate downsizing, but more worrying for the HR function is that outsourcing may also have been fuelled by senior management concerns about the quality and responsiveness of in-house HR functions (Greer *et al.*, 1999). For example, drawing from survey evidence from UK private sector organisations, Guest reports that chief executives and personnel managers both give low ratings to the performance of the HR department and the effectiveness of HR practices in the company (Guest and Baron, 2000).

Table 1.3 Functions performed by the HR department

- Job analysis
- Human resource planning
- Recruitment and selection
- Training and development
- Pay and conditions of employment
- Grievance and disciplinary procedures
- Employee relations and communications
- Administration of contracts of employment
- Employee welfare and counselling
- Equal opportunities policy and monitoring
- Health and safety
- Outplacement

Thus the rising recognition that HR issues are vitally important in organisations has, paradoxically, not been all good news for the HR department, given their 'Cinderella' image. It seems many senior managers may be of the view that people management is far too important to be left to the HR department. In a *Fortune* article one commentator urged CEOs to 'Blow the sucker (HR) up' (Stewart, 1996). Whilst others have not been as forthright as this, the HR function appears to be at a dangerous crossroads, with some suggesting ascendancy to a full business partner whilst others predict a painful demise. On the one hand, the ascendancy school sees the rise of HR following hard on the success of SHRM and the creation of competitive advantage for organisations. In contrast, the formula for demise often involves the failure of HR to understand the broader business agenda. The literature typically sees a need for the 'reinvention' of HR along such lines, and that HR must simply evolve or die. However, Ulrich (1997) has also warned that the literature is replete with premature death notices of the HR function.

What then is the 'formula' for HR success? Firstly, in addressing this question there is a real danger of slipping into unrealistic, wishful thinking – of which there is already an ample supply in the prescriptive HR literature. Secondly, there is rather more consistency in the literature on what the future for HR should *not* be based on than that on what it should be. Thus Rucci (1997) has suggested that the worst-case scenario for HR survival is a department that does not promote change, does not identify leaders, does not understand the business, does not know customers, does not drive costs and does not emphasise values. According to Pfeffer (1998: 195) 'if human resources is to have a future inside organisations, it is not by playing police person and enforcer of rules and policies, nor is it likely to be ensured by playing handmaiden to finance'.

In contrast, there are a wide variety of suggestions for what the HR department should do in the future. According to Brockbank (1997) the future agenda is that a successful HR department needs to be involved in framing not only HR strategy but also business strategy, promoting growth rather than downsizing and building more credible relationships with key shareholders and board members. Beer and Eisenstat (1996) emphasise the need for a comprehensive HR vision, stressing that in the future HR managers will require co-ordination skills across functions, business units and borders following the increased globalisation of business, and general management, communication leadership, creativity and entrepreneurship competencies. Research by Eichinger and Ulrich (1995) on the top priorities that HR professionals believe need to addressed in the future emphasises organisational redesign, attracting new leaders, customer focus, cost containment, rejecting fads, addressing diversity and becoming a more effective business partner with their line management customers. Ulrich (1998) also reports the results of survey research on the key competencies managers believe will be necessary for future success in HR roles – see Table 1.4. The ability to manage culture and change coupled with personal credibility is seen as critical.

Table 1.4 Key competencies of HR professionals

Relative importance to effectiveness	%
Understanding of business	14
Knowledge of HR practices	17
Ability to manage culture	19
Ability to manage change	22
Personal credibility	27

Source: Ulrich (1998: 20–1)

Thus a key theme in much of the work is that HR needs to earn its place at the top, i.e. senior management, table. One danger in these accounts is that the emphasis is very much on the strategic and business aspects of the HR role. In particular the 'bread and butter' issues of effectively managing the recruitment, selection, appraisal, development, reward and involvement of staff have been rather pushed to the periphery. What is interesting about Table 1.4 is the relatively low rating of knowledge of HR practices. There is thus a real concern that HR managers could be neglecting 'the basics' in their search for legitimacy and status with senior managers. In short, HR could be accused of ignoring employees. Indeed, HR 'futurologists', it seems, need to be reminded of Giles and Williams' (1991) rejoinder to accept that the HR role is to serve their customers and not their egos. We feel that there is a danger that the senior management and shareholder customers will be getting rather better service than the 'employee customer' in the HR department of the future.

One of our aims in the presentation of material in this book has been to balance the discussion in terms of both employee expectations and management expectations of the HR function. So, for example, in accounts of topics such as downsizing, empowerment, performance management, reward, flexibility, etc. the approach has been not only to critically examine HR's strategic role in the process but to also review the impact of these practices on employees. The last section of this chapter now discusses in more detail the layout of the book and some suggestions on its use.

The book

This book has been written primarily as a text for students of business and management who are studying HRM. It aims to be critical but pragmatic: we are wary of quick fixes, slogans, prescriptive checklists, and bullet points of 'best practice'. The authors are all prominent researchers and draw from a considerable depth of research in their field. Each chapter provides a critical review of the topic, bringing together theoretical and empirical material. The emphasis is on analysis and insight and areas of growing significance are also included in each chapter. At the same time we wish to look at the implications of HRM research and theory development for practice and to do so in a readable, accessible manner. The book does not assume prior knowledge on the part of the reader but seeks to locate issues in a wider theoretical framework. It is suitable for MBA students, and undergraduates who these days may be doing business studies alongside degrees in engineering, humanities, social science, etc. As such, this is appropriate for modular degree courses.

The book is divided into two parts; the first one: *Fundamentals of HRM* examines the core elements of HR practice (see Table 1.3 above). In this section there are chapters on selection and assessment, performance appraisal, employee development, reward, grievance and discipline, employment relations. The second half of the book: *Contemporary Themes and Issues* addresses some key areas of rising importance in HRM practice. Here there are chapters on flexibility, careers, downsizing, empowerment, ethics, diversity management and HRM practice in the increasingly important small and medium-sized business sector.

Each chapter is accompanied by a combination of case studies, role-plays and exercises for students. The intention is that students should be actively involved in the study of HRM. We believe that in this respect the book is unique in the UK, where the trend has been for the publication of separate text and case books. Our aim in combining these elements in a single volume is to permit a smoother integration of the topic material and supporting cases and exercises. In all chapters the authors have provided both text and cases, although in some we also include additional material from other authors. The cases and exercises are of different lengths, levels and type in order to serve different teaching and learning purposes, e.g. a long case study for students to read and prepare prior to seminars/tutorials as well as shorter cases and exercises which can be prepared in the session itself. The aim is to provide a good range of up-to-date, relevant material based upon actual practice in HRM.

References to Chapter 1

Armstrong, M. (1987) 'Human resource management: a case of the emperor's new clothes?', *Personnel Management*, August.

Arthur, J. (1994) 'Effects of human resource system on manufacturing performance and turnover', *Academy of Management Journal*, 37: 670–87.

Barney, J. (1991) 'Firm resources and sustained competitive advantage', *Journal of Management*, 17 (1): 99–120.

Barney, J.B. (1995) 'Looking inside for competitive advantage', *Academy of Management Executive*, 9 (4): 49–61.

Beardwell, I. (1998) (ed) *Contemporary Industrial Relations*, Oxford: Open University Press.

Beer, M. and Eisenstat, R. (1996) 'Developing an organisation capable of implementing strategy and learning', *Human Relations*, 49 (5).

Boxall, P. (1992) 'Strategic human resource management: beginnings of a new theoretical sophistication?', *Human Resource Management Journal*, 2 (3), Spring: 60–79.

Boxall, P. (1996) 'The strategic HRM debate and the resource-based view of the firm', *Human Resource Management Journal*, 6 (3): 59–75.

Boxall, P. and Purcell, J. (2000) 'Strategic human resource management: where have we come from and where should we be going?', *International Journal of Management Review*, 2 (2): 183–20.

Boxall, P. and Steenveld, M. (1999) 'Human resource strategy and competitive advantage: a longitudinal study of engineering consultancies', *Journal of Management Studies*, 36 (4): 443–63.

Brockbank, W. (1997) 'HR's future on the way to a presence', *Human Resource Management*, 36 (1): 65–69.

Clark, I. and Clark, T. (1990) 'Personnel management and the use of executive recruitment consultancies', *Human Resource Management Journal*, 1 (1): 46–62.

Collinson, M., Edwards, P., Rees, C., and Innes, L. (1997) *Involving Employees in Quality Management*, DTI report.

Cully, M., Woodland, S., O'Reilly, A. and Dix, G. (1999) *Britain at Work*, London: Routledge.

Delaney, J.T., Lewis, D. and Ichniowski, C. (1989) *Human Resource Policies and Practices in American Firms*, Washington DC: US Government Printing Office.

Delery, J. and Doty, D. (1996) 'Modes of theorizing in strategic human resource management: tests of universalistic, contingency and configurational performance predictions', *Academy of Management Journal*, 39 (4): 802–35.

Dent, M. (1995) 'The new National Health Service: a case of postmodernism?', *Organization Studies*, 16 (5): 875–99.

Donovan (1968) *The Royal Commission on Trade Unions and Employers' Associations, 1965–1968: Report*, Cmnd. 3623.

Drucker, P. (1961) *The Practice of Management*, London: Mercury.

Eccles, R. and Nohira, N. (1992) *Beyond the Hype: Rediscovering the Essence of Management*, Boston, Mass: Harvard Business School Press.

Eichinger, B. and Ulrich, D. (1995) 'Are you future agile?', *Human Resource Planning*: 30–41.

Ferris, G., Hochwarter, W.A., Buckley, M.K., Harnell-Cook, G. and Frink, D.D. (1999) 'Human resource management: some new directions', *Journal of Management*, 25 (3): 385–416.

Fowler, A. (1987) 'When the Chief Executive discovers HRM', *Personnel Management*, January: 3.

Gennard, J. and Kelly, J. (1997) 'The unimportance of labels: the diffusion of the personnel/HRM function', *Industrial Relations Journal*, 28 (I): 27–42.

Giles, E. and Williams, R. (1991) 'Can the personnel department survive quality management?', *Personnel Management*, April: 28–33.

Greer, C.R., Youngblood, S.A. and Gray, D.A. (1999) 'Human Resource Management outsourcing: the make or buy decision', *Academy of Management Executive*, 13 (3): 85–96.

Guest, D. (1987) 'Human resource management and industrial relations', *Journal of Management Studies*, 24 (5), September: 503–21.

Guest, D. (1991) 'Personnel management: the end of orthodoxy?', *British Journal of Industrial Relations*, 29 (2).

Guest, D. (1998) 'Beyond HRM: commitment and the contract culture' in M. Marchington and P. Sparrow (eds) (1998) *Human Resource Management: the New Agenda*, London: FT/ Pitman.

Guest, D. (1999) 'Human resource management: the workers' verdict', *Human Resource Management Journal*, 9 (3): 5–25.

Guest, D. and Baron, A. (2000) 'Piece by piece', *People Management*, 6 (15): 26–31.

Guest, D. and Conway, N. (1999) 'Peering into the black hole: the downside of the new employment relations in the UK', *British Journal of Industrial Relations*, 37 (3): 367–90.

Hendry, C. and Pettigrew, A. (1992) 'Patterns of strategic change in the development of human resource management', *British Journal of Management*, 3: 137–56.

Hendry, C., Pettigrew, A. and Sparrow, P. (1988) 'Changing patterns of human resource management', *Personnel Management*, November: 37–41.

Heriot, P. and Pemberton, C. (1995) *New Deals: the Revolution in Management Careers*, London: Wiley.

Huselid, M. (1995) 'The impact of human resource management practices on turnover, productivity and corporate financial performance', *Academy of Management Journal*, 38 (3).

Ichniowski, C., Kochan, T., Levine, D., Olsen, C. and Strauss, G. (1996) 'What works at work: overview and assessment', *Industrial Relations*, 35 (3): 299–333.

Keenoy, T. (1990) 'HRM: rhetoric, reality and contradiction', *International Journal of Human Resource Management*, 1 (3): 363–84.

Kochan, T., McKersie, R. and Cappelli, P. (1983) 'Strategic choice and industrial relations theory', *Industrial Relations*, 23 (I): 16–39.

Legge, K. (1989) 'Human resource management: a critical analysis' in J. Storey (ed) *New Perspective on Human Resource Management*, London: Routledge.

Legge, K. (1995) *Human Resource Management: Rhetorics and Realities*, Basingstoke: Macmillan.

Lengnick-Hall, C.A. and Lengnick-Hall, M.L. (1988) 'Strategic human resources management: a review of the literature and a proposed typology', *Academy of Management Review*, 13 (3): 454–70.

Mabey, C., Clark, T. and Skinner, D. (eds) (1998) *The Experience of Human Resource Management*, Milton Keynes: Open University Press.

MacDuffie, J. (1995) 'Human resource bundles and manufacturing performance: organisational logic and flexible production systems in the world auto industry', *Industrial and Labour Relations Review*, 48 (2): 197–221.

Marchington, M. and Wilkinson, A. (2000) *Core Personnel and Development*, London: CIPD.

McKinlay, A. and Starkey, K. (1992) 'Competitive strategies and organizational change', *Human Resource Strategies*, G. Salaman (ed) London: Sage.

Miller, P. (1987) 'Strategic industrial relations and human resource management – distinction, definition and recognition', *Journal of Management Studies*, 24 (4) July: 347–61.

Mueller, F. (1996) 'Human resources as strategic assets: an evolutionary resource based theory', *Journal of Management Studies*, 33 (6): 757–85.

National Association of Citizens' Advice Bureaux (1997) *Flexibility Abused: A CAB Report on Empowerment Conditions in the Labour Market*, London: NACAB.

Noon, M. and Blyton, P. (1998) *The Realities of Work*, London: Macmillan.

Patterson, M., West, M., Hawthorn, R. and Nickell, S. (1998) 'Impact of people management practices on business performance issues', *People Management*, 22, London: IPD.

Pfeffer, J. (1994) *Competitive Advantage through People*, Boston, Mass: Harvard Business School Press.

Pfeffer, P. (1997) 'Does human resource have a future?' in Ulrich, D., *Tomorrow's Human Resource Management*, New York: Wiley.

Pfeffer, P. (1998) *The Human Equation*, Boston, Mass: Harvard Business School Press.

Porter, M. (1985) *Corporate Advantage*, New York: Free Press.

Purcell, J. (1989) 'The impact of corporate strategy on human resource management', *New Perspectives on Human Resource Management*, ed. J. Storey, London: Routledge.

Purcell, J. (1999) 'Best practice and best fit: chimera or cul-de-sac?', *Human Resource Management Journal*, 9 (3): 26–41.

Rocha, J.A.O. (1998) 'The new public management and its consequences in the public personnel system', *The Review of Public Personnel Administration*, Spring, 18 (2): 82–87.

Rucci, A.J. (1997) 'Should HR survive? A profession at the crossroads', *Human Resource Management*, 36 (1): 169–75.

Schuler, R.S. and Jackson, S.E. (1989) 'Determinants of human resource management priorities and implications for industrial relations', *Journal of Management*, 15 (1): 89–99.

Scott, A. (1994) *Willing Slaves?*, Cambridge: CUP.

Sheppeck, M.A. and Militello, J. (2000) 'Strategic human resource configurations and organizational performance', *Human Resource Management*, 39 (1): 5–16.

Sisson, K. (1990) 'Introducing the *Human Resource Management Journal*', *Human Resource Management Journal*, 1 (1): 1–11.

Snape, E., Wilkinson, A. and Redman, T. (1993) 'Human resource management in building societies: making the transformation?', *Human Resource Management Journal*, 3 (3).

Sparrow, P. and Hilltrop, J. (1994) *European Human Resource Management in Transition*, London: Prentice-Hall.

Stewart, T. (1996) 'Taking on the last bureaucracy', *Fortune Magazine*: 105–108.

Storey, J. (1992) *Developments in the Management of Human Resources*, Oxford: Blackwell.

Thompson, P. and O'Conner Davidson, J. (1995) 'The continuity of discountinuity: managerial rhetoric in turbulent times', *Personnel Review*, 24 (4): 17–33.

Torrington, D. (1993) 'How dangerous is human resource management?', *Employee Relations*, 15 (5): 40–53.

Torrington, D. (1998) 'Crisis and opportunity in HRM: the challenge for the personnel function', in Sparrow, P. and Marchington, M. (eds) *Human Resource Management: The New Agenda*, London: Prentice Hall.

Torrington, D. and Hall, L. (1998) *Personnel Management* (3rd edn), London: Prentice-Hall.

Tyson, S. (1987) 'The management of the personnel function', *Journal of Management Studies*, 24 (5), September: 523–32.

Tyson, S. (1995) *Human Resource Strategy Towards a General Theory of Human Resource Management*, London: Pitman.

Ulrich, D. (1997) *Tomorrow's Human Resource Management*, New York: Wiley.

Ulrich, D. (1998) *Human Resource Champions*, Boston, Mass: Harvard Business School Press.

Whitfield, K. and Poole, M. (1997) 'Organizing employment for high performance', *Organization Studies*, 18 (5): 745–64.

Wickens, P. (1987) *The Road to Nissan*, London: Macmillan.

Williams, A., Dobson, P. and Walters, A. (1989) *Changing Cultures*, London: IPD.

Wood, S. (1995) 'The four pillars of human resource management: are they connected?', *Human Resource Management Journal*, 5 (5): 49–59.

Wood, S. (1999) 'Getting the measure of the transformed high performance organisation', *British Journal of Industrial Relations*, 37 (3): 391–417.

Wood, S. and de Menezes, L. (1998) 'High commitment management in the UK', *Human Relations*, 51: 485–515.

Chapter 2

Selection and assessment as an interactive decision–action process

Sue Newell and Viv Shackleton

Introduction: selection from a decision-making perspective

A given topic can always be viewed from a number of different perspectives. Traditionally, selection and assessment has been viewed from a psychometric perspective. It is treated as representing a measurement problem. There are clearly individual differences (both physical and psychological), which mean that certain people will be more suited to some jobs than others. From a psychometric perspective then, selection and assessment is concerned with finding methods to measure these individual differences more accurately so that individuals and jobs can be appropriately matched.

In this chapter, while not ignoring this psychometric tradition, we will adopt a rather different perspective, which can help us to explore some issues in selection and assessment that may be underemphasised by the traditional perspective. We will view selection and assessment from a decision-making perspective (Brunsson, 1982), where a decision is a conscious choice between at least two alternative actions. In this chapter we will consider decisions that are made in respect of both selection and development, both of which involve making decisions based on the assessment of individuals. Thus, in terms of selection, a representative (or group of representatives) of the recruiting organisation chooses between a number of candidates in order to select the individual who best fits the requirements of a particular job for which there is a vacancy. These decisions are made on the basis of some kind of assessment of the suitability of a group of potential individuals who might fill the vacancy.

While selection involves decisions about who will best fit a particular job vacancy, the same or similar processes of assessment are also increasingly used within organisations to make developmental decisions related to the promotion potential of internal employees. Thus, it is recognised that it is necessary to pre-pare current employees for taking on more senior roles within the organisation, so that leadership crises are averted. However, it is also recognised that not all exist-ing employees will be suitable for these more senior roles. Assessment methods are therefore used to identify the developmental potential of existing employees. The result is that choices are made about who will be groomed and developed and for which senior jobs.

The emphasis in the selection literature has typically been on the decision made by the recruiting organisation. However, it is also the case that candidates are making decisions – to apply (or not) for a particular job vacancy, to turn up (or not) to an interview, or to take (or decline) an offered job. In terms of assessment for developmental purposes there has always been more recognition that the can-didate is making decisions as well as the assessors. Indeed, with the increasing emphasis on self-direction, assessment exercises are used as much to provide the individual with evidence to make career path choices as they are for the organisa-tion to make promotion decisions. In this chapter we will consider the selection and assessment decision-making process from the perspective of both the organisa-tion and the candidates.

The decision-making perspective has been dominated by normative research, which prescribes how decisions should be made (Brunsson, 1982). This assumes that the desire is to make decisions as 'rational' as possible. The prescription for making decisions rational is to follow a sequence of specified steps: understand the situation and identify the problem(s); generate potential solutions to the problem(s); systematically evaluate each solution; select the best solution; monitor and evaluate the results; identify the problem(s) etc. This rational decision-making model has also implicitly underpinned selection and assessment research. Thus, in selection or development decisions, the objective has been to make this decision as objective and rational as possible in order to select the 'right' or 'best' person for the job. It is possible therefore to look at the steps prescribed in the rational deci-sion-making process and apply them to the literature on selection and assessment.

Selection and assessment as a rational decision-making process?

Each of the steps in the rational decision-making model can be applied to the steps in selection and assessment:

1. Understand the situation and identify the problem(s): organisational review and job analysis

The first step typically identified in the selection process is to undertake a review of the situation to determine that a recruitment need actually exists. Even if an individual has left a job, this should not automatically mean that a job vacancy is presumed. It is necessary to establish that there are not alternative and more effective ways of filling the gap left by the departing employee. For example, it may provide the opportunity for reassigning these tasks to other employees. Alternatively, the tasks may be automated so that human resources are no longer required. Prior to developmental assessment, the rational model would see the need for succession planning to identify the predicted gaps at senior levels for which people need to be groomed.

Once the situation has been reviewed to ensure that a job vacancy or succession gap does actually exist, the next step is to conduct a thorough analysis of the particular job. Job analysis is used to gather information about a job in order to determine the key tasks and role requirements and so specify the kind of person most likely to be successful in that job. A problem with traditional job analysis is that it collects information about the job as it currently exists on the assumption that it will be similar in the future (Schneider and Konz, 1989). Unfortunately, given the dynamic environment in which organisations operate, this is increasingly an unwarranted assumption. As a result, there is a need to develop new methods of job analysis which can identify the key tasks and the associated knowledge, skills and abilities (KSAs) that are required for jobs that are changing (Landy *et al.*, 1995). In this light, Landis *et al.* (1998) describe the process of conducting a future-oriented job analysis. This begins with a traditional job analysis, collecting relevant information about the target jobs as they currently exist and then using panel discussion groups to develop a comprehensive list of tasks and KSAs. Then subject-matter expert groups are involved to identify how these tasks and KSAs are likely to change in the future.

The traditional person specification has given way to a focus on competencies (Boam and Sparrow, 1992). Competencies are behavioural indicators that have been identified as relevant to a particular context. There are a number of different approaches to identifying competencies, but they have a common focus on specifying 'outputs'. These are 'couched in terms of what an individual achieves and produces from a situation by managing it effectively' (Sparrow and Bognanno, 1993: 51). The advantage of using a competency framework is that the focus is on actual behaviour – what a person can do or needs to be able to do – and there is no need to make inferences about personal qualities that might underpin this. Theoretically, this should allow for the fact that different individuals can achieve the same output, but using a rather different approach because of different knowledge, skills and abilities. Unfortunately, while this is true in theory, in practice competency approaches are often used in ways which specify process criteria as well as output or task criteria. In other words, the person is assessed not simply in terms of whether they successfully completed the task but also in terms of dimensions that are 'normally' expected to underpin successful task completion. This means there is a presumption of 'the right way' to complete a task, and the individual will be assessed against this 'right way', as well as against the task output itself.

Nevertheless, whether a job analysis (traditional or future-oriented) or competency analysis is undertaken, the goal is to describe the particular job, identify the task requirements and specify the kind of person most likely to fulfill these requirements.

2. Gather information and materials to help solve the problem: identify appropriate assessment methods

Once the job analysis has been completed, the next step is to identify methods that will allow individuals to be assessed and compared on the various KSAs or competencies identified as crucial for job success. Much effort has been devoted to this step from the psychometric perspective. The reason for this is that traditional assessment methods – unstructured interviews and references – have, until recently, been shown to be very poor at measuring these important individual differences. The development of newer methods of assessment is considered in more detail below.

3. Generate potential solutions to the problem: recruitment

Once this initial phase has been completed and there is a clear idea about the kind of person wanted and the methods to be used to assess individuals, the next step is to attract a pool of applicants from which the 'right' person can be chosen. Where assessment is used for developmental purposes, recruitment will be internal and typically based on information gathered during appraisals as to which individuals are 'ready' and have the potential to be developed. Where an organisation is selecting for a particular job vacancy recruitment can be internal or external. External recruitment is expensive. In the UK, over £1 billion was spent in 1997 on recruitment advertising (Merrick, 1997). Matthews and Redman (1998) found that, despite such a large amount being spent on recruitment advertising, recruiters were not making the most effective use of it, because generally the ads were not well tailored to managerial requirements. In particular, they argue that recruitment advertisements need to be more specifically targeted to the group they are trying to attract. They advocate that this targeting should be done on the basis of market research to identify what the potential applicant is looking for in a recruitment advertisement. With regard to the content of advertisements they suggest that many do not contain enough information to attract the initial interest, especially of the casual job seeker. For example, they found that one in five advertisements gave no details of salary level and job location, which have been shown to be key to gaining attention. Once attracted, potential applicants then seek further information from the advertisement to decide whether to apply. However, 59 per cent of the advertisements gave no information on minimum qualifications, which is useful to help applicants self-screen. At the same time, 71 per cent did give information on personal attributes required, despite this being condemned by prescriptive models of 'good' adverts (Redmond, 1989).

Increasingly, companies have started to use information and communication technologies (ICTs) for recruitment purposes. For example, the internet is now a common medium for advertising job vacancy information, having the advantage of reaching a global audience, at least of potential recruits with access to this technology. Similarly, applicants are using the internet to submit their CVs, thus potentially speeding up the process of applying. A key advantage of such electronic applications is that CVs can be coded (e.g. in terms of the applicants' competencies) and stored electronically so that they can be easily searched, both for current job vacancies and for jobs in the future. This search can be done on a global basis provided that a company has a shared electronic database for storing and retrieving applicant information. The use of ICTs for both advertising and applying is likely to increase as accessibility and familiarity with this medium grow (Batram, 2000).

4. Systematically evaluate each solution: assessment methods applied to candidates

Once a pool of recruits has been attracted, the assessment methods are applied in order to evaluate each individual against the KSAs or competencies identified as important for job success. For selection, presuming that there are more applicants than vacancies, a first step will be to pre-select those applicants who look potentially suitable. This is done typically on the basis of the application form and/or CV that has been sent in. Despite the widespread use of such pre-screening methods, research evidence suggests that they are not designed or used systematically (Keenan, 1995). A growing trend is to use telephone interviews as a more interactive and potentially valid method of pre-selecting. Evidence about the effectiveness of this method is not yet very clear. From this initial screening, a smaller number of applicants will be assessed more fully, using whatever is considered to be the appropriate assessment method(s). The different methods of assessment are considered more fully later in the chapter.

5. Select 'best' solution: selection or development decision

This step in the decision-making cycle is seen to be the logical outcome of the previous steps. Once each candidate has been measured using the particular assessment methods the data can be evaluated in a logical manner in order to select the 'best' candidate. Each candidate can be rated against the person specification or competency profile. The candidate who has all the specified essential characteristics and the most desirable characteristics should be selected for the job. Where assessment is used for developmental purposes the decision is more about which candidates are suitable for which senior positions within the organisation. Nevertheless, there is the same assumption that this can be done rationally and logically on the basis of the data accumulated from the assessment exercises.

6. Monitor and evaluate results: validation

Ratings of employee potential estimated during the selection or developmental assessment process can be compared with subsequent performance on the job. This provides the measure of validity. High correlations between the selection or development ratings (referred to as the predictor) and performance ratings (referred to as the criterion) would indicate that the decisions made during the assessment process were valid (and hence rational). Low correlations would indicate that decisions were not valid. Evidence of the criterion-related validity of traditional methods used to make selection decisions, i.e. the unstructured interview and references, suggests that neither of these methods results in valid predictions.

One particular problem with such validity studies is that the criteria against which the selection or development decisions are compared (i.e. measures of job performance) may themselves be inaccurate (Campbell, 1990). The most typical criterion used is supervisory ratings, but research has demonstrated that these may vary widely in terms of accuracy. For example, Sundvik and Lindeman (1998) found that accuracy was dependent on the opportunity the supervisor had to observe the subordinate, especially in terms of the length of the supervisor–subordinate relationship. They also found that female supervisors are more accurate at rating than are males.

From the rational decision-making perspective, however, the key issue is to identify where selection or development decisions have been made that have not been good (i.e. where validity is poor) and to take this as the starting point for repeating the decision-making cycle in order to improve validity.

7. Identify problem

And so the circle repeats itself!

The selection and assessment decision-making process in practice

While the rational decision-making model can be applied to the selection and assessment process, and indeed underpins much of the literature on improving the validity of such decisions, research evidence suggests that, in practice, the decision process is often far removed from this ideal. This is true for decisions of all kinds, not just selection and development decisions. Thus, research has demonstrated that such rational decision-making does not equate with reality. Rather, empirical research gives mostly examples of irrational decisions when compared to the normative standard (Cyert and March, 1963; March and Olsen, 1976; Nisbett and Ross, 1980). This is the case even where the decision is taken by a group rather than an individual. Indeed, Janis (1972) demonstrated how groups making extremely important strategic decisions failed to adopt the rational, normative approach. Janis used the term 'groupthink' to refer to the fact that, within the decision-making groups he observed, disturbing information was suppressed, immense and unjustified risks taken, and individuals censored their own concerns. The result was an illusion of unanimity for the decision taken, despite individual group members not really agreeing.

Given that research evidence does not support a rational decision-making process in practice, other models have been developed which attempt to mirror reality rather than idealism. Simon (1960) introduced the concept of bounded rationality, which acknowledged the fact that decision-makers, in practice, were under pressure to make decisions so that they did not have time to search exhaustively for all possible solutions. He coined the term 'satisficing' to describe how the search for solutions was not exhaustive, but continued only until a satisfactory solution had been found. Another model of decision-making that has attracted attention recently has been the intuitive decision-making model (e.g. Agor, 1989; Behling and Eckel, 1991). This assumes that managers make decisions by relying on past experiences and their general sense of the situation. Intuition is essentially an unconscious process created out of distilled experience. When managers face complex decisions and cannot get accurate information, they tend to rely on hunches, intuitions and general experiences. As Bazerman (1994) concludes: 'Most significant decisions are made by judgement, rather than by a defined prescriptive model'. Such intuition, however, is not really acceptable in cultures where rational analysis is the approved way of making decisions, such as North America and the UK. So intuition is often disguised or hidden. For example, one of the executives in the study by Agor (1986) commented: 'Sometimes one must dress up a gut decision in "data clothes" to make it acceptable or palatable, but this fine-tuning is usually after the fact of the decision.'

A final, non-rational model of the decision-making process is the garbage can model developed by Cohen *et al.* (1971). They described decision-making processes in terms of a 'garbage can', rather than a rational process. This model suggests that decisions have a random and haphazard element to them – that is, decisions are sometimes made from the random interaction of problems, solutions, choice situations and participants, rather than from intentions, plans, and consistent decisions. Various kinds of problems, solutions and energy ('garbage') are dumped into a garbage can by participants. The decision process may then just as well start with the solution as the problem.

These models of decision-making acknowledge the limits or 'bounds' to rational decision-making, including:

1. Perceptual limitations and biases
2. Limited availability of information
3. Prediction is an art not a science so it is not possible to evaluate options as rationally as proposed
4. Organisational goals constrain decisions
5. Conflicting goals of different stakeholders mean that interpersonal conflicts, personal biases and power struggles are an inherent part of the decision process.

The irrationality of the selection and assessment decision-making process

The irrationality of decision-making processes has been confirmed in studies focusing on selection and assessment decisions. A brief look at the steps in the decision-making cycle and evidence of what happens at each stage highlights the continued 'irrationality' of the selection process in practice.

1. Understand the situation and identify the problem

The idea that someone leaving an organisation should be used as an opportunity to rationally consider whether or not a replacement is 'really needed', ignores the political realities of organisations (Pfeffer, 1981). Power within organisations is at least partly a function of resources that are controlled, including human resources. While individuals are recruited to work for a particular company, in reality they are recruited to particular departments or divisions. A department is unlikely to admit voluntarily that they do not need to replace a particular person since that will diminish their 'empire'. The department may actually be more likely to argue that they 'need' two people to replace the one leaver! Someone leaving may be an opportunity for a renegotiation of resources within the organisation, but this needs to be understood as an inherently political process. 'Need' is not something that can be established as fact, but is socially constructed through a process of negotiation and sense-making until a 'workable version of reality' is produced (Weick, 1990).

2. Gather information and material to help solve the problem

Despite the extensive effort put into developing new, more valid methods to measure and assess individuals during the selection process, evidence suggests that unstructured interviews and references remain the most dominant methods (Shackleton and Newell, 1991; Keenan, 1995). This can be related to the human fallacy of us each believing that we are a 'good judge of people', despite evidence to the contrary (see section below on person perceptions errors). Later in this chapter we will also consider another reason for the continued use of the interview – that is, that selection is not simply about 'valid' selection, but also about commitment and motivation to follow up the decision with behaviours that encourage the individual selected to integrate into the organisation. A recruiter who feels that s/he has personally selected the candidate is much more likely to feel committed and motivated to helping achieve that integration. Similarly, the selected candidate may well be more committed to the organisation because unstructured interviews are more likely to provide the opportunity to negotiate a 'mutually agreeable psychological contract' (Dipboye, 1997).

3. Generate potential solutions

While the rational model of selection suggests that the recruitment stage is about generating the widest search possible in order to ensure the 'best' pool of applicants, evidence suggests that, in reality, the alternatives considered are often less than exhaustive. For example, some organisations only go to Oxford and Cambridge universities to recruit graduates. While these universities may well have some of the brightest graduates, there will certainly be bright graduates at other universities. Other evidence suggests that the so-called 'old boy network' is still actively used across organisations (Coe, 1992). In other words, it is very often personal contacts that provide job openings rather than systematic recruitment and selection procedures.

4. Systematically evaluate each solution

The evidence suggests that assessors, whatever method they are using, do not systematically use the evidence that is collected. For example, the evidence about assessment centres, reviewed below, suggests that assessors are unable to distinguish between different aspects of behaviour within a given exercise, but instead give ratings based on their overall assessment of the candidate's performance on that particular exercise. Research on interviews suggests that decisions are often made very quickly and are subjective, unreliable and vulnerable to bias (Arvey and Faley, 1992; Dipboye, 1992; Janz, 1989).

5. Select best solution

A truly rational decision process would have assessors numerically rate each candidate on each dimension or competency; give the different dimensions or competencies specific weightings depending on their relative importance for the job in question; and then total the score for each candidate, taking into account the relative weightings. The candidate with the highest total would be selected. This can be described as the actuarial method as it is based purely on a numerical calculation of the collected data (although the ratings themselves are subjective). In practice, however, the decision is much more likely to be based on a process of clinical judgement. The ratings may be numerical but these will be evaluated subjectively by the assessors and weightings will be assigned to justify decisions rather than to make the decisions. So leadership skills become more important than numerical skills, if this allows the favoured candidate to come out top! As Beach (1990: xiii) states: 'most decisions are made quickly and simply on the basis of "fittingness", and only in particular circumstances are they made on the basis of anything like the weighing and balancing of gains and losses that is prescribed by classical decision theory'.

6. Monitor and evaluate results

In practice it seems that very few organisations carry out a systematic evaluation of their selection process (or indeed any other human resource practice). Moreover, where validity studies have been conducted, they demonstrate low levels of validity even when using methods that can potentially provide reasonable or good levels of validity (see below). These results confirm that selection methods are not used in the prescribed way and that efforts to improve validity have had rather limited impact on actual practice.

The conclusion drawn from such research is that the prescriptive, rational decision-making process does not typically equate with what happens in practice and that methods of selection actually used by practitioners are often not high on criterion-related validity. Exactly the same points could be made with reference to decisions made during developmental assessment processes. The response from those researching and writing about selection and assessment has been to attempt to improve the validity of the methods used to measure individual differences. In other words, the focus has been on trying to find ways of improving the extent to which the rational, normative decision-making model is actually followed.

Improving the validity of selection and assessment decisions

In particular, attention has focused on introducing methods which provide a better basis on which to make rational decisions. Considerable progress has been made here, which demonstrates how the validity of the selection and assessment decision-making process can be improved.

Structured interviews

The interview is the most common selection tool used within organisations across many countries (DiMilia *et al.*, 1994; Shackleton and Newell, 1994). Early research demonstrated that the traditional unstructured interview had very low validity (e.g. Mayfield, 1964; Ulrich and Trumbo, 1965). Given the ubiquity of the interview, effort has been devoted to improving its validity, primarily by increasing the structure of the interview, so that at least all candidates are asked the same sorts of questions (if not the identical questions) and all interviewers use the same dimensions to assess candidates. Research looking at the validity of structured interviews suggests that they can indeed improve validity. For example, McDaniel *et al.* (1994), in a large meta-analytic study, reported that structured interviews were more valid than unstructured interviews. Structuring interviews can therefore potentially improve the quality of decisions made, although there appears to be a ceiling on this, beyond which increasing structure does not improve validity (Heffcutt and Arthur, 1994).

Biographical measures

Biographical measures, or biodata, attempt to capture directly the past behaviour of a person and use this as the basis for predicting future behaviour. Since they are based on actual behaviour, the idea is that they are less prone to misinterpretation, resistance and distortion (Stricker and Rock, 1998). Research has indeed demonstrated that biographical measures can produce good levels of predictive validity (e.g. Mumford and Stokes, 1992; Stokes *et al.*, 1993; Hesketh, 1999). Nevertheless, there remain a number of concerns about the appropriate item content and about test construction methods (Mael, 1991). For example, in terms of content many biographical measures contain questions which are indistinguishable from items on an attitude scale (e.g. What is your attitude towards working mothers?); or items that call for subjective judgements (e.g. How punctual are you?); or items that are not under the control of the assessee and so are dubious on ethical grounds (e.g. How many sisters and brothers have you got?). In terms of test construction, a key problem is that because most measures are empirically keyed to predict particular criteria, they cannot be used in different settings. There is also the problem that this method can produce a very homogeneous workforce, since those selected will have very similar backgrounds and experiences. This may be problematic in a dynamic environment where the ability to adapt to change is important.

Psychometric tests

Essentially, there are two kinds of tests used for selection or developmental assessment – cognitive and personality tests. Cognitive tests, especially tests of general intelligence, have typically been found to have high predictive validity across a wide range of jobs (Hunter and Hunter, 1984), but it is debatable how much additional information they provide since there are other ways of estimating ability, especially from academic qualifications.

Personality tests have typically been found to have a low validity for predicting job performance (Ghiselli, 1973; Schmitt *et al.*, 1984). However, more recently, evidence has been established to suggest that personality measures can be valid predictors of job performance (e.g. Day and Silverman, 1989; Robertson and Kinder, 1993; Salgado, 1996). One reason for the early pessimism was that there was no generally accepted model of personality. More recently, the so called 'Big 5' have emerged around which there is substantial agreement. Research using the Big 5 model has shown that measurement of these five traits can help to predict job performance. For example, Barrick and Mount (1991) found that conscientiousness is a valid predictor for all occupational groups and all criterion types. And Hough *et al.* (1990) found that neuroticism is negatively related to general performance measures. Moreover, researchers have begun to consider more thoughtfully the relationship between particular aspects of personality and particular aspects of performance that might logically be related; not assuming that a measure of personality will be related to just any criterion measure.

Assessment or development centres

Assessment or development centres make use of a variety of exercises over a period of time (typically 2 days) to assess a small group of candidates on a number of dimensions (often defined in terms of competencies) that are deemed relevant to the particular job and organisation. Ratings are made by a small group of trained assessors who observe the candidates on the different exercises. Exercises might include: a group decision-making exercise, a presentation, a role play, an in-basket test, psychometric tests, and interviews. In the UK, the use of assessment centres is increasing more rapidly than any other selection procedure, with 65 per cent of large firms (over 1,000 employees) using them (Industrial Relations Service, 1997). Research evidence using meta-analysis demonstrates that they can have a relatively high level of predictive validity (Gaugler *et al.*, 1987) and are seen as fair and thorough by candidates (Macan *et al.*, 1994).

Despite this good predictive validity, research has demonstrated that assessment and development centres do not have good construct validity (Kauffman *et al.*, 1993). In particular, research has demonstrated that within each exercise, ratings across the different dimensions are not clearly differentiated, while correlation of a given dimension across exercises is low (Joyce *et al.*, 1994; Kaufman *et al.*, 1993; McCredie and Shackleton, 1994). One suggested reason for this is that the information-processing load on assessors is too high, so that they selectively attend to only certain behaviours, misinterpret key behaviours, and/or confuse categorisation of behaviours by dimensions (Fleenor, 1996; Thornton, 1992). Schema-driven theory suggests that this occurs because people use established schemata to interpret and evaluate the observed behaviour of others (Fiske and Taylor, 1991; Zedeck, 1986). Schemata refer to the mental representations that an individual has built up over time to structure and cluster their understanding of perceived phenomena. Any new input will be interpreted on the basis of the assumptions which underpin these schemata. Traditionally, the recommended way to overcome this problem has been to separate the steps of observation and classification – recording behaviours longhand while observing, classifying behaviours according to the defined dimensions for the exercise, and only then rating the individual on each dimension (Bray and Grant, 1966; Boyle *et al.*, 1995). While this does help to overcome some of the perceptual problems of assessors, the requirement to write detailed notes of the observation can be a distraction and means that the assessor might miss some behavioural information.

Hennessy *et al.* (1998), in an attempt to overcome this problem, experimented with the use of a Behavioural Coding method of assessment. This provides a list of key behaviours for each of the dimensions rated and requires observers to code the frequency of behaviours as they occur. They are not required actually to note the behaviours per se, but only tally the frequency of the specified behaviours. This has the advantage that information-processing demands are reduced and also limits the extent to which personal schemata will direct the observation. The results of their research demonstrated that this Behavioural Coding method was as accurate as the traditional method of assessment and reduced differences between raters in their judgements. They suggest that its simplicity in comparison with the traditional method, and its theoretical basis in schema-driven theory, may make this a preferred method for overcoming the construct validity problem of assessment or development centres.

On the basis of reviewing a number of studies which have attempted to improve the construct validity of assessment and development centres, Lievens (1998) makes a number of practical recommendations. For example, in terms of:

1. Dimensions: use only a small number of conceptually distinct dimensions and define these in a concrete and job-related way.
2. Assessors: ensure assessors are trained, especially in relation to understanding the dimensions and categorisation schemes used.

3. Situational exercises: develop exercises which generate a large amount of dimension-related behaviour and avoid exercises which elicit behaviours potentially relevant to many dimensions.

4. Systematic observation, evaluation and integration procedures: Provide assessors with an observation aid (a checklist), which operationalises each dimension with 6–12 key behaviours.

The rhetoric versus the reality of the selection and assessment decision-making process

These newer assessment methods appear to offer significant benefits since they can improve objectivity and criterion-related validity. However, as seen, research into actual practice suggests that, in reality, selection and development decisions continue to be dominated by more subjective approaches. Moreover, even where so-called 'objective' approaches are used, their interpretation remains highly subjective. That is, the fact that a structured interview or an assessment centre has the potential to reach high levels of validity does not mean that it will be used in ways to guarantee this. For example, DiMilia and Gorodecki (1997) evaluated the reliability and use of a commercially available structured interviewing system. They found that, in practice, the reliability achieved was much lower than considered in the literature to be an acceptable level. This was because there was a lack of role clarity for interviewers, interviewers had different expectations of the job specification and there was inconsistency in the application of the rating system. They conclude that: '. . . whilst an interviewing system can have a number of features described in the literature as necessary conditions for better validity, the actual result of the system is in the hands of the user' (DiMilia and Gorodecki, 1997: 198).

Similarly, while psychometric tests can potentially add valid information to the selection or development decision, it is also clear that this will only occur if tests are used appropriately (Newell and Shackleton, 1993). Rees (1996) identifies a number of common misunderstandings among test users which suggest that tests are not always used in a valid and ethical way. For example, a frequent misconception is that it is acceptable to use a poor test to structure a subsequent interview. Rees concludes that such misunderstandings may, over time, undermine the case of those attempting to use psychometric tests 'effectively and appropriately in the occupational setting'. He argues that there are too many test users who are unable to recognise technically poor test material and so use such tests inappropriately to help them make decisions that affect both individuals and organisations.

These observations are not confined to selection decision methods. Other attempts to improve the rationality of decision-making, for example by introducing cost-benefit analysis, computer-based information systems or other decision support systems, demonstrate that, in practice, these solutions are not used in the prescribed way (e.g. Ackerman *et al.*, 1974; Argyris, 1977). Essentially, the normative model of the selection and assessment decision-making process does not equate to reality because selection and assessment is a process that inherently depends on an interaction between two or more parties. Such interpersonal *interactions* involve two (or more) parties who are simultaneously providing input (which the other is evaluating) and evaluating the other. Such interactions are inherently subjective, involving processes of impression management and interpretation.

Impression management

Decisions made about candidates during selection and assessment depend on the concrete experiences that are provided. These experiences of the 'target person' (i.e. the candidate) may be indirect (e.g. information from an application form or a personality test) or direct (e.g. behaviour exhibited during an interview). The newer methods of assessment attempt to ensure that the event provides assessors with an accurate reflection of the person being assessed. This assumes that the candidate is passively responding to the various assessment experiences. In reality, of course, candidates are actively attempting to create a certain image of themselves. This is especially the case in the 'high stakes' selection situation. Candidates will attempt to create and maintain a particular impression of themselves which coincides with what they believe the assessor is looking for. Thus, to some extent at least, the assessor only sees what the target person wants him/her to see. This is referred to as Impression Management (Rosenfeld *et al.*, 1995). Arnold *et al.* (1997) identify a variety of techniques that can be used to convey a particular impression. For example, ingratiation ('I have always wanted to work for this firm'), selective description of events (candidate ignoring details of failed examinations they have taken), positive descriptions of self ('I am a very hard-working person'). While it might be obvious to appreciate that candidates are engaging in impression management tactics, it is also the case that assessors are simultaneously attempting to 'create an impression' because they want to attract or retain the 'best' candidates.

Interpretation

The assessor has to make sense of the data that is accumulated about the candidate and this sense-making process is inherently subjective. At the same time, the candidate is also trying to 'make sense' of the situation – what would it be like to work for this company, or what would my colleagues be like, or what are my implied career opportunities? For both parties, there is a stimulus ('evidence' from the candidate to the assessor and vice versa) and a response (a job offer or an acceptance of a job offer). However, the key to understanding this is that between these two observable phenomena are the unobservable processes of perception.

Perception, by definition, is a subjective process by which individuals attend to, organise and so interpret their sensory input in order to give meaning to their environment. Subjective processes, including selective attention, personal judgement and interpretation, will therefore affect the decision. Behaviour is based on

the world as it is perceived and a number of factors operate to shape and sometimes distort perception, including personal characteristics, motives, interests, past
experiences, and expectations. This will result in biases, such as:

1. *Selective attention* – as we cannot attend to everything, we only attend to some
   things, but this is not random. Rather, what we attend to is chosen according
   to our interests, background, experience and attitudes. This allows us to draw
   conclusions from an ambiguous situation.
2. *Halo/horn effect* – we tend to draw a general impression about an individual
   on the basis of a single characteristic, such as intelligence.
3. *Contrast effects* – evaluations of a person's characteristics can be affected by
   comparisons with other people recently encountered. So, in an interview situation, if someone has just been interviewed who was judged very poor, the next
   candidate may be more positively evaluated in contrast. Conversely, following
   a very good candidate, an average candidate may be rated poorly.
4. *Projection* – there is a tendency to attribute one's own characteristics to other
   people. So if I want challenge and responsibility in a job, I assume that others
   want the same.
5. *Stereotyping* – this involves judging someone on the basis of one's perceptions
   of the group to which that person belongs.
6. *Heuristics* – these are judgemental short cuts in decision-making. Two common
   heuristics are availability and representativeness. The availability heuristic is
   the tendency for people to base their judgements on information that is readily
   available to them. For example, if there is an internal and an external candidate, the internal candidate may be preferred simply because more information
   is readily available about him/her ('better the devil you know!'). The representative heuristic is the tendency to assess the likelihood of an occurrence by
   drawing analogies and seeing identical situations where they do not exist. So,
   for example, if four graduates from the same college had all been recruited but
   none had been very satisfactory, then another applicant from this college might
   be rejected on the assumption that they also would not be good.

   It is just these sorts of impression management problems and perceptual biases
that 'new' assessment methods have attempted to overcome. They structure and
standardise the information gained during the assessment process, so that decisions are less likely to be biased by these perceptual short cuts that we use in our
everyday judgements of other people, to a greater or lesser extent. To the extent
that these new assessment methods can reduce these biases, they can improve
validity. The research evidence presented earlier suggests that this is indeed the
case. However, as we have also seen, while newer, more valid assessment methods
have been developed, and can improve the validity of selection and development
decisions, in practice they are often not used in quite the 'rational' way anticipated. Human subjectivity and the political reality of organisations mean that the
normative decision model can never be an entirely realistic account of decision-
making in practice.

Unfounded assumptions: selection as an interactive process

While human perception and organisational politics limit the extent to which a selection or development decision can ever be entirely rational, there is an even more fundamental problem with the normative decision model. The normative approach makes the assumption of a 'right' or 'best' person for the job and assumes that there is one key decision, i.e. to select or reject the candidate, which is the crucial point. The important issue is to select the 'right' person and then this will solve the organisational problem because this person will be able successfully to carry out the particular tasks where there is currently a vacancy (although this may be only after training has been given). However, this ignores the fact that successful performance on a job is rarely, if ever, dependent solely on a particular individual. The individual job exists within a complex network of structures, processes and relationships, which will affect and interact with the actions of the particular individual employee. So a potentially very competent recruit can be thwarted in their ability to perform to a high standard by a whole multitude of events – a lack of adequate resources, poor training, an unhelpful supervisor, colleagues who are not supportive, etc. On the other hand, a barely competent recruit can perform to a high standard if she/he is exposed to a supportive or benign situation.

In other words, it is not helpful to look at the selection decision itself in isolation from the stream of events that occur both before and after this. Vaughan (1996, 1997) made a similar point in analysing the Challenger space shuttle disaster. She points out that the explosion should not be viewed as the unfortunate result of one bad decision to launch on that day in January 1986. Rather, it was the outcome of an accumulation of many launch decisions over the course of the shuttle programme. So instead of focusing on single decisions, she advocates the analysis of cycles of decisions or networks of decisions. This is equally the case in terms of analysing selection or development decisions. Thus, whether a decision to select (or reject) can be described as 'good' or 'bad' is the result of a network of interacting decisions. These decisions are made by both the individual and the organisational representatives, over a period of time, starting well before the actual advertisement of a job. For example, individuals will form an impression of a particular company based on what they know about its products and services or what they know about the organisation itself. These impressions may be formed either on the basis of direct experience (e.g. good or bad experience of service as a customer) or indirect experience (e.g. reading something good or bad about the company in the press). These impressions will influence how an individual responds to a recruitment advertisement. So a potentially ideal candidate may not even apply if s/he has formed a negative impression. Moreover, decisions made subsequent to the selection decision, will have a considerable impact on the extent to which the recruit performs the job effectively. Particularly important in this respect is the socialisation experience of the new recruit (Anderson and Ostroff, 1997). This suggests the need to see selection as an interactive process in which the expectations of both parties are intertwined in a process of continuous exchange, which does not begin and end at the point of the selection decision. Again, exactly the same points can be made with reference to development decisions. Whether the 'right' career path is chosen for and by a particular individual on the basis of evidence from a development centre will depend on a host of decisions made prior and subsequent to this choice.

What this analysis implies is that the normative, rational model of decision-making isolates the decision from subsequent action, including subsequent decisions (Brunsson, 1982). Brunsson argues that the normative decision-making perspective fails to recognise that a decision is not an end product but simply a step towards action of some kind. In the case of selection, this equals the effective deployment of human resources. More importantly, Brunsson points out that rational decisions are not always good bases for appropriate and successful actions: 'Since decision processes aim at action, they should not be designed solely according to such decision-internal criteria as the norms of rationality; they should be adapted to external criteria of action' (1982: 32). The selection or development decision per se is only one episode in the successful integration of the individual in the organisation. Successful integration is more likely to occur where there are positive expectations, motivation and commitment from both parties. Thus, the stronger the expectation, motivation and commitment expressed in a decision, the more power that decision exerts as a basis for action. However, Brunnson argues that to achieve such expectation, motivation and commitment breaks all the rules for rational decision-making:

1. Few alternatives should be considered: while the rational model assumes that many (all) alternatives should be considered, from a decision-action perspective parsimony is more appropriate. Considering multiple alternatives generates uncertainty and this reduces commitment and motivation.
2. Only positive consequences of the chosen decision should be analysed: the rational model advocates considering all consequences of a decision, both positive and negative. From a decision-action perspective it may be more sensible to search for consequences in only one direction since this reduces inconsistency which can stimulate doubt.
3. Objectives should not be predefined: the rational model assumes that objectives should be predefined so that all alternatives can be considered against these objectives. For producing action, a better strategy may be to start from the consequences and invent the objectives afterwards (Lindblom, 1959).

This action-oriented perspective can help to explain some of the research findings on the selection and assessment decision process, which suggest that it remains less rational than prescribed best practice would advocate. Examples of this are given below.

1. Continued use of unstructured interviews – the belief that 'I am a good judge of character' allows the interviewer to be confident in his/her decision and so increases commitment and motivation to make the chosen individual 'fit'.

2. Continued use of subjective (clinical) rather than objective (actuarial) choice criteria – again this empowers the assessor to believe that they were influential in the decision and so makes him/her more committed to ensuring the decision translates into effective action – i.e. successful integration of the chosen candidate within the organisation.

3. Less than exhaustive search of alternatives – making decisions quickly makes life more comfortable for managers. It allows them to use heuristics or 'short-cuts' to solving problems. Predefined recipes for successful selection decisions can increase confidence in the decision and so raise expectations of subsequent success by the candidate.

4. Little systematic evaluation of selection decision – while academic research has focused on establishing the predictive validity of selection decisions, in practice few organisations systematically monitor the success of their decisions. Again, from an action perspective this is sensible since it allows those involved to be confident in their decision-making qualities and so more confident about and committed to the decisions they make. It also reduces the possibility of cognitive dissonance (Festinger, 1957). Cognitive dissonance is the uncomfortable feeling that occurs when people hold inconsistent or conflicting beliefs – I made the decision to hire this person, I am good at making these kinds of decisions, this person is not a good employee. Cognitive dissonance can be avoided if systematic evaluation of selection decisions is avoided.

5. Overemphasis of negative data – research has demonstrated that negative information about a candidate is given more weight than positive information. Many of the newer assessment methods are aimed at reducing this effect. However, from a decision-action perspective this is entirely rational. Negative information raises doubts about the suitability of a candidate and so will undermine confidence that the person can be successful. So if there are two candidates, and from an objective evaluation of the evidence, candidate A is 'best', having more of the essential and desirable characteristics than candidate B, then rationally that candidate should be selected. However, if there is also one piece of negative information about candidate A (for example a question mark over their willingness to collaborate), while there is nothing negative about candidate B, then from an action-decision perspective, candidate B would be preferable. If candidate A were selected there would remain doubts, which might undermine motivation and commitment to the decision.

In each case, the decision-action criteria improve the positive expectations of those involved over the purely rational decision criteria. This is important since expectations can become self-fulfilling prophecies. For example, Eden and Shani (1982) informed the instructors of a command course for the Israeli Defence Forces that one-third of the 105 soldiers on the course had high potential, one-third had normal potential and the rest were of unknown potential. In reality, the soldiers had been randomly assigned to one of these three groups. However, at the end of the 15-week course, those trainees who were given the high potential label

scored significantly higher on objective achievement tests and exhibited more positive attitudes to the course and the instructors, than did the rest.

Interactive action-oriented perspective, fairness and justice

One particular problem in selection and development decisions has been the issue
of 'fair' discrimination. Thus, while selection is based on making discriminations
between people, the objective has been to make these discriminations on the basis
of relevant criteria, i.e. ability to do the job effectively, rather than irrelevant criteria like sex, ethnicity, and disability. One of the key benefits of the psychometric
perspective is that it presents a very rational and objective view of the whole
process. It assumes that the 'best' person for the job can be clearly specified in
advance, with selection and assessment processes essentially presented as a set of
'rational' choices based on objective evidence gained about the candidates from
the various selection methods deployed. This allowed companies to defend against
claims of unfair discrimination. Essentially, the traditional approach may be considered to have a high level of procedural justice (Lind and Tyler, 1988) since it
theoretically treats everyone the same. In this chapter, we have argued that this
semblance of rationality is actually a myth. Moreover, it could be argued that the
psychometric perspective actually increases the opportunity for distributive injus-
tice (Singer, 1993), because its starting premise is that there is one 'best' way to do
the job. This 'best' way is likely to be a reflection of the way previous job incumbents have done the job. So if the previous job incumbents have all been white
males who have adopted fairly autocratic management styles, worked long hours,
relied on a lot of electronic communication, etc., then the assumption will be that
these are the characteristics to look for in a replacement. This may perpetuate the
status quo and thus the segregation that exists within organisations, although the
process may look procedurally 'fair'.

Adopting the interactive, action-oriented perspective provides the opportunity
to break through this barrier by recognising that people can do jobs in very different ways but equally effectively. The problem with this perspective, however, is
that it acknowledges the subjectivity of the selection process and so could be used
as a vehicle to increase unfair discrimination even more. This is entirely true but it
will depend on the motives of those involved. If there is a belief in equal opportunities, or, perhaps even better, in the advantages of diversity in the workforce, then
this perspective can help to increase these opportunities. The psychometric perspective simply hides behind a façade of objectivity so that it remains easy to
perpetuate discrimination even while presenting the whole process as fair. The
interactive action-oriented perspective does not have this façade to hide behind so
that any continuation of segregated workforces must, by implication, be the result
of prejudice and unfair discrimination.

Conclusion

Understanding the selection and assessment process from a decision-making perspective highlights issues that are otherwise not brought into focus. In this chapter, this perspective has been used to contrast the traditional psychometric perspective with its implicit acceptance of the normative rational decision-making model, with an interactive decision-action perspective. The decision-action perspective leads us to recognise both that the process of selection and assessment can never be entirely rational and objective and that the decision per se (to accept or reject) is not necessarily the crucial point in the process. Rather, it is a stage in the ultimate goal of achieving the effective integration and socialisation of an individual within the organisation. Effective integration is clearly unlikely if an entirely unsuitable person is chosen for a job. However, the assumption that there is a fixed type of person for a particular job and that the only goal of selection and assessment is to ensure accurate measurement in order to be able to identify this right type, is inappropriate. It is inappropriate both because of its assumptions about individual differences and our ability to assess these accurately in a selection or development situation and because it ignores the criteria for translating the decision into action.

Successful performance on the job is dependent on motivation as well as ability. Ability is dependent not only on fixed characteristics, but also on opportunities for training and development that are provided. An 'ideal' person selected for a job but then given no training or development opportunities is more likely to fail than a moderately suitable person who is given such opportunities.

More importantly, in terms of motivation, success or failure will depend on both the individual's own self-beliefs and on the beliefs of those around him/her. If these significant others have been involved in the selection and assessment process and believe that the person selected is 'the best', then they will be committed to ensuring he/she is successful, regardless of whether or not he/she is best according to some objective rational decision criteria. An entirely rational, actuarial evaluation of data collected during an assessment centre that results in the selection of a person that those involved do not 'like' or do not think is 'best' (for whatever reason), is unlikely to translate into active commitment aimed at helping that individual succeed. As seen, such commitment is more likely to follow a selection decision-process that is less than entirely rational, but that gives those involved the belief that they have chosen someone who will be successful. Similarly, motivation is likely to be high if the selection or development experience results in positive but realistic expectations on the part of those assessed. Self-efficacy beliefs, an individual's belief that s/he is capable of performing the task selected for (Bandura, 1977), will be high and these beliefs have been shown to be important in influencing the persistence and effort that someone will put into ensuring success (Gist, 1987).

An action-decision perspective can help to identify those selection and assessment processes that can generate such high levels of self- and other belief and expectation that lead, in turn, to high levels of commitment and motivation. Of course, measurement of individual differences will remain important in selection and development decisions. However, the recognition that accurate measurement per se is not enough (even if it were possible), can help us focus on the ultimate goal of successful person-organisation fit, rather than just valid and rational decisions that might not readily translate into action. The decision-action perspective, therefore, compliments the more traditional psychometric perspective and can help to ensure not only that decisions are made on the basis of reasonably good individual assessment but also that those decisions get translated into successful organisational performance.

Assessment at Newsco, Pharmco and Retailco

Sue Newell and Viv Shackleton

Taking a decision-action perspective suggests that processes involved in selection and assessment should differ depending on the particular context and, in particular, on the intended action outcome. In order to demonstrate this diversity, we consider three separate cases in the following section. Each had a different objective and so a different design.

Newsco

Introduction

The first example of the application of the assessment techniques we have talked about in this chapter concerns Newsco, a large and successful company in the business of selling news and information. It is a truly international company, operating as it does in most countries of the world. It divides the world up into three zones. We are concerned here with the European part of the operation.

The brief

The company decided to assess the top 50 or so of its managers in this region. The stated purpose was assessment for development. That is to say, the managers would go through a development centre (an assessment-type centre designed with development in mind) in order for them to assess what sort of development they needed. 'Development' is a word that is frequently misunderstood. Here, it does not necessarily mean promotion or acquiring new responsibilities. It means training in techniques or skills, or acquiring new information, that would help them in their present or future roles. The traditional 'sheep dip' approach to management development, training and learning, where everyone receives the same training, regardless of need, is often not appropriate at any level in an organisation. It can be particularly inappropriate for senior people where the opportunity cost of having them away from their desks on a course is very high. This organisation wanted to target training only on those who needed it, in the areas they most needed.

The role of those participating in the development centre was mostly that of 'country manager', the people who headed up the business in each country, although there were also specialists of various kinds.

The design

The start of the process of designing the development centre began with an assessment of competencies, just as we described in the section on the traditional approach to assessment in this chapter. This involved interviewing people in the organisation to establish what the competencies were, both for the present job and for the ways in which the jobs might develop. The interviews were based on in-depth reviews of the role in question and how the organisation might develop. Two other kinds of interview were also used, the repertory grid technique and the critical incident technique. The repertory grid technique asks the interviewee to think of a number of people known to him or her who do, or have done, the job and to compare the way that they perform that role. From this information, the interviewer can work out the key skills, knowledge, abilities or competencies that effective job holders need and which differentiate the effective from the less effective. The critical incident technique asks interviewees to think of times in the job when they or their team were particularly successful or unsuccessful. The interviewee is encouraged to say what it was that made this particular incident successful or unsuccessful. From this evidence, the experienced interviewer can work out some of the competencies needed in the job.

Some of the competencies in this case were:

- *Managing change*
    - Continually challenging the status quo
    - Generating innovative ideas and solutions
    - Driving change through and overcoming resistance

- *Thinking for the future*
    - Anticipating future trends and identifying new opportunities
    - Thinking strategically
    - Retaining a global perspective

- *Working with customers*
    - Building partnerships with customers by knowing their business
    - Consulting with customers to understand needs and provide the best service
    - Promoting a positive image of the company

Exercises were then designed to give the opportunity to assess these and the other competencies. Exercises included:

- a role play with a customer, where the customer had a serious complaint about the level of service and support he or she was receiving
- a competitor analysis, where participants were given information about three competitors and asked to do a SWOT (strengths, weaknesses, opportunities and threats) analysis of their own organisation and the competition
- giving a presentation on issues of their own choosing from their own country business to the top management from the head office

- a group discussion on a strategic issue facing the whole organisation
- some psychometric tests

The workshop

Each development centre lasted two days. Managers from all corners of Europe and North Africa arrived, eight at a time, for the programme. There were external consultants and managers from head office running the programme and assessing the participants on the competencies. A crucial element of the two days was a one-to-one feedback, lasting around an hour, conducted by the external consultant with each of the participants. The purpose of this meeting was to review the performance of the participant on each of the exercises and competencies, and to get his or her agreement to the accuracy of the assessment. Most importantly, it was also an opportunity to discuss what the participant proposed to do about developing the strengths and remedying the weaknesses exposed by the programme.

The outputs

Following the workshop, the consultant wrote a report on the participant, summarising his or her performance and outlining a development plan. In effect, the report summarised and formalised the one-to-one discussion at the end of the centre. The report was sent to the participant and to his or her human resources manager. Participants themselves only showed it to their line manager or others in the organisation if they so wished. It was a confidential report and the recommendations were to be implemented by the participant in the manner most likely to achieve the development proposed. Development methods included secondments, job shadowing, training courses, self-directed learning, distance learning, job changes, and even withdrawal from the organisation if this was what the participant wanted.

After the development centre, there was no follow-up to check that the participants at the workshop had done any development after the event, and no attempt to evaluate the benefits of the programme. It was sufficient for the participants to say that the workshop had been useful and enjoyable. The feedback was essentially positive. This is not to say that the development centre was anodyne. There was some indication of how they could do even better. It pointed out that, where the participant had demonstrated excellent skills, he or she might coach others in these skills or seek opportunities to use them even more. Where there were skills that needed improving, suggestions were made on how this might be accomplished. But the whole development centre, and the feedback in particular, was geared to reinforcing, motivating and encouraging, rather than assessing and measuring. The participants were generally very positive about the event, after some initial reservations. They pointed out the many considerable advantages of the programme, including the opportunity to meet others in similar roles, to reflect on their own progress in the organisation, to think about themselves for a change, rather than the job in hand, and to consider how they might change or reinforce certain aspects of their own behaviour. In summary, the opportunity to reflect and learn was very motivating and satisfying for them.

Pharmco

Introduction

The second case concerns a long-established German corporation, Pharmco. Its early beginnings were in the traditional 'smokestack' industries of iron and steel, but since the Second World War it has moved into pharmaceutical manufacture and retail, along with the manufacture of medical and other technical equipment and a number of other businesses. In the more recent past, it has also started to expand beyond its national border and acquire and develop businesses in other European countries, including Britain, France and Spain. It is still predominantly a German company, though, with 90 per cent of its manufacturing and retail business conducted within the country.

The brief

We meet up with the company at the point when it was thinking of investing in the development of its young managers to groom them for more senior appointments. In typical German style, it placed great emphasis on the importance of formal, high-quality education. It planned to offer the chance for some of the young managers to broaden their education and experience out of their technical and functional expertise and into a general management education. They would offer the opportunity to enrol in a part-time MBA at a prestigious international business school for those who were assessed as having the potential to profit from it. But who would benefit?

The design

The method they chose to select those who would be offered the opportunity was an assessment centre. Germany, like Britain and America, has a long tradition of using assessment centres, right back from the days of officer selection in the Second World War. But here, there was the additional complication of having to design an assessment centre for candidates from a number of different European countries. Although the language of the centre would be English, the exercises would be taken by people from four or five different countries. Of course, Newsco was a very international group, and consideration was given to designing exercises that would not favour one culture rather than another. But here, the cultural fairness issue was considered even more carefully by the designers. This is because this centre was seen as more akin to a traditional assessment centre, where fairness of treatment and equal opportunity to display skills are paramount. As we will discuss shortly, though, this objectivity and equal treatment were more apparent than real.

Once again, the first issue was what knowledge, skills and abilities should be assessed. And again, the favoured means of acquiring that knowledge was a competency analysis. Methods adopted to decide on the required competencies were very similar to those already described for Newsco. Competencies included:

- *Cross-cultural sensitivity*
  - Demonstrating curiosity and open-mindedness about other national cultures
  - Acting to promote mutual understanding of other cultures
  - Demonstrating sensitivity when working with people from other cultures

- *Leadership*
  - Focusing a group on generating a range of new ideas and possibilities
  - Demonstrating confidence and a sense of responsibility
  - Developing subordinates by making demands on them

- *Orientation to the task*
  - Agreeing clear and realistic actions
  - Prioritising
  - Taking decisions
  - Reviewing progress towards achieving the task

Participants were nominated by their line managers and by human resource professionals in their separate companies, in whichever country they worked. Participants were assessed at the centre by both company managers and by outside consultants, using competency-based rating scales.

Exercises were designed with the multicultural audience in mind. They included one on cultural sensitivity, where participants discussed their perception of their own culture and the German culture, as they had experienced it. They had to meet to discuss what recommendations they would make to improve cross-cultural working and how they would know if their recommendations were effective.

When designing assessment centre exercises, it is important to keep these and other cultural dimensions in mind. So, for example, it is important to make sure that exercises have many routes to success for a participant. An example of this need to provide many routes to success (and failure) in a multicultural environment is provided by an exercise used in this case. The exercise involved a customer service manager who was new to the post, and a subordinate, a customer service team leader, who had been in post for a long time. This was a role play exercise. An 'actor', a manager who had been in that post in the past, played the team leader. The participant played the superior, the customer service manager. There was some written material on the team leader, such as previous performance appraisal reports and statistical data on the subordinate's performance, available to the new boss. The issues were that the team leader was very good with customers, being liked and respected by them, but not good at developing his or her team, in part because s/he spent so much time with customers. In addition, they were not good at organising the work of the team since they were too busy doing the work themselves. The exercise could be done in a number of ways. It could be done from a relationships-building point of view, where, for example, the new boss could coach or mentor the old hand into new ways of working. Or it could be done from a very task-focused point of view, such as saying that this style and level of performance is not accept-able and you should be working in a different way and here are some targets and a timetable to achieve a different level of achievement. Or it could be successfully tackled in ways between those two extremes, such as helping the individual to explore alternative ways of doing the job over the next month and coming back to discuss progress after that time interval. What was important was that the individ-ual was guided to seeing that the job involved two sets of customers, internal and external, and that it was important for the team leader to give attention to both. How participants achieved that aim was up to them.

Retailco

Introduction

The third case is a British-based retailer, Retailco. Like many large retailers in Britain, it was finding organic growth within Britain hard to achieve. It was already market leader, with the market dominated by about five players. Growth in its main market was less than 5 per cent a year, with it achieving this or a little more, year by year. This was likely to be the case for the foreseeable future. It was innovative in expanding in other businesses, but its main core business was unlikely to grow substantially.

An obvious route for a company in this position is growth by acquisition. While this was an option, a few big players dominated the market, so, realistically, a major acquisition in its home market was unlikely. Another route was expansion into other markets, and this it was pursuing. A third route was expanding over-seas, and it is this route which concerns us here.

Recently, the markets of Eastern Europe have opened up considerably. Our case organisation saw this as an opportunity. In four or five countries in that part of the world, it acquired small businesses in its market sector, or, in some cases, developed those businesses from scratch.

The brief

But this presented the organisation with a difficulty from a human resources point of view. It was completely new to the issue of recruiting and employing a non-British workforce. To start with, it sent experienced, specialist managers from Britain and recruited skilled and semi-skilled workers locally. But this was only a stopgap measure. For the longer term it needed to develop indigenous managers. In Britain, it had a well-designed and long-standing assessment centre for the selec-tion of graduates who would become the senior managers of the future. This selection centre was regularly revised and checked for criterion validity. But could this centre be used for the assessment and selection of foreign graduates?

The design

The answer was a firm 'no'. The exercises and tests were not appropriate for can-didates from outside of Britain. It was not just the obvious differences, such as use of the English language or measurements in miles and gallons rather than kilo-metres and litres. It was the nature of the exercises themselves. Topics for group discussion, such as use of drugs by young people, have different meanings and importance for people from other cultures. Exercises dealing with the design of supermarkets are unlikely to work as well in countries less familiar with them. Tests not only have to have local norms and validation studies, but may not be as appropriate in countries where the whole concept of testing is unfamiliar and even disapproved of.

There was also the issue of whether the competencies were the same for gradu-ates being selected for a post within their own country and for a well-established, brand name company in its local market, compared to a start-up enterprise for a company which was small and unknown in its local market. Obviously, the compe-tencies were different. A competency analysis, similar to that described in the first two cases, was conducted. This revealed that being able to be independent of much day-to-day support was important. These managers would be big fish in small ponds, the opposite of new recruits in Britain. So they needed considerable confi-dence to back their own judgements and to act independently, when they were hundreds or thousands of miles from their head office in England. Similarly, the capacity for innovation and entrepreneurialism was much more important in Eastern Europe than it was in the home country. In effect, these managers would be in charge of their own business in a more fundamental way than they would be if running a store in Britain. Finally, a capacity for cultural awareness was important. The candidates would be groomed for the role of international manager. They would spend time in Britain, getting to know the business. They would spend time in their home country, learning about and, hopefully, expanding the business there. But this organisation had big expansion plans. It was considered likely that the European managers would often be transferred to foreign postings outside of their home market. So it was important for them to have not just the capacity to work in English, the international business language, but to be able to have some cultural sensitivity and awareness to be able to relate to, and work with, people from a wide range of different cultures. This was not a fundamental requirement for most of the British graduates being recruited in the organisation's home country.

So the whole assessment process was redesigned. Out went those stalwarts of the assessment centre, psychometric tests, since appropriate norms of sufficient sample size were not available. In addition, there were doubts about their accept-ability in cultures unfamiliar with such things.

Exercises which could assess the required competencies, such as cultural sensi-tivity, entrepreneurialism and independence, were designed. An exercise designed for the cultural issue was a group discussion, which involved candidates describing how they saw their own culture and the cultures represented in the group. Observers were trained to look for behaviours which indicated that a candidate was open-minded towards different views of his or her own culture, and aware of the ways in which his or her own culture could be viewed. Defensiveness about others' negative perceptions of one's own culture was a contraindication.

This approach is very much in the psychometric tradition: job analysis, followed by description of the job in competency terms, then design of exercises to assess that competency. What is different from the usual approach to the design of selection centres, though, is the cross-cultural dimension. This brings enormous challenges, as described in the case of Pharmco. Once again, the exercises were designed so that there was more than one route to success. How candidates tackled the exercise was much less important than the outcome.

Even here, though, the rational decision-making model was not adopted to the full. Candidates were expected to gain an 'acceptable' score on all competencies, but this was not always adhered to. Rules were 'broken' when a candidate was seen to perform exceptionally well in one or two exercises. There was no attempt to base decisions on a statistical or mathematical calculation of marks (sometimes called the actuarial method) whereby scores given for each competency are summed or weighted in some way. The decision was much more an intuitive feel (sometimes called the clinical approach) for what final grade a candidate should be given based on an impression of the suite of marks. In the early centres the assessors were a mix of expatriates and indigenous managers. The power and influence in contentious decisions about a certain candidate tended to lie with the expatriate. As the company became more established in the foreign market, and more and more expatriates became replaced with indigenous managers, the power shifted. So, even in this more traditional example, the rational decision-making model is found not to explain all purposes and outcomes.

Questions

1. Compare the three cases according to how far they conform to the rational decision-making perspective (i.e. the psychometric tradition) or to the interactive action-oriented perspective described in this chapter.

2. On the surface, the case of Newsco illustrates the design of a fairly standard assessment for development workshop in the psychometric tradition. What evidence is there to suggest that assessment is not the sole purpose? What other purposes might the centre serve?

3. In what ways is Pharmco an example of an assessment centre, a development centre, or a mix of the two?

4. Why is it important to consider the national/cultural dimension in the design of centres?

References to Chapter 2

Ackerman, B., Ross-Ackerman, S., Sawyer, J. and Henderson, D. (1974) *The Uncertain Research for Environmental Quality*, New York: Free Press.

Agor, W. (1986) 'The logic of intuition: How top executives make important decisions', *Organizational Dynamics*, Winter: 5–15.

Agor, W. (1989) *Intuition in organizations*, Newbury Park, CA: Sage.

Anderson, N. and Ostroff, C. (1997) 'Selection as socialization', in Anderson, N. and Herriot, P. (eds) *International Handbook of Selection and Assessment*, Chichester: Wiley.

Argyris, C. (1977) 'Organizational learning and management information systems', *Accounting, Organizations and Society*, 2: 113–123.

Arnold, J., Cooper, C. and Robertson, I. (1997) *Work Psychology: Understanding Human Behaviour in the Workplace*, London: Financial Times/Pitman Publishing.

Arvey, R.D. and Faley, R.H. (1992) *Fairness in Selecting Employees* (2nd edn), Reading, Mass: Addison-Wesley.

Bandura, A. (1977) 'Self-efficacy: Toward a unifying theory of behavioural change', *Psychological Review*, May: 191–215.

Barrick, M. and Mount, M. (1991) 'The big five personality dimensions and job performance: A meta-analysis', *Personnel Psychology*, 44: 1–26.

Batram, D. (2000) 'Internet recruitment and selection: kissing frogs to find princes', *International Journal of Selection and Assessment*, 8(4): 261–74.

Bazerman, M. (1994) *Judgement in managerial decision-making* (3rd edn), New York: Wiley.

Beach, L. (1990) *Image Theory: Decision Making in Personal and Organizational Contexts*, Chichester: John Wiley.

Behling, O. and Eckel, N. (1991) 'Making sense out of intuition', *Academy of Management Executives*, February: 46–54.

Boam, R. and Sparrow, P. (1992) *Designing and Achieving Competency: A Competency-Based Approach to Managing People and Organizations*, London: McGraw-Hill.

Boyle, S., Fullerton, J. and Wood, R. (1995) 'Do assessment/development centres use optimal evaluation procedures?', *International Journal of Selection and Assessment*, 3: 132–140.

Bray, D. and Grant, D. (1966) 'The assessment centre in the measurement of potential for business management', *Psychological Monographs*, 80(17) (Whole No. 625).

Brunsson, N. (1982) 'The irrationality of action and action rationality: decisions, ideologies and organizational actions', *Journal of Management Studies*, 19(1): 29–44.

Campbell, J.P. (1990) 'Modeling the performance prediction problem in industrial and organizational psychology', in Dunnette, M.D. and Hough, L.M. (eds) *Handbook of Industrial and Organizational Psychology* (2nd edn), Vol. 1, Palo Alto, CA: Consulting Psychologists Press.

Coe, T. (1992) *The Key to the Men's Club: Opening the Doors to Women in Management*, Corby: IM Foundation.

Cohen, M., March, J. and Olsen, J. (1971) 'A garbage can model of organizational choice', *Administrative Science Quarterly*, March: 1–25.

Cyert, R. and March, J. (1963) *A Behavioural Theory of the Firm*, Englewood Cliffs, NJ: Prentice Hall.

Day, D. and Silverman, S. (1989) 'Personality and job performance: Evidence of incremental validity', *Personnel Psychology*, 42: 25–36.

DiMilia, L., Smith, P. and Brown, D. (1994) 'Management selection in Australia: A comparison with British and French findings', *International Journal of Selection and Assessment*, 2: 80–90.

DiMilia, L. and Gorodecki, M. (1997) 'Some factors explaining the reliability of a structured interview at a work site', *International Journal of Selection and Assessment*, 5(4): 193–199.

Dipboye, R. (1992) 'Selection interviews: Process perspectives', Cincinnati, Oh.: South-Western.

Dipboye, R. (1997) 'Structured selection interviews: Why do they work? Why are they underutilized?' in Anderson, N. and Herriot, P. (eds) *International Handbook of Selection and Assessment*, Chichester: John Wiley.

Eden, D. and Shani, A. (1982) 'Pygmalion goes to boot camp: Expectancy, leadership and trainee performance', *Journal of Applied Psychology*, April: 194–199.

Festinger, L. (1957) *A Theory of Cognitive Dissonance*, New York: Harper Row.

Fiske, S. and Taylor, S. (1991) *Social Cognition*, New York: McGraw Hill.

Fleenor, J. (1996) 'Constructs and developmental assessment centres: Further troubling empirical findings', *Journal of Business and Psychology*, 10: 319–333.

Gaugler, B., Rosenthal, D., Thornton, G. and Bentson, C. (1987) 'Meta-analysis of assessment centre validity', *Journal of Applied Psychology*, 72: 493–511.

Ghiselli, E. (1973) 'The validity of aptitude tests in personnel selection', *Personnel Psychology*, 26: 461–77.

Gist, M. (1987) 'Self-efficacy: implications for organizational behaviour and human resource management', *Academy of Management Review*, July: 472–485.

Heffcut, A.I. and Arthur, W. (1994) 'Hunter and Hunter (1984) revisited: interview validity and entry level jobs', *Journal of Applied Psychology*, 79: 184–190.

Hennessy, J., Mabey, B. and Warr, P. (1998) 'Assessment centre observation procedures: an experimental comparison of traditional, checklist and coding methods', *International Journal of Selection and Assessment*, 6(4): 222–31.

Hesketh, B. (1999) 'Introduction' to the *International Journal of Selection and Assessment* special issue on biodata: *International Journal of Selection and Assessment*, 7(2): 55–56.

Hofstede, G., (1984) *Culture's Consequences: International Differences in Work-Related Values*, Sage Publications: London.

Hough, L., Eaton, N., Dunnette, M., Kamp, J. and McCloy, R. (1990) 'Criterion-related validities of personality constructs and the effect of response distortion on those validities', *Journal of Applied Psychology*, 75: 581–585.

Hunter, J. and Hunter, R. (1984) 'Validity and utility of alternative predictors of job performance, *Psychological Bulletin*, 96: 72–98.

Industrial Relations Service (1997) 'The state of selection: an IRS survey', *Employee Development Bulletin*, 85: 8–18.

Janis, I. (1972) *Victims of Groupthink*, Boston, Mass: Houghton Mifflin.

Janz, T. (1989) 'The patterned behaviour description interview: the best prophet of the future is the past', in Eder, R.D. and Ferris, G.R. (eds) *The Employment Interview: Theory and Practice*, London: Sage.

Joyce, L., Thayer, P. and Pond, S. (1994) 'Managerial functions: An alternative to traditional assessment centre dimensions?', *Personnel Psychology*, 47: 109–121.

Kauffman, J., Jex, S., Love, K. and Libkuman, T. (1993) 'The construct validity of assessment centre performance dimensions', *International Journal of Selection and Assessment*, 1: 213–23.

Keenan, T. (1995) 'Graduate recruitment in Britain: A survey of selection methods used by organizations', *Journal of Organizational Behaviour*, 16: 303–17.

Landis, R., Fogli, L. and Goldberg, E. (1998) 'Future-oriented job analysis: A description of the process and its organizational implications', *International Journal of Selection and Assessment*, 6(3): 192–97.

Landy, F., Shankster-Cawley, L. and Moran, S. (1995) 'Advancing personnel selection and placement methods', in Howard, A. (ed.) *The Changing Nature of Work*, San Francisco, CA: Jossey-Bass.

Lievens, F. (1998) 'Factors which improve the construct validity of Assessment Centres: A review', *International Journal of Selection and Assessment*, 6(3): 141–152.

Lind, E. and Tyler, T. (1988) *The Social Psychology of Procedural Justice*, New York: Plenum Press.

Lindblom, C.E. (1959) 'The science of "muddling through"', *Public Administration Review*, 19: 79–88.

Macan, T.H., Avedon, M.J., Paese, M. and Smith, D.E. (1994) 'The effects of applicants' reactions to cognitive ability tests and an assessment centre', *Personnel Psychology*, 47(4): 715–38.

Mael, F. (1991) 'A conceptual rationale for the domain and attributes of biodata items', *Personnel Psychology*, 44: 763–92.

March, J. and Olsen, J. (1976) *Ambiguity and Choice in Organizations*, Bergen: Universitetsforlaget.

Matthews, B. and Redman, T. (1998) 'Managerial recruitment advertisements – Just how market-orientated are they?', *International Journal of Selection and Assessment*, 6(4): 240–48.

Mayfield, E.C. (1964) 'The selection interview: A re-evaluation of published research', *Personnel Psychology*, 17: 239–60.

McCredie, H. and Shackleton, V.J. (1994) 'The development and interim validation of a dimensions-based senior management assessment centre', *Human Resources Management Journal*, 5(1): 91–101.

McDaniel, M.A., Whetzel, D.L., Schmidt, F.L. and Maurer, S.D. (1994) 'The validity of the employment interviews: a comprehensive review and meta-analysis', *Journal of Applied Psychology*, 79: 599–616.

Merrick, N. (1997) 'Big thaw shows up on recruitment market', *People Management*, 3(2): 10–11.

Mumford, M. and Stokes, G. (1992) 'Developmental determinants of individual action: Theory and practice in applying background measures', in Dunnette, M. & Hough, L. (eds) *Handbook of Industrial and Organizational Psychology*, 2nd edn, Vol. 3, 61–138), Palo Alto, Ca: Consulting Psychologists Press.

Newell, S. and Shackleton, V. (1993) 'The use (and abuse) of psychometric tests in British industry and commerce', *Human Resource Management Journal*, 4(1): 14–23.

Nisbett, R. and Ross, L. (1980) *Human Inference*, Englewood Cliffs, NJ: Prentice-Hall.

Pfeffer, J. (1981) *Power in organisations*, Marshfield, Mass: Pitman Publishing.

Redmond, S. (1989) *How to Recruit Good Managers*, London: Kogan Page.

Rees, C. (1996) 'Psychometrics: Topical misunderstandings amongst test users', *International Journal of Selection and Assessment*, 4(1): 44–48.

Robertson, I. and Kinder, A. (1993) 'Personality and job competences: The criterion-related validity of some personality variables', *Journal of Occupational and Organizational Psychology*, 66: 225–44.

Rosenfeld, P., Giacalone, R.A. and Riordan, C.A. (1995) *Impression Management in Organizations*, London: Routledge.

Salgado, J. (1996) 'Personality and job competences: a comment on Robertson and Kinder's (1993) study', *Journal of Occupational and Organizational Psychology*, 69: 373–75.

Schmitt, N., Gooding, R., Noe, R. and Kirsch, M. (1984) 'Meta-analyses of validity studies published between 1964 and 1982, and the investigation of study characteristics', *Personnel Psychology*, 37: 407–22.

Schneider, B. and Konz, A. (1989) 'Strategic job analysis', *Human Resource Management*, 28: 51–63.

Shackleton, V. and Newell, S. (1991) 'Management selection: a comparative survey of methods used in top British and French companies', *Journal of Occupational Psychology*, 64: 23–26.

Shackleton, V. and Newell, S. (1994) 'European selection methods: a comparison of five countries', *International Journal of Selection and Assessment*, 2: 91–102.

Simon, H. (1960) *The New Science of Management Decision*, New York: Harper and Row.

Singer, M. (1993) *Fairness in Personnel Selection*, Aldershot: Avebury.

Sparrow, P. and Bognanno, M. (1993) 'Competency requirement forecasting: issues for international selection and assessment', *International Journal of Selection and Assessment*, 1(1): 50–58.

Stokes, G., Hogan, J. and Snell, A. (1993) 'Comparability of incumbent and applicant samples for the development of biodata keys: the influence of social desirability', *Personnel Psychology*, 46: 739–62.

Stricker, L. and Rock, D. (1998) 'Assessing leadership potential with a biographical measure of personality traits', *International Journal of Selection and Assessment*, 6(3): 164–184.

Sundvik, L. and Lindeman, M. (1998) 'Performance rating accuracy: convergence between supervisor assessment and sales productivity', *International Journal of Selection and Assessment*, 6(1): 9–15.

Thornton, G. (1992) *Assessment Centres in Human Resource Management*, Reading, Mass: Addison Wesley.

Trompenaars, F. (1993) *Riding the Waves of Culture: Understanding Cultural Diversity in Business*, Nicholas Brealey Publishing: London.

Ulrich, L. and Trumbo, D. (1965) 'The selection interview since 1949', *Psychological Bulletin*, 53: 100–116.

Vaughan, D. (1996) *The Challenger Launch Decision: Risky Technology, Culture, and Deviance at NASA*, Chicago, Il: University of Chicago Press.

Vaughan, D. (1997) 'The trickle-down effect: policy decisions, risky work and the Challenger tragedy', *California Management Review*, 39(2): 80–102.

Weick, K.E. (1990)'Technology as equivoque: sensemaking in new technologies', in Goodman, P.S., Sproull, L.S. and Associates, *Technology and Organisations*, Oxford: Jossey-Bass.

Zedeck, S. (1986) 'A process analysis of the assessment centre method', in Shaw, B. and Cummings, L. (eds) *Research in Organizational Behaviour*, 8: 259–96, Greenwich, CT: JAI Press.

Chapter 3

Performance appraisal

Tom Redman

Introduction

The practice of performance appraisal has undergone many major changes over the last decade or so. In the main developments have been driven by large-scale organisational change (see Chapter 1) rather than theoretical advances in the study of performance appraisal. Particularly prominent here are the advent of downsizing, decentralisation and delayering, flexibilisation of the workforce, the move to teamworking, and wave after wave of culture change programmes and new managerial initiatives such as TQM, BPR, competency and in particular Investors in People. The most recent WERS data finds that organisations which are recognised as an Investor in People were significantly more likely to have a performance appraisal scheme in use (Cully *et al.*, 1999). Changes in payment systems have also fuelled the growth and development of performance appraisal. Developments in integrated reward systems, harmonisation and the increased use of merit- and performance-based pay have been strongly associated with the growth of performance appraisal.

Two main implications for performance appraisal practice arise from the new organisational context. Firstly, it would be clearly inappropriate to expect that those appraisal schemes operating ten years or so ago could be effective in many organisations today (see Case Study 3.1). Secondly, rather than new developments heralding the end of performance appraisal or diminishing its importance, they appear to have enhanced its contribution to helping achieve organisational objectives and stimulated considerable experimentation and innovation in its practice. Performance appraisal, as we discuss below, has in fact become more widespread. It has grown to include previously untouched organisations and occupational groups. In particular, performance appraisal has moved down the organisational hierarchy to encompass blue-collar, secretarial and administrative staff, and from the private to the public sector. New forms of appraisal have also emerged. We thus now have competency-based appraisal systems, staff appraisal of managers, team-based appraisal, customer appraisals and the so-called '360°' systems.

This chapter's main aim is to review some of the key developments in the practice of performance appraisal. Firstly, a brief history of performance appraisal is presented and its current practice examined by considering how widespread it is, what it is used for, and its role as a managerial control tool within broader performance management systems. Secondly, we review some of the major innovations in the practice of performance appraisal. Thirdly, some of the problems of performance appraisal in practice are considered – in particular, we examine here the compatibility of performance appraisal with TQM and customer service initiatives. Finally, in light of the growing criticisms, we conclude by considering whether performance appraisal has a future in HRM practice.

Development of performance appraisal

Informal systems of performance appraisal have been around as long as people have worked together; it is a universal human tendency to make evaluations of our colleagues at work. Formal performance appraisals have a shorter but still considerable history. Grint (1993) traces it back to a third-century Chinese practice. In the UK Randell (1989) identifies its first use via the 'silent monitor' in Robert Owen's textile mills. Here a multi-coloured block of wood was hung over the employee's workspace with the front colour indicating the foreman's assessment of the previous day's conduct, from white for good through to black for bad. Owen also recorded a yearly assessment of employees in a 'book of character'.

Since these early developments performance appraisal has now become a staple element of HRM practice, although personnel managers have tended to be much keener on it than their line manager colleagues (see below). Accompanying practitioner interest in performance appraisal has been a mushrooming of academic research, notably by occupational psychologists. A key thrust of much of this research has been on improving performance appraisal's effectiveness, and in particular, its accuracy in assessing employee performance. We know rather less about a more strategic use of performance appraisal as an organisational change lever and managerial control tool. There is now a wealth of academic studies on performance appraisal. A computer literature search of one year alone in the USA reports a 'conservative' figure of 11 articles per month appearing with 'performance appraisal' in their titles (Halachmi, 1993). Despite the large and growing volume of research work on the subject, however, it is debatable how much influence such studies have had on the actual practice of performance appraisal (Maroney and Buckley, 1992). It seems that managers are peculiarly reluctant to heed the advice of researchers in this area of business practice and there is an increasing gap between research and practice (Banks and Murphy, 1985).

This lack of impact of research on practice is not simply a question of general managerial indifference to the academic researcher, especially when compared to the wide influence of consultants and popular management gurus. Rather, one explanation is that little of the research has considered the implications for practitioners who are faced with a plethora of organisational constraints not encountered in the research laboratory. More damning perhaps is the view that much of the research has had little to offer HR managers, except for the recommendation to train appraisers, as it has generally been unable to provide much improvement – in terms of accuracy at least – over the simplest of supervisory ratings systems (Giffin, 1989).

The practice of performance appraisal

How widespread is performance appraisal?

Performance appraisal has become more widespread in Western countries. For example, surveys report performance appraisal in the USA increasing from 89 per cent of organisations surveyed in the mid-1970s to 94 per cent by the mid-1980s (Locher and Teel, 1988). Similar surveys in the UK by the Institute of Personnel and Development report increasing coverage of formal appraisal arrangements (Long, 1986; Armstrong and Baron, 1998). Performance appraisal is also now more common in many other non-Western countries, such as China (Chow, 1994), Hong Kong (Snape et al., 1998), Japan in the form of Satei (see Endo, 1994); Africa (Arthur et al., 1995) and India (Lawler et al., 1995).

Appraisal is particularly prominent in some industrial sectors in the UK, such as financial services (IRS, 1994, 1999), and it has grown rapidly in the public sector of late. The last decade has seen its introduction in schools, hospitals, universities, local authorities, the civil service, etc. For example, some 80 per cent of local authorities surveyed either operated or were currently introducing performance appraisal (IRS, 1995a). It has also grown from its main deployment in the middle of organisation hierarchies, particularly in middle management and professional occupations, to include a much broader group of manual and clerical employees (Cully et al., 1999). Increasingly it seems, in line with harmonisation policies, that all employees in an organisation are included in the performance system appraisal. An IRS survey found that 39 per cent of organisations applied appraisal to every employee (IRS, 1994) and a replication of the survey five years later found 75 per cent to do so (IRS, 1999). The coverage of employees in the public sector, given the relative infancy of many schemes, is still rather more limited than the private sector. The IRS found only 17 per cent of public sector organisations surveyed included all employees in the scheme. However, these claims can be misleading. Employers who include the growing numbers of 'contingent' or 'peripheral' workers, such as part-time and contract staff, in performance appraisal schemes appear to be the exception rather than the rule (Syrett and Lammiman, 1994).

How is appraisal conducted?

A wide range of methods are used to conduct performance appraisals, from the simplest of ranking schemes through objective-, standard- and competency-based systems (see below) to complex behaviourally anchored rating schemes (see Snape *et al.*, 1994). The nature of an organisation's appraisal scheme is largely a reflection of its managerial beliefs (Randell, 1994), the amount of resources it has available to commit, and the expertise it possesses. Thus, smaller organisations with limited HR expertise tend to adopt simpler ranking and rating schemes whilst the more complex and resource consuming systems, such as competency-based and 360° appraisal, are found mainly in larger organisations.

Most employers use only one type of appraisal scheme, often a 'hybrid form' of a number of methods and a few companies even provide employees with a choice of methods in how they are appraised. The IRS surveys (IRS, 1994, 1999) found many organisations with more than one system of performance appraisal operating. The main reason behind multiple systems was the wish to separate out reward and non-reward aspects of appraisal, and to provide different systems for different occupational groups (e.g. managerial and non-managerial employees), and separate systems for different parts of the organisation.

What is it used for?

Organisations use performance appraisal for a wide range of different purposes. Surveys commonly report the use of performance appraisal for clarifying and defining performance expectations; identifying training and development needs; providing career counselling; succession planning; improving individual, team and corporate performance; facilitating communications and involvement; allocating financial rewards; determining promotion, motivating and controlling employees, and achieving cultural change (Bowles and Coates, 1993; IRS, 1994, 1999).

Recent trends suggest that the more judgmental and 'harder' forms of performance appraisal are on the increase and that 'softer', largely developmental approaches are declining (Gill, 1977; Long, 1986; Armstrong and Baron, 1998). Thus there has been a shift in performance appraisal away from using it for career planning and identifying future potential and increased use of it for improving current performance and allocating rewards. Here the arrival of flatter organisations has given rise to the need to uncouple to some extent performance appraisal and promotion whilst competitive pressures have emphasised the need to incentivise improvements in short-term performance.

There are both advantages and disadvantages to such broad demands upon performance appraisal systems. A wide use helps to integrate various, often disparate, HRM areas into a coherent package of practices. For example, by providing a link between performance and rewards, and development needs and succession planning, more effective HRM outcomes are possible. However, it also gives rise to the common criticism that performance appraisal systems are simply too ambitious in that managers expect them to be able to accommodate a very wide range of purposes. The breadth of use thus results in appraisal becoming a 'blunt instrument that tries to do too much' (Boudreaux, 1994).

Further, many of the above purposes of appraisal are seen as being in conflict. Thus, recording the past and influencing future performance is difficult to achieve in a single process. The danger is that appraisal, particularly given the trends identified above, concentrates on the past at the expense of the future performance, with a common analogy being that this is rather like using the rear view mirror to drive future performance. Similarly, allocating rewards and identifying training needs are often seen as being incompatible objectives in a single appraisal scheme. The openness required for meaningfully assessing development needs is closed down by the need for the employee to 'explain away' performance problems in order to gain a merit rise. However, the danger of disconnecting reward allocation from appraisal is that appraisers and appraised would not treat the process as seriously because without it appraisal lacks bite and 'fires blank bullets' (Lawler, 1994). Increasingly, as we now examine, performance appraisal is used as one element of a much broader performance management system.

Performance management

Performance management, like many HRM innovations, is an American import that has been a major driver in the increased use of performance appraisal by British organisations. Performance management has been defined as 'systems and attitudes which help organisations to plan, delegate and assess the operation of their services' (LGMB, 1994). Bevan and Thompson (1991) describe a 'textbook' performance management system thus:

- a shared vision of the organisation's objectives communicated via a mission statement to all employees
- individual performance targets which are related to operating unit and wider organisational objectives
- regular formal review of progress towards targets
- a review process which identifies training and development needs and rewards outcomes
- an evaluation of the effectiveness of the whole process and its contribution to overall organisational performance to allow changes and improvements to be made.

A principal feature of performance management is thus that it connects the objectives of the organisation to a system of work targets for individual employees. In such models of performance management objective setting and formal appraisal are placed at the heart of the approach. The development of performance management systems has had major implications for performance appraisal. A key trend has been away from stand-alone performance appraisal systems and towards individual appraisal becoming part of an integrated performance management system. Bevan and Thompson's survey for the IPM found some 20 per cent of British organisations had introduced performance management systems.

There is a growing critique of performance management systems. Firstly, they are seen as adding more pressure to a short-term view amongst British managers, which may well hamper organisational performance over the long term. Secondly, they are often proffered in a very prescriptive fashion, with many writers advocating a single best way for performance management, to the neglect of important variables such as degree of centralisation, unionisation, etc. This is in contrast to the actual practice of performance management in the UK, which is 'extremely diverse' (Fletcher and Williams, 1992). The real danger is that performance management systems cannot be simply borrowed from one organisation and applied in another, as many advocates appear to suggest. Thirdly, although performance management is supposed to be line management 'driven' (Fowler, 1990), case studies of its practices report the motivating forces in organisations as being chief executives and HR departments with often questionable ownership and commitment from line managers (Fletcher and Williams, 1992). Fourthly, there is a growing concern that performance management systems, because of their dedicated focus on improving the bottom line, have added unduly to the pressures and stresses of work-life for many employees. Many systems have been introduced with scant regard for employee welfare (see Box 3.1). Lastly, and perhaps more damning, is the view that it is ineffective. The main driver of performance management is the improvement of overall organisational effectiveness. However, there is little support from various studies that performance management actually improves performance. For example, Bevan and Thompson's survey of performance management in the UK found that there was no relationship between high-performing UK companies (defined as those demonstrating pre-tax profit growth over a five-year period) and the operation of a performance management system.

Performance appraisal as managerial control

With the decline of careers in the flat, delayered organisation, HRM techniques such as performance appraisal have become more significant managerial tools in motivating and controlling the workforce. Appraisal is now seen by some commentators as being much more significant in maintaining employee loyalty and commitment than in directly managing performance (Bowles and Coates, 1993). Its use provides managers with a major opportunity to reinforce corporate values and attitudes and so it appeals as an important strategic instrument in the control process. Thus, we find a growing use of appraisal systems for non-managerial employees that are based on social, attitudinal and trait attributes (Townley, 1989). Employees are increasingly being appraised not only on 'objective' measures such as attendance, timekeeping, productivity and quality but also on more subjective aspects such as 'dependability', 'flexibility', 'initiative', 'loyalty', etc.

Recent analyses of performance appraisal, based upon the work of Foucault, have given particular emphasis to the power relations implicit in performance appraisal. For Townley performance appraisal has the potential to act as the 'paper equivalent' of the panopticon with its 'anonymous and continuous surveillance'

BOX 3.1

Stretching the American workforce

A new approach to performance management in the USA is the so-called 'stretch management'. Instead of a traditional approach of generating more output by committing more input 'corporate America seems to be trying to get more output just by demanding more output' (Sherman, 1995: 231). It is being applied in US companies such as Boeing (to drive down costs) and 3M (to improve product innovation). Stretch management involves setting demanding objectives – 'stetch targets' – for the organisation.

Accounts chronicle its success in achieving major performance improvements in areas such as return of investment, product innovation, productivity, capital utilisation (Tully, 1994). Alcoa, the world's largest aluminium company, provides a good example. Following the appointment of a new chief executive, a large scale TQM programme was initiated in 1987 and, by many standards, proved highly successful (Kolesar, 1993). However, by 1991 a new strategy emerged due to the CEO's frustration with the slow pace of TQM. The new strategy demanded intense and focused commitment to 'quantum leap' rather than continuous improvement management.

Given its recent introduction it is perhaps too early to write off 'stretch management'. Nevertheless, its sustainability must be open to question and critics view it simply as one of the latest and most intense forms of 'management by stress'. Indeed, early reports show an especially high casualty rate amongst middle managers, with estimates of between a third and a half of managers being unable to cope (Tully, 1994). Some companies have now 'softened' their stretch programmes. At General Electric its role is seen as an 'artificial stimulant' for new and more effective ways of working and employees are not punished for failing to achieve demanding targets (Sherman, 1995). This leads to a particular problem with stretch management: its demotivation potential. The danger is that such a system of performance management which sets truly stretching goals, which employees thus often fail to achieve, results in high-performing staff feeling like losers. In an attempt to get employees to buy into stretch programmes some companies are now linking the achievement of targets to gainsharing programmes.

(1993: 232). Recent developments in appraisal, which have both broadened the range of, and increased the number of appraisers, via 360° appraisal, upward appraisal and the use of external customers (see below), have increased the potential for managerial control and the utilisation of the panoptical powers of performance appraisal. In such systems the employee is now continually exposed to the appraiser's 'constant yet elusive presence' (Fuller and Smith, 1991: 11). Every customer, peer, subordinate and colleague is now also a potential appraiser. Thus it is hardly surprising that employees have nicknamed peer reviews of performance 'screw your buddy' systems of appraisal.

Managers themselves are not immune from the disciplinary 'gaze' of performance appraisal (see next section). Managerial attitudes, especially at middle management levels, have often been identified as a barrier to the introduction of new ways of managing, such as employee involvement and empowerment. The use of upward appraisal of managers by staff is increasingly being used to link managerial behaviour more closely with corporate values and mission statements by incorporating questions on these into appraisal instruments which are completed by the employee (Redman and Snape, 1992). Thus at one and the same time organisations promote their required values to their employees and evaluate the commitment of their managers to these. Managers scoring badly in such appraisals are often 'culled' (see Redman and Mathews, 1995). Thus, for example, at Semco, the much-discussed Brazilian company, managers are upwardly appraised every six months using a scale up to 100. The results are then posted on a notice board and those who consistently underperform are squeezed out or simply 'fade away'.

Recent developments in performance appraisal

As we noted in the introduction, there have been many innovations in performance appraisal practice. In this section we discuss some of the more influential of these.

Upward appraisal

Upward appraisal is a relatively recent addition to performance appraisal practice in the UK. Although it is still far from common, the 1990s have witnessed the introduction of upward appraisal in a range of UK companies. Upward appraisal is more common in the USA and appears to have spread from US parent companies to their UK operations (e.g. at companies such as Federal Express, Standard Chartered Bank, and AMEX) and from these to UK companies such as WH Smith, The Body Shop and parts of the UK public sector (see Redman and Mathews, 1995). Upward appraisal involves the employee rating their manager's performance via, in most cases, an anonymous questionnaire. The process is anonymous to overcome employees' worries about providing honest but unfavourable feedback on managerial performance. Anonymity limits the potential for managerial retribution or what is termed the 'get even' factor of upward appraisal.

Advocates claim significant benefits for upward appraisal (see Redman and Snape, 1992) including improved managerial effectiveness and leadership through 'make-you-better' feedback and increased employee voice and empowerment. Equally, upward appraisal is seen as being more in tune with the delayered organisation where managerial spans of control are greater and working arrangements much more diverse. In such situations employees are in much greater contact with their manager than is the manager's manager and thus traditional top-down boss appraisal is seen as being less effective. Upward appraisal, because of the use of multiple raters, is also seen as being more robust to legal challenge of performance judgements. Given the increasingly litigatious culture in the UK, Townley (1990) has noted that it is surprising that performance appraisal methods and the systems in which they are embedded are not attacked in the courts more often.

Managers have been reported as not being especially fond of upward appraisal systems. In part this may stem from the career-threatening use of upward appraisal schemes in some organisations. For example, one of BP Exploration's objectives in introducing upward appraisal was to return to individual contribution roles those managers 'clearly not cut out to manage people' (Thomas *et al.*, 1992). Often it appears to the manager on the receiving end of upward appraisal that, according to Grint (1993), '. . ."the honest opinions" of subordinates look more like the barbs on a whale harpoon than gentle and constructive nudges'. Such a lack of managerial acceptance of upward appraisal, especially at middle and junior levels of management, may go some way to explaining its relatively low uptake in the UK after a flurry of activity in the early 1990s.

360° performance appraisal

The so-called 360° appraisals appear to be taking root and becoming an established form of appraisal in the UK (see Box 3.2). A survey by consultants Pilat reported up to 40 per cent of FTSE companies are now using it. Although considerable, such a usage rate is somewhat behind the three-quarters of Fortune 500 companies reported as employing 360° appraisal in a similar US survey (*Personnel Management*, July, 1995 p. 15). Dudgill (1994) traces the origins of 360° appraisal to the US army in the 1970s. Here military researchers found that peers' opinions were more accurate indicators of a soldier's ability than those of superiors were. The term '360°' is used to describe the comprehensive nature of feedback derived from a composite rating from peers, subordinates, supervisors and occasionally customers. Again, it is normally conducted via an anonymous survey, although some recent innovations include the use of audio and videotape to record feedback answers. Some organisations also use on-line computerised data-gathering systems as well as more informal systems where managers simply pass a disk around a number of appraisers. One management consultancy, in order to encourage responses, is experimenting with 'fun' methods of collecting data such as using short statements comparing individual managers with well-known characters (CPCR, 1995).

There is a wide variation in what is appraised in 360° feedback. Many companies use fully structured questionnaires based upon models of managerial competency. Others, such as Dupont, which uses 360° appraisal in its Individual Career Management programme, employ a much less structured approach. Here appraisers respond to open questions, which ask for descriptions of the appraiser's 'major value-adding areas for the year'; summaries of the manager's strengths; descriptions of key improvement needs, and a request for other general comments. Unstructured systems of appraisal have advantages in tapping into key aspects of managerial performance. Nevertheless, the danger of using an unstructured approach is that the popular but incompetent manager may well fare better than one who is highly effective but not particularly pleasant. Mostly the appraisers remain anonymous but some systems, such as Dupont's, leave the option open to

---

BOX 3.2

360° appraisal at Northumbrian Water

Following the hot dry summer of 1995 and accompanying water shortages, adverse public relations and intense media interest, life has been particularly difficult for managers in the newly privatised water companies. One company, Northumbrian Water, has been helping its managers to cope with a range of management development practices, including 360° appraisal.

Northumbrian Water introduced a 360° feedback programme for its managers in 1990 via a pilot group of 35 managers. A key reason behind the introduction was to provide data for the company's development centre for senior managers. The development centre was designed to enable managers to move to a position of managing their own career development. It was considered important that individual managers should have a view from their colleagues about their performance, potential and development needs in order to facilitate sound career decisions. The 360° appraisal instrument consists of a bank of questions asking respondents to comment on the effectiveness and performance of the appraised manager against three main categories: competence, style and role. Appraisers, for example, are asked to say how often they see the candidate behave in a particular fashion which is consistent with the behaviours listed for a senior manager. Space is also provided for open comments on the manager's performance and the company feels it is often these which prove the most enlightening.

The system is based upon a refined competency model originally developed in 1981. The competencies model was further developed following privatisation of the industry as the roles and styles of management appropriate to the company's new values were developed. For example, commercial awareness and customer care were not present in the original formulation. A study of HRM practices in the post-privatization water industry considers Northumbrian Water to have introduced the 'most dramatic changes' of all the companies (IRS, 1992).

The feedback forms are distributed to 10–12 of the manager's colleagues in some form of distribution such as two above, five sideways and four below the individual manager. Internal customers are often part of the process but the company has yet to incorporate external customers. The forms are returned directly to the company's consultants who produce a summary data booklet, discuss the results with the manager, and help prepare them for the development centre.

The main benefit the company perceives it has obtained from 360° feedback is in providing individual managers with vital insights into some of their shortcomings, which would otherwise remain unaddressed. Although it has been somewhat of a shock for some, managers are considered to be much more self-aware about their leadership qualities and are felt to be working better with their staff. 360° appraisal is also seen as making a valuable contribution in encouraging managers to engage in continuous professional development and encouraging an approach where performance problems can be positively tackled through training and development. One of the main problems the company has found with its implementation is that in the early programmes there was some difficulty in convincing managers that such feedback was of value because their development and career planning was within their own remit rather than that of their boss. A few individuals also had great difficulty in accepting the feedback and searched for reasons to rationalise it.

Source: interviews with managers

the appraiser whether or not to add their name to the appraisal form. However, unless a composite rating only is presented to the manager – and this tends to counter the value of having multiple perspectives in 360° – it is very difficult to provide the immediate supervisor with anonymity.

It seems that 360° appraisal is edging away from a management development tool and towards a broader organisational role. Increasingly, and controversially, it seems that organisations are also experimenting with linking 360° appraisal and managerial remuneration. The press has recently reported companies such as 3M and British Aerospace as introducing 360° appraisal and feeding the results into the formula for performance-related pay for managers. Rather a lot is claimed for 360° appraisal and, as in the case of many new initiatives, we have seen a rash of articles announcing how it can 'change your life' (O'Reilly, 1994), and deliver competitive advantage for the organisation (London and Beatty, 1993). Because of its use of multiple raters with different perspectives – a sort of safety in numbers approach – it is often suggested that it provides more accurate and meaningful feedback. However, as Grint (1993) notes, this often simply replaces the subjectivity of a single appraiser with the subjectivity of multiple appraisers.

Undoubtedly, many organisations have gained some advantages from using 360° appraisal, particularly in management developmental terms. It has proved especially useful for providing feedback for senior managers who are often neglected at the top in appraisal terms. A strength of 360° appraisal is that management consultants proffering systems will tailor a basic questionnaire to meet the organisation's characteristics such as culture, mission, business values, and structure and management practices. It remains to be seen whether the benefits gained are outweighed by the considerable time, effort and costs involved. Indeed it seems some management consultants are 'gravy training' on the back of the current enthusiasm for 360° appraisal with week-long feedback courses, facilitated by themselves, recommended to debrief managers.

One key advantage of the broad group of appraisers used in this method is that it can provide a more meaningful appraisal for employees with little contact with their workplace. In such situations traditional top-down appraisals are of little value. A good example is provided by Burger King, which in a recent re-organisation, now has over half of all managerial staff working in the field (*Financial Times*, 13 September, 1995, p. 15). Such managers are based at home and communicate with head office via computerised telecommunications equipment. The aim of the reorganisation was to force managerial staff into closer contact with the restaurant staff. Clearly, top-down appraisal is of little value in such a low-contact working relationship. Thus Burger King introduced 360° assessment whereby up to 10 colleagues provide an assessment of the manager against some 83 behavioural characteristics. Although the system is not perfect – one manager described the process as having your personality dissected by ten people you have hardly met – the company feels that it provides a more meaningful assessment process for its field managers.

A number of questions remain unanswered about 360° appraisal – not least whether the data generated is accurate, valid and, more importantly, meaningful for the appraisee and whether the organisation stands to benefit from it. Ratings are only as good as the questions asked and often the interpretation of question wording is far from clear in many instruments. Such questions as 'Does the manager deal with problems in a flexible manner?' are not uncommon in appraisal instruments. Items need to be clear, easy to understand and easy to rate given the rater's contact with the appraisee. One particular criticism of many 360° systems is that all raters are given the same instrument, despite the different nature of the contact with the appraisee. Some issues are clearly more visible to the rater from different vantage points and questionnaires should ideally be constructed accordingly. Items based on actual behaviours, key organisational competencies, or critical incidents observed in the workplace indicative of superior-performing managers tend to be more effective. However, respondents will usually provide ratings on whatever questions are asked, whether they are in a position to do so or not.

There is also a tendency to produce overly bureaucratic systems. The danger here is that one common cause of failure in performance appraisal – that of requiring participants to fill in large quantities of paperwork – is being ignored. Making the feedback meaningful is also a challenge to which many users of 360° appraisal fail to rise. To ensure meaningful feedback a process of self-appraisal, comparison against other managers' ratings and follow-up with facilitators and those who provided the ratings are the minimum required. Also there is an implicit expectation on the part of those providing the ratings that such feedback will lead to improvements and that managers will change their behaviour for the better. However, there is as yet little evidence that this actually occurs (e.g. Redman and McElwee, 1993).

Lastly, many so called 360° appraisal systems are far from an all-round view of managers; the external customer as a reviewer is often left out but, as we discuss in the next section, customers are an increasingly heard voice in the assessment of employee performance. 360° appraisal, it seems, is also only a starting point and as management consultants 'discover' new sources of raters we can look forward to such innovations as 450° and even 540° appraisal.

Customer appraisal

TQM and customer care programmes are now very widespread in both private and public sectors in the UK. One impact of these initiatives is that organisations are now increasingly setting employee performance standards based upon customer care indicators and appraising staff against these. A mix of 'hard' quantifiable standards such as 'delivery of a customer's first drink within two minutes' and soft qualitative standards such as 'a warm and friendly greeting', as used at Forte Roadside Restaurants, are now used in performance appraisal systems (IRS, 1995b). Employee performance standards, when linked into customer care policies, need to be realistic, achievable, and measurable. The use of service guarantees, which involve the payment of compensatory moneys to customers if the organisations do not reach the standards has also led to a greater use of customer data in performance appraisal ratings.

Customer service data for use in appraising employees is gathered by a variety of methods. Firstly, there is the use of a range of customer surveys, via the completion of customer care cards, telephone surveys, interviews with customers, postal surveys, etc. Organisations are now using such surveys more frequently and are increasingly sophisticated in how they gather customer views (Silvestro, 1990). Secondly, there is a range of surveillance techniques used by managers to sample the service encounter. Here the electronic work monitoring of factory workers is being extended into the services sector (Laabs, 1992). For example, customer service managers at Mercury Communications spend some 30 hours of their time each month reviewing staff performance by taping staff–customer conversations and giving immediate feedback as well as using the data for the regular formal review process.

Third, and even more controversial, is the increasing use of the so-called 'mystery shopping'. For some commentators customer service can only be really effectively evaluated at the boundary between customer and organisation and this view has fuelled the growth of shopping as a data capturing process (Miles, 1993). Here staff employed by a specialist agency purport to be real shoppers and observe and record their experience of the service encounter. It is now commonly used in banks, insurance companies, supermarkets and parts of the public sector (see Moores, 1990; Ring, 1992). For example, an element of the Citizen's Charter requires the setting of performance indicators on answering telephone calls and letters. Some local authorities evaluate the quality of telephone responses by employing consultants to randomly call the authority and assess the quality of the response (IRS, 1995b).

Mystery shopping is argued to give a company a rich source of data that cannot be uncovered by other means, such as customer surveys. Such surveys, although useful for some purposes, are often conducted many months after the service encounter and thus exact service problems are difficult to recollect. Mystery shopping is also seen as being particularly useful in revealing staff performance that causes customers to leave without purchasing. In many service sector organisations a natural consequence of the use of mystery shoppers has been to utilise the data in the performance evaluations of staff (Fuller and Smith, 1991).

These data gathering methods are, as one could well expect, not very popular with staff. Employees often question the ethics of introducing shoppers and feel that it represents a distinct lack of managerial trust in them. Thus employees describe shoppers in terms of 'spies' and 'snoopers' and react with hostility and 'shopper spotting' to their introduction. The introduction of mystery shopping for the largely negative reason of catching staff performing poorly only fuels such reactions. Cook (1993) advises that using shoppers as a means to reward staff for good performance, rather than to punish staff for poor performance, can help their acceptance. Staff who obtain good mystery shopping ratings should be rewarded and recognised whilst those who obtain poor ones should use them as a way of identifying training needs.

In an increasing number of organisations internal service level agreements are also being established. The introduction of compulsory competitive tendering has given considerable impetus to such agreements in the public sector. Often in such agreements there is an internal customer-service 'guarantee' stating what level and the nature of services the supplier will provide. It has been a natural progression of such a development for organisations such as Federal Express and Digital to incorporate performance data from service level agreements into the appraisal process (e.g. Milliman *et al.*, 1995). A key advantage claimed for using internal customers in this way is that joint goal-setting helped to give both internal customer and provider a greater understanding of the roles that individuals and departments fulfil. It thus helps in breaking down internal barriers between departments.

Team-based appraisal

Work is increasingly being restructured into highly interdependent work teams, yet, despite this, performance appraisal often remains stubbornly based on the individual. In some cases teams are being given more responsibility for allocating work tasks, setting bonuses, selecting new staff, and even disciplining errant members. For such organisations it has thus been seen as entirely appropriate that performance appraisals should also be based upon and even conducted by the team themselves.

Two main variants of team appraisal can be identified. In some approaches the manager appraises the team as a whole. Targets are set, performance measured and assessments made, and rewards are allocated as with traditional individual appraisals. The manager makes no attempt to differentiate one member from another in performance terms, in fact, the creation of internal inequity with respect to rewarding performance is a deliberate aspect (Lawler, 1994). Equal ratings and rewards ensue for all the team, regardless of performance. The team are then encouraged to resolve internally any performance problems or competence deficiencies in order to facilitate overall team performance and development. Team members themselves may then provide informal awards or recognition of superior performance. The other main variant is where individual appraisals of each team member are still made but not by management. Rather, in a form of peer appraisal, team members appraise each other, usually via the use of anonymous rating questionnaires.

Competency-based appraisal

Interest in the concept of competency has been one of the major HR themes of the last decade. Connock (1992) describes it as one of HRM's 'big ideas'. One consequence of this has been the attempt by some organisations to use the competency approach to develop an integrated human resource strategy. This has been particularly pronounced in HR practices targeted at managers but is also growing for non-managerial groups. A consequence of the development of organisational competency models has been that employers have increasingly extended their use from training and development, selection and reward uses into the area of appraisal (e.g. Mitrani *et al.*, 1992). For example, the most widely reported innovation in performance appraisal systems during the 1990s has been the linking of appraisals to competency frameworks (IRS, 1999).

The assessment of competencies in the appraisal process has a number of benefits. The evaluation of competencies identified as central to a good job performance provides a useful focus for analysing the progress an individual is making in the job rather than the static approach of many ability- or trait-rating schemes. Thus competency-based assessment is especially useful in directing employee attention to areas where there is scope for improvement. The use of competencies broadens appraisal by including 'How well is it done' measures in addition to the more traditional 'What is achieved measures'. It also helps to concentrate the appraisal process on the key area of performance and effectiveness and provides a language for feedback on performance problems (Sparrow, 1994: 9). This latter benefit overcomes one of the problems of traditional objective-based appraisal systems in which the appraiser is often at a loss as to how to counsel an employee on what they should do differently if the appraisal objectives have not been achieved. However, these benefits must be set against the development and running costs involved and the wider critical debate surrounding the 'competency movement' in general.

Problems of performance appraisal

Performance appraisals appear to be one human resource activity that everyone loves to hate. Carroll and Schneier's (1982) research found that performance appraisal ranks as the most disliked managerial activity. It is frequently suggested in the popular management literature that most managers would prefer to have a dental appointment rather than conduct a performance appraisal. Many appraisees, it seems, would also prefer this! According to Grint (1993: 64) 'rarely in the history of business can such a system have promised so much and delivered so little'.

The critics of performance appraisal claim that it is expensive; causes conflict between appraised and appraiser; has limited value and may even be dysfunctional in the improvement of employee performance; and, despite the rhetoric its use contributes little to the strategic management of an organisation. It is also held to be riddled with so many distorting 'effects' that its accuracy in providing an indicator of actual employee performance must also be called into question (see Box 3.3). Some appraisal systems, especially the more judgmental, those tied in to merit pay systems and those with forced distributions are argued to be especially problematic in these respects. Thus, for many writers performance appraisal is 'doomed' (Halachmi, 1993); a managerial practice 'whose time has gone' (Fletcher, 1993; Bhote, 1994) and whose end is imminently predicted (Roth and Ferguson, 1994).

Why does performance appraisal not work? One reason is that, despite their widely held belief to the contrary, most managers are not naturally good at conducting performance appraisals. According to Lawler (1994: 17), it is an

---

BOX 3.3

Cronies and doppelgangers in performance appraisal

The search for accurate performance appraisals is a seemingly illusory one, with many pitfalls and distorting effects strewn in the appraiser's path. Some of the main ones are:

- *Halo effects* – This is where one positive criterion distorts the assessment of others. Similarly the *horns effect* is where a single negative aspect dominates the appraisal rating.

- *Doppelganger effect* – This is where the rating reflects the similarity between appraiser and appraised.

- *Crony effect* – This is the result of appraisal being distorted by the closeness of the relationship between appraiser and appraised.

- *Veblen effect* – This is named after Veblen's practice of giving all his students the grade C irrespective of the quality of their efforts. Thus all those appraised received middle-order ratings.

- *Impression effect* – This is the problem of distinguishing actual performance from calculated 'impression-management'. The impression management tactics of employees can result in supervisors liking them more and thus rating their job performance more highly. Employees often attempt to manage their reputations by substituting measures of process (effort, behaviour, etc.) for measures of outcome (results), particularly when the results are less than favourable.

'unnatural act' for managers, with the result that, if they are not trained properly, it is done rather poorly. Appraisal meetings are thus reported as being short-lived, ill-structured and often bruising encounters. Studies find that appraisers are ill-prepared, talk too much, and base much of the discussion on third-party complaints with many of the judgements made on 'gut feelings' (e.g. Finn and Fontaine, 1993). It is then of little surprise when we find reports of how it takes the average employee six months to recover from it (Peters, 1987).

Appraisals are also discredited by being subject to 'political' manipulation (Tziner, 1999). Managers, it seems, frequently play organisational games with performance ratings (Snape *et al.*, 1994). Longenecker's (1989) research found that managers' appraisal ratings are often manipulated to suit various ends. Sometimes ratings were artificially deflated to show who was the boss; to prepare the ground for termination; to punish a difficult and rebellious employee and even to 'scare' better performance out of the appraisee. One manager we interviewed described how he deflated the performance ratings of all new graduate trainees for their first few years of employment in order to 'knock some of the cleverness out of them' and show them that they 'did not know everything'. Equally, a poor performer may be given an excellent rating so that they will be promoted up and out of the department and managers may inflate ratings in the hope that an exemplary set of appraisals reflects favourably on the manager responsible for such a high-performing team.

The move to more objective forms of performance appraisal, particularly encouraged by performance management models, and increasingly reported for managerial grades is often argued to overcome some of the above 'subjective' problems. Legal challenges to personality- and trait-based performance appraisal schemes, particularly in North America and increasingly in the UK (Townley, 1990) have also encouraged the move away from personality- and trait-based systems. However, the so-called objective-based schemes are not without difficulties. Firstly, measurement is often difficult and according to Wright (1991) 'there are a number of jobs where the meaningful is not measurable and the measurable is not meaningful'. The tendency is also to simplify measurement by focusing on the short rather than the long term. Secondly, since objectives are set for individual employees or teams under such systems, it can be especially challenging to achieve equitable ratings. Equally problematical is that the actions of the employee may account for little of the variability in the outcomes measured (a key criticism of the quality gurus – see below) and thus the extent to which they are achievable is not within the employee's control. This has posed real problems with appraisals in industries such as financial services where the economic climate and general business cycle arguably affect outcomes far more than individual effort. The potential here is thus for employee demotivation and disillusionment, especially when many such systems are now linked to reward structures.

Kessler and Purcell (1992) identify a range of further specific problems with objective-based systems. These include the difficulty in achieving a balance between maintenance and innovator objectives; in setting objectives that cover the whole job so that performance does not get skewed to part of it; and the lack of flexibility to redefine objectives as circumstances change during the appraisal cycle. The introduction of performance appraisal into the public sector has also given rise to many concerns. In particular there are worries about its potential to undermine professional autonomy, with this concern being strongly expressed by clinicians in the NHS. A more general concern is that such a 'managerialist' intervention would undermine the public service values and public accountability of employees (Redman et al., 2000).

A range of more practical difficulties also results in problems with performance appraisal. Often the paperwork used to support the system can become excessive and give rise to a considerable bureaucratic burden for managers, particularly as spans of control grow. Some organisations have attempted to reduce this problem by designing paperless systems (Anderson et al., 1987), requiring the employee to complete the bulk of the paperwork (Wilson and Cole, 1990) or moving to computer-based systems (Angel, 1989). A real danger in many systems is that the paperwork dominates and the process is reduced to an annual 'cosy chat' and a ritual bureaucratic exercise devoid of meaning or importance for all concerned. Thus, according to Barlow (1989: 503), the performance appraisal of managers is little more than the 'routinized recording of trivialities'. Appraisers and appraised go through the motions, sign the forms and send them to a central personnel department who simply file them away rather than utilising the data in a meaningful way (Snape *et al.*, 1994). Given the lack of follow-up in many appraisal systems, it is hardly surprising when they fall into disrepute and eventual decay.

Lastly, the growth of TQM and customer care programmes has triggered a considerable debate and a reassessment of the organisational value of appraisal. On the one hand, there has been a high-profile barrage of criticism rejecting appraisal as being incompatible with TQM. In its strongest formulation it is suggested that managers face a stark choice between choosing either TQM or performance appraisal (Scholtes, 1993; Bowman, 1994). On the other hand, some have suggested that appraisal may play a key role in developing, communicating and monitoring the achievement of quality standards (Deblieux, 1991; Fletcher, 1993) and many organisations have been spurred by the introduction of TQM to revise their appraisal schemes in more customer-focused ways.

TQM has thus highlighted both old and new problems with performance appraisal. In relation to old problems some of the quality gurus, most notably Deming (1986), maintain that performance appraisal is inconsistent with quality improvement. He argues that variation in performance is attributable mainly to work systems rather than to variations in the performance of individual workers. Quality improvements are thus found mainly by changing processes rather than people, and the key is to develop co-operative teamwork. This, he claims, is difficult to do where the focus is on 'blaming' the individual, as in traditional appraisal, and where, as a result, there is a climate of fear and risk-avoidance, and a concern for short-term, individual targets, all of which undermines the co-operative, creative, and committed behaviour necessary for continuous improvement.

Deming is careful to argue, in rejecting performance appraisal, not that all staff perform equally well but that appraisers are incapable of disaggregating system effects from individual staff effects. Thus, what is needed for TQM is a shift away from the traditional focus on results and individual recognition, towards processes and group recognition. The TQM critics also raise some new problems with performance appraisal, in particular that it 'disempowers' employees by reducing variety and increasing homogenisation of the workforce whereas for meaningful customer care we need the 'empowered' employee.

Conclusions

Performance appraisal is now more widespread than at any time in its history and the organisational resources consumed by its practice are enormous. At the same time its critics grow both in number and in the ferocity of their attacks. It is thus tempting to adopt a somewhat sceptical view of the value of performance appraisal. Following the rise of TQM and the prominence of its, mainly American, management gurus, it has become rather fashionable of late to reject performance appraisal outright. Pathological descriptions of performance appraisal as a 'deadly disease' and an 'organisational virus' are increasingly common.

However, it would appear that the danger here is that such views are often based on little more than anecdote rather than solid empirical research. For example, one survey of employer reasons for introducing appraisal systems in the UK found that in over a third of cases they were developed to provide support for quality management initiatives (IRS, 1994). Our studies of managers' actual experience of being appraised finds many reporting its overall value to them and the organisation, with few suggesting that it should be discarded altogether (e.g. Redman and Mathews, 1995; Redman *et al.*, 2000). Many of the criticisms are based upon a hard and uncompromising model of performance appraisal that is now less commonly found in practice, and on the ineffective way in which many organisations implement appraisal. The critics all too often have rather conveniently ignored many of the new developments we discuss above, which act to alleviate some of these problems. Many of the problems of performance appraisal can be ironed out over time as experience with its practice accumulates. Indeed, there is some evidence to suggest that employers who have used performance appraisal for longer report fewer problems (Bowles and Coates, 1993).

Further, performance appraisal's detractors are usually silent on what should replace it. A common response is to suggest that this is an unfair question in that it is the organisational equivalent of asking, 'What you would replace pneumonia with?' (e.g. see *People Management*, 13 July 1995, p. 15). The question of how to assess individual performance, determine rewards and promotion, provide feedback, decide training and career needs and link business and individual goals without a performance appraisal system, however, cannot be so easily shrugged off.

Performance appraisal emerged in the first place to meet such needs and employees still need guidance in focusing their skills and efforts on important organisational goals and values. Hence we would suggest that performance appraisal will continue to have an important role in HRM practice. A good example here is that organisations often struggle to get managers committed to taking health and safety management as seriously as other aspects of their jobs. Tombs (1992) reports that 'safety leaders' in the chemical industry ensure that managers give safety management the attention it deserves by developing a 'safety culture', a key part of which is achieved by incorporating safety objectives into their performance appraisals. Thus the first objective of all ICI plant managers is always a safety one.

This is not to argue that the current practice of performance appraisal is unproblematic. Certainly some of the evidence presented above would suggest that there are many concerns with its application. However, although these problems are persistent they are certainly not insurmountable and it is argued strongly that organisations should think very carefully before abandoning performance appraisal altogether. Rather, the evidence would seem to support the view that the key task facing most organisations in the new millennium is the upgrading, renewal and reinvention of performance appraisal such that it is more compatible with new business environments. The evidence above and elsewhere (e.g. IRS, 1999) suggests that many employers are rising to such a challenge.

> ### Case study 3.1
>
> # Performance appraisal at North Trust
>
> Tom Redman, Ed Snape, David Thompson and Fanny Ka-ching Yan

Organisation background

This case study examines the practice of performance appraisal in an NHS trust hospital. North Trust (NT) is a whole district trust in the North-east of England serving a community of quarter of a million people. It provides 32 major health care services, including the full range of inpatient, day case and outpatient services alongside a comprehensive primary care service including health visiting and district nursing services. It employs some 2,200 'whole time equivalent' (wte) staff. The trust has recently been relatively successful, meeting all its financial targets thus far. However, at the time of the study (1995–97), it was, like many other trusts, experiencing increasing difficulties in meeting the demand for healthcare services within the constraints of its current resources.

The development of appraisal at NT

Appraisal at North Trust, a variant of the national Individual Performance Review scheme, was first implemented for senior managers in 1988. Between 1988 and 1994 it was largely restricted to managerial and senior professional groups. In 1994 a review of IPR was conducted. An initial analysis found patchy coverage of IPR and a half-hearted commitment to it. Following the review, a decision was taken to revise and relaunch the IPR scheme and roll it out to a wider group of staff. There were two key influences underpinning this decision. Firstly, a new chief executive with a much greater belief in the value of performance management was appointed. Secondly, a decision to pursue the Investors in People award resulted in a decision to commit more time and effort to making IPR work. The next 18 months thus saw the revising of policy, the redesigning of supporting paperwork, and the committing of major training resources to IPR.

Final written agreement was secured in March 1995 and the new policy and procedure were approved by the chief executive in June 1995. The key aims of IPR at NT were articulated in the new policy document as ensuring that all staff understand the trust's goals and strategic direction; are clear about their objectives, how these fit with the work of others and the organisation as whole and are aware of the tasks they need to carry out; are given regular feedback and explicit assessment of performance; and are developed to improve their performance. The revised policy document made an explicit commitment to implement IPR for all employees.

The revised IPR policy at NT placed greater emphasis on measurability as a key aspect of the setting of individual objectives. The policy document outlines the principles underpinning individual objective setting as following the acronym 'SMART'. Here objectives should be specific, measurable, agreed/achievable, realistic and time-bound with the form of measurement for each objective to be agreed at the time when they are set. According to the CEO, when he first arrived, this aspect was perceived as being very weak in practice:

> Most people didn't know what an objective was if it sat up and bit them on the backside. Objectives here tended to be half-a-dozen or so generalised statements with no measurable outcome, no timescale, no agreement about how something is to be judged and whether it has been done or not with the result that there is little accountability.

For the CEO the result of this was major problems in 'getting things done' at the trust:

> We don't have a performance culture here. This place was just great for talking about things. Only talking about things, not actually doing them.

Thus, a key aim for the CEO was to 'toughen up' IPR. This was to be attained in part by an increased emphasis on the evaluation of the achievement of work objectives and to encourage detailed measures to be established for all new objectives. However, the CEO's view of the direction in which IPR should go did not seem to be shared by its 'owners' – the personnel department. Here a softer, more developmental focus for IPR was envisioned:

> What is important is the manager taking the time out to talk to the individual about how they are progressing. How they feel things are going. And talk about training and development. These things really help morale. Forget the form filling and objectives, and all the other bits. It is these things that really make the difference.

In the remainder of this case study we describe the practice of performance appraisal in North Trust.

The IPR process

Mechanics

IPR at NT is designed to cascade downwards through the organisation. The business plan is formulated by December/January each year and reviews conducted during February and March for senior managers. The majority of appraisals for other staff take place during April and May. A minority of managers, because of the large number of appraisals they conducted, in one case over 50, scheduled the appraisals over the full year, which, in effect, largely undermined the direct link with business planning for the majority of their staff. However, linkages with the business plan, especially for lower levels of staff, were also difficult to discern in the accounts of the IPR reviews conducted by those managers who did these in phase with the business planning process. Here managers' descriptions of how they appraised healthcare assistants, porters, domestics, catering staff, laundry workers, nurses rarely mentioned anything other than the loosest of connections with the business plan.

The IPR policy specifies very much a 'top-down' process, noting that only occasionally it might be beneficial to involve another manager closely concerned with the objectives being measured (such as a project manager). In practice, no examples of this were found. A particular problem reported by the interviewees was that of continuity of appraisers between appraisal cycles. Due to high levels of managerial turnover, caused by resignations, promotions, transfers, and secondments, etc. of both appraisees and appraisers, nearly a third of interviewees reported having different appraisers from one cycle to the next. This level of managerial change, because of the need for a close working relationship between manager and employee for appraisal to be effective (see below), was felt to generally limit IPR's potential. Interviewees described how continuity between appraiser and appraisee was important because reviews were generally perceived as improving as both parties got to know each other better and the discussion became more useful and open.

Coverage

There was an uneven application and use of IPR. Despite the avowed intention of the new policy to roll out IPR uniformly over the trust, its use appeared to be distinctly patchy. The personnel department estimated that only around 25–30 per cent of staff received a performance review and that below management levels 'huge swathes' of staff were not involved. One of the tools to encourage its greater uptake was that senior managers were now being given personal objectives in their own appraisals to introduce IPR for all their staff. However, this strategy alone did not seem sufficient to gain their commitment to making IPR process effective. As one manager explains:

> Appraisal for lower-level staff is a five-minute wonder, get it out of the way. The supervisors say . . . 'I have got to go through this with you. You haven't been too bad a lad this year, have you? See you next year.' We get the odd constructive thing coming out of it but the main thing is that the director will be happy that he can report we have now appraised all the staff in our department when he has his next IPR.

Such cynical attitudes were a source of irritation to the majority of managers who spent considerable time and effort in conducting IPRs in their departments. Here it was particularly resented that their managerial colleagues either did not conduct appraisals ('It's not fair that I have to do it if others don't'; 'Other staff feel they are missing out because they are not getting it') or gave mere lip service to them ('It brings the whole IPR process into disrepute and makes it much more difficult for me to get my staff to take it seriously').

Documentation

The standard trust documentation was used for fewer than half of our interviewees' appraisals. The standard forms were felt to be too cumbersome and somewhat of an administrative chore, especially for use with employees at lower levels in the organisation. Thus, those responsible for IPR often tailored the forms, usually reducing their length. A problem with some of the customised forms was that questionable performance categories, such as an appraisee's 'personality', featured prominently in these versions. In contrast, some professional groups found the forms rather too simplistic to capture the nature of their roles and again customised the standard forms to suit their needs. In a number of departments reviews were conducted without the aid of either customised or standard forms, and in one case an appraiser admitted that this was because he had never got round to actually reading them.

The IPR encounter

The heart of the IPR process, and the main source of participants' evaluation of it as either a success or failure, is the face-to-face meeting between appraiser and appraisee. Here for IPR is its 'moment of truth'. Table 3.1 shows that the majority of our appraisees reported interviews of at least 30 minutes, with 47 per cent having interviews of more than an hour. Judging from Table 3.2, appraisers were not usually dominating the interviews. The impression gained is that the majority of appraisees were having a sufficiently long and participative appraisal interview, an encouraging finding when we note that those who reported longer and more participative interviews also tended to report greater satisfaction with the appraisal process.

Table 3.1 How long did the appraisal interview last?

Time	Percentage of total appraisals
Less than 30 minutes	11
Between 30 minutes and an hour	43
Between one and two hours	35
More than two hours	12

Table 3.2 During the appraisal interview approximately what proportion of the time did you and the appraiser talk?

Proportion of time spent talking	Percentages of total appraisals
Mainly me (more than 75%)	13
Approximately 60% me	26
Approximately equal	48
Approximately 60% appraiser	12
Mainly the appraiser (more than 75%)	1

Table 3.2 sets out the extent to which various issues were discussed during the appraisal, as reported by our appraisees. The main emphasis appears to be on the achievement and planning of work objectives and on the planning of training and

Table 3.3 To what extent were the following issues covered in your appraisal?

Issue	Percentage of total appraisals		
	3 *Thoroughly discussed*	2 *Briefly discussed*	1 *Not discussed at all*
Your achievement of work objectives	63	32	5
Your future work objectives	65	31	4
Your personality or behaviour	17	42	42
Your skills or competencies	35	52	13
Your training and development needs	45	43	12
Your career aspirations and plans	30	43	27
Your pay or benefits	3	12	85
Your job difficulties	24	57	19
How you might improve your performance	16	40	44
How your supervisor might help you to improve your performance	15	45	40
Your personal or domestic circumstances	4	20	76

development. Not surprisingly, given the absence of performance-related pay for most staff, pay and benefits were only discussed in any detail during the appraisal interview. Overall, the approach seems to be one of performance management and development rather than of judgement and reward allocation.

A strong theme in the accounts of those who were positive about the overall IPR process was the notion that the interview represented 'quality time' between manager and managed. For some it was an 'employee's right' to have meaningful 'one-on-one time' with their manager and:

> People value quality time to talk through with their immediate manager what they are doing, why they are doing it, and what they need to do in the future.

As we have seen, in these 'quality-time' appraisals, which were often two to three hours in duration for managers, appraisees reported that a broad range of issues were discussed.

In contrast, the focus for lower-level grades was much more restricted and our in-depth interviews suggested that for such staff the time spent on the IPR's interview varied between 10 and 45 minutes. Typical descriptions of the nature of appraisals for lower-grade staff were:

> I discuss with them how they have worked this year. I say 'You've been a bit slack in these things. You are bloody good at that. You are one of my key workers for this. But your time-keeping wants pulling up a bit and your general attitude is not what it should be.

> To be honest there is very little to say to someone who feeds sheets into a machine five days a week. I have found it hard to think of positive things.

One manager reported the difficulty of getting lower-grade staff to relax during their review because prior to IPR's introduction the only time such staff were called to her office was for a 'rugging'. Perhaps unsurprisingly given such an approach, lower-grade staff were often reported as being 'indifferent' to and 'disinterested' in the IPR process.

> It's the lower grades that feel 'Do I have to go through this again? I don't know why. I only want to do the job I'm doing and get my money at the end of the week.' These tend to be short interviews, most are less than 10 minutes.

Managers appeared to be coping with this lack of interest via a number of strategies. Firstly, by renewing efforts to encourage active staff participation and using developmental 'carrots'. Secondly, individual sceptics were labelled 'lost causes' and managers simply went through motions in IPR and waited for such staff to leave. A more difficult problem was with clusters of IPR-resistant employees. Here a coping strategy, often sold under the guise of self-development, appeared to be one of 'sharing the misery' more evenly with more junior managers and supervisors. The responsibility for conducting IPRs for 'difficult', 'obstructive', and 'awkward' staff was spread between the managerial team.

Generally, appraisees felt that their managers were good at giving performance feedback but fewer felt that they received regular feedback on their progress towards objectives (Table 3.4). The need for appraisal to be an ongoing, year-round exercise was emphasised in the IPR system (see below). It seems that at NT, significant minorities of appraisers were neglecting to do the expected follow-up. Judging from our interviews, constructive feedback was especially welcomed by the appraisees in providing direction ('You realize you are getting there'; 'Gives me some comfort I am getting there') and helping to boost confidence ('You know what you are doing is being done correctly'). Critical feedback was also valued but not often received by the interviewees, who in part blamed appraisal training here, which overly emphasised the positive nature of IPR. Around a third of interviewees said they often watered down their feedback in the reviews to ensure a positive IPR event and harmony within their work-teams. Appraisees, especially female managers, emphasised the value of constructive criticism and 'meaningful' appraisals, with cosy chats being seen as a waste of their time.

Sound personal relationships between appraiser and appraised were emphasised by our interviewees as being a necessary but not sufficient condition for the review to be effective. The large majority of appraisees considered that their managers were professional enough not to reward favourites, thought that appraisers were objective, felt they could talk freely, were confident enough to challenge their appraisal, and believed that keeping on good terms with their manager was not a requirement in order to obtain a good appraisal (see Table 3.4). However, this still leaves a minority of appraisers whose appraisal behaviour was less positively rated by appraisees. Thus, some interviewees reported a poor relationship with their manager, describing IPR reviews in terms of conflict, verbal confrontation, point-scoring,

Table 3.4 Perceived supervisor behaviour

	Percentage of total appraisals				
	5 Strongly agree	4 Agree	3 Neither agree nor disagree	2 Disagree	1 Strongly disagree
Positive aspects					
My supervisor is good at giving me feedback on my performance.	7	51	19	19	4
I receive regular informal feedback from my supervisor regarding my progress towards agreed targets and objectives.	4	37	19	30	9
My supervisor takes my appraisals very seriously.	21	50	15	12	2
My supervisor takes my career aspirations very seriously.	5	50	24	17	3
I am confident that my supervisor is as objective as possible when conducting appraisals.	10	60	20	8	1
Negative aspects					
I have to keep on good terms with my supervisor in order to get a good appraisal rating.	2	10	21	52	14
Supervisors use appraisals to reward their favourites.	2	6	16	54	23
I am not entirely happy about challenging my supervisor's appraisal of my performance.	3	18	17	52	11
I found it difficult during my performance appraisal to talk freely with my supervisor about what I wanted to discuss.	4	14	9	52	21

and 'edging about the real issues'. At its worst, this reduced appraisers using IPR to list what the appraisee had done wrong or badly over the year. A few appraisers, particularly those in clinical posts, described the problems of achieving an appropriate environment for conducting appraisal in a busy, emergency-led hospital.

> When I had my IPR the phones were going, people were coming in and out of the office, the manager got called away. It spoke volumes to me about the value that was attached to IPR here.

> Conducting IPRs on nights, at 2 am, when people are not at their best, is hardly conducive to a quality process.

Mini-reviews

The formal annual reviews are supported by mini reviews. The policy document sees these as a 'crucial element' of IPR, providing constant review and monitoring such that the annual review itself becomes 'mainly a confirmation of agreements made during the year', or, as the title of the IPR training video suggests, appraisees should experience *No Surprises*. However, these appear to be rather sporadic in practice and, as we saw in Table 3.4, only 41 per cent of survey appraisees said that they received regular feedback from their supervisor on their progress towards their objectives.

A few departmental heads formally scheduled three-monthly reviews for all employees. The norm for the mini-reviews was a six-monthly, informal discussion, with a minority of interviewees receiving only the annual appraisal. Below management and professional levels, the impression gained was that mini-reviews were extremely rare or very ad hoc and rushed at best – 'corridor and canteen chats' – with managers struggling to find the time to conduct even the annual appraisal for some groups. However, the interviewees themselves often stressed the value of mini reviews, not only in providing a measure of progress and attainment but in a general updating of performance objectives. Several interviewees reported requesting, and receiving, additional mini reviews. Here mini reviews were especially useful to fine-tune, and often to replace personal objectives that had been rendered obsolete by a rapidly changing organisational environment. Given the current level of change and 'churn' in the NHS, we suggest that it may now be appropriate to consider it a 'high-velocity' environment requiring fast strategic decision-making. In such circumstances static yearly objectives are clearly inappropriate. Interviewees reported how objectives set in April of one year were often irrelevant and obsolete by the following year. Mini reviews allowed for individual objectives to be kept in line with changes in business strategy.

Objective setting

As we have seen, the increased emphasis on work objectives and measurability desired by the CEO is reflected in the issues covered in the appraisal process, with appraisees reporting that the achievement and planning of work objectives were the most thoroughly discussed issues in the appraisal meeting. Generally, appraisees found the emphasis on objectives a useful part of the IPR process. A picture that emerges from the survey findings is that objectives are generally clear, cover the most important parts of the job, and that appraisees are actively involved in the objective-setting process (see Table 3.5). Interviewees reported being reassured they were on the 'right track', 'working along the right lines', 'on-line', and 'knowing where they stood' ('You might think you are doing a good job but you need some one to tell you that and vice versa') in their jobs. For example:

> Without IPR it would be so easy for you to drift and not do anything. It keeps you on your toes. It keeps you focused. You know exactly what you are aiming for. It makes you look at what you do and what the organisation's trying to achieve. If you didn't have appraisal it would be so easy just to not do anything. You'd just drift. It makes you think about where you are going and where you would like to be.

Table 3.5 Objectives and feedback

	Percentage of total appraisals				
	5 Strongly agree	4 Agree	3 Neither agree nor disagree	2 Disagree	1 Strongly disagree
The goals that I am to achieve are clear.	8	61	13	15	2
The most important parts of my job are emphasised in my performance appraisal.	3	58	24	13	2
The performance appraisal system helps me understand my personal weaknesses.	5	48	19	26	3
My supervisor allows me to help choose the goals that I am to achieve.	13	65	10	10	1
The performance appraisal system helps me to understand my job better.	3	37	27	31	1
The performance appraisal system gives me a good idea of how I am doing in my job.	6	55	23	14	2

The setting of objectives provided direction in an increasingly complex and fast-moving organisational environment. The view of one manager was that, by appraising her staff, she:

> Gives them something to hang onto. The job description is so vast and we are facing so many changes. The objectives give direction. It's a stepping stone for them. They give staff guidance and something to aim for, something constructive to aim for.

Interviewees reported how they often tended to 'push' and 'challenge' themselves to make 'progress', attain 'personal development' and 'growth' via the objective-setting process. The general view was that in this respect the objectives they set for themselves were more challenging (and interesting) than those produced by their managers. For example:

> Generally, I can take them in my stride. There are one or two demanding ones but they are actually objectives I have brought forward myself. I probably tend to push myself harder than the organisation does.

> I always put a new really challenging one in each time, like reducing sickness absence. I tend to challenge myself.

However, for some interviewees their accumulated experience of objective-setting had taught them not to challenge themselves 'too much' and restrict both the scope and the number of the objectives they set for themselves. Here we find managerial appraisees becoming sensitised to the objective-setting 'game'. For example:

What I've learnt, as time goes by, is you've got to be careful, right at the outset, how you set your objectives because you can be overoptimistic, unrealistic. There's a danger of sitting down and thinking of all the things you'd love to do, or ideally should do, forgetting that you've got lots of constraints and you couldn't in a month of Sundays achieve it. So I think quite a few of us have learnt there is a skill in setting objectives which are reasonable and stand a chance of being achieved. I think that that bit is probably more important than anything else. There is nothing more demoralizing than being measured against something which you yourself have declared as being in need of being done and finding that you couldn't possibly do it.

Some appraisees felt that objectives were 'imposed' on them but most accepted that this was 'just part of the job'. Occasionally, though, this caused considerable irritation and anger, particularly in the clash with IPR's espoused developmental focus. One manager described 'ending up with nothing you really wanted to do' from his IPR and another described how, when she pushed her appraiser to include a particular objective that she perceived as being a key issue for the department and which fitted well with her personal development needs, she was told '...either forget it or fit it into your own time'. The danger with imposing objectives on staff reluctant to accept them was that all that was achieved was lip service and half-hearted commitment, accompanied by subsequent 'fudge' in the appraisal review on the measures of achievement. For example:

> I've got to do them (objectives). I don't not do them but I don't give them the commitment they need if I don't feel it's right. And it never gets picked up at the next appraisal.

Measuring achievement

The use of data in measuring and evaluating individual performance was reported by interviewees as being very reactive on the part of appraisers. Here if the appraisee did not produce data there tended to be very little use of anything other than informed opinion in assessing whether objectives had actually been achieved. An effect of this lack of data use appears to be that although a majority of appraisees felt that IPRs represented an accurate measure of their performance, a substantial number were unclear on the standards used to evaluate performance (see Table 3.6).

Some appraisees were prolific in their use of data in the IPR process. Interviewees who had also undertaken NVQ management programmes described a considerable use of reports and the production of memorandums to measure their achievement of objectives. It seems that the NVQ requirement to produce a portfolio causes managers to start to document their work – at least until they attain the award. Our findings suggest this new-found enthusiasm for the memorandum and report generated by NVQs found a further outlet in the IPR process. Further, such documentation and the generally greater level of preparation on the part of the appraisee enabled them to control, to a considerable extent, the content and outcomes of the IPR process. For example:

> I took lots of things along (to the IPR meeting). One of my objectives was to set up team objectives on the ward. I copied examples of these objectives and took them along. I

Table 3.6 Measuring performance

	Percentage of total appraisals				
	5 Strongly agree	4 Agree	3 Neither agree nor disagree	2 Disagree	1 Strongly disagree
My performance appraisal for this year represents a fair and accurate picture of my job performance.	7	68	11	13	1
My supervisor and I agree on what equals good performance in my job	6	67	14	12	1
I know the standards used to evaluate my performance	2	40	26	29	4

showed reports I had done on the empowerment of patients and gave her copies of patients' meetings. I used information to show that I had done things. I used these things to prove to her that I had achieved them.

In contrast, other managers usually reported a much less documented measuring process under IPR. The effective use of documentation by this group of managers and professionals thus raises the issue of 'impression management' in the performance measurement process. Impression management is a process by which people attempt to create and sustain desired perceptions of themselves in the eyes of others. In the employment context such others are colleagues, peers, internal customers, clients, and especially bosses. The theory of impression management suggests that employees attempt to control, sometimes consciously and sometimes unconsciously, information on themselves which positively shapes others' perceptions of them. The performance appraisal process is a particularly important arena for the creation of favourable impressions at work. The effective use of performance documentation on the part of appraisees thus appears to be a very powerful tool in the production of an overall favourable impression of their managerial capability. A number of appraisers appeared to be very aware of staff's attempts at impression management via the IPR process. Such appraisers reported how they supplemented data from the IPR interview with views from an appraisee's peers and the 'grapevine'. Some declared that they were very wary of the accuracy of views offered by 'mouthy' and 'gobby' staff. For example:

A nurse who's an extrovert, who does a lot of mouthing off, may give the impression that they are doing a really wonderful job and the lass who is quiet could be doing an even better job. But because she's not there selling herself, telling you how wonderful she is, she often loses out here.

I am always wary of the gobby ones. Those who are always telling you how wonderful [they are] and how hard worked [they are].

It appears that the key for managers in measuring individual performance under IPR was distinguishing between 'real' and 'created' performance achievements, the danger being that managers may actually measure an employee's ability to perform in a 'theatrical' rather 'task-orientated' sense.

Objectives and teamwork

The CEO was also keen to encourage wider sharing of objectives, particularly between managers. Here the IPR policy's emphasis on the confidentiality of the appraisal process and its individual nature was seen as discouraging the formal communication of personal objectives with others. The individualistic nature of IPR thus fitted rather uneasily with the considerable growth in teamwork across the trust. For example, according to one manager:

> My boss knows how my objectives fit in with my colleagues', but I don't because I never see them.

The CEO was attempting to introduce change here by leading by example and then encouraging other managers to do the same. After setting objectives for his executive directors, all objectives for each manager, including his own, were circulated to the entire senior management team and also sent out to the clinical divisions. However, generally there did not seem to be much formal sharing of objectives amongst other managers and professionals. Many of our interviewees felt that greater sharing of objectives would be valuable, not least in creating a better understanding of performance priorities within and between departments. On an informal level some staff were actively sharing objectives. One manager describes how she encourages this at team meetings with her managers and supervisors:

> I'll say at meetings 'Have you looked at your IPR lately? Who's got that in their IPR? Somebody's got that in their IPR.'

Interviewees expressed how they found it easier to prepare their own objectives when their appraising manager provided copies of his or her own objectives in advance of the review process. Appraisees also reported that much of their work was now conducted in teams, and many felt that more team-based appraisals and the setting of team objectives would helpfully supplement the individualistic nature of IPR. For example:

> I think IPR needs to achieve a better balance between individual performance and team performance. We need a much greater emphasis on team performance. Nowadays at NT we are all about teamwork. The IPR approach is too preoccupied with individual performance. It can become too narrow and it is often divisive.

A number also suggested that wider collaboration on the setting of objectives with other managers, project leaders, working parties, etc. would be beneficial in encompassing the full range of their activities.

IPR outputs

In this last section we report our findings on what the IPR process actually achieves. Here we structure our discussion under four main headings: management control; employee motivation; training and development; and rewards.

Management control

Clearly, as we discuss above, the setting and measuring of work objectives facilitates a direct form of managerial control over the labour process. Despite the rhetoric and policy of development, appraisers seemed to use IPR to exert their managerial authority. Occasionally, this was done in a very crude way. For example, a number of interviewees reported problems with managers waiting for the IPR to settle scores for past conflicts. IPR was thus perceived by some appraisees as a vehicle for the line manager to 'tell me what I should be doing', and to ' tell me what I am not doing right in my job'. There is also evidence that IPR acts as a less obvious and more indirect form of managerial control. Here IPR appears to act as a means to encourage self-discipline and responsibility amongst staff and thus to promote the reshaping of staff attitudes to fit new managerial values and beliefs in line with the changing form of work organisation. Even some of the sternest critics of IPR noted its subtle effects on them:

> I achieve nothing from it. I suppose the main benefit is I actually discipline myself more with my time management. I think 'Oh I have got to do so and so' and I chart out my work better so that I'll take all that in. I give myself deadlines for my work, saying 'I'll achieve that by March.'

The direction of control in the IPR process, however, is far from one-way. Some managers described how their staff turned the IPR tables on them:

> The cooks use IPR to say 'This is why I cannot do my job. This is why I cannot achieve this objective.' And then they trot out a great list of problems with the job.

One manager described why he hated doing appraisals with lower-level staff because they were reduced to 'a managerial witch-hunt and a general gripe and groan session about what I had or hadn't done over the year'. The manager became so fed-up with being on the receiving end of this that he had written to all staff reminding them of the nature of the IPR process and asking for a more positive attitude and less moaning about perceived managerial inadequacies. However, the memorandum had only served to highlight his discomfort with the process and to increase the level of complaining behaviour from appraisees, such that he now admitted to merely '. . .going through the motions with IPR to get it over with as quickly as possible'.

'It's good to talk': motivation and morale

IPR, as we discuss above, was often perceived by appraisers and appraised as a good opportunity for managers and managed to talk meaningfully, and engage in 'quality time' together. Not only did IPR visibly and symbolically demonstrate to staff their value and importance to the organisation but that the manager also personally cared about their wellbeing. In some of the accounts of appraisers there were classic human-relations descriptions of the IPR encounter going well beyond the boundaries of work relations. Here interviewees reported appraisals discussing broader personal and social issues and referred to this as 'getting to know your staff'.

> IPR helps people in knowing where their professional career and their lives are going.

> It's your time that you devote to them. And some of them have aspirations that you wouldn't know about until you sit down and talk to them. You show that you are genuinely interested in them as people as well as nurses.

The language used to describe these encounters was often heavily redolent of the unitary ideology of human relations. Appraisees' and appraisers' stories were littered with references to 'progress', 'going forward together', 'participation', 'empowering the appraisee', 'boosting morale', 'becoming a proactive team', 'harnessing our collective energies' via IPR. Interviewees emphasised the importance of good communication, listening and being listened to particularly, as being a manager was often described as being a 'lonely job'. Thus some two-thirds of interviewees felt that they performed the duties of the post better and that IPR contributed positively to their personal motivation and job satisfaction:

> If they scrapped it tomorrow, I don't think I would go home in tears but I would miss it. It helps me keep going, helps me keep motivated. It gives me some comfort, considering all the problems we have at the moment – I've got a service with a lot of problems – that I am achieving what I am supposed to do in my job.

In contrast, other managers, again especially in relation to lower-level staff, were not convinced that IPR reviews delivered much other than a lot of 'hot air' and wasted time that could have been much more profitably employed doing other things. For example:

> I have 49 staff. Appraisal takes at least 30-40 minutes each. That's a lot of man-hours to get nothing out of it other than hot air.

> Senior management would like to think that if you appraise everybody it would instil in them some kind of belonging, some kind of corporate feeling. But for the rank and file they are just not interested.

Training and development

Despite the emphasis of IPR on training and development by the personnel department, as we can see from Table 3.3, the discussion of an appraisee's training needs takes second place to that on work objectives. Some 12 per cent of appraisees reported that training and development issues were not discussed at all. The majority of those interviewed emphasised training and development as an outcome of the IPR process. All interviewees claimed to have discussed their own 'personal development plan' (PDP) during the interview. However, this was often reported to be a relatively unfocused and vague discussion. Indeed, few interviewees, under persistent probing, could actually give details of what was in their PDP. The impression gained was that the PDP title signified a much more formalised, more detailed and rather grander training and development document in theory at least if not in practice. Many of the interviewees described a rather mechanical process whereby training and development was discussed as a distinct, almost stand-alone issue. The appraiser was often perceived as running through a check list of items to be covered in the interview, of which training and development was one, rather than the identification of training needs emerging from a grounded discussion of appraisee performance. The large majority of interviewees felt that much of the training and development that was taking place would still have occurred without the use of IPR but possibly less systematically and at a slower pace.

Managers reported problems with the IPR process – especially coupled with the decision to pursue the IiP award – giving rise to appraisees producing training and development 'wish lists' . Here the key difficulty was finding the training resources to fund costly external courses in the face of increasingly tight training budgets. The demand for degree and diploma courses – particularly amongst nursing staff – fuelled in part by IPR, was causing managers problems in maintaining staff commitment to the appraisal process, given that few employees could be supported in this way. Managers described a coping strategy here of encouraging employees to consider alternative, and less costly, development activities such as short secondments, work shadowing and job exchanges. Interviewees were also critical of the personnel department pushing the current training 'flavour of the month' via the IPR process. At the time of our study this was reported as being the managerial NVQ programme running in-house in conjunction with a local university.

Rewards

The PRP element of IPR was not particularly popular with either appraisers or appraisees. Whereas the general view of IPR was that a majority of both appraisees and interviewees considered it to be an overall positive experience, at least for managers and professionals, the views expressed in relation to performance-related pay were all negative. A strong view from those receiving PRP was that it was: a lot of 'hassle' for little reward; more influenced by quotas than real performance; did little to motivate yet was often demotivating; unfair; arbitrary; inequitable; highly subjective; bias-laden; ineffective and detrimental to professionalism; created dysfunctional interpersonal competition; and undermined the developmental focus of IPR. For some IPR was 'sullied' by its linkage with PRP. At best, appraisees felt that PRP might possibly work with better and more stringent guidelines, where performance targets were clear and easily measurable rather than subject to an assessment based on ratings, and when they got on well with their line-manager. PRP also ensured that appraisals were treated seriously. Many of these issues are very familiar 'moans and groans' from the growing PRP literature. A particular problem identified at NT was that performance was highly dependent on team effort and work was increasingly being reorganised along teamwork lines yet PRP was individually based. The team–individual conflict in

PRP may be at least partially resolved by including teamwork objectives in the appraisal process but as we discuss above this was rarely done at NT. Thus:

> To achieve my objectives I have to rely on all my heads of departments. I have to rely on people outside of our division to co-operate or to take things on board. It's a team effort, yet I receive an individual reward that's largely determined on things beyond my control

Equally, those who did not receive PRP were not keen to be subject to it. This seems to contradict the view that PRP is like an extra-marital affair where those with no experience of such things think they are missing out on something terribly exciting and rewarding whilst those who were involved simply felt miserable. For example:

> I don't need someone wielding a financial stick to tell me how to do my job or push myself.

> PRP wouldn't affect me in the slightest. A few hundred pounds is neither here nor there for me.

Only one of the non-PRP managers was concerned that he was not receiving PRP. In essence, this stemmed from his belief that it was unfair for some managers to receive PRP whilst others (such as himself) did not, rather than any great desire to be subject to it himself:

> IPR was first introduced here for senior managers and was linked to their pay. Then they brought it down to other managers. This is not sour grapes, but when it got down to my level of management the pay was wiped out and just the appraisal was left.

> *Note* This case study draws on four main sources of data: interviews with managers and professionals; a fully structured postal questionnaire administered to a sample of 270 managers and professionals; the analysis of internal documents and procedures manuals and fourthly, the observation of training workshops on appraisal and several senior management meetings reviewing appraisal practice in the organisation (see Redman *et al.*, 2000).

Questions

1. Is IPR a failure at North Trust?

2. Should IPR be retained by the organisation? If you recommend retention, what changes would you advise? If you recommend that it should be scrapped, what would you advise should replace it?

3. According to Wright (1991) a paradox of performance management systems is that the meaningful is rarely measurable and the measurable is rarely meaningful. What evidence is there to support such a criticism in North-Trust?

4. A key for managers in measuring individual performance under systems of performance appraisal is distinguishing between 'real' and 'created' performance achievements, the danger being that managers may actually measure an employee's 'ability to perform in the theatrical rather than task-oriented sense' (Randle and Rainne, 1997). What evidence is there that this is a problem at North Trust? How can the problems of impression management be minimised?

5. It has been suggested that the key challenge now facing performance appraisal systems is their upgrading, renewal and reinvention such that they are more compatible with business environments. To what extent does IPR fit the business environment of the 'new, modern and dependable NHS' (Department of Health, 1997)?

6. Some analysts have suggested that the NHS is moving from a bureaucratic mode of organisation to a network mode of organising. What are the implications of such a development for IPR practice?

References

Department of Health (1997) *The New NHS: Modern, Dependable*, London: The Stationery Office.

Randle, K. and Rainnie, A. (1997) 'Managing creativity, maintaining control: a study in pharmaceutical research', *Human Research Management Journal*, 7(2): 32–46.

Redman, T., Snape, E., Thompson, D. and Ka-ching Yan (2000) 'Performance appraisal in an NHS hospital', *Human Resource Management Journal*, 10(1): 1–16.

Wright, V. 1991. 'Performance related pay' in Neale, F. (ed) *The Handbook of Performance Management*, London: Institute of Personnel Management.

Appraisal at Bankco

Tom Redman and Adrian Wilkinson

Jim is a branch manager at Bankco, a large retail bank. The branch comprises 20 staff with a mix of front desk, sales and back office roles. There has been a lot of pressure on the bank in the last two years or so with threats of takeover and merger, and branch managers have had rigorous financial targets to meet. Jim has managed to achieve these but at the cost of bearing down on staff. He is known as a strict disciplinarian and is known to berate staff in front of customers if they have failed to meet targets. The result is low morale and increasing staff turnover. A branch inspection has raised HR issues. Jim has not done much induction or many appraisals this year and few staff have been on training programmes. Staff see his manner to them as offhand and very directive. At the same time the bank has promoted 'a profits through people' philosophy and has a mission statement which places great emphasis on staff value to the organisation and how the organisation will treat them with respect.

Corporate principles refer not only to business objectives and shareholders but also to the organisation's commitment to its employees, the community, customers and the environment. The section on employees in the booklet which is issued to all staff places great stress and emphasis on teamworking, involvement and communication, training and development and welfare. In particular, the booklet states that:

- We will seek to achieve an atmosphere conducive at all levels to effective teamwork.
- We will encourage involvement in decision-making within the scope of an employee's responsibilities.
- We will ensure that each employee receives all relevant information necessary for the performance of duties and an understanding of how these relate to the Bank as a whole.
- We will provide for the possibility of developing the potential of employees by means of training and development, education, job rotation, and performance appraisal.
- We treat employees fairly and with dignity.

You (the Divisional Head, Fred) are now appraising Jim. You are anxious to be sympathetic as he is an experienced and capable manager, but at the same time you need to put the message across that he has to change his attitude to staff. Jim has a reputation for being confrontational and aggressive. You are not looking forward to this meeting.

Instructions for exercise

Carry out an appraisal role play with Fred and Jim. The observing group should review the following issues:

1. Did Fred put the message he wanted across?
2. Did Jim accept this? If not, what was the resolution? If so, what were the required standards for the future?
3. How well did Fred question and listen?

References to Chapter 3

Anderson. G.C., Young, E. and Hulme, D. (1987) 'Appraisal without form-filling', *Personnel Management*, 19(2), 44–7.

Angel, N.F. (1989) 'Evaluating employees by computer', *Personnel Administrator*, November: 67–72.

Armstrong, M. and Baron, A. (1998) *Performance Management*, London: IPD.

Arthur, W., Woehr, D.J., Akande, A. and Strong, M.H. (1995) 'Human resource management in West Africa: practices and perceptions', *International Journal of Human Resource Management*, 6(2): 347–67.

Banks, C.G. and Murphy, K.R. (1985) 'Toward narrowing the research–practice gap in performance appraisal', *Personnel Psychology*, 38: 335–45.

Barlow, G. (1989) 'Deficiencies and the perpetuation of power: latent functions in management appraisal', *Journal of Management Studies*, 26(5): 499–517.

Bevan, S. and Thompson, M. (1991) 'Performance management at the crossroads', *Personnel Management*, November: 36–39.

Bhote, K.R. (1994) 'Boss performance appraisal: a metric whose time has gone', *Employment Relations Today*, 21(1): 1–8.

Bowman, J.S. (1994) 'At last, an alternative to performance appraisal: total quality management', *Public Administration Review*, 54(2): 129–36.

Bowles, M.L. and Coates, G. (1993) 'Image and substance: the management of performance as rhetoric or reality', *Personnel Review*, 22(2): 3–21.

Boudreaux, G. (1994) 'What TQM says about performance appraisal', *Compensation and Benefits Review*, 26, 3: 20–24.

Carroll, S.J. and Schneier, C.E. (1982) *Performance Appraisal and Review Systems: The Identification, Measurement and Development of Performance in Organisations*, Glenview, Il: Scott Foresman.

Chow, I. (1994) 'An opinion survey of performance appraisal practices in Hong Kong and the Peoples' Republic of China', *Asia Pacific Journal of Human Resources*, 32: 62–79.

Coates, G. (1994) 'Performance appraisal as icon: Oscar-winning performance or dressing to impress?', *International Journal of Human Resource Management*, 5(1): 165–191.

Connock, S. (1992) 'The importance of "big ideas" to HR managers', *Personnel Management*, 21(11): 52–56.

Cook, S. (1993) *Customer Care*, London: Kogan Page.

CPCR (1995) *The Right Angle on 360-degree Feedback*, Newcastle: CPCR.

Cully, M., Woodland, S., O'Reilly, A. and Dix, G. (1999) *Britain at Work*, London: Routledge.

Deblieux, M. (1991) 'Performance reviews support the quest for quality', *HR Focus*, November: 3–4.

Deming, W.E. (1986) *Out of the Crisis: Quality, Productivity and Competitive Position*, Cambridge: Cambridge University Press.

Dent, M. (1995) 'The new National Health Service: a case of postmodernism?', *Organisation Studies*, 16(5): 875–99.

Dugdill, G. (1994) 'Wide angle view', *Personnel Today*, 27 September: 31–32.

Endo, K. (1994) 'Satei (personal assessment) and interworker competition in Japanese firms', *Industrial Relations*, 33(1): 70–82

Finn, R.H. and Fontaine, P.A. (1983) 'Performance appraisal: some dynamics and dilemmas', *Public Personnel Management Journal*, 13(4): 335–43.

Fletcher, C. and Williams, R. (1992) 'The route to performance management', *Personnel Management*, October 24(10), 42–47

Fletcher, C. (1993) 'Appraisal: an idea whose time has gone?', *Personnel Management*, September: 25(9), 34–38.

Fowler, A. (1990) 'Performance management: the MBO of the 1990s?', *Personnel Management*, July: 47–51.

Fuller, L. and Smith, V. (1991) 'Consumers' reports: management by customers in a changing economy', *Work Employment and Society*, 4(1): 1–16.

Giffin, M.E. (1989) 'Personnel research on testing, selection and performance appraisal', *Public Personnel Management*, 18(2): 127–37.

Gill, D. (1977) *Appraising Performance: Present Trends and the Next Decade*, London: IPD.

Grint, K. (1993) 'What's wrong with performance appraisals? A critique and a suggestion', *Human Resource Management*, 3(3): 61–77.

Halachmi, A. (1993) 'From performance appraisal to performance targeting', *Public Personnel Management*, 22(2): 323–44.

Illes, P. and Salaman, M. (1995) 'Recruitment, selection and assessment', in Storey, J. (ed) *Human Resource Management. A Critical Text*, London: Routledge.

IRS (1992) 'Industrial relations developments in the water industry', *Employment Trends*, 516: 6–15.

IRS (1994) 'Improving performance? A survey of appraisal arrangements', *Employment Trends*, 556: 5–14.

IRS (1995a) 'Survey of employee relations in local government', *Employment Trends*, 594: 6–13.

IRS (1995b) 'The customer is boss: matching employee performance to customer service needs', *Employment Trends*, 585: 7–13.

IRS (1999) 'New ways to perform appraisal', *Employment Trends*, 676: 7–16.

Kessler, I. and Purcell, J. (1992) 'Performance related pay: objectives and application', *Human Resource Management Journal*, 2(3): 16–33.

Kolesar, P. (1993) 'Vision, values and milestones. Paul O'Neil starts total quality at Alcoa', *California Management Review*, 35(3): 133–65.

Laabs, J. (1992) 'Measuring work in the electronic age', *Personnel Journal*, 71(6): 35.

Lawler, E.E. III (1994) 'Performance management: the next generation', *Compensation and Benefits Review*, May–June: 16–28.

Lawler, J.J., Jain, H.C., Ratnam, C.S.V. and Atmiyanandana, V. (1995) 'Human resource management in developing economies: a comparison of India and Thailand', *International Journal of Human Resource Management*, 6(2): 320–46.

LGMB (1994) *Performance Management and Performance Related Pay. Local Government Practice*, London: LGMB.

Locher, A.H. and Teel, K.S. (1988) 'Appraisal trends', *Personnel Journal*, 67(9): 139–43.

London, M. and Beatty, R. W. (1993), '360-degree feedback as a competitive advantage', *Human Resource Management*, Summer/Autumn: 353–72.

Long, P. (1986) *Performance Appraisal Revisited*, London: IPD.

Longenecker, C. (1989) 'Truth or consequences: politics and performance appraisals', *Business Horizons*, November–December: 76–82.

Maroney, B.P. and Buckley, P.P.M. (1992) 'Does research in performance appraisal influence the practice of performance appraisal? Regretfully not.' *Public Personnel Management*, 21(2): 185–196.

Miles, L. (1993) 'Rise of the mystery shopper', *Marketing*, 29 July: 19–20.

Milliman, J.F., Zawacki, R.A., Schulz, B., Wiggins, S. and Norman, C. (1995) 'Customer service drives 360-degree goal setting', *Personnel Journal*, June: 136–41.

Mitrani, A., Dalziel, M.M., and Fitt, D. (1992) *Competency Based Human Resource Management*, London: Kogan Page.

Moores, B. (1990) 'The service excellence experience', *Marketing Intelligence and Planning*, 8(6): 19–24.

O'Reilly, B. (1995) '360-degree feedback can change your life', *Fortune*, October 17: 55–58.

Peters, T. (1987) *Thriving on Chaos*, London: Macmillan.

Randell, G. (1994) 'Employee appraisal', in Sisson, K. (ed) *Personnel Management in Britain*, Oxford: Blackwell.

Redman, T. and Snape, E. (1992) 'Upward and onward: can staff appraise their managers?,' *Personnel Review*, 21(7): 32–46.

Redman, T., and McElwee, G. (1993) 'Upward appraisal of lecturers: lessons from industry?', *Education + Training*, 35(2): 20–26.

Redman, T. and Mathews, B.P. (1995) 'Do corporate turkeys vote for Christmas? Managers' attitudes towards upward appraisal', *Personnel Review*, 24(7): 13–24.

Redman, T., Snape, E., Thompson, D. and Ka-ching Yan, F. (2000) 'Performance appraisal in the National Health Service: a trust hospital study', *Human Resource Management Journal*, 10(1): 1–16.

Ring, T. (1992) 'Managing quality: efficiency on the line', *Personnel Today*, 14 July: 25–26.

Roth, W. and Ferguson, D. (1994) 'The end of performance appraisals?', *Quality Digest*, 14(9): 52–57.

Scholtes, P.R. (1993) 'Total quality or performance appraisal: choose one', *National Productivity Review*, Summer: 349–63.

Sherman, S. (1995) 'Stretch goals: the dark side of asking for miracles', *Fortune*, November: 231–32.

Silvestro, R. (1990) 'Quality management in service industries', *International Journal of Service Industry Management*, 1(2): 54–56.

Snape, E., Redman, T. and Bamber, G. (1994) *Managing Managers*, Oxford: Blackwells.

Snape, E., Thompson, D., Ka-ching Yan, F. and Redman, T. (1998) 'Performance appraisal and culture: practice and attitudes in Hong Kong and Great Britain', *International Journal of Human Resource Management*, 9(5): 841–61.

Sparrow, P. (1994) 'Organizational competencies: creating a strategic behavioural framework for selection and assessment', in Anderson, N. and Herriot, P. (eds) *Assessment and Selection in Organizations*, Chichester: John Wiley.

Syrett, M. and Lammiman, J. (1994) 'Developing the "peripheral" worker', *Personnel Management*, July: 28–31.

Thomas, A., Wells, M. and Willard, J. (1992) 'A novel approach to developing managers and their teams: BPX uses upward feedback', *Management Education and Development*, 23(1): 30–32.

Tombs, S. (1992) 'Managing safety: could do better...', *Occupational Safety and Health*, 9–12.

Townley, B. (1989) 'Selection and appraisal: reconstituting "social relations"', in J. Storey (ed) *New Perspectives on Human Resource Management*, London: Routledge.

Townley, B. (1990) 'A discrimination approach to appraisal', *Personnel Management*, December: 34–37.

Townley, B. (1993) 'Performance appraisal and the emergence of management', *Journal of Management Studies*, 30(2): 221–38.

Townley, B. (1994) *Reframing Human Resource Management*, London: Sage.

Tully, S. (1994) 'Stretch targets', *Fortune*, 14 November: 83–90.

Tziner, A. (1999) 'The relationship between distal and proximal factors and the use of political considerations in performance appraisal', *Journal of Business and Psychology*, 14(1): 217–31.

Wilson, J. and Cole, G. (1990) 'A healthy approach to performance appraisal', *Personnel Management*, June: 46–49.

Winstanley, D., Dawson, S., Mole, V. and Sherval, J. (1995) 'Under the microscope: performance management and review for senior managers in the NHS', paper presented at BUIRA annual conference, Durham.

Wright, V. (1991) 'Performance related pay', in Neale F. (ed) *The Handbook of Performance Management*, London: IPM.

Chapter 4

Reward management

Philip Lewis

Introduction

Reward has traditionally been thought of as the poor relation of personnel management. It has been seen as part of 'the turgid, unimaginative and inflexible world of wage and salary administration' (Smith, 1993: 45). But this world has changed in recent years for many organisations. This chapter reflects this new thinking about reward. Indeed, many writers have argued that thinking about wage and salary administration is in itself new. Livy (1988) typifies this scepticism in describing most reward systems as 'chaotic' with 'employers having little idea about what their pay systems are supposed to achieve'. Smith (1983: 12) is equally sceptical:

> Repeated questions to managers and employees about why they pay and accept certain levels of remuneration usually result in replies which boil down to the same answer: that is the pay level is as it has always been or, in harsher terms, we don't really know. There are very few organisations where the answer is clear and positive.

Pay does not have to be so 'chaotic'. The orthodoxy which has arisen in recent years under the heading of 'new pay' (Lawler, 1990; Schuster and Zingheim, 1992) argues that the business strategy of the organisation determines the behaviours employees need to demonstrate in order that the strategy may be implemented effectively. These behaviours may, in part, be delivered by the reward strategy. Lawler (1995) notes that the reward strategy consists of three key elements: the values which underpin the reward strategy; the reward structures and reward processes.

This chapter uses the 'new pay' approach, and in particular Lawler's theory. This serves as a point of departure and a device for structuring the chapter. Using this perspective ensures that the emphasis is upon the major concern of many organisations: the role that reward strategy redesign may play in contributing to organisational change.

Strategic reward management

Consideration of the relationship between reward management and changing employee behaviours in order to complement business strategy must begin with a clarification of what it is the organisation wishes to change and why. It was pointed out at the beginning of this chapter that a logical starting point for this process is to clarify what it is that the organisation wishes employees to do which may be different from what they are currently doing. Equally logical is the rationale for such changed employee behaviours: that is, they should be consistent with what the organisation is seeking to achieve through its business strategy. This sits easily with the strategic HRM literature (see, for example, Mabey, Salaman and Storey, 1998).

The strategic reward model in Figure 4.1 below suggests that reward strategy starts with a consideration of the business strategy. This is based upon the organisation's external and internal operating environments. (Armstrong (1993) notes that the internal environment consists of the organisation's culture, structure, technology, working arrangements, processes and systems.) The business strategy implies the need for the development of particular employee behaviours appropriate to the strategy. This may be, for example, the acquisition of more 'commercially aware' attitudes and behaviours and greater preparedness and ability to undertake a wider range of tasks.

Lawler's model proposes that the compensation strategy can make a valuable contribution to the development of these employee behaviours. As such, compensation is, of course, only part of the wider HR strategy. Lawler (1984) argues that there should be congruence between these various aspects of the HRM strategy in that the reward system needs to fit the other features of the HR strategy, such as job design and managers' leadership styles, to ensure that total human resource management congruence exists.

According to Lawler (1995) the reward strategy consists of three components:

- the organisation's core reward values
- structural issues
- process features

The organisation's core reward values are what the organisation stands for, which informs the principles on which the reward strategy is founded. Structural issues include the strategy features (e.g. performance-related or profit-related pay) and the administrative policies surrounding these features. Process features include principally how the strategy is communicated and implemented and the extent to which employees are involved in the design and implementation of the strategy.

Each of these is considered in the remainder of this chapter. Lawler makes the point that the stronger the alignment between the core reward values, structural features and processes, the more effective the reward strategy will be. He argues that the key consideration is the level of consistency between what organisations say and what they do. In the event of inconsistency, Lawler notes that there is likely to be employee misunderstanding about how the reward strategy works, with a consequence being a failure to generate the required behaviours.

Challenging the assumptions underlying strategic reward management

On first examination this model of strategic reward management seems highly rational, but it makes significant assumptions. First, consider the main driving force of the reward strategy – the business strategy. Two of the complications are well rehearsed in the literature. First, the assumption that business strategy is a rational, top-down process rather than emerging as a result of a pattern of management actions over time (Mintzberg and Waters, 1989; Whittington, 1993). Even if the business strategy is clearly formulated, it is by no means certain that the HRM strategy will follow this lead. Indeed, if this is contemplated, it is often not possible to promote wholesale changes to, for example, recruitment and selection, training, appraisal and career development. What is more likely is that such changes happen incrementally over time.

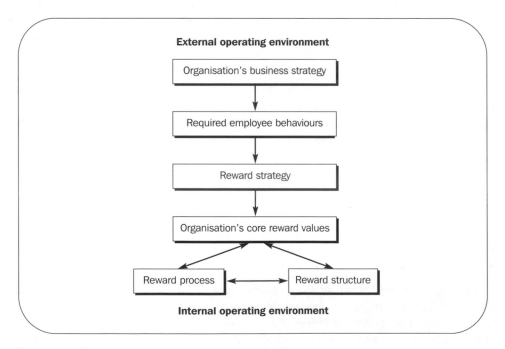

Figure 4.1 Key elements of reward system design
Source: developed from Lawler, 1995

In addition, the model is essentially unitarist in that it assumes employees will endorse the business strategy and wish to demonstrate the behaviours it implies. Moreover, it assumes that they will accept the organisation's reward strategy if the values, structure and process are consistent. This may be the case if the employees' interests are not threatened. But such reward changes under the heading of 'new pay' may not be received favourably by employees. Indeed, if, as is often the case, one of the strategic driving forces is cost saving, such a threat is almost inevitable.

As well as being unitarist, the strategic reward management model is highly deterministic. It reflects a very 'bottom line' orientation (Beaumont, 1993: 205) which assumes that an effective reward strategy will have a beneficial effect upon the performance of the organisation. This is a significant assumption because of the difficulty in subjecting it to empirical test. The model masks the complexities of organisational life. To think that simply designing the reward strategy in accordance with the prescription will yield 'success' ignores the host of variables which may conspire to render such an outcome unlikely. Managers often take 'short cuts' due to the pressure to produce quick results exerted by senior managers obsessed with short-term goals (Storey and Sisson, 1993; Monks, 1998). There is often opposition to changing reward strategies from trade unions as well as managers who feel their interests threatened. In short, the deterministic perspective is based on assumptions of rationality and unitarism which disregard the political realities of organisational life (Keenoy, 1990).

There is also a major assumption which dominates reward management thinking in general and the model in Figure. 4.1 in particular. This is that pay has the ability to motivate employees to behave in a way in which they might not otherwise behave. The theory that tends to dominate is that of the rational economic person. This has its roots in the work of F.W.Taylor (1911) who assumed that workers were lazy and needed money to motivate them to expend greater effort. The prevalence of payments-by-results schemes this century, in particular for blue-collar workers, testifies to the influence of this way of thinking about the relationship between pay and employee effort. Later, this approach was questioned by the human relations school, which queried the overreliance on money as a motivator and argued that social relationships were an important determinant of employee productivity.

The theories of Maslow (1943) and Herzberg (1968) are equally well known. Maslow's 'hierarchy of needs' suggests that people's needs change as they ascend a hierarchy which has basic needs for food, security, etc. at the lowest level, ranging to self-actualisation at the highest. Herzberg argued that employees were more likely to be motivated by factors such as achievement and the work itself rather than simply money. While money has only limited power to motivate, it does have the ability to demotivate employees if they are dissatisfied with the amount they receive or the way in which this amount is determined.

It is beyond the scope of this chapter to go into detail on these and the many other motivation theories. What is clear is that the relationship between pay and motivation is highly complex. Perhaps the best that can be said is that money may motivate some people to behave in particular ways some of the time, in some circumstances. What cannot be assumed is a clear relationship between pay and motivation. Indeed, as Pfeffer (1998) suggests, overreliance on pay to secure the motivation of employees may be at the cost of more powerful motivators such as meaningful work in a high-trust, friendly environment.

Clearly, caution needs to be exercised in assuming that the implementation of strategic reward management will lead to a reward strategy that will automatically change employee behaviours in line with the organisation's business strategy. There are far too many variables which may conspire against such a straightforward cause–effect relationship. However, it would be foolish to abandon the possibility that reward strategy may play a role in contributing to organisational change.

Ethical concerns of strategic reward management

In addition to the assumptions of rationality, unitarism and determinism, the strategic reward management model promotes ethical concerns. Heery (1996) argues that there are three concerns with new pay. First, strategic reward management poses a threat to the wellbeing of employees. New pay advocates suggest reducing the proportion of pay that is fixed, thus putting a proportion of the pay packet 'at risk' through techniques such as performance-related pay or profit-related pay. Wellbeing is threatened by an increased amount of insecurity and unpredictability that is potentially harmful both economically and psychologically. Additionally, putting a proportion of employees' income at risk may lead to such behaviours as overwork which may damage both mental and physical health.

Second, Heery argues that new pay may be unjust. This may be at two levels. It may be procedurally unjust in terms of the way in which the element of pay at risk is determined, usually by line managers. This is considered later in this chapter under the heading of individual performance-related pay. It also may be unjust in a distributive sense. New pay theory has it that employees take their share of the hardship when the organisation is doing less well, for example, through lower or non-existent profit-related pay. In this way employers are transferring an element of risk from their shareholders to their employees. But as Heery points out, shareholders are often better equipped to spread their risks than employees, who often are dependent on their salary as the sole source of income.

Thirdly, Heery (1996: 62) suggests that new pay 'affords little scope for the exercise of democratic rights by citizens at the workplace'. It is suggested earlier in this chapter that new pay has a highly unitarist ring. If it is assumed that there is no essential conflict of interest between employer and employees then the right of employees to have their views represented is of little importance. Indeed, trade unions and collective bargaining have little coverage in the new pay literature. On the other hand, there is emphasis on employee involvement, but this tends to focus on securing commitment of employees to the goals of the organisation and new pay rather than representing the interests of employees. In this sense, new pay may be seen as part of a sophisticated edifice to marginalise the democratic rights of employees at the workplace and the mechanisms for securing those rights. There is little evidence, however, of such a sophisticated level of strategic thinking in the UK. Wood's (1996) survey of UK manufacturing plants found little systematic association between pay systems such as performance-related pay and profit-related pay and so-called high commitment work practices such as teamworking, quality circles, employee communication, multiskilling and single status terms and conditions. These are the sort of HR practices, when aligned with new pay techniques, which one would expect to see if management were making concerted efforts to ensure that employees adopted the goals of the organisation.

The remainder of this chapter examines the components of Figure 4.1. The purpose of the analysis is to explain how integration between the HRM strategy and the reward strategy, and integration between the three components of the reward strategy itself, may contribute to changed employee behaviours.

The analysis starts with a consideration of the employee behaviours employers may wish to encourage. The relationship between HRM strategy and reward strategy is then examined briefly. The main part of the analysis is devoted to a consideration of the reward strategy's values, structure and processes.

What employee behaviours may organisations wish to encourage?

The strategic HRM literature (e.g. Beer *et al.*, 1984; Guest, 1987) reflects the desire for certain key goals: employee commitment to the organisation's aims; employee competence; flexibility and the production of quality goods and services. The way in which many organisations have sought to ensure the acquisition of appropriate employee behaviours is through the definition of key competencies for particular jobs. Typical of this approach is the competencies required by Standard Chartered Bank (IDS, 1992). Box 4.1 (overleaf) lists the generic competencies employees are expected to develop if they are to perform their jobs satisfactorily and generate individual performance-related pay awards.

At the end of this chapter is a case study of Lincoln Insurance. It is clear in this case that Lincoln wished to develop the range of skills of its employees to make them more flexible. This was a response to the need to restructure the work processes to provide a better service to customers

What part do reward management values, structures and processes play in changing employee behaviour?

The importance Lawler (1995) placed on consistency between the three components of reward strategy, values, structure and processes, is noted above. In particular, Lawler claimed that an inconsistency between what the organisation says and does in its reward strategy may lead to employee discontent. It follows from this that the reward values which employers espouse are of great significance.

BOX 4.1

Generic competencies used by Standard Chartered Bank for performance-related pay awards

- *Job and professional knowledge* which includes keeping abreast of the latest technology developments in the employee's professional field and knowledge of other areas of the bank.

- *Commercial customer awareness*, including understanding the financial and competitive forces affecting the bank and keeping informed of customer needs.

- *Communication*, which includes speaking and writing clearly.

- *Interpersonal skills*, which include interacting effectively with colleagues and responding productively to constructive criticism.

- *Teamwork*, including fully contributing to the team effort by relating well to others.

- *Initiative/adaptability/creativity*, which includes seeking out opportunities for innovation, setting priorities and goals.

- *Analytical skills/decision-making*, including understanding data and information in order to solve problems.

- *Productivity*, which assesses the quantity of performance such as volume of work.

- *Quality*, for example, freedom from errors.

- *Management/supervision*, which includes reviewing performance, counselling and staff development and delegation.

- *Leadership*, including the ability to inspire, motivate and give confidence.

(IDS, 1992)

This section analyses four values which organisations may consider in reward management design. These are the degree to which the organisation believes in:

- paying for performance
- equity
- employees sharing in the organisation's success
- combining financial and non-financial rewards

The analysis that follows considers each of these values and the ways in which the values are reflected in the pay structure. There is also some consideration of key implementation processes.

The value of paying for performance

Paying for individual job performance is, for many organisations, at the heart of a reward strategy. This raises what for many employees is a highly contentious issue: the putting at risk of a proportion of their salary. Most employees think about pay in terms of base pay (Schuster and Zingheim, 1992): the fixed amount which traditionally has increased yearly to reflect inflation and, often, length of service. Base pay will also change, of course, upon promotion to a more responsible job. This embodies the values of predictability, security and permanency – none of which are characteristics consistent with the desire to change employee behaviours. From a managerial perspective, it is not necessarily the best form of reward strategy. The very permanency which employees value is expensive. Increasingly employers are asking themselves why they should build into their fixed salary costs a permanent salary bill which takes little account of changing external, organisational and individual circumstances. Pay strategies which rely exclusively on base pay enshrined in salary scales through which employees move annually until the top of the scale is reached, or promotion achieved, are typical in the public sector. Such strategies assume that length of service equates with experience and loyalty. Neither tends to be as prized by organisations now as in the past. Such is the pace of change that yesterday's experience may be an impediment to change. It is accepted that loyalty to one employer, typified by a career spent with that employer, is an increasingly outdated concept in an age where employees may have a number of different careers as well as employers. In addition, pay strategies which rely on promotions for employees to grow their salaries do not take into account the fact that organisations now have flatter structures, with the consequence that promotion is less available. The desire of employees only to move to jobs within their own organisation which result in a minor promotion, and therefore, regrading, is a major obstacle to developing employees into different roles where they learn new skills. This was precisely the problem which Lincoln experienced. It proved a major incentive for the company to reduce the amount of levels in its pay structure.

For some organisations base pay is of declining importance. This raises the question: 'How can the traditional reward objectives of attracting, retaining and motivating people be achieved while making the pay budget more cost-effective?' The answer for many organisations has been to make base pay reflect the market rate for the job and to supplement this with a variable pay element related to individual performance, team performance, organisational performance and individual competence acquisition – or a combination of these. One of the key decisions that needs to be taken into account is whether to pay the variable element as a lump sum bonus or to consolidate this into salary. The trend in the USA has been for variable pay to be one-off cash bonuses (Kanter, 1987). This is hardly surprising given the cost saving that the organisation enjoys. By not raising base pay, one-off cash bonuses do not affect future base pay increases or other associated payments such as overtime and, of course, pensions.

A shift from all base pay to a combination of base and variable pay does, of course, signal the organisation's desire to move from paying for the job to paying the person. Therefore, the reliance on traditional bureaucratic forms of job evaluation is less pronounced. However, job evaluation is still relevant. Base pay still needs to be set at a level consistent with the external labour market. Therefore, some method of determining the relative importance of jobs is needed. It is that definition of importance that is likely to be different in the organisation which places more significance in a combination of base and variable pay. Such a definition is likely to reflect the changed employee behaviours the organisation wishes to encourage in order to meet its changed organisational circumstances. What is clear, according to Schuster and Zingheim (1992), is that internal equity will no longer be the dominant consideration. The market value of jobs, and employees' skills and their impact on the organisation's strategy will take precedence over internal equity. Such a strategy, however, runs the risk of contravening the legislation on equal pay if, for example, women are systematically disadvantaged in that they have fewer opportunities to demonstrate good performance or achieve competence. This may be, for example, as a consequence of the greater likelihood of women working part-time.

Below is a brief consideration of some of the main structural and process issues in relation to two pay for performance initiatives: individual performance-related pay and competence-based pay (pay linked to organisational performance is considered in the section on employees sharing in the organisation's success). Both of these are exemplified in the Lincoln case study at the end of this chapter.

Individual performance-related pay

Individual performance-related pay (PRP) is defined by ACAS as: 'a method of payment where an individual employee receives increases in pay based wholly or partly on the regular and systematic assessment of job performance' (ACAS, 1990: 2). It has been adopted with great enthusiasm in many areas of white-collar employment, for example local government and financial services.

PRP has been introduced in many organisations to change the culture to reflect the 'new' values which senior managers think are necessary. Lawler (1984: 128) argues that reward systems can 'cause the culture of an organisation to vary quite widely. For example they can influence the degree to which it is seen as a human-resource oriented culture, an entrepreneurial culture, an innovative culture, a competence-based culture, and a participative culture'. There is also a strong thread of felt-fairness about PRP. Most employees (Kessler, 1994) agree with the principle of PRP: that the able and industrious employee should be rewarded more generously for that ability and industry than the idle and incompetent.

However, it is the implementation of PRP that seems to cause problems of perceived unfairness. Lewis (1998), in a study of PRP for first-level managers in three financial services organisations found evidence of their managers imposing objectives upon them, with the result that the objective-setting process was 'something that was done to them rather than something in which they played an active part'

(Lewis, 1998: 70).The employees interviewed by Procter *et al.* (1993) in an electronics plant expressed concerns about favouritism, in particular, the arbitrary way in which managers applied measurement criteria and the ways in which grades were distributed. In two of the three organisations Lewis (1998) researched he noted little attention paid to the giving of performance feedback to employees. There were similar implementation problems in the pharmaceutical company studied by Randle (1997: 198) such that performance-related pay emerged as 'one of Pharmex's most consistently disliked management practices'.

An important part of the implementation of PRP is that managers are put in a position where they must differentiate between the level of reward of their team members. This decision process effectively creates increased dependency of the team member on the line manager, and less dependency on, for example, the trade union (Kessler, 1994). Consequently, some organisations have seized this opportunity to expect greater management accountability. ACAS (1990: 8) point out that the role of managers and supervisors is critical to the implementation of PRP. It is they who must define the required standards of performance and behaviour; explain these to their team members; take tough decisions about assessments; communicate these decisions to team members and defend their judgements if asked (Storey and Sisson, 1993). But often managers find this differentiation difficult, with the result that they produce statistical distributions that concentrate on the middle rank of performance, thus defeating the object of paying for differentiated performance. Kessler and Purcell (1992: 22) found evidence of the desire to 'make managers manage' in their research. They note, 'PRP is often seen as a means of forcing a manager into a direct one-to-one, usually face to face relationship with their employees'.

The outcome of these implementation weaknesses is that the value of paying for performance is not practised. What seems a good idea in principle becomes overtaken by perceived problems, with the result that employees lose faith in the concept. It seems that teachers have learned the lessons from other employment sectors in developing their opposition to PRP (*The Guardian*, 1999).

Competence-related pay

Competence-related pay can be defined as 'a method of rewarding people wholly or partly by reference to the level of competence they demonstrate in carrying out their roles' (Armstrong and Murlis, 1998). It is predictable that interest in competence-related pay should grow in view of the enormous amount of attention given to the definition of competencies for purposes of selection, training and appraisal in recent years.

One of the frequent complaints of the first-line managers in a bank (Lewis, 1998) was that it was really only the 'hard' outputs (e.g. the number of mortgages sold) rather than the 'soft' processes (e.g. the way in which they led their branch team) that counted when performance measurement was carried out. Their managers were not too concerned with how the job was done, provided that results were achieved. Competence-related pay overcomes this alleged weakness of PRP by ensuring that, usually, both processes and outputs are taken into account when pay-related measurement is made.

Armstrong and Murlis's (1998) definition of competence-related pay captures the most important difference between competence-related pay and PRP. This is that PRP is essentially retrospective in that it measures performance over the past pay period (often one year). However, competence-related pay is more forward-looking. It identifies those competencies that are likely to be associated with effective job performance.

Flannery *et al.* (1996: 92) define competencies as 'sets of skills, knowledge, abilities, behavioural characteristics, and other attributes that, in the right combination and for the right set of circumstances, predict superior performance'. So the technical skill to do the job is clearly not enough. The successful job-holder must ally this skill (e.g. introducing clients to new products) with other attributes (e.g. the desire to enhance the performance of the branch or team). In other words, competence-related pay is highly contextual. It also has, potentially, strong links to organisational strategy. The question which may be asked at business strategy level is 'What competencies do we want our people to demonstrate in order that we may achieve our business goals?'

Managers concerned with 'hard' outputs would be comforted by the fact that many organisations introducing competence-related pay accompany competence-related ratings with performance output measurements, the market rate for the job, and the position of the individual on the pay scale in determining salary level. As can be seen in the following case study, this is the case at Lincoln.

With PRP, it was noted that managers can apply measurement criteria in an arbitrary way, which creates in employees problems of a lack of felt-fairness. This is no less true of competence-related pay. In fact, the more the approach moves from one where identifying discernible skills and outputs is possible, the more subjective the measurement process becomes. As yet, little empirical research has been done on the operation of competence-related pay, but it would be surprising were it to uncover anything other than the same sort of employee dissatisfactions as PRP. However, the measurement criteria themselves may be more acceptable to employees than in the case of PRP. This is often because there is some form of employee involvement in the development of the competence statements (Armstrong and Murlis, 1998), albeit that line managers are making the assessment of the extent to which they have been demonstrated. This is unlike PRP, where it is usually the manager who defines the performance objectives and assesses performance.

The value of equity

It would be an exaggeration to say that the value of equity may be a major contributor to the promotion of changed employee behaviours. But if employees feel their pay to be inequitable then the changed employee behaviours managers hope for in their new reward strategy are unlikely to materialise. Employee acceptance is a key determinant of reward strategy success (Lawler, 1990) and perceived inequity by employees will lead to a lack of employee acceptance of the reward strategy.

There are two ways in which employees may feel their pay is inequitable. First, there is the issue of external equity and internal equity. External equity refers to the extent to which the employee feels his/her pay is fair in relation to those doing similar jobs in other organisations. Internal equity relates to the same feeling in comparison with those doing similar jobs in his/her own organisation. Armstrong (1993) points out that in many organisations there is a tension between the two. The desire to be competitive in the labour market for some jobs, thus ensuring external equity, may lead to feelings of lack of internal inequity among those employees whose external labour market appeal does not afford them similar power. What is implied here is the necessity for the employer to take a clear policy decision on the value it places in equity and the way in which this value is expressed.

The second way in which employees may feel their pay is inequitable is less about the amount of pay than the way in which it is determined. This raises issues concerning structure and process, which are considered below.

One of the most potent symbols of perceived inequity which has gained considerable publicity in recent years is that of directors' pay. The image of directors gaining huge pay increases at a time when their organisations have been declaring redundancies and trimming general pay costs is one that has created significant employee and trade union discontent. The facts appear to justify this discontent. Armstrong (1996) notes that in the period between 1985 and 1990, according to a survey by the UK National Institute of Economic and Social Research, directors' pay rose in real terms by 77 per cent while the equivalent figure for all employees was 17 per cent. Reports from the Cadbury and Greenbury committees of the mid-1990s, which were designed to secure greater openness and accountability, seem to have done little to improve the public perception of unfairness. Clearly, employee acceptance of reward strategy change is unlikely if the general impression is that 'fat cats' are getting an unfair share of organisational rewards.

But it is not just directors' pay that fed the impression of inequity. Inequality between the pay of men and women is such that, despite the three decades of equal pay legislation, the gross hourly earnings of women in 1998 were significantly lower than men's. Manual women earned 71.6 per cent of the equivalent gross hourly figure for men. For non-manual women the figure was 69 per cent (*Labour Market Trends*, 1998).

Less often discussed is the possibility of perceived inequality in the comparison between white- and blue-collar workers. This is a wider issue than simply pay. It relates to a range of terms and conditions of employment. Many organisations which have been at the forefront of change, in particular Japanese manufacturing companies, have featured initiatives designed to harmonise terms and conditions of employment between white- and blue-collar workers in an attempt to foster a greater feeling of 'community' in their workforce (Price and Price, 1994).

There may be a similar feeling of inequity among these employees who may be called 'solid citizens'. These are the employees who add a good deal to every organisation but who do not pursue promotion. The move to broad banding has the capacity to reduce some of these feelings of inequity. Broad banding is defined by Armstrong (1996: 224) as 'the compression of pay grades and salary ranges into a small number (typically four or five) of wide bands. Each of the bands will therefore span the pay opportunities previously covered by several separate pay ranges'. The advantages of broad banding noted by Armstrong (1996) suggest that this pay reform has, potentially, a powerful role to play in complementing, if not generating, organisational change. Among these are:

- facilitation of movement of employees across the organisation without the necessity for promotion to a higher grade to be obtained
- development of employees' skills and competencies by removing perceived barriers to movement
- the support of multiskilling and teamwork by removing barriers to lateral movement
- enabling line managers to accept greater responsibility to reward with salary increases those employees who demonstrate a greater 'contribution' (however defined) to the organisation.

Wider pay ranges give the 'solid citizens' the opportunity to 'grow' their salaries without hitting the barriers imposed by narrower bands which can only be surmounted by promotion. The role broad banding plays in changing employee behaviours is potentially very important. It complements the efforts which many organisations are currently making to achieve greater flexibility in the organisation of work. The Lincoln case study at the end of this chapter is an excellent example of an organisation introducing broad banding for this purpose.

The value of employees sharing in the organisation's success

Organisations that wish to promote a high level of employee identification with the pursuit of success are likely to have an element of sharing in that success built into their reward strategy. The most popular form this has taken is profit-related pay, although other forms of profit-share schemes are explained below. These schemes may not play the major role in changing employee behaviours due to the remote connection between effort and reward. However, they are likely to form an increasingly significant portion of the employee's pay and have the potential to foster a greater bond between employers and employees.

Profit-related pay

Profit-related pay has grown considerably in recent years to the point where in 1994 1.8 million private sector employees were covered by such a scheme (IDS, 1994). Such schemes are most popular in the utilities sector (water, gas and electricity) and financial services where 81 per cent and 80 per cent of workplaces reported their existence in the 1998 Workplace Employee Relations survey (Cully *et al.*, 1999). Overall, the survey noted that 47 per cent of private sector workplaces had profit-related pay schemes.

The reasons for this are easy to guess since it has been possible for employees to have as much as £4,000 of salary per year free of income tax. This tax advantage was introduced by government to promote a stronger awareness of the commercial performance of the employer among employees and to encourage employees to greater effort. It is doubtful if it has achieved that effect since many organisations have seen it as little more than a tax-efficient way of structuring salary. However, the last Conservative budget in 1997 announced the gradual withdrawal of the tax advantage by the year 2000. This may see the growth of other forms of profit-sharing and share option schemes which have the capacity to enhance employee awareness of profit performance.

Profit-sharing schemes

The concept of the profit-sharing scheme is quite simple: the company pays a bonus to eligible employees, based on company profits, which the employee must use to buy shares in the company. Unlike profit-related pay, this is not a part of the employee's salary – it is a discretionary bonus. However, like profit-related pay, it gives tax advantages to the employee because the share bonus is tax-free provided that the scheme is approved by the Inland Revenue. In order for the scheme to meet this approval the employer must meet a number of criteria including:

■ the necessity to set up a company-wide scheme
■ the payment of bonuses must be in free shares of the company, not in cash
■ the necessity to set up a special trust with appointed trustees. (The trust purchases the shares for employees and sets these aside)
■ the stipulation that no more than £3,000 p.a. per employee or, if it is a greater amount, 10 per cent of salary, up to a maximum of £8,000 in any tax year (at 1999) must be set aside as bonus.

The employee has no tax liability if the bonus shares are not sold for at least three years. To gain Inland Revenue approval, all employees who have been employed by the company for five years must be eligible, although in many cases companies allow employees to participate with much shorter service periods (e.g. six months at Severn Trent Water (IDS, 1998)). Payments are made from a profit-related pool. This pool may be determined by a published formula or be at the discretion of the directors at the time of the payout. For example, at Barclays Bank in 1997, 5 per cent of company profits made up the profit-share pool (IDS, 1998).

In his November 1999 pre-Budget report, the Chancellor announced that companies will be able to give their employees £3,000-worth of shares tax free with no capital gains to pay after 5 years. This can be restricted to a single department, division or subsidiary of the company. In addition, employees will be able to buy another £1,500-worth of shares out of their pre-tax pay. If they do so the company can give them another £3,000-worth of shares (*Daily Telegraph*, 1999).

Profit-sharing schemes are likely to become more widespread in future years. In 1995/6 around 740,000 UK employees were enjoying the benefits of profit-sharing schemes (IDS, 1998). The 1998 Workplace Employee Relations survey (Cully *et al.*, 1999) reported that 25 per cent of private sector workplaces had some sort of employee share ownership scheme. According to IDS (1998) the average value in shares allocated as bonus to each participant was £640.

Savings-related share option schemes

Unlike the typical profit-sharing scheme, the savings-related share option scheme requires a contribution from the employee. In a savings-related share option scheme the employee saves for a specified period (three, five or seven years). The scheme specifies that employees can buy shares at the end of the savings period with the savings fund accumulated. The price of the shares will be the market price at the start of the savings contract or at an agreed discount, that discount rate being agreed at the start of the contract. The shares bought at the end of the savings contract attract tax relief.

With the three-year savings contract the employee saves a fixed amount monthly (it cannot exceed £250) and at the end of the term a cash bonus of 2.75 months' payments is added. At the end of a five-year contract a cash bonus of nine months' payments is added. At the end of the three or five year term the employee uses the amount saved and the bonus to buy shares in the company. For employees who have saved for five years there is the option of saving for seven years, in which case 18 months' payments are added as a cash bonus. However, this means that the employee can still only buy shares with the amount saved after five years.

The price at which employees have the opportunity to purchase shares must not be below 80 per cent of the market value at the start of the contract. This seemed to be the typical price determined by employers in an IDS study (IDS, 1998).

As with profit-sharing schemes, all employees who have been employed by the company for five years must be eligible to participate in savings-related share option schemes if the scheme is to gain Inland Revenue approval. However, one year appears to be a more usual minimum service period (IDS, 1998). In 1995/6, 610,000 employees were in 1,305 schemes.

Company share option plans

Inland Revenue approval may also be gained for schemes that grant share options to employees. These have usually been aimed at directors and senior managers and have therefore become known as 'executive share options'. However, some companies, like Kingfisher, run all-employee share option schemes. The scheme allows employees to buy shares at a future date but at prices operating at the time the share option is granted. There is a £30,000 limit on the amount of shares that may be granted under this and other approved share option schemes. In addition, the Inland Revenue rules forbid the granting of shares at a discount.

At Kingfisher (IDS, 1998), all full-time and part-time employees employed on the date at which the company results are announced are included in the scheme and therefore have the option to buy. All eligible Kingfisher employees were granted 200 shares (companies may also base the grant allocation on a percentage of salary) at a price of £6.57 per share in April 1997. In order to gain tax relief on the shares Kingfisher employees must take up the option to purchase shares from their allocation of 200 between April 2000 and April 2007 (i.e. between three and ten years after the date of the grant). Kingfisher employees are able to buy and sell the shares and take any gain at no cost to themselves.

Gainsharing

Gainsharing is more popular in the USA than in Britain. In a gainsharing scheme the relationship between employees' efforts and their eventual reward is more direct than with profit-related pay. Gainsharing plans are designed so that employees share the financial results of improvements in productivity, cost saving or quality. The resultant payment is paid from costs savings generated as a result of such improvements. Employees participating in the gainsharing plan are normally part of a discernible group who have had a direct effect upon the cost savings. The gainshare plan payment to them may be made in three ways: as a percentage of base pay; as a one-off cash bonus or as a payment per hour worked. Schuster and Zingheim (1992) make the point that the same payment would normally go to all members of the group. They are also careful to point out that the organisation must design safeguards to ensure that it derives financial value from the results generated from the project linked to gainsharing. This type of gainsharing differs from more traditional forms of gainsharing which have operated in manufacturing under the heading of Scanlon and Rucker plans. The principal difference is that the foundation of this new type of gainsharing is the future goals of the organisation whereas that of more traditional gainsharing plans is the historical performance standards of the participating employees. The key point here, of course, is that historical performance standards may be achieved or exceeded while the organisation's overall goals are not met.

The value of combining financial and non-financial rewards

The extent to which an organisation combines financial and non-financial rewards in its reward strategy reflects a clear value position. Overreliance on pay as a motivator is likely to be accompanied by other human resource policies which assume a scientific management perspective (e.g. no involvement in management decisions, minimum employee control over the way in which jobs are performed). Recognition by the employer that non-financial rewards may play an important part in attracting, and more particularly retaining, employees suggests a view of humanity which recognises that individuals require more for their efforts than monetary reward.

Armstrong (1996) notes that there are five areas where employees' needs may be met by non-financial rewards: achievement, recognition, responsibility, influence and personal growth. Of these, it is likely that the first two, achievement and recognition, will apply to virtually all employees. Responsibility, influence and personal growth will apply to many more than may be realised. Everyone likes to feel that they have achieved something in their work – pride being derived from a job well done. In addition, most managers realise that a simple 'thank you' and a pat on the back for a job well done have enormous motivational power. It has to be recognised that not all employees seek greater responsibility in their jobs, or greater influence over decisions which directly or indirectly influence those jobs. This may be related to the individual's personal characteristics. But it may also be a consequence of a history of organisations not giving people the opportunity to exercise responsibility or influence. Semler's (1993) account of the management style in his Brazilian company is an excellent example of how employees accept responsibility when they are treated in such a way that they are obviously valued. The desire of many individuals to seek opportunities for personal growth through their work is very powerful. It may seem odd that this could be termed an employee reward rather than a vital prerequisite of organisational success. Yet many individuals rate the opportunity for personal growth more highly than financial reward.

Non-financial rewards may be particularly important as motivational tools for some employees. Noted below are some of the structures which may need to be in place in order for employee needs for achievement, recognition, responsibility, influence and personal growth to be realised. Meeting these needs increases the possibility of more positive employee attitudes and behaviours.

The first of these structures is probably the easiest to put in place. This is a communication strategy which broadcasts the successes of individuals and teams. Many organisations do this through their in-house magazines. This combined with special 'thank you' prizes (e.g. a weekend in Paris) often will have more motivational influence than direct financial rewards. Most of us like our colleagues to know when we are successful!

Performance appraisal systems also have a significant role to play in meeting employees' needs for recognition and a feeling of achievement. Goal-setting and giving feedback to employees about their performance in pursuit of those goals are key performance appraisal activities. A developmental perspective to performance appraisal rather than seeing it as a management control mechanism is likely to result in employees defining their own training and career development needs. However, this approach to performance appraisal does depend on line managers having the appropriate attitudes and skills to manage in such a way that the individual is given sufficient autonomy for personal growth to be developed. This implies a clear training need for managers to shed the 'technician' label they often possess and embrace new ways of managing which have leadership and facilitation as their guiding principles. These 'new ways of managing' are central to the concept of change, given the key role line managers play in managing the change process.

Employees' needs for responsibility, influence and personal growth may also be met through imaginative job design. Among the elements of job design which Armstrong (1993) advocates to enhance the interest and challenge of work are:

greater responsibility for employees in deciding how their work is done; reducing task specialisation; allowing employees greater freedom in defining their performance goals and standards of performance and introducing new and more challenging tasks. In addition, more opportunities for employee involvement may also foster responsibility, influence and personal growth among employees. They may be achieved through such activities as quality circles and problem-solving groups.

Conclusions

'New pay' is the philosophy which underpins this chapter. It is a useful way of thinking about reward management because it has the potential to complement, if not generate, organisational change.

Organisational change begins with a clarification of what it is the organisation wishes to change and why. A starting point is to clarify what it is that the organisation wishes employees to do which may be different from what they are currently doing. Such changed employee behaviours should be consistent with what the organisation is seeking to achieve through its business strategy. The aim of the reward strategy is to contribute to the generation of these changed employee behaviours.

If the reward strategy is to contribute to changing employee behaviours it must contain three key components: the values which underpin the strategy; the structures which are in place to promote these values and the processes involved in the design and implementation of the strategy.

The four values which underpin the reward management strategy are: the degree to which the organisation believes in: paying for performance; equity; employees sharing in the organisation's success and combining financial and non-financial rewards.

Important structures to promote the reward values are: making a clear division between base pay and variable pay; individual performance-related pay; team-based pay; broad banding; profit-related pay; gainsharing; performance appraisal and job design. It is important that the way in which these structures are communicated and implemented is consistent with the values which the organisation is seeking to pursue.

Many of the concepts in this chapter are being introduced in a piecemeal fashion by UK organisations. But Lincoln Insurance is introducing them in an integrated way. An examination of that organisation's reward strategy is conducted below.

Case study 4.1

Introducing a new pay structure at Lincoln

Philip Lewis

Background to Lincoln

In the UK, Lincoln is a leading provider of life assurance, pensions and investment plans. The company has grown quickly, both through acquisition and putting customers first. At the time of writing Lincoln has assets of over £4.9 billion and there are more than one million client policies in existence. The UK group is owned by Lincoln National Corporation, whose business was founded in the USA in 1905. The company was named after the former American President, Abraham Lincoln. It manages total assets of nearly $134 billion and at March 1999 had $6 billion in annual revenues. In the UK Lincoln sells its range of financial services through self-employed financial advisers. It has approximately 1,500 UK employees, based primarily on two operational sites in Uxbridge and Gloucester and 60 branch offices.

The company operates a divisional structure, the main divisions being finance, actuarial, legal, operations (e.g. customer services, IT), sales, investment and HR. Some of these divisions, e.g. HR and operations, operate on both sites.

In common with most financial services organisations, Lincoln is going through a period of significant change. This is due to its growth and the necessity to seek competitive advantage in an increasingly aggressive product market. Lincoln's principal goal is to grow sales faster than the industry average. To achieve this it aims to be more customer-focused, to develop products in line with customer requirements and to embrace new technology.

The way in which HR in general, and pay in particular, can contribute to achieving Lincoln's aims is through generating greater employee flexibility. As the introductory details for managers on the new pay structure note:

> . . . we need to create an environment which encourages the development and utilisation of each employee's skills so they can achieve results for us by becoming multi-skilled and flexible.

Nowhere illustrates this need for flexibility and multiskilling better than the image and workflow system which has been introduced in Customer Services. In essence, this means that paper is only evident at two stages in the work process: at the beginning and the end. Initially, the client's paper post is scanned on to the computer system, indexed with the policy number and a process number and delivered into an electronic 'pot' of work. Work is then taken electronically from the 'pot', sent to employees' screens and processed. At the end of the process relevant completed documents are printed in paper form and mailed to the client. This system means that employees need to possess both a wide range of skills and knowledge of technical processes because managers require them to perform a variety of functions on the client's policy work. For example, staff who have only worked on applications enquiries are required in the new system to deal with renewals or payments. In addition, staff also need to be accomplished in their operation and knowledge of the software necessary to perform the various processes.

The major benefits of the image and workflow system are that instant data retrieval will be possible on any post received and replies sent in the past six months, meaning that client enquiries can be handled more quickly and efficiently. The system also means that work can be balanced between the two operational sites more effectively. Employees on both sites have been trained to operate the system, thus enabling work to be allocated to the site where resources are best able to deal with the work.

The 'old' pay structure

The pre-1998 pay structure was a hierarchical, incremental ladder which had 16 grades. Pay progression for individuals was through moving up to the next rung on the ladder, provided that there was a job available. The consequence was that staff became, as the compensation and benefits manager put it, 'grade-fixated'. This was because jumping to the next grade not only generated a salary increase but sent a powerful message to the Lincoln world that 'here was someone on the way up'. Managers too saw upgrading as the only way of achieving salary increases for their staff outside the annual review. This was particularly important in times of low inflation and low general pay awards.

Often the means by which managers secured such upgradings was by claiming that the job had grown and this warranted an increase. Agreeing to such requests created the problem of 'leap frogging' where an upgrading in one area created pressure elsewhere for another to maintain a perceived differential status. Over time this had the effect of undermining the integrity of the grade structure. This led to senior managers asking 'Why should we feel we have to promote someone every time we want to reward them?'

The old system also paid employees more on the basis of their length of service and, therefore, experience in the company. It was clear that this was no longer a sustainable basis for the pay structure, given the amount of change that was taking place. In fact, 'unlearning' traditional ways of doing jobs was becoming even more important than adhering to old methods.

The new pay structure

The old pay structure was characterised by paying for jobs rather than paying the person and it was felt that it encouraged a value of 'job ownership'. Lincoln wished to change the pay structure so that employees defined themselves in terms of the contribution they could individually make to achieving the company's business aims. As the guidance notes for managers put it:

> We want to reward people for the knowledge and skills they have and how they apply them, not simply for the job they do. Of course, the make up of duties, tasks and responsibilities remains important but we want to move towards rewarding people for the results they achieve. Carrying out a series of rigidly defined jobs is not, we believe, the best way for people to develop and grow.

Lincoln's principal aim is to create a pay structure that complements business needs more effectively. In people terms these business needs are for a more flexible organisation, flexible work patterns with expanded job roles requiring broader skills and competencies and greater responsiveness to client demands. In addition, managers are to be given greater scope to reward good performance by their employees and respond more swiftly to changes in individual employee contribution and responsibility.

The specific objectives of the new pay structure are to:

- create a clearer, flatter structure with fewer grades which would be simpler to manage
- put greater emphasis on the individual, not the job
- increase the focus on individual growth and lateral career development
- motivate individuals to acquire new skills and responsibilities to enhance their career progression
- empower managers to make decisions about pay to reward good performance and increased responsibilities
- streamline the job evaluation process, making it more responsive to business needs.

Decreasing the amount of grades

The new grade structure reflects the process of broad banding. It consists of eight broad-banded levels rather than sixteen. Each of the eight levels contains roles with common responsibilities and a comparable impact upon organisational success. Thus, the grade levels reflect what the company calls 'value added tiers'. Roles add value to the organisation's success to an increasing degree as the levels ascend.

For each level there is a general statement of the responsibilities entailed and skills required. The responsibilities are illustrated in Table 4.1. opposite. Role titles are harmonised within each division to ensure consistency with the role holder's role and responsibilities and with general industry practice.

Each level has defined key skills and behaviours (KSBs). These are deemed necessary requirements for effective completion of the role. These KSBs effectively change the emphasis from the content of the role to the way in which the role is performed. More detail on the role of these KSBs is given opposite.

Determining the pay level of the individual employee

One of the key principles of the new pay structure is the flexibility it affords managers to make their own decisions about the pay of individual employees for

Table 4.1. Definition of responsibilities for each of the grades in the new pay structure at Lincoln

Level A	Former grades 1–4	Responsibility for processing a variety of high-volume, well-defined activities in a variety of contexts under direct supervision.
Level B	Former grades 5–6	Responsibility for processing a variety of high-volume, well-defined and some less well-defined activities in a variety of contexts. Requires close supervision for some of the time.
Level C	Former grades 7–8	Responsibility for processing a variety of high-volume, non-routine activities in a variety of contexts. Requires some supervision as well as being capable of some independence. May have responsibility for leading a small team.
Level D	Former grades 9–10	Responsibility for a variety of complex non-routine activities. Capable of a large degree of independence. Performs some specialist or professional activities and/or has responsibility for the direction and guidance of a team.
Level E	Former grade 11	Involves some accountability and autonomy. Performs specialist or professional activities and/or has responsibility for the direction and guidance of a team.
Level M1	Former grades 12–13	Involves significant accountability and autonomy. Competence in a broad range of complex specialist or professional activities and/or has responsibility for the direction and guidance of others.
Level M2	Former grades 14–15	Involves comprehensive accountability and autonomy. Competence in an extensive range of complex specialist or professional activities, including accountability for analysis and diagnosis, design, planning, execution and evaluation. Has responsibility for the direction and guidance of others and for substantial resources.
Level M3	Former grade 16	Involves the allocation of a significant range of fundamental principles and complex techniques across a wide and often unpredictable variety of contexts. Complete personal autonomy and responsibility for the work of others and for the allocation of substantial resources.

Source: Lincoln internal document.

whom they have responsibility. Consequently, there are no rigid guidelines which managers must follow. An example of this is the lack of mid-points in the new salary ranges, which means that managers and employees do not have an immediate reference point that indicates the 'typical' salary of a 'typical' employee. However, within each level there is a benchmark role. There is a target salary rate set for each benchmark role. The benchmark role is intended to be useful in providing guidance to managers on locating the position of job roles in the new structure and determining individual salaries.

Target rates are based on an assessment of four considerations:

- the local labour and, where appropriate, national market rate for comparable roles
- the average basic salary for staff undertaking the same or a similar role within the same department or division

- the average basic salary for staff undertaking the same or a similar role within Lincoln
- budgetary considerations.

Target rates are set by HR. They are deliberately not called market rates because this does not capture the full range of criteria used. It also prevents employees asserting that the company is paying less than market rate by producing job advertisements for similar roles in other companies which are, in all probability, selectively chosen. Target rates are based, in part, upon data from specialist pay consultancies such as Hay, Watson Wyatt and Remuneration Economics. In addition, the compensation and benefits manager attends a number of HR forums on a regional and national basis where pay is the main agenda item.

Further assistance is given to managers in that a pay zone is defined for each benchmark role. This pay zone is based on the target rate for a fully competent performer. The pay zone establishes a *minimum* recommended salary for a given role which is below the target rate. The pay zone figure is regularly reviewed by HR in order that it may remain competitive. Lincoln's policy is to pay a fully competent employee within the pay zone for any role. The fact that there is a minimum recommended salary for a given role which is below the target rate means that there is scope for the employee to grow his or her salary dependent on individual circumstances. The level of this pay zone will be influenced by the amount of time the employee needs to achieve target rate related to a fully competent employee. The more technical the role content, the longer the period necessary to become fully competent. The aim is to enable employees to achieve target rate as soon as full competence is demonstrated. This contrasts sharply with the old pay structure where salary was grown through length of service. It is important to note in this respect that there are no maxima to the pay zones. Therefore individuals can progress their salaries in a way that was not possible under the old structure. In that case employees had to secure promotion to progress their salaries beyond the grade maximum. The pay zone is useful for two additional reasons. First, it provides managers with a useful reference point to help guide pay decisions. Second, it serves as a valuable means of assuring internal equity.

Salaries at Lincoln are reviewed on February 1 each year. It is more likely that employees progress their salaries through horizontal moves across their existing grade level than by being promoted to a new level. Examples of the ways in which an individual employee's salary may be enhanced are:

- permanent additional responsibilities
- sustained high-quality performance
- development of competencies and/or the acquisition of experience leading to more effective role performance or the ability to assume greater responsibilities
- acquisition of full or part professional qualification.

The extent to which each of these is applicable is dependent upon the individual employee and the role that employee is performing.

In the event of the first of these, permanent additional responsibilities, it is necessary for the line manager to make a case for the employee. This case is made to the job evaluation committee, which consists of two representatives from HR (the compensation and benefits manager and the HR director) and four managers from different parts of the business. It is important to note here that the claim must be made on the basis of permanent role responsibility growth rather than because the line manager wishes to secure an increase for the employee. The intention of the new pay structure is to give line managers sufficient flexibility to increase the salary of individuals without the necessity to 'bid up' the importance of the role. The key question for the job evaluation committee to ask is: 'Has the role changed significantly such that it warrants an upgrading?' The old argument of needing to pay more to retain an employee is no longer applicable given the breadth of the pay bands.

Sustained high-quality performance relates to the performance of the role holder against predetermined objectives. Each individual employee has role objectives set between that employee and the line manager. The employee is measured against these objectives. There are three reviews per year. But objectives need not necessarily change three times in the year. This depends on the level of the role. Level A and level B role objectives may change more frequently than the more all-embracing objectives of higher-level roles.

The third way in which an individual employee may enhance salary is the development of competencies and/or the acquisition of experience leading to more effective role performance or the ability to assume greater responsibility. Lincoln put a great deal of work into the development of these competence statements. This involved pilot groups involving over 100 managers and employees, and structured questionnaires and interviews with members of the workforce. As noted above, the development of these competencies is seen as the key to creating the multiskilled, flexible workforce Lincoln need.

As noted above, the competence statements are based on the principle of key skills and behaviours (KSBs). There are four areas in the company where all employees need to excel. These are grouped under four general headings:

- developing the business (the KSBs necessary to ensure the successful planning and co-ordination of work)
- developing the role (the KSBs necessary to ensure that tasks are completed in the most efficient and effective way)
- developing relationships (the KSBs necessary to work effectively with colleagues, customers and other stakeholders)
- developing self (the KSBs necessary to develop continually both professionally and personally).

Each employee has an information pack which describes all the competence statements related to his or her level. Table 4.2 is an example from level B (roles with responsibility for processing a variety of high-volume, well-defined and some less well-defined activities in a variety of contexts and which requires close supervision for some of the time). It relates to the second KSB area of 'developing the job'.

Table 4.2 Competence statements relating to the KSB area 'developing the job'

Key behaviours	Examples of how my customers will know I am achieving this are when I . . .	Key skills
Ensuring communication is clear and simple	Speak and write clearly Avoid or explain jargon Adhere to company written and telephone standards	Telephone techniques Written communications
Resolving problems and passing on information	Reach solutions that take account of others' needs Refer queries or complaints above my authority level	Customer care
Supporting colleagues to achieve objectives	Help colleagues to meet deadlines Achieve my personal and departmental goals Highlight tasks not allocated	Problem solving
Paying attention to detail	Adhere to company standards Plan time to check my work Keep mistakes to a minimum	Adaptability
Approaching all tasks conscientiously and with a sense of urgency	Undertake all tasks with enthusiasm Accept responsibility for non-routine tasks Accept responsibility for completing tasks Undertake all work professionally and with equal effort Don't avoid doing the tasks I dislike	Accuracy Planning
Sharing and requesting information	Seek and distribute information as appropriate Update correspondence and files	Handling information

Source: Lincoln internal document

Underpinning the move to competence development is the principle that employees should take charge of their own development. This is important if they are to progress their salaries and their careers. Lincoln has set up a learning centre with a full set of learning resources (e.g. self-learning packs in technical and management development skills) in order to assist employees.

These competence statements form the basis of the performance reviews. They cover all Lincoln's employees from levels A–M3. Employees are defined as 'fully competent' when they use their knowledge and skills effectively and possess the personal attributes required to achieve the results managers expect from them. It is possible for individuals to progress beyond the salary which relates to 'fully competent'. This would be the consequence of the acquisition and application of additional competencies as the individual's career develops.

In the view of the compensation and benefits manager, success of the change in the pay structure depends on two principal factors. First is the willingness and ability of managers to recognise the extent to which employees are displaying the competencies in their work. In addition, managers need to become skilled at working with the employee to ensure that competencies which have not been achieved are developed. The second factor is the readiness with which employees grasp the importance of competencies, both to Lincoln's success and to the development of their own careers both with Lincoln and, in the longer term, other employers.

The fourth way in which an individual employee can progress salary is through the acquisition of full or part professional qualifications. This may be, for example, in accountancy, actuarial, IT or taxation. The company pays the relevant fees and gives necessary time-off for study.

Maintaining the pay structure

Job evaluation still has a role to play at Lincoln, despite the assertion by the compensation and benefits manager that the technique is insufficiently sensitive to market pressures and places undue emphasis upon measuring the job rather than the person. Job evaluation remains useful in ensuring internal equity by measuring the relative worth of jobs through defining the boundaries of the eight levels. In addition, it is useful in deciding whether roles should be allocated to new levels, although the role of job evaluation in deciding on grading appeals has diminished, as is explained later. The compensation and benefits manager is also mindful of the role job evaluation plays in the avoidance of claims under the 1970 Equal Pay Act. At Lincoln the scheme is sufficiently analytical to merit the basis of a defence against claims brought under the legislation. This may be where a woman (for example) claims that her work is equivalent to a man's if her job and his have been given equal value in a job evaluation study undertaken to evaluate the jobs done by the organisation's employees.

The job evaluation committee meets monthly. Its role is to decide on the appropriate level for new jobs and jobs that may need upgrading. For upgradings, managers make a claim to the committee based upon significant permanent change to the responsibilities of the job. In the event of a job not reflecting significant permanent change to merit an upgrading, the flexibility given to managers under the new structure means that managers may award an increase in pay.

Communication of the new pay structure

The initial stage in the communication process took place during April 1998. This involved a series of two-day workshops for managers, which focused on the new pay structure in general and the KSBs in particular. It was then for managers, with the aid of a briefing pack, to brief their staff. All staff attended KSB briefings run by the HR team. This included an explanation of KSBs, the rationale for their introduction, a video and role plays of a performance review and an introduction to broad banding.

All employees received a letter informing them of their level and salary range together with their new role title as from July 1, 1998.

Progress so far

As with any major change, some employees greeted the new pay structure with caution. They had become familiar with the old structure and understood the principle of being rewarded for length of service and promotions. Reducing the number of grades from sixteen to eight meant that promotions were no longer the frequent occurrence that they had been. Employees voiced the fear that they had lost their familiar 'signposts' – the steps on the promotional ladder. With that had gone the opportunity to gain public esteem through highly visible promotions. Some employees were more positive about the new structure. Those in more pre-scribed and constrained roles – in particular, those at level A – had traditionally seen little prospect of promotion in the old structure. However, the new structure meant that they could grow their salary through acquiring new competencies. As the new pay structure complemented the introduction of the new image and work-flow system, it meant that the development of new individual competencies was not only a realisable ambition, but also an organisational necessity.

Similarly, some managers have adopted a very positive attitude to the new pay structure while some have been more circumspect. This is best illustrated in the way in which managers have used their allocated pay 'pot'. Some have, as the compen-sation and benefits manager said, 'bitten the bullet' and given a wide range of awards, including zero increase. Other managers have given virtually all their employees the average increase, which in February 1999 was 3.6 per cent. Employees given a zero increase were typically those being paid in excess of the maximum salary for their level or those who were not effective performers. This suggests that they may receive zero increases in the foreseeable future unless perfor-mance or competence acquisition merits otherwise. High performers have received increases paid for by the zero increases applicable to less effective performers.

HR managers have welcomed the fact that the job evaluation committee has seen a marked drop in the number of submissions from line managers for job upgradings. Prior to the introduction of the new structure, managers would go to the committee with outdated job descriptions and incomplete data on the revised content of the job. The real reason for the upgrading appeal was often that the manager would fear losing the employee if a salary increase was not forthcoming, and an upgrading was the way to secure an increase. The compensation and bene-fits manager gave a typical example:

> A manager came to me and said that he wanted to promote one of his old level 8 (new level C) employees to a level D role because he was afraid of losing him. It was clear that the person warranted an increase but the role did not. I encouraged him to use the flexi-bility of the new structure to award a salary increase based on contribution, which the manager willingly accepted.

It is too early to judge the overall effectiveness of the new pay structure at Lincoln. However, early evidence suggests that managers are using the greater flex-ibility offered them because they are awarding increases outside the annual review cycle. This is the result of giving managers an annual pay budget which they have the power to spend as they think fit, although the compensation and benefits man-ager sees all managers' increase decisions and has the authority to recommend rejection of some of these. This has appeased some employee grumbles because they see that it is now possible to earn increases other than as a consequence of the annual review or promotion.

Savings-related share option scheme

The aim of the Lincoln savings-related share option scheme is to encourage a sense of employee ownership. According to the published set of shared values this means that:

> employees should feel a strong sense of ownership of their work and be proud of, and committed to, the company. One tangible way to make that commitment is to have a financial stake in it. Lincoln UK encourages its staff to own shares in the parent company, LNC, so that they can gain from the growth and prosperity of the group.

In addition, the scheme provides enhanced benefits for employees, thus making the benefits package more competitive.

Employees may save £10–£250 monthly: the average contribution is £90 per month. The scheme is administered by Abbey National, who invest the employee's savings in a fund which, at the end of three years, can be used to buy shares at the price operative at the start of the savings contract. Abbey National add to this fund a bonus of 2.75 times the monthly savings amount (e.g. £275 for the employee saving £100 per month.)

Approximately 40 per cent of Lincoln UK employees have joined the scheme, distributed evenly across the levels.

Note: Phil Lewis would like to thank Steve Glover, Compensation and Benefits Manager at Lincoln, for his valuable help in preparing this case study.

Questions

1. What do you think are the potential strengths and weaknesses of Lincoln's new pay structure?

2. The case explains that target rates are based on an assessment of four considerations: the local labour and national market rate for comparable roles; the average basic salary for staff undertaking the same or a similar role within the same department or division; the average basic salary for staff undertaking the same or a similar role within Lincoln and budgetary considerations. What tensions do you think these may produce and how may these tensions be resolved?

3. One consequence of Lincoln's new pay structure is that employees are less likely to be promoted. What problems may that create and how may the impact of these problems be lessened?

4. The measurement of competencies may cause particular problems for line managers. What techniques may be used by managers in establishing the extent to which employees are displaying competencies in their work?

5. If you had to develop a training programme for Lincoln line managers in order to ensure they implemented the new pay structure effectively what would be the programme's objectives and content?

References to Chapter 4

ACAS (1990) *Appraisal-related Pay*, London: ACAS.

Armstrong, M. (1993) *Managing Reward Systems*, Buckingham: Open University Press.

Armstrong, M. (1996) *Employee Reward*, London: Institute of Personnel and Development.

Armstrong, M. and Murlis, H. (1998) *Reward Management: A Handbook of Remuneration Strategy and Practice,* 4th edition, London: Kogan Page.

Beaumont, P.B. (1993) *Human Resource Management : Key Concepts and Skills*, London: Sage.

Beer, M., Spector, B., Lawrence, P.R., Mills, Q.N., and Walton, R.E. (1984) *Managing Human Assets*, New York: Free Press.

Cully, M., Woodland, S., O'Reilly, A. and Dix, G. (1999) *Britain at Work*, London: Routledge.

Daily Telegraph (1999) 'Green budget maps out the way ahead', 15 November.

Flannery, T., Hofrichter, D. and Platten, P. (1996) *People, Performance and Pay*, New York: Free Press.

Guest, D. (1987) 'Human resource management and industrial relations', *Journal of Management Studies*, 24(5): 503–21.

Heery, E. (1996) 'Risk, representation and the new pay', *Personnel Review*, 25(6): 54–65.

Herzberg, F. (1968) *Work and the Nature of Man*, London: Staples Press.

Income Data Services (1992) *Skill-based Pay*, Study No. 500, February.

Income Data Services (1994) *Profit-related Pay*, Study No. 564, October.

Income Data Services (1998) *Profit-sharing and Share Options*, Study No. 641, January.

Kanter, R.M. (1987) 'The attack on pay', *Harvard Business Review*, March–April: 60–67.

Keenoy, T. (1990) 'Human Resource Management: rhetoric, reality and contradiction', *International Journal of Human Resource Management*, 1(3): 363–84.

Kessler, I. (1994) 'Performance pay', in Sisson, K. (ed) *Personnel Management*, Oxford: Blackwell.

Kessler, I. and Purcell, J. (1992) 'Performance-related pay: objectives and application', *Human Resource Management Journal*, 2(3): 16–33.

Labour Market Trends (1998), 'Patterns of pay: results of the New Earnings Survey 1998', December: 623–34.

Lawler, E.E. (1984) 'The strategic design of reward systems', in Fombrun, C., Tichy, N.M. and Devanna, M.A., *Strategic Human Resource Management*, New York: John Wiley.

Lawler, E.E. (1990) *Strategic Pay: Aligning Organisational Strategies and Pay Systems*, San Francisco: Jossey Bass.

Lawler, E. (1995) 'The new pay: a strategic approach', *Compensation and Benefits Review*, July–August: 14–22.

Lewis, P. (1998) Managing performance-related pay based on evidence from the financial services sector', *Human Resource Management Journal*, 8(2): 66–77.

Livy, B. (1988) *Corporate Personnel Management*, London: Pitman.

Mabey, C. , Salaman, M. and Storey, J. (1998) *Human Resource Management: A Strategic Introduction*, 2nd edition, Oxford, Blackwell.

Maslow, A. (1943) 'A theory of human motivation', *Psychological Review*, 50: 370–96.

Mintzberg, H. and Waters, J. (1989) 'Of strategies deliberate and emergent', in Asch, D. and Bowman, C., *Readings in Strategic Management*, Basingstoke: Macmillan.

Monks, J. (1998) 'Trade unions, enterprise and the future', in Sparrow, P. and Marchington, M., *Human Resource Management: the New Agenda*, London: Financial Times Pitman Publishing.

Pfeffer, J. (1998) 'Six dangerous myths about pay', *Harvard Business Review*, May–June: 109–119.

Price, L. and Price, R. (1994) 'Change and continuity in the status divide', in Sisson, K. (ed) *Personnel Management,* Oxford: Blackwell.

Procter, S., McArdle, L., Rowlinson, M., Forrester, P. and Hassard, J. (1993) 'Performance-related pay in operation: a case study from the electronics industry', *Human Resource Management Journal*, 3(4): 60–74.

Randle, K. (1997) 'Rewarding failure: operating a performance-related pay system in pharmaceutical research', *Personnel Review*, 26(3): 187–200.

Schuster, J. and Zingheim, P. (1992) *The New Pay: Linking Employee and Organisational Performance*, New York: Lexington.

Semler, R. (1993) *Maverick! The Success Story Behind the World's Most Unusual Workplace*, London: Arrow Business Books.

Smith, I. (1983) *The Management of Remuneration: Paying for Effectiveness*, London: Institute of Personnel Management.

Smith, I. (1993) 'Reward management: a retrospective assessment', *Employee Relations*, 15(3): 45–59.

Storey, J. and Sisson, K. (1993) *Managing Human Resources and Industrial Relations*, Buckingham: The Open University Press.

Taylor, F.W. (1911) *Principles of Scientific Management*, New York: Harper and Row.

The Guardian (1999) 'A stick in carrot's clothing', 9 April.

Whittington, R. (1993) *What is Strategy and Does it Matter?*, London: Routledge.

Wood, S. (1996), 'High commitment management and payment systems', *Journal of Management Studies*, 33(1): 53–77.

Chapter 5

Employee development

Stephen Gibb and David Megginson

Introduction

Issues and challenges in contemporary employee development (ED[1]) are considered here in relation to two sets of factors. First are learning issues about how the knowledge, skills and attitudes required for employment are formed and are linked to career, organisational and economic success. The main challenges raised are those involved in responding to the onset of the knowledge economy, the continuing interest in achieving 'skill revolutions', and the demands involved in managing employment 'cultures'. The theory and practice of contemporary ED, its strengths and weaknesses, are bound up with meeting each of these challenges.

The second set of factors concern the stakeholders involved in ED. The issues here are related to the contribution of individuals, employers and government as participants in ED. Challenges here include the dynamics of individual motivation to learn and participation in ED; the role of employers and training providers in supplying effective ED, and finally the challenge to government, in the form of policy development and implementation of initiatives in the promotion of ED.

The practice of ED needs to be analysed in the context of all these issues and challenges; managing effective learning through stakeholder interactions and partnership. Employers are certainly the 'hub' of the whole system, given employees'

---

[1] Many commentators seek to distinguish between training, education and development. While there are sometimes good reasons for this, for example when compiling survey data, the semantics of these distinctions can become unwieldy and intrusive. The essence of employees being 'trained', professionals being 'educated' and managers being 'developed' amounts to the same; support of learning for and at work. For this chapter the term 'Employee development' (ED) will be used to cover training at work and training for work, work-related vocational education and work-based on-job and off-job development, and what is generally thought of as soft 'development' in the employment context.

dependence upon them as suppliers of ED and the government's voluntarist approach in this aspect of HRM. A description of the different approaches to ED which can exist in employing organisations is provided in conclusion, as a focus for analysing and evaluating cases at an organisational level.

The context of employee development

The purpose of ED can be defined as developing human potential to assist organisations and individuals to achieve their objectives. The question of what exactly is meant by developing human potential needs to be considered more fully if the theory and practice of ED, and the challenges it faces, are to be properly defined. A common way of expanding upon this is to argue that in order to realise their potential in the context of employment people need to develop, in balance, their knowledge, skills and emotions/attitudes/values[2] (EVA). The capacity to learn and become competent, to be able to achieve the performance standards expected in employment, is fulfilled through integrated development of these three aspects of human potential. In this respect development in and for employment is the same as development in any other context.

The most evident form this takes is the standard organisation of learning experiences in and for employment into programmes which specify objectives in all these three aspects. The trinity of development in knowledge, skills and EVA is to be explicitly found in some form in many systems of human potential development, and is implicit in most others. Each aspect will be considered here in turn to explain what they involve and to raise key issues for evaluating contemporary ED.

The first types of objective in realising human potential in the context of employment are those relating to cognitive capacities: the development and extension of knowledge. The cognitive aspects of ED are concerned with the extent to which employees need to obtain and use information, models and theories to enable development and effective performance in jobs and their employing organisation. Bloom's taxonomy of cognitive categories (Bloom, 1956), given in Table 5.1, provides a continuum against which jobs can be measured.

---

[2] Conventionally, it is 'attitudes' which are defined as the third element of the learning trinity 'KSA'. Attitudes are defined as the positive or negative orientations people have with regard to themselves, others and the world – their likes and dislikes, conventionally studied within social psychology. Forming or changing people's attitudes is certainly a part of development in the context of employment. But this is too narrow to encompass the contemporary concerns of development in employment. Forming and developing values, people's core ideas on what is right and wrong, is a concern as well – often illustrated by organisations making their values explicit and requiring employee behaviour congruent with them in work. Supporting and using 'emotions', the psychology of people feeling 'mad, bad, sad or glad' also matters in developing effective performance. Indeed, emotional factors are often given the 'executive' role in controlling human behaviour; to shape and influence human behaviour in employment it is then possible – and, for some, necessary – to acknowledge and work with developing emotions and values, not just attitudes.

Table 5.1 Bloom's cognitive categories

Type	Evidence	
Knowledge	state, list, identify	*Simple*
Comprehension	explain, give examples	
Application	demonstrate, solve, use	
Analysis	describe, break down, select	
Synthesis	combine, design, create	
Evaluation	appraise, contrast, criticise	
		Complex

Different occupations will require different types and levels of cognitive development. All human potential development in the context of employment involves knowledge; the issue is the extent to which performance depends upon knowledge, and the type of knowledge involved. Occupations can be mapped against Bloom's types, to profile where the cognitive demands are. The difference which most starkly highlights this point is the distinction made between occupations where performance greatly depends on knowledge and other cognitive capacities and areas where knowledge and cognitive capacity appear to be of little relevance and concern. With the former, knowledge-intensive development for the 'professions', such as medicine, law, engineering, teaching and social work is seen as typical, requiring several years of university-level education followed by a long period of supervised practice before becoming fully licensed. As that education progresses, the cognitive capacities required become more complex. In the case of the latter, development for relatively routine forms of programmed service provision, for example serving in a fast-food outlet or administration in a call centre, is seen as requiring little cognitive complexity and that is of the more basic kind. What is required depends only upon basic education and can be supplemented by the instruction of the employer in the course of basic training within the company.

Cognitive capacities in occupational performance also vary on a continuum of certainty – from occupations where knowledge is certain and complete to jobs where knowledge is uncertain and partial. Schön (1987) makes the distinction between what he calls 'determined practice' and 'indeterminate practice'. In the former, cognition is fixed and prescribed, and used to deal with routine circumstances. In the latter, cognition is not fixed and prescribed, it comes into operation to support creative problem-solving needed to deal with unique circumstances. This distinction is not new, but it is arguably more relevant now. In a time of new sciences, new technologies, and 'new organisations' demands on the creative use of cognition rather than its prescriptive application are greater; demands in occupations are increasingly at the complex end of Bloom's categories. The cognition involved in occupations and employment is evolving and changing fast, and it is therefore more likely to be uncertain and partial even among the most 'experienced'.

This also affects the practicalities of developing human potential in employment more than the familiar distinction between cognition-intensive and low-knowledge occupations. This is because, where knowledge is felt to be certain and complete, the most appropriate form of developmental support is clearly through the instruction and 'conditioning' of those who need the knowledge by those who currently possess the knowledge. These tend to be intermediaries – whether that mediation arises in the forms of knowledge present in books, or lectures, or the Internet. Where knowledge is uncertain and fragmented the appropriate form of learning needs to be more 'experiential'. By 'experiential' is meant a process of learning that is based on direct personal experience and reflection, undertaken in a 'community' of others who have experience of synthesis and evaluation. Only cognitive skills developed in this unmediated context, rather than knowledge gained through mediated information-processing in formal education, is of any substance and value. Such knowledge cannot be effectively codified and transmitted through systems of mediated instruction. In a sense, but not entirely, the former lends itself to being learnt as a 'science'[3], a coherent package of principles, concepts and methods; while the latter lends itself to being learnt as an 'art', requiring creativity on the part of the learner while learning.

In occupations where knowledge is becoming more certain there can be an increase in both 'science'-based pedagogy and instruction-based forms of learning. The role of Information and Communications Technologies (ICT) in supporting efficiency and effectiveness in this area of learning could be central. Where knowledge is becoming more uncertain and partial then expanding forms of experiential learning, centred on long-term learning relationships in communities of practice, may become much more important. The increase in systems of mentoring (Gibb, 1999) is one indicator of this trend in many different occupational contexts.

The fundamental issue relating to knowledge in the context of employment is the question of the extent to which cognition is forming a greater or lesser part of the development of human and organisation potential in any event, regardless of how that is categorised or learned. On the one hand there are claims for the onset of the 'knowledge economy' and the 'knowledge worker' (Tapscott, 1996); this era is supposed to be characterised by the increasing importance of 'intellectual capital' (Stewart, 1997) in many occupations and organisations. 'Knowledge management' (Davenport and Prusak, 1998) is then the latest strategic aspiration and focus for reviewing organisational effectiveness. The structure, design and culture of organisation needs to be built around managing knowledge. This suggests, in essence, that cognition is more important than ever before in employment. The implication is that the possession and use of knowledge permeates all productive activity, at all levels in an organisation, and therefore the

---

[3] The distinction between science and art as paradigms for occupational development is potentially useful and stimulating. Science is characterised by organised bodies of knowledge derived from methods which enable theories to be developed and tested. Arts are characterised by organised performances derived from methods which enable symbol systems to be developed and enjoyed. Most employment and occupations can be seen to share elements of a scientific base and an artistic base in effective performance. A recent illustration of this abstract point would be the involvement of musicians in facilitating management development (Pickard, 1999). The parallels between conducting an orchestra or playing in a jazz band are investigated to illuminate the challenges facing managers and to propose some solutions for meeting those based on musicians' experiences.

development of human potential in this respect forms a greater part of ensuring organisational effectiveness than in the past. More people need to learn more knowledge than ever before. It has been commonplace to hear of skills shortages as a potential threat to economic and business development; in the future it may be that it is cognitive deficits which cause economic and business development problems.

On the other hand there are arguments that the whole knowledge economy and knowledge worker concepts have been vastly overhyped. There is less scope for knowledge work, as information technologies enable everything from the whole systems running complex plants down to interpersonal transactions between customers and the organisation's representatives to be automated. Knowledge has migrated to computer systems, leaving people in employment to tend the computers. And when the key 'knowledge'-based institutions, particularly schools, colleges and universities, are considered there is contradictory evidence about what is happening. While education is becoming a more significant and greater part of everyone's future, there is, nevertheless, pressure for these institutions to become more concerned with helping to develop basic skills and competence. This is because the absence of basic skills among the labour force is currently the greatest problem experienced by employers, not the absence of smart 'knowledge' workers. This is a finding highlighted in, for example, employer concerns about the quality of young people's and graduate recruits' employability.

The second type of objectives in human potential development are those relating to developing psychomotor skills, through practice. The more commonplace term in use now is 'competence' rather than psychomotor skills; 'competence' being defined as the ability to do things to the standards required in employment and in practice. The difference between 'knowing how' to do something and actually being able to perform effectively is the skills or competence gap. Many people 'know how' to do many things; they can appreciate the elements of cooking and follow the recipes in cookbooks, or appreciate the principles of playing certain sports. But only some are competent enough, skilled enough, to do these well enough to produce excellent meals or compete with the best on actual playing fields.

Again there is a stark distinction between areas of human development in employment which are relatively low-skilled and areas which are highly skilled. Low-skill activities require little human potential development in the form of development through practice. These are jobs where most typical mature adults would be able to achieve a successful performance without needing much practice. For example, most people could serve behind a fast-food counter, stock shelves in a supermarket, or pack mobile phones into boxes. The main performance issue in such circumstances is usually ensuring a standard performance to set guidelines and procedures; it is about managing basic competence as conformity to procedures in the occupation.

On a bigger stage the issue of skill development raises economic development and political policy questions (Crouch, Finegold and Sako, 1999). A predominance of low-skill jobs and organisations creates a low-skill economy. This is an economy in which there are few driving forces to develop human potential in this respect. A vicious cycle then arises, where that lack of interest in human potential development means that only low-skill industries and jobs can be supported and managed, and then the preponderance of low-skill jobs and industries means that there is little demand for investing in skills development. In such conditions skills shortages are unlikely to be a problem, as the development of basic 'threshold' competence is an integral part of normal human development, and needs little in the way of additional time and investment devoted to practice. The main HR problem in these circumstances is the potential shortage of people prepared to take and stay in such low-skill jobs, and the degree of problem is contingent upon prevailing labour market conditions.

High-skill activities require significant human potential development, through substantial and continuing periods of guided practice in order to create a successful performer. This initial interest in high levels of human development for employment is further reinforced by the fact that skilled performance cannot be 'stored'; it either has to be in use and therefore constantly refreshed, or it will be lost. For example, continuing the sporting theme, professional footballers may only play once a week, but they spend all week practising. Armed forces may only encounter actual active duty irregularly, but professional armies are more effective as they constantly take part in exercises to prepare for the 'real thing'. The main performance issues in such circumstances are then ensuring a quality of 'apprenticeship' prior to licensing people to practise, and maintaining sufficient practise to keep skill levels at their peak. Such an emphasis on apprenticeship and 'Continuing Professional Development' is then one necessary hallmark of a 'true' profession. The net effect is to require sophisticated and substantial support for human development related to employment.

In high-skill economies there needs to be much investment in developing human potential through skills development. In traditional professions, such as medicine and law, skills development has long been integrated with professional development as a period of supervised practice after study and before licensing. In many modern professions, of which 'HRM' and management are two relevant examples, similar systems are being developed. Without effective foresight and planning there is great potential for skills shortages to develop and become a factor constraining economic growth. The biotechnology and software development sectors provide good contemporary examples of sectors where skill shortages throughout the range of jobs involved, not just at the top professional levels, can constrain economic development. Employers' and public policy concerns are then with 'skills revolutions'; how to attain a high-skill, high-value economy and avoid the traps of being, or becoming, a low-skill economy and having skills shortages which constrain economic and business development.

The general view is that the UK has been much in need of such a skills revolution to overcome its historically low skill levels, and to avoid skills shortages in key developing industries. Yet much has been made of the absence of even the 'basic skills' of literacy and numeracy among large parts of the labour force, needed to sustain even a low-skill economy. This situation has arisen for a variety of reasons, and many commentators look at both employers and an educational system in the UK which together have failed to manage the effective development of skills over decades. Remedying this aspect of developing human potential has been the central feature of policy development in recent times, exemplified in the development of national competence frameworks defining skills in occupations and in gearing educational systems to help develop competence.

Many of the government initiatives outlined later are responses to this central issue. Whether in any event 'skills are the answer' is, as Crouch *et al.* (1999) suggest, a claim that needs to be further debated. The logic that skills are a necessary element of future economic and social development is, they argue, fair. But skills increases in themselves are not going to be sufficient to achieve the employment and economic goals seen to be associated with these policies: job creation, high levels of employment, social inclusion, increasing living standards and equal opportunities. Critics of the use of skills revolutions as the main tool argue that there are a number of reasons for this. One is that occupations requiring truly advanced skills are still a small proportion of all jobs. Many jobs just do not require high skills, and never will. Another consideration is that the skills revolution depends on the actions of firms who have no real interest in carrying the burden for 'up-skilling' on behalf of other organisations or society in general. In this situation it is actually government that is being left to deal with the problems of development for employment; in particular to deal with the problem of unemployment. This undermines the credibility of the initiatives they develop, as they are seen as solutions to unemployment, not as integral to economic and business development and useful for employers. Finally, the necessary links between firms and employers and control of skills development is still a problem. Ideally, employers should be taking the lead, as it is their interests and experience which need to be met, but in practice it is still 'detached' government departments which have the main role. Even with the best intentions public servants cannot be a substitute for employer leadership.

The final objectives involved in developing human potential in employment are those related to developing and enhancing emotions, and values and attitudes. It is arguable that the essential difference between superior performance and ordinary, or indeed incompetent, performance is linked to emotions, attitude and values. People with emotional 'intelligence' (Goleman, 1999), 'positive' attitudes and the right values will be more effective than those lacking emotional intelligence, with negative attitudes or without the right values. Certainly, different occupations call upon some common and some particular elements of emotional intelligence, attitudes and values (Johnson and Indvik, 1999). For example, when facing difficult customers staff are meant to be equable and 'professional', rather than letting their personal feelings show. More often the crucible of the workplace as a whole can provide many spurs to interpersonal and intergroup conflict in the course of normal working life between employees, and between employers and employees.

Maintaining emotional intelligence and positive attitudes in that context of performance in a job is a perpetual challenge.

Instilling, reinforcing and leveraging emotions, values and attitudes is then an integral and inescapable part of development for employment. Pinker suggests the importance of emotions is that 'the emotions are mechanisms that set the brain's highest level goals' (1997: 373). Deliberate control of emotions is a route to managing behaviour; whether that control is personal and internal or is exerted from other sources. As far as values are concerned, Rokeach (1970) points out that many organisations explicitly identify their 'core values' with the aim of encouraging employees to behave in tune with them. These may be instrumental values, relating to the appropriate modes of conduct desired from and expected of employees in the course of their work as individuals, in groups and with customers. For example, employers will seek to enhance the ethics of amity within the workforce, often through the means of team building. There may be relationship skills involved in this, but most crucial is often the development of a team spirit, co-operation and trust between the team members. Values may also be 'terminal values', relating to the types of goals and ends which organisations wish their employees to pursue; the values which will govern their behaviour in achieving a successful performance. A concern with achieving 'quality' standards, for example, is partly based on good knowledge of systems, partly on skills developed through practice, and partly on being guided by the value of achieving quality.

The argument is that where emotions, attitudes and values are not effectively developed in an employee there is a high probability that performance standards will not be attained, even though employees may have the right knowledge and appropriate skills developed through practice. Developing human potential in the context of employment invariably raises issues about emotions, values and attitudes. These may be about harnessing and reinforcing an individual's, group's or organisation's emotions, attitudes and values in the context of jobs and work. They may be about challenging and changing the emotional intelligence, attitudes and values of individuals, groups and, on occasion, entire organisations.

Another way of thinking of this aspect of development for employment is that it is about the development of the whole person, and the development of the whole organisation. Effective development requires more than the 'digestion' of knowledge and the acquisition of skills through practice to underpin effective performance; it also depends upon the effective development of the whole person in the context of the whole organisation. There needs to be a congruence of emotions, values and attitudes with the occupational role, supported by an organisational environment which nurtures and rewards those emotions, values and attitudes. For instance, the emotions, values and attitudes which underpin performance in a caring role and organisation are not the same as those underpinning an entrepreneurial role in a profit-oriented organisation.

Sometimes, then, the development issue is about broader personal or organisational concerns. From the shelves of 'transform your life' self-help books to the most recent examples of analysing organisational values (Wickens, 1999) to catalyse change, this aspect of development for employment provides a rich seam of activity. It is most evident in, and related to, the concern with 'culture' change and culture management in the workplace that has been a high-profile concern in recent years as a focus of organisational change and development. The extent to which cultures can be controlled and changed is also open to debate. There is, however, no doubt that many organisations aspire to mould individual behaviours and the overall 'culture'.

The stakeholders: individuals, employers and government

There is, then, an agenda concerning the new and changing requirements of the knowledge economy, the old and continuing need for a skills revolution and the evergreen issues of managing behaviour and cultures in occupations and the workplace. These create the environment in which ED theory and practice has been and is evolving. Responses to this environment, in the form of actual strategies for supporting human potential development for employment, depend upon the actions of a variety of stakeholders. The primary stakeholders in ED are individuals, employers and the government. Problems or successes are not due to one set of agents alone; it is how they all interact which produces either an effective outcome or a problematic situation.

Individuals

Individual factors supporting effective ED are the levels of motivation and participation which lead employees or prospective employees themselves to seek to develop their potential in employment. Options range from opting out of the world of employment altogether, and pursuing alternative lifestyles, to consistently and extensively developing oneself with the aspiration of achieving success in employment. One career survey recently classified young people in terms of those 'getting on', those getting by and those getting nowhere (ESRC, 1999). Motivators that all these will share may include seeking greater job security through enhancement of knowledge, skills and self-development and improving personal performance for its own sake, for the pleasure of competent performance. There will be differences in people's response to seeking successful career development through enhanced knowledge, skills and self-development; seeking work enrichment, through being able to do more. The net effect is to spur active and interested participation in learning or to curtail enthusiasm for and participation in development for employment.

Developing their own potential may indeed have helped many 'getting on' individual employees or prospective employees meet these objectives in the past. Now many more employers wish to encourage their employees towards self-activated and self-directed development, to planning and managing their own development. This is a natural development of more general and focused processes of performance appraisal which are concerned with development needs. It also fits with the general trend towards employees becoming active and free agents rather than being dependent upon others to be told what to do – an aspect of the whole 'empowerment' movement and the 'new deal' in employment more generally. One difficulty with this, however, is that with the declining prospect of achieving their core goals in the organisation, such as job security or career development, the natural motivators for self-directed development may be missing for everyone; whether they are 'getting on' or 'getting by'.

There are other potential problems with relying more on self-driven potential realisation. Individuals may have misconceptions of their own potential, rating themselves incorrectly as unable to achieve some objectives when they can, or as able to achieve some objectives when they cannot. And the need to be seen as competent may lead individuals to present themselves as being competent instead of accurately assessing their own learning needs. Finally, there is the influence of the course, or ontology, of human development, and the different life-styles which accompany life stages. There are varying degrees of interest in learning and different types of concern with learning at different life stages and in different lifestyles. Individuals will be more motivated to realise their potential for employment at some stages of life than at others. Some lifestyles will emphasise the importance of development for employment more than others. Conventional ideas about the normal patterns of learning and life stages and lifestyles are being challenged, with an emphasis on lifelong learning, not just learning in youth, and a need to achieve a better 'life – work' balance (Foster, 1999) across the spectrum from those socially excluded to those who may be seen as 'workaholics'.

Employers

For employers ED is a means to an end – the end being to ensure achievement of the organisation's goals and the means being basic competence in the workforce. To achieve this employers may work in partnerships with schools, colleges and universities to develop courses that relate to the needs of businesses. They will also provide development for their own employees, through the induction of new employees, basic job training and closing any 'training gaps' identified by managers or others in reviewing the performance of staff. There may also be other organisational objectives beyond ensuring competence. These include increasing competitiveness through providing more or better ED than competitors. Employers will seek to improve product and/or service quality through more investment in ED. Continuous improvement requires continuous learning. The quality of ED provided can help by attracting the best people, by using more of their potential and productivity, and by maintaining their satisfaction as employees because they are being invested in. There can also be a concern with achieving 'culture changes' through ED interventions. Finally, there is a general concern to promote the habit of learning: keeping people 'fit' to learn. The logic and provision of many Employee Development and Assistance Programmes (EDAPs) reflects this.

Developing the potential of their workforces can help organisations meet these objectives by providing more competent, adaptable and committed employees. There are typical difficulties facing employers as they do this. One is simply a lack of resources to invest in ED, with a consequent basic failure to take up the responsibility to promote human potential development even in its most rudimentary forms, such as employee induction and health and safety training. This may be due to an assumption that development for employment has been achieved elsewhere, and the employer has no interest in incurring unnecessary further expenditure. For example, why should an employer send an employee who has become an HR manager on a long and expensive course of professional development leading to a professional qualification if they already have their own set HR systems and policies in place? Another difficulty is a narrowness of concern, seeing developing human potential only in as far as it can be 'justified' by direct and explicit benefits for the employer. This normally translates into 'hard' development for the knowledge and skills required for the specific job, to the neglect of other aspects of knowledge and skill, and the whole issue of values. The problems with analysing the costs and benefits of ED are a perennial issue, and the effect can be to preclude effective development. Lastly, there are concerns with the quality of the provision of ED provided. The quality of ED, as a service, is tied to the quality of the staff providing it. Confidence in the competence of trainers or training providers must be at the heart of the system. In many organisations this is recognised, and there is confidence in trainers who are themselves well trained in their roles, or reputable providers are used. In other circumstances bad experiences with trainers or training providers can mean that confidence in investing in ED is low.

A review of companies who have invested in ED (see Table 5.2) suggests that they gain in all key business success measures. From the employers' perspective such figures appear to suggest unambiguously that effective ED is indeed a key to business success.

Table 5.2 Learning pays: the value of learning and training to employers

	Average company	IiP accredited company	Gain
Rate of return on capital (RRC)	9.21%	16.27%	77%
Pre-tax profit margins	2.54%	6.91%	172%
Average salary	£12,590	£14,195	13%
Turnover/sales per employee	£64,912	£86,625	33%
Profit per employee	£1,815	£3,198	76%

Note: The data compare average UK companies with Investor in People (IiP)-accredited companies. The IiP standard will be explained later; in essence it is awarded to organisations which can prove that they are effectively supporting ED.

Source: National Advisory Council for Education and Training Targets 1999

Organisations will evolve systems and processes of their own to manage learning and ED to at least some extent. These will range from developing induction systems for new employees, through job-specific training, to retraining and career development. Research suggests that many companies have continued to develop and retain their own in-house training function, but a number have also been cutting back in recent years. The explanations for this decrease in internally managed ED vary from it representing straightforward cost-cutting to it representing the planned outsourcing of ED. It certainly seems that many more organisations are faced with the decision of choosing an external training provider as at least a partner, if not the major provider of ED. Much ED in organisations is managed in partnerships with others. These may be private sector providers, or public sector providers, or associated with private–public initiatives such as IiP.

The main reasons for selecting an outside provider are to obtain the best training available, and because the required training cannot be supplied in-house (The Industrial Society, 1998). Other key factors influencing the choice of provider include the availability of training facilities and the quality of the training design. A dedicated training company is likely to have broad experience in designing different courses for the various needs of different clients. An in-house training department is unlikely to have this breadth of knowledge and experience. Accreditation is also gaining importance, in part due to an environment where continuing career development and the workplace as a competitive internal labour market become more important. There are also factors which make in-house training more attractive. The two factors that seem to play a crucial role in persuading companies to develop their internal ED provisions are price and the ability to tailor a course to company needs.

So organisations develop ED strategies, deliberately and in a planned way and also as events unfold in the business; this involves developing and using some in-house provisions and also using external providers. Determining exactly which approach to ED they will invest in is still an issue, given the many different options available, and these will be considered in conclusion.

The role of government

In this area of HRM there is little substantive 'legal context',[4] in a way that parallels what is found in the legal regulation of employment through employment contracts or in specific employee relations legislation in industrial relations and areas like health and safety or managing discipline. Voluntarism still provides the main philosophy in ED in the UK – in other words, it is down to the people concerned to make decisions and develop initiatives as they see fit. Rather, the role of government is to promote the supply of ED through a number of initiatives, using a number of agencies. These agencies tend to change their name, if not their nature, with bewildering frequency. At the moment the central focus is on achieving a range of National

---

[4] One rare example would be the 1998 Teaching and Higher Education Act which amends the Employment Rights Act 1996; 16- and 17-year-old employees who have not achieved a certain standard of education/training will be entitled to reasonable paid time off during normal working hours to pursue approved qualifications. To be able to pursue learning and get an NVQ Level 2 or equivalent at least is therefore now a right for any individual. (http:www.hmso.gov.uk/acts/acts1998)

Training Targets, through the work of *Learning and Skills Councils* (LSCs) and Learning Partnerships and the initiative *Investors in People* (IiP).

From a government perspective the problems arising are ultimately about the implementation of economic and social policy. The nuts and bolts are about raising and allocating resources for ED. The balance of responsibility for paying for ED between individuals, companies, and government remains a constant concern. It seems that everyone aspires to achieve a high knowledge-based and high-skill economy, but would like to see someone else pay for it. One important aspect of this is that for the current government the challenge of dealing with groups facing social exclusion also provides a social agenda for ED, a social aspect to learning for and at work. Social exclusion includes a wide range of concerns. In the ED context it means dealing with the problems experienced by the long-term unemployed, women returners, alienated young people, and ethnic minority groups, in achieving their human potential through work and employment. In this context schools, colleges and universities, indeed education in general at all stages of life, can help drive the development of human potential to an extent. But it is often only in the context of employment, inside organisations, that many people have the opportunity to concentrate on developing their potential in the context of job experience and working with experienced practitioners.

The government's spending on training is an integral part of its broader economic and social policy. It is hard to quantify as it is bound up with its education programmes (see Table 5.3). This has become more pronounced since the Department of Education and the Department for Employment were merged in 1995/96, to form the Department for Education and Employment (DfEE). The amount being spent on training programmes in 1998/99 was £2.36 billion, excluding £951million being spent on the Welfare to Work programme. There is also some training included under the broad initiative of encouraging 'people to continue throughout their lives to develop their knowledge, skills and understanding and improve their employability in a changing labour market'.

Table 5.3 Expenditure by the Department for Education and Employment and OFSTED (£m), 1993/94–1998/99

	1993/ 94	1994/ 95	1995/ 96	e1997/ 98	†1998/ 99
Total expenditure	13 616	14 364	14 449	14 794	14 023
Expenditure on employment and training programmes of which‡:	2392	2394	2198	2496	3311
Welfare to Work	-	-	-	172	951
work-based training for young people	640	647	635	731	741
work-based training for adults	760	693	502	439	340
European Social Fund	96	108	181	270	308

Note: e – estimated, † – planned, ‡ – these are the largest single categories of expenditure – including the Welfare to Work programme OFSTED – Office for Standards in Education

Source: Department for Education and Employment Expenditure Plans 1998–99

There are a number of national training targets (see Table 5.4), whose achievement is meant to concentrate the minds of all those involved in the provision of ED.

Table 5.4 Training targets

Targets for 11-year-olds	80% reaching standards in literacy and 75% reaching standards in numeracy
Targets for 16-year-olds	50% getting 5 higher grade GCSEs and 95% getting at least 1 GCSE
Targets for young people	85% of 19-year-olds with a level 2 qualification and 60% of 21-year-olds with a level 3 qualification
Targets for adults	50% with a level 3 qualification, 28% with a level 4 qualification, and a learning participation target (still to be set)
Targets for organisations	45% of medium and large organisations recognised as IiP, and 10 000 small organisations recognised as IiP

Note: These are the targets for England for 2002; targets for Scotland are currently being consulted upon.
Source: DfEE, 1998c

Provisions for young people in England and Wales are being reorganised into a new 'Connexions' Service (http://www.connexions.gov.uk). This will involve a host of initiatives based on eight key principles:

- raising aspirations – setting high expectations of every individual
- meeting individual need and overcoming barriers to learning
- taking account of the views of young people, individually and collectively, as the new service is developed and as it is operated locally
- inclusion – keeping young people in mainstream education and training and preventing them from moving to the margins of their community
- partnerships – agencies collaborating to achieve more for young people, parents and communities than agencies working in isolation
- community involvement and neighbourhood renewal – through involvement of community mentors and through personal advisors brokering access to local welfare, health, arts, sport and guidance networks
- extending opportunity and equality of opportunity – raising participation and achievement levels for all young people, influencing the availability, suitability and quality of provisions and raising awareness of opportunities
- evidence-based practice – ensuring that new interventions are based on rigorous research into and evaluation of 'what works'.

The emphasis is on the evolution of a broad and integrated service to give young people 'the best start in life', not just on initiatives to train them in vocational skills.

Youth training and youth credits

The problem of developing skills in young people has attracted policy attention for some considerable time. The context is one of abiding problems with youth unemployment, general disaffection with learning and training among some youth groups, and helping people cross the bridge from school to work and careers. From the government's perspective, there are clearly both economic and social concerns wrapped up in this. Youth Training and Youth Credits were launched in 1990. Under the Youth Training scheme, the DfEE guarantees the offer of a suitable training place to all 16–17-year-olds who 'are not in full-time education, are unemployed and seeking training'. Youth Training is offered via a Youth Credits system. 16- and 17-year-old school leavers (and sometimes other special groups) can use Youth Credits to buy training to N/SVQ standard from an employer or from a specialist provider of training.

Modern Apprenticeships

The 'old' system of ED, of apprenticeships managed by companies and craft unions, has been seen to have died out over time; with a decline of the industries and often organisations in which young people were apprenticed. Modern Apprenticeships were introduced in 1995. According to the DfEE, the purpose of Modern Apprenticeships is to develop technical, supervisory and craft-level skills among 16–18-year-olds. These schemes are designed to overcome the weaknesses of other attempts to improve ED for these occupations in industry, because they are industry-specific, and have been created by industry representatives in consultation with the DfEE. At the beginning of 1998, more than 150,000 young people had begun a Modern Apprenticeship, and there are now 75 Modern Apprenticeships, covering different sectors of industry and commerce.

Of all the government schemes, the Modern Apprenticeship scheme seems to be currently the most successful, attracting a rising number of entrants. However, these figures may have been inflated by some employers who have been using the scheme to train graduates, gaining a subsidy for these training costs. The government was sufficiently concerned to formally ban graduates from Modern Apprenticeship courses.

The DfEE has been considering the possibility of introducing a separate scheme for university students, whereby company-sponsored students would be able to qualify for a new type of Modern Apprenticeship scheme, where students would leave university with both a degree and a vocational qualification.

National Traineeships

National Traineeships were introduced in 1997. They offer young people who have left compulsory education a high-quality, work-based route to qualifications at intermediate level. They operate to agreed national criteria and standards set by industry and employers. In addition to specific vocational skills National Traineeships are meant to include all the key skills and components which will help young people progress in their chosen careers. National Traineeships currently cover more than 25 sectors of industry and commerce with plans for expansion into other sectors.

Work-Based Training for Adults

In 1998/1999, a new scheme called Work-Based Training for Adults was introduced to replace existing provisions. The aim of this new scheme is to help long-term unemployed adults, particularly those at risk of exclusion from the job market, to secure and sustain employment or self-employment, through an individually tailored combination of guidance, structured work experience, training and approved qualifications. The programme has some key features. It offers a combination of pre-vocational and occupational training. It provides occupational training which significantly improves skills in demand in the labour market. It provides lifelong learning facilities following Work-Based Training for Adults.

Investors in People

The aim of Investors in People (IiP) is to encourage employers to take training more seriously and improve their levels and quality of training. Employers satisfying the criteria become IiP-accredited companies. In essence, IiP provides a national 'benchmark' standard that helps employers to look at their training needs and links investment in training to the achievement of business goals. This standard is based on four principles:

- top-level commitment to develop all employees
- a regular review of the training and development of all employees
- action to train and develop individuals on recruitment and provide training throughout their employment
- evaluation of the outcome of training and development as a basis for continuous improvement.

Companies that adopt HRM practices that satisfy these four principles will be awarded IiP accreditation by Investors in People UK. By October 1998, around 10,000 firms had achieved IiP accreditation. The government provides £1.6 million to help firms achieve this accreditation. In recent times a focus upon small firms (i.e. firms employing up to 50 people) and medium-sized firms has become evident. The IiP standard, as with many other government initiatives, is currently being reviewed. Changes in the standard and the process for achieving it are expected.

This brief empirical review of IiP would suggest that an enhancement of the positive driving forces supporting employers' activities in ED and learning at work and an elimination of the negative restraining forces in order to more effectively and efficiently promote ED is still needed. That, in most accounts, would seem to involve a range of actors, from employers and their training departments, government and quasi-governmental organisations, and training providers working with individuals, groups and organisations to improve ED. Effective and efficient ED depends upon relationships and collaboration among employers, government, and training providers.

For employers these collaborations can begin with links to education, particularly the final years of secondary education, further education and Higher Education (HE), and professional development based in HE. Arguably, most centrally it involves assuring the right quantity and quality of ED in the workplace. This involves more than doing more training; it is about ED being an integral part of major business developments and company changes. This is exemplified in the UK presently by the IiP initiative. In IiP the core issues of ED, commitment to training, the planning and actions involved in training, and the need to evaluate training are seen as central business development concerns.

Improving the training market

The DfEE has a number of programmes which are aimed at encouraging individuals' investment in learning and at improving the quality and market responsiveness of training and vocational education. Current initiatives include promoting and making more accessible the benefits of lifelong learning; promoting the use of flexible learning; establishing mechanisms to achieve greater responsiveness of the further education sector to the needs of employers and promoting continuous improvement in the performance of bodies charged with supporting and delivering employee development

Welfare to Work

Welfare to Work is based on the 'New Deal' scheme for young and long-term unemployed people. Features of the scheme include helping young people, aged 18–24, who have been unemployed for more than six months to find work. It involves offering employers who take on a young unemployed person for six months a subsidy of £60 per week, providing full-time education and training for a year, and providing work in the voluntary sector or on the Environmental Task Force for up to six months. There are also a set of initiatives aimed at helping long-term unemployed people aged over 25 to find work. These include the opportunity to study while claiming the job seeker's allowance and offering a subsidy to companies which employ the long-term unemployed for six months.

National/Scottish Vocational Qualifications

National/Scottish Vocational Qualifications (N/SVQs) were launched in 1986. There are now more than 900 N/SVQs, representing different economic sectors and industries. They are divided into five ascending levels of competence:

- Level 1 – performance of routine work activities and/or achievement of a broad foundation of work competence as a basis for progression
- Level 2 – broader range of activities involving greater responsibility
- Level 3 – skilled activities involving greater responsibility
- Level 4 – complex, technical and specialised activities, including supervision and management
- Level 5 – pursuit of a senior occupation or profession, including the ability to apply a significant range of fundamental principles and techniques.

The take-up of N/SVQs varies enormously between commerce and industry sectors. Companies that have used these qualifications consistently report an improvement in product and service quality, increased staff motivation and more targeted training. Yet estimates are that only 7 per cent of employers are using N/SVQs and that only 5 per cent of the workforce have gained an N/SVQ award.

There have been other government initiatives on education and training since the election of the Labour government in 1997 to introduce what is being called 'The Learning Age' (DfEE 1997). The four main proposals are:

- a University for Industry (UFI) based on a network of local learning centres and access points to put 'learning on the High Street'
- Individual Learning Accounts (ILAs) – study and learning vouchers, with which people can buy the education and training that they need
- childcare support for those who need to take courses during the day or evening
- Learning Direct – a helpline through which people can obtain information on courses available.

As government reform of ED continues three main issues are evident: establishing the overall costs of reforms for lifelong learning; defining how much employers should contribute; and identifying what kind of learning technologies should be supported. These issues reprise the fundamental and abiding problems with all and any policy: being able clearly to identify costs and benefits among a range of options in order to structure optimum investment in people. The issue is less 'making training pay' than 'How much will it actually cost?' and 'Who pays for it?'.

During the last decade, there have also been significant changes within the framework and institutions supporting ED. To some this amounts to a revolution in training policy since 1988; to others it smacks of reorganisation in the face of uncertainty about what to do for the best when facing the challenges of improving ED. All of the UK's ED industry's major current institutional landmarks have been developed since 1988. In particular, there is continuing uncertainty about the type of system needed to ensure there is effective liaison in the development, marketing and evaluation of supply-side and demand-side initiatives. This is a common theme in the 'revolutions' – institutional and cultural – that have been heralded several times in the last two decades. How best to get everybody working together, making optimum use of limited resources, to achieve a range of stakeholder goals is a problem that has not yet been solved. This chapter can only briefly mention the main bodies involved.

At the top stands some form of national body: in England and Wales it is the National Advisory Council for Education and Training Targets (NACETT), which monitors the progress of training in relation to national targets across the range of concerns addressed above, as well as advising the DfEE on current performance and the effect of policies designed to achieve the targets. It draws its members from the Confederation of British Industry (CBI), the Trades Union Congress (TUC), the fields of education and training, and government departments. Its equivalent in Scotland was the Advisory Scottish Committee on Training Targets

(ASCETT), though, with constitutional change and a devolved parliament taking responsibility for these matters, a new institutional system is currently being developed in Scotland. A Skills Task Force advises the DfEE on the National Skills Agenda. Its purpose is to analyse and forecast skills shortages and to propose solutions. Its recommendations do affect education and training policies.

At the next level down are National Training Organisations (NTOs). The key responsibilities of the NTOs are to identify the industry sector's training needs, establish occupational standards and qualifications for their sector, provide the sector with information on training capacity, and to ensure that the sector has relevant training capacity. NTOs are larger than previous industry bodies with a similar role, covering bigger industry sectors, and are, therefore, fewer in number. In autumn 1998, there were 55, but a total of 75 are planned. They are also required particularly to look at skills requirements in their industry. The NTO National Council has devised a programme called Skills Foresight, which the NTOs are to use in order to assess skills needs. They will make use of tools like benchmarking and scenario planning, as well as local focus groups, rather than just using the old centralised forecasting of skills demands characteristic of the old systems.

Downstream there are also geographically based bodies. Until recently these were the Training and Enterprise Companies (TECs) in England and Wales and Local Enterprise Companies (LECs) in Scotland. These were set up in 1990, to improve vocational training for young people, to raise training levels in smaller businesses, and to promote local economic growth. These are being superseded by new bodies in England from 2000, and the LECs are under review, given the devolution of government in Scotland. The principles will remain; they have been run by boards of executives, made up of members from industry, local government and the training industry. This tripartite structure is likely to remain in some form, however the actual organisations evolve. They are required to work closely with the NTOs, as their responsibilities overlap. The balance between central control and local initiative will continue to be a tension in the system whatever new forms of body emerge.

The context for the evolution of ED in this aspect in the UK is continuing institutional and policy change. All these factors increase demands for more spending on ED. Whether that is forthcoming, and whether this amounts to a government-inspired institutional and cultural revolution that is preparing the UK to face the challenges of the future is still very much open to question. Whether there is enough investment, and whether it is directed at the areas of most importance to 'UK plc' are questions different stakeholders would answer quite differently.

Employers' approaches to employee development

We conclude by briefly reviewing here the practice and the theory of ED within companies. It is at the workplace where the issues involved in managing skills, knowledge and values, and the stakeholders who are concerned with ED, interact and can be evaluated. Many employers provide much ED themselves, through having and using their own trainers and training departments. Some large organisations even aspire to create their own 'universities'. It is also employers who use the substantial and strong 'private sector' concerned with ED, in the form of companies which provide training services for organisations. And it is employers who use the substantial public sector input to the development of ED, in the form of public policies and government-backed development schemes and programmes. The hub of the whole system has to be what happens within workplaces. According to an Industrial Society survey, the most common subjects that development in employment focuses upon within companies are health and safety (68 per cent), communication (61 per cent), and customer care (53 per cent)(Industrial Society 1998). Much less common are financial (14 per cent) and leadership aspects (6 per cent).

Much training is of very short duration. Surveys of employers report that a third of all training courses last less than three days (*Employment Gazette*, 1995). Of employees who received job-related training the primary clusters of activity are around very brief courses and also around longer-term, more substantial programmes.

Table 5.5 shows that two- to three-day courses remain the most popular form of training provided by external sources, suggesting that this is the form of training most in demand when organisations seek partners to provide ED. The apparent low demand for some high-profile innovative approaches, such as mentoring and even distance learning, suggests that the short course structure is consistently appealing to organisations.

Table 5.5 Training approaches used regularly for external training (% of employers citing use of these approaches), 1998

2- to 3-day courses	82
Up to 1 day courses	79
Day release	69
Residential training	63
Evening classes	55
Distance/open learning	42
Computer-based learning	24
Outdoor training	24
Coaching/mentoring	12
Video-based learning	9
Learning resource centres	6
Action learning sets	7

Source: The Industrial Society, *Training Trends*, May/June 1998

In sum, ED typically involves organisations providing one-day courses for their own employees from a menu of options, with external private providers offering two- or three- day courses, and also with organisations providing or working in partnership with accrediting institutions to offer long programmes of study and development. These are the three primary fields of development within employment: 'short and sharp' courses, extended short courses and longer programmes.

Different approaches to ED have been identified among employers. These can be classified historically, as they have changed over time in response to new demands and priorities. An example of this (Megginson, Banfield and Joy-Matthews, 1999) is to review past 'leading ideas'.

- 1964–70 Systematic approach to diagnosis of training
- 1968–75 Standardisation of training for job categories by industry. Thorough off-job basic education for skilled occupations
- 1970–75 Systematic planning of training for all categories of employee
- 1974–80 Company contribution to training for young people and long-term unemployed to meet national needs
- 1979–90 Business-orientated training directed at improving organisational effectiveness
- 1988–present Personal development with individualised plans for which each employee and their line manager take responsibility
- 1990–present Learning company development with a focus on a conscious, systemic, whole-organisation perspective
- 1998–present Knowledge management focus with knowledge workers and their intellectual properties seen as the core significant assets of the organisation

These approaches were around for some organisations before the dates suggested above as the start, and they continue in use long after their 'heyday'. Old approaches also emerge in new forms in each era. So, for example, the standardisation of training for job categories, characteristic of the systematic approach in the late 1960s, has had a rebirth with the development of the Management Charter Initiative (MCI). MCI seeks to specify management training, as does the development of National/Scottish Vocational Qualifications (N/SVQs) for other categories of employee competence.

Survey methods to find out what is being advocated by practitioners also provide a way of categorising what is involved in ED. This methodology has the advantage of being grounded in experience, but has the disadvantage of being less neat and tidy than more conceptually elegant frameworks. A complex and detailed outline of a huge range of training ideas and their development over time in the view of 633 practitioners, is spelled out in the *Developing the Developers* report (Boydell *et al.*, 1991). A more recent example of the practitioner survey (Megginson, Banfield and Joy-Matthews, 1999) surveyed very experienced developers active in the Association of Management Education and Development (AMED) and elicited a long list of 16 possible leading ideas. The surveyors asked a wider group of human resource development (HRD) practitioners to rank this long list. They calculated the proportion of respondents listing each idea as one of their top two, and the proportion listing it as one of their bottom two. Table 5.6 shows the ideas listed according to the size of the difference between these two percentages; those at the top of the list are the ideas seen as being of highest priority in the balanced view of their respondents.

Table 5.6 Leading ideas listed in order of the size of the gap between the proportion given top two priority and the proportion given bottom two priority (N=61), listed in order of size of gap.

Leading idea	% giving top 2 ranks	% giving bottom 2 ranks	% difference between top and bottom
1. Linking development to the organisation's strategy	35	5	+30
2. Focus on company or organisation learning	21	2	+19
3. Improved communication / briefing	18	0	+18
4. Linking learning to work	22	7	+15
5. Involving and participative management	15	0	+15
6. Focus on development rather than training	19	7	+12
7. Empowerment of staff	9	2	+7
8. Learners responsible for their own development	10	5	+5
9. Building balanced lives	16	16	0
10. Learning between organisations	9	10	−1

Source: Megginson, D., Banfield, P. and Joy-Matthews, J. (1999) *Human Resource Development*, (2nd edn) Kogan Page, London (p.19).

An interesting feature of this list is that it excluded from an earlier version of the survey 'accreditation and competence'. Although quite a number of the sample rated this very highly, a much larger number rated it very low. These 'low raters' were disproportionately concentrated among the more experienced of the sample of respondents.

Reviewing the historical and the survey data the dominant approaches to ED in the UK can be classified as:

- the systematic approach
- business orientation
- competencies and accreditation
- self-development
- the learning organisation
- knowledge management.

Each of these theories and approach is briefly considered here in turn.

The systematic approach

In spite of its 'antiquity' and persistent critiques, the systematic training approach maintains a remarkable hold in the world of ED. One reason for this is that many books on training, development and HRD offer it as a core 'intellectual property', organising their text around a (usually) four-stage cycle, as shown in Figure 5.1

Another reason is its simplicity in suggesting a cycle of activity which can be managed in practice, breaking down into discrete parts. A deeper question about the persistence of this approach might be, 'Why do *authors* continue to use this framework?' One reason for the continuation of this strand of thinking about ED may be that it gives a professional identity to trainers as well as to writers on

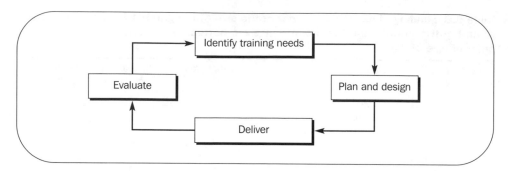

Figure 5.1

training. It provides a framework for what trainers do and enables them to describe their professional practice in a coherent way. Some of the components of this expertise are mapped in Box 5.1.

This model, however, is limited. It is a map of the 'internal content' of ED: what happens within employee development as a practical management activity; how to identify training needs, how to design and deliver training events, and how

---

BOX 5.1

The training cycle

Identify training needs
- Company and business needs
- Job and performance need
- Individual and personal need
- Self-determined needs (wants)

- Training plans and training policies
- Job analysis
- Performance appraisal
- Knowledge, skill and attitude (KSA)

Plan and design
- KSA linked to programme elements
- Learning methods linked to type of need
- Learning materials and resources
- Setting learning objectives

- On-job, at-job or off-job
- Internal or external
- Tutored or open learning resource

Deliver
- Use of range of learning methods
- Facilitation skills
- Engagement of internal providers
- Sourcing of external providers

- Instruction, coaching, mentoring
- Manage groups and teams
- A professional job role
- Being a broker of services

Evaluate
- Reactions, learning, job behaviour, organisation effects
- Feedback to learners
- Evaluating programme/strategy effectiveness

to evaluate them. The training cycle is also an essentially prescriptive model; it presents an ideal of what should be done, and does not reflect or describe what is actually done and the problems encountered.

Business orientation

The advent of the National Training Awards in Britain 1985 was the occasion when the business-oriented approach and theory were first formally advocated as a coherent framework, though of course many would have claimed prior to this that ED was integrated with business needs. The design of the awards required applicants to describe what had been done in terms of the four stages of the training cycle, outlined in the section on systematic training above, and they also required that the training must be preceded by identification of a business need and that the training outcome be shown to lead to a business outcome.

This approach was congruent with the spirit of the times, with businesses demanding 'bottom-line' contributions from all service functions if they were to survive deep cuts and downsizing. Arguably, the whole IiP approach, the central initiative in ED at the moment in the UK, is an incarnation of this approach.

The Institute of Personnel and Development (IPD) and Investors in People (IiP), arguably the two most notable proponents of ED in the UK, together launched a booklet called *Making Training Pay* (1997). This makes the business case for training and gives examples of how companies have benefited from training. The Confederation of British Industry also issued a survey-based report, which showed that, as well as putting more effort into training, two-thirds of employers were training their staff 'beyond the skills necessary for their jobs' (CBI, 1998).

Such reports are each small waves in a tide of change which has seen ED become a focus for effective business development and competitive success. Another survey claims to reveal that there is now a substantial attempt to link training with business objectives 'delivering human resource development in line with business objectives' (IPD, 1999: 11). This somewhat begs the question of what has been going on for the past several decades. The overemphasis in current times on having a business orientation may sometimes be seen as avoiding the specific challenges of evaluating exactly which approach is most effective and efficient and best provides value for money in different contexts.

Competencies and accreditation

An interesting 'mutation' of the business-oriented approach came when the UK government chose to put its authority behind approaches that advocated the identification of standardised competencies for occupations. The Management Charter Initiative (MCI) was one such initiative. This kind of set of competence statements specifying what it requires to 'do things well' in order to be effective in employment has, in fact, been a feature of training from the advent of systematic training. However, systematic training had offered the perspective that the particular needs of any specific group of managers (or any other group) needed to be identified. 'Universal' models of competence can thus seem to be a step back from this insight.

The government chose to put its weight behind the accreditation of individual competence because of a need to document progress towards the achievement of National Training Targets in the UK. The achievement of accredited qualifications gave the policy makers something to measure. From this emerged the whole panoply of N/SVQs. These qualifications were seen as having a number of advantages, discussed elsewhere in this chapter. A principal advantage was seen to be their portability – they could be related to other similar qualifications in other organisations and even in other EU countries.

The original work of Boyatzis (1982) on competencies had been based on finding out what behaviour led to superior performance by some individuals in a population. This work was therefore situated in particular contexts, and also provided a focus on what was required in order to 'do things better'. It was adopted by many large organisations in order to paint a vision of what was required in a major change project – and thus sought to encourage 'doing better things'; companies like BP and Boots developed such approaches. Many companies have now developed their own 'maps' of competence, though these are in essence, and often in detail, very similar.

Competencies were also proposed as providing a coherent framework for the integration of various HRM processes and initiatives. Some companies, including Commercial and General Union (see Case Study 5.1 at the end of this chapter) and Royal Bank of Scotland, had vigorous HR departments concerned with creating a set of initiatives bound together with a set of managerial behaviours which would lead to some future desirable state. Thus, selection, performance management, development and pay could all be tied down to some common framework. We have also identified cases, where having originally embraced competencies, senior HR people came to see that the model they imposed companywide did not capture the unique and crucial capabilities and contributions of a diversity of managerial roles and styles.

Self-development

This approach is grounded on two axioms:

- Any learning is a good thing as it leads to the embracing of the new and the extension of skills and capability.
- Learning which has the most potency to create these effects is that chosen and specified by the learners themselves.

The first axiom leads to the practice of employee development schemes, of which the most famous is the Ford's Employee Development and Assistance Programme (EDAP). Here a personal budget is provided to enable individuals to learn whatever they want in order to initiate or reawaken the habit of learning, and to offer a commitment on behalf of the employer to making this happen.

Recently some authorities (Hamblett and Holden, 2000) have been suggesting that employee-led development has a component that makes a difference – namely, the fact that overall control of the scheme is in the hands of the workforce or their representatives. This participation ensures effective development.

The second axiom leads to an approach to development where the learner is given central responsibility for and control over the process of identifying and meeting learning needs, and others have roles to support this development. Often personal development plans (see the CGU case study at the end of this chapter) are a part of the process, and line managers can have an important role in supporting and stimulating the consideration of development. Training functions are seen as enablers and can provide advice on the resources to deliver training or development opportunities. The experience of the authors in designing and supporting such programmes (in, for example, Texaco and ICL) is that competencies are sometimes used and found helpful in the first round of need-identification. However, they are often rejected in favour of a more individual expression of need once the learner gains confidence in expressing their own needs (Megginson and Whitaker, 1996).

The learning organisation

Ideas of organisational learning, which had been present in the literature for more than 20 years, became popular in the early 1990s with the publication of Senge (1990) in the USA and Pedler, Burgoyne and Boydell (1991) in the UK. Essentially, both advocated a systemic rather than a systematic approach to development. By this we mean that they saw that everything was connected to everything else. Simple cause and effect models (we sometimes call them 'boxes and arrows' approaches) do not capture the complex interactions between components of a system. Learning, if it is to generate new possibility for action, needs to recognise that most of our actions are grounded in basic assumptions of which we may not be aware. These assumptions limit our thinking and acting, and at the same time seal off from us the awareness that we are thus limited (Argyris and Schön, 1978).

Many trainers claim to be adopting this approach by following a recipe of pre-scriptions (such as Pedler *et al*.'s (1991) eleven characteristics of a learning company). Trainers do this in spite of the authors' clear advice to the contrary, and without the systemic perspective of Senge (1990). They also often lack the willingness and skill required to question basic assumptions inherent in the writing of Argyris and Schön (1978). This approach is, it would seem, much less commonly adopted than the rhetoric of its adherents would suggest.

Knowledge management

An emerging approach, which may establish itself and displace the systematic training approach, is the approach to learning via the concerns of knowledge management. Knowledge management gurus argue that knowledge held by knowledge workers creates intellectual capital which represents the intangible assets of modern organisations. These intangible assets have often far greater worth than the tangible assets of buildings and machinery. Development is therefore crucially concerned with the management and enhancement of these knowledge assets. As the field develops, there seem to be contributions from three currents of thinking. The first is the information systems (IS) perspective, which emphasises the capture, store and retrieval of knowledge. The second is the organisation learning (OL) perspective, which focuses on learning as being mediated, situated, provisional, pragmatic and contested (Easterby-Smith *et al.*, 1999). The third is a strategic perspective, which emphasises the value of intellectual capital and the worth of knowledge as embodied in patents and corporate core competencies (Davenport and Prusak, 1998). The prospect of a fusion of these perspectives is beguiling for developers, who find that conversations about learning often do not engage the attention of strategic management in the way that a hard-headed concern for tangible assets can.

Conclusion

There are a variety of approaches to achieving development in employment, with no single best way being evident in theory or practice. In a prescriptive sense, as outlined in the beginning, ED is concerned with learning for and learning at work to help individuals and organisations achieve their full potential. Individuals have development needs throughout their lives. These range from gaining basic knowledge and basic skills in education and pre-employment vocational development, through to induction and initial job-related training with an employer, and on to their lifelong performance and career development up to leaving the employer on redundancy or retirement. Employers are concerned with ensuring that their workforce is competent and that the development activities used to achieve competency are effective and efficient. This requires employers' involvement in a range of activities, from influencing and shaping government policy on education through to organising their own development activities for individuals, specific job roles and the organisation as a whole. While some issues come to more prominence in some contexts than others, there is no settled, universal and dominant prescriptive approach.

In terms of evidence for a positive evaluation of employers' activities in ED in the UK, many UK work organisations have often looked to ED as an integral part of becoming and remaining efficient and more effective. There is a long and substantial tradition of investing in ED in many UK organisations, and those which it has been quick and easy to accredit as Investors in People (IiPs) reflect that. This is simply and logically because, other things being equal, an organisation with well-developed and therefore competent employees will be more efficient and effective than an organisation with poorly developed and therefore incompetent employees.

In the light of greater challenges to be 'excellent' in order to compete successfully or to provide better-quality public services, a greater concern with ED among employers has been reinforced as a route to helping achieve these aspirations. In partnership with employers, the government has reformed the education and training system that underpins ED in the UK, to make it better fit the country's economic and social needs. The development of employees and the promotion of learning at work are now seen as a means of transforming organisations from struggling businesses or services into world-class and successful organisations. All the driving forces in the business environment push most employers towards greater levels and improved quality of ED. Evidence in the form of organisations who adopt this philosophy and succeed is plentiful; see Case Study 5.2.

However, investment in effective ED does not appear to be the norm among UK employers seeking to develop their businesses. The need for promotional initiatives like IiP, raises questions about the extent to which there is indeed a general, common-sense and logical case for transforming organisations through employers increasing their investing in ED. As exemplary employers in this respect are not the norm, either employers are ignorant of the returns to be achieved, or are led to other conclusions in reality. Perhaps the 'unambiguous' data supporting the returns on ED is discounted as unrealistic. Kellaway (2000) claims that there is

---

BOX 5.2

Chase Advanced Technologies Ltd

In 1996 Chase Advanced Technologies won a major contract to provide electronic components for fruit machines across the UK. But the contract led to problems for the company, including poor pass rates and high levels of reworking. At one point things were so bad that internal pass rates fell to 38 per cent.

An intensive training programme to tackle the immediate crisis was devised which involved 60 employees undertaking basic training in printed circuit board assembly. Quality levels began to rise, reaching 80 per cent in a few months. The company then introduced a skills training and National Vocational Qualification (NVQ) initiative and an in-house workmanship training culture, set up with support from a local college and Electronic ITEC, Bradford College's electronic training centre. A multimedia computer-based training package to support the delivery of the NVQ was also developed.

Finally the change management team began to lay the foundations for a genuine training culture. They made a commitment to the Investors in People standard and offered staff access to a nationally recognised qualification.

After 2 years of heavy losses Chase returned to profit in 1998 and the company is now a thriving organisation with a skilled and committed workforce. Managing director Eugene Martinez commented 'The training programme has led to a new spirit of enthusiasm among our staff. Having been given an opportunity to learn, many have developed a real hunger for knowledge. A working grandmother was one of the first people to gain a NVQ and has recently gained a level 3 qualification in manufacturing support. Many staff are so keen that they are even undertaking NVQ work in their own time.'

Source: DfEE Employment News, December/January 2000, p.5. Quoted in full with permission.

indeed much hype and inflation surrounding ED. As a trenchant critic of UK employers' susceptibility to management fads and fashions, she asserts that:

> Some of the dullest days I have spent in my 18 years as a wage slave have been on training courses. Training is only good if it succeeds in teaching you something useful. But most of it doesn't or doesn't do it very effectively.

(Kellaway, 2000: 81)

It seems that many employers share her views, rather than being gulled, as she supposes, by the 'nonsense' claims that ED can transform a company. A negative evaluation of employers' activities in ED in the UK would also be supported by the fact that many work organisations have failed to make ED a priority. Investment in ED in companies in the UK is consistently lower than in other countries. Employers continue either to operate inefficiently and ineffectively, or seek to become more efficient and effective by other means – the primary strategy being through deskilling work and minimising costs by actually neglecting ED. While the high-quality development of a few professionals and managers may be achieved in some companies, the limited ED that is provided by employers, and their influence on schools, colleges and universities, is of dubious quality and value. This has resulted in systematic problems in achieving even basic competence amongst the general labour force and in specific workforces, which leaves UK employers at a disadvantage. Effects range from poor health and safety standards, through poor standards of customer service and up to ineffective strategic management of the organisation as a whole. This leads to the UK being saddled with a 'low-skill, low-wage' economy. It is also badly placed to restructure and meet the demands of the knowledge economy and society.

The apparent failure of employers to support ED is compounded by governmental failures to challenge them. Government has actively handed responsibility over to employers to lead the 'skills revolutions' they seek, but employers have been found wanting. Government has thus failed to identify and resource properly the priorities and institutions needed to break free from the 'low-skill, low-wage' economy the UK is seen to have. Skills shortages cause problems not only for immediate business and service development, the main concern of employers; they can also constrain longer-term economic growth and social restructuring, a primary concern of government. As a result, UK organisations are falling further and further behind their competitors in the rest of the world. Other nations' greater governmental emphasis on investment in ED pays general economic and social dividends, while in the UK the gaps between those who are successful and those who are 'socially excluded' widen and deepen (Hutton, 1995).

The truth would seem to lie somewhere between the simplified and exaggerated negative and positive evaluations of employers' activities in ED in the UK. One estimate (Keynote, 1998) was that the total amount spent on training by the private sector in 1998 was £13.2 billion, spent on a workforce of around 21 million where around 3 million people in the year were participants in off-job training. In

BOX 5.3

Skills shortages

For 42% of employers with hard-to-fill vacancies the main reason given is not enough suitable skilled people.

<table>
<tr><td>

Areas
- Catering occupations
- Road transport
- Miscellaneous sales and services
- Engineers and technologists
- Health and related occupations
- Health associate professionals
- Miscellaneous clerks
- Receptionists and telephonists
- Computer analysts and programmers
- Telephone sales
- Specialist managers

</td><td>

Effects
- Increased running costs
- Loss of quality
- Restrict business developments

</td></tr>
</table>

Changes in skill needs

68% of employers say skills needed are increasing due to changes in processes, technology and management practices.

Skills that matter

Technical and practical skills
Computer literacy
General communication skills
Customer handling skills
Management skills
Teamworking skills
Problem-solving skills
Managing own development

Source: IRS ED Bulletin 110:*Skill Needs in Great Britain and NI 1998*

the UK the average spend is then £62 per person if all employees are considered, or £440 per person for those who actually received off-job training.[5]

The negative evaluators would be challenged by this trend, but not the basic fact. They would still wonder whether this level of activity and the development it involves are good enough. And questions about the efficiency and effectiveness of investments in ED remain in any event. The pessimist would also question where resources invested in ED are actually going. Research (DfEE: *Labour Market Trends*, 1998) shows that there is a marked bias towards younger age groups as

---

[5] There are no available estimates for similar figures on ED in the public sector.

participants in ED. This makes sense as the early career stages are when learning needs would seem most evident. But in an era where the promotion of 'lifelong learning' is important, and where organisational and job changes are so prevalent, it seems that ED needs to be – but is not yet in practice – a lifelong activity.

There are also significant variations in the occupational characteristics of ED activity (ONS, 1996). Professional employees are the most likely to receive ED, while regular training is lowest among manual workers. Again these statistics seem to reflect a 'reality' where professional jobs require more learning, and therefore attract more resources. However, many commentators argue that the provision of ED for all is a precondition of successful performance for any organisation, and in the UK it is problems with basic and intermediate ED (or vocational education and training (VET)) which present the greatest areas of need. The concentration of resources and activity among certain occupational groups may reflect an anomaly inherited from history rather than an effective allocation of resources.

There are also sector variations. Some sectors invest more in ED than others. One survey (Industrial Society, 1998) shows, for example, that off-the-job training is more widespread in the financial sector than in manufacturing. This discrepancy may reflect greater use of on-the-job ED in manufacturing rather than the financial sector, so the balance of overall investment in ED may be more equal than it first seems. It may also be the case that there are greater ED needs in the financial sector than in manufacturing; for example, due to the introduction of legislation and the demand for improved levels of competence in the selling of financial services. The pessimists' suspicion would be that ED in manufacturing is neglected because it is a low-skill, low-wage sector, thus contributing to the overall decline of that sector within the UK economy. They may also suspect that much of the investment in ED in the financial sector is of dubious value.

So learning in and for the workplace depends upon the outcome of complex interactions between individuals, employers and government. The hope is that optimum investment by each in development brings maximum gains: individuals gain attractive and useful employment, employers gain business success in high-skill industries, and governments achieve the social and economic goals they were elected to pursue. There is then a weight of expectation hanging on ED, exerted by the dependence of all these stakeholders upon it. Whether, in principle, ED can deliver on these expectations, and whether, in practice, one approach is better than another, are questions which have exercised many in HRM in recent times and which need to be pursued further.

This chapter has described and evaluated the nature of ED, what it involves and what the issues and challenges are, particularly from an employer's perspective. Seeing employers' activities as the hub of the matter is, indeed, only one way of concluding a review of ED; but it has the merit of leading on to theoretical case study analysis of workplace and employer examples, rather than to specialist theories and matters of motivation and involvement in learning, or to the evaluation of government policies and initiatives in the broader context of evaluating social and economic goals and aspirations.

From an employer's perspective the context is one of achieving their goals through creating a competent workforce. This involves them in a range of activities, from organising their own employees' development, to influencing education and development policy and taking the lead in evolving supportive national policies and systems. In all these respects the evaluation of employers' activities in ED can be positive: education is being reformed to meet the economic and social needs of the contemporary workforce, employers are investing more in ED, with gains for all; and as a result of these activities, broader social and economic goals and aspirations can be met. Changes and restructuring in companies are bringing about changes in people's tasks and responsibilities, with a subsequent need for more ED. All sectors appear to be supporting change: companies are reviewing their internal provisions, government provides new and salient frameworks which are funded and a dynamic private sector provides a range of ED options 'for all tastes and budgets'. Changes in markets, in customer requirements, and in approaches to ED are forcing providers to review their products and services, which leads to better products and services. For the government there are continuing economic, social and political gains to be made in promoting 'supply-side' policies that involve motivating employers and individuals to increase skills and employability rather than achieving economic and social aims by 'taxing and spending'.

The evaluation can also be negative: education is becoming too vocationalised and losing its fundamental purpose; insufficient investment in development in organisations is the stubborn norm; policies and institutions which are employer-led fail to deliver on longer-term economic and social goals and aspirations. The three main stakeholders arguably continue to underfund their rhetoric. Companies are still prone to limiting ED budgets; the government does not follow through on funding for its initiatives; and individuals are reluctant to pay themselves for ED. In addition, ED standards vary considerably. Internal provisions, and those offered externally by the private and public sector, are often criticised. There appear to be a significant proportion of ED programmes that are poorly planned and structured, despite decades of established advice on how to do it properly. There are continuing critiques of the success and viability of government programmes – for example, the merits of the IiP initiative. Evaluating the worth of ED, in terms of costs and benefits, has never been easy; its higher profile further exposes this, paradoxically leading to greater criticisms of ED as it grows in popularity as a business development tool. Also, current investment in ED is concentrated among the large companies, whose share of total employees is declining, and in certain employment categories and age groups.

There is then a huge demand for ED: within companies, from competent external providers, and in the form of public sector initiatives designed to support individuals and organisations. Computer-based learning is gaining popularity and may be particularly suited to some sectors which involve jobs that are heavily dependent on using IT. School, university and personal use of ICT systems is clearly growing, and this whole aspect of the design and delivery of training will be a major concern in the future. The shift towards self-managed learning offers the prospect of better focused and greater personal and professional development. New entrants to the ED market, such as computer companies and publishers, are expanding the range of courses available and offering cheaper training. Non-profit organisations are competing strongly against the commercial training companies.

Yet in companies there is a threat to training budgets and initiatives in the face of cost reduction factors and the imperatives of production/service delivery in lean organisations concerned to maintain limits to working hours. Greater use in companies of learning resource centres may increase the demand on internal company training, but may not deliver the goods without trained trainers there to facilitate. Governments are struggling to sort out the 'Who pays?' part of the equation. Getting bogged down in this, or making decisions that prove unpopular with major stakeholders, can undo all the efforts that have hitherto been made.

In many respects there is a great deal of inertia in the system. Despite promulgating and promoting the benefits of ED, it takes time and a lot of resources to establish and co-ordinate efforts which can bring real business and social benefits. Dissatisfaction with the quantity and quality of ED provided, both by the public sector and the private sector as well as within companies, can be expected to spur the further evolution of innovative approaches to ED and further restructuring of the overall system. The potential of technologies, for example, has yet to be fully realised. All this means that further, and perhaps greater, change is likely in the future. Such changes can be expected to succeed or fail according to how well they engage individuals, employers and government in partnerships as much as they will depend upon the relevance and accuracy of the substantive knowledge, skill and values identified as priorities for future human potential development.

Where that interaction involves individuals motivated to learn, able to access learning within employment and elsewhere, supported by investing employers and guided by principled economic and social policy being effectively implemented, then a synergy is possible with all benefiting. Where that interaction involves people unwilling or unable to participate in learning, compounded by employers who fail to invest in ED and there is a lack of principle or effective implementation in economic and social policy then a vicious cycle will exist, with all paying the price. These realities of providing development for employment present human, organisational and political challenges which are at the heart of HRM.

Employee development in Commercial & General Union

Stephen Gibb and David Megginson

The context

Commercial Union, a large British general insurance company, initiated a strategic change project, called Best Place to Work (BPTW), in 1996. BPTW aimed to change beliefs about working relationships and performance towards a more competitive and customer-focused set of values. Current management styles were to be challenged, structures were to become more customer-focused, and processes would be redesigned to enable more front-line decision-making. Reward systems were to become more performance-focused and awareness of the redefined brand was to be increased. A BPTW survey showed that staff wanted 'to grow and develop', and felt that opportunities were scarce. A Personal Development Planning (PDP) process was set in train to meet this aspiration, and to reinforce other aspects of the BPTW programme.

ED in the company before this point was focused upon:

- Professional insurance industry qualifications, with relatively little attention paid to N/SVQs
- IiP, which was being pursued by various parts of the business
- A tradition of attendance on residential courses at the company's training centre – Douce's Manor, in Kent.

During 1997 a relationship was established with Cranfield Business School, which delivered residential training for senior managers. During 1998 a Certificate, Diploma and MBA programme was set up with the Open University Business School for people who self-nominated and were supported by their managers.

The aims of the PDP initiative were to enable staff to:

1. Take personal responsibility for acquiring the right technical, interpersonal and business skills to do the job now, and to gain management support for this process.
2. Think ahead about their career and future possibilities – and start to chart a way forward; to see patterns in what they had done, and rethink whether they wanted them to continue or change.
3. Tune into the changes going on around them, recognise the impact of change on them and develop coping/success skills.
4. Recognise the value of developing outside of work, and gain management support for this.

The scheme had been launched and rolled out to the 8,000 staff in CU(UK) when, in February 1998, a merger was announced with another UK insurer, General Accident (GA). This merger was realised in June 1998, to form Commercial and General Union (CGU). Thereafter, attention was diverted from the PDP scheme to more pressing concerns of creating new structures and roles, and implementing a voluntary redundancy scheme.

Processes

The company's approach to the project:

- Initial research was carried out to find out what had worked elsewhere.
- Leading outside consultants were brought in to challenge thinking and assist in development of workshop design, workbooks and video.
- There was close liaison with other HR system developments, especially an emerging competency framework, IiP and a performance management system.
- Communication with stakeholders in the business was important during the development of the process.
- Champions were sought at each of the company sites, and they were trained in PDP principles and practices, and briefed in how to train managers in supporting the PDP process.
- Champions trained the managers at their site in how to support staff in preparing PDPs.
- Managers worked with their staff in supporting the development of their PDPs.
- Staff worked on developing and implementing their own PDPs.

Workbooks were produced for the workshops, outlining the process and the format for a PDP. A video was produced describing CU staff's reactions to such a process. It showed endorsement of PDPs by senior managers.

The stages in the PDP process described in the staff's 'Guide to personal development planning' were:

- Identify your 'here and now' needs – from the performance management system and from feedback from others.
- Develop for future business needs – from the competency framework, from expected role changes within BPTW, from business changes in CU, and from personal awareness of changes in business.
- Set goals based on recognising past success, get in touch with your own dream for your development, and identify an extraordinarily realistic self-image.
- Create your own plan, with prioritised needs, development goals and development actions.
- 'Do it and review it', including logging learning and learning from experience. They were given a checklist for a personal development review.

Outcomes

All the above processes had taken place for the vast majority of CU(UK) staff before the merger with GA was confirmed. Plans had been made for embedding the scheme and ensuring its continuation over subsequent years. However, these plans were put on hold in the flurry of activity surrounding the merger.

Informal soundings of HR staff involved in supporting staff through the changes necessitated by the merger indicate that ex-CU staff may have been better equipped to make choices for themselves and for the new CGU Insurance.

It is difficult to evaluate the absolute success of the PDP programme, as it was never intended to be a discrete product, but was part of a wider (BPTW) process of change. However all three sets of workshops were very well received, and managers' workshops had an average rating of 3.25 on a scale of 1–4, where 3 = Well and 4 = Very well, in response to a range of questions asked. The staff workshops had average ratings of 3.40.

Typical comments about the workshops were:

> *'Interesting and well presented'*
>
> *'Whilst enjoyable – a long day, lots to take in'*
>
> *'Enjoyable, fun – but could have been condensed slightly'*
>
> *'Facilitators assisting and guiding during activities was helpful'*
>
> *'Overall a good course. Showed the importance of PDPs. Ran in a relaxed manner with plenty of activities. Plenty of motivation'*
>
> *'We managers need more help in ensuring that expectations are not raised too high'*
>
> *'Interesting – not as boring as I thought it would be'*
>
> *'Good variety of activities and facilitator participation'*
>
> *'Nice to know that CU is committed to the development of staff'*
>
> *'Useful to apply in my private life'*

Questions

1. Which approach to ED is this employer using ?
2. Which concern seems uppermost in this example: knowledge development, skills development or EVA development ?
3. In what ways does the example reflect a use of the three sectors: internal ED, adoption of public initiatives and use of external providers/partners ?
4. Do the evaluation findings suggest that this ED initiative achieved the objectives the company had in mind ?
5. What else might you want to evaluate to analyse the efficiency and the effectiveness of this ED initiative ?

Case study 5.2

External training providers

Stephen Gibb and David Megginson

The effectiveness of ED overall depends in large part on the effectiveness of private providers. Private training providers work in a very fragmented industry, supporting a large number of training providers, which range from sole practitioners to some very large training companies. Estimates of the number of private providers vary. There appear to be around 400 principal training organisations in the UK, with many more organisations, companies, partnerships and sole practitioners which provide training. The number of value-added tax (VAT)-based enterprises listed as training providers totals 4,475 (Keynote, 1998). In addition, there are many smaller training providers who escape VAT categorisation, either because their turnover is too low or because their main business is not in training. According to the Association for Management Education and Development (AMED), there are around 10,000 independent trainers. The majority of providers fall into the categories shown below.

- **Independent, commercially run training companies** – there seem to be around 400 of these in the UK, including some long-established firms.
- **Professional/institutional bodies** – most professional bodies offer some form of training, which often complements their role as accreditation bodies. Examples include the Institute of Personnel and Development, the Chartered Institute of Marketing, and the Institute of Directors.
- **Business schools/universities** – there are over 100 training providers in this category. Business schools and universities are now heavily promoted as centres of vocational learning and training.
- **Colleges of further education** – supplying mainly vocational training.
- **Product/service companies**; for example computer companies who provide training along with hardware and software purchases.
- **Open learning providers** – there are many examples, including, of course, the Open University. The uptake of multimedia and internet systems means many open learning providers are leading the way in technological developments.
- **Sole practitioners** – many ex-company in-house trainers set themselves up as independent trainers. They may work totally independently, in collaboration with other sole practitioners, or as subcontractors of training companies.
- **Management consultancies** – some consultancies offer training, although this tends to form only a small part of their activities.

Being able to tailor a course to a company's needs is obviously of primary importance for external training providers (The Industrial Society, 1998). Training companies are increasingly offering 'tailored' courses rather than off-the-shelf options. Quality and perceived value for money are also seen to be extremely important. For an employer it is argued that price is less important (i.e. differentials between one training company and another) than the company's image and professionalism. The need for a course to be 'locally' based is no longer a consideration for most companies; the quality and subject matter are the main determinants. Even the location of local colleges and universities as external partners is less important, in view of the availability of distance learning and internet technologies. This opens up the market for the provision of ED on a global basis; providing both a threat and opportunity to private providers of ED in the UK.

The most popular choice of external partner for employers is a private sector trainer, followed by an educational institution, a professional association/institute or a non-profit making training body (Table 5.7).

Table 5.7: External training providers – percentage of organisations using each source

Type of training provider	1997	1998
Private sector trainers/providers	73	78
University/college/other FE body	56	68
Professional association/institute	45	55
Non-profit-making training body (e.g. The Industrial Society)	51	48
Equipment supplier	32	33
Training and Enterprise Council/ Local Enterprise Council	25	24
Informal employers' network/club	10	10

Note: FE – further education

Source: The Industrial Society, *Training Trends*, May/June 1998

Around a third of all training still takes place at an employer's workplace or training centre. This proportion is likely to rise as employers increase the amount of in-house training that they purchase. Further education and technical colleges are also important sites of learning, as are adult education centres and universities. Educational/academic institutions are becoming more important as sources and places of training. Figure 5.2 shows the main location of face-to-face teaching for all taught learning episodes in England and Wales during 1997 (DfEE: *Labour Market Trends*, 1998).

With only a few exceptions, private suppliers and partners are wholly UK-owned and UK-staffed. Arguably, this is because the involvement of foreign companies is problematic in the context of the specific needs of the workforce skills, knowledge and values within a nation or region. Moreover, the educational and cultural framework of each country is different, and this is reflected in training approaches and

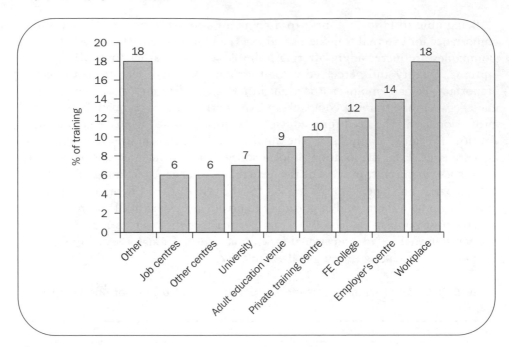

Figure 5.2 Venues for training

content. Management practice and style also vary from one country to another, as indeed does HRM practice. As a result, ED tends to be indigenous to each country. Partnerships between organisations in different parts of Europe may emerge with further Europeanisation, and harmonisation in economic and social matters.

The major exception at the moment to this national specialisation is the development of 'European managers' by some of the multinational companies. However, this type of training tends to be influenced by the corporate style emanating from the company headquarters, which, in some cases, is still culturally oriented towards one country. There is also the traditional 'North American' influence on much personal and management development. As Europe becomes more integrated, there are likely to be increased calls for some kind of mechanism by which qualifications in one country can be equated with those of another. The first step towards this is the Europass, a passport-type document which will contain details of the owner's training and the government training schemes they have been on.

Questions

1. What are the advantages and disadvantages of using external training providers?
2. What factors explain the increasing use of external training providers in the UK?
3. What factors influence an organisation's choice of external training providers?

References to Chapter 5

Argyris, C. and Schön, D. (1978) *Organizational Learning*, Reading, Mass: Addison-Wesley.

Bloom, B.S. (ed) (1956) *Taxonomy of Educational Objectives: The Classification of Educational Goals: Handbook 1, Cognitive Domain*, New York: Longman.

Boyatzis, R. (1982) *The Competent Manager*, New York: Wiley.

Boydell, T., Leary, M., Megginson, D. and Pedler, M. (1991) *Developing the Developers*, London: AMED.

Blackler, F. (1995) 'Knowledge, knowledge work and organizations', *Organization Studies*, 16(6): 1021–46.

CBI (1998) *Employment Trends*, London: CBI.

Crouch, C., Finegold, D., Sako, M. (1999) 'Are skills the answer? The political economy of skill creation in advanced industrial countries', Oxford: Oxford University Press.

Davenport, T. and Prusak, L.(1998) *Working Knowledge*, Boston, Mass: Harvard Business School.

DfEE (1995) 'Length of training courses', *Employment Gazette*, 103 (7): 37.

DfEE (1996) *Labour Force Survey*, London: DfEE.

DfEE (1998a) *The Learning Age: a New Renaissance for a New Britain*, London: DfEE.

DfEE (1998b) *Labour Market Trends*, London: DfEE.

DfEE (1998c) *National Learning Targets for England 2002*, London: DfEE.

Easterby-Smith, M., Burgoyne, J., Avaujo, L. (eds) (1999) *Organizational Learning and the Learning Organization*, London: Sage.

ESRC (1999) 'Twenty-Something in the 1990s', ESCR briefing.

Foster, J. (1999) 'Looking for balance', London: The National Work-Life Forum.

Gibb, S. (1999) 'The usefulness of theory: a case study in evaluating formal mentoring schemes', *Human Relations*, 52(8): 1055–75.

Goleman, D. (1996) *Emotional Intelligence: Why it can Matter More than IQ*, London: Bloomsbury.

Hamblett, J. and Holden, R. (2000) 'Employee-led development: another piece of left luggage?', *Personnel Review*, 29(4): 509–20.

Hutton, W. (1995) *The State We're In*, London: Jonathan Cape.

Industrial Society (1998) *Training Trends*, May/June, London: Industrial Society

IPD (1997) *Making Training Pay*, London: IPD/IiP.

IPD (1999) *Training and Development in Britain 1999*, London: IPD.

Johnson, P. and Indvik, J. (1999) 'Organizational benefits of having emotionally intelligent managers and employees', *Journal of Workplace Learning*, 11(3): 84–88

Kellaway, L. (2000) *Sense and Nonsense in the Office*, London: FT/Prentice Hall.

Keynote (1998) *Training*, Keynote marketing report.

Megginson, D., Banfield, P. and Joy-Matthews, J. (1999) *Human Resource Development*, 2nd edition, London: Kogan Page.

Megginson, D. and Whitaker, V. (1996) *Cultivating Self-development*, London: IPD.

ONS (1996) *Social Trends*, London: HMSO.

Pedler, M., Burgoyne, J. and Boydell, T. (1991) *The Learning Company*, Maidenhead: McGraw-Hill,

Pickard, J. (1999) 'Keynote speakers', *People Management*, 5(11).

Pinker, S. (1997) *How the Mind Works*, London: Penguin.

Rokeach, M. (1970) *Beliefs, Attitudes and Values: A Theory of Organisation and Change*, San Francisco: Jossey-Bass.

Schön, D. (1987) *Educating the Reflective Practitioner*, San Francisco: Jossey-Bass.

Senge, P. (1990) *The Fifth Discipline*, London: Century.

Stewart, T. (1997) *Intellectual Capital*, London: Nicholas Brealey Publishing.

Tapscott, D. (1996) *The Digital Economy: Promise and Peril in the Age of Networked Intelligence*, New York: McGraw Hill.

Wickens, P. (1999) 'Values added', *People Management*, 5(10): 33–38.

Chapter 6

Grievance and discipline

Douglas Renwick and John Gennard

Introduction

Within organisations' HR strategies, one of the areas seen by managers as being most difficult to comprehend, manage, and deliver effectively is that of grievance and discipline handling. That this is the case is a common admission of many managers, practitioners and students of employee relations alike. This chapter does not intend to repeat general guidance on 'good practice' in grievance and discipline handling, or indeed to produce a complex discussion of the issues within employment law, as these have been covered comprehensively elsewhere, (e.g. Gennard and Judge, 1997; Lewis, 1997; and Suter, 1997). This chapter limits itself to a number of key themes: (1) the rights and responsibilities of the employer and employee, (2) the role of the HR professional, (3) current research findings, and (4) issues for the future. The general focus of this chapter is to examine issues and strategies that surround the operation of grievance and discipline policies and procedures within the workplace, and highlight existing and new concerns that have emerged. The general focus of the case studies is to reinforce the need for five tests to be satisfied in grievance and discipline handling: fairness, reasonableness, consistency, operating with just cause, and operating within the law.

Rights and responsibilities

That there *are* issues surrounding grievance and discipline handling in the workplace is a logical consequence of the employment relationship itself. Not all of the interests of both employers and employees necessarily coincide, and inappropriate actions and transgressions on either side raise the issue of the satisfactory resolution of those differences within the parameters of both the organisational context and the law. These interests are expressed in both parties' rights and responsibilities to each other in legal contracts of employment and in their informal expectations of each other.

Clearly, both sides to the employment relationship have expectations that need to be met if that relationship is to succeed. The expectation from employees of employers is that they will be treated in a reasonable, fair and consistent manner and act against them only on the basis of just cause after thorough investigation. Employers look to employees to perform satisfactorily for them. If employee performance is not seen to be acceptable to the employer then the employer will look to discipline the employee. Hence the importance of HR interventions to resolve differences, and facilitate the more effective and smoother running of organisations. As employer and employee, both parties to the employment relationship are not only bound ethically, morally and socially to seek such a resolution of differences, but there is a clear business case for the resolution of their differences also. That business case rests on the assumptions that if discipline and grievance issues are dealt with properly, employee dissatisfaction should decrease and motivation increase, labour turnover should decline and retention rates increase, and a reservoir of discontent from employee against employer would thus be avoided. If employers are too harsh in disciplining employees, grievances from employees against arbitrary management action may arise. If employers are too soft, enforcing future discipline of employees may be difficult. Additionally, if employee representatives tolerate lapses in discipline from employees, then resolving their members' future grievances with managers may become more difficult, whilst too strict a stance from representatives may well raise accusations of them being 'in bed with management'. Klass *et al.* (1999) have charted line manager perceptions of organisations' disciplinary systems and found:

> *Our results suggest that it is possible to introduce some level of restrictiveness to protect employee rights without adversely affecting managers.* At some point, however, adding further restrictions affects managerial perceptions of disciplinary system effectiveness. Thus, at higher levels of restrictiveness, consideration must be given to the tradeoffs between protecting employee rights and the effect of restrictions on managers. Results also showed that investment in employee training, monitoring costs, grievance systems, unionization, and pressure to perform also were significantly associated with managerial evaluations of disciplinary system effectiveness
>
> (Klass *et al.*, 1999: 547, my emphasis)

In the absence of the option for managers to recruit and select a new workforce, or the ability of employees to find a new employer to work for, both are engaged in the process of conflict resolution. Both sides, if they are serious in looking for a resolution to the issues raised may well be advised to find the common interest between them. The same process can be seen between these two parties in other areas of employee relations, most notably in negotiations over pay, terms and conditions and provisions for employee development. Both issues of grievance and discipline handling are seen to be linked and often share one set of procedures in organisations. This is because:

one can be given disproportionately greater status, and be taken more seriously than the other. No matter which is favoured, if the balance is lost there are potential problems.

(IPM, 1992: 8)

The issue of getting the balance right is now put further under the microscope as we are entering a perceived era of increased line management responsibility in employee relations (Storey, 1992; Poole and Jenkins, 1997; Cunningham and Hyman, 1999). That all managers need to be trained properly to handle grievance and discipline cases is crucial because these managers have to ensure that a distinction is drawn between employee complaints which managers see as unjustified, and those that are justified under the organisation's procedure, collective agreement or works rule (Gennard and Judge, 1997: 198–9). Where a dismissal of an employee has occurred, in investigating whether or not an employee has a grievance against their employer, tribunals test the issues of fairness and reasonableness by asking whether procedures that the employer has applied actually 'conform to the concepts of natural justice' (IPM, 1992: 26). The purpose of having a procedure is to ensure that standards are maintained. Procedures are implemented via a number of stages, with a manager's objective being to settle each one as close to its origin as possible. Realistically, time pressures may constrain a manager's ability to stall in carrying out a full investigation quickly, as the employee requires the issue to be solved urgently (Gennard and Judge, 1997: 202–3). But managers need to be careful. Recent research has identified cases where some disciplinary hearings took place without a long time delay – giving the impression that managers had retributional or punishment motives foremost in their minds (Rollinson *et al.*, 1997: 298–9). Depressingly, a full investigation of the facts is still absent in some disciplinary cases cited by industrial tribunals (Earnshaw *et al.*, 1998: 15). The responsibility of the employer is that any professional management team conducts a full and proper investigation of the facts of each case, which often requires some time to achieve, as witnesses need to be interviewed and their statements assessed.

At present, most work surrounding discipline handling lies with the personnel function (IRS, 1995). If, however, line managers are increasingly involved in the process of grievance and discipline handling, (in the context of outsourcing, downsizing and delayering of management functions, including HR), a 'nightmare scenario' may arise where line managers do not know how to operate grievance and discipline procedures correctly, because they may not have received adequate training in this area, or may not have received adequate advice from their HR department as to how to operate these procedures effectively. The most extreme form of this scenario would occur with the HR specialist being 'absent' – i.e. no HR manager is employed for the line to consult with (see Thornhill and Saunders, 1998), or where HR engage in 'sitting back' – i.e. HR managers are present, but sit at corporate headquarters not wishing to get involved in 'operational' HR work (see Proctor and Currie, 1999). Such scenarios may well be too pessimistic, as they both presume that line manager skill is low in grievance and discipline handling, and that the line is ineffective on a day-to-day level so that grievance and discipline issues are not solved at their point of origin quickly. However, if line manager skill is high, then their training becomes less of an issue. The main requirement is that HR advice to line managers would have to be expert, and that advice would have to be 'on tap', if not necessarily 'on site'.

As we already know, line skill and competence in handling personnel/IR matters is questionable – this is openly admitted by line managers themselves (Marsh and Gillies, 1983). This concern persists today (see Cunningham and Hyman, 1995, 1999; and McGovern *et al.*, 1997), but often takes the form of allegation rather than proven empirical fact. Indeed, recent research has indicated somewhat of a 'mixed bag' in line skill in HR matters, as it depends on the HR initiative being devolved to the line (see for example Proctor and Currie, 1999). Certainly, although line managers have been enthusiastic about embracing more HR work, this is offset by them feeling 'dumped on' as they deem it to be a result of cost-cutting. Working on HR initiatives is seen as a luxury that often gets lost when the pressure is on (see for example Holden and Roberts, 1996). However, the overall concern remains, as to whether line managers are skilled and competent in HR matters, and in grievance and discipline handling in particular. Further research is needed to provide us with a fuller answer to this question.

In coping with grievance and discipline issues, HR managers will need either to maintain or develop the skills essential to gain and record accurate information, so as to provide a record of events to pass up through the procedure. A question here is whether these skills are being developed fully. Such skills include interviewing, questioning, listening, writing, and record keeping. That records are completed, and done so accurately, is essential for organisations to secure legal compliance. Although a formal grievance procedure is not legally required, employers who do not have a formal grievance procedure can fall foul of the law (as per W.A. Goold (Pearmack) Ltd *v* McConnell (1995)), but:

> The benefits of having procedures for handling employee grievances are also clear from the case of Chris Metcalf Ltd *v* Maddocks (1985). The industrial tribunal ruled that a grievance procedure would have enabled employees to articulate their worries and anxieties, and would thus have prevented the problem's occurring. An appeal by the firm against the decision failed.
>
> (Gennard and Judge, 1997: 210–11)

Within both grievance and discipline handling, there is a need for HR and line managers to ensure that mutual trust between the employee and employer is maintained. This requires both employers and employees to honour their side of the employment relationship so that both of their rights can be exercised, while at the same time they also acknowledge their responsibilities to each other. The law has effectively enshrined 'good practice', and Codes of Practice from ACAS and employers' associations reaffirm this. The fact that good practice is not always observed and is not always common practice is simply another reason for it to be observed. Organisational 'good practice' in grievance and disciplinary handling raises issues of integration and 'fit' with other HR policies and procedures, and ensuring consistency of action in this integration is normally the responsibility of the HR professional.

The role of the HR professional

HR managers are employed by organisations to run their people management side, but that is not necessarily how they may see it. Some may be inclined to take sides with employees over specific issues against their management colleagues, or to promote a 'welfare' or paternalistic approach, and see their role as one where they act as an 'arbitrator' or 'go-between' between management and employees. Such a situation sharply illustrates the contradictory nature of the employment relationship. What then is the role of the HR professional today? The IPM argued that the responsibility of the personnel professional is ultimately 'to their employer', and recommended that where personnel's responsibilities to employer and employee conflict, personnel practitioners might wish to record their reservations to their employer on decisions they have to implement by resignation from their job (1991: 1). Hence the HR professional is caught in the middle. Would they contemplate resigning from an organisation if they felt that its senior management and/or employee representatives had behaved arbitrarily in a grievance or discipline case, or would they continue to work for this same employer, to whom they were ultimately responsible? The IPM's position on this question was that:

> The organisation expects the personnel department to advise it on policies and to provide procedures which conform to the law and maintain optimum employee relations. Hands-on involvement, though, should always be limited. The role of personnel derives from the fact that grievances and disciplinary matters should be dealt with on the line, by the line managers.
>
> (IPM, 1992: 51)

The formation of the Institute of Personnel and Development (IPD) in 1994 saw the people management profession propose a new perspective on the HR professional's role:

> IPD members are expected to adopt in the most appropriate way, the most appropriate people management processes and structures to enable the organisation to best achieve its present and future objectives.
>
> (IPD, 1997: Clause 4, 4.1.4.)

Thus the IPD's conception of the role of the HR professional is to support the organisation's objectives in employee relations in general, and in grievance and discipline handling in particular (IPD, 1995). Some authors identify a specific obligation by HR professionals to their employer as members of the management team (see Martin and Jackson, 1997), and not to act as an umpire in disputes. Problems may arise for HR managers if they abuse their advisory role to senior management and overstep their authority by handling grievance and discipline cases themselves – rather than leaving them to line managers. HR advice may be ignored if it is not seen as being useful to senior managers or as adding value to organisational goals. A concern here is whether HR advice is useful and/or adds value, or whether it merely gains the organisation compliance with employment law. The latter approach may not necessarily undermine partnership approaches to employee relations, but can restrict the right of managers to manage within a framework of fairness, justice and legal compliance. Such issues are raised by the introduction of the new *Employment Relations Act (1999: Bill 36, 52/2)*, whose provisions we will discuss later. First though, we examine current research findings in grievance and discipline handling.

Current research

Usage of grievance and discipline policies, procedures and rules

Grievance procedures

WERS 4[1] (Cully *et al.*, 1999) gives perhaps the most comprehensive and extensive set of findings on the use of grievance and discipline policies and procedures in British workplaces. Cully *et al.* found that in respect of grievance procedures, nine out of ten workplaces (91 per cent) had a formal procedure in place for dealing with individual grievances raised by non-managerial employees, with stand-alone sites at 74 per cent of workplaces, and nearly all public sector workplaces having a procedure in place (90 per cent). In the one in twelve workplaces without a grievance procedure, managers said that problems were resolved by 'they come to me and we sort it out', with grievance procedures 'invariably' covering all non-managerial employees at the workplace. It was usual for employees to be made aware of the existence and content of grievance procedures through some form of written documentation, namely: a letter of appointment (47 per cent), a staff handbook (55 per cent), or a notice board (10 per cent). In 13 per cent of workplaces procedures were not written down, and most managers said employees were made aware 'either at the time of their entry into the workplace or at some other time by their line manager or supervisor' (1999: 77). Cully *et al.* concluded:

> The general impression, then, is that most employees had access to a formal procedure to take forward any grievances they might have. There was relatively little use made of grievance procedures in the year preceding the survey. One reason for this might be that employees had nothing to complain about. Another might be that the procedure is not a particularly effective mechanism for resolving problems, consistent with case study evidence from Earnshaw *et al.* (1998). Both were commonly advanced by managers when asked why they thought the procedure had not been used.
>
> (Cully *et al.*, 1999: 77)

---

[1] WERS 4 in this chapter refers to the Workplace Employee Relations Survey, as detailed by Cully *et al.* (1998, 1999).

Disciplinary procedures

Cully *et al.* found disciplinary procedures 'as evident as grievance procedures' – operating in 92 per cent of workplaces, and indeed 'distributed on an almost identical pattern'. Of workplaces with a grievance procedure, 97 per cent also had a disciplinary procedure, were nearly identical in workforce coverage, and the means by which employees were made aware of the procedure. They also found that even workplaces without a procedure might allow an employee to appeal, and across all workplaces, 96 per cent did so 'against decisions concerning discipline or dismissal'. The pattern was that almost all workplaces with procedures allowed appeals (99 per cent) compared with 71 per cent of workplaces with no procedures (1999: 78).

Accompaniment

Cully *et al.* examined accompaniment in both grievance and disciplinary handling 'and found a near identical pattern between the two'. Only 4 per cent of workplaces do not allow employees to be accompanied by a third party in actions taken to discipline or dismiss them, and a further 2 per cent only allow the option of bringing a supervisor or line manager along. But, where employees are allowed to be independently accompanied, 41 per cent of workplaces allow them to choose whoever they wish to accompany them, and the remaining half of workplaces specified various options, including 'trade union representatives (45 per cent), full-time union officials (27 per cent), and nearly all permit colleagues to join the employee (87 per cent)' (1999: 98).

Dismissals, sanctions and industrial tribunal applications

Cully *et al.* found that over 60 per cent of workplaces had sanctioned one or more employees in the last year, with greater incidences in larger workplaces than smaller ones. Dismissals were less likely to have occurred in all organisations, with the highest rate of sanctions made in transport and communication, than wholesale and retail, with education using them the least. The average workplace in the hotel and restaurant sector dismissed the most employees – the rate being three times higher than for any other industry, and unionised workplaces were seen to have lower rates of both sanctions and dismissals. Overall, the impression from WERS was that most workplaces had 'clean' records – reflected in the fact that 71 per cent of them had had no industrial tribunal claims made against them in the last five years (Cully *et al.*, 1999: 127–9).

Union role and non-union issues

Research into the role of unions by Hodson (1997) characterised them as regulating workplace conflict by 'informal forms of resistance' rather than through strike action and grievance procedures, and as helping 'to discipline workers and keep them on the job' with the quid pro quo being rights to collective bargaining. Edwards (1995) analysed three outcomes of personnel practice – rates of discipline, quitting and absence, and found 'no firm association with measures of practices associated with HRM', but 'by contrast, unionisation was strongly associated with the low use of discipline and low quit rates' (1995: 204). Edwards argues that numerous writers chart a long-term shift from authoritarian regimes which use sanctions frequently to more corrective models where discipline is rarely used to maintain organisational rules. Several styles of discipline are found, i.e. the frequent use of penalties in small firms practising 'simple control'; a lower reliance on sanctions in large proceduralised firms, and the more recent models of 'self-discipline' where workers are encouraged, through HRM techniques, to take responsibility for their own actions and in which overt sanctions are expected to be rare (1995: 206). Edwards concluded from his analysis of WIRS3[2] that:

> In short, the overall use of discipline increased, and the increase seems to have affected all types of firm. There is no evidence that HRM has changed this picture. Disciplinary systems have a degree of stability. Far from overt punishment becoming less important, it seems to be of growing significance. In particular the stabilising effects of unionisation are being weakened which may make discipline a more intractable issue in the 1990's.
>
> (Edwards, 1995: 219)

Research into grievance and discipline handling in non-union firms has not indicated that they have adopted a 'new' approach compared to unionised firms (McLoughlin and Gourlay, 1994: 80), but work in this area is still a relatively underresearched subject (Rollinson *et al.*, 1997: 288). Guest and Conway (1999) examined employee experiences of working in 'so-called "black hole" organisations' (i.e. where there is neither a set of progressive HRM practices nor a recognised trade union), and found that they reported more negative attitudes and work experiences with respect to job satisfaction, organisational commitment, and in judgements about experiences of fairness of treatment and trust in management than 'in settings where there is either HRM, a trade union presence or both'. They concluded that:

> the most negative views about employment relations are reported by those who belong to a union in workplaces with little HRM. The findings indicate that it is HRM practices rather than trade union membership that have the major impact on attitudes and experiences. Even in black hole organisations some employees report satisfaction. This can be largely explained by a positive psychological contract between individual and organisation
>
> (Guest and Conway, 1999: 367)

Handling style

Research on managerial behaviour in grievance and discipline handling has developed from the use of metaphors to indicate best practice and managerial inadequacies (Fenley, 1998: 362), to more sophisticated modelling, most notably

---

[2] WIRS3 in this context refers to the third Workplace Industrial Relations Survey (Millward *et al.*, 1992)

by Hook *et al.* (1996) and Rollinson *et al.* (1996) on managers' *preferred handling style* in grievance and discipline cases and latterly on *actual handling style* in disciplinary cases (Rollinson *et al.*, 1997). Hook *et al.* focused on examining whether or not a common preferred style was used for both grievance and discipline issues (1996: 20). For discipline, Hook *et al.* found that handling styles 'tend to be concentrated in the categories of tell to improve and tell and sell', whilst for grievance they found that 'the major concentrations were in "tell and sell" and "joint problem solving" respectively' (1996: 27–9).

Hook *et al.* deduced that managers' preferred style for discipline 'shows a steady rise in involvement of person with the issue seriousness', but that with grievance, 'there is a trough in the category of medium seriousness' and the handling style used on other issues 'tended to be less prescriptive'. They saw this anomaly in handling issues of medium seriousness as being down to the degree of personal challenge to the manager involved and concluded that little support existed for a thesis that managers would adopt the same handling styles for grievance and discipline issues, as there appeared to be 'no clear relationship' between the preferred styles used to handle grievance and those styles used to handle discipline (1996: 29, 30).

Rollinson *et al.*'s (1996) study found that for discipline cases by far the most influential variable lay in 'the degree of inconvenience to the manager'. Where the seriousness of the issue was seen to be low, there was a tendency for the preferred style to contain a large element of 'telling'. Where the seriousness of the issue was seen to be high, the preferred handling style tended to move 'towards joint problem solving or ask and listen' (1996: 46–7). Rollinson *et al.* found that, regardless of the issue type, it was employees with the longest service records that were more likely to have any breaches 'explored in a joint problem solving or ask and listen approach' (1996: 46–7). Rollinson *et al.* found similar results in grievance handling, except that if the challenge is seen to be either 'high' or 'low', the preferred style seemed to move towards 'joint problem solving or ask and listen', and that sex had some influence on generating different outcomes, (female managers had a 'slight tendency' to use prescriptive handling styles), but experience of working in personnel had 'no discernible effect' on handling either grievance or discipline cases (1996: 49). In their follow-up study of 1997, Rollinson *et al.* examined the perceptions of the disciplinary process from employees *who had* been formally disciplined and received some sanction of some sort and found:

> discipline can achieve the outcome of rule internalisation and/or observation, but it does so for only about half of those formally disciplined; for the remaining half, there are ongoing tendencies towards rule breaking.
>
> (Rollinson *et al.*, 1997: 283)

They explained these findings by arguing that the internal dynamics of the disciplinary process handling used a 'conditioning by punishment' paradigm which was applied in a context which was ineffective in shaping behaviour. Managerial styles added to the problem, as they gave the impression to the subjects 'that retributional motives are at work' (Rollinson *et al.*, 1997: 283). Moves from punitive to corrective discipline along a progressive historical continuum are thus limited – the punitive approach is still in use by some employers – although 'straight autocracy' is still seen as rare (Edwards, 2000: 326, 330).

General concerns in grievance and discipline handling

Earnshaw *et al.* (1998) have specifically focused on the problem of the influence that workplace disciplinary and grievance procedures have as a variable (among others) in contributing to applications to industrial tribunals, and in particular, instances of unfair dismissal claims. Their research over 33 case study firms was located in three industries: hotel and catering, transport and communication, and engineering – i.e. those that tend to generate the highest numbers of industrial tribunal claims – and found that conduct was 'the most common reason for dismissal' where employers that lost were found to be at fault for 'procedural shortcomings', whilst successful industrial tribunal defences were those where it was noted that 'a fair procedure had been followed' (1998: 479–80). Interestingly, the research by Goodman *et al.* from a sample of managers found 'no one simple variable' that might explain the incidences of unfair dismissal cases that they investigated (1998: 541, 548).

Such findings raise issues of employers being 'fair and reasonable' in their use of procedures, and illustrate the difficulties and problems inherent in grievance and discipline handling. That employers are not necessarily fair and reasonable in their treatment of cases is a major concern, as the 1971 Industrial Relations Act gave employees the right not to be *unfairly dismissed* without sanction against the employer of a monetary payment, if the employer is deemed to have acted unreasonably and unfairly in doing so. The use of managerial prerogative has not been removed, but it is clear that such prerogatives exist within defined limits. Earnshaw *et al.*'s findings on recruitment and employment practice were that the 'key features that distinguished companies who had faced recent IT cases from those who had not' were 'managerial style, managerial method, managerial quality, and "the respect they commanded"', (as well as the more expected general methods and care taken over the process as a whole) (1998: 481). Thus the concern that managers display *fairness and reasonableness* in grievance and discipline handling is highlighted by these findings.

Other difficulties and problems already exist. The 1996 Employment Rights Act (Section 98 (4) (a)), gave employees the right to a statement of their employment particulars, containing a specific definition of disciplinary rules that were applicable to them or referring the employee to a document and its contents that specified them, to which the employee's access is seen to be reasonable. The 1996 Act also stated that the statement of particulars must give details as to who an employee can appeal to if they are dissatisfied with any discipline decisions that are made (Gennard and Judge, 1997: 176, 183). The use of the ACAS Code of Practice on

'Disciplinary Practices and Procedures in Employment' has the twin aims of providing a mechanism through which employees are to be encouraged to 'achieve and maintain standards of conduct, attendance and job performance', and ensuring 'consistent and fair treatment for all'.

The 1975 Employment Protection Act (Section 6(11)), states that the ACAS Code will 'be admissible in evidence', and its provisions will be 'taken into account', if it appears to be 'relevant to any question arising'. Hence the scope and purpose of procedures should be clear (Gennard and Judge, 1997: 176, 178, 183). The goal here then, in terms of drawing up and operating an effective procedure, thus becomes one of consistency, and managers have the ACAS booklet *Discipline at Work* for a survival kit on how to produce and enact such a procedure. The rules of employment need to be made explicit, i.e. it must be clear to both managers and employees what the difference between gross misconduct and ordinary misconduct is, and whether the former will result in dismissal or not. The concern that managers display *consistency* in grievance and discipline handling is highlighted by these findings.

Another problem is the extent to which British workers are dissatisfied and seek resolution by airing grievances against their employer. Guest and Conway (1999)[3] gave a general indication that most workers were satisfied at work, but that there was a significant minority who were not, and a profile could be drawn of them as 'most likely to be traditional male, blue-collar workers who are trade union members' (1999: 30–1). Further work needs to be done to establish whether employees in these groups are involved in the bulk of grievance cases against employers. It is certain that many employees may have grounds for airing grievances, as mutual trust and confidence in the employment relationship have been recently undermined by the emergence of 'zero hours contracts' in the UK, most notably in retailing and fast-food restaurants. The omission to outlaw such working practices in the *Employment Relations Act (1999)* may be a major opportunity missed. Indeed, the Secretary of State for Trade and Industry's written reply to the House of Commons gives it little attention (see Section 6, 1998). The relative lack of rights that workers in the 'zero hours contracts' have compared to workers who are organised collectively is a major issue, especially as concerns continue over the lack of protection for casual workers in the hotel and catering industries (Price, 1993), and the working practices of employment agencies which have come under close scrutiny recently (Walsh, 1999b). Recent work by Edwards found that employer moves towards generating increased levels of trust and establishing employee 'self-discipline' in the employment relationship remain rare (even under HRM initiatives), due to unfavourable conditions 'and employee ingenuity in

---

[3] Which examined the findings of the following surveys: The General Household Survey (GHS), The British Social Attitudes Survey (BSA), The Eurobarometer Survey (EURB), The 1998 Workplace Employee Relations Survey (WERS), The Employment in Britain Survey (EIBS), and The Institute of Personnel and Development Annual Survey of the State of the Employment Relationship (IPD) (1999: 7).

developing their own standards of behaviour' (2000: 337). Thus, the extent of employee trust in their employer becomes a critical issue to examine in the context of debates on the break-up of the 'psychological contract' (see for example Sparrow and Marchington, 1998).

Issues for the future

New legislation

The current Labour government's approach on how grievance and discipline are handled has been outlined in a series of publications, most notably in its pre-election document *Building Prosperity: Flexibility, Efficiency and Fairness at Work*. This raised the issue of exercising employee rights at work, and the fact that employers wanted to limit them. Such issues were discussed in the White Paper *Fairness at Work*, and included in the *Employment Relations Act (1999)*. The basic principle which underlies *Building Prosperity* is to encourage moves toward greater labour market flexibility 'based on minimum standards and security of employment for all employees' (Gennard, 1998: 12). With regard to the issue of grievance and discipline handling this entails commitments to:

> give individuals the right to representation, including by a trade union, to permit unfair dismissal claims by those dismissed for participating in lawful industrial action, and streamline industrial tribunal procedures and promoting the use of alternative dispute resolution by the use of voluntary arbitration.
>
> (Gennard, 1997: 12–13)

The concept of employer-employee partnership (IPD, 1995) is at the heart of the Labour government's approach. The *Employment Relations Act (1999)* makes some specific proposals regarding grievance and discipline handling. Walsh documents four main changes: a reduction in the qualifying period for unfair dismissal claims from two years to 12 months, the ceiling on unfair dismissal awards to be raised to £50,000, tribunal awards and redundancy payments to be index-linked, and an outlawing of waiver clauses in fixed-term contracts to prevent unfair dismissal claims (1999a: 18). Such provisions relate to the issue of natural justice in employee relations. Managers are required to operate with 'just cause' and in ways that reinforce their right to manage, as most clearly expressed in the law on unfair dismissal (Gennard and Judge, 1997: 183). The provision on removing the ceiling on unfair dismissal awards provides an incentive for managers to manage properly and not to behave in an arbitrary fashion.

Within the Act itself, the clauses on the point of 'disciplinary and grievance hearings' contain three main provisions, of representation, employment tribunals and detriment. On the issue of representation, the Act states that a worker has the 'right to be accompanied' by a 'single companion' who is 'chosen by the worker', a worker being defined as 'an official of a trade union or another of the employer's workers' (Clause 11, parts 1, 2 and 3). On the use of employment tribunals, under

the provisions in the Act, a worker can 'present a complaint' to an employment tribunal if 'his employer has failed, or threatened to fail' to comply with the
provisions above. If the tribunal finds such a complaint to be well founded then it
can order the employer to pay compensation to the worker of 'an amount not
exceeding two weeks' pay' (Clause 12, parts 1 and 3). And on the issue of 'detriment and dismissal', the Act gives workers the right 'not to be subjected to any
detriment' (including the right not to be unfairly dismissed) by the employer by
exercising the worker's right to be accompanied, or for having 'accompanied or
sought to accompany another worker' regardless 'whether of the same employer or
not' (Clause 13, parts 1, 2 and 3). Thus the concern that managers *operate with
just cause* in grievance and discipline handling is highlighted by the enactment of
this legislation.

The right to be accompanied

On the issue of an employee's right to be accompanied at a grievance and/or disciplinary hearing, the exact extent of workers' representation rights has been limited
to those 'concerning serious issues' (see Walsh, 1999a). Whilst the phrase 'serious
issues' does not feature prominently in the Act itself, it is indeed central to the government's intent, as the Secretary of State for Trade and Industry indicated:

> Employees in firms of all sizes will have the right to be accompanied by a fellow
> employee or a trade union official in disciplinary hearings and grievance hearings about
> serious issues. There will be a Code of Practice to give guidance to employers and
> employees on how the right should be applied in practice.
>
> (1998, Section 13)

Thus, the *Employment Relations Act (1999)* looks at first sight set to curtail
and restrict employees' rights to representation at work in grievance and discipline
cases. Concerns have arisen as to what is deemed a 'serious issue' and what is not,
and who decides these matters. However, the Act also opens up the prospect of
extended employee rights at work in grievance and discipline cases, as employees
can choose an individual of their choice to represent them – which can include a
trade unionist (or even, in some cases, a lawyer – if they are another of the organisation's employees). Although the latter scenario looks a rare one, it needs to be
considered by practising HR professionals. The consequences of a lack of a thorough investigation and poor preparation for grievance and disciplinary meetings
by HR professionals could be quite far-reaching for the organisation as a whole if
legal wrangling ensues. Thus, the concern that managers *operate within the law* in
grievance and discipline handling is raised by this new legislation.

The issue of the right to be 'accompanied' in grievance and disciplinary procedures draws from *Building Prosperity* (Wilmore, 1997) which proposed to give the
general right for employees to be represented by an individual of their choice
(including individuals who belonged to a trade union). The phrase 'serious issues'
has been included in an attempt to respond to employers' objections that allowing
trade unions in at the local stage undermines the principle that grievance and

discipline matters should be settled at the lowest level of managerial authority and by the local players, which has been a fundamental principle for a long time. The representational concern raised by the phrase 'serious issues' may effectively reinforce the 'local' principle above. The importance of the proposal on representation rights lies in the fact that it does still guarantee (albeit to a more limited extent) that employees will be on an equal footing with managers if they are represented. The provision in the Act on 'detriment and dismissal' raises the general issue of employees' rights to appeal against disciplinary penalties, and the move to enacting the disciplinary procedure by a manager if an employee's alleged misconduct is seen to be serious enough for them to do so. Related issues include those of the length of time for which warnings stay 'live', and their scope (Gennard and Judge, 1997: 178–9). Overall, the proposals of the Act illustrate related concerns over the key role that individual managers play in handling grievance and discipline cases, as the Act gives management teams an element of discretion in defining which cases are 'serious' and which are not.

The need for skilled HR professionals

The *Employment Relations Act (1999)* reinforces requirements from existing legislation that the HR professional investigate grievance and disciplinary issues thoroughly as a matter of course, and to hone their skills in being able to do so. Persuading other managers of the need to satisfy the five tests of fairness, reasonableness, consistency, operating with just cause and operating within the law is a huge task and requires the HR professional to learn and develop a number of interpersonal skills. Other skills are also needed, including situation analysis, report writing, knowledge and understanding of the ACAS code, the workings of the CAC and the law. Demonstrating excellence in these skills may help to solve day-to-day grievance and discipline issues before they escalate further. If day-to-day contact between a line manager and an employee breaks down in enforcing discipline, then counselling can be used by HR managers as a mechanism of pre-empting the need to enact the disciplinary process. However, caution is advised and it is recommended that expert advice is sought in this regard, perhaps from an independent third-party counselling service (Gennard and Judge, 1997: 184).

Help is at hand for managers in handling extremely difficult situations like unfair dismissal claims, as the provisions laid out in the Employment Rights (Dispute Resolution) Act of 1998 have been added to by moves towards an alternative system for unfair dismissal case resolution in the new 'ACAS Scheme'. This scheme gives all parties a further option to pursue in the settling of discipline and grievance issues as the scheme uses voluntary but binding arbitration, whilst both parties will need to forgo their rights under law to enact it. There is certainly an issue from both parties' perspective in that they will not jointly select the arbitrator (as this will be done by ACAS), and that if a decision goes against them they have no appeal on points of law or fact, except a right to challenge if there has been a 'serious irregularity'. In the instances of reinstatement or non-reinstatement of employees, the outcomes for employer and/or employee may well not be what they expected. However, the scheme is arguably cheaper, speedier, more informal and more private than using employment tribunals.

Employee stress

As employers are looking for new ways to be innovative in employee relations, reorganising the work patterns and processes involved through teamworking and empowerment programmes in the search for increased organisational commitment from employees, the particular issue of employee stress and employer liability for it has come to the fore (Earnshaw and Cooper, 1996). One of the legal issues raised revolves around claimed breaches of the implied terms contained within contracts of employment which place a clear responsibility on employers to ensure that managers avoid such breaches.

Threats to employees from supervisors and managers raise the issue of bullying in the workplace, which has received increased attention via the TUC's 'bad bosses hotline' – a helpline for employees who feel they have been bullied by their boss, or by another employee. Recent (preliminary) research has also revealed that bullying and/or intimidation by employees *against* their superiors is also occurring, and that some of this is made against 'personnel professionals by resentful employees' (Welch, 1999: 10). Managerial handling style of grievance and discipline cases needs to be exemplary so that cases of constructive dismissal are not pursued by employees as a result of managers seeming to undermine 'trust and confidence' in the employment relationship by alleged intimidation and/or bullying. The prospect of 'voluntary quitting' by employees who find the pace of work too onerous (Edwards, 2000: 326) is also a scenario managers should investigate and guard against so that 'mutual trust and confidence' is maintained. As Lewis states, in cases of constructive dismissal 'a refusal to act reasonably in dealing with grievances, matters of safety or incidents of harassment could all give rise to a claim', but:

> Given the consequences of being found to have been dismissed at law, it was to be expected that employers would seek to establish the notion of 'constructive resignation'. However, the Court of Appeal has refused to accept such a concept. The contract will be regarded as terminated only if the employer has expressly or impliedly accepted the repudiation.
>
> (Lewis, 1997: 153)

Thus the overall responsibility to provide a safe working environment lies with the employer. Although, as Fenley argues, labour and product markets, union and workforce strength, social values and employment law 'all have a bearing on managers' actions' (1998: 363), when all of these factors are taken into account, managers' actions can still be decisive in making or breaking 'good practice' in grievance and discipline handling.

Conclusion: a series of evolving concerns

The importance of concentrating attention on the outcomes generated in grievance and discipline handling is highlighted by negative employee responses to poor management practice, and the deleterious effects such poor practice has on the confidence and legitimacy of management teams themselves to manage modern organisations successfully. It is the outcomes that all employees and managers focus on as they not only set precedents for the future, but also reflect the balance of rights and responsibilities of the employment relationship itself. That managers have had due training, follow an organisation's procedures and best practice, and are aware of the implications of their actions, are all issues that can be clearly seen in the decisions that they arrive at in the grievance and discipline cases they manage. Thus, current issues in grievance and discipline handling form a set of *evolving concerns*, linked to past issues, but with new emphasis and direction. Managers' decisions can be examined and used to assess their knowledge, understanding and competence in this field. All managers involved in the process of grievance and discipline handling need to pay due regard to the issues raised above via the use of existing procedures (or indeed via the use of codes of conduct if these are used instead by employers), as it is important that good practice becomes common practice.

The theme of good practice is illustrated in the cases and exercises that follow. We see that there are five main tests that any management must pass if they are to manage grievance and discipline issues effectively. These five tests are those of fairness, reasonableness, consistency, operating with just cause, and operating within the law. If managers do not observe these five tests, the law may well make them adjust their practice in the future. We see that outcomes can provide a useful barometer to measure whether the five criteria above have been satisfied, and it is these issues that our case studies seek to test.

Grievance and discipline handling: two cases

Within the literature on managing grievance and discipline three key themes emerge. The first is that poor practice dominates in particular industries, as seen in the cases referred to industrial tribunals (Earnshaw *et al.*, 1998: 479). The industries that stand out particularly in this respect are: hotel and catering, transport and communication, and engineering (Earnshaw *et al.*, 1998: 479), and construction and public administration (Cully *et al.*, 1998: 25). The two case study role plays included in this chapter examine transport (grievance), and construction (discipline).[4] The second theme is that outcomes are a critical indicator as to whether best practice is indeed common practice. The final theme is that the way

---

[4] For some contextual background on transport see Smith (1999) and on construction Druker and White (1995).

in which HR and other managers handle grievance and discipline cases is a crucial factor, amongst others, in determining the outcomes produced.

The approach we have adopted in the cases reflects a call in the literature to focus on manager and supervisor justifications for their actions (Rollinson *et al.*, 1996: 51). The actual decisions that are taken and their rationale are, in our view, the litmus test in ascertaining and benchmarking managers' knowledge, understanding and competence in this field, as they give the observer a trail of evidence which is useful in pinpointing errors made. Have managerial decisions passed the five tests mentioned in this chapter? Employee representative and union roles have been included in the cases, so as to provide a useful context within which the *Employment Relations Act (1999)* occurs.

Grievance handling at TransCo

John Gennard and Douglas Renwick

Background

Thompson Ltd of Woodbridge produce components parts for a major car manufacturer. The Woodbridge depot of TransCo is the sole transport operator for Thompson, this work supplying 60 per cent of the total business to the TransCo Woodbridge depot. TransCo are based in a relatively prosperous area although unemployment is relatively high, and thus there is a shortage of good experienced drivers qualified to work on the articulated vehicles. This situation is exacerbated by the relatively low wages paid at TransCo, and the depot is consequently undermanned. Another reason for undermanning is that the company has a policy of using overtime to meet unexpected surges in demand. For example, management at TransCo have been in the practice of using overtime on Saturdays to ensure that the quota of deliveries from Thompson is completed. In addition, Thompson frequently request TransCo to expedite special deliveries ('specials') outside the agreed schedule. TransCo have executed the 'specials' by using drivers not normally engaged on the Thompson contract. The following is a clause from the TransCo employee handbook (given to each employee) which includes all the conditions of employment:

> C1. 10 – Employees will be expected to work a reasonable amount of overtime at the request of the management.

Situation

This afternoon Mr Jones returned to the TransCo Woodbridge depot at 3.30 pm. When he had parked his vehicle a colleague told him that the team leader, Mr Brown, wanted to see him. Mr Jones went directly to Mr Brown where he was informed that due to Thompson requesting a special delivery he should report for work at 8.00 am tomorrow (Saturday) to carry this out. Mr Jones refused the request, saying, 'United are playing their first match of the season tomorrow and I have no intention of missing it, but I could work on Sunday.'

Mr Brown was annoyed at this, and pointed out that Mr Jones had not worked overtime for over two months, during which he had twice refused to work on a Saturday. Mr Brown had warned him regarding these refusals. Mr Jones replied, 'My contract is for 37 hours Monday to Friday and I have no wish to work overtime and certainly not on a Saturday, this one or any other.'

Mr Brown then pointed out that Mr Jones's contract of employment stated that he should work reasonable amounts of overtime at the request of management. Mr Brown further added that, 'In my opinion you are no use to me because of your reluctance to work overtime.'

Mr Jones replied, 'In my opinion overtime is up to me and if I don't want to work it there is nothing you can do about it.'

Mr Brown then explained why it was necessary, saying, 'Thompsons are our major customer, we need their business and this load is urgently required by their customer for Saturday lunchtime. It is an "artic" load and two drivers are off sick, the remainder are all booked for other work on Saturday or having their rest day (certain rest days are legally required to ensure drivers do not exceed a specified number of driving hours during a working week), which only leaves you.'

Mr Jones replied, 'I'm not interested,' and walked out of the office. Twenty minutes later, Mr Brown called Mr Jones to the office and informed him that from next Monday he would be driving one of the three-ton trucks permanently.

Mr Jones said, 'We will see about that,' and went directly to discuss the matter further with his Employee Representative, Mr Fairman.

A meeting has been called by Mrs Young, the HR Manager, for next Tuesday morning at 9.00 am with Mr Brown, Mr Fairman, Mr Jones and Mrs Young regarding the transfer of Mr Jones.

Company information

TransCo fleet: 15 twenty-ton articulated lorries ('artics'), 3 fifteen-ton, six-wheeler lorries, and 4 three-ton trucks.

Drivers: Total of 16: 12 Class 1; 2 Class 2; 2 Class 3.

Essential requirements: 5 articulated lorries daily on Thompson contract. (plus 3 on a Saturday), 2 fifteen-ton, six-wheelers daily on Smith contract, 3 three-ton trucks daily on Henderson contract.

Notes: Mr Michaels on Henderson contract, Mr Smith on Thompson contract.

There is seldom any overtime requirement for the three-ton truck.

Weekly rates of pay: twenty-ton £300 (37 hours), fifteen-ton £275 (37 hours), three-ton £250 (37 hours).

Due to staff shortages the company has on occasions requested a driver to operate a vehicle of a lower class than he would normally. When doing so the company has paid the driver his normal wage.

Grievance handling – role briefs

Mr Jones: You do not like working overtime, preferring to pursue your hobbies and other leisure interests at the weekends, which you feel are your own time. You have only worked five Saturdays since you joined the company two years ago, the last one being nine weeks ago.

Mr Fairman – Employee Representative: Mr Jones has just informed you of Mr Brown's decision to transfer him. This transfer will result in a drop in Mr Jones's earnings from £300 to £250 per week. Mr Jones insists that Mr Brown is always picking on him. As a single man he feels that he should be able to enjoy his weekends however he sees fit, not work them.

Mr Brown – Team Leader: You have decided to transfer Mr Jones in order to release another driver (Mr Michaels) from the three-ton trucks to employ him on the artic lorries. Mr Michaels is 22 and passed his Class 1 test only two weeks ago. He has been in your employ for only two months but has been very obliging in working overtime whenever asked. He has in fact agreed to do the 'special' for Thompson's tomorrow, although he did say to you last Monday that he would like this Saturday off to watch the first football match of the season.

Mrs Young – HR Manager: You are in receipt of some of the information of the case, as Mr Fairman called you late on Friday afternoon protesting on behalf of Mr Jones about Mr Brown's actions. You have scheduled a meeting next week to sort this matter out before it gets out of hand, and have asked Mr Jones, Mr Brown and Mr Fairman to attend it. You have been with the organisation for 20 years.

Case study 6.2

Discipline handling at CityBuilding

John Gennard and Douglas Renwick

Background

This is the case of a labourer, Mr Smith, and his actions on Friday 4 June this year, which resulted in his dismissal by the team leader the following Monday morning, 7 June. Briefly, the facts are as follows:

A 19-year-old labourer named Mr Andrews was trying out a water hose before he used it to mix some cement, which he was using to rebuild a wall of a council building. Mr Smith was working in the immediate area and unfortunately was drenched, as Mr Andrews was not concentrating on what he was doing. Like most of these incidents it was amusing to the onlookers, but not the recipient. Mr Smith threw a trowel at Mr Andrews which missed him and struck the newly rebuilt wall he was working on causing no damage. This not being sufficient to restore his dignity, Mr Smith immediately searched around and found a brick. Mr Smith then threw the brick at Mr Andrews and missed again, but this time smashed a window in one of the council buildings, and just missed a fellow worker.

Mr Andrews reported the first incident and Mr Smith was reprimanded by his team leader, Mr Jenkins. Unfortunately, Mr Smith taunted Mr Andrews before they both left the site at the end of the day's work, and Mr Andrews retaliated with the threat that he would kill Mr Smith if 'he ever tried that again'. The second incident was also reported by Mr Andrews and on investigating the whole affair, CityBuilding's Administrator, Mrs Campbell, dismissed Mr Smith the following Monday, 7 June, at 10.00 am in the presence of his shop steward. The union branch to which Mr Smith belonged were dissatisfied with the dismissal decision, and reported the matter to the union divisional officer. An urgent meeting has been arranged for today – Tuesday, 8 June – by the Council Administrator from a request by the Union Divisional Officer to reinstate Mr Smith. Management have made it clear to all parties that this is an opportunity for all parties to discuss the matter further.

Additional information

Mr Smith has been with CityBuilding for 10 years. During that time he has never had any complaints laid against him, and had never appeared before management on any disciplinary charge. He has the reputation of being a very docile man, and is married with two children. Subsection 4 of the CityBuilding policy and procedure on 'Grievance and Discipline Handling at Work', which was redrafted and agreed by the Union at 5 pm on 3 June, states:

> (Subsection 4): Any employee, whether of a staff or management grade, will be dismissed for any act of gross misconduct. Gross misconduct is defined as acts of violence or threatened violence, assault, theft, swearing, or drunkenness directed at any employee (whether management or not), the organisation's customers, suppliers, shareholders or any other relevant third party which management deem relevant for inclusion in acts of this nature. The punishment for an offence of gross misconduct is summary dismissal, and any appeal against such action will be made through the appeals procedure as contained in the company handbook.

The appeal procedure states:

> The management reserves the right to override the agreed grievance and discipline appeals procedure in search of common-sense solutions to all organisational issues if exceptional circumstances dictate that due use of the appeals procedure is too time-consuming and both union and management are agreed that simpler solutions can be reached by dialogue between the two parties instead.

CityBuilding is a building services and repair contractor and its major work is for local authorities in the local area. The majority of its employees are former workers of the local authority who were made redundant five years ago (although some have been there for longer), and are heavily unionised. The union favours a 'partnership' approach with the employer.

Discipline handling – role briefs

Mr Andrews – Labourer: You could not believe Mr Smith's reaction to a bit of water sprayed at him. Such incidents, you feel, are part and parcel of your work, as you like 'to have a bit of a laugh' with the lads.

Mr Smith – Labourer: You are a married man with two children. You have worked for CityBuilding for 10 years. You are extremely concerned about health and safety on building sites, and have extensive knowledge of the risks associated, however caused and however small, with working in this environment.

Mr Jenkins – Team Leader: You were alerted to both incidents concerning Mr Andrews and Mr Smith initially by a fellow worker, who has asked to remain anonymous. You asked both Andrews and Smith for their sides of the incident, and felt you had 'no choice' but to reprimand Mr Smith.

Mrs Campbell – Administrator: You were alerted to the first and second incidents concerning Mr Andrews and Mr Smith by the Team Leader last Friday afternoon, after they had both finished work. You have thought hard about the issues the incidents raised over the weekend. You have worked for CityBuilding for 10 years.

Mr Jones – Union Divisional Officer: The shop steward called you on the telephone to tell you of Mr Smith's dismissal, and you asked that the steward come and see you straight away. You are keen to pursue Mr Smith's case, and have requested a meeting with management to seek his reinstatement.

References to Chapter 6

Bingham, L.B. (1995) 'Is there a bias in arbitration of non-union employment disputes? An analysis of actual cases and outcomes', *International Journal Of Conflict Management*, 6(4): 369–86.

Bohlander, G.W. (1994) 'Why arbitrators overturn managers in employee suspension and discharge cases', *Journal of Collective Negotiations in the public sector*, 23(1): 73–89.

Bouwen, R. and Salipante, P.F. (1990) 'Behavioural analysis of grievances: episodes, actions and outcomes', *Employee Relations*, 12(4): 27–32.

Cully, M., O'Reilly, A., Millward, N., Forth, J., Woodland, S., Dix, G. and Bryson, A. (1998) *The 1998 Workplace Employee Relations Survey: First Findings*, London: DTI/ESRC/ACAS/PSI.

Cully, M., Woodland, S., O'Reilly, A. and Dix, G. (1999) *Britain At Work: As Depicted by the 1998 Workplace Employee Relations Survey*, London: Routledge.

Cunningham, I. and Hyman, J. (1995) 'Transforming the HRM vision into reality: The role of line managers and supervisors in implementing change', *Employee Relations*, 17(8): 5–20.

Cunningham, I. and Hyman, J. (1999) 'Devolving human resource responsibilities to the line: Beginning of the end or a new beginning for personnel?', *Personnel Review*, 28(1/2): 9–27.

Department of Trade and Industry (1998) *Fairness At Work* (May) Cm 3968.

Druker, J. and White, G. (1995) 'Misunderstood and undervalued? Personnel management in construction', *Human Resource Management Journal*, 5(3) (Spring): 77–91.

Earnshaw, J. and Cooper, C. (1996) *Stress and Employer Liability*, London: Institute of Personnel and Development.

Earnshaw, J., Goodman, J., Harris, R., and Marchington, M. (1998) 'Industrial tribunals, workplace disciplinary procedures and employment practice', *Labour Market Trends*, September: 479–81.

Edwards, P.K. (1995) 'Human Resource Management, union voice and the use of discipline: an analysis of WIRS3', *Industrial Relations Journal*, 26(3): 204–20.

Edwards, P.K. (2000) 'Discipline: towards trust and self-discipline?', in Bach, S. and Sisson, K. (eds) *Personnel Management: A Comprehensive Guide To Theory And Practice*, Oxford: Blackwell, 317–37.

Employment Relations Bill 1999, Bill 36, 52/2, Norwich: HMSO.

Fenley, A. (1998) 'Models, styles and metaphors: understanding the management of discipline', *Employee Relations*, 20(4): 349–64.

Gennard, J. (1998) 'Labour government: change in employment law', *Employee Relations*, 20(1): 12–25.

Gennard, J. and Judge, G. (1997) *Employee Relations*, London: Institute of Personnel and Development.

Goodman, J., Earnshaw, J., Marchington, M. and Harrison, R. (1998) 'Unfair dismissal cases, disciplinary procedures, recruitment methods and management style: Case study evidence from three industrial sectors', *Employee Relations*, 20(6): 536–50.

Guest, D. and Conway, N. (1999a) *How Dissatisfied and Insecure Are British Workers? A Survey of Surveys*, London: Institute of Personnel and Development.

Guest, D. and Conway, N. (1999b) 'Peering into the black hole: The downside of the new employment relations in the UK', *British Journal of Industrial Relations*, 37(3), September: 367–89.

House of Commons Official Report (1999) Parliamentary Debates (Hansard), vol. 328, no.65, Tuesday 30 March.

Hodson, R. (1997) 'Individual voice on the shop floor: The role of unions', *Social Forces*, 75(4): 1183–1212.

Holden, L. and Roberts, I. (1996) *European Middle Managers: the Search for Identity in a Conflicting Role and an Uncertain Role*, Paris: Editions ESKA.

Hook, C.M., Rollinson, D.J., Foot, M. and Handley, J. (1996) 'Supervisor and manager styles in handling discipline and grievance: Part one – comparing styles in handling discipline and grievance', *Personnel Review*, 25(3): 20–34.

Institute of Personnel and Development (1995) *People Make The Difference: an IPD position paper*, (January), London: IPD.

Institute of Personnel and Development (1997) *The IPD Code of Professional Conduct and Disciplinary Procedures*, London: IPD.

Institute of Personnel Management (1991) *IPM Code of Professional Conduct and Professional Conduct Regulations*, (October), London: IPM.

Institute of Personnel Management (1992) *Handling Grievances*, London: IPM.

IRS (Industrial Relations Services) (1995) 'Discipline at work: the practice', *Employment Trends*, 591 (September): 4–11.

Klass, B.S., Gainey, T.W. and Dell'omo, G.G. (1999) 'The determinants of disciplinary system effectiveness: a line-management perspective', *Industrial Relations*, 38(4), October: 542–49.

Lewis, D. (1997) *Essentials of Employment Law*, 5th edn, London: IPD.

Mandelson, P. (1998) 'The policy on fairness at work', written reply from the Secretary of State for Trade and Industry to the House of Commons, 17 December 1998, London: DTI.

Marsh, A.I. and Gillies, J.G. (1983) 'The involvement of line and staff managers in industrial relations', as quoted in Thurley, K. and Wood, S. (eds) *Industrial Relations and Management Strategy*, Cambridge: Cambridge University Press.

Martin, M. and Jackson, T. (1997) *Personnel Practice*, London: IPD.

McGovern, P., Gratton, L., Hope-Hailey, V. and Truss, C. (1997) 'Human resource management on the line?', *Human Resource Management Journal*, 7(4): 12–29.

McLoughlin, I. and Gourlay, S. (1994) *Enterprise without Unions*, Milton Keynes: Open University Press.

Mesch, D.J. (1995) 'Arbitration and gender – an analysis of cases taken to arbitration in the public sector', *Journal of Collective Negotiations in the Public Sector*, 24(3): 207–18.

Morrill, C. and Thomas, C.K. (1992) 'Organizational conflict-management as disputing process – the problem of social escalation', *Human Communications Research*, 18(3): 400–28.

New Labour (1996) *Building Prosperity: Flexibility, Efficiency, and Fairness at Work*, (September) Conference paper.

Piskorski, T.J. (1993) 'Reinstatement of the sexual harasser – the conflict between federal labor law and Title-VII', *Employee Relations Law Journal*, 18(4): 617–23.

Poole, M. and Jenkins, G. (1997) 'Responsibilities for human resource management practices in the modern enterprise', *Personnel Review*, 25(5): 333–56.

Price, L. (1993) 'The limitations of the law in influencing employment practices in UK hotels and restaurants', *Employee Relations*, 15(2): 16–24.

Proctor, S. and Currie, G. (1999) 'The role of the personnel function: roles, perceptions and processes in an NHS trust', *International Journal of Human Resource Management*, 10(6), December: 1077–91.

Rollinson, D. (1992) 'Individual issues in industrial relations – an examination of discipline, and an agenda for research', *Personnel Review*, 21(1): 46–57.

Rollinson, D., Hook, C., Foot, M., and Handley, J. (1996) 'Supervisor and manager styles in handling discipline and grievance: Part two – approaches to handling discipline and grievance', *Personnel Review*, 25(4): 38–55.

Rollinson, D., Handley, J., Cook, C. and Foot, M. (1997) 'The disciplinary experience and its effects on behaviour: an exploratory study', *Work, Employment and Society*, 11(2): 283–311.

Smith, P. (1999) 'Exclusion and disarticulation: the Transport and General Workers' Union in the road haulage industry, 1979–1998', *British Journal of Industrial Relations*, 37(4), December: 615–36.

Sparrow, P. and Marchington, M. (1998) *Human Resource Management: The New Agenda*, London: Financial Times/Pitman Publishing.

Storey, J. (1992) *Developments in the Management of Human Resources*, Oxford: Blackwell.

Suter, E. (1997) *The Employment Law Checklist*, 6th edn, London: IPD.

Thornhill, A. and Saunders, M.N.K., (1998) 'What if line managers don't realize they're responsible for HR? Lessons from an organization experiencing rapid change', *Personnel Review*, 27(6): 460–76.

Wagar, T.H. (1994) 'The effect of lawyers on non-discipline discharge arbitration decisions', *Journal of Labor Research*, 15(3): 283–93.

Walsh, J. (1999a) 'The employment relations bill at a glance', *People Management*, 5(3): 18–19.

Walsh, J. (1999b) 'TUC attempts to promote rights of agency workers', *People Management*, 5(8): 15.

Welch, J. (1999) 'HR staff bear the brunt of bullies' fury over bad news', *People Management*, 5(3): 10.

Wilmore, I. (1997) 'New bible offers rotten bargain', *The Guardian*, 29 September.

Zirkel, P.A. and Breslin, P.H. (1995) 'Correlates of grievance arbitration awards', *Journal of Collective Negotiations in the Public Sector*, 24(1): 45–54.

Chapter 7

Employee relations

Nick Bacon

Introduction

The terms 'employee relations' and, more traditionally, 'industrial relations' are used to indicate those areas of the employment relationship in which managers deal with the representatives of employees rather than managing employees directly as individuals (Edwards, 1995). Where employees seek collective representation they generally join trade unions and the reaction of managers to this potential challenge to management authority provides valuable insights into the nature of employment. As the membership of trade unions has declined over the past two decades a critical debate has developed around the nature of employment relations in non-union workplaces. The purpose of this chapter is to chart the changes in the collective regulation of labour and consider the implications of the increasing number of workers who are not represented by trade unions.

Management frames of reference and management style

The suggestion that employees may need some form of collective protection from employers provokes a strong response in many managers. Behind this response is a set of assumptions about the right to manage (frequently termed the management prerogative) and the correct power balance in the employment relationship. These assumptions held by managers are the mixture of a complex blend of experiences, predispositions, learned behaviour and prejudice. They combine to create management frames of reference (Fox, 1966, 1974) that capture the often deeply held assumptions of managers towards a labour force. Three separate frames of reference can be identified: unitarist, pluralist and radical. Each of these differ in their beliefs about the nature of organisations, the role of conflict and the task of managing employees. Managers holding a unitarist frame of reference believe the natural state of organisations is one of harmony and co-operation. All employees are thought to be in the same team, pulling together for the common goal of organisational success. The employee relations task of management is to prevent conflict arising from misunderstandings that result if they fail adequately to communicate organisational goals to employees. Any remaining conflicts are attributed to mischief created by troublemakers. A pluralist frame of reference recognises that organisations contain a variety of sectional groups who legitimately seek to express divergent interests. The resulting conflict is inevitable and the task of managers is to establish a system of structures and procedures in which conflict is institutionalised and a negotiated order is established. The radical critique of pluralism is not, strictly speaking, a frame of reference for understanding management views of the employment relationship. It draws upon Marxism and explains workplace conflict within a broader historical and social context and places a stress upon the unequal power struggle of opposing social classes.

There are no simple methods to assess the frame of reference held by managers – indeed, they usually hold a complex set of ideas rather than falling neatly into a single and possibly oversimplistic frame of reference. However, insights into management attitudes can be gained through their responses to questions about trade unions. From comparable questions posed to managers at the start of the 1980s and 1990s, Poole and Mansfield (1993) suggested the underlying pluralistic preferences of British managers were remarkably consistent. Another question posed more recently indicated that a majority of workplace managers do not have a single frame of reference. In the 1998 Workplace Employee Relations Survey (WERS 98) most managers (54 per cent) were 'neutral' about union membership, whereas 29 per cent were 'in favour' with 17 per cent 'not in favour' (Cully *et al.*, 1999: 87). However, when managers are asked more directly whether they prefer to manage employees directly or through unions then unitarist preferences emerge. For example, 72 per cent of managers agreed with the statement 'we would rather consult directly with employees than with unions', whereas only 13 per cent disagreed (*ibid.*: 88). Consequently, management approaches to industrial relations are often characterised as a mixing and matching between unitarism and pluralism in the 'time-honoured' British fashion (Edwards *et al.*, 1998). Many managers accept such a view on the grounds that it merely reflects the reality of managing employees who may at times need representation. The evidence suggests, however, that managers can deter or encourage employees from joining trade unions. In the 1998 Workplace Employee Relations Survey pro-union management attitudes were significantly associated with union presence in the workplace (Cully *et al.*, 1998: 19).

Frames of reference are also important because they underlie the management style adopted in organisations towards the workforce. Many authors have attempted to classify management styles (Fox, 1974; Purcell and Sisson, 1983; Purcell and Ahlstrand, 1994; Storey and Bacon, 1993) and as the resulting models have become increasingly complex some now doubt the usefulness of producing yet more typologies (Kitay and Marchington, 1996). The most recent typologies attempt to highlight the interaction between HRM and industrial relations. The central question raised is the extent to which HRM and industrial relations are alternative or complementary systems for managing employees. Whether managers recognise trade unions indicates the extent to which a 'collective' approach to managing employees is preferred and it does capture a key factor in distinguishing between management approaches. In addition, the extent to which managers invest in and develop employees indicates the extent to which they stress 'individualism'. In Figure 7.1 Purcell and Ahlstrand (1994) use the dimensions of 'collectivism' and 'individualism' to identify six different management styles of employee relations.

Individualism and collectivism have recently become popular terms in employee relations. In comparison with the traditional management frames of reference – unitarism and pluralism – these concepts have 'common-sense' meanings and appear grounded in everyday management vocabularies and thinking about employee relations. Individualism in employment relations is traditionally used to denote non-unionism and/or a HRM-style investment approach to employees (Marchington and Parker, 1990; Purcell, 1987; Storey and Sisson, 1993). Correspondingly, collectivism in industrial relations in the 1970s is counterposed

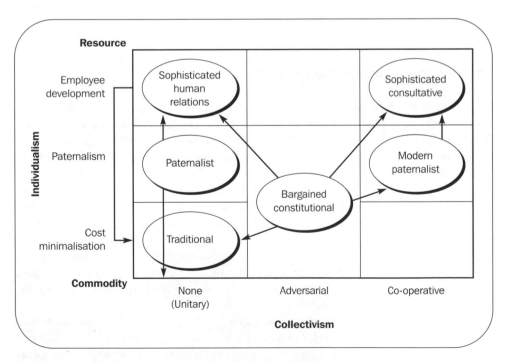

Figure 7.1 Movements in management style in employee relations

Source: Storey and Sisson, 1993, adapted from Purcell and Ahlstrand, 1994

with individualism and HRM in the 1990s (Storey and Sisson, 1993). The 'collectivism' dimension includes a unitarist position where trade unions are not recognised, an adversarial position of conflict with unions and a co-operative position of partnership with unions. The 'individualism' dimension includes a cost minimisation approach to employees, a 'paternalist' position of care for employee welfare and an employee development scenario.

Initial studies of the adoption of HRM policies in unionised workplaces (Storey, 1992) suggested little fit between HRM and industrial relations as managers attempted to bypass industrial relations processes and deal directly with employees. This comes as no great surprise as personnel management in the UK is commonly described as pragmatic and largely opportunistic (Sisson and Marginson, 1995). In seeking the appropriate recipe for managing employees during the 1980s many managers saw an opportunity to reduce the influence of unions. This involved a secular (if disputed) shift towards unitarism as managers reasserted their prerogative over employees at work. Initially, in the 1980s this appeared in an aggressive form of 'macho-management' as senior executives, often in state-owned industries, attacked unions and the customs and practices entrenched in many workplaces (Purcell, 1982). However, most companies did not derecognise unions and commentators noted that 'the lack of clarity about how industrial relations fits with the new initiatives will sooner or later have to be addressed' (Storey and Sisson, 1993: 27). In short, the main issue on the employee relations agenda appeared to be how to combine the individual and collective approaches in a complementary fashion.

The decline of collective regulation

As employment relations transformed we appear to have witnessed 'the end of institutional industrial relations' (Purcell, 1993). The third Workplace Industrial Relations Survey (WIRS 3) in 1990 underlined the extent to which the nature of British employee relations had changed and was no longer characterised by adversarial collective bargaining at workplace level (Millward *et al.*, 1992). Recent data confirm a further decline in the collective regulation of the employment relationship in the UK. Table 7.1 illustrates this change as captured by the Workplace Industrial Relations Surveys in terms of changes to union presence (the presence of one or more union members in a workplace), union membership density (percentage of employees who are union members), union recognition for negotiating pay and conditions of employment, coverage of collective bargaining (the proportion of employees in workplaces with recognised unions covered by collective bargaining) and joint consultative committees.

As almost one half of workplaces are effectively union-free a 'representation gap' (Towers, 1997) may have developed where managers operate without any independent employee voice. Three in five workplaces have no worker representatives at all (either union or non-union representatives), and this increases to nine out of ten workplaces where unions are not present (Cully *et al.*, 1999: 95).

Table 7.1 The decline of collective regulation in the Workplace Industrial Relations Surveys (figures related to percentages of workplaces)

	1980	1984	1990	1998
Union presence	73	73	64	54
Union membership density	65	58	47	36
Union recognition	65	65	53	42
Coverage of collective bargaining	–	70	54	41
Joint consultative committees	34	34	29	29

Source: Workplace Industrial Relations Surveys, see Cully *et al.*, 1999.

The decline in union recognition during the 1980s was in part due to changes in industrial relations law. However, the number of companies which have actively sought to derecognise existing trade unions in established workplaces has remained relatively small (Claydon, 1996). Although trade unions were out of favour with the UK government there was little evidence that union members wanted trade unions to abandon their traditional roles. In a survey of almost 11,000 union members conducted by Waddington and Whitston (1997) employees revealed they continued to join unions for collective protection and to improve terms and conditions (Table 7.2).

Table 7.2 What reasons do employees give for joining unions?

Reason	%
Support if I had a problem at work	72
Improved pay and conditions	36
Because I believe in trade unions	16
Free legal advice	15
Most people at work are members	14

Source: Waddington and Whitston, 1997: 521.

A more convincing explanation for union decline during the 1980s was the changing nature of the economy, with an increase in the service sector and reductions in the number of large manufacturing plants, manual work and the public sector. The traditional habitat for the UK's system of industrial relations based on adversarial collective bargaining was disappearing (Millward *et al.*, 1992). Although the decline in trade union representation continued throughout the 1990s there is evidence that the explanation has changed as 'almost all of the change arose because workplaces that joined the WIRS population between 1990 and 1998, even controlling for their sector and employment of part-time workers, were less likely to recognise unions than similar workplaces that had dropped out of the population' (Cully *et al.*, 1999: 241).

However, when we consider the scope and depth of joint consultation and bargaining trade union influence appears lower than current levels of union recognition indicate. It is difficult to assess the extent to which managers rely upon collective agreements with trade unions in workplaces. One study comparing collective agreements at the start and end of the 1980s outlined a relative stability in procedural agreements covering how issues are handled between management and labour (Dunn and Wright, 1994). A rather different picture emerged from case studies at plant level, indicating that managers were increasingly exercising their prerogative to make important changes, particularly in working methods (Geary, 1995). The latest data from the 1998 Workplace Employee Relations Surveys indicates a deeper 'hollowing out' of collective agreements. In workplaces where union representatives are present only a 'modest' level of joint regulation occurs. No negotiations occurred over any issues in one half of the workplaces with worker representatives present (Cully *et al.*, 1999: 110). In a further 13 per cent of workplaces negotiations only occurred on non-pay issues, in 17 per cent negotiations only covered pay and in 22 per cent negotiations occurred over pay and one other issue. Managers in many workplaces appear to regard certain HR issues as 'off limits' to union representatives and do not even involve unions in providing information. In 53 per cent of workplaces with union representatives, representatives played no role at all in performance appraisals, in 52 per cent no role in recruitment, in 46 per cent no role in payment systems and in 43 per cent no role in training. This evidence suggests that in many cases trade union influence has 'withered on the vine' and where union representatives remain in place this resembles a unionised approach to industrial relations which in fact is little more than a 'hollow shell' (Hyman, 1997). Given these findings traditional debates on the most appropriate levels for collective bargaining (at the workplace, corporate or industry levels) and the balance between collective bargaining and joint consultation are giving way to the broader question of whether and on what terms trade unions are involved in any degree of joint workplace governance. The central role played by collective industrial relations has certainly declined but what types of non-union workplaces have emerged?

Non-union workplaces

According to one estimate the majority of UK workplaces had become non-union by 1995 (Cully and Woodland, 1996). In the classic account by Fox (1974) it was necessary for managers to enforce management prerogative by coercive power to justify a unitarist ideology and non-union status. Managers have often used a wide-ranging web of defences against unionisation that in their more extreme variants in the United States could combine 'sweet stuff' to make management policies more acceptable to employees, 'fear stuff' to discourage union joining and 'evil stuff' to demonise unions (Roy, 1980). A unitarist ideology can therefore include a variety of different management techniques. Returning to Figure 7.1 we can see that Purcell and Ahlstrand (1994) classify three non-union management styles in terms of whether an organisation recognises and develops individual employees. Companies adopting a 'sophisticated human relations' approach invest in staff development and use a wide range of human resource management policies to substitute for the services unions provide for members (a union substitution approach). Other non-union companies adopt a 'paternalist' approach and seek the loyalty and commitment of staff through consideration for employee welfare. Finally, some organisations maintain a 'Bleak House' strategy of cost minimisation and avoid union recruitment.

Several key commentators in the late 1980s identified the non-union sector as the most likely location for the development of HRM in the UK, foreseeing a growth in the 'sophisticated human relations' approach (Sisson, 1989). As some HRM models, but not all, are fundamentally unitarist, a non-union environment appeared well suited to the demands of developing committed and flexible employees as demonstrated by several large non-union US multinationals such as IBM, Hewlett Packard and Mars (Foulkes, 1980; Kochan *et al.*, 1986). For example, IBM had combined corporate success, a positive employee relations climate of low conflict, low labour turnover and long service, with good pay and conditions. In addition, the company provided procedures to fulfil many of the functions met by unions, including a complex array of alternative procedures (a no redundancy policy, single status, equal opportunities policies, merit pay and performance assessments), a strong emphasis on internal communications and a grievance system.

Empirical support for the apparent link between sophisticated HRM and non-unionism was also provided by several case studies in the UK outlining a union substitution approach. In the case of 'Comco' explored by Cressey *et al.* (1985) employees identified strongly with the company and enjoyed 'greater benefits' and 'less disciplinary pressure'. Most employees working at an IBM plant in the UK studied by Dickson *et al.* (1988) were positively attached to the individualistic ethos of the company and perceived little need for union protection. Scott (1994) outlined a 'golden handcuffs' approach whereby employees in a chocolate works received good terms and conditions in return for accepting a high rate of effort and strict rules. Despite this evidence, initial studies indicated that non-union companies with a sophisticated approach to managing employees may remain the exception. A study of high-tech companies in the Southeast of England where we might expect companies to reproduce the IBM non-union model uncovered little evidence of sophisticated HRM, with companies either opportunistically avoiding unions or adopting the style of 'benevolent autocracies' (McLoughlin and Gourlay, 1994). Furthermore, the assumed benefits of a 'sophisticated human relations' approach have more recently come under closer scrutiny. Blyton and Turnbull (1994) suggest that Marks and Spencer, so often held up as an exemplar non-union company, simultaneously pursued a 'union substitution' strategy in retail outlets while forcing suppliers into a cost minimisation approach. In another case study, a steel plant had widely publicised the introduction of a HRM approach and subsequently derecognised trade unions. However, employee gains proved illusory, with managerial strategy geared towards attitudinal compliance, work intensification and the suppression of any counterbalancing trade union activity (Bacon, 1999).

HRM: a union or non-union phenomenon?

The evidence from the latest UK workplace survey (WERS98) confirms the finding of the 1990 survey (WIRS3, see Sisson, 1993: 206) that sophisticated HRM practices are to be found alongside union recognition mainly in larger workplaces and those in the public sector. In short, these surveys indicate that 'an active and strong union presence is compatible with the broad suite of high commitment management practices' (Cully *et al.*, 1999: 111). Furthermore, higher union density (the proportion of employees who are trade union members) is also associated with greater joint regulation and more high commitment management (HCM) practices. Figure 7.2 indicates that of the workplaces with no recognised unions, 41 per cent had none to three HCM practices, 54 per cent four to seven HCM practices, and 5 per cent eight or more. This compares unfavourably with 25 per cent of workplaces with recognised unions reporting eight or more high commitment management practices.

However, only 4 per cent of workplaces in the workplace survey combine a majority of the workforce in unions, collective negotiations over issues and at least one half of the measured list of high commitment work practices in place. There

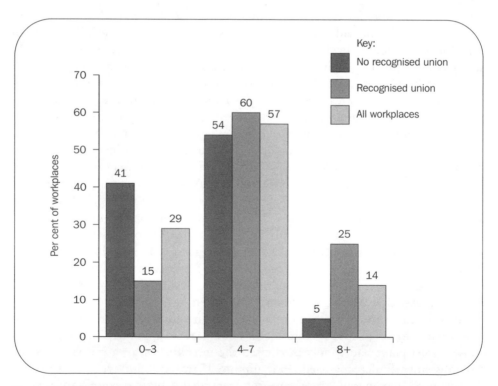

Figure 7.2 Number of high commitment management practices, by trade union recognition

Source: Cully et al., 1999

is, nevertheless, evidence from WERS98 that the combination of union recognition and HCM practices has a powerful effect on workplace performance. In the words of the WERS98 team 'workplaces with a recognised union and a majority of the HCM practices . . . did better than the average, and better than workplaces without recognition and a minority of these practices' (Cully *et al.*, 1999: 135). Sceptics of the impact of trade unions may still like to believe that adopting a wide range of HCM practices in a non-union environment may lead to even higher performance, but the fact that WERS98 could find so few such organisations casts some doubt upon this belief. In organisations where managers continue to recognise unions and are seeking to develop staff new approaches to industrial relations are developing involving 'partnership agreements'.

Partnership and the 'new unionism'

The election of 'New Labour' in 1997 has resulted in a new public policy environment. The government's Employment Relations Act 1999 and '*Fairness at Work*' programme have introduced new rights for trade unions and individual employees (Undy, 1999; Wood and Godard, 1999). In sum, this legislative programme involves a statutory route for union recognition, an extension of rights for individual employees, a national minimum wage and closer engagement with the social policies of the European Union. A central aim of this legislative programme is to 'replace the notion of conflict between employers and employees with the promotion of partnership in the longer term' (HMSO, 1998). The influence of a European approach was already felt as legislation obliged companies to establish a European works council if they employed over 1,000 employees in Europe and a minimum of 150 employees in at least two different member states. In sum, it is now commonplace to call for less destructive conflict and more co-operation to improve organisational productivity.

The issue of the balance between co-operation and conflict in union–management relations is a long-standing tension in employee relations. As the employment relationship encapsulates both shared and contrary interests the relationship between management and unions will contain elements of conflict and co-operation. As management and unions have begun to use the word 'partnership' it has become a contested term that appears inherently ambiguous and at times has no agreed meaning (Undy, 1999; Ackers and Payne, 1998). As Undy (1999: 318) has pointed out, 'What one party, or commentator, means by "partnership" is not necessarily shared by others.' As with so many terms in the area of employment relations, key pressure groups such as the TUC, the CBI and the Institute of Directors (IoDs) have sought to provide widely 'differing interpretations' of partnership (Undy, 1999: 318), defining the term for their own ends. The Institute of Personnel and Development, for example, explains that partnership 'has more to do with an approach to the relationship between employers and employees, individually and in groups, than it has to do with trade unions' (IPD, 1997: 8). Partnership can therefore be defined in both unitarist and pluralist terms. Rather unsurprisingly, the definition favoured by the TUC is pluralistic, with the stress placed on respecting union influence, whereas the IoD prefers a unitarist definition, whereby employees identify with the employer and trade unions are compliant to the wishes of management.

The Involvement and Participation Association, an independent pressure group, developed an influential definition of 'partnership' with leading companies and trade union leaders. This approach was endorsed by leading figures, including representatives from J. Sainsbury plc, the Boddington Group, the Post Office and the leaders of several trade unions (Involvement and Participation Association, 1992). This definition requires managers to declare security of employment as a key corporate objective; 'gainsharing' the results of success, and recognise the legitimacy of the employees' right to be informed, consulted and represented. In return, trade unions are required to renounce rigid job demarcations and commit to flexible working; give sympathetic consideration to the Continental model of representation of the whole workforce by means of election of representatives to new works councils, and recognise and then co-promote employee involvement methods. Case 7.2 invites you to consider the extent to which you feel companies and unions are able to sign up to a partnership agenda.

Given the lack of a general consensus on the meaning of industrial relations partnerships, it may be surprising that the term has acquired such a topical currency. A principal reason why the concept has taken hold is that it offers an industrial relations solution to the low competitiveness of much of UK industry. In this respect, partnership is no different from previous legislative changes that have sought to improve organisational performance through changes in industrial relations. Influential US literature suggests that in some companies managers may be able to forge a strategic linkage between industrial relations and HRM initiatives to create 'mutual gains enterprises' (Kochan and Osterman, 1994; Appelbaum and Batt, 1994). In such enterprises important changes are introduced in the organisation of work to enhance productivity, to the mutual benefit of employees, unions and management acting in coalition.

The signing of partnership agreements is of potential importance (IRS, 1997) although to date there is little evidence that they have become spread beyond around 40 companies. If partnerships are to become further established in UK industrial relations then managers and unions must find a workable balance between a number of key tensions beyond the above-mentioned disputes as to the meaning of the concept. The first tension is that workable partnership agreements appear to require a strategic and long-term commitment by managers to working closely with unions in the tradition of companies labelled 'sophisticated moderns' by Fox (1974). If managers are simply behaving in a short-term, contradictory or opportunistic manner then genuine industrial relations partnerships are unlikely to endure. For example, at the Royal Mail several partnership initiatives have struggled, primarily because some managers in the company are not firmly behind the partnership approach (see Bacon and Storey, 2000; Bacon and Storey, 1996).

The second tension, not unconnected to the first, is to what extent management and unions are able to commit fully to a single strategy of co-operative industrial relations. If partnerships do not secure the types of compliant trade unionism required in the CBI's definition of partnership then management commitment to such agreements may prove half-hearted. Similarly, at the same time as the TUC is supporting partnership agreements it is also pursuing an organising and campaigning approach to membership growth (Heery, 1998). It may prove difficult for unions to convince a company to sign a meaningful partnership agreement in one plant while actively recruiting union members against the wishes of the same or a similar company in another plant.

The third tension is whether partnership agreements form part of a longer-term strategy to marginalise trade unions rather than an alternative. Many observers critical of the co-operative relationships between managers and unions that are central to partnership agreements have highlighted continued employer attacks on unions (Claydon, 1989, 1996; Gall and McKay, 1994; Kelly, 1996; Smith and Morton, 1993). Although partnerships are frequently presented as a step away from attempts to derecognise trade unions this may not be the case. Evidence on this matter is not yet conclusive. Whereas one recent review of partnership agreements in six organisations reported that 'none gave serious consideration to ending recognition' (IDS, 1998: 4), a study of management attempts to restructure industrial relations in ten organisations (Bacon and Storey, 2000) revealed that derecognition had been more seriously explored. In the latter study, the new agreements signed with trade unions did not appear to reflect long-term commitments to working with trade unions nor sophisticated moves towards derecognition. Managers appeared to display unitarist preferences. However, for pragmatic reasons – for instance, the desire to maintain the trust of employees – they were willing to involve unions in joint regulation albeit within parameters managers attempted to control. In many workplaces union representatives feel they have no option but to accept management terms and union support for partnership resembles a resigned compliance. For example, in the case of United Distillers trade unions either signed the partnership agreement on offer or faced 'de facto derecognition' (Marks *et al.*, 1998: 222).

Finally, it is not yet clear whether partnership agreements will deliver greater returns for managers and trade unions. If returns are not forthcoming for either party then enthusiasm for the partnership approach may wane. Kelly (1996) has argued that, a priori, a union strategy of moderation is inferior in many respects to a militant stance. Union moderation is associated by Kelly with: eroding the willingness and capacity of union members to resist employers; inhibiting the growth of workplace union organisation; generating apathy among union members; involving union 'give' and management 'take'; resulting in attempts to drive down terms and conditions of employment and failing to genuinely represent member grievances. The key differences between militant and moderate union positions are highlighted in Case 7.3.

The extent to which Kelly is correct and neither unions nor employees will benefit from partnership agreements is an interesting question. Certainly, the number of partnership agreements signed between unions and management has increased, but remains low overall. There is little evidence that employers are able to offer the job security guarantees that unions seek or that trade unions are able to prevent managers unilaterally imposing changes in work organisation in order to bring managers to sign partnership agreements.

Conclusions

In this chapter we have argued that managers in the majority of workplaces no longer appear to support or utilise collective industrial relations in their employee management strategies. Sisson and Storey (2000: x) have recently restated that 'managing the employment relationship will demand both an individual and a collective perspective' in forthcoming years. However, recent evidence suggests that managers in few workplaces have sought to balance an individual and collective approach to employee management. Figure 7.3 presents a summary drawing upon the findings from WERS98 of the current pattern of employee relations. The predominant employee relations style in the British workplace is not to manage both individualism and collectivism, it is to manage neither. Considering all the

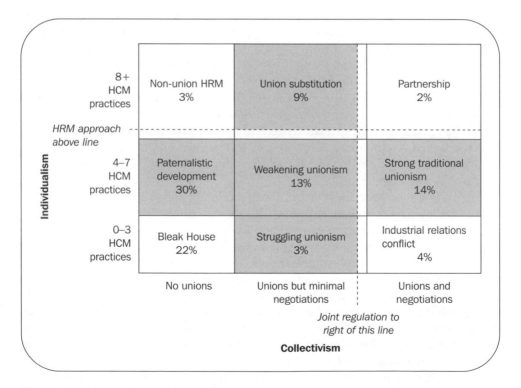

Figure 7.3 New patterns of employee relations.

workplaces which fall into the bottom left-hand quadrant of the dotted lines, approximately seven in ten (68 per cent) operate fewer than one-half of 15 high-commitment management practices and do not involve trade unions in negotiations on matters other than pay. Fifty-two per cent of workplaces in this quadrant do not recognise trade unions.

Approximately 14 per cent of workplaces could be described as pursuing a HRM approach but only 5 per cent appeared to combine individualism with either a union exclusion or partnership approach. The majority of workplaces appear to be marginalising unions, and although they remain present significant negotiations do not occur. It is tempting to classify organisations falling into the four corner boxes as having an apparently settled employee relations strategy that is unlikely to change in the near future. The numerous workplaces which fall into the 'Bleak House' classification (approximately 22 per cent) are focused upon cost reduction and will resist any attempts at unionisation. They are likely to be smaller workplaces in such sectors as wholesale and retail, hotels and restaurants. The small number of organisations which negotiate with unions but eschew developing employees ('industrial relations traditional') may be resigned to dealing with unions in the absence of a more sophisticated approach to managing employees. A few genuine examples of partnership may flourish in the current political climate but the overall number of such workplaces remains small. Companies adopting non-union HRM are likely to feel they have permanently resolved the union issue.

This leaves approximately 69 per cent of organisations (in the shaded areas of Figure 7.3) which currently operate with an opportunistic mixture of labour management policies. Organisations currently occupying these different positions face somewhat different dilemmas. Those currently using HRM policies to substitute for negotiating with unions but still recognising unions ('union substitution') may at some point in the future sign partnership deals with trade unions to share more decision-making and/or further erode union influence. Companies with 'strong traditional unionism' may further develop HR policies either to substitute for unions or develop a partnership approach. From an industrial relations perspective the most significant developments may occur within the 'weakening unionism' category. Although trade unions in these workplaces are involved in fewer negotiations managers have not developed high-commitment management practices to replace the services unions provide for members in terms of voicing collective grievances and seeking to improve terms and conditions. It would appear to be in this category of workplaces that trade unions may target recruitment to increase union density and exert greater influence. The Employment Relations Act 1999 encourages union recruitment and organising efforts as it provides a statutory recognition procedure. As so few organisations appear to have resolved the issue of managing employees through individual or collective means they are likely to face continued pressure from individual employees for increased training and more satisfying work and from employee representatives for a greater say in workplace governance.

| Case study 7.1 |

The UK's largest private sector employers

Nick Bacon

Below is a list of the largest private sector employers in the UK taken from *Labour Research*. Which do you think:

(a) Do not recognise trade unions;
(b) Recognise and negotiate with trade unions;
(c) Recognise trade unions but only for the purposes of consultation or to represent individual employees?

Explain your decisions.

Table 7.3

Tesco	153,800	Retail – supermarkets
J Sainsbury	150,700	Retail – supermarkets
BT	125,800	Telecommunications
Lloyds-TSB	82,000	Banking and finance
Whitbread	80,000	Food and drink
Boots Co.	75,000	Retail and pharmaceuticals
Asda Group	73,700	Retail – supermarkets
Safeway Group	70,400	Retail – supermarkets
Kingfisher	69,600	Retail
Bass	67,500	Brewing and leisure
National Westminster	66,000	Banking and finance
Rentokil Initial	65,000	Business services
Barclays	60,800	Banking and finance
Granada Group	58,000	Leisure
Marks and Spencer	54,900	Retail
General Electric Co.	52,300	Electronics
HSBC Holding (Midland Bank)	50,000	Banking and finance
British Airways	47,700	Banking and finance
Allied Domecq	46,500	Food and drink
Somerfield	45,700	Retail – supermarket
Burton Group	43,700	Retail
British Steel	43,400	Steel Manufacturers
Ladbroke Group	42,000	Leisure
John Lewis Partnership	41,100	Retail – department stores
BMW – Rover Group	39,000	Motor manufacture
Scottish and Newcastle	39,000	Brewing and leisure
British Aerospace	38,500	Aerospace and engineering
MacDonald's Restaurants	36,700	Food retail
Halifax	36,000	Banking and finance
Ford	35,900	Motor manufacturing
Compass Group	35,700	Catering
Co-operative Wholesale Society	35,000	Banking, insurance, retail
OCS Group	35,000	Cleaning
Sears	32,600	Retail
Rolls Royce	31,200	Aerospace and engineering
Rank Organisation	30,300	Leisure and films
Greenhalls Group	30,100	Brewing, food, hotels
WH Smith	30,000	Retail
Royal & Sun Alliance	27,800	Insurance
Securicor Group	27,500	Security services
Wm Morrison Supermarkets	27,000	Retail – supermarkets
Unigate	27,000	Food manufacture
Lucas Varity	26,800	Engineering
BTR	26,600	Industrial conglomerate
Kwik Save Group	26,000	Retail

The principles and practices of partnership with trade unions

Nick Bacon

As explained in Chapter 6, one option for managers and trade unions is to establish a partnership agreement. However, successful agreements depend upon a serious commitment to the principles and practices of partnership. Thinking of the last organisation you worked for, an organisation you know well or your own personal 'frame of reference', to what extent do you agree or disagree with the following statements? Your answers indicate whether organisations could be committed to a partnership agreement. *(Circle one number for each statement)*

	Agree	Neutral	Disagree
Personnel managers worry about trade unions, most other senior managers would rather they disappear.	1	2	3
Trade unions don't have a useful function in organisations.	1	2	3
All managers should share all information, however sensitive, with unions.	1	2	3
Managers can get employees to work hard without making concessions to unions.	1	2	3
Job security is a myth in today's world.	1	2	3
To attract top managers organisations have to offer extra incentives such as private health insurance that are too expensive to give to all employees.	1	2	3
Companies should train all employees to a high level even though some will leave.	1	2	3

Case study 7.3

What should trade unions do?

Nick Bacon

In Chapter 7 we outlined Kelly's (1996) argument that trade unions would benefit from a militant rather than a moderate stance. Reading through the following statements, indicate the extent to which you believe trade unions should adopt a moderate or militant stance. Explain your choices.

Trade unions should:

Union militancy		Union moderation
Make ambitious demands	or	Make moderate demands
Offer few concessions	or	Offer many concessions
Rely on members' activity	or	Rely on managers' good will
Rely on collective bargaining	or	Rely on consultation
Frequently threaten industrial action	or	Rarely threaten industrial action
Believe in a basic conflict of interests	or	Believe in a basic common interest

Employee relations at North Fire Brigade

Tom Redman and Ed Snape

Background

North Fire Brigade has a current establishment of 700 whole-time operational fire-fighters located in twelve fire stations across the region with a non-uniformed support staff of 100. In addition there are 72 part-time retained firefighters located in a further six stations. Firefighting in the UK is still virtually an exclusively male occupation when compared to the slow but steady inroads of women firefighters in some other countries. North Brigade is no different in this respect, not employing a single woman firefighter. The number of firefighters per station varies from around 30 in the smallest to over 100 in the largest. Each firefighter is a member of one of four watches (red, white, blue, and green), with each watch working for two day and two night shifts on a 42-hour week duty system. Despite the introduction of new managerial practices in the 1990s the organisation of fire fighting remains hierarchical and bureaucratised, with ten levels separating the chief officer and qualified firefighter posts.

The nature of the firefighters' job makes heavy demands in terms of personal discipline and commitment to teamwork and results in a strongly collectivist work ethic. In the words of a previous general secretary of the FBU:

> When all is said and done, at the end of it firefighting comes to this: that a small number of people will go into a darkened smoke-logged building not knowing what they are going to meet, having faith in each other, in the long run prepared to risk their lives to save the lives of other people. In the long run, no matter what transformation we effect in the Fire Service, firefighting in its final stages remains just that. And we do not forget it.

This collectivist work ethic imparts high levels of loyalty and discipline to the union. North Brigade has a union density rate of nearly 100 per cent amongst uniformed staff. The TUC-affiliated FBU is the dominant trade union for firefighters, particularly for lower grades, with the NAFO (and CACFOA) having very limited representation amongst higher-grade employees at station officer and above. Non-uniformed staff are represented by Unison. The FBU has ambitions to be an industrial union for firefighting, with its first object being 'to organise all uniformed employees'. There has been a recent history of competition between the fire service unions, with some acrimonious disputes arising over representation rights.

Collective bargaining is organised through a National Joint Council composed on the employer's side of representatives made up of various local authority bodies. However, the national bargaining system was under pressure from management initiatives to increase the range of local bargaining, in particular to reduce the scope of the National Scheme of Conditions of Service or 'Grey Book'. Here a critical report from the Audit Commission in 1995 added momentum to a move to more local bargaining. The report suggested the national framework was constraining brigade effectiveness by preventing some possible improvements in efficiency. However, the FBU see this less as a need for local flexibility and more as a simple prelude to a concerted attack on the levels of terms and conditions provided by national bargaining arrangements. Local bargaining currently occurs between four key union representatives (from a brigade committee of some 12 representatives) and the Deputy Chief Fire Officer and Assistant Chief Officers. Typical bargaining issues include changes to 'detached' duties (terms for redeploying staff between stations), the duty mix of whole-time and retained firefighters, and meal arrangements.

Cost containment

Although the fire service has probably not been on the receiving end of some of the more drastic cutbacks in public spending over the last decade, there is now considerable pressure for cost containment and 'efficiency' within the sector. According to one senior and long-serving manager:

> In the past people accepted we put out fires and that somehow was enough. Now with the general closer scrutiny we have from auditing and performance indicators and the like, it is not sufficient. We have to be much more efficient and service-minded nowadays.

Such pressures are occurring at a time of increasing demand for fire services. The FBU estimates an increase of 87 per cent in calls to the fire service between 1979 and 1998. The funding for fire services in England is calculated by the Standard Spending Assessment (SSA) formula. The majority of English County Councils, particularly rural ones, exceed their SSA allocation. North Brigade is no exception, with 1998 seeing a budget shortfall of over £2 million needed to support the current establishment and existing levels of service provision. In particular, the physical characteristics of North Brigade's geographical location, with a large concentration of heavy chemical industries, are felt to necessitate a higher level of spending than the SSA allocation.

More recently, the cost and efficiency pressures generated by 'Best Value' were occupying managerial attention. Here the brigade had set up task teams to investigate the cost reduction potential of greater collaboration with other regional brigades in areas such as the purchasing of uniforms and equipment, training, the provision of payroll services and, more controversially, the use of joint control centres. Task teams had also been set up to examine the potential for generating income by providing training courses for industry and other fire services where

North Brigade had particular expertise, for example, in relation to dealing with hazardous materials. Increasingly, the mounting pressure for cost containment and efficiency was impacting on the industrial relations climate of the industry as management attempted to reduce costs but at the same time improve service quality levels.

Industrial relations

Industrial relations in the brigade were perceived as being typical for the industry with fewer disputes occurring in North Brigade than some other more 'militant' brigades, recent protracted disputes over terms and conditions and establishment level having occurred in Merseyside, Derbyshire and, most recently, Essex. The latter three and a half-month dispute involved over 20 strikes. Following the resolution of the dispute, the Essex MP Teresa Gorman, in an open letter to Essex Fire Brigade committee, accused the FBU of 'blackmailing' and 'shroud-waving' to protect outdated practices and overgenerous terms and conditions:

> All Britain's fire services are far too overstaffed. It is one of the last of the dinosaur industries clinging to feather bedding, using shroud-waving and blackmail to prevent the modernisation of the service. The Algarve is stuffed with healthy young British males, living comfortably, their incomes supplemented by disabled pensions from the fire service. In Arizona, when the fire service was privatised, it became obvious that 80 per cent of all 'calls' could be dealt with by two men in a fast car. And the cost of the service was halved. Who will be the first council to have an open debate on privatising its fire services and let some fresh air in to the argument?

Managers at North Brigade felt the relatively dispute-free recent past could be explained by an open relationship with the union and more 'responsible' union leaders.

> We accommodate them (the union) with whatever information they want with regard to budgets. There is a standing instruction that the union can have whatever information the Brigade has. If they want information on, say, the capital or revenue budgets they can go and get it with my authority. There are no secrets here. It comes from us being able to say to the union 'We have not got the money to do this or that. There are the figures. If you can find X thousand pounds, you can have it'.

Senior management emphasised the importance of good communication with their employees, and the need for it, given a generally better-educated workforce. Employee involvement mechanisms include a brigade Intranet, newsletters, senior management visits and informal talks 'with the troops in the stations'. The latter was seen to be particularly important to counter the perceived gulf between headquarters and the stations. According to one manager, North Brigade now had 'thinking union officers rather than the table bangers of the past'. Trade union interviewees also reported that the current senior management was, to a large extent, more willing to listen to their concerns, particularly when compared to some previous senior managers, who were reluctant even to speak to other managers below a certain rank, let alone union representatives. Union–management co-operation had extended in the recent past to a joint delegation to lobby Parliament on SSA levels.

An index of the generally positive industrial relations climate of the 1990s in North Brigade was the low level of formal grievances, with few grievances reaching the 'failure to agree' stage. This was seen as a considerable achievement when set against a backcloth of cost containment, the level of organisational change and the high potential for conflict in the character of firefighting disputes. Here the nature of an emergency led to 'life or death' service results in many disputes, according to both union representatives and managers, involving some very emotional and moral arguments being thrown around. Thus, the brigade had successfully managed to reduce its establishment levels by about 10 per cent over the last eight years without any industrial action occurring. Most recently in 1998 the brigade had removed two fireboats from service and this had resulted in the loss of 15 jobs through natural wastage. Here the union officers felt they had provided 'realistic opposition' to the cuts – the original management proposal had been to lose 43 jobs through compulsory redundancy.

However, several developments were underway which had high potential for straining future management–union relationships. In particular, a number of industry-wide issues, such as the 1998 review of the national pension scheme and the move to local bargaining, were causing concern for local relationships between management and unions. The new pension proposals contained a recommendation for a two-tier scheme with considerably reduced benefits for new starters and a diminution of terms for existing staff. Equally, increasing attempts by various brigades to renegotiate and in some cases 'buy-out' 'Grey Book' conditions was a major source of instability which was seen as eventually posing considerable problems for industrial relations in North Brigade. Local issues included managerial attempts to introduce performance appraisal; appraisal-related pay, revised duty systems and a capability procedure, all of which the union had strongly resisted. Union representatives also reported increasing interest by management in the performance of individual firefighters and increased pressure on sickness levels via the introduction of formal interview panels. A key union concern here was that such pressure resulted in some employees coming to work in an unfit state and thus becoming a danger to themselves and their colleagues. Firefighters in North Brigade had also traditionally had two days' extra annual leave above the national minimum and management was being subjected to increasing pressure from the district Audit Office to reduce this.

As a result there had been a recent increase in grievance activity in disputes, with several of these reaching the 'failure to agree' stage. Here disputes varied from the cutback of hot meals on weekend shifts; a demarcation dispute (with the ambulance service) over the use of defibrillators and basic trauma life support and management's attempt to obtain a 'seamless ambulance and fire fighting service'; management attempts to get full-time staff to undertake duties traditionally carried out by retained firemen, and more flexible rostering. Union representatives reported that they were currently working very hard to hold back the members and a senior manager lamented that, given the current IR climate, a capability procedure he had been working on for two years was 'not worth the hassle of getting it out of the drawer'. According to one union representative:

> We may have been guilty of crying wolf with the members in the past. You know, always telling them that this year the management are coming for us. But now it looks like it is probably going to happen.

Thus, the industrial relations climate was generally perceived as deteriorating somewhat under the wider pressures on the industry. For example, the union representatives reported that they were becoming increasingly more sceptical of management's espoused rhetoric of seeking a 'partnership' with the union. One union representative described management's claim of having an open door policy as being 'just words' as union concerns were now more often met by 'shoulder shrugging' and 'There is no alternative' statements. Union interviewees also reported the organisational culture of the brigade changing under the creeping use of business language and new managerial 'speak'. Here the language of 'customer service' was seen as a veil for management pushing through desired organisational changes in the search for efficiency and cost cutting. Thus:

> We used to have the feel of being a big family doing a key public service. Now it very much feels like we are working for a business. (union representative)

The 'us and them' divide in the brigade was thus perceived by union representatives as increasing. For example, in relation to the meal dispute one union representative commented that 'It now seems we cannot get a meal but they can have big cars'.

Note: The amount of funding allocated to run fire services in England is calculated using a formula know as the Standard Spending Assessment. In Scotland it is the Grant Aided Expenditure, in Wales the Revenue Support Grant and in Northern Ireland a block grant for the funding of all services.

Questions

1. Management at North Brigade is very concerned that a worsening national IR environment will undermine their relatively good local IR climate. What would you advise them to do in order to protect local relationships in such conditions?

2. Many commentators have suggested that the right to strike should be removed from essential public services, such as firefighting. Do you agree with this view? What issues would be raised by such a development?

3. Fire brigades are currently under considerable pressure to increase the number of women firefighters in the service. What IR issues would be raised by the increased recruitment of women firefighters?

References to Chapter 7

Ackers, P. and Payne, J. (1998) 'British trade unions and social partnership: rhetoric, reality and strategy', *International Journal of Human Resource Management*, 9: 529–50.

Appelbaum, R. and Batt, R. (1994) *The New American Workplace*. Ithaca: ILR Press.

Bacon, N. (1999) 'Union derecognition and the new human relations: a steel industry case study', *Work, Employment and Society*, 13(1): 1–17.

Bacon, N. and Storey, J. (1996) 'Individualism and collectivism and the changing role of trade unions' in Ackers, P., Smith, C. and Smith, P. (eds) *The New Workplace and Trade Unionism*, London, Routledge, 1–40.

Bacon, N. and Storey, J. (2000) 'New employee relations strategies: towards individualism or partnership', *British Journal of Industrial Relations*, forthcoming.

Blyton, P. and Turnbull, P. (1994) *The Dynamics of Employee Relations*, London: Macmillan.

Claydon, T. (1989) 'Union de-recognition in Britain in the 1980s', *British Journal of Industrial Relations*, 27: 214–23.

Claydon, T. (1996) 'Union recognition: a re-examination', in Beardwell, I. (ed) *Contemporary Industrial Relations*, Oxford: Oxford University Press.

Cressey, P., Eldridge, J. and MacInnes, J. (1985) *Just Managing: Authority and Democracy in Industry*, Milton Keynes: Open University Press.

Cully, M. and Woodland, S. (1996) 'Trade union membership and recognition: an analysis of data from the 1995 Labour Force Survey', *Labour Market Trends*, May: 215–25 (Norwich: HMSO).

Cully, M., Woodland, S., O'Reilly, A., Dix, G., Millward, N., Bryson, A., and Forth, J. (1998) *The 1998 Workplaces Employee Relations Survey: First Findings*, London: Department of Trade and Industry.

Cully, M., Woodland, S., O'Reilly, A. and Dix, G. (1999) *Britain at Work*, London: Routledge.

Dickson, T., McLachlan, M.V., Prior, P. and Swales, K. (1988) 'Big blue and the union: IBM, individualism and trade union strategy', *Work, Employment and Society*, 2: 506–20.

Dunn, S., and Wright, M. (1994) 'Maintaining the "status quo": An analysis of the contents of British collective agreements 1979–1990', *British Journal of Industrial Relations*, 32: 23–46.

Edwards, P. (1990) 'The politics of conflict and consent', *Journal of Economic Behaviour and Organization*, 13: 41–61.

Edwards, P. (1995) 'The employment relationship', in P. Edwards (ed) *Industrial Relations*, Oxford: Blackwell, 3–26.

Edwards, P. *et al.* (1998) 'Great Britain: from partial collectivism to neo-liberalism to where?', in Ferner, A., and Hyman, R. (eds) *Changing Industrial Relations in Europe*, Oxford: Blackwell, 1–54.

Flanders, A. (1970) *Management and Unions: The Theory and Reform of Industrial Relations*, London: Faber.

Foulkes, F. K. (1980) *Personnel Policies in Large Non-union Companies*, Englewood Cliffs, NJ: Prentice Hall.

Fox, A. (1966) 'Industrial sociology and industrial relations', *Royal Commission Research Paper* No. 3, London: HMSO.

Fox, A. (1974) *Beyond Contract: Work, Power and Trust Relations*, London: Faber and Faber.

Freeman, R.B. and Medoff, J.L. (1984) *What Do Unions Do?*, New York: Basic Books.

Gall, G. and McKay, S. (1994) 'Trade union de-recognition in Britain 1988-94', *British Journal of Industrial Relations*, 32: 433–48.

Geary, J. (1995) 'Work practices: the structure of work', in P. Edwards (ed) *Industrial Relations*, Oxford: Blackwell, 368–96.

Guest, D. (1987). 'Human resource management and industrial relations', *Journal of Management Studies*, 24(5): 503–21.

Guest, D. (1989) 'Human resource management: its implications for industrial relations and trade unions', in J. Storey, (ed) *New Perspectives in Human Resource Management*, London: Routledge, 41–55.

Guest, D. (1990). 'Human resource management and the American Dream', *Journal of Management Studies*, 27(4): 378–97.

Guest, D. (1995). 'Human resource management, trade unions and industrial relations', in Storey, J. (ed) *Human Resource Management: A Critical Text*, London: Routledge, 110–41.

Guest, D. and Hoque, K. (1994) 'The good, the bad and the ugly: Employment relations in new non-union workplaces', *Human Resource Management Journal*, 5: 1–14.

Heery, E. (1996) 'The new new unionism', in Beardwell, I. (ed) *Contemporary Industrial Relations*, Oxford: Oxford University Press, 175–202.

Heery, E. (1998) 'The re-launch of the Trades Union Congress', *British Journal of Industrial Relations*, 36: 339–60.

HMSO (1998) *Fairness at Work*, White Paper.

Hyman, R. (1987) 'Strategy or structure? Capital, Labour and Control', *Work, Employment and Society*, 1(1): 25–55.

Hyman, R. (1997) 'The future of employee representation', *British Journal of Industrial Relations*, 35(3): 309–36.

IDS (1998) 'Partnership agreements', *IDS Study 656*, October.

Institute of Directors (1994) Evidence presented to the Employment Committee Enquiry, *The Future of Trade Unions*, HC 676-II, London: HMSO.

Involvement and Participation Association (1992) *Towards Industrial Partnership: A New Approach to Management Union Relations*, London: IPA.

IPD (1997) *Employment Relations into the 21st Century*, London: Institute of Personnel and Development.

IRS (1997) Partnership at work: a survey. *Employment Trends*, 645, December: 3–24.

Kelly, J. (1996) 'Union militancy and social partnership', in Ackers, P., Smith, C. and Smith, P. (eds) *The New Workplace and Trade Unionism*, London: Routledge, 41–76.

Kitay, J. and Marchington, M. (1996) 'A review and critique of workplace industrial relations typologies', *Human Relations*, 49(10): 1263–90.

Kochan, T. and Osterman, P. (1994) *The Mutual Gains Enterprise*, Cambridge, Mass: Harvard Business School Press.

Kochan, T., Katz, H. and McKersie, B. (1986) *The Transformation of American Industrial Relations*, New York: Basic Books.

Marchington, M. and Parker, P. (1990) *Changing Patterns of Employee Relations*, Hemel Hempstead: Harvester Wheatsheaf.

Marks, A., Findlay, P., Hine, J., McKinlay, A. and Thompson, P. (1998) 'The politics of partnership? Innovation in employment relations in the Scottish spirits industry', *British Journal of Industrial Relations*, 36(2): 209–26.

McLoughlin, I. and Gourlay, S. (1994) *Enterprise Without Unions: Industrial Relations in the Non-Union Firm*, Milton Keynes: Open University Press.

Millward, N., Stevens, M., Smart, D. and Hawes, W.R. (1992) *Workplace Industrial Relations in Transition*, Dartmouth: Aldershot.

Monks, J. (1998) 'Trade unions, enterprise and the future', in Sparrow, P. and Marchington, M. (eds) *Human Resource Management: The New Agenda*, London: Pitman, 171–9.

Poole, M., and Mansfield, R. (1993) 'Patterns of continuity and change in managerial attitudes and behaviour in industrial relations 1980–90', *British Journal of Industrial Relations*, 31(1): 11–36.

Purcell, J. (1982) 'Macho managers and the new industrial relations', *Employee Relations*, 4(1): 3–5.

Purcell, J. (1987) 'Mapping management styles in employee relations', *Journal of Management Studies*, 24(5): 533–48.

Purcell, J. (1991) 'The rediscovery of management prerogative: the management of labour relations in the 1980s', *Oxford Review of Economic Policy*, 7(1): 33–43.

Purcell, J. (1993) 'The end of institutional industrial relations', *Political Quarterly*, 64(1): 6–23.

Purcell, J. and Ahlstrand, B. (1994) *Human Resource Management in the Multi-Divisional Company*, Oxford: Oxford University Press.

Purcell, J. and Sisson, K. (1983) 'Strategies and practice in the management of industrial relations', in G. Bain (ed) *Industrial Relations in Britain*, Oxford: Blackwell.

Roy, D. (1980) 'Fear stuff, sweet stuff and evil stuff: management's defences against unionization in the South', in T. Nichols (ed) *Capital and Labour: A Marxist Primer*, Glasgow: Fontana, 395–415.

Scott, A. (1994) *Willing Slaves?*, Cambridge: Cambridge University Press.

Sisson, K. (1989) 'Personnel management in transition?', in Sisson, K. (ed) *Personnel Management in Britain*, Oxford: Blackwell.

Sisson, K. (1993) 'In Search of HRM', *British Journal of Industrial Relations*, 31(2): 201–10.

Sisson, K. (ed) (1994) *Personnel Management*, Oxford: Blackwell.

Sisson, K. (1995) 'Human resource management and the personnel function', in Storey, J. (ed) *Human Resource Management: A Critical Test*, London: Routledge, 87–109.

Sisson, K., and Marginson, P. (1995) 'Management: systems, structures and strategy', in Edwards, P. (ed) *Industrial Relations*, Oxford: Blackwell, 89–122.

Sisson, K., and Storey, J. (2000) *The Realities of Human Resource Management*, Buckingham: Open University Press.

Smith, P. and Morton, G. (1993) 'Union exclusion and decollectivization of industrial relations in contemporary Britain', *British Journal of Industrial Relations*, 31(1): 97–114.

Storey, J. (1992) *Developments in the Management of Human Resources*, Oxford: Blackwell.

Storey, J., and Bacon, N. (1993) 'Individualism and collectivism: into the 1990s', *International Journal of Human Resource Management*, 4(3): 665–84.

Storey, J., Bacon, N., Edmonds, J. and Wyatt, P. (1993) 'The new agenda and human resource management: a roundtable discussion with John Edmonds', *Human Resource Management Journal*, 4(1): 63–70.

Storey, J. and Sisson, K. (1993) *Managing Human Resources and Industrial Relations*, Milton Keynes: Open University Press.

Towers, B. (1997) *The Representation Gap*, Oxford: Oxford University Press.

TUC (1993) Evidence presented to the Employment Committee Enquiry, *The Future of Trade Unions*, HC 676-II, 18 October, London: HMSO.

Undy, R. (1999) 'Annual review article: New Labour's "Industrial Relations Settlement": The Third Way?', *British Journal of Industrial Relations*, 37(2): 315–36.

Waddington, J. and Whitston, C. (1997) 'Why do people join unions in a period of membership decline', *British Journal of Industrial Relations*, 35(4): 515–46.

Wood, S. (1997) *Statutory Union Recognition*, Institute of Personnel and Development, London.

Wood, S. and Godard, J. (1999) 'The statutory union recognition procedure in the Employment Relations Bill: A comparative analysis', *British Journal of Industrial Relations*, 37: 203–44.

Part 2

Contemporary themes and issues

Chapter 8

Flexibility

Stephen Procter and Stephen Ackroyd

Introduction: what do we mean by flexibility?

Flexibility is a concept that can be understood in many different ways and at many different levels. At its broadest it is perhaps best understood as the quality by which an entity adapts itself to a change in the demands made upon it. The appeal of flexibility as a concept can be seen by a consideration of its opposites – inflexibility, rigidity, etc. – all of which carry a quite negative connotation. However, before portraying flexibility as something which should be welcomed in all cases, we need to raise two simple questions: flexibility of what and flexibility for whom?

(a) Flexibility of what?

In answer to the first question, we can identify four basic areas in which the idea of flexibility has been applied:

- **Flexibility of labour** – this in turn can be understood in two different ways: as the ability and willingness of individual workers to perform a wider range of tasks, jobs or skills; and as the ability of organisations to vary the amount of labour they use in accordance with fluctuations in demand.
- **Flexibility of technology** – technology here can include both physical technology and the broader ideas of technique and know-how; flexibility refers to both the range of things technology can do and the ease with which it can move between them.
- **Flexibility of organisations** – this might include the flexibility of both labour and technology, but refers to the more general ability of organisations to adapt themselves to the demands made upon them.

■ **Flexibility of systems** – at a broader level still, we are concerned with the systems within which organisations operate. A system might thus be a national economy, a region or even the world economy as a whole. Again, to understand what form this might take, we must take into account the other forms of flexibility.

(b) Flexibility for whom?

The nature of the present volume means that our focus is on the flexibility of labour. As we shall see, however, it is impossible to understand this in isolation from the other types of flexibility we have described. What we shall also see is that – in answer to our second basic question – flexibility is defined from the point of view of those who run and those who own organisations. In terms of the employment relationship, it is flexibility *for* the employer, which, in all likelihood, is likely to mean flexibility *of* the employee. While in some circumstances this will also mean flexibility *for* the employee, the nature of the employment relationship means that the interests of employer and employee will not always coincide. From the point of view of the employee, flexibility cannot unequivocally be seen as a good thing (see also Legge, 1998).

(c) The structure of this chapter

The chapter is structured as follows. We look first at flexibility in historical perspective, showing how the idea of the flexibility of labour needs to be understood against the background of longer-term trends in how work is organised. We turn then to how labour and organisational flexibility have been conceptualised in recent and current UK debates. We shall see that although the so-called 'flexible firm' model has much to commend it, it cannot offer a full explanation of the developments we observe. A consideration of technological flexibility leads us on to the 'new flexible firm' model, which combines labour, technological and organisational flexibility in a way which offers us much greater insight. The 'new flexible firm' is then compared to a rival configuration which is based on the idea that British organisations have attempted to achieve flexibility through the emulation of their Japanese counterparts. All this, as we shall see, involves a quite structural account of flexibility; one which emphasises the constraints within which HR and other managers are working. In the final main section of the chapter we therefore turn to areas in which managers are able to exercise more discretion.

Flexibility in historical perspective

Although we can trace the history of job or work design back to 1776 and Adam Smith's enunciation in *The Wealth of Nations* of the benefits of a highly developed division of labour, it is only really since the end of the nineteenth century that these and other ideas have been applied systematically in organisations. According to Buchanan's (1994a) account, we can divide this more recent history roughly into three main phases:

- the period up to around 1950, which was dominated by the ideas of scientific management
- the period from the middle of the twentieth century to around 1980, which, in reaction against scientific management, saw a concern with designing jobs with workers' motivation and satisfaction in mind
- the period since the late 1970s/early 1980s, in which we have seen the emergence of what Buchanan describes as team-based 'high performance work systems' (1994a: 85).

Although it is in the last of these three periods that flexibility takes on a central role, we need first to say something about the historical background against which it developed (for a fuller account, see Buchanan 1994a; Parker and Wall, 1998).

(a) Scientific management

The first of Buchanan's three periods centres on the development and influence of the ideas of Frederick Taylor (1856–1917; see Taylor, 1911). Taylor's concern was to eliminate what he saw as systematic inefficiencies in the manner in which work was organised and managed. Doing this, he claimed, would be to the benefit of both workers and employers. Under Taylor's ideas of scientific management, work was to be fragmented into its most basic components, each of which would be undertaken in a manner deemed to be the most efficient. Just as important was the idea that work should be the exclusive responsibility of managers: there was thus a separation between those who did the work – the workers – and those who determined how it should be done – the managers.

The extent to which these ideas were used, and the nature of their impact on people's work and lives, are issues which have generated a great deal of research and discussion. Much of this has centred around Harry Braverman's (1974) 'deskilling thesis', which was based on Marxist ideas of the 'labour process'. In this account, Taylor's ideas had proved to be overwhelmingly the dominant force in the organisation and control of work since the beginning of the twentieth century. The fragmentation of work and the removal of worker responsibility for its organisation had thus led to it being progressively deskilled or degraded.

Subsequent research has sought to modify Braverman's basic thesis. Littler (1982), for example, showed how scientific management or Taylorism developed in different ways in different countries. More pertinent for our purposes is Friedman's (1977) distinction between 'direct control' and 'responsible autonomy'. His argument was that management interests would not in all cases be best served by the 'direct control' of the workforce which scientific management involved. Where workers were skilled and work was more complex, it might be better to acknowledge and exploit this through pursuit of a more trust-based strategy of 'responsible autonomy'.

(b) Away from scientific management

New developments in thinking on how work should be organised were in any case already well established by the mid-1970s. Problems associated with the simplified and repetitive nature of work under scientific management had from an early stage led to such measures as job rotation – the movement of workers between tasks – and job enlargement – the creation of jobs combining larger numbers of tasks (Parker and Wall, 1998). From the 1950s onwards more fundamental concerns began to be addressed, as the design of jobs began more systematically to take into account the motivation and satisfaction of employees (Parker and Wall, 1998). Thus Herzberg's (1966) two-factor theory of worker motivation led to the idea that jobs should be not merely rotated or enlarged but 'enriched' by the provision of scope for personal achievement and development; while Hackman and Oldham's (1976) job characteristics model provided for the design of jobs on the basis of such principles as skill variety, task identity and task significance.

Also influential was the sociotechnical systems approach. Of key importance here was the work of the London-based Tavistock Institute, whose principles, based on the idea of the 'joint optimisation' of the social and technical subsystems in organisations, gave rise to their proposing the development of autonomous working groups of employees (AWGs). Trist and Bamforth's (1951) study of the post-war British coal-mining industry showed how automation had brought with it the introduction of a version of scientific management, the 'longwall' method, which displaced the autonomous multiskilled groups which had operated under the old 'hand-got' system. Later work (Trist *et al.*, 1963) revealed the development of a compromise 'composite shortwall' method, based on multiskilled, self-selecting groups, responsible on one shift for the whole of the coal-getting cycle. Sociotechnical ideas were picked up in several countries, most notably in Scandinavia (Benders and Van Hootegem, 1999). It is here that we find the most celebrated and most controversial example of the use of AWGs: the Kalmar and Uddevalla plants of the automotive manufacturer, Volvo (Berggren, 1993).

The flexible firm

(a) The flexible firm model

In the period since the early 1980s, UK debates on the flexibility of work and organisation have centred on the model of the flexible firm. Put forward by John Atkinson and others (Atkinson, 1984; Atkinson and Meager, 1986; NEDO, 1986), it claimed that firms were increasingly seeking and achieving greater flexibility from their workforce. This flexibility was of two main kinds:

- **numerical** – 'This is concerned with enhancing firms' ability to adjust the level of labour inputs to meet fluctuations in output' (NEDO, 1986: 3–4). It thus covers such practices as the employment of part-time, temporary or contract workers.

■ **functional** – '[This] consists of a firm's ability to adjust and deploy the skills of its employees to match the tasks required by its changing workload, production methods and/or technology' (NEDO, 1986: 4). It is thus concerned with the ease with which employees can move or be moved between tasks or jobs.

As part of these developments, it was argued, the workforce was being divided into two basic groups. Represented diagrammatically in Figure 8.1, the two groups are:

■ **core workers** – members of this group would be expected to display functional flexibility in return for security of employment
■ **peripheral workers** – members of this group would be expected to provide the firm with the numerical flexibility it required. This group would in fact be made up of a number of subgroups – part-time workers, contract workers, and so on – each of which would exhibit a particular type of numerical flexibility.

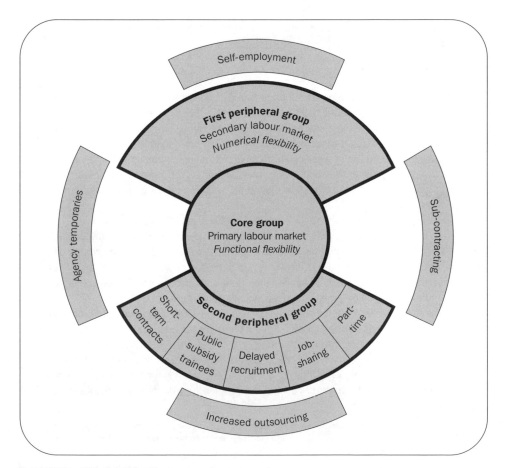

Figure 8.1 The flexible firm

Source: Atkinson, 1984

(b) Debate over the flexible firm

Since the model of the flexible firm was first developed in the mid-1980s, it has been at the centre of an extensive and often heated debate. There certainly was enough evidence to offer the model at least *prima facie* support. With regard to numerical flexibility, besides the NEDO (1986) study itself, the work of Hakim (1990), Casey (1991), Marginson (1991) and Penn (1992) all contributed to establishing its continued importance. Evidence for functional flexibility was less easy to gather from survey data, but what evidence there was supported the idea that it was on the increase (Daniel, 1987; Cross, 1988). There were also a large number of case studies of individual industries and companies. Although this work tended to be concentrated in a small number of sectors (Elger, 1991), and although too the nature of this form of flexibility was not so easy to pin down, here again moves towards a greater degree of functional flexibility were in evidence. An example of the form functional flexibility might take is provided in Box 8.1.

BOX 8.1

Functional flexibility

In his book, *Managing Innovation and Change* (1995), Jon Clark looks at Pirelli's creation and operation of a cable manufacturing plant in Aberdare, South Wales over the period 1984–92. Work within the plant was divided into 'skill modules', each of which set out the skills and knowledge required to perform an activity. It was envisaged that each worker would acquire between six and ten of these modules, each attracting a supplement of 4 per cent on basic pay. Workers were divided into three main groups – producers, maintainers and administrators – and it was expected that they would acquire at least one module from outside their own area.

Responsibility for developing and awarding the modules passed eventually to line managers, but the inconsistencies this generated became a serious source of dissatisfaction amongst employees. Wide disparities became evident between the three main groups of workers, and, eventually, separate settlements had to be arrived at with each of them. For producers, this involved 'capping' or limiting the number of modules employees could acquire and allocating them 'primary' and 'secondary' work areas.

Thus the 'full flexibility' of employees which Pirelli had aspired to was not achieved. Clark (1995: 153) sets out six reasons for this. Among them are the advantages of specialisation and the realisation that skills may not be retained by employees if they are not used regularly. In fact, the 'full flexibility' of employees was considered unnecessary. As Clark expresses it, Pirelli 'achieved what they set out to achieve, namely full flexibility to do what they wanted. In practice, however, to do what they wanted they did not need full flexibility' (1995: 153).

Source: Clark, J. (1995) *Managing Innovation and Change: People, Technology and Strategy*, London: Sage. Another useful source of information on flexible working arrangements are the publications of Incomes Data Services. See, for example: 'Multi-skilling', *IDS Study* 558, 1994.

What critics of the flexible firm took issue with was the idea that the different forms of flexibility were part of a concerted or 'strategic' move on the part of employers. Wood and Smith (1989), for example, found that only around 11 per cent of a large sample of companies saw themselves as following a 'core–periphery' strategy with regard to the employment of labour. As Procter *et al.* (1994) demonstrated, however, such findings were based on a rather restricted view of what constituted a strategy – one which saw it as an explicit decision, made at the top of an organisation and then communicated to and implemented by managers at lower levels. More recent conceptions would see strategy as a 'pattern' rather a 'plan', and would thus take account of its 'emergent' as well as its 'deliberate' aspects (see, for example, Mintzberg, 1978). As Hyman (1987: 39) argued, while firms' attempts to accommodate fluctuations in demand might have led to the opening up of divisions in the workforce, 'this does not entail that such divisions were designed, let alone the primary motive'. Looked at in this way, the flexible firm could still appear to provide a useful framework within which changes in employment and work organization could be analysed.

(c) Beyond the flexible firm

As the debate moved towards the end of the century, the different categories of numerical flexibility continued to grow. The fourth Workplace Employee Relations Survey (WERS4) showed part-timers to account for 25 per cent of all UK employment in the workplaces they surveyed in 1998 (Cully *et al.*, 1999: 32), a figure supported by the household-based Labour Force Survey (LFS) (Emmott and Hutchinson, 1998: 232). On the other hand, the *growth rate* in part-time employment had never matched the levels achieved in the 1960s and 1970s, and a large part of the growth could be accounted for by changes in the sectoral composition of the economy (Emmott and Hutchinson, 1998: 232–3). The use of temporary workers, however, did increase markedly in the 1990s, as employers moved out of the recession of the early part of the decade. Although the LFS showed temporary workers to account for only around 7 per cent of the workforce by 1996, what was more significant was the growth in the use of fixed-term contracts and the fact that temporary jobs accounted for almost one-third of all engagements since 1984 (Emmott and Hutchinson, 1998: 234). To back this up, the 1998 WERS showed fixed-term contracts being used in 44 per cent of workplaces and temporary agency workers in 28 per cent (Cully *et al.*, 1999: 35).

Although increases could be discerned in functional flexibility as well, it was less easy to associate each of the two forms of flexibility with a particular group of employees. In other words, there was little evidence that the workforce was being divided between a core of highly trained multi-skilled workers and a less-skilled, dispensable periphery. This is illustrated most clearly by the findings of WERS4. These showed that for each occupation, the proportion of workplaces using fixed-term contracts was greater when this was the largest occupational group: 'It appears,' Cully *et al.* (1999: 38) conclude, 'that the use of the non-standard forms

of labour is more closely related to employment *within* the core than outside it'
(emphasis in original).

In any case, the idea of a functionally flexible 'core' worker taking the form of a
polyvalent super-craftsperson has proved to be a wildly optimistic one. As O'Reilly
(1992: 370) argued, there is a distinction between a functional flexibility 'accompanied by an increase in training and upgrading' and a functional flexibility 'used in
an *ad hoc* manner to meet shortages and intensify work'. While we might disagree
with the idea that the latter was 'non-strategic', this contrast between the positive
and the negative interpretations of functional flexibility is an important one.

What the evidence suggests is that in the UK, functional flexibility is better represented by the negative interpretation. Two bodies of evidence support this claim.
The first of these centres on the idea that this form of flexibility represents simply
the breaking down of demarcations between different crafts or between production and maintenance work (Daniel, 1987), and that, in many cases, this
breakdown is of a marginal nature (Cross, 1988). This is to be taken together with
more indirect evidence on training and skill. On training, Gospel (1995), for
example, has pointed to the continued decline in traditional ways of training and
recruiting skilled workers, and Keep and Rainbird (1995) note that between 1970
and 1990 the number of apprenticeships fell by around three-quarters. What evidence there is of new forms of training suggests the widespread use of cut-down,
on-the-job, company-based skill appraisal and training schemes (Poole and
Jenkins, 1997).

On the nature of skill, we have the evidence of the Social Change and Economic
Life Initiative (SCELI). Gallie's (1991) account of its findings shows that, at first
sight, they support the idea of an up-skilled workforce: in all but the lowest occupational classification (non-skilled manual workers) a majority of respondents
reported an increase in skill over the five-year period of the study, and in all classi-
fications the proportion of respondents reporting an increase was very much
greater than the proportion reporting a decrease. Interpretation of this data, however, very much turns on what we define as skill. As Gallie points out, those
inclined to see a movement in the direction of up-skilling argue that rather than
being seen simply in a 'craft' sense, of which the key indicator is the amount of
task-specific training required, account needs to be taken of such things as general
educational level and the ability to exercise responsibility. The correspondence in
SCELI between respondents' answers on skill and their answers on levels of
responsibility suggests that it is more this latter definition that they had in mind.

What we have is a picture in which, in so far as they ever existed, the boundaries between 'core' and 'peripheral' workers are being broken down and all
workers are being made subject to a greatly heightened insecurity. It is in this context that Legge (1998) points to how a 'degraded' employment relationship can be
masked by the language of flexibility. She offers up instead 'two cheers' for the
security and predictability offered by the employment relationship characteristic of
more traditional, bureaucratic organisations. This theme is explored in greater
depth by Sennett (1998). In his view, the change in the nature of work means that

it can now be said that, 'The qualities of good work are not the qualities of good character' (1998: 21). The impact on individuals and society as a whole can be profound: in the words of the title of Sennett's book, flexibility is associated with 'the corrosion of character'. Something of this can be seen in Box 8.2, which describes what flexibility can involve for those in an already vulnerable position.

BOX 8.2

The abuse of flexibility

A report by the National Association of Citizens Advice Bureaux, *Flexibility Abused* (1997), shows how flexibility can too often take the form of 'worker insecurity'. Using evidence drawn from Citizens Advice Bureaux (CAB) throughout the country, the report identifies two broad categories of abusive action by employers: their introduction of contractual arrangements which severely disadvantage workers, and their withdrawal entirely from the responsibilities of the employment relationship. The former may take the form of variable hours contracts, fixed-term and casual employment, or the replacement of full-time by part-time work; withdrawal from the employment relationship might involve the imposition of 'self-employed' status on employees, the taking on of agency workers, and the use of 'contracting out'. The two broad categories are illustrated by the following cases, which are drawn directly from the report (pp. 12–13 and 36).

> A CAB in Oxfordshire reported two typical clients. The first was looking for full-time work but had only been able to obtain a zero hours contract collecting and delivering cars for a car rental company. He had to ring every day to find out what work was available. His weekly earnings averaged £70 but some weeks he earned nothing. The second client worked as a chef. His written particulars stated his normal hours as 39 per week, but went on to say that 'your total hours of work and time of work may vary in accordance with the needs of the business'. The client came to the bureau because his hours had been cut drastically, to the extent that he had only been given one day's work in the last week, and the equivalent of two days per week over a full month.

> A CAB in Dorset reported a client who had worked for a company as a skilled manual worker for several years. He had no written contract, but he had always worked regular hours for regular pay – so, although he paid his own tax and National Insurance, his pattern of work appeared to qualify him as an employee. He had now been presented with a contract which stated that he was an independent contractor; he was not guaranteed work at any time; he was not entitled to sick pay; and was not entitled to take any holiday. The employer was pressurising the client, and about ten colleagues, to sign the contracts, implying that there would be no further work if they did not do so.

Source: NACAB (National Association of Citizens Advice Bureaux) (1997) *Flexibility Abused: a CAB Evidence Report on Employment Conditions in the Labour Market*, London: NACAB.

Labour-centred and technology-centred flexibility

(a) Technology-centred Flexibility

But how can we conceptualise all this? The original model of the flexible firm, although perhaps somewhat unjustly maligned, does seem to have little purchase on these developments in flexibility, training and skill. To understand them better, we have first to take a step backwards and look at another aspect or version of flexibility — the flexibility attained or aspired to through the development of production technologies. A distillation of the large amount of work that has been undertaken in this area (see, for example, Slack, 1983, 1987, 1990) reveals that this type of flexibility takes two main forms: flexibility in volume and flexibility in product. Of these, the former is the more straightforward, referring to the ability of a production system to deal with fluctuations in demand. Product flexibility, on the other hand, can be broken down into four main types. These concern a production system's ability to

- produce a certain mix of products
- change the mix of a certain set of products
- deal with changes in the design of existing products
- deal with new products.

While this body of literature – drawn chiefly from the area of operations or production management – is of great interest in a number of ways, our concern here is its various attempts both to establish the relationship between different types of flexibility and to see where these fit with an organisation's objectives more broadly defined. In fact, accounts of technology-centred flexibility have almost nothing to say about its relationship with the flexibility of labour. For the most part, labour flexibility is ignored completely; where it is referred to, it assumes a position of subsidiary importance. This applies even to the most systematic analyses, such as Gerwin's (1987) attempt to take into account both the social and technological factors in production system design.

(b) Technology-centred flexibility in the UK

If we extend our analysis from the conceptual to the empirical, we see that UK firms have not, on the whole, pursued a strategy of technology-centred flexibility. An examination of the adoption and operation of advanced manufacturing technology (AMT) shows that, even in its more primitive forms, it remains rare in British industry and, where it is used, it appears unable to achieve the level of flexibility expected of it. This can be seen by an examination of four major types of AMT:

- **numerically controlled (NC) and computer numerically controlled (CNC) machine tools** – Tidd (1991) shows that the proportion of machine tools of this pre-programmed form was half in the UK what was in Japan, and that no improvement in flexibility was evident

- **robotics** – Tidd (1991) paints a similar picture here: proportionate to the number of employees, the use of robotics was ten times greater in Japan than in the UK. Their use in the UK, moreover, was often confined to the performance of a single task
- **flexible manufacturing systems (FMS)** – Rush and Bessant (1992) estimate that there were no more than 100 of these systems in the UK by 1990; while Jones (1988) reports on the difficulties firms have had in using them to achieve greater flexibility
- **computer-integrated manufacturing (CIM)** – even the potential component parts of CIM, such as computer-aided design (CAD), are difficult to detect (Edquist and Jacobsson, 1988); while McLoughlin (1990) demonstrates the difficulties firms have encountered in the use of CAD.

(c) Explaining the failures of technology-centred flexibility

This catalogue of failure has not, of course, gone unnoticed. Attempts at explanation have focused on the 'barriers' or 'obstacles' to successful adoption – the implication being that if only these impediments could be overcome, the situation would resolve itself satisfactorily. The barriers or obstacles can be considered under three headings:

- **trade union or workforce resistance** – although a long-running theme in writings on British organisations (Nichols, 1986), more recent evidence suggests that workers tend to welcome technical change for its association with progress and success (Daniel and Hogarth, 1990; Hogarth, 1993).
- **the technological hardware itself** – this might refer to the technical limitations of such things as FMS (Tidd, 1991) or to the initial design of systems (Jones, 1989).
- **management failures** – at worst, the lack of success with technology-centred flexibility is put down to simple managerial incompetence (Burnes, 1988); though a more sophisticated version of this argument is that AMT may require more flexible organisational structures (Fjermestad and Chakrabarti, 1993; Lei and Goldhar, 1991).

All this leaves a very dismal impression. Even if we accept that worker resistance plays little part, we still have a picture of widespread managerial incompetence in both technical and organisational matters. At worst, this is no more than a truism: if managers were more competent they would manage better. Even with more sympathetic interpretation, it does not cut very deep: if the only barrier in the way of achieving success is the provision of managerial and technical training, why have firms not undertaken it?

In order to understand this we need to go beyond the level of the individual organisation and instead focus on the institutional constraints within which it operates and makes decisions. Of key importance in this regard is industry's relationship with finance. Hutton (1995) has provided a clear account of this, placing emphasis on the financial system's need for liquidity, and showing how this is reflected in its lack of commitment to industry. He sets out in detail how the operation of the banking system leaves industry dependent on expensive short-term funding; whilst reliance on the stock market forces it into the actions necessary to satisfy shareholders and fend off the threat of takeover.

This impacts on investment in flexible production technologies in a number of ways. The most basic argument is that conventional means of investment appraisal are inadequate for dealing with such technologies because they have no way of taking into account their 'strategic' nature (Boer, 1994). Thus the broader benefits of such systems are ignored because it is impossible to value them precisely (Pike *et al.*, 1989). In any case, if this kind of investment does take place, it is likely that the technologies will be misused in order to make them financially viable. Thus, rather than being used for low-volume, high-variety manufacture, FMS, say, are pressurised by utilisation targets into producing on a mass standardised basis. Jones (1989: 116), for example, points to the 'pronounced Fordist bias' of the objectives of British management, and shows that it was in these terms, rather than in terms of flexibility, that the advantages of FMS are sought. The pressures under which flexible production technologies can come in even the most propitious circumstances are illustrated in Box 8.3.

BOX 8.3

Flexibility through technology

The story of the Pirelli cable manufacturing plant (see Box 8.1) begins with the 1984 decision to establish an experimental plant whose level of automation would provide an example to the rest of the company of how low-cost competition from firms in newly emerging nations could be countered. Jon Clark's book, *Managing Innovation and Change* (1995), documents how, although the experimental plant was accepted by Pirelli, the vision was eventually sacrificed to more short-term considerations.

A small project team was charged with investigating the concept of computer-integrated manufacturing (CIM) and with preparing a case for the investment needed to put the idea into practice. Although it was largely in technical and strategic terms that the project had been envisaged, the team also contained a member whose task it was to provide the detailed costings. An initial consideration of the team's work generated concerns about the project's cost and payback period. Other, financially more acceptable, courses of action were thus also considered, but the idea of the new high-tech factory was accepted in principle in 1985. Final authorisation of the necessary investment came only after the financial case had been revised so as to incorporate an increase in the assumed rate of capacity utilisation.

Installation of the computer-controlled plant operation management system (POMS) began in 1987. The plant's software requirements soon proved to be more complex than the system anticipated, however, and further problems were caused by modifications undertaken to certain machines. With financial and production pressure mounting, an internal troubleshooter was called in in 1989. He proposed the reinforcement of the managerial hierarchy within the plant, and this, combined with the much more direct involvement of the parent company, marks the beginning of what Clark calls 'the retreat from full automation'. With the recognition that greater human intervention in the process was necessary, the objectives of POMS were scaled down. Under pressure from senior management outside the plant, the vision of CIM was sacrificed, and a more traditional 'production orientation' reasserted itself.

Source: Clark, J. (1995) *Managing Innovation and Change: People, Technology and Strategy*, London: Sage.

(d) Technology-centred and labour-centred flexibility

Our purpose here is not simply to provide an explanation of British firms' inability to introduce and operate flexible production technologies. Indeed, our primary concern is to explain why flexibility has taken on a labour-centred rather than this technology-centred form. The two issues are inextricably linked, since it is the same conditions that both discourage the latter and encourage the former. In Hutton's (1995) account, for example, the terms on which finance is offered have direct implications for the way in which labour is managed. Standards of employment need to be undemanding, he argues, 'because without that flexibility [British companies] are much more likely to get into financial difficulty than their competitors whose debt structure is more longterm' (1995: 150). Though long-standing in nature, this emphasis on labour-centred flexibility can be said to have increased as short-term pressures on firms have intensified over the last 20 or so years. At the same time, forces which might have militated against these pressures have been weakened. The analysis presented here is certainly in line with those such as Nolan (1989), who maintains that increased productivity growth needs to be seen against the shift in the balance of power in industrial relations in favour of employers. The effect this had has to encourage the intensification of labour rather than the deployment of multiskilled workers and advanced production techniques.

As we have seen, there has been little consideration of the link between labour-centred and technology-centred flexibility. To the extent that there has, the general presumption seems to be that the two go together. In Piore and Sabel's (1984) 'flexible specialisation', for example, flexible production technologies are associated with a highly skilled flexible workforce. The analysis presented in the present chapter, however, suggests that the two forms of flexibility should be regarded not as complementary but as substitutes for each other. The question of how we can represent this is the subject of our next section.

The new flexible firm

(a) Flexibility through technology and labour

As the previous section showed, there is very little evidence to suggest that flexibility in British industry is based on technologically sophisticated, flexible production systems. What appears to be emerging instead is a system of cell- or group-based production, in which, rather than on functional lines, production is organised so as to bring together in one place the people and equipment needed to produce a certain range of goods or services. Particularly in manufacturing industry, cellular working has quite quickly become widespread. In 1990 the Ingersoll Engineers (1990) consultancy's survey of engineering companies with turnovers in excess of £10 million found what they described as a 'quiet revolution': 51 per cent of their sample had introduced some form of cellular manufacturing, most of them in the previous few years. By 1993, they found that the proportion had increased to 73 per cent (Ingersoll Engineers, 1994).

Cellular production will often be introduced on the initiative of production managers and for what seem largely technical reasons. A major advantage of organising production in this way is that it cuts down the time part-made products spend 'travelling' around the organisation from function to function (Hill, 1991). Nonetheless, the implications from a human resource management point of view are likely to be profound. For one thing, the operation of cellular production will both encourage and be encouraged by the kind of flexibility in labour we explored in the previous sections. The introduction of a product 'focus' to the organisation of work will militate against too strong a reliance on functional specialisation, especially if, as has happened in a number of cases, the reorganisation of production is accompanied by a reduction in workforce numbers, thus effectively forcing functional flexibility onto those remaining (Turnbull, 1988). This relationship between cellular production and flexibility is shown in Box 8.4.

BOX 8.4

Flexibility through cellular production

Cellular manufacturing was central to the programme of change introduced by Engineering Industries, a large UK-based manufacturing group, which, in common with many other manufacturing organisations, attempted to restructure itself in the aftermath of the recession of the early 1980s. Each business unit in the group had to submit its own Business Action Plan, which laid down business targets on the basis of the unit's leading international competitor. As part of this, each unit's products were to be divided into 'families'. These were translated, first, into broad categories known as 'modules', and then, within each module, into more tightly defined cells. Each cell, typically employing between 15 and 20 people, was to be given responsibility for its own scheduling, planning, quality control, set-up activities and maintenance diagnostics. The aim was that each cell would include members of a new breed of 'super-craftsmen', proficient in various skills and able to work in a highly flexible manner.

The introduction and operation of cellular production in two of Engineering Industries' business units were examined by Stephen Procter and his colleagues (Procter *et al.*, 1995). In the first, Company A, cellular production demanded changes in working practices which some were unwilling to adopt. Some who saw themselves as, for example, millers or turners, were unwilling to perform other operations. With the removal of support staff, moreover, operators had to begin sweeping up around their own machines – something which caused great resentment. Flexibility was not absolute. One cell leader estimated that only 50 per cent of his cell had the level of ability necessary to perform the full range of tasks that flexible working demanded. The less able 50 per cent were thus restricted to a narrow range of relatively simple jobs.

A similar situation arose in Company B. Within each cell there were to be only two grades of worker – craftsmen and operators. This system was a major change for craftsmen who were used to specific job titles and numerous skill gradings. Under the cellular system, craftsmen, in addition to the specialist tasks, were required to do maintenance, inspection, cleaning, and to move work around – all work which demarcation agreements had previously ruled out. What was achieved was not complete flexibility but a degree sufficient for the new system to work satisfactorily.

Source: Procter, S., Hassard, J. and Rowlinson, M. (1995) 'Introducing cellular manufacturing: Operations, human resources and high-trust dynamics', *Human Resource Management Journal*, 5(2): 46–64.

A second major factor is the association of cellular production with teamworking. In the case of cellular production, what is important from a human resource management perspective is that when equipment is brought together, so too are the workers who operate it. As Benders and Van Hootegem (1999) argue, cellular production has been important in reintroducing the idea of semi-autonomous work teams into the UK, where, as we have seen, they were first identified. Certainly, the use of teamworking has extended beyond certain narrow areas of production. A survey of manufacturing companies undertaken by the Institute of Work Psychology found team-based working being used to some extent by 70 per cent of their respondents (Waterson *et al.*, 1997); and this was backed up by the 1998 WERS, which, on its broadest definition, found 65 per cent of all workplaces reporting that most of those employed worked in formally designated teams (Cully *et al.*, 1999: 38).

What characterises this current wave of interest in teamworking is its strategic nature. Thus, rather than being concerned with improving the quality of working life for employees, teamworking – and work design more generally – has come to be seen as crucial to the questions of how organisations deal with their customers and competitors (Buchanan, 1994b). As Buchanan (1994a: 86) expresses it, 'It has … become increasingly unrealistic to distinguish between work design on the one hand and organizational design on the other. The former now typically implies the latter.' Perhaps the most important aspect of this is that the team becomes the basic organisational unit. We have, in Jenkins' (1994: 851) words, 'organizations *built around* – and not just including – autonomous teams' (emphasis in original). The implications of this for flexibility are taken up in Box 8.5, but the more general point is that, as well as technology and labour, our account of flexibility needs to consider broader issues of organisation and management.

(b) Flexibility through management and organisation

How, then, is flexibility managed and organised? The short answer is that this takes the form not of direct control based on high levels of surveillance – a line of argument to which we return below – but of indirect control based on the allocation of costs. From the second Company-level Industrial Relations Survey (CLIRS), carried out in 1992, we get some idea of how large British firms use a range of budgetary controls in managing the relationship between the corporate centre and the operating or business units (Armstrong *et al.*, 1996). Perhaps most important for our purposes is the relationship Armstrong *et al.* establish between the extent of labour flexibility and the use of budgetary controls based on labour cost. Companies using these measures at business unit level were found to employ more part-time and female workers than those which did not. Using the original flexible firm model, Armstrong *et al.* argue that because of the relative ease with which it is possible to change the numbers or tasks of these 'flexible' workers, labour cost budgets were more likely to be used. 'The implication', they claim, 'is that these labour cost ratios are used to impose numerical and/or temporal flexibility on the workforces of large UK companies' (Armstrong *et al.*, 1996: 19).

BOX 8.5

Teamworking and flexibility

At first sight we might expect teamworking to be associated with a greater degree of specialisation amongst employees. The popular view of a team in such areas as medicine and sport is of a group that brings together individuals with complementary skills. The form of teamworking that has been introduced in many organisations in recent years is thus in some ways counterintuitive, for what we see amongst team members is a tendency towards flexibility (see Procter and Mueller, 2000).

Paul Edwards and Martyn Wright studied the operation of teamworking in Alcan's aluminium smelter in Lynemouth, Northumberland. One objective of their study was to see whether a 'continuous process' production technology was one that was suitable for teamworking. They observed what they described as a relatively advanced form of teamworking, 'which involved the eventual elimination of supervisors and the delegation of responsibility to teams, which were organized by team leaders who remained essentially part of the work group' (1998: 274–5).

Edwards and Wright found that the workforce responded to teamworking in a broadly positive way. A survey of workers revealed greater interest in the job, more scope to take decisions, and better relations with other workers. Workers, said Edwards and Wright (1998: 278), were not more skilled in the sense of having new technical abilities. What workers did report was an increase in the number of tasks they performed, and this was backed up by a more systematic approach to training. Although teamworking appeared on the whole to be working well at Lynemouth, a number of remaining tensions could be identified. Among these was that the work group were not ready to take on all new tasks. Production workers on the night shift, for example, would not take samples of metal for testing, something which was normally the job of a technician. As Edwards and Wright (1998: 280) express it, 'There were thus limits to flexibility.'

Source: Edwards, P. and Wright, M. (1998) 'HRM and commitment: a case study of teamworking', in Sparrow, P. and Marchington, M. (eds) *Human Resource Management: the New Agenda*, London: Financial Times/Pitman, 272–84.

But how do these corporate-level strategies translate into workplace-level decisions? Here, although the evidence is less systematic, a pattern can tentatively be identified. The survey data of Armstrong *et al.* (1996) shows a definite association between the use of labour cost targets and the declaration of redundancies in operating units which fail to meet them. Other evidence is provided by Hunter *et al.* (1993), whose analysis of the flexible firm concluded that there was no tendency on the part of employers to effect horizontal segmentation by levels of skill. What we have instead is a vertical segmentation on the basis of the team or a group of teams. For each of these product-focused segments a calculation of costs and benefits can be made, and this allows firms to make decisions about discrete areas of activities. In other words, a form of numerical flexibility is achieved by taking on and dispensing with sections not of a peripheral workforce but of the workforce as a whole.

We can combine all these elements – labour, technology, management, organisation – into a model of the 'new flexible firm' (Ackroyd and Procter, 1998). The main features of the model are summarised in Box 8.6. This is represented in diagrammatic form in Figure 8.2, which should be compared directly with the original flexible firm model portrayed in Figure 8.1. In the terms of the original flexible firm, the core of the new flexible firm is of almost negligible proportions; the distinction between core and periphery has disappeared; and flexibility is achieved through the manipulation of product-focused segments of activity.

BOX 8.6

The new flexible firm: summary of features

■ Production is organised through the arrangement of machines and workers as cells capable of producing 'families' of components or products.

■ Advanced manufacturing technology is little used, except as additions to existing configurations of equipment.

■ Employed labour contributes to flexibility as teams of semi-skilled workers performing a range of specific tasks and given on-the-job training.

■ Employees do not enjoy privileged status or high employment security, but compete with subcontracted labour and alternative suppliers.

■ Production operations are considered as dispensable separate 'segments', about which calculations of cost are regularly made.

■ Management takes the form of intensified indirect control based on the allocation of costs.

Japanisation and the high-surveillance firm

Although the flexible firm model has been the focus of debate in the UK, and although the 'new flexible firm' appears to offer a better way of conceptualising the changes that have been taking place, we also need to look at other attempts to describe and explain the restructuring of work and organisation. One very popular idea is that British organisations have been restructuring themselves along the lines of their Japanese counterparts – a process known as Japanisation, perhaps the best known exponents of which are Oliver and Wilkinson (1992). Two main forms of Japanisation can be identified: direct and mediated (Ackroyd *et al.*, 1988); we shall look at each of them in turn.

(a) Direct Japanisation

Direct Japanisation refers to direct investment by Japanese companies in British industry. Although it is possible to identify certain high-profile cases such as

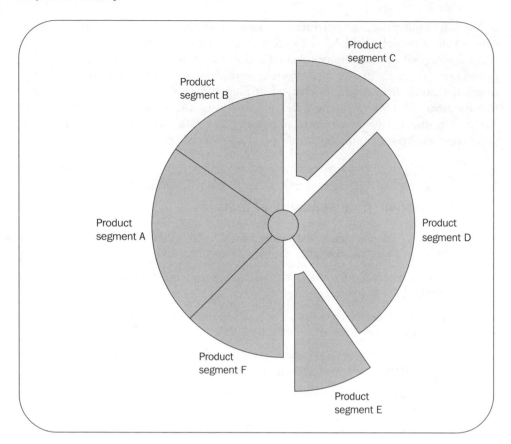

Figure 8.2 The new flexible firm.

Nissan, Toyota and Honda, the Japanese-owned sector remains very small. Even by the mid-1990s, the number of people employed in Japanese manufacturing plants in the UK was only 70,000, a figure that represented just 9 per cent of the total employed in the foreign-owned manufacturing sector (Munday and Peel, 1998). Moreover, there is little evidence to suggest that Japanese-owned plants offer an example to their British counterparts in terms of efficiency or effectiveness in management and organization (Munday and Peel, 1998). Little is known about how capital is allocated by the Japanese parent company and about what returns are expected from its foreign operations.

(b) Mediated or indirect Japanisation

In contrast to direct Japanisation, the mediated or indirect form refers to the adoption of Japanese-style policies and practices by indigenous UK companies. Surveys conducted at the end of the 1980s and the beginning of the 1990s did suggest that certain techniques were being picked up and used by British companies (Oliver and Wilkinson, 1992). This data, however, carried with it a number of problems. The first was that it was never clear what was 'Japanese' in this context. Thus cellular production, for example, could be included as part of the Japanese model, even though its origins and adoption could be explained in quite different terms. Second, the way in which the surveys were conducted was itself a cause for concern (Procter, 1995).

Most fundamentally, the idea of mediated Japanisation focused attention on how the conditions in which British companies were operating made anything but the superficial adoption of Japanese methods very unlikely. Their effective adoption implies a high level of investment, the willingness and capacity to reconfigure technology on a continuous basis and a commitment to high levels of training and employee involvement. As we have seen, the institutional conditions in which British companies operate are very different. In these circumstances they are likely to be very selective about which aspects of the Japanese model to adopt, taking only those that were cheap to implement and which would meet their immediate needs; or they would be even more pragmatic than this, making cosmetic use of Japanese ideas in order to introduce changes they would have made in any case (Ackroyd *et al.*, 1988; Procter and Ackroyd, 1998).

(c) The high-surveillance firm

What the focus on Japanese investment and Japanese practice has given rise to is a model of organisation that we can call the high-surveillance firm. In this model, emphasis is put on the ability of specific procedures and techniques to secure increased quality and variety of production (Delbridge *et al.*, 1992; Sewell and Wilkinson, 1992). Control is exerted over individuals and groups by constantly monitoring, measuring and reporting their performance. This is achieved in part through the discipline imposed by such techniques as just-in-time production (JIT) and total quality management (TQM), but supplementing these are more recent developments which make use of the ability of IT-based systems to record and provide information on work performance. At the extreme, such systems are held to exercise an absolute control over employees, thus representing the modern-day application of the idea of the 'panopticon', the principles underlying which had previously applied to the design of prisons (Sewell and Wilkinson, 1992).

These ideas are powerful ones and have exerted a considerable influence on debates surrounding work and technology. They have been developed most recently in attempts to describe and understand the operation of telephone call centres. These have been portrayed as the apotheosis of panoptical control, the success of which is achieved ultimately by its 'internalisation' by workers as a result of its ubiquitous nature (Fernie and Metcalf, 1997). There are, however, a number of reasons to cast doubt on such conclusions. Quite apart from the institutional conditions which we have already referred to on a number of occasions, there must still be doubts about the willingness and ability of British managers to condense, interpret and make use of the vast amount of information such systems can generate. Perhaps more importantly, the idea of absolute control disregards the notion of worker resistance, the different forms such resistance can take, and the effects it can have (Thompson and Ackroyd, 1995; Taylor and Bain, 1999). This is illustrated in Box 8.7.

BOX 8.7

Flexibility, surveillance and resistance

Phil Taylor and Peter Bain's study of work in Scottish call centres set out to test the idea that the centres allowed management to exercise absolute control over employees. Their description of work in call centres is worth quoting in full (Taylor and Bain, 1999: 115):

> The typical call centre operator is young, female and works in a large open plan office or fabricated building, which may well justify the white-collar factory description. Although probably full-time, she is increasingly likely to be a part-time permanent employee, working complex shift patterns which correspond to peaks of customer demand. Promotion prospects and career advancement are limited so that the attraction of better pay and conditions in another call centre may prove irresistible. In all probability, work consists of an uninterrupted and endless sequence of similar conversations with customers she never meets. She has to concentrate hard on what is being said, jump from page to page on a screen, making sure that the details entered are accurate and that she has said the right things in a pleasant manner. The conversation ends and as she tidies up the loose ends there is another voice in her headset. The pressure is intense because she knows her work is being measured, her speech monitored, and it often leaves her mentally, physically and emotionally exhausted.

As Taylor and Bain make clear, however, all this does not mean that work in call centres is best understood as the application of a modern form of panoptical control. As well as being able to exert collective resistance through their membership of trade unions, workers have open to them a number of less formal, more individual courses of action. They find ways of removing themselves from waiting queues of calls, for example, or can merely pretend to be involved in making a call. Management, say Taylor and Bain, 'would certainly be surprised to discover that they exercise total control over the workforce' (1999: 115). What the enhanced means of surveillance offers management is not a solution but a dilemma: while it cannot be abandoned altogether, 'intense surveillance can be counterproductive, costly in terms of workforce motivation and commitment' (1999: 116).

Source: Taylor, P. and Bain, P. (1999) '"An assembly line in the head": Work and employee relations in the call centre', *Industrial Relations Journal*, 30(2): 101–17. For a fictional account of work in a call centre see Matt Thorne's novel, *Eight Minutes Idle* (Sceptre, 1999).

Although the ideas underlying the idea of the high-surveillance firm deserve to be treated with respect, they offer little insight into the way British organisations are restructuring work and technology in order to achieve an enhanced flexibility of operation. A summary of this and our other two models of flexibility is presented in Table 8.1. As we have argued, the original model of the flexible firm is useful to the extent that it focuses attention on labour as the main route through which flexibility is achieved; less useful is its neglect of technology and its division of the workforce into core and peripheral elements. The 'new flexible firm' attempts to overcome some of these deficiencies. Although still focusing on the role of labour, this is combined with a low-technology, product-based organisational restructuring and an indirect, cost-based form of control. The high-surveillance firm shares some of this concern with technique and organisation, but stresses also the ability of high-technology IT systems to effect direct control over the workforce.

Table 8.1 Dimensions of the three models: original flexible firm, high-surveillance firm, and new flexible firm

	Labour	Technology in use	Sources of flexibility	Management	Network	Problems/sector
Original flexible firm (OFF)	*Requirements:* High-skill and low-skill groups *Policy:* Segmentation	Little or nothing specified	Labour	*Objective:* Rapid changes in direction and scale of production *Strategy:* Labour segmentation	Little or nothing specified; independent producer	Does it exist anywhere?
High-surveillance firm (HSF)	*Requirements:* Semi-skilled *Policy:* Progressive training	Medium to high investment in productive technology	Mix of technical and labour flexibility	*Objective:* Medium to large batch production *Strategy:* High quality/low price	Japanese parent	Electronics and automotives
New flexible firm (NFF)	*Requirements:* Mostly unskilled/ semi-skilled *Policy:* Limited on-the-job training	Low to medium technology; cell-working	Labour and selection of product markets	*Objective:* Medium batches of related products for specific niches *Strategy:* Short term profit	Specialist provider to supply chains	General manufacturing

Human resource management and human resource managers

(a) Managing HRM strategically

Our approach so far has been a rather structural one. In other words, rather than the options open to HR and other managers in the area of flexibility, we have stressed how the constraints within which managers operate are more likely to give rise to certain courses of action than to others. While in the next section we want to shift the focus towards the discretion which managers can exercise in this area, we have first to explain and contextualise our overall approach.

The approach we have taken here is very much in line with that of Storey and Sisson (1993). As they demonstrate, although the new models of HRM – especially in their insistence on its strategic importance – appeared to open up tremendous possibilities, few organisations could be said to have fully realised their potential. The question of why this ideal should be so difficult to attain carried with it a more specific question: 'What are the factors which limit its attainment in the British context?' (1993: 73). As well as factors that relate to particular technologies and industries, Storey and Sisson identify what they call 'the more generic impediments' (1993: 75). The first of these is the 'short-termism' which limits managerial performance horizons and encourages expedient solutions. This, in turn, is related to the way in which, in Goold and Campbell's (1987) terms, multi-divisional structures are used to effect a system of financial control rather than one of strategic planning. As we have seen throughout this chapter, it is these underlying conditions that encourage the adoption of particular forms of flexibility.

(b) The role and standing of the personnel profession

It is perhaps worth stressing one other aspect of the constraining structures within which decisions about flexibility are made. Reflecting and reinforcing the short-term, finance-driven mode of operation is the relationship between different professional groups. In many British organisations it is accountants who form the dominant group. Following Armstrong (1987a, 1987b, 1989), we can say that this results from their ability to capture the strategic functions of organisations. In the conditions we have described, it is accounting logic that has defined organisational performance and, therefore, it is accounting-based policies that provide the basis for organisational decisions. In terms of the introduction and management of technology, for example, accountants are able to dominate the logic of engineers (Jones *et al.*, 1994).

For the personnel or HR profession this is all part of a long-running debate about its own role and standing. The origins of the personnel profession and its inability to exercise power in organisations have long been a matter of concern (Legge, 1995). Thus even in areas like technological change, the success of which has been shown to depend on the manner of implementation and the way in which organisational and human resource issues are dealt with, the personnel role is very much a subsidiary one (Clark, 1993a).

The rise of HRM appeared to bring with it the opportunity to change this situation. Although the pessimistic interpretation was that the integration of HR issues into wider issues of business strategy would lead to HR managers losing what little specialist expertise and power they possessed, even this could be portrayed as the giving up of the more prosaic parts of personnel work in return for, in Storey's (1992) terms, the opportunity to act at the apex of the organisation as a 'strategic change-maker'. More recently, we have seen the work of Ulrich (1997) emerge as the focus for debate. His line is that 'HR professionals' can – and should – take on multiple roles: they must be concerned with both strategic and operational matters and with both people and processes.

How this works out in practice is less clear. Within the constraints we have outlined, there is still scope for personnel managers to develop their own role and enhance their influence. Recent work by one of the present authors supports Ulrich's argument that this is best done through a consideration of the multiple roles the personnel function can perform (Procter and Currie, 1999). What this work also shows is that two other things need to be taken into account: first, how these multiple roles relate to specific issues that personnel managers face within organisations, and, second, how these roles emerge from the process of interaction with other organisational actors. It is in this context that we can best understand the management of flexibility and the role of the personnel function within it. This is a theme explored in Box 8.8 and in Case Study 8.1 attached to this chapter.

BOX 8.8

Managing flexibility

Among the issues raised by the case study attached to this chapter is the role played in flexibility initiatives by human resource or personnel managers (Procter and Currie, this volume). Flexibility in this case takes the form of the introduction of new, harmonised terms and conditions for two groups of staff – nurses and Operational Department Practitioners or Assistants – working in operating theatres in a large acute hospital. The two groups of staff had worked closely together – and in some tasks were interchangeable – but their different terms and conditions posed immense problems for the management of the operating theatres.

For the hospital's human resources (HR) department, the so-called Theatres Project represented a pilot project for a system of local pay that they had intended – and still hoped – would apply to the hospital as a whole. They were involved in each stage of the process of implementation: the drawing up of the new pay scales; the calculation of the offers that were made to individual members of staff; the putting of the new terms and conditions to the operating theatre staff through a series of mass meetings; and the negotiation of agreements with individuals.

The Theatres Project thus involved the HR department in a variety of roles, some of which brought them into conflict with the operating theatres' management. It was felt, for example, that in negotiating deals with certain individuals, the HR department was concerned more with the financial implications for the hospital as a whole than with the day-to-day needs of the operating theatres. On the other hand, the presence of an HR adviser at the individual interviews was welcomed as providing an objective observer. The case thus illustrates both the range of functions personnel managers can be expected to take on and how these functions depend on their relationships with other organisational actors (see also Procter and Currie, 1999).

Source: Procter, S. and Currie, G. (2001) 'Managing flexibility: the Theatres Project in Midland City Hospital Trust' (this volume)

Managing flexibility

(a) Negotiating flexibility

Although in some eyes the objective and effect of the shift in the industrial relations balance of power over the past 20 or so years was to allow the reassertion of
the 'managerial prerogative', there is little evidence to support the cruder versions
of the idea that 'macho management' has emerged as dominant (Legge, 1988).
Certainly, we have seen no improvement in areas where traditionally there has
been little legal or collective protection of employee interests, but, in other areas,
settlements on such things as workforce flexibility have been the result of agreement rather than unilateral imposition. Marsden and Thompson (1990), for
example, found that although the number of formal working practice agreements
was fairly small, more significant were the associated changes in working methods, which were settled largely informally. Dunn and Wright (1994) also provided
evidence to suggest that working practices were being negotiated through existing
provisions. In certain sectors at least, therefore, there remains open to personnel
managers a traditional role in industrial relations negotiations.

(b) Implementing flexibility

In many cases, just as important as the content of work reorganisation is the
process by which it is introduced. Using Fox's (1974) terminology, we can say that
if flexibility is assumed to take on the characteristics of a 'high discretion syndrome' – trust, encouragement and participation – then its introduction, not just its
operation, requires the use of high trust management. As Geary (1994) argues,
management in British organisations find it all too easy to adopt a strategy based
on 'the availability of a cheap and dispensable workforce', one which is 'most likely
to induce a low trust relationship' (1994: 656). Procter *et al.*'s (1995) study of the
introduction of flexible team-based working in two parts of a large engineering
concern shows how its failure in one of these was associated with a closed and
uncommunicative style of management. While there is no necessary connection
between success and the manner of introduction, the chances of successfully operating a work system based on a high discretion syndrome will certainly not be
reduced by a process based on the same assumptions. Studies of change episodes
have tended to focus on technical change, but they do suggest that personnel managers' involvement is often peripheral and, at best, a belated response to foreseeable
organisational problems (Legge, 1993). Although this is itself explicable in terms of
the constraints we have already identified, this process of introduction is one part
of the management of flexibility in which personnel might take on a greater role.

(c) Paying for flexibility

Paying for flexibility can be considered under two headings: the pay settlement
associated with the introduction of flexible working arrangements; and the

payments system under which they operate. On the first of these, Ingram (1991) looked at the extent to which changes in working practices were linked to pay settlements. Of a panel of 160 groups, 80 per cent of those with collective bargaining had experienced such change in working arrangements at some time over the period 1979–90. What this showed, he argued, was that change was more effective if linked to pay.

As for payment systems, those which might be thought to be most consistent with the development of flexibility have not proved to be the most popular and successful. If anything, the trend in payment systems has been towards the adoption of performance-related pay based on individual appraisal (Kessler, 1994). While in itself this does not run contrary to the idea of flexible working arrangements, an explicitly skills-based system would appear to offer more positive encouragement. Such systems have proved difficult to operate. Mueller and Purcell's (1992) study of the European automotive engine industry found that it was in this area of work restructuring that firms had made the least progress. Likewise, to the extent that flexibility is associated with teamworking, team-based systems of pay have been found to encounter severe problems. Ezzamel and Willmott's (1998) study of a UK-based clothing manufacturer shows clearly the conflicts and issues such systems can raise.

Conclusions

This chapter carries a mixed message for specialist HR managers and general managers with HR responsibilities. On the one hand, there exist severe constraints within which they have to operate. This means that with regard to flexibility – as with other issues – some courses of action are more likely to be taken than others. Thus, in their pursuit of flexibility, organisations are likely to place the emphasis on the flexibility of labour. The type of flexibility required of labour may be of a negative form: we are much less likely to see securely employed, highly trained, multiskilled workers than we are their insecure, semi-trained, multi-tasked counterparts. At the level of the individual manager or the individual organisation, there is little opportunity to change the conditions which bring this situation about. This is not to say, however, that there is nothing at all that can be done. We have highlighted in our final section a number of areas in which HR managers might intervene in order to steer change in a particular direction. HR managers might at least make an attempt to shift the emphasis of the employment relationship from areas in which the interests of employers conflict with the interests of employees, to areas in which the interests of the two coincide.

| Case study 8.1 |

Managing flexibility: the Theatres Project in Midland City Hospital NHS Trust

Stephen Procter and Graeme Currie

Organisational setting

The theatres directorate of Midland City Hospital NHS Trust

Our case study organisation, Midland City Hospital NHS Trust, is an acute NHS hospital based in a city in the English Midlands. It has an annual budget of over £100 million and employs around 5,000 staff. It is divided into 30–40 departments or 'directorates'.

Within the hospital, our main focus is the theatres directorate, which consists of a total of 15 operating theatres. In addition to the eight theatres in the main block, there are more specialist facilities in the areas of urology, maternity, day surgery and burns. Over 200 people were employed in the directorate at the time of the study. Its annual budget was over £6 million, of which around half was accounted for by pay. The mission statement of the theatres directorate described its role as follows:

> To provide a multi-disciplinary team using the holistic approach to care. To provide and maintain professional assistance in the anaesthetic, theatre and recovery areas within the resources available until patients are in a safe state prior to their return to intensive care or ward areas.

Head of the directorate was the clinical director, who had taken up the post partway through 1997, after 20 years in the NHS working as an anaesthetist. Two other key members of staff were the theatre manager and the speciality manager. The former, a senior nurse, had joined the hospital in the early 1970s, and her chief concern was staff management within the directorate. The speciality manager had been in the job eight years. His own role he described as 'really processes, money, ensuring things happen . . . I do lots of the linking with the rest of the hospital and linking with other directorates.'

The human resources department

The trust's human resources (HR) department has a total of around 20 staff. At its head is the director of human resources, who sits on the trust's board. Amongst those reporting to the director are the management development manager and the personnel manager, who also serves as deputy to the director. Reporting to the personnel manager are three personnel advisers, each of whom is responsible for a particular area of the trust. It is these personnel advisers who are the main point of day-to-day contact with the trust's managers and staff.

The trust's HR strategy for the period 1998–2003 was contained in a written document. The first of its 'key themes' was 'a competent and flexible workforce'. This and other key themes were each backed up by a series of more specific 'objectives'. In the case of flexible working, these included:

(a) To introduce new patterns of working appropriate to service needs, reducing overtime where necessary.
(b) To introduce local harmonised terms and conditions on a phased basis, linked with local need, robust costing procedures and affordability.
(c) To define roles through definitions based on competencies required to do the job. To review these competencies regularly and where appropriate, link progression within local pay scales to the acquisition of competencies.

(HR Strategy document)

Background to change

Local pay

From the point of view of the HR department, local pay was an issue of great importance. The original intention had been to address this situation on a trust-wide basis. When the idea began to be encouraged by the Conservative government from 1995/96 onwards, local pay meant the operation of an 'X+Y' formula, under which the national pay awards (X) could be supplemented according to local discretion (Y). According to the personnel manager, Midland City's experience of this notion of local pay had not been a favourable one. Although financial scope to make discretionary awards was severely limited, it was decided to push forward with a corporate project. In consultation with the main trade unions, and with HR driving the process, a trust-wide programme of job evaluation was undertaken. This was followed by HR working closely with the finance directorate in order to arrive at a detailed idea of how this would translate into pay.

This whole process then became subject to the uncertainties surrounding the general election of 1997. It was felt that it was best to wait until the new government's position became clear. It was at this stage that the Theatres Project emerged. 'From there [Theatres]', as the HR director expressed it, 'the managers were screaming.' 'So,' said the personnel manager, ' we developed what was a very corporate project into a Theatres project.'

Nurses and ODPs/ODAs

The problems faced by the theatres directorate arose from the co-existence of two groups of staff – nurses and Operational Department Practitioners or Assistants [ODPs/ODAs] – who worked very closely together and who, in some aspects of work, were interchangeable, but who were trained, paid, progressed, managed and organised quite separately from each other. The reason for this was that the nurses' role had been to assist the surgeons, and the ODPs' to assist the anaesthetist.

The two groups of staff each had their own management and organisation within the directorate:

> [the ODP manager] used to meet with his team and he used to deploy them, agree training needs with them and agree a roster; and then there used to be the G grades [nurses] that are basically team leaders . . . and each month they'd get together and decide what they were going to do.
>
> (Personnel adviser)

Not only were there two different duty rosters; terms and conditions for the two groups of staff were very different. This could give rise to some anomalous situations. In particular, the relative position of the ODPs meant that it was felt they should be given greater opportunity to work at overtime rates of pay: 'You had to pay them overtime to make their pay up to the normal level,' said the speciality manager:

> . . . to allow ODPs to get equivalent earnings, all the overtime was in their favour . . . their normal shift would stop at 5.15 and they were allowed to stay until 6 o'clock in the evening. So each night they were picking up three-quarters of an hour overtime . . . and when they came at the weekends it was all as additional overtime.
>
> (Personnel adviser)

It was not just that this in itself caused managerial and organisational problems. The differences were held to generate conflict between the nurses and the ODPs:

> . . . you could have somebody working alongside each other, let's say for a Bank Holiday, and getting two entirely different rates of pay, one walking out saying, 'Thank you very much,' and the other a little dissatisfied.
>
> (Theatre manager)

The theatres directorate began to take action by introducing a common work rota for nurses and ODPs at the beginning of 1997. Although this was seen as a move in the right direction, it did not address what were, from the management point of view, the more fundamental problems. With the situation a long-standing cause for concern, the prevarication over the organisation-wide local pay programme had led to demands from the theatres directorate that it be proceeded with at least in their area:

> A long time ago we wanted to do something about it, and we were told, 'Wait for local pay.' And we sat back and waited. There was a campus-wide group that looked at local pay, which then did not progress, but we said, 'Could we be the pilot for local pay, because we really need to sort it?'
>
> (Theatre manager)

It was against this background that 'harmonised' terms and conditions for nurses and ODPs eventually came into effect. The process by which these terms and conditions were worked out, agreed upon and introduced was known as the Theatres Project.

The Theatres Project

Objectives

The official position on objectives was stated in the 'Harmonisation' document, which set out the proposed new terms and conditions:

> For some considerable time the Theatres Directorate has been wanting to recognise the contribution made by all the staff working within the service but who are paid on a range of different scales and allowances and are on different terms and conditions.

The provision of a common pay scale and common terms and conditions would, it was claimed, have the following advantages:

- an increase in flexibility of relevant staff
- to enable a positive movement to equal pay for equal contribution to the service
- to encourage the development of knowledge and skills amongst theatre staff
- to ensure the most effective and efficient provision of cover at particular times during the week . . .   ('Harmonisation')

The project's concern for flexibility was made clear in interviews with the directorate's managers. In reference to the nurses and ODPs, the clinical director said, 'We wanted to get them multi-skilled for flexibility.' 'The purpose of doing it', said the speciality manager, 'was so that we could use the staff interchangeably . . . and so that we could make savings.'

Outcomes

The terms of the agreement eventually arrived at came into effect on 1 January 1998. The clinical director described its essence: 'We call everybody a theatre practitioner now; you're not a nurse, you're a theatre practitioner.' Its chief elements were:

- single pay spine for nurses and ODPs
- new seven-day single duty rota
- common 37.5-hour week
- pay enhancements for commitment to working 'non-core' hours
- managers encouraged to avoid use of overtime
- overtime rate of time-and-a-third
- competence-based system of progression

The new 'harmonised' grades can be seen in Table 8.2. Alongside each of the eight grades are the basic salary range it covers, and the number and type of staff within it. As the table shows, the majority of trained theatre staff are to be found on Grade 6. This covers the old nursing grades of D and E and the equivalent grades on the ODPs' pay scales.

What did these changes imply for the two groups of workers? The 37.5-hour week, although leaving the hours of nurses unchanged, meant an increase in hours for the ODPs. At the same time, unsocial hours pay was abolished, managers were encouraged to 'continue to develop operational processes and policies which

Table 8.2 The Theatres Project: new grades and their Whitley equivalents

Basic Salary	Grade	Points/ bars	Scale	Whitley equivalent	No. staff
27,297– 21,549	8	3/0	Operational manager		2
			Resources manager		1
			Pain control nurse		1
20,921– 15,567	7	11/1	Team leader	G Grade nurse	13
			Relief team leader	F Grade nurse	6
			Assistant co-ordinator		1
16,515– 12,289	6	11/2	Senior theatre practitioner	E Grade nurse/ MTO 2+3 ODP	58
			Theatre practitioner	D grade nurse/ MTO 2 ODP	45
13,428– 11,246	5	7/1			
12,289– 10,292	4	7/1			
10,918– 9,144	3	7/1			
9,992– 8,368	2	7/1	Theatre support worker	A Grade nurse	33
9,144– 6,606	1	12/1	Student ODP		7

Notes:
1. Basic salary excludes 5 per cent and 8 per cent enhancements.
2. Staff numbers based on full-time equivalents.
3. MTO = Medical Technical Officer.
4. Full grid would also include eight clerical staff (three on grade 2 and five on grade 3) and nine ancillary staff (eight on grade 2 and one on grade 3).

avoid using overtime', and the overtime rate was cut from the previous standard rate of time-and-a-half. As we saw above, it was the ODPs who had the most to lose in these respects as well. Against this, with core hours defined as between 6 am and 8 pm, seven days a week, staff with a contractual commitment to work regularly outside these hours received a flat 5 per cent enhancement of basic salary. Staff with a contractual commitment to work rotational shifts received an 8 per cent enhancement.

The competence-based system of progression was designed to replace a system in which progression had been based largely on time served. Under the new system, progression through a grade was to be done on the basis of 'performance/contribution/competency'. It was intended that this be fully in place by January 1999. For movement within Grade 6, for example, the general principles upon which the first bar could be crossed meant that the new theatre practitioners would have to 'demonstrate competency in both areas of work – anaesthesia and surgery – and willingness to work flexibly in both' and 'demonstrate level of specialist knowledge in "base" area.' ('Harmonisation')

Financial implications

The trust, said the personnel manager, was under great pressure to break-even financially: 'It's about the bottom line today; it's about this year's accounts and this year's income and expenditure.' In these circumstances it could be very difficult to make a case for this kind of flexibility agreement:

> If I said to you that by introducing harmonised terms and conditions in nursing, I believe that we could save hundreds of thousands of pounds over the next five or six years on recruitment, retention, induction, training, etc., it's hard to put that up and show you, and say, 'Well, if we reduce turnover from 20 per cent to 10 per cent, that's 10 per cent less vacancies and that equates to [£]10,000 a vacancy and that means it's this amount of money' – it may be, but it isn't real money this year.
>
> (Personnel manager)

This trust's director of finance had called for this kind of justification. According to the HR Director,

> It was a very pure bottom-line approach to, 'So, convince me of the benefits, HR', but the project was able to go forward on this basis: . . . we went to the trust board with that Theatres Project fully costed, and it was £30,000 best case, £60,000 worst case; 1 per cent of the pay budget of [£]3,000,000, and it went in.

Nonetheless, it was felt that a longer term, more strategic view should be taken:

> For me, the benefits of harmonised terms and conditions . . . are lost in the 'Let's look at the bottom line cost' issue, are lost to a certain extent in the wider strategic view of what are the long-term benefits of actually doing certain things within the organisation.
>
> (Personnel manager)

The change process

We thus have some idea of what flexibility looks like in this case and what its financial implications were. But how had all this come about? What, in other words, was the process of change? With the unified terms and conditions coming into effect on 1 January 1998, all new staff in the theatres directorate are now appointed on that basis. For the directorate and trust management, of course, the main problem was how existing staff could be moved across. The principle contained in the official documentation was that staff transferring would be dealt with as follows:

> [they] will assimilate to the next point above their current salary within the appropriate section of the new grade. Where this assimilation is less than the individual's current salary, a personal offer may be made.
>
> ('Harmonisation')

Perhaps most importantly, there was no attempt to impose the new terms and conditions on employees; it was to be done through a process of consultation and negotiation. 'We said,' said the theatre manager, '"You have a choice of remaining where you are or you take up the offer."'

Differences and issues

The Theatres Project had begun with the establishment of a working group. Consisting of representatives of the human resources department and both management and staff of the theatres directorate, compromises had to be made. In particular, there was the issue of the extent to which a scheme designed for the hospital as a whole should be modified so as to fit better the conditions in theatres. 'There were times', said one team leader involved in the consultation process, 'when HR had very different ideas to us.' The theatres directorate felt themselves to be unique.

> [Other directorates] don't have a similar situation, said the Clinical Director, they have wards that are staffed by nurses. They don't have two separate groups of people working side by side on different conditions . . . They [HR] kept saying it was for the whole hospital, and we said, 'Well, it won't work for us. We'll have to be an exception on that one, and anyway you're not using it for the whole hospital' . . . there was the feeling that they'd designed it for the whole hospital and they didn't want us to come in and change it all, so it then was useless for the rest of the hospital – but equally it wasn't any use to us in the state it was in . . .
>
> (Clinical director)

On this basis, for example, it was agreed that a permanent night-time staff, consisting of around ten people, should be retained.

Another issue was the harmonisation of night-time breaks. Under the existing terms and conditions, both groups of workers had one hour's break but, while ODPs were paid for theirs, nurses were not. The original proposal was that there would be an hour's break, half of which would be paid and half unpaid. The initial reaction from staff was that they would make themselves unavailable for the half-hour for which they were not being paid, but in the end agreement was reached:

> The unions were involved, and said, 'You're not going to get very far here, because you're not actually entitled to any lunch-break time in the middle of the night, it's just that it happens to have evolved like that. If I were you, I'd take the half an hour and shut up.' I think that's what happened in the end, and in the end I think that is the sort of messy compromise, that everybody gets half an hour break in the night paid for and half an hour not paid for.
>
> (Clinical director)

This and other issues and compromises brought home the fact that the starting point for the project was not a blank sheet of paper but formal and informal practices built up over a number of years:

> We are still left with some anomalies which will fade away in about ten years, with retirement. You cannot substantially alter someone's earning capacity overnight, so I suppose the word is assimilation.
>
> (Theatre manager)

Mass meetings and individual offers

Once something approaching agreement had been reached, in the autumn of 1997, the proposed changes were put into booklet form and submitted to the theatres staff as a whole. This was done in three stages, the first being a series of meetings – 16 in number, according to the speciality manager – which were open to all staff. The meetings continued until it was felt that demand for them had been satisfied:

> . . . we had big meetings, we had meetings at every time of day and night in small groups . . . You got down to as many as four people in a group or you had a room full of 20-odd . . . [The speciality manager] put out e-mails saying, 'Do you want to come any more?', and when we got the nil replies, we stopped.
>
> (Theatre manager)

The second stage was the drawing up of each individual's terms and conditions:

> We had to get everybody's earnings over the last couple of years and then make decisions and decide on what we were going to offer people and what they were capable of.
>
> (Theatre manager)

Because nobody was being forced to move on to the new terms and conditions, said the speciality manager, 'everybody was made an offer that actually was slightly better or considerably better for them'.

The trade-off between the costs involved and the desire to extend the new terms and conditions as far as possible was most acutely felt in the cases of a group of around 12 key staff who did not come out well from the original calculations. Not only did they have a great deal of experience, it was argued, but there was a danger of their influencing other members of staff against accepting the new terms and conditions:

> They were people that we had to make sure were well provided for, but they didn't fit into the pay scale, so there were major arguments over that. And in the end we brought in a once-and-only, accept-it-this-time, if-you-decide-not-to-come-over-onto-local-pay-now-you-won't-get-as-good-an-offer-again, and we made them an off-the-scale offer of . . . I can't remember the figure but it was more than [£]1,000 [more] than they would have been normally offered . . .
>
> (Clinical director)

In the third stage of this part of the project, the offers were discussed in individual interviews with all staff. 'We interviewed about 240 people at 20 minutes a time,' said the theatre manager. The interviews could be quite fraught:

> A lot of the hassles we saved ourselves in the one-to-one by the open meetings, but there were still some that wanted every 'i' dotted. And although we kept saying, 'This is a personal offer to you,' [they would say] 'Why has Joe Bloggs got . . . ?' – 'We're not here to discuss Joe Bloggs, we're here to discuss you.'
>
> (Theatre manager)

The role of the HR department

As the theatre manager recognised, the HR department had a vested interest in the success of the Theatres Project:

> It was the project for the hospital; they were concerned that we sold it to the staff, we got the take-up. Otherwise we would have ended up with egg on our face . . . And the fact was that as a directorate we wanted to do it, so it was their role to support us in getting it in, which they did.

We have already seen something of their role in the working group that thrashed out the terms and conditions that were to be put to theatres staff; their involvement, however, did not end there. The speciality manager described the part they played in the series of open meetings:

> . . . I tended to lead, but the human resources person was always there to answer any complex questions – which was rarely the case, but it's also quite good if you're leading it, to say, 'We also have here . . .', so that they could see that the local management wasn't doing something just that they'd thought of, but it was the whole hospital.

They were also fully involved in the drawing up of individuals' offers:

> . . . they [HR] also, for every individual member of theatre staff, which is well over 200, prepared – in conjunction with ourselves, people working in Theatres . . . – prepared individual offers for everybody, looking at their circumstances, how many years they'd worked there, what their incremental date was, etc.
>
> (Clinical director)

In sorting out a number of special deals, the clinical director felt that the HR department had been concerned with the financial rather than the operational implications:

> I got the feeling that they [HR] were coming from the organisation's point of view that the cost had to be kept down, whereas we were coming from the point of view that these people who we (a) rely on, and (b) work with . . . So there were two points to it: (1) we wanted to retain them so that Theatres didn't fall apart; and (2) they were people we worked with on a personal day-to-day basis, and we didn't want to see them done out of anything.

The HR department's input was carried into the individual interviews with staff. The theatre manager did most of the interviews on her own: 'But if there was a dodgy one I made sure I had a personnel adviser with me':

> People turned up with their pay slips. [The personnel adviser] sat there with his calculator and said, 'This is OK.' Some of the information we got from Finance was not easily interpretable and, yes, we did make some mistakes . . .
>
> (Theatre manager)

The presence of the personnel advisor could be welcomed by the staff:

> I think some of them appreciated Personnel being here . . . some of them wanted to know which would be the best advantage for them when they went on maternity leave – so, 'Over to you, [personnel adviser].'
>
> (Theatre manager)

The theatre manager also described how she could be protected by the HR department. She might be asked, for example, 'Is that the best deal if you have sickness?', to which her response was, 'I'm not allowed to advise you what to do. I can give you the options; you make up your own mind.' In these circumstances, said the theatre manager, the presence of the personnel adviser meant that, 'At least you had a witness to say that you had said that.' The speciality manager made similar observations about the individual interviews:

> . . . we always . . . had a human resources adviser with us, to see fair play, . . . to answer any questions; but also that a totally consistent approach was taken along these lines. Then we had all the changes, after all the interviews, and then Human Resources did all the contract issuing.

Overall, it was held by some that the HR input had been essential to the success of the project: 'We could not have done all that without a great deal of support from HR,' said the theatre manager. The clinical director expressed similar views:

> We relied heavily on them to compose the pay scales, obviously, and to offer us advice about what we could and couldn't do. They did put a lot of effort into the individual offer stage, so they played quite a big part in it. I think they also played a part of being an external body as well, rather than Theatres staff feeling that their pay depended on how [the theatre manager] viewed them . . .

Others were inclined to play down the role of the HR Department:

> I think if the HR department had just tried to introduce it themselves without negotiating with Theatres and without involving them, then it wouldn't have worked so well. It's very important for those people that are working within that environment to feel a part of it, to gain ownership of what's happening in their own workplace.
>
> (Team leader)

Evaluating the project

Take-up of new terms and conditions

As a first consideration, the project was judged to have been successful because of the proportion of theatres staff that had elected to take up the new terms and conditions. Although there were small differences between the figures given by different respondents, it seemed that over 70 per cent of existing staff had moved over. Typical was the personnel manager: '75 per cent of people have actually moved over, so that was a real success story'. A 100 per cent take-up had not been expected. According to the speciality manager:

> There are some that we never expected would [agree to the new terms and conditions]; the permanent night staff, you can't possibly offer them the sort of basic pay that they can get . . .

The clinical director made a similar point:

> I thought it was probably quite a reasonable deal for a lot of people. But there were years' worth of bitterness from being underpaid and under-graded that all came out at the same time. I think for the organization it was a success, and for most individuals it was.

New working arrangements

It was not just a case of how many staff had moved over; more important to the trust and directorate management was what the Theatres Project implied for the way in which work was organised. The creation of the new position of theatre practitioner was seen by some to have facilitated a great improvement. Under the new structure, the ODP manager had disappeared, and the teams of theatre practitioners were each responsible to a team leader, who in turn reported to the theatre manager. What the changes had allowed was the much more effective operation of these teams:

> Before the changes we would often have the right number of staff, but not the right mix of skills, so we had to cancel operations. Now it is a lot easier to fill gaps and we don't cancel lists as often because we can find someone either to scrub or to assist the anaesthetist, as staff do both on a regular basis. Throughput is smoother, there is more flexibility, we have better motivated teams and lower staff turnover.
>
> (Clinical director, quoted in professional journal)

This echoed the clinical director's earlier comments to us:

> [I]t has enabled us to be much more flexible with working, because you can ask people to do extra hours without worrying about what their conditions are. A team leader has a team of people and she can say who stays after six [o'clock]. Previously there were rules that the ODAs couldn't stay until after six o'clock or they had to stay until after six o'clock so many days a week to get their planned overtime.
>
> (Clinical director)

From the perspective of some of those working in the teams, the changes in working arrangements had been welcomed or at least accepted. According to a team leader:

> . . . teething problems seem to have sorted themselves out now, in that the rota certainly is running quite smoothly, and the staff seem to accept it; those who obviously signed over to local pay have accepted that.

In particular, it was felt that the distinction between the two main groups of staff was beginning to be broken down in practice:

> Certainly now we've got more nurses doing anaesthetics as well as the scrub side; and a lot more technicians working the scrub side. So, certainly, there's been a lot more of interchange between the roles . . . There was always, amongst some of the staff, this 'them and us' scenario. It's still there to a certain extent but not as much as it was before.
>
> (Team leader)

It was recognised that not all had welcomed the new arrangements and their implications. According to the clinical director, some of the senior nurses had regarded it as a 'levelling down' or regrading exercise designed simply to cut costs. This she had found 'a bit annoying', given what she saw as the efforts that had been made to get as good a deal as possible for all staff. Nonetheless, even the fact that some would gain more than others might be the source of resentment:

It wasn't a regrading exercise at all; it was changing people onto a different set of scales, and some people got a couple of thousand [pounds] a year out of it and some people got £30. Because it depended on what level they were previously, they had to move across to the one up. They didn't all move across . . . they moved to the next point on the scale. So obviously some people who were nowhere near that point did not get so much out of it. And that was where a lot of the bitterness came from.

(Clinical director)

Later interviews with staff – carried out in late 1999 – revealed that, for some, divides between staff were still important: 'I think there's a nurse/ODA divide in theatre … ,' said one theatre practitioner, 'I don't know why it is but when you first come in you notice it.' This seemed to be felt particularly strongly by the former nurses:

ODAs and nurses do exactly the same job now but with different training. And nurses are … I can't really explain it, but it's because we're no longer classed as nurses, morale has plummeted and that's the main thing.

(Theatre practitioner)

Competencies and progression

As we have already noted, the new, unified pay spine was to be supplemented by a competence-based system of progression. These competencies, developed for introduction at the beginning of 1999, were the responsibility of the management development manager. Interviewed towards the end of 1999, she pointed to the benefits this had brought:

Where staff previously said that they didn't want to do something that was not part of their role, now they say they need that experience to progress on the pay scale. This means we now have a pool of people who can do two or three jobs. With better rostering, this means we have greater efficiency, and that is providing a payback on the costs incurred for training.

(Management development manager, quoted in professional journal)

Opinions were divided amongst those working in the new system. Some welcomed it as providing clear and achievable targets:

It gives people direction to work in, and I think it is quite clear-cut what needs to be done to work your way up. Traditionally people have reached the top of the grade and they haven't done much for it, but with this scheme they really have got to work to achieve top of the grade.

(Theatre practitioner)

Others felt it had made little difference or might even be counterproductive:

You can get someone who's absolutely brilliant practically, you know, who could run rings round people practically . . . but can't get the qualifications. If they don't get them, they can't progress. You can get somebody who has just scraped through, who's wonderful with pen and paper, who will get up there. It's, as I say, too much reliance on some of the academic stuff.

(Theatre practitioner)

Beyond the Theatres Project

As well as management in theatres considering the project a success in terms of their ability to manage and deploy staff, the HR department were keen to exploit its wider implications. The personnel manager said that it was now planned to apply the principles of the project in other areas of the trust. Previously, he said, the corporate project had not been seen as capable of meeting operational needs. The difference now was that:

> it's started to be bottom-up-driven, whereas when we set out with the project it was very HR-top-driven. It's started to be bottom-up driven because they've seen the benefits of the Theatres Project.
>
> (Personnel manager)

The HR director felt that the appeal of the project was further strengthened by its *not* being the result of central government initiative. It could be justified as concerted, long-term strategy, something that should not be dispensed with on the basis of political whim. If anything, he maintained, the rest of the NHS would now be following them.

Note: Most of the research for this case study was carried out in 1998. The authors would also like to acknowledge two other sources of data: an article in a professional journal which was published in late 1999; and a small number of interviews with theatres staff carried out by Nottingham University MBA student, David Giddings, at around the same time. Where data is drawn from the former, this is noted in the case study, although the precise reference is not given in order to preserve the anonymity of the case study organisation.

Questions

1. From where did the Theatres Project emerge? What issues did it address? If you had been looking at the project at the time of its emergence, would you have said that it was likely to be a success?

2. How is flexibility understood by, respectively, the management of the theatres directorate, theatres directorate staff and the human resources department?

3. What does the harmonisation agreement imply for the terms and conditions of the two main groups of staff involved? Would you welcome the new terms and conditions if you were formerly (a) a nurse, and (b) an ODP?

4. How well was the process of change managed?

5. What were the main concerns of the HR department? What pressures and difficulties did they face? What role or roles did they take on?

6. On what criteria would you judge the Theatres Project? Would you say that it has been successful? Are there any lessons that might be learned by other NHS trusts and other organisations more generally?

Further reading

On the management of reform in the National Health Service and the public sector in general, see:

Ferlie, E., Ashburner, L., Fitzgerald, L. and Pettigrew A. (1996) *The New Public Management in Action*, Oxford: Oxford University Press.

On the role of the HR function, see:

Procter, S. and Currie, G. (1999) 'The role of the personnel function: Roles, perceptions and processes in an NHS trust', *International Journal of Human Resource Management*, 10(6): 1077–91.
Ulrich, D. (1997) *Human Resource Champions*, Boston, Mass: Harvard Business School Press.

References to Chapter 8

Ackroyd, S., Burrell, G., Hughes, M. and Whitaker, A. (1988) 'The Japanization of British industry?', *Industrial Relations Journal*, 19(1): 11–23.

Ackroyd, S. and Procter, S. (1998) 'British manufacturing organization and workplace industrial relations: Some attributes of the new flexible firm', *British Journal of Industrial Relations*, 36(2): 163–83.

Armstrong, P. (1987a) 'Engineers, managers and trust', *Work, Employment and Society*, 1(4): 421–40.

Armstrong, P. (1987b) 'The rise of accounting controls in British capitalist enterprises', *Accounting, Organizations and Society*, 12(5): 415–36.

Armstrong, P. (1989) 'Limits and possibilities for HRM in an age of management accountancy', in Storey, J. (ed) *New Perspectives on Human Resource Management*, London: Routledge, 154–66.

Armstrong, P., Marginson, P., Edwards, P. and Purcell, J. (1996) 'Budgetary control and the labour force: Findings from a survey of large British companies', *Management Accounting Research*, 7(1): 1–23.

Atkinson, J. (1984) 'Manpower strategies for flexible organizations', *Personnel Management*, August: 28–31.

Atkinson, J. and Meager, N. (1986) 'Is flexibility just a flash in the pan?', *Personnel Management*, September: 26–29.

Benders, J. and Van Hootegem, G. (1999) 'Teams and their context: Moving the team discussion beyond dichotomies', *Journal of Management Studies*, 36(5): 609–28.

Berggren, C. (1993) *The Volvo experience: Alternatives to lean production in the Swedish auto industry*, London: Macmillan.

Boer, H. (1994) 'Flexible manufacturing systems', in Storey, J. (ed) *New Wave Manufacturing Strategies*, London: Paul Chapman, 80–102.

Braverman, H. (1974) *Labor and Monopoly Capital: the Degradation of Work in the Twentieth Century*, New York: Monthly Review Press.

Buchanan, D. (1994a) 'Principles and practice in work design', in Sisson, K. (ed) *Personnel Management: a Comprehensive Guide to Theory and Practice in Britain*, 2nd edn, Oxford: Blackwell.

Buchanan, D. (1994b) 'Cellular manufacture and the role of teams', in Storey, J. (ed) *New Wave Manufacturing Strategies*, London: Paul Chapman.

Burnes, B. (1988) 'New technology and job design: the case of CNC', *New Technology, Work and Employment*, 3(2): 100–111.

Casey, B. (1991) 'Survey evidence on trends in "non-standard" employment' in Pollert, A. (ed) *Farewell to Flexibility?*, Oxford: Blackwell, 171–99.

Clark, J. (1993a) (ed) *Human Resource Management and Technical Change*, London: Sage.

Clark, J. (1993b) 'Personnel management, human resource management and technical change', in Clark, J. (ed) *Human Resource Management and Technical Change*, London: Sage, 1–19.

Clark, J. (1995) *Managing Innovation and Change: People, Technology and Strategy*, London: Sage.

Conti, R. and Warner, M. (1993) 'Taylorism, new technology and just-in-time systems in Japanese manufacturing', *New Technology, Work and Employment*, 8(1): 31–46.

Cross, M. (1988) 'Changes in working practices in UK manufacturing 1981–88', *Industrial Relations Review and Report*, 415: 2–10.

Cully, M., Woodland, S., O'Reilly, A. and Dix, G. (1999) *Britain at Work: as Depicted by the 1998 Workplace Employee Relations Survey*, London/New York: Routledge.

Daniel, W. (1987) *Workplace Industrial Relations and Technical Change*, London: Pinter.

Daniel, W. and Hogarth, T. (1990) 'Worker support for technical change', *New Technology, Work and Employment*, 5(2): 82–93.

Delbridge, R., Turnbull, P. and Wilkinson, B. (1992) 'Pushing back the frontiers: Management control and work intensification under JIT/TQM factory regimes', *New Technology, Work and Employment*, 7(2): 97–106.

Dunn, S. and Wright, M. (1994) 'Maintaining the status quo: an analysis of British collective agreements, 1979–1990', *British Journal of Industrial Relations*, 32: 23–46.

Edquist, C. and Jacobsson, S. (1988) *Flexible Automation: The Global Diffusion of New Technology in the Engineering Industry*, Oxford: Blackwell.

Edwards, P. and Wright, M. (1998) 'HRM and commitment: a case study of teamworking', in Sparrow, P. and Marchington, M. (eds) *Human Resource Management: the New Agenda*, London: Financial Times/Pitman.

Elger, T. (1991) 'Task flexibility and the intensification of labour in UK manufacturing in the 1980s', in Pollert, A. (ed.) *Farewell to Flexibility?*, Oxford: Blackwell, 46–66.

Emmott, M. and Hutchinson, S. (1998) 'Employment flexibility: Threat or promise?', in Sparrow, P. and Marchington, M. (eds) *Human Resource Management: the New Agenda*, London: Financial Times/Pitman, 229–44.

Ezzamel, M. and Willmott, H. (1998) 'Accounting for teamwork: a critical study of group-based systems of organizational control', *Administrative Science Quarterly*, 43: 358–96.

Fernie, S. and Metcalf, D. (1997) '(Not) hanging on the telephone: payment systems in the new sweatshops', London: Centre for Economic Performance, London School of Economics.

Fjermestad, J. and Chakrabarti, A. (1993) 'Survey of the computer-integrated manufacturing literature: a framework of strategy, implementation and innovation', *Technology Analysis and Strategic Management*, 5(3): 251–71.

Fox, A. (1974) *Beyond Contract: Work, Power and Trust Relations*, London: Faber & Faber.

Friedman, A. (1977) *Industry and Labour*, London: Macmillan.

Gallie, D (1991) 'Patterns of skill change: Upskilling, deskilling or the polarization of skills', *Work, Employment and Society*, 5(3): 319–51.

Geary, J. (1994) 'Task participation: Employees' participation enabled or constrained?', in Sisson, K. (ed) *Personnel Management: a Comprehensive Guide to Theory and Practice in Britain*, 2nd edn, Oxford: Blackwell.

Gerwin, D. (1987) 'An agenda for research on the flexibility of manufacturing processes', *International Journal of Operations and Production Management*, 7(1): 38–49.

Goold, M. and Campbell, A. (1987) *Strategies and Styles: the Role of the Centre in Managing Diversified Corporations*, Oxford: Blackwell.

Gospel, H. (1995) 'The decline in apprenticeship training in Britain', *Industrial Relations Journal*, 26: 32–44.

Hackman, J. and Oldham, G. (1976) 'Motivation through the design of work: Test of a theory', *Organizational Behaviour and Performance*, 16: 250–79.

Hakim, C. (1990) 'Core and periphery in employers' workplace strategies: Evidence from the 1987 ELUS survey', *Work, Employment and Society*, 4(2): 157–88.

Herzberg, F. (1966) *Work and the Nature of Man*, Cleveland, OH: World.

Hill, T. (1991) *Production/Operations Management*, 2nd edn, Hemel Hempstead: Prentice Hall.

Hogarth, T. (1993) 'Worker support for organizational and technical change: Workplace industrial relations in UK manufacturing – the case study evidence', *Work, Employment and Society*, 7(2): 189–212.

Hunter, L., McGregor, A., MacInnes, J. and Sproull, A. (1993) 'The "flexible firm": Strategy and segmentation', *British Journal of Industrial Relations*, 31(3): 383–407.

Hutton, W. (1995) *The State We're In*, London: Jonathan Cape.

Hyman, R. (1987) 'Strategy or structure? Capital, labour and control', *Work, Employment and Society*, 1(1): 25–55.

IDS (Incomes Data Services) (1994) 'Multi-skilling', *IDS Study*, 558.

Ingersoll Engineers (1990) *Competitive Manufacturing: the Quiet Revolution*, Rugby: Ingersoll Engineers.

Ingersoll Engineers (1994) *The Quiet Revolution Continues*, Rugby: Ingersoll Engineers.

Ingram, P. (1991) 'Changes in working practices in British manufacturing industry in the 1980s: a study of employee concessions made during wage negotiations', *British Journal of Industrial Relations*, 29: 1–13.

Jenkins, A. (1994) 'Teams: from "ideology" to analysis', *Organization Studies*, 15(6): 849–60.

Jones, B. (1988) 'Work and flexible automation in Britain: a review of developments and possibilities', *Work, Employment and Society*, 2(4): 451–86.

Jones, B. (1989) 'Flexible automation and factory politics: the United Kingdom in current perspective', in Hirst, P. and Zeitlin, J. (eds) *Reversing Industrial Decline?*, Oxford: Berg, 95–121.

Jones, B. (1991) 'Technological convergence and limits to managerial control: Flexible manufacturing systems in Britain, the USA and Japan', in Tolliday, S. and Zeitlin, J. (eds) *The Power to Manage?*, London: Routledge, 231–55.

Jones, O., Green, K. and Coombs, R. (1994) 'Technology management: Developing a critical perspective', *International Journal of Technology Management*, 9(2): 156–71.

Keep, E. and Rainbird, H. (1995) 'Training', in Edwards, P. (ed.) *Industrial Relations: Theory and Practice in Britain*, Oxford: Blackwell, 515–42.

Kessler, I. (1994) 'Performance Pay', in Sisson, K. (ed) *Personnel Management: a Comprehensive Guide to Theory and Practice in Britain*, 2nd edn, Oxford: Blackwell.

Lee, B. (1996) 'The justification and monitoring of advanced manufacturing technology: an empirical study of 21 installations of flexible manufacturing systems', *Management Accounting Research*, 7(1): 95–118.

Legge, K. (1988), 'Personnel management in recession and recovery: a comparative analysis of what the surveys say', *Personnel Review*, 17: 3–72.

Legge, K. (1993) 'The role of personnel specialists: Centrality or marginalisation?', in Clark, J. (ed) *Human Resource Management and Technical Change*, London: Sage, 20–42.

Legge, K. (1995) *Human Resource Management: Rhetorics and Realities*, London: Macmillan.

Legge, K. (1998) 'Flexibility: the Gift-wrapping on employment degradation?', in Sparrow, P. and Marchington, M. (eds) *Human Resource Management: the New Agenda*, London: Financial Times/Pitman, 286–95.

Lei, D. and Goldhar, J. (1991) 'Computer-integrated manufacturing (CIM): Redefining the manufacturing firm into a global service business', *International Journal of Operations and Production Management*, 11(10): 5–18.

Littler, C. (1982) *The Development of the Labour Process in Capitalist Societies*, London: Heinemann.

Marginson, P. (1991) 'Change and continuity in the employment structure of large companies', in Pollert, A. (ed) *Farewell to Flexibility?*, Oxford: Blackwell, 32–45.

Marsden, D. and Thompson, M. (1990) 'Flexibility agreements and their significance in the increase in productivity in British manufacturing since 1980', *Work, Employment and Society*, 4: 83–104.

McLoughlin, I. (1990) 'Management, work organization and CAD: Towards flexible automation?', *Work, Employment and Society*, 4(2): 217–37.

Mintzberg, H. (1978) 'Patterns in strategy formation', *Management Science*, 24(9): 934–948.

Mueller, F. and Purcell, J. (1992) 'The drive for higher productivity', *Personnel Management*, 25(2): 28–33.

Munday, M. and Peel, M. (1998) 'An analysis of the performance of Japanese, US and domestic manufacturing firms in the UK electronics/electrical sector', in Delbridge, R. and Lowe, J. (eds) *Manufacturing in Transition*, London: Routledge, 53–78.

NACAB (National Association of Citizens Advice Bureaux) (1997) *Flexibility Abused: a CAB Evidence Report on Employment Conditions in the Labour Market*, London: NACAB.

NEDO (National Economic Development Office) (1986) *Changing Working Patterns: How Companies Achieve Flexibility to Meet New Needs*, London: NEDO.

Nichols, T. (1986) *The British Worker Question: a New Look at Workers and Productivity in Manufacturing*, London: Routledge & Kegan Paul.

Nolan, P. (1989) 'The productivity miracle', in Green, F. (ed) *The Restructuring of the UK Economy*, London: Harvester Wheatsheaf, 101–21.

Oliver, N. and Wilkinson, B. (1992) *The Japanization of British Industry*, 2nd edn, Oxford: Blackwell.

O'Reilly, J. (1992) 'Where do you draw the line? Functional flexibility, training and skill in Britain and France', *Work, Employment and Society*, 6(3): 369–96.

Parker, S. and Wall, T. (1998) *Job and Work Design: Organizing Work to Promote Well-being and Effectiveness*, London: Sage.

Penn, R. (1992) 'Flexibility in Britain during the 1980s: Recent empirical evidence', in Gilbert, N., Burrows, R. and Pollert, A. (eds) *Fordism and Flexibility: Divisions and Change*, London: Macmillan, 66–86.

Pike, R., Sharp, J. and Price, D. (1989) 'AMT investment in the larger UK firm', *International Journal of Operations and Production Management*, 9(2): 13–26.

Piore, M. and Sabel, C. (1984) *The Second Industrial Divide: Possibilities for Prosperity*, New York: Basic Books.

Poole, M. and Jenkins, G. (1997) 'Developments in HRM in manufacturing in Modern Britain', *International Journal of Human Resource Management*, 8: 841–56.

Procter, S. (1995) 'The extent of just-in-time manufacturing in the UK: Evidence from aggregate economic data', *Integrated Manufacturing Systems*, 6(4): 16–25.

Procter, S. and Ackroyd, S. (1998) 'Against Japanization: Understanding the reorganization of British manufacturing', *Employee Relations*, 20(3): 237–47.

Procter, S. and Currie, G. (1999) 'The role of the personnel function: Roles, perceptions and processes in an NHS trust', *International Journal of Human Resource Management*, 10(6): 1076–90.

Procter, S., Hassard, J. and Rowlinson, M. (1995) 'Introducing cellular manufacturing: Operations, human resources and high-trust dynamics', *Human Resource Management Journal*, 5(2): 46–64.

Procter, S. and Mueller, F. (2000) 'Teamworking: Strategy, structure, systems and culture', in Procter, S. and Mueller, F. (eds) *Teamworking*, London: Macmillan, 3–24.

Procter, S., Rowlinson, M., McArdle, L., Hassard, J. and Forrester, P. (1994), 'Flexibility, politics and strategy: in defence of the model of the flexible firm', *Work, Employment and Society*, 8: 221–42.

Rush, H. and Bessant, J. (1992) 'Revolution in three-quarter time: Lessons from the diffusion of advanced manufacturing technologies', *Technology Analysis and Strategic Management*, 4(1): 3–19.

Sennett, R. (1998) *The Corrosion of Character*, London: Norton.

Sewell, G. and Wilkinson, B. (1992) 'Someone to watch over me: Surveillance, discipline and the just in time labour process', *Sociology*, 26(2): 271–89.

Slack, N. (1983) 'Flexibility as a manufacturing objective', in Voss, C. (ed) *Research in Production/Operations Management*, Aldershot: Gower, 101–19.

Slack, N. (1987) 'The flexibility of manufacturing systems', *International Journal of Operations and Production Management*, 7(4): 35–45.

Slack, N. (1990) 'Flexibility as managers see it', in Warner, M., Wobbe, W. and Brodner, P. (eds) *New Technology and Manufacturing Management: Strategic Choices for Flexible Production Systems*, Chichester: John Wiley, 33–48.

Storey, J. (1992) *Developments in the Management of Human Resources*, Oxford: Blackwell.

Storey, J. and Sisson, K. (1993) *Managing Human Resources and Industrial Relations*, Buckingham: Open University Press.

Taylor, F.W. (1911) *The Principles of Scientific Management*, New York: Harper.

Taylor, P. and Bain, P. (1999) '"An assembly line in the head": Work and employee relations in the call centre', *Industrial Relations Journal*, 30(2): 101–17.

Thompson, P. and Ackroyd, S. (1995) 'All quiet on the workplace front? A critique of recent trends in British industrial sociology', *Sociology*, 29(4): 615–33.

Tidd, J. (1991) *Flexible Manufacturing Technologies and International Competitiveness*, London: Pinter.

Trist, E. and Bamforth, K. (1951) 'Some social and psychological consequences of the longwall method of coal-getting', *Human Relations*, 4(1): 3–38.

Trist, E., Higgin, G., Murray, H. and Pollock, A. (1963) *Organizational Choice: Capabilities of Groups at the Coal Face under Changing Technologies: the Loss, Rediscovery and Transformation of a Work Tradition*, London: Tavistock.

Turnbull, P. (1988) 'The limits to "Japanization": Just-in-time, labour relations and the UK automotive industry', *Industrial Relations Journal*, 17(3): 193–206.

Ulrich, D. (1997) *Human Resource Champions*, Boston, Mass: Harvard Business School Press.

Waterson, P., Clegg, C., Bolden, R., Pepper, K., Warr, P. and Wall, T. (1997) *The Use and Effectiveness of Modern Manufacturing Practices in the United Kingdom*, Sheffield: Institute of Work Psychology.

Wood, D. and Smith, P. (1989) 'Employers' labour use strategies: First report of the 1987 survey', Department of Employment Research Paper No. 63, London: Department of Employment.

Chapter 9

Careers

Laurie Cohen

Father Tadeusz was sixty-two years old, tall and thin. He had spent a career in the priesthood in small parishes, despite a lifelong desire for an assignment in a city, with libraries and museums and theatres ... he thought of his career as a priest – as measured against his early ambitions – as a lackluster disappointment, if not an outright failure.

(from *In the Memory of the Forest*, Powers, 1997: 41)

When my children grow up I don't want them to have a job, I want them to have a career.

(Prime Minister Tony Blair on a visit to the Sheffield Job Centre, *The Sheffield Star*, 5 February 1998: 1. Cited in Mallon, 1998: 48)

Introduction

This chapter is about career: how we can understand the concept of career, and how we might go about managing our own careers and other people's. Academics have examined career in a whole range of ways: from psychological and sociological perspectives, as objective reality or subjective construction, from individual and organisational points of view. Similarly, in everyday language career has a number of different meanings and is used in a variety of contexts: the career of the footballer, the bureaucrat, the politician or the patient; career education, career breaks, career mentoring. If we were to analyse what career means in each of these cases, we would come up with a rich, diverse and probably ambiguous picture. In spite of this diversity, though, what many of these examples have in common is a relationship between an individual and an organisation. The nature of this relationship, and in particular the ways in which this relationship is managed so that both individual and organisational aims and aspirations can be realised, is a fundamental issue within HRM.

It has been suggested that, with today's emphasis on flexibility, flatter organisational structures and the increase in temporary and part-time work, careers are in a state of flux. The first section of this chapter examines this changing context and raises questions about the implications of these changes for people's thinking about career, and for career management. The second section focuses more explicitly on the concept of career, considering a number of academic and popular definitions and usages. It will examine the nature of the relationship between individuals and organisations suggested by these definitions, and evaluate their relevance to our current social and economic circumstances. Third, the chapter will explore the way in which academic thinking about career has developed, considering traditional psychological and sociological approaches, as well as interdisciplinary and interpretive perspectives. The next section focuses on careers and diversity. Mainstream career theory has been widely criticised for its failure to account for the diverse ways in which people construct their careers. In particular, feminist theorists have argued that such theory is based on the experiences and perceptions of men, and that it does not take into account the often different ways in which women think about and manage their careers. In addition, other scholars have suggested that within career theory there is an assumption that careers happen in large organisations, that it does not attempt to account for careers in small businesses, or self-employment. This section considers the different forms that careers take, and in particular, the suggestion that new capitalism is heralding new kinds of career. The final section in the chapter examines organisational interventions in career management, considering these in light of current debates about changing careers.

Changing organisations

Today the phrase 'flexible capitalism' describes a system which is more than a permutation on an old theme. The emphasis is on flexibility. Rigid forms of bureaucracy are under attack, as are the evils of blind routine. Workers are asked to behave nimbly, to be open to change at short notice, to take risks continually, to become ever less dependent on regulations and formal procedures. This emphasis on flexibility is changing the very meaning of work . . .

(Sennett, 1998: 9)

There is an emerging consensus that we are experiencing an irreversible change in the organisation of our working lives. Terms such as flexible capitalism, new capitalism, post-and neo-Fordism have all been used to describe a transformation from an economy based on huge bureaucracies and mass production to flexible arrangements which emphasise small product runs, high levels of skill and technological expertise, flexible specialisation and the production and dissemination of knowledge (Piore and Sabel, 1984; Sennett, 1998; Heckscher, 1995). The related processes of increasing globalisation and rapid technological change are frequently cited as reasons for this transformation, heralding in their wake an emphasis on the market: an orientation to customer needs and wishes, quality, innovation and competition (Arnold, 1997a). Doubts have been raised (Hutton, 1995; Heckscher, 1995) about the extent to which these phenomena can actually be held responsible. However, while this is in itself a fascinating debate, for our purposes what is perhaps more significant are the ways in which changes in the structures and cultures of our working environments are impacting on our perceptions and experience of career.

Arnold (1997a) cites a number of key changes which he sees as particularly relevant to individuals' understandings of career and career management, including macro-level changes in demography and the labour market, as well as at the level of the organisation. As regards the former, he highlights the significance of growing numbers of women in the labour force. Recent Labour Force Survey statistics reveal a 6 per cent increase in women's participation in the labour market between 1984 and 1999, during which time men's rates of participation decreased by 4 per cent (Office for National Statistics, 1999), a trend which is echoed in other European countries and North America. At the same time, our labour force is ageing, with increased economic activity of both women and men in the 50–64 age bracket forecast to increase until at least 2011 (Office for National Statistics, 2000). As the labour force becomes more diverse, the structures of opportunity afforded to people are changing significantly. For example, consistent with the growing representation of women is the increase in part-time and temporary work (Thair and Risdon, 1999). With more people involved in paid work, and changing structures of employment opportunities, it follows that individuals' and organisations' expectations of career and career development are also undergoing some transformation.

At the level of the organisation, widespread restructuring initiatives – downsizing and delayering – have had a significant impact on large numbers of people. For some this has meant redundancy, while for others such initiatives have resulted in significant increases in workloads and levels of responsibility. In addition to change programmes which seek to reduce costs have been those focusing on making more effective use of the remaining workforce. This has typically been attempted through decentralising and devolving responsibility, and through the replacement of conventional functional arrangements with the establishment of more flexible task-based teams – sometimes operating in direct competition with one another. For individuals these changes have meant working in a whole range of contexts, with different people, and have required the acquisition of new skills:

> . . . a worker has to bring to short-term tasks an instant ability to work well with a shifting cast of characters. That means the social skills people bring to work are *portable*, you listen well and help others, as you move from team to team, as the personnel of the team shifts – as though moving from window to window on a computer screen.
>
> (Sennett, 1998: 110)

At the same time, from a cultural dimension it has been argued that within organisations traditional paternalistic relationships between employers and employees are being eroded in favour of more contractually based arrangements (Heckscher, 1995: 6). Thus, cultures based on trust, loyalty, protection and security are being replaced by cultures of empowerment and short-term, legalistic relationships. Handy (1996) uses the metaphor of the shamrock to describe what he sees as an increasingly common organisational configuration: the three leaves represent core, contract and temporary employees. Core employees are central to the organisation, performing strategically important functions and thus helping to ensure its long-term creativity and viability. These employees experience the greatest job security – their arrangements most closely approximate to traditional employer/employee relationships. Conversely, contract employees work outside and alongside the organisation, performing functions which are seen as peripheral, and building up their own portfolios of clients and skills. The experiences of such workers will be discussed more fully in the section on emerging careers. Here, though, it suffices to say that while for some individuals contract work represents an opportunity to negotiate their own terms and conditions, to develop their careers in their own unique ways, for others it is experienced quite differently – as financially and emotionally precarious, resulting in a loss of job security and sense of belonging. Finally, temporary employees are taken on to perform specific, usually lower-skilled tasks as and when they are needed by the organisation. This group of workers is not a new phenomenon, but is particularly vulnerable to the vagaries of economic and social change.

Evidence of a new employment relationship based on a contingent workforce is mixed. On one hand, Templar and Cawsey argue that the 'so-called alternative work arrangements are not so alternative anymore – rather, they are becoming the new norm' (1999: 71). However, they insist that 'contingent workers' must not be considered a monolithic group; rather, they represent a diversity of employment arrangements. In contrast, other scholars maintain that the case for a radical transformation in people's experience of work is overstated. Thus Guest and Mackenzie Davey (1996) argue that a significant number of people have always worked in 'alternative' ways. The difference is that now middle-class people are being affected (Arnold, 1997a: 23) – and so the issue has become newsworthy.

It must not be assumed, though, that careers are necessarily enacted either within large organisations or alongside them. On the contrary, many people have always built their careers in small business contexts. That such contexts are often eclipsed in both academic and conventional definitions of career is an interesting point that will be considered in the discussion on diverse careers. However, in the last two decades, in the wake of the organisational restructuring initiatives discussed above and the celebration of the enterprise culture (Musson and Cohen, 1998), small businesses have been heralded as the cornerstones of economic activity and have gained prominence.

The causes and extent of change in today's world of work are still a subject of vigorous debate. Nevertheless, in contrast to the (mythical?) job for life, careers today are characterised by uncertainty and frequent change – of organisation, role, colleagues and required skills. It is a world of movement: 'the more gaps, detours, or intermediaries between people in a network, the easier it is for individuals to move around' (Sennett, 1998: 84). While for some individuals these 'gaps' and 'holes' represent opportunities for career advancement and development, for others they result in increasing insecurity and a loss of identity and affiliation.

Definitions of career: diverse understandings

The term 'career' conjures up an array of images. We might use it to refer to a life-time of service in a bureaucracy, or to a professional career like law or medicine. In contrast, we could talk about the much more temporary career of a footballer, or a professional athlete. In years gone by 'career girl' was used to differentiate a woman in paid employment from housewives and mothers. We could refer to a career in crime, or the career of a drug addict or of a patient. We could even talk about the career of an academic subject, for example, the career of organisational analysis (Mallon, 1998). In short, it is a term we use every day, unproblematically, in a whole variety of situations and contexts. But what do we actually mean by career? Is it just another way of talking about paid employment? Could any job be described as a career, or is the term exclusive to a particular type of position? And finally, what role, if any, does one's life outside of work play in the definition of career? An academic analysis of career and career management clearly requires some consideration of these questions. A traditional view of career is illustrated in Wilensky's (1961) classic definition:

> Let us define career in structural terms. A career is a succession of related jobs arranged in a hierarchy of prestige, through which persons move in an ordered, (more or less predictable) sequence.
>
> (Wilensky, 1961: 523)

A number of interesting points emerge here. First, implicit within this definition is the idea of career as paid work. The reference to 'hierarchy of prestige' suggests a bureaucratic context. Second, Wilensky describes career as a structural phenom-enon – that is, it seems to have its own existence independent of the individual. This view implies that careers are real things, prescriptions, available for people to take part in in a particular, set way. A more recent take on this perspective is intro-duced by Leach and Chakiris (1988):

> Careers flow from jobs . . . jobs need not lead anywhere, it is just something a person gets paid for. Careers, on the other hand, are continuous behavioural episodes, leading to a path or ladder that ends, optimally, in some sort of career capstone experience.
>
> (Leach and Chakiris, 1988: 50)

The notion of hierarchy, of *moving up* is emphasised in this definition. Also interesting here is the idea that one can reach the top of the career – that the career has an ultimate goal or destination. This notion of the career as a journey which leads somewhere definable is reiterated in the path metaphor, while upward movement is suggested by the familiar ladder image. Other popular metaphors for describing careers include tracks and arrows (and of course, the much more cynical rat race). As Mallon (1998: 48) suggests, such definitions 'reflect a widespread (although highly debatable) conjunction of career with advancement through an occupational hierarchy . . . [it is] based on employment within a vertically integrated organisation which actively manages career opportunities'. In addition, they are exclusive, applying *only* to those who participate in the sequence, and according most value to those who get to the top.

In contrast are those definitions of career which extend beyond the domain of paid employment, to the sequence of an individual's life experiences more generally. In the 1930s Chicago sociologist Hughes (1937) explained:

A career consists, objectively, of a series of statuses and clearly defined offices . . . subjectively, a career is the moving perspective in which the person sees his [sic] life as a whole and interprets the meaning of his various attributes, action, and the things that happen to him.

(Hughes, 1937: 413)

While acknowledging the structural, objective dimension of career, Hughes' definition also highlights the notion of the career as situated within the individual, thus emphasising its subjective dimension. Thus it is not the case that a person simply acts out a prescribed career pattern, instead, they construct their career in dynamic negotiation with their social/economic/cultural context. Hughes' work stimulated research into career in a whole variety of social situations: from funeral directors to tubercular patients and marijuana users. In a later generation Goffman further developed Hughes' notion of career, subverting conventional definitions which equated career with occupational advancement:

Traditionally the term career has been reserved for those who expect to enjoy rises laid out within a respectable profession. The term is coming to be used, however, in a broadened sense to refer to any social strand of any person's course through life. . . Such a career is not a thing that can be brilliant or disappointing; it can no more be a success than a failure. One value of the concept is its two-sidedness. One side is linked to the internal matters held dearly and closely, such as image of self and felt identity; the other side concerns official position, jural position and style of life and is part of a publicly accessible institutional complex. The concept of career, then, allows one to move back and forth between the personal and the public, between the self and its significant society.

(Goffman, 1961: 127)

What strikes me as particularly notable here is, first, the extension of the career concept way beyond the context of paid employment: indeed, much of Goffman's own work focused on the careers of institutionalised psychiatric patients. Second is his insistence that the notion is not value-laden – a career is neither good nor bad, it just *is*. Finally, Goffman, like Hughes, uses the notion of career to explore the relationship between objective and subjective dimensions of life, between the individual and her social world.

More recent definitions, put forward by academics writing in the fields of HRM and career guidance, echo this broader, more inclusive approach:

> accumulations of information and knowledge embodied in skills, expertise and relationship networks that are acquired through an evolving sequence of work experiences over time.
>
> (Bird, 1996: 150).

> the individual's development in learning and work throughout life.
>
> (Collin and Watts, 1996: 393)

While they contain subtle differences, central to both conceptualisations is an emphasis on work and non-work experience and the notion of career as moving and sequential – though not necessarily hierarchical. In addition, each can be used to explore both objective and subjective aspects of career, and their interrelationship.

Understanding career: theoretical perspectives

Traditional studies tended to approach career from the perspective of a single academic discipline – typically sociology or psychology: 'While psychologists say "people make careers", sociologists claim "careers make people" and the career literature shows a dearth of cross referencing between these two frames of reference' (Derr and Laurent, 1989: 454). Although these approaches have been criticised for being partial and fragmented, given their prominence within career theory, they are a really useful and important starting point.

Sociological approaches see the career as something which is organisationally based, planned, progressive and enacted by rational individuals (Inkson, 1995). This literature typically explores careers in terms of particular occupational paths, and as stages within organisations, and focuses on issues such as turnover patterns, organisational demographics and internal labour markets (Mallon, 1998). Such perspectives are based on the concept of the career as objective, external to the individual. 'Individuals are portrayed as if they join the organisation practically as lumps of clay, ready to be shaped by all those around them' (Bell and Staw, 1989: 232). This view, reminiscent of Wilenksy's definition above, emphasises social structures over individuals' ability to act and effect change. It sees the career as something with its own prescribed existence, as something real and external to the individual.

The notion of the career as something which exists within the organisation, and can be managed by the organisation, is central to many HRM approaches to career (Mayo, 1991), and is manifest in practices including recruitment, training and development and performance evaluation (Mallon, 1998). The managerialist perspective explicit within much HRM, emphasising the role of the organisation over that of the individual in developing and managing careers, has been criticised (Herriot and Pemberton, 1996). On one hand, scholars have suggested that such approaches fail to acknowledge the extent to which careers are constructed by individuals themselves. In addition, others argue that HRM practices must recognise the changing contexts of career, and acknowledge the current emphasis on flexibility, movement and employability.

In contrast, early psychological work on career focused on the individual, and on the notion of the career as subjective, situated within the individual. This literature is concerned with issues such as personality traits and their implications for occupational choice, and the importance of person–environment 'fit' for occupational stability (Super, 1973; Holland, 1973). Psychological approaches were influenced by trends in developmental psychology. Consistent with psychologists' interest in adult change and development (Hall, 1976; Levinson, 1978), career development theorists study the ways in which careers develop over the span of an individual's adult life. Here the work of Super (1957) has been particularly influential. His original five-stage model, from 'growth' to 'decline', though criticised for its exclusivity and its apparent lack of flexibility, has been the basis of much thinking and theorising about career development over the last 40 years. Indeed, Super himself reworked this model in 1985, in order to accommodate greater diversity in the form and timing of individuals' career development (this revised model is illustrated in Table 9.1).

While they continue to influence academic and popular thinking about career, questions have been raised about the adequacy of psychological models of understanding. Scholars have criticised personality traits approaches for being too static and determining, and for their failure to account for social processes and contexts (Nicholson and West, 1989; Potter and Weatherell, 1987). As regards life stage

Table 9.1 Super's adult career concerns

Exploration

Crystallisation	Developing employment ideas
Specification	Turning general preference into specific choice
Implementation	Planning to enter occupation, executing plan

Establishment

Stabilising	Settling into occupation and adopting a lifestyle consistent with it
Consolidating	Making oneself secure in occupation
Advancing	Increasing earnings/responsibility

Maintenance

Holding	Retaining position in face of change and external pressure
Updating	More proactive than holding
Innovating	Finding new ways of approaching tasks

Disengagement

Decelerating	Reducing workload and pace
Planning for retirement	Finance and lifestyle
Retirement	Learning to live without work

Source: Adapted from Super, Thompson and Lindeman, 1985

models, academics have taken issue with the fact that much of this research was conducted exclusively on men, thus failing to take account of women's experiences of life and career. In addition, they have been criticised for their overemphasis on age, and for not taking social and organisational change into account (Arnold, 1997b). However, despite these criticisms, on a practical level, computer packages which help people to make career decisions are typically based on psychological models of person/occupation fit and career development (Arnold, 1997b).

Holistic perspectives: new metaphors for thinking about career

Arrows, ladders, paths and ceilings. Reflecting on our own careers, and those of others, our language is metaphorical: successful careers are described in terms of climbing to the top, reaching targets and being at the pinnacle, while unsuccessful careers are attributed to losing one's sense of direction, getting lost or hitting the glass ceilings. It has been suggested that metaphors 'are used to make sense of the situations we find ourselves in' (Grant and Oswick, 1996: 1); they are 'a way of thinking and a way of seeing' (Morgan, 1986: 12). These familiar metaphors which we use to talk about career are no accident. Rather, underpinning them are fundamental assumptions about what a career is and is not, about career success and failure. These assumptions are typically based on notions of career as external to the individual, organisationally based and prescribed, linear and hierarchical.

In contrast to scholars who see career as either external or internal, residing within the organisation or within the individual, are those who seek to explore career more holistically, as an on-going process central to which is the relationship between the invidual and the organisation. Here Schein (1978, 1993), Driver (1982) and Derr (1986) are notable examples. All three attempt to look at careers, not as static entities caught at a moment in time, but as they unfold and develop through time, and seek to understand what gives a career its continuity. It is interesting that in doing so, each theorist uses a different metaphor for describing their approach: for Schein it is the anchor, Driver's 'career concepts' are based on shapes and patterns, and Derr's work focuses on 'career logics'. Schein, for example, used the anchor image to describe what he saw as those fundamental, unwavering and unchanging ideas around which individuals construct their careers. Through his research into male Masters students at a prestigious American business school, he identified eight such anchors: technical/functional competence, general management competence, autonomy/independence, security/stability, entrepreneurial creativity, service/dedication, pure challenge and lifestyle (Schein, 1996). In contrast to the solidity of the anchor, Driver's 'concept' model is about shapes and patterns: transitory, steady-state, linear and spiral, while Derr's five 'career logics': getting ahead, getting secure, getting free, getting high and getting balanced, are based on the idea of career development as a fundamentally rational process.

It could be argued that these approaches are now somewhat dated, reminiscent of an employment context which offered more choice and opportunity than many experience in today's labour market. Nevertheless, I find them interesting in their attempt to integrate the individual and the organisation, and their radical departure from the idea of career as necessarily linear and hierarchical. Instead, they acknowledge the diverse ways in which individuals construct their careers, and recognise the significance of non-work aspects of life in the experience of career.

Interpretive approaches: individuals making sense of their careers

As discussed in the section on definitions above, Hughes and the Chicago sociologists were interested in the subjective dimension of career, the ways in which people make sense of their careers. While these interpretive approaches were to some extent eclipsed by more mainstream sociological and psychological research, they have persisted and, to my mind, provide an illuminating, and often missing, perspective on the ways in which individuals construct and experience their careers. Examples of interpretive work include Cohen and Mallon's research into individuals' transition from organisational employment to self-employment (Cohen, 1997; Mallon, 1998; Cohen and Mallon, 1999), Fournier's (1998) research on careers and the discourse of enterprise, and Collin and Watts' (1996) study of career guidance. Such perspectives are centrally concerned with the ways in which individuals account for their careers, recognising that 'the story may well change as individuals move through the twists and turns of their own working life, reconstructing the past to come to terms with the present and the future' (Mallon, 1998: 68).

Diverse careers: women's careers and men's theories

Although theories like those of Schein, Driver and Derr offer insights into people's experiences of career, they are nevertheless based on middle-class, white men, failing to take account of the significance of gender, class or ethnicity for an individual's career story. To take gender as an example, in recent years feminist career theorists have taken issue with this persistent male orientation, and have sought to develop frameworks for understanding which more adequately reflect women's lives.

Apart from a few early studies which suggested that the process of career development is essentially the same for women and men (Fitzgerald and Crites, 1980), there is a general consensus that women's lives are fundamentally different from men's, and that they construct their careers in different ways. For example, feminist psychologists take issue with theories of adult development based on male experiences, while feminist sociologists emphasise the significance of gender in an individual's experience of life. Research on gender and careers focuses on a whole array of issues including women's career aspirations (Martin et al., 1987); the significance of family background (Boardman et al., 1987); family roles and responsibilities (White, 1995; Howard, 1992), women's careers in management (Cassell and Walsh, 1992; Marshall, 1984, 1989, 1995), and women's experience of career transition (Cohen, 1997). These studies offer illuminating insights into the day-to-day issues which women confront as part and parcel of their unfolding careers.

However, central to this developing literature is a more fundamental point about the inadequacy of existing career theory for women. It is argued that what is needed is not simply to include more women in our research samples, but to completely rethink our taken-for-granted definitions of careers and assumptions about what constitutes career success. For example, in her study of the career development of 'successful' women White (1995) makes a plea for a change in attitudes and understandings which would allow women more flexibility and would take greater account of women's responsibilities. Gallos (1989) too calls for a separate theory of women's career development, suggesting, like White, that any rethinking must involve a challenge to accepted definitions. In her view, despite increasing attention to women's careers, traditional understandings persist, connoting images of linearity and steady advancement. Any deviation is interpreted, not as a viable alternative, but as 'opting out':

> Women who limit work time to parent children or refuse to prove themselves during early career years by assuming the standard workaholic stance easily look less committed to their careers. Women who find it hard to define clearly their professional goals or plan a long-term career strategy because of unsureness of what relationships and home demands may bring certainly can look unfocused . . . Women who leave successful organisational positions and clearly defined career tracks to gain more control over their lives can look foolish and misdirected.
>
> (Gallos, 1989: 124)

Marshall (1989: 282) too is critical of developments in women's career theory which have simply 'modified its basic arrow design', arguing that instead we need to 'recreate it at the core'. Marshall's approach is based on two related concepts: agency and communion. In her view, traditional career theory is based on male, *agentic* principles – with an emphasis on control, individualism and action oriented towards the achievement of personal goals. Such an approach, she maintains, is inadequate for men as well as women. Marshall argues that change in career thinking involves recognising the value of the female principle of *communion*, with its emphasis on co-operation, relationships and integration.

The emergence of new kinds of careers – and new ways of thinking about career

As discussed in the section on contexts, there is a growing consensus that careers are changing, from traditional, hierarchical, linear and organisationally bound models to more fluid arrangements, based on the accumulation of skills and knowledge and the integration of personal and professional life. It is notable that, in spite of the very different ways in which individuals' careers develop, much of career theory remains staunchly bureaucratic in its orientation, emphasising (albeit implicitly) linearity, hierarchy and the division of work and home life. Kanter (1989), in a challenge to this traditional perspective, offers a very different model for understanding career development and change. Her starting point is that as bureaucratic forms of organisation are beginning to wane, so too are bureaucratic careers. Kanter identifies three career 'forms', 'organising principle[s] around which a career logic unfolds' : bureaucratic, professional and entrepreneurial' (1989: 508). To Kanter, bureaucratic careers are characterised by:

> the logic of advancement. [It] involves a sequence of positions in a formally defined hierarchy of other positions. 'Growth' is equated with promotion to a position of higher rank . . . 'progress' means advancement within the hierarchy . . . In the typical bureaucratic career, all of the elements of career opportunity – responsibilities, challenges, influence, formal training and development, compensation – are all closely tied to rank in an organisation.
>
> (Kanter, 1989: 509)

As suggested previously, the bureaucratic career form is central to popular and academic understandings of careers, and has been the basis of much HRM thinking about career management. On the other hand, Kanter defines professional careers as:

> craft of skill, with monopolisation of socially valued knowledge the key determinant of occupational status, and 'reputation' the key resource for the individual . . . Career 'growth' for professionals does not necessarily consist of moving from job to job, as it does for bureaucrats . . . Opportunity in the professional form, then, involves the chance to take on ever more demanding or challenging or important or rewarding assignments that involve greater exercise of the skills that define the professional's stock-in-trade.
>
> (Kanter, 1989: 510–11)

Kanter maintains that, unlike a bureaucrat, whose career is inextricably linked to the organisation, a professional's relationship with their organisation is more complex. Several intriguing questions emerge from Kanter's categorisation. From an individual perspective one might ask to what extent and in what ways professionals are able to fulfil their career aspirations within organisational boundaries. From an organisational perspective, questions arise about how best to manage the career development of professionals in order to fulfil both individual and organisational aims and objectives. Research into professional careers includes issues such as the meaning and enactment of professional careers, provision of career guidance, performance monitoring and evaluation, professional career structures, and the relationship between the professional work and management (Arnold, 1997a; Raelin, 1986).

Finally, Kanter sees the entrepreneurial career as:

> one in which growth occurs through the creation of new value or new organisational capacity. If the key resource in a bureaucratic career is hierarchical position, and the key resource in a professional career is knowledge and reputation, then the key resource in an entrepreneurial career is the capacity to create valued outputs . . . Instead of moving UP, those in entrepreneurial careers see progress when the territory grows BELOW them . . . Freedom, independence, and control over not only one's tasks . . . but also one's organisational surroundings, are associated with the entrepreneurial career.
>
> (Kanter, 1989: 515–16)

There is a striking neglect of entrepreneurship (and indeed of self-employment more generally) in the careers literature – a neglect which is all the more notable given the current plethora of work on the emergence of new career forms, many of which are essentially varieties of self-employment. Why this is the case is an intriguing question. It could be argued that this lack of recognition makes sense, given the bureaucratic orientation of much career theory. As for its absence within the literature on new careers, it may be that with its emphasis on newness, originality and a late-twentieth-century world view, self-employment seems old-fashioned and out-of-date. In any case, it is a curious omission.

In so far as Kanter takes a broad, macro view, she does not examine in detail the processes through which these career patterns are constructed: she does not explore the way in which individuals come to identify with one or another of these patterns, and she does not consider the implications of gender for an individual's experience of these career forms. Also, Kanter identifies three principal forms, but there could be more. For example, in her study of women who left organisations and set up their own businesses, Cohen (1997) identified 'personal growth and development' as a fourth career form, and it has been suggested that the portfolio could constitute a fifth (Cohen and Mallon, 1999). Nevertheless, Kanter's model provides a very valuable starting point for examining career and career diversity as at the start of a new millennium. Her suggestion that we need to know more about these forms and the ways in which they are enacted in organisational contexts is a significant issue for HRM.

Kanter's work is based on the idea that the bureaucratic career is indeed beginning to falter. Scholars have argued that not only are such careers seen as less and less likely, but they are also less and less appealing. In the literature on emerging careers, organisations are frequently depicted as 'stultifying individuals' initiative and creativity and promoting an unhealthy dependence on organisations for the conduct of one's working life' (Cohen and Mallon, 1999: 333). People are encouraged to weaken their links with organisations, and to develop relationships based on short-term contracts and financial arrangements. It has been argued that within this brave new world the boundaries between work and other aspects of people's lives are changing: thus Mirvis and Hall (1994) introduced the term 'boundaryless career' to describe career patterns based on cyclical rather than linear patterns of movement, periods of reskilling, of lateral rather than upward movement and of change – of job, company, even occupation. Within such careers identity is no longer organisationally determined, but is constructed through 'cumulative work experiences and career achievement, [and] also through "work" as a spouse, parent and community member' (Mirvis and Hall, 1994: 387). Their work thus echoes those feminist calls for rethinking career discussed earlier. Research into emerging career forms and boundaryless careers has focused on a wide range of areas, from understanding and enacting boundaryless careers, to the wider social implications of emerging career forms.

While the idea of the new career is widely celebrated, voices have been raised about its potentially negative implications for both individuals and organisations. And questions are raised about the concept of 'boundarylessness' itself: 'the stories we heard were less about breaking free than about *reconstructing* the boundaries

. . . It appeared that participants were attempting to establish new employment contexts which in some ways approximated those that they had only recently left. Each merit of portfolio working was constructed as a drawback and vice versa' (Cohen and Mallon, 1999: 346).

As discussed in the section on changing organisations, the extent to which careers have changed is still open to question. However, Arnold (1997b: 20) maintains that, notwithstanding this divergence of views, 'what has changed is that few people can look forward to a predefined sequence of jobs roles within one general line or work . . . with periodic promotion. In truth, this kind of career was always the preserve of a minority of people (not everyone wanted one like this), but now it is even rarer'. These changes clearly have consequences for the individual. They also have consequences for the organisation. It has been suggested that in today's world of movement, diversity, flexibility and short-term relationships, organisations need to rethink their approaches to human resource development and career development. This issue is considered in the section which follows.

Managing careers: implications for HR practice

Assumptions about how we might define career (whether careers are objective, existing within and defined by organisations, or subjectively constructed by diverse individuals) are embedded within organisational approaches to career management and development. Indeed, current debates on the nature and extent of organisational change have thrown the whole issue of HR intervention in career management into sharp relief. Some scholars have argued that in a world of organisational restructuring, outsourcing and a growing contingent workforce, traditional approaches to career management, based on notions of lifelong employment and hierarchical development, have become obsolete. However, others maintain that employees continue to attach real importance to managed career development initiatives and the concept of employment security. Indeed, Sparrow and Marchington (1998) suggest that after a decade of 'organisational anorexia', 'trust and commitment are increasingly seen as key business drivers and they are unlikely to flourish within short-term and precarious employment relationships'.

Central to these debates is the issue of the changing psychological contract between employees and employers. Arnold describes the psychological contract as the 'informal, unwritten understandings between employers and employee(s). From the employees' point of view, the psychological contract is the agreement that they think they have with their employer about what they will contribute to their employer via their work, and what they can expect in return' (Arnold 1997a: 38). Herriot and Pemberton (1995: 58), and other commentators, suggest that in recent years the terms of this implicit 'deal' have changed beyond all recognition: that industrial leaders have 'set in motion a revolution in the nature of the employment relationship'. Whereas traditionally the psychological contract was based on long-term commitment, trust and mutual respect, the 'new deals' are short-term, flexible arrangements based on fixed contracts and financial transactions. Theoretically, this distinction has been described in terms of a move from relational to transactional contracts. Relational approaches 'entail long-term social exchange between parties, mutual trust, interpersonal attachment and commitment'. In contrast, transactional contracts involve a 'formal, adversarial relationship . . . in which integration and control are achieved through the implementation of contractual specifications and the discipline of (quasi)-market forces' (Darwin *et al.*, 1999: 4). In exchange for greater uncertainty, instability and longer hours, the new psychological contract offers employees higher rates of pay, reward for performance, flexibility (the positive gloss on what can also be described as uncertainty) and, Arnold (1997a) somewhat cynically adds, a job.

The psychological contract is relevant to HR career management practice because it impacts on employees' and employers' expectations of how an individual's sequence of work experiences will unfold and develop. Indeed, scholars working in this area have argued that the extent to which stakeholders see their psychological contract as either relational or transactional will influence their perceptions of who should take responsibility for an individual's career development (Arthur and Rousseau, 1996; Robinson and Rousseau, 1994). Amongst employers, employees and academics there is considerable ambiguity about the role and purpose of organisational career management. Some commentators argue that the changing psychological contract has heralded a shift in responsibility from the organisation to the individual: 'It is less viable than it was to look toward your employer for future development. Some employers have withdrawn entirely from career management, and some are concerned with short-term profitability to the exclusion of virtually all else' (Arnold, 1997a: 41). Likewise, writing in *The Wall Street Journal*, Lancaster announces: 'the social contract between employees and employers, in which companies promise to ensure employment and guide the career of loyal troops, is dead, dead, dead' (1994, cited in Thomas and Higgins, 1996: 268).

Notwithstanding this current emphasis on self-managed careers, many organisations do make an attempt to intervene in individuals' career development. Arnold (1997a) identifies a number of such interventions, illustrated in Table 9.2.

Of the techniques and approaches listed, research shows that internal vacancy advertising, mentoring and the provision of formal career path information are increasingly common (Iles and Mabey, 1993). This chapter does not offer the scope for a full debate on these interventions (see Chapter 5 in this volume for a discussion of training, development and learning, and Chapter 3 on performance appraisal). However, it is important to point out that there is still considerable uncertainty about how often these interventions are used and to what effect. Despite this lack of consensus about the precise impact of career management initiatives, the literature suggests that they could offer a number of benefits to individuals and organisations. These include increasing employee commitment, satisfaction, and productivity; identifying employees with potential, strategic

Table 9.2 Career management interventions in organisations

Internal vacancy notification	Details about jobs available within the organisation prior to external advertising. Should include necessary experience and qualifications, and a job description.
Career paths	Information about the sequence of jobs that people can do, or competencies they can acquire within the organisation, with details of how high the path goes, potential lateral moves, required qualifications/skills/experience.
Career workbooks	Exercises designed to guide individuals in analysing their own strengths and weaknesses, identifying opportunities and assessing action necessary to achieve goals.
Career planning workshops	Deal with similar issues to workbooks, but in a more 'managed' way, offering opportunities for discussion and feedback. Sometimes include psychometric testing.
Computer-assisted career management	Packages which help employees to assess their skills, interests, and values, and translate these into employment options. Sometimes these are organisationally specific.
Opportunities for training and development	Information, financial support and sometimes delivery of courses. Could be within or outside of the organisation. Designed to enable employees to update, or to acquire new skills and knowledge. Often used in preparation for seeking promotion.
Personal development plans	Statements of how an individual's skills and knowledge might develop, given a particular employment context and timescale. Often arise from performance appraisal or development centre assessment.
Career action centres	Resources (paper, video and electronic) available to employees on a drop-in basis. Sometimes also offer counselling.
Development centres	Employees are assessed on the basis of their performance in a number of different exercises and tests. Focus on identifying an individual's strengths and weaknesses for the purpose of development.
Mentoring programmes	Attaching employees to more senior colleagues who act as advisors, advocates, counsellors.
Job assignment/rotation	Careful use of work tasks can help a person to stay employable. Organisation will benefit from staff adaptability, flexibility.
Outplacement	Purpose is to support people who are leaving organisation, to help them clarify future plans. May include a variety of the above interventions.

Source: Adapted from Arnold, 1997a

development of staff, in line with organisational goals more generally, and sociali-sation of employees into the organisation (London and Stumpf, 1982; Gutteridge *et al.*, 1993).

Arnold (1997a) concludes that career management interventions are most likely to have their desired effect in situations where, first, there is openness and trust. Although one could argue these are becoming increasingly rare in these days of flexibility and changing psychological contracts, Macauley and Harding (1996) maintain that it is precisely in this context that such qualities are needed most. They report on the development of a career management programme in a computer software firm, the first step of which was a diagnosis of employees' perceptions and expectations. Macauley and Harding argue that where psychological contracts are being redefined, an understanding of employees' perspectives is vital if motivation and commitment are to be maintained, and if career management interventions are to achieve their desired results – in this case increasing learning and development opportunities. Macauley and Harding emphasise the importance of communication and feedback within such processes.

Second, Arnold suggests that the goals of career management processes must be clear and explicit. Such clarity will be most easily achieved if there are a limited number of interventions, and if they are compatible. Also, it is important that interventions stay in existence long enough to become established. Related to this is Summers' (1999) insistence that such initiatives must not be seen as once-a-year events which take place in isolation from other HR activities. Rather, he argues that such programmes must be fully integrated into HR functions on a daily basis.

Third, the way in which these processes are managed and delivered is crucial. On a theoretical level, Arnold (1997b) suggests that, given current changes in career patterns and expectations, providers of careers guidance and counselling need to be more aware of process, rather than focusing exclusively on outcomes (which are becoming increasingly difficult to predict and/or realise). He maintains that in view of these fundamental changes, more attention should be given to the 'cognitive processes employed by individuals in managing their careers' (1997b: 447), particularly the extent to which individuals think about their careers in advanced, wise and expert ways. Not only do Arnold's propositions relate to individual career management, but they likewise have implications for those involved in managing the careers of others:

> Counsellors have perhaps always been encouraged, or even trained, to adopt multiple perspectives, recognise dissonance between thoughts and emotions, and develop and use heuristics for classifying career problems. Here the emphasis is very much on encouraging the client to do the same. This might mean a rather more controlling and pedagogic orientation than some counsellors are accustomed to using.
>
> (Arnold, 1997b: 452)

On a more practical level, managers should themselves be appraised on how well they carry out career interventions, and top management should be seen as actively supportive of such initiatives (Mayo, 1991). Here again, it is vital that career management programmes are seen as integrated in the organisation's daily practices, and consistent with its more general strategic orientation. Finally, it is essential that career management interventions are not perceived as only available to a select few: rather, organisations should be seen to take an interest in the careers of all their employees.

It is interesting to consider HR interventions in career management in the light of current debates on changing careers. As noted earlier, traditional approaches to career management were based on the notion of the career as lifelong, existing within and defined by the organisation, and sought to establish the right 'fit' between the person and the position. In this case the role of the HRM practitioner 'became one of defining position requirements, identifying and selecting individuals capable of meeting those position requirements and assisting organisational members to progress through a sequence of positions within the organisation' (Templar and Cawsey, 1999: 72). However, the emerging discourse on new careers sees the career as situated within the individual, focusing on individual choice, self-development and 'employability' (see also Ball and Jordan, 1997). From this perspective, career management is contract-oriented, concerned with defining core competencies and identifying the 'core' workforce, and is short-term in focus. Templar and Cawsey describe these, respectively, as 'position-centred' and 'portfolio-centred' career development procedures. Whereas the former sees HR practitioners as having a central role to play in the employees' long-term training and development, within a portfolio perspective individuals are responsible for their own training and career growth. In this case, HR managers must ensure that individuals have the requisite skills needed to fulfil the terms of a specific contract.

Given these two perspectives, we can ask where the interventions outlined in Table 9.2 can be situated. In other words, do they reflect position-centred or portfolio-centred approaches to career management? Although certain interventions (such as career planning workshops and job assignment/rotation) are often associated with an individual's long-term relationship with the organisation, this does not have to be the case (Ball and Jordan, 1997). Taking opportunities for training and development as an example, in certain cases such programmes could be offered by the organisation to help individuals prepare for promotion. However, in other cases individuals might opt into particular training courses as a way of updating their knowledge and skills – thereby enhancing their personal portfolio. Thus, it is not the intervention *per se* which is significant, but the way in which it is used and understood.

There is a cynical view that from the point of view of the organisation the self-managed career is a cheap option – that rhetoric about emerging career forms and self-development offers a justification for cost cutting. However, in their research into self-development, MacKenzie Davey and Guest (1994) found that some organisations take a much more proactive stance, sponsoring a range of activities from career workbooks to mentoring schemes and career workshops. Similarly, in their evaluation of two open learning career management initiatives, Ball and Jordan (1997) describe a high level of organisational involvement and commitment. Indeed, participants in these programmes felt that the support they received from highly trained and skilled tutors was an 'essential ingredient in the process' (Ball and Jordan, 1997: 515):

> Working in partnership, careers advisers became facilitators and enablers rather than guidance gurus . . . Careers advisers became part of a developmental programme in which participants were encouraged to make and revise decisions about life goals and which reinforced the notion of career management as a life skill rather than a single decision.
>
> (ibid: 514)

Likewise, although the programme described by Macauley and Harding (noted above, 1996) is based on the principle of individual career management and self-development, this is not to suggest that employers can simply duck out of their responsibility. Rather, their key point is that employers have a vital role to play in facilitating this development.

Conclusion

This chapter began with two quotes about career: one poignant and retrospective, the other looking ahead, full of promise and opportunity. In the first, career is seen as the sum of an individual's working life. Here, an elderly priest looks back on his life and finds it lacking. He has not fulfilled his youthful aspirations. He has had a disappointing, unsuccessful career. Conversely, in the second quote Tony Blair uses the word 'career' *in contrast* to job to express his high hopes for his children's future. There is a sense of purpose and meaning embedded in the term. Together these quotes raise some fascinating questions about what careers are, the relationship between personal and work life, about where careers are located and the extent to which (and by whom) they can be managed. While not aiming to provide definitive answers, this chapter explored these questions, considering in particular emerging debates on changing careers, and the implications of these debates for HR practice.

The chapter began by discussing the changing contexts in which careers are enacted, considering changes in the demography of the labour force, and also at the level of the organisation. While the precise nature and extent of change is still an open question, there is a growing consensus that careers are increasingly characterised by uncertainty and instability. One way of engaging with these debates is by considering how career thinking has developed – examining traditional definitions and theories, and the extent to which these are being reproduced/challenged or transformed in current employment contexts. While some might argue that conventional definitions, with their emphasis on hierarchy and linearity, are outdated, metaphors of ladders, arrows and getting to the top continue to send powerful messages about career success and failure. In addition to these traditional conceptualisations, broader, more inclusive definitions were introduced, emphasising both subjective and objective dimensions of career, and the integration of professional and personal life.

The chapter then briefly discussed the theoretical frameworks on which these definitions are based, considering their relevance to real people's lives, and with particular reference to women's experiences. Not only were conventional definitions found to be wanting, failing to account adequately for the diverse patterns and rhythms which different individuals' working lives can take, but also within these approaches there is often an implicit assumption that careers take place in large organisations and are based on bureaucratic notions of success. Alternatives to this traditional model were introduced, including emerging notions of boundaryless careers, which carry in their wake very different ideas about the relationship between the individual and the organisation, and have significant implications for HR approaches to career management. The final section of the chapter focused on organisational intervention in career management, in the light of current ideas about changing psychological contracts between individuals and organisations. In particular, this section considers the role of the HR practitioner in the context of current debates on changing careers.

Understanding your career

Laurie Cohen

- Working in a group, compile a list of 20–30 jobs – make your list as wide-ranging as possible.

- Which of these jobs would you consider to be 'careers'? Which would not be careers? Why?

- Construct a definition of career that justifies your categorisation. How does this definition compare to those introduced in the chapter?

- Apply this definition to your own experiences. Which aspects of your life would it include? Which aspects would be excluded from this definition? Based on this definition, would you say that your experiences constitute a career?

- Make a 'time-line' of your career to date. Choose an appropriate shape, and include significant events, decisions, people, transitions. Should aspects of personal life be included? What about voluntary or community activities, education, training? Who have been the key stakeholders in your career development?

- Consider this time-line in terms of the theoretical approaches introduced in this chapter.
  - Do you see your career as objective or subjective? Who 'owns' your career?
  - To what extent do sociological/psychological approaches shed light on your career experiences?
  - Explore the relevance of career anchors, shapes or logics. What are the relative merits/weaknesses of these approaches in relation to your own experience of career?
  - Consider the issue of career diversity in terms of your experience of career. To what extent do feminist calls for 're-visioning' the career concept have resonance for you?
  - How does your career compare to traditional, bureaucratic conceptualisations?
  - Consider Kanter's model in light of your career time-line. Would you say that your career could be described in terms of one of her career forms? Could more than one of these forms apply? Simultaneously or at different times? How might you account for movement between these career forms?

- Describe any career interventions you have experienced (in terms of your own career, or in terms of managing the careers of others). Critically examine the apparent strengths/weaknesses of this intervention, for the individual and the organisation.

- Using your accumulated understanding of careers, develop a metaphor that describes your career and reflects key concepts introduced in the chapter.
- Based on your experience and observations, to what extent and in what ways do you think careers are changing? What are the implications of these changes for individuals and organisations?

Moving from organisational employment to self-employment: the stories of Deborah and Yasmin

Laurie Cohen

Deborah

Deborah is fifty-five years old, and is the owner/manager of a nursing home. A nurse, she worked as a night sister in a large teaching hospital in a northern city for 20 years. She has been in business for herself for three years.

Deborah describes nursing as her vocation. She completed her professional training within the NHS, and from the outset of her career she anticipated lifelong employment within that organisation, seeking out opportunities for professional development and promotion wherever possible. She spoke of her early days in the NHS as challenging but rewarding; at that time she strongly believed in what the NHS was trying to do and felt that she belonged there. To Deborah, what is most important is providing high-quality, personal attention for her patients, and she explained how this approach used to be valued and indeed promoted by the Health Service. As a night sister for many years, she had considerable responsibility, both with respect to doctors (many of whom were very junior), and to her own nursing staff. In the light of this senior position and extensive experience, however, it is interesting that Deborah never described herself as a manager.

In the last few years of her employment within the NHS, Deborah became increasingly disillusioned. She explained how the Health Service was changing, becoming less caring and more business-like, and she found herself increasingly at odds with the organisation and its direction. She felt that within the NHS she could no longer practise the highest-quality nursing, the sort of nursing that she was trained for, and vividly described the constraints of the new regime. In particular Deborah spoke of the difficulty of trying to reconcile her commitment to patients with the new emphasis on financial control, efficiency and accountability to managers. After an incident during which she felt that her performance was unfairly criticised, it appeared to Deborah that she had lost the support of her managers and of the organisation generally. At that point, she decided to resign from the NHS.

However, she did not leave straight away. Having made the decision to buy her own nursing home, where she felt she would be able to get back to 'real nursing', Deborah spoke of a two-year transition period. During that time her husband prepared detailed business plans, negotiated with banks and building societies and sorted out the financial aspects of the new venture. While this was going on in the background, Deborah carried on with her Health Service position. As a demoralised night sister, Deborah had a vision of the high-quality, one-to-one care she would be able to offer to the elderly residents in her future nursing home. She was well aware of her abilities as a nurse and these skills, together with her husband's meticulous financial planning and the bank's eagerness to lend, gave her the confidence that her business ideas were sound, that this venture would be a success.

Deborah completed the purchase of the home, inheriting, of course, its residents and their families, and continued to work in the NHS for three more months. During these months, Deborah worked night and day, stopping only occasionally to catnap on the floor, 'under the buzzers so that if anybody needed me I could hear it'. She describes those early days as 'your worst nightmare. [Because] I didn't have a clue how to run the place . . . It was horrific . . . If anyone had said to me after three months, I'd have said we made the most awful mistake of our lives.' Although she had always seen herself as a very well-organised person, she felt 'totally and utterly out of control'.

Apart from the problems of doing two jobs, there were aspects of the venture that Deborah had not considered. She was unprepared to deal with HR issues, including recruitment, training and development of staff; operational matters such as the ongoing maintenance of the building, food preparation and laundry; and the social dimension of business life, which involved extensive networking with families, doctors and outside agencies. 'Everything about it was new . . . I mean, I didn't know what the daily routine was, how they got people out of bed, who did what . . . I'd met these people once, for an hour on the Saturday, and then Monday morning at 8 o'clock it was mine.' At the time, Deborah was overwhelmed by what she saw as these new and ever-increasing demands on her time, energy and personal resources – she was having to do things far beyond the view of nursing and identification of herself as a nurse that had motivated her thus far. 'I mean, here was me, a dead organised person, but I had so much thrown at me, I just literally went to pieces. I couldn't speak, if anybody gave me a kind word I just cried, 'cos I couldn't cope. I was very tired, and you're thinking about this enormous debt that's hanging over your head.'

As time went on, Deborah regained her sense of control and during her interview spoke proudly and confidently of her achievements. She described her home as happy and caring, and felt that she offered her residents and their families high-quality provision. She had the respect and support of her staff and had established very positive working relationships with professionals and agencies outside the home. It is interesting that although Deborah had become a successful owner/manager of a small business, she continued to describe herself as a nurse: speaking of 'one-to-one care', 'not minding night work', not minding 'getting her hands dirty'. When asked directly, Deborah acknowledged that she has certain management skills, but it was not until this issue was probed more deeply that she began to make links between these and what she was already doing as a night sister in the NHS (earlier in the interview she had asserted that at the time of leaving, 'my skills were nursing, they were my only skills'). Perhaps some recognition of these tacit abilities and competencies *beforehand* might have facilitated Deborah's transition from work within a large organisation to self-employment.

Yasmin

Yasmin is thirty-five years old, the single mother of two young daughters. At the time of interview, she had been working as an independent management consultant for two years. Yasmin never considered her career in terms of a single organisation, or indeed a single occupation. Instead, she explained how she had always envisaged her working life as an ongoing developmental process: acquiring a range of skills, knowledge and experiences, and applying these to a whole variety of employment contexts. Since obtaining her degree and training as a teacher, Yasmin has had various positions within several different local authorities, working in the field of race relations. In addition, she had a short stint of self-employment, running a small clothing business together with her former husband. Her last organisational position, before embarking on her work as a management consultant, was a senior role within the policy department of a northern local authority.

Yasmin described how after two and a half years in this post, she began to feel stuck. It was a highly politicised local authority, both internally and publicly, and the issue of race relations was contentious and deeply sensitive. Her brief was to initiate policy change, and although she was given considerable responsibility, she felt largely ineffective. As a black woman coming from another city to work in a largely white, male organisation, an 'outsider' in an organisation in which many senior managers had spent their entire working lives, she described her feelings of marginalisation and powerlessness. In addition to these frustrations with the work itself, Yasmin described the incompatibility of her roles and responsibilities as a local authority employee and as a mother. In particular, she explained how the excessively bureaucratic culture within that organisation did not allow her the flexibility she needed to manage her domestic life, and to care for her children. Not only was she 'failing to thrive' professionally, but she felt that her daughters were likewise stifled by the arrangements. As her levels of stress and frustration grew, she realised that it was time to leave. 'I got to a point where I thought I'm becoming deskilled here, I'm not developing further and I'm not getting a sense of achievement . . . Then I looked at where am I going to go, and I looked around at the organisation, I mean the next tier up would have been applying for director level, and it just seemed that people had to work so hard . . . I mean there's work life, and there's the rest of your life, and there are your children. The balance would've been all wrong.'

During her notice period, Yasmin enrolled in a Masters course in Organisational Development, a programme oriented to management consultancy. Although she had not made a decision to become a consultant, she felt that such a course would give her the opportunity to gain a more theoretical understanding of organisation in the light of her own employment experiences. She explained how during that time she reflected on her career achievements and considered where to go next. 'What the course did for me is it made me realise that I had a lot of good experience, it made me realise that I'd already got consultancy skills, in fact, I was already a consultant. Without realising it I had been working as an internal consultant for several years. Only I called it something different then.' Upon completing the course, Yasmin decided not to go back into organisational employment, and to embark on a portfolio career as a consultant in organisational development.

Yasmin did not describe the move to portfolio work as a radical change; rather it was part of an ongoing process, a way in which she could build on her experience and knowledge, continuing to grow and learn, as she has striven to do throughout her working life. 'It's interesting about my life. I grew up with the idea that I would have an education, that I would have a degree. I grew up with the idea that I'd be self-sufficient regardless of whether I was married or not . . . But I never really had a career plan as such. I knew I'd be working, but I didn't know where. So I mean, even now I don't really have a career plan beyond the next year or two . . . I couldn't tell you now what I'll be doing in ten years time'. Yasmin thus described her career as 'emergent' rather than 'planned'. However, she insisted that this did not mean that it was in any way ad hoc. Rather, at the time of interview she had in place firm plans for continued professional development (which is often problematic for consultants and other portfolio workers), and a network of contacts that she saw as a crucial resource. Notwithstanding these networks, however, Yasmin said that at times her new arrangements can be lonely and isolating, that she does miss the sense of belonging that can develop when one is a member of a department within an organisation.

On a personal level, Yasmin explained how her domestic responsibilities are more easily accommodated within the flexible patterns of portfolio employment. In charge of her own schedule, she can organise work to fit around her daughters' school year. While such arrangements were untenable within the local authority, amongst portfolio workers a greater integration of personal and professional life is seen as the norm. However, she maintained that this sort of synthesis does have its costs. In particular, there is no strict delineation between work and home life, each encroaches on the other, resulting in a lack of clarity and feelings of underachievement in both. In addition, she explained that when one is based at home, it is very difficult to stop working. However, Yasmin explained that as she has become more used to the rhythm of management consultancy, she has been able to find ways of managing the tension between these two contexts.

Although she is satisfied at the moment, Yasmin insisted that OD consultancy would definitely not be her last career move. She spoke of herself as 'essentially a change person. I've always had this willingness to take risks with my career. I'm not one of these people who has a clear plan. I have a sense that I'll always be working, and I'll always be doing something that I'm interested in, but I don't know what it is. As far as management consultancy goes, I'll probably do it for a couple of years, then I'll move on to something else. That's just how I am.'

Questions

1. Would you say that Deborah and Yasmin's careers could be described as external, having an objective existence, or internal, subjectively constructed by the individuals themselves?

2. To what extent can Schein's career anchors be applied to Deborah and Yasmin's accounts?

3. Refer back to the quote from Joan Gallos on p. 273. Do you think her comments have any resonance for Deborah or Yasmin's career stories?

4. Examine Deborah and Yasmin's stories in light of Kanter's bureaucratic, professional and entrepreneurial career forms. Does Kanter's model work? To what extent to you think it can accommodate the transitions described by these two women? Is there a fourth (or even a fifth) career form which you feel would enhance Kanter's framework?

5. To what extent would you say Deborah and Yasmin's careers have been affected by changing social/economic, and organisational contexts?

6. Would you say Deborah and Yasmin's stories are more about change or continuity?

Organisational interventions in career management: experiences of performance appraisal schemes

Laurie Cohen

Debbie

My first experience of performance appraisal was when I was working in the retail sector. The organisation I was employed by at that time used performance appraisal as a key tool in their performance-related pay scheme. However, rather than being seen as part of an ongoing developmental process, in that firm performance appraisal was a one-off yearly event, conducted in an almost tokenistic way, with no objectives or development plans. It was a really frustrating and demotivating experience, which I think had a lot to do with my decision to resign.

My current organisation, an insurance company, has been using performance appraisal for at least a decade, but in my view it has only become effective in the past five years. A corporate-wide framework has been adopted by all managers responsible for conducting half-yearly appraisals, part of this framework is the personal development plan (PDP). This plan is used to address an individual's development needs beyond their specific group or department, in the context of the whole organisation. Alongside the PDP are performance objectives, devised by the individual in consultation with their line manager. Objectives are intended to be both task and behaviourally oriented, designed to fulfil the needs both of the individual and the organisation. I think that when it is conducted well, performance appraisal is a valid and beneficial intervention.

However, I must say that my experience of this process has been erratic. The people who conduct the appraisal are really pivotal to its success. Unfortunately, though, I do not think that my company has fully appreciated the importance of this role, and as yet has not invested enough time and money in ensuring that managers are adequately prepared for it. This is disappointing, particularly given that salary increases are typically based on the outputs of the performance appraisal.

In addition, in order for the potential of the appraisal process to be realised, appraisal needs to be used regularly and consistently. Where they have become established, and where they are used thoughtfully, conducted by well-trained managers, they can be an extremely effective performance management tool. In particular, as project and contract work increase, the performance appraisal can be a useful way to align organisational and individual objectives.

Vince

On the first day of my first job I was provided with a log book in which to record my daily training and work experiences. I was required to set out my observations on the work I undertook on each assignment. My assignment supervisor was obliged to give me instant feedback on my performance, and to record this in the log. In addition, this supervisor was required to assess whether I exhibited any particular skills or strengths during the assignment that might be useful to the firm. On a quarterly basis, I was then required to produce an assessment of my training in the period, and to present this for discussion with my principal/mentor. He, too, was required to give me feedback on my career to date, with an assessment of my potential within the firm. On an annual basis, throughout my 'training contract' period of three years, an assessment of my performance was carried out through a structured appraisal process. This, too, was confirmed in writing.

My early training could possibly be described as a combination of 'developmental work assignments', 'career counseling', 'appraisal' and 'mentoring'. As my experience grew, each assignment I undertook increased in complexity. Each task would test me a little further. I believe . . . [that] my overall performance improved the more challenging the assignments became. I learned a great deal about my profession by being 'dropped in at the deep end'.

. . . Needless to say, I found the whole process valuable. Over this time my personal log became a key reference point from which both my employer and I were able to evaluate my strengths and weaknesses. I was able to see how changes and improvements to my technique and skills were taking shape over time. The process placed solid structure and order into what otherwise could have been a greatly bewildering time for me. It allowed my employer to determine whether I was able to meet each of the early stages in my career, from raw trainee, to responsible assignment supervisor and manager. It gave me the chance to bargain with my employer over my responsibilities and remuneration.

Paul

The process of career management intervention in my organisation, a leading aeronautical engineering firm, involves four distinct, but interrelated phases: staff appraisal, the development cell (the management follow-up of the appraisal), personal development plans and the 360° appraisal.

As regards staff appraisal in particular, the system used in my firm, and in fact most of the engineering departments of the civil airline business, has been in place for many years. The appraisal typically takes place in the form of a private discussion between the individual and his or her immediate supervisor or functional manager. The structure of this discussion is directed towards the completion of a formal appraisal form which, upon completion, is entered into the individual's company record. Following this discussion, the appraisal form is passed on to the departmental senior manager for comment. Finally, the individual adds any relevant comments, and signs the form in acceptance. In cases where problems or discrepancies arise, these are discussed by the relevant individuals, and hopefully resolved.

In the past, the frequency of appraisals, and both the quality of the initial discussion and subsequent activities have been somewhat erratic. This, I think, resulted in some degree of cynicism amongst the participants in the process. However, project leaders have recognised these problems, and have worked to rectify them, and to provide a more coherent, and consistent process. It is intended that everyone should be formally appraised on an annual basis. Individuals' performance is measured against the targets outlined through the appraisal process, and this information is made available to all project members, in an attempt to raise the status of the scheme, and to signal the importance placed upon it by senior managers. In addition, in an attempt to create greater coherence between appraisals, the form itself has been modified, such that it now provides an opportunity to reflect on an individual's success at the year end, as well as setting clear goals for the future. In contrast to those who argue that evaluation of past performance and the review of development needs should be separated, I think that the way in which these are synthesised in the current appraisal scheme is a real strength. However, the appraisal mechanism is seen as totally independent from the pay review process, a split that in my view is very important. Likewise, I agree entirely with my department's policy of not using appraisal to rank members of staff. Thus, within the appraisal there is no mechanism for comparing one individual's performance with another's. This is a real strength, as the appraisal does not get stuck on whether a certain individual should be given a 4 instead of a 3, but instead can develop into a meaningful and constructive dialogue.

The development cell is the next step in the staff appraisal. In this forum, the individual is excluded. Instead, it comprises the appraiser, the function manager, and the HR representative aligned with that function. The focus of this discussion is the individual's career, in particular issues such training and development needs, readiness for promotion, and possible job rotations and options. In addition, an assessment is made as to where in the organisation the individual might eventually aspire (e.g. staff technologist, management, company senior staff). Although in the past members of staff felt that this process was too secretive, it has become more open. The individual can now view their completed form, although they can not remove it from the HR department.

As regards my own experience of the development cell, in the very early years of my career I was, somewhat naively, satisfied if the front page summary reflected a successful year. However, after the novelty of a manager's 'nice words' wore off I, like many others, became somewhat cynical that, regardless of the contents of the appraisal, nothing seemed to ever happen as a result. In those days, the development cell seemed more of a 'smoke and mirrors' exercise carried out by management, with the individual excluded from many of the key issues and conclusions. However, I feel that there has been some improvement – although this change in my perception could be a result of the fact that I am now involved in conducting appraisals and development cells myself, and thus have new insights into the process. As an appraisee as well as an appraiser, I am sure there is still room for improvement. In particular, the form should be less prescriptive, and mechanisms should be put in place to ensure that the target of at least one yearly appraisal for all members of staff is realised.

Questions

1. Compare and contrast the stories of Debbie, Vince and Paul. If you have been involved in performance appraisal processes, to what extent do these stories resonate with your own experiences?

2. What would you say are the key advantages and disadvantages of these three schemes?

3. Would you describe these three performance appraisal schemes as 'position' or 'portfolio-centered' career management interventions?

Note: These three case studies are adapted from the work of Paul Borton, Vince Elder and Debbie Hodge, MBA students at The Business School, Loughborough University.

References to Chapter 9

Arnold, J. (1997a) *Managing Careers into the 21st Century*, London: Paul Chapman.

Arnold, J. (1997b) 'Nineteen propositions concerning the nature of effective thinking for career management in a turbulent world', *British Journal of Guidance and Counselling*, 25(4): 447–62.

Arthur, M. and Rousseau, D. (1996) *The Boundaryless Career*, Oxford: Oxford University Press.

Ball, B. and Jordan, M. (1997) 'An open-learning approach to career management and guidance', *British Journal of Guidance and Counselling*, 25(4): 507–16.

Bell, N.E. and Staw, B.M. (1989) 'People as sculptors versus sculpture: the roles of personality and personal control in organisations', in Arthur, M.B., Hall D.T. and Lawrence, B.S. (eds) *Handbook of Career Theory*, New York: Cambridge University Press.

Bird, A. (1996) 'Careers as repositories of knowledge: Considerations for a boundaryless career', in Arthur, M.B. and Rousseau, D.M. (eds) *The Boundaryless Career. A New Employment Principle For A New Organizational Era*, New York: Oxford University Press, 150–68.

Boardman, S.K., Harrington, C.C. and Horowitx, S.V. (1987) 'Successful women: a psychological investigation of family, class and education origins', in Gutek, B.A. and Larwood, L. (eds) *Women's Career Development*, London: Sage.

Cassell, C. and Walsh, S. (1992) 'Being seen but not heard: barriers to women's equality in the workplace', *The Psychologist*, 5: 55–60.

Cohen, L. (1997) *Women's Move from Employment to Self-Employment: Understanding the Transition*, Unpublished PhD thesis, Sheffield Hallam University.

Cohen, L. and Mallon, M. (1999) 'The transition from organisational employment to portfolio working: perceptions of boundarylessness', *Work, Employment and Society*, 13(2): 329–52.

Collin, A. and Watts, A.G. (1996) 'The death and transfiguration of career – and of career guidance?', *British Journal of Guidance and Counselling*, 24(3): 385–98.

Darwin, J., Duhaley, J. and Johnson, P. (2000) 'Contracting in ten English local authorities: preferences and practices', in *International Journal of Public Sector Management*, 13(1): 48–57.

Davidson, M.J. and Cooper, C.L. (1992) *Shattering the Glass Ceiling*, London: Paul Chapman Publishing.

Derr, C.B. (1986) *Managing the New Careerists*, San Francisco, Ca: Jossey-Bass.

Derr, C.B. and Laurent, A. (1989) 'The internal and external career: a theoretical and cross-cultural perspective', in Arthur, M.B., Hall, D.T. and Lawrence, B.S. (eds) *Handbook of Career Theory*, New York: Cambridge University Press.

Driver, M.J. (1982) 'Career concepts: a new approach to career research', in Katz, R. (ed) *Career Issues in Human Resource Management*, Englewood Cliffs, NJ: Prentice-Hall.

Fitzgerald, L.F. and Crites, J.O. (1980) 'Toward a career psychology of women: What do we know? What do we need to know?', *Journal of Counselling Psychology*, 27: 44–62.

Fournier, V. (1998) 'Stories of development and exploitation: Militant voices in an enterprise culture', *Organization*, 5(1): 55–80.

Gallos, J.V. (1989) 'Exploring women's development: implications for career theory, practice and research', in Arthur, M.B., Hall, D.T. and Lawrence, B.S. (eds) *Handbook of Career Theory*, New York: Cambridge University Press.

Goffman, I. (1961) *Asylums*, New York: Anchor.

Grant, D. and Oswick, C. (eds) (1996) *Metaphor and Organization*, London: Sage.

Guest, D. and Mackenzie Davey, K. (1996) 'Don't write off the traditional career', *People Management*, 22 February: 22–25.

Gutteridge, T.G., Leibowitz, Z.B. and Shore, J.E. (1993) *Organisational Career Development*, San Francisco, Ca: Jossey Bass.

Hall, D.T. (1976) *Careers in Organizations*, Pacific Palisades, Ca: Goodyear.

Handy, C. (1996) *Beyond Certainty*, Boston, Mass: Harvard Business School Press.

Heckscher, C. (1995) *White Collar Blues. Management Loyalties in an Age of Corporate Restructuring*, New York: Basic Books.

Herriot, P. and Pemberton, C. (1995) *New Deals*, Chichester: Wiley.

Herriot, P. and Pemberton, C. (1996) 'Contracting Careers', *Human Relations*, June, 49(6): 757–90.

Holland, J.L. (1973) *Making Vocational Choices*, Englewood Cliffs, NJ: Prentice-Hall.

Howard, A. (1992) 'Work and family crossroads spanning the career', in Zedeck, S. (ed) *Work, Families and Organisations*, San Francisco: Jossey-Bass.

Hughes, E.C. (1937) 'Institutional office and the person', *American Journal of Sociology*, 43: 404–13.

Hutton, W. (1995) *The State We're In*, London: Cape.

Iles, P. and Mabey, C. (1993) 'Managerial career development programmes: effectiveness, availability and acceptability', *British Journal of Management*, 4(3): 11–16.

Inkson, K. (1995) 'Effects of changing economic conditions on managerial job changes and careers', *British Journal of Management*, 6: 183–94.

Kanter, R.M. (1989) 'Careers and the wealth of nations: a macro-perspective on the structure and implications of career forms', in Arthur, M.B., Hall, D.T., and Lawrence, B.S. (eds) *Handbook of Career Theory*, New York: Cambridge University Press.

Lancaster, H. (1994) 'Managing your career: a new social contract to benefit employer and employee', *Wall Street Journal*, 29 November.

Leach, J.L. and Chakiris, B.J. (1988) 'The future of work, careers and jobs', *Training and Development Journal*, April: 48–54.

Levinson, D. (1978) *The Seasons of a Man's Life*, New York: Knopf.

London, M. and Stumpf, S. (1982) *Managing Careers*, Reading, Mass: Addison-Wesley.

Macauley, S. and Harding, N. (1996) 'Drawing up a new careers contract', *People Management*, 4 April: 34–5.

Mackenzie Davey, K. and Guest, D. (1994) 'Self-development and the career: a review of some issues', Paper prepared for the Careers Research Forum, available from the authors at Birkbeck College, University of London.

Mallon, M. (1998) *From Managerial Career To Portfolio Career: Making Sense of the Transition*, Unpublished PhD thesis, Sheffield Hallam University.

Marshall, J. (1984) *Women Managers: Travellers in a Male World*, Chichester: Wiley.

Marshall, J. (1989) 'Re-visioning career concepts: a feminist invitation', in Arthur, M.D., Hall, D.T. and Lawrence, B.S. (eds) *Handbook of Career Theory*, New York: Cambridge University Press.

Marshall, J. (1995) *Women Managers Moving On*, London: Routledge.

Martin, J., Price, R.L., Bies, R.J. and Powers, M.E. (1987) 'Now that I can have it, I'm not so sure I want it: the effects of opportunity on aspirations and discontent', in Gutek, B.A. and Larwood, L. (eds) *Women's Career Development*, London: Sage.

Mayo, A. (1991) *Managing Careers in Organisations*, London: IPM.

Mirvis, P.H. and Hall, D.T. (1994) 'Psychological success and the boundaryless career', *Journal of Organisational Behaviour*, 15: 365–80.

Morgan, G. (1986) *Images of Organization*, London: Sage.

Musson, G. and Cohen, L. (1998) 'Making sense of enterprise: identity, power and the enterprise culture', in Ram, M., Deakins, D., and Smallbone, D. (eds) *Small Firms. Enterprising Futures*, London: Paul Chapman.

Nicholson, N. and West, M. (1989) 'Transitions, work histories and careers', in Arthur, M.B., Hall, D.T. and Lawrence, B.S. (eds) *Handbook of Career Theory*, New York: Cambridge University Press.

Office for National Statistics (1999) *Labour Force Survey Quarterly Supplement*, Spring.

Office for National Statistics (2000) *Labour Market Trends*, April.

Piore, M.J. and Sabel, C.F. (1984) *The Second Industrial Divide: Possibilities for Prosperity*, New York: Basic Books.

Potter, J. and Wetherell, M. (1987) *Discourse and Social Psychology*, London: Sage.

Powers, C. (1997) *In the Memory of the Forest*, London: Anchor.

Raelin, J. (1986) *The Clash of Cultures: Managers and Professionals*, Boston, Mass: Harvard Business School Press.

Robinson, S.L. and Rousseau, D.M. (1994) 'Violating the psychological contract: not the exception but the norm', *Journal of Organisational Behaviour*, 15: 245–59.

Schein, E.H. (1978) *Career Dynamics*, Reading, Mass: Addison-Wesley.

Schein, E.H. (1993) *Career Anchors: Discovering your Real Values*, 1st edition, London: Pfeffer and Co.

Sennett, R. (1998) *The Corrosion of Character: the Personal Consequences of Work in the New Capitalism*, New York: W.W. Norton & Co.

Sparrow, P. and Marchington, M. (1998) *Human Resource Management: the New Agenda*, London: Financial Times/Pitman.

Summers, J. (1999) 'How to broaden your career management programme', *HR Focus*, 76(6): 26–32.

Super, D.E. (1957) *The Psychology of Careers*, New York: Harper and Row.

Super, D.E. (1973) 'The work values inventory', in Zytowski, D.G. (ed) *Contemporary Approaches to Interest Measurement*, Minneapolis: University of Minnesota Press.

Super, D.E., Thompson, A.S. and Lindeman, R.H. (1985) *The Adult Careers Concern Inventory*, Palo Alto, Ca: Consulting Psychologists' Press.

Templar, A.J. and Cawsey, T.F. (1999) 'Rethinking career development in an era of portfolio careers', *Career Development International*, 4(2): 70–76.

Thair, T. and Ridson, A. (1999) 'Women in the labour market: results from the Spring 1998 Labour Force Survey', *Labour Market Trends*, March: 103–13.

Thomas, D. and Higgins, M. (1996) 'Mentoring and the boundaryless career', in Arthur, M. and Rousseau, D. (eds) *The Boundaryless Career*, Oxford: Oxford University Press.

White, B. (1995) 'The career development of successful women', *Women in Management Review*, 10(3): 4–15.

Wilensky, H. (1961) 'Work, careers and social integration', *International Social Science Journal*, 12(4): 543–74.

Chapter 10

Downsizing: the dark side of HRM

Tom Redman and Adrian Wilkinson

Introduction

In this chapter we introduce the subject of organisational downsizing by discussing its extent and potential for causing problems when mismanaged. The breadth and depth of organisational restructuring seen in the industrialised economies has been significant in recent years. Secondly, we review the methods by which downsizing occurs and consider a range of alternatives to its use. Thirdly, we examine the processes involved and focus in particular on consultation, redundancy selection and support for both those made redundant and the survivors of downsizing. Lastly, we conclude by asking whether the costs of downsizing, in both financial and human terms, are too high a price to pay for the organisational gains. Here we address the view that downsizing translates simply into 'increased stress and decreased job security' (De Meuse *et al.*, 1997: 168). In short, we ask, does lean mean mean?

Downsizing: the reality of HRM?

> The lack of labour market protection, the weakness of unions and the intense pressure on private and public sector companies alike to improve their profitability and efficiency have meant that the fashionable doctrine of downsizing has spread like a contagion.
>
> (Hutton, 1997: 40)

The above comment from Hutton reflects that organisational downsizing, defined as a 'planned elimination of positions or jobs' (Cascio, 1993), is thus now firmly established as a central aspect of HRM practice in the UK. However, after a perusal of the growing numbers of textbooks on HRM a reader could be forgiven for thinking that HRM practice is largely associated with a positively virtuous image in the organisation. Righteous HRM managers recruit, train, devise strategies, manage rewards and careers, involve employees, improve labour relations, solve problems, etc, for the mutual benefit of the organisation and workforce (see, for example, Torrington and Hall, 1998; Armstrong, 1997; Hendry, 1994). Most management books take an upbeat tone with little reference to the more unpalatable aspects of downsizing and redundancy. References are to the 'ascendant' organisations (Wickens, 1995) and 'beyond world class' (Morton, 1994). Revitalising change is an entirely positive process to do with 'rooting out inertia', promoting efficiency and fostering innovation (Fombrun, 1992). Peters' *Liberation Management* (1992) makes no mention of downsizing in over 800 pages of text! Downsizing is more apparent in the Dilbert books (Adams, 1996), the Doonesbury cartoons (Anfuso, 1996) and novels of HRM (Kemske, 1996). When managers do discuss downsizing it tends to be couched in very euphemistic terms (see Box 10.1). However, an examination of managerial practice over the last decade or so also finds a darker side to HRM in organisational downsizing.

BOX 10.1

The sanitisation of dismissal: sacking goes out of fashion

Redundancy and dismissal are one area of HRM practice that particularly suffers from euphemistic jargon. Some of the terms HRM managers use include:

building down	exiting	releasing
career reappraisal	headcount reduction	resizing
compressing	involuntary quit	restructuring
decruiting	lay-off	retrenchment
dehiring	letting-go	rightsizing
dejobbing	non-retaining	severance
delayering	outplacing	slimming
demassing	payroll adjustment	streamlining
deselection	rationalising	termination
disemploying	rebalancing	wastage
downscoping	reduction in force	
downsizing	re-engineering	

The motor industry seems especially afflicted in this respect, perhaps as a result of the large scale of recent workforce reductions For example, General Motors described one plant closure as a 'volume-related production schedule adjustment', Chrysler referred to 'a career alternative enhancement program' whilst Nissan introduced a 'separation program'. Two motor industry personnel managers interviewed about the effects of lean production methods talked of 'increasing the velocity of organizational exit' and 'liberating from our organisation' those who could not accommodate the new system. One also talked of getting rid of the PUREs (Previously Unrecognised Recruitment Errors). In contrast, the language of the shopfloor is much more direct and includes being: sacked, canned, given your cards, axed and sent down the road.

Despite its importance and growing prominence, this aspect of HRM rarely merits treatment in the texts (Wright, 1994). According to Cameron (1994), it is the 'most pervasive, yet understudied' phenomenon in the business world (1994: 183). In those few texts that recognise its existence the focus is usually on a discussion of how to avoid the legal pitfalls when reducing the workforce or a simple attempt to quantify its use. Much rarer is any discussion that examines the nature, significance and aftermath of making people redundant. This neglect is a serious and somewhat puzzling one.

One possible explanation for the neglect of this issue lies in the view that workforce reduction is considered to be an isolated and unpleasant element of HRM practice and one that is best hurriedly carried out and quickly forgotten: the so called 'Mafia model' of downsizing (Stebbins, 1989). The statistics for redundancy and dismissal in Britain would, however, suggest that, unpleasant though it may be, workforce reduction is not an isolated event, rather it is a central aspect of HRM practice in recent years (see Table 10.1). In the IRS survey of redundancy two-thirds of organisations had reduced their staff over the last two years with the number of jobs lost ranging from 4 to over 10,000 (IRS, 1998a; 1998b). Individual UK-based companies have undergone massive layoffs, for example, BT shed 88,000 out of 237,000 (37 per cent) between 1990 and 1994, BP 118,050 to 66,500 (44 per cent) and Rolls Royce 65,900 to 43,500 (34 per cent). In the 1980s the brunt of job reductions were borne by the manufacturing sector, with services suffering particularly in the 1990s. For example, financial services alone lost 150,000 jobs between 1990 and 1995 (IRS, 1995a). The public sector has also suffered, with privatisation and outsourcing leading to large-scale redundancies in the former privatised industries and in the public sector more generally (Deakin and Wilkinson, 1999).

In Europe, in the early 1990s the Cranfield surveys found that over 30 per cent of firms in all but two countries (Germany and the Netherlands – where the level was 20 per cent) reported reductions in the workforce (Papalexandris, 1996). In some of the central and eastern European countries surveyed, this was over 80 per cent. In the USA, surveys report more than 85 per cent of Fortune 1,000 companies having downsized between 1987 and 1991 and in the early 1990s 100 per cent were planning to continue to do so in the next five years. There has also been little abatement in the levels of job loss in the USA, with record levels of announced job cuts being posted in 1998 (Vanderheiden *et al.*, 1999). Particularly worrying here is the numbers of organisations downsizing who are actually making healthy profits (Storey *et al.*, 1999). Organisational size is no longer a measure of corporate success (Cameron, 1994). Western managers, it seems, have a bent for sacking employees. Indeed, some have suggested that the role of HR professional has undergone a significant transformation during this period. According to Hunt (1984: 6):

> The personnel role has undergone a radical re-alignment from finding, training and developing human beings to excluding, exiting and retiring them.

Table 10.1

Year	Number of redundancies (000's)
1977	158
1978	173
1979	187
1980	494
1981	532
1982	398
1983	324
1984	245
1985	235
1986	238
1987	144
1988	108
1989	144
1990	181
1991	391
1992	331
1993	267
1994	209
1995	222
1996	212
1997	208
1998	208

Note: Figures for 1977–1990 are based on the Department of Employment's statutory returns measuring confirmed redundancies – whilst those after 1990 are based on individual returns from the Labour Force Survey which are on average around 30 per cent higher (see Deakin and Wilkinson, 1999). This stems from the exclusion in the earlier years of redundancies of 10 employees or fewer from a single establishment.

Source: various editions of the *Employment Gazette* and *Labour Market Trends*.

One trigger for increasing interest and attention for downsizing, above and beyond its greater extent and scale than in the past, is that as Sennett (1998:18) notes: 'Downsizings and reengineerings impose on middle class people sudden disasters which were in an earlier capitalism much more confined to the working classes.' Heckscher argues that it is because job reductions now transcend hierarchical levels and occupational types, including many professional workers, that it will lead to greater interest than in the past:

> The current restructuring cuts managers adrift from the stable communities that formerly framed their career prospects and threatens to throw them into a world of fierce competition. The reduction of security, the threat to poor performers, and the general diminution in numbers have raised the stakes for those who remain. There is great pressure for harder work, higher productivity and beating out fellow workers. As the ranks of management have thinned, opportunities for advancement have necessarily declined; thus promotion is no longer a predictable reward for steady work. Indeed, the downsizing trend has begun to erase the key distinction between managers and workers: for the first time managers are being treated as a variable cost rather than a part of the fixed base.
>
> (Heckscher, 1995: 4)

Effectively managing workforce reduction is thus of increasing importance in HRM practice, not only because of its greater scale and frequency but also because of the potentially serious negative effects of its mismanagement. The mismanagement of workforce reduction can clearly cause major damage to both the organisation's employment and general business reputations. Damage to the former can seriously affect an organization's selection attractiveness with potential future employees by producing an uncaring, 'hire and fire' image. Similarly, bad publicity over retrenchment can cause customers to worry that the firm may go out of business or give rise to problems in the continuity or quality of supplies and services, and so on.

There have also been increasing recent concerns about the organisational effectiveness of the post-downsized 'anorexic organisation'. The benefits which organisations claim to be seeking from downsizing centre on savings in labour costs, speedier decision-making, better communication, reduced product development time, enhanced involvement of employees and greater responsiveness to customers (De Meuse *et al.*, 1997: 168). However, reports suggest that the results of downsizing are 'illusory' and the long-term effects 'terrifying' (Mason, 1997). Downsizing, it seems, can have a damaging effect on corporate performance. Cole, drawing from learning theory, points out that employee turnover (whether voluntary or involuntary) hurts organisational memory in so far as individual organisational members have 'a primary repository of an organisation's operational knowledge and trust' which cannot be easily replaced as it is impossible to document. This is especially relevant in terms of customer contact as bonds are built with individuals (Cole, 1993: 14–15).

Paradoxically, restructuring has also been seen as a sign of corporate virility and stock market prices boomed in the context of such plans. Barclays Bank shares soared after its announcement of the axing of 6,000 staff (Garfield, 1999). However, there is some suggestion from the literature that, while shares of downsizing companies have outperformed the stock market for six months or so after downsizing, three years later they lagged behind (Mitchell *et al.* cited by Mickthart and Hardy,: 35). Equally, other studies have found downsizing has an adverse effect on innovation (Dougherty and Bowman, 1995) and on the bottom line (McKinley *et al.*, 1995). Empirical research has found that companies using lay-offs as a strategy for financial improvements failed to achieve this, and profit margins, return on assets and return on equity continued to deteriorate but at an even faster rate than pre-downsizing (De Meuse *et al.*, 1994).

Industrial conflict and workforce resistance (e.g. via strikes, sit-ins, work-ins, etc) are also potential problems that arise in periods of retrenchment. However, given the unparalleled levels of workforce reductions, the relatively low level of disputes overall is perhaps surprising. It may reflect not only reduced trade union and worker power but also the fact that redundancy is now so commonplace and woven into the fabric of industrial life that it is seen as an inevitable consequence of work in hypercompetitive times. It is thus no longer as frequently resisted via industrial action, especially when we find that in the cases where unions have taken action in the past they have rarely been successful in resisting job losses (Dickson and Judge, 1987).

Thus, in 1990 redundancy was less likely to be mentioned as an issue for any form of industrial action amongst any section of the workforce (Millward *et al.*, 1992: 288). The latest WERS data report any form of industrial conflict over downsizing as a very rare event (Cully *et al.*, 1999). According to Guest and Peccei (1992: 36), conflict over redundancy is now reduced to the level of 'a ritual protest' from unions with workers enticed into acceptance by generous severance terms. The form of union resistance to redundancy has thus changed to one of attempting to secure the best deal possible for members via job security agreements which incorporate consultation mechanisms, severance payments and supportive measures, alongside a general lobbying and campaigning role, with industrial action a very rarely used last resort (e.g. see IRS, 1995b; Storey *et al.*, 1999).

The potential negative impact of downsizing is not restricted to those who leave but it has also a major effect on the remaining employees. Such employees are, by their very nature, now much more important to the employer, but are often over-looked in downsizing situations. The impact of downsizing on the remaining employees is such that commentators now talk of 'the survivor syndrome' (Brockner, 1992). This is the term given to the collection of behaviours such as 'decreased motivation, morale and loyalty to the organization, and increased stress levels and skepticism' that are exhibited by those who are still in employment fol-lowing restructuring (Doherty and Horstead, 1995).

Given this rather damning account, the question arises why it is that organisations still seem so fond of downsizing? According to Hutton, in the UK this is because of:

> The bias in the system to financial values over those of production and innovation, so that at the margin a dividend pay-out is preferred to an additional pound of research and development, an extra profit now is preferred to higher profits in the future. This is why British companies tend to look for higher returns over shorter periods than their international competitors and why, under intense pressure to minimize their costs, they are under such constant pressure to downsize and reduce their core labour force.
>
> (Hutton, 1997: 47)

We return to this question in our concluding section.

Methods of downsizing

There are a number of ways in which organisations can reduce the size of the workforce. In this section we firstly examine the ones employers use the most: nat-ural wastage, compulsory and voluntary redundancy, and early retirement (see Table 10.2) Secondly, we consider a range of alternatives to dismissing workers, in particular redeployment and wage reduction.

Table 10.2 Methods of reducing the workforce (%)

Method	1990	1998
Natural wastage	67	57
Redeployment	45	32
Early retirement and voluntary redundancy	47	37
Compulsory redundancy	30	27

Source: Millward *et al.*, 1992; Cully *et al.*, 1999

Natural attrition/wastage

Natural wastage is often proffered as the most positive and humane method of workforce reduction. It is seen as giving individuals a free choice in whether to leave or stay and thus reduces the potential for conflict and employees' feelings of powerlessness. Evidence suggests that it is not the exact equivalent of normal labour turnover. It appears that in a redundancy situation both the rate and nature of labour turnover change. Early research reported that labour turnover increases in retrenchment situations (Bulmer, 1971; Wedderburn, 1965) but this may reflect more on the nature of the labour market, with alternative jobs easier to obtain during this period. This form of workforce reduction poses problems for management in that it is unplanned and uncontrollable. Some evidence also suggests that it depresses workforce morale more than the short sharp shock approach of redundancy. Research by Turner (1988) in mining found it creates uncertainty over a much longer period and results in a greater intensification of work for those who remain. Natural wastage is also a form of job loss that is much more difficult for employees and unions to resist because of its incremental nature.

Voluntary redundancy

This method is increasingly most employers' preferred method of downsizing. Some common concerns are that it is expensive, because employees with long service find it attractive, and that the best workers leave because there is demand for their skills whilst poorer workers stay because they are less marketable. There is little evidence on which to base a judgement here but Hardy's (1987) research suggests the reverse actually occurs in practice. Marginal performers are more likely to take up voluntary redundancy packages because of either disillusionment with the job or the fear of dismissal without any financial cushion at a later date. Savery *et al.* (1998) report that high absenteeism and low commitment are associated largely with those who have expressed an interest in voluntary redundancy. The main advantages are that at least employees are given a choice and this destigmatizes, to some extent, the loss of the job. Although voluntary redundancy is much preferred to compulsory forms it is sometimes seen by unions as 'selling jobs' (Barrar and Sullivan, 1988).

There is, however, considerable evidence that voluntary redundancy is often far from a willing choice on the part of employees, with many reports of managers 'leaning' on targeted employees, leading to the question of whether they jumped or were pushed. Westergaard *et al.* (1989) followed up a sample of redundancy volunteers and found that 40 per cent subsequently felt they had been coerced into accepting redundancy. Research on teacher lay-offs also found a wide range of informal and very threatening tactics used by managers to 'encourage' particular teachers to volunteer. In one case this included a manager threatening to disclose to an employee's spouse his extramarital affairs if the teacher did not 'volunteer' for redundancy (Sinclair *et al.*, 1995). Lewis suggests managers can encourage volunteers by targeting particular groups, using persuasive communications and by presenting overpessimistic manpower forecasts. Such tactics are aimed at pressurising employees and reducing morale in order to elicit more volunteers by 'sickening them into submission' (Lewis, 1993: 34). Research by Wass (1996) on the coal industry showed how extra-statutory redundancy payments were effective in obtaining the 'voluntary' acceptance by targeted groups and the voluntary system was used to 'control selection for redundancy'.

Compulsory redundancy

Compulsory redundancy – where no choice is presented to the departing employee – is normally a 'last resort' strategy for employers and is usually seen as the least acceptable face of downsizing. However, as it is based on managerial decision-making, it gives employers the opportunity to design and implement criteria based on business needs. For example, the increasing emphasis on research in UK universities has meant that 'publish or perish' has never been taken so literally. One effect of the periodic assessment of research quality in UK universities, via the Research Assessment Exercise, has been that some universities have been targeting research-inactive lecturers for compulsory redundancy (BBC Online News, 17 January 1999).

Compulsory redundancy is also more common where downsizings are large-scale or involve complete plant closures. According to WERS data, compulsory redundancy is also much more common in the private sector than in the public sector (Cully *et al.*, 1999). However, it has also been suggested that compulsory redundancy is becoming more frequent in the public sector as the potential for voluntary redundancy and early retirement has been exhausted and, more generally, because of doubts about the latter's effectiveness.

Early retirement

Early retirement schemes are usually utilised alongside other methods of workforce reduction, although it is often sufficient of itself to generate the required cuts. It is often seen less as a method of redundancy and more as a way of avoiding it (Casey, 1992: 426). The mechanics differ from other methods in one key respect: employees opting for early retirement are less likely to seek to re-enter the workforce. The increasing use of early retirement can be detected in surveys, which measure the declining economic activity rates of older employees. Although considerable reduction has occurred in the participation rates of male workers aged over 55 in the UK the decline has been steeper in countries such as Finland, France, Germany, and the Netherlands. For example, in Germany the employment rate of men aged 55–65 dropped from 65.5 per cent to 60.1 per cent over the decade 1982–92 and in France from 59.8 per cent to 44 per cent (Manpower Argus, 1995). In Germany the so-called 59er actions (59er Aktionen), whereby employees who are over the age of 59 are dismissed and thus become eligible for early pensions, have greatly increased.

Ill-health (see below) is one cause for the increase in early retirement, but other developments at both company and national level also lie behind the increase. At national level there has been a desire by governments in the USA and Europe as well as other industrialised countries to increase work opportunities for younger workers. At company level the expansion of occupational pension schemes and the inclusion of standard arrangements for redundancy retirement have facilitated the use of early retirement as a method of workforce reduction (McGoldrick and Cooper, 1989). The use of enhanced early retirement benefit makes it more palatable. It would also appear that many managers, usually with little supporting evidence, associate increasing age with declining levels of productivity and poorer-quality performance. Ageism in managerial circles, it seems, is rife and some companies even have formal 'first in first out' redundancy policies (IRS, 1994). The view that older workers have critical experience and expertise with 'seasoning', an asset rather than a liability, is not widely shared (Clabaugh, 1997). The main exception here appears to be senior managers themselves. The increasing age profile of directors has caused some to question whether there should be a 'sell-by' date for such a group (Weyer, 1994). A further incentive to dismiss older workers is provided by the nature of some payment systems, such as the incremental schemes common in the public sector, whereby cost savings can be made by replacing older and more expensive employees by younger and cheaper ones.

There are a number of advantages of early retirement ('downsizing with dignity' – Barbee, 1986). In particular, it is seen as carrying less stigma than other forms of redundancy; 'retired' is a much more socially acceptable 'r' word than 'redundant'. However, there are also a number of drawbacks. The decline of 'last in first out' (LIFO) redundancy selection criteria (see below), which protected older workers by virtue of seniority, has left them disproportionately vulnerable to enforced early retirement under employers' labour-shedding policies.

People are now living longer and retiring earlier and thus need sound financial provision if demeaning financial dependency is to be avoided. The adequacy of early retirement benefits is under increasing question. A growing number of ex-employees who were persuaded to take early retirement are experiencing financial difficulties (Mallier and Shafto, 1994). A particular problem concerns the fall in the real value of pensions in Britain, not least because of indexing to prices rather than, as in Germany, wages. Early retirees who may be happy with their level of income when they leave work may find their absolute position deteriorating over time and thus become more dependent on means-tested public benefits (Casey, 1992: 438).

It is unclear whether current trends in early retirement will continue, not least because of uncertainty over the capacity of pension funds to sustain the costs. Unions, although they perceive a number of real benefits to early retirement, are also starting to question the appropriateness of using pension funds to reduce employers' redundancy costs via early retirement.

Ill-health retirement

There has been a major increase in level of ill-health retirements in the 1990s (IRS, 1995c). A commonly voiced argument is that this is a consequence of intensification of work and associated increases in stress levels which result in more long-term sickness. The teaching profession provides us with an illustrative example of this widespread trend. In teaching the advent of initiatives such as the national curriculum, standard assessment tests, local management of schools, formula funding, inspections, performance league tables, performance appraisal (and, imminently, performance-related pay) amongst others has led to increasing class sizes, increased work loads, lay-offs and a declining morale. One effect was a doubling of teacher retirements on ill-health grounds between 1987 and 1993 (Sinclair *et al.*, 1995).

Alternatives to redundancy

Employers are often encouraged to consider alternatives to redundancies and to view compulsory redundancy especially, only as a last resort. For example, the House of Commons Employment Committee's report *The Management of Redundancies* urged employers to devise more imaginative alternatives rather than mechanically resorting to lay-offs. There is a wide range of possible alternatives to redundancy. These include redeployment, freezing recruitment, disengaging contractors and other flexible workers, reducing overtime, secondments, career breaks, and introducing more flexible working patterns such as job-sharing and part-time work. For example, in the USA, Delta Airlines, Lincoln Electric and Rhino Food are often-cited exemplars of how adjustments can be made in the use of temporary workers, subcontracting, etc, to reduce the impact of downsizing on core staff (De Meuse *et al.*, 1997: 172).

However, despite such calls, there is little evidence for any widespread development of redundancy alternatives in Britain. For some commentators an explanation lies in the ease with which British employers can dismiss their workers without having to consider alternatives. Turnbull and Wass (1997) argue that deregulation has made redundancy, or what the EU terms 'collective dismissal', easier than other forms of workforce reduction. It seems that, as a consequence of a more protracted dismissal process, other countries have a much greater emphasis on avoiding redundancy. Japan and Scandinavian countries have the most developed forms of employment protection with graded steps for cost reduction. In the case of Japan, this includes redeployment, relocation, retraining, transfer and even the suspending of dividends and cutting the salaries of senior managers. As Turnbull and Wass (1997) acutely point out, this is the exact reverse of the British picture, where dividends and the bonus payments of senior managers are boosted by making workers redundant in the pursuit of short-term profit improvements. Following an analysis of redundancy in steel, coal and port-transport industries, Turnbull and Wass (1997) call for the 'reconversion' of employees rather than their redundancy. Reconversion is seen as a socially and economically more effective alternative to redundancy via the redirection of workers to more productive activities either within the firm or other industries. Such a change in emphasis requires more resources to be devoted to retraining rather than to compensate for job loss.

Some of the main alternatives to redundancy are now briefly discussed.

Wage reductions

Wage cuts as an alternative to job cuts tend to be sparingly used, although there have been a number of prominent examples in the UK, as a method of cost reduction. The case of the attempted reduction of wages for British Gas showroom workers, which coincided with the controversial pay increases awarded to senior managers, is a good example. Following a much-publicised campaign, pay cuts were not fully implemented. Instead a 'two-tier deal' was agreed, combining pay freezes for existing staff and lower market-oriented rates and conditions (levelled down to competitors' rates/conditions in the 'white goods' market) for new recruits (IRS, 1995a).

Pay freezes or cuts, so the pain is shared as in the above example, are not widespread. A particular use has been in the introduction of US concession-style bargaining arrangements wherein employees forgo a wage increase for some form of job security agreement. For example, such agreements were reached in local government at Sheffield in the late 1980s. In 1994 Tate and Lyle agreed a major restructuring of its pay and productivity arrangements in an attempt to achieve a fully flexible, multiskilled and 'restriction-free' workplace. The agreement included a security of employment deal involving redeployment, outplacement support and retraining elements (IRS, 1994).

This phenomenon that wages are 'sticky' downwards and labour markets respond to falls in demand by employment adjustments is well established in economic theory. Sullivan has researched the implications for HRM policy in such diverse situations as R&D (Sullivan and Hogge, 1987) and the wire industry (Barrar and Sullivan, 1988). What Sullivan terms 'wage fix/employment flex' was found to operate widely, with managers faced by a recession seeking to control labour costs (via redundancies), improve productivity and maintain employment reputation and workers' morale. The mechanisms that best achieved this were adjustments to employment rather than wage levels. Neither management nor unions sought to negotiate on maintaining employment as an alternative to real wages as this would damage the 'implicit contract' between workers and managers. An alternative might be reducing hours as VW did in the early 1990s. Rowlinson (1996) also argues that rather than downsizing senior staff in an ageist way (because of the high cost), a policy of salary reduction may make more sense, both for the employer (keeping experienced staff) and the employee who is likely to have to accept a wage reduction if they go elsewhere. However, the implications for those in final-salary pension schemes may make such a prospect financially unattractive over the longer term.

Redeployment

Although employers' attempts to secure more flexible workforces have been subject to a great deal of debate of late, the concept of spatial flexibility and the redeployment of workers has received little attention. In the USA redeployment – or 'inplacement' (Stuller, 1993) – is well established. In some cases employers have even been reported as temporarily redeploying by 'loaning' excess staff to other companies (Francis *et al.*, 1992). There are some examples in the UK where a number of companies have developed redeployment policies and practices. For example, Ford run a central clearing house which ensures that the details of all vacancies are circulated. John Lewis claim to have virtually avoided redundancy situations altogether by extensive use of redeployment. The nature of redeployment makes it more readily applicable to lower-level grades of employees than higher-graded posts such as managers, not least because there tend to be more opportunities available at this level. In the recession of the mid-1970s, Japanese corporations maintained as many as four million permanent employees despite the lack of work for them to do, with redeployment easier, given the tendency to straddle several industries (Hill, 1989: 51). As Bamber (1999) notes 'even in the 1990s when Japanese weaknesses were identified, plant closure and sell-offs were rarely carried out, and while the Japanese method of labour handling during a recession makes it difficult to instigate quick turnarounds in bleeding companies; on the other hand it also means that companies have resources at hand for a rapid expansion when there is a business turn up'.

Redeployment is not an easy option for managers. It requires considerable co-operation between different divisions, plants and departments within a firm and brings a number of often costly implications. A common need is for redeployed workers to be retrained and reskilled. Relocation and/or travelling costs can be incurred. A key issue in supporting redeployment is the degree of pay protection given to such workers. The reality of redeployment is that most workers are redeployed to lower-graded posts. Many employers protect the existing income of redeployed workers for a specified period, e.g. at British Steel (now Corus) it was three years.

Redeployment can also be problematic for the employee, and counselling – not least to help workers overcome a sense of loss – is recommended (Lane, 1988). As well as changes in terms and conditions and location it can involve disruptive changes in the pattern of work, for example, a move to shift working. Guest and Peccei's (1992) study of a British plant closure found that redeployed workers often felt coerced into moving and unwelcome at the new sites. Workers redeployed from the South of England to northern plants faced particular difficulties in integration as they were seen as taking the jobs away from the local community in areas of high unemployment. Some employers, while outwardly appearing to promote redeployment by having pools for displaced workers, make little effort to actually place staff in new jobs. The workers in the pool quickly become disillusioned and demoralised and opt for redundancy.

The redundancy process

Redundancy, despite the practice that managers have had in implementing it of late, is often badly managed, with many negative consequences. In part this may stem from the rarity of formal redundancy procedures. The large majority of employers do not have an agreed and written redundancy procedure. Recent notions of partnership have begun to address such concerns. Some agreements have embodied no compulsory redundancy guarantees. The recent WERS data reported that 14 per cent of workplaces (with 25 or more employees) had a guaranteed job security or no compulsory redundancy policy (Cully *et al.*, 1999). In contrast, an IRS survey (1998a, 1998b) of Japanese plants in the UK reported that 20 out of 23 provide some form of job guarantee.

There is much to be gained from a humane, planned and strategic approach to downsizing. According to Cameron (1994, 1998), the way downsizing is implemented is more important than the fact that it is implemented. He reports on three approaches to downsizing.

Workforce reduction strategies are focused primarily on reducing headcount and are usually implemented in a top-down, speedy way. However, the downside of such an approach is that it is seen as 'equivalent to throwing a grenade into a crowded room, closing the door and expecting the explosion to eliminate a certain percentage of the workforce. It is difficult to predict exactly who will be eliminated and who will remain' (Cameron, 1994: 197). Secondly, *work redesign strategies*, aim to reduce work (in addition to or instead of reducing the number of workers) through redesigning tasks, reducing work hours, merging units, etc. However, these are difficult to implement swiftly and hence are seen as a medium-term strategy. Thirdly, *systemic strategies* focus more broadly on changing culture, attitude and values, not just changing workforce size. This involves 'redefining downsizing as an on-going process, as a basis for continuous improvement; rather than as a programme or a target. Downsizing is also equated with simplification of all aspects of the organization – the entire system including supplies, inventories, design process, production methods, customer relations, marketing and sales support, and so on' (Cameron, 1994: 199). Again, this strategy requires longer-term perspectives than that of workforce reduction.

Table 10.3 Three types of downsizing strategies

	Workforce reduction	Work redesign	Systemic
Focus	Headcount	Jobs, levels, units	Culture
Eliminate	People	Work	Status quo
Implementation time	Quick	Moderate	Extended
Payoff target	Short-term payoff	Moderate-term payoff	Long-term payoff
Inhibits	Long-term adaptability	Quick payback	Short-term cost savings
Examples	Attrition	Combine functions	Involve everyone
	Lay-offs	Merge units	Simplify everything
	Early retirement	Redesign jobs	Bottom-up change
	Buy-out packages	Eliminate layers	Target hidden costs

Source: Cameron, 1994

To what extent is such advice heeded in reality? 'Good practice' suggests that three elements of the redundancy process are often critical: consultation with employees, the selection decision and pre-post-redundancy support both for those made redundant and for those who remain. We deal with each of these in turn.

Consultation

Consultation with unions and employees is emphasised in most accounts of downsizing. Employees need to understand the rationale for downsizing and also how the process will be managed. Breaks in communication are seen as sinister and lead to rumours (Kettley, 1995). There is, however, a concern that much consultation is often only a token effort, with many managers seeing it as a 'time-wasting charade' (Fowler, 1993: 6). Recent research for the Department of Trade and Industry suggests that this is perhaps too harsh a judgement. Consultation with unions over redundancies can make a difference to the nature of the redundancy process used, and, occasionally, to the numbers of jobs lost (Edwards and Hall, 1999). The downsizing process is often characterised by secrecy and swiftness and is thus often poorly planned and executed with little scope for employee involvement. To some extent this reluctance to consult over workforce reduction stems from it being seen as part of a deeply entrenched managerial prerogative about the right to hire and fire and close down businesses.

Legislative restrictions on managerial prerogative in redundancy are extremely limited in the UK. Firstly, the requirement is to consult rather than negotiate over redundancies (for a minimum of 30 days in cases of 20–99 redundancies and 90 days for more than 100), although this should include examining ways of avoiding dismissal. Secondly, this consultation used to be limited to recognised unions only and in the increasing non-union sector there was no such statutory requirement. However, following a ruling against the UK by the European Court of Justice in June 1994 under the *Acquired Rights* and the *Collective Redundancies* Directives, UK Regulations were issued in 1995 to provide for consultative mechanisms with 'appropriate' (employee) representatives in non-union organisations. The *Collective Redundancies and Transfer of Undertakings (Protection of Employment) Regulations*, which came into force on 28 July 1999 and have been applied from 1 November 1999, strengthened the 1995 regulations. The new regulations lay down specific requirements for electing employee representatives to be consulted in non-union organisations at times of redundancy. Thirdly, redundancy consultation is often not complied with in practice, with managers choosing to make additional payments in lieu of notice so as to shed workers quickly via the short sharp shock approach of a sudden announcement and a quick lay-off. Here the new regulations have buttressed and simplified the remedies that employees and their representatives may obtain in cases where employers fail to provide the required consultation. It remains to be seen how effective these new regulations are in practice.

Despite this lack of use, there is some evidence that extensive consultation and employee involvement, although they do little to reduce the stress caused by job loss, can help in its smooth implementation. US studies indicate that increased communication and participation of employees in the downsizing process were associated with improvement (Cameron, 1994). Lloyds Bank's downsizing of 15,000 jobs since 1990 led to low morale and trust and a business change programme to explain the direction of the organisation was introduced. Unfortunately, the merger with TSB meant that this was put on hold (Purcell and Hutchinson, 1996: 28). BP Chemicals in the mid-1990s was seen as a 'good case' with a reduction in headcount of 21,000 (1990) to 9,500 (1994/5) facilitated by managers acting as carriers of information and easing the pain with generous terms (Kennedy, 1996).

Guest and Peccei's (1992) research into a major plant closure by British Aerospace found that a strategy of managing redundancy by high employee involvement had many benefits for both employees and managers. Managers approached the plant closure with five main objectives: achieving a smooth rundown; avoidance of industrial action; transfer and retention of key managerial, professional and skilled staff; the maintenance of goodwill towards the company from transferees, leavers and the local community, as well as testing out the value of employee involvement in a redundancy situation. The closure programme involved considerable communication efforts, a range of nine special measures of help with job search, counselling, training, etc, and the unusual one of giving employees a degree of choice over leaving date. The overall evaluation of the use of employee involvement under conditions of redundancy was positive. Managers achieved most of their objectives and the provisions were widely used and valued by most employee groups. The main cause of concern was the inability of the strategy to keep the goodwill of the workers who transferred to other plants, many of whom felt coerced into moving and unwelcome at the new sites. Survivors, as we discuss below, are often forgotten.

Selection

Whatever methods are used to reach redundancy decisions the notions of fairness and 'organisational justice' are key issues. Here the process of the decision-making on redundancy is just as important as the outcome if not more so. Research on the perception of organisational justice by employees has been found to be related both to how the decision was made and how much 'voice' they felt they had in the process. The other important factors in the selection process, which also help to increase employees' perceptions of fairness, are that it should be clear and appropriate.

There are some noteworthy general trends within selection criteria. First is the distinct move away from seniority and the reduction of LIFO and towards selection based on an assessment of skills and performance (IRS, 1998a, 1998b). Despite the advantages of LIFO, which, according to ACAS, are that it is an 'objective, easy to apply, readily understood, and widely accepted' criterion, it now tends to be used as a criterion of last resort when others fail to produce a clear-cut decision. There can also be problems of unfair discrimination in its application. The most common criteria are requests for voluntary redundancy, skill levels, performance assessments, and job ability or attendance records. The issue of employers using sickness absences as a criterion for redundancy, such as at National Westminster and Barclays, has caused much concern amongst unions, not least because of the worry that employees will now be frightened to take time off work when genuinely sick.

The criteria are applied by some form of appraisal/assessment, either by formal appraisal schemes, personnel records, competency-based assessments, skill matrixes, points systems or against personnel specifications. In some cases interviews are used, as at Birmingham Midshires (Wood, 1990), selection committees, and even assessment centres. Often, though, the assessment is made on the sole basis of managerial judgement. A recent and somewhat controversial development has been the use of psychometric tests in redundancy selection (see Box 10.2).

Despite the outwardly 'objective' nature of many of these selection criteria and mechanisms, we can also find considerable evidence of subjective manipulation of a redundancy situation by managers. Those who use downsizing as a raw form of managerial control again illustrate the dark side of HRM practice. In the search for 'committed' workers employers appear to use workforce reduction for a variety of ends. Often, it seems, a redundancy situation is used, or in some cases even engineered, to edge out 'troublemakers' and periodically get rid of 'dead wood'. Troublemakers are variously defined as the shirkers, union activists and the non-believers in new managerial philosophies and programmes. For example, the Personnel Director of Co-Steel Sheerness, a British-based but Canadian-owned steel mill, described how they dealt with employees who were unhappy with the new practices of 'total team culture' and union derecognition thus:

> When it became clear that there were employees who became increasingly dissatisfied with our new philosophies . . . we bit the bullet with those employees and put in place termination programmes. About 5 to 6 per cent of employees were terminated.
>
> (Personnel director quoted in *The Guardian*, 6 September 1995: 19)

BOX 10.2

Redundant personalities

One controversial development in redundancy selection surrounds the use of psychometric tests, especially personality tests, in deciding who goes or stays. Tests have largely been used in redundancies involving white-collar jobs, for example, at Anglian Water, Southwark and Brent Councils, Coventry Healthcare NHS Trust and Wyeth Laboratories. Their use has caused considerable concern among the employees and trade unions involved.

At Anglian Water around a third of the staff (around 900 employees) were to be made redundant. Instead of keeping the staff whose jobs remained, all employees undertook personality testing designed to measure conceptual thinking, innovation, teamwork, initiative, people-orientation and flexibility. The test was said to influence around 30 per cent of the final redundancy decision but the union believes it carried more weight. Whatever weight the tests were given in eventual termination decisions and despite their 'objective' nature, they became a focus of staff resentment. Unison claimed that the company determined the competencies to be tested before it identified what characteristics and skills were needed. Those dismissed felt unfairly deprived of their jobs and tribunal claims for unfair redundancy have ensued. Concerns about racial discrimination have also arisen with the use of tests for redundancy and downgrading. At the Coventry Healthcare NHS Trust five nurses won an out-of-court settlement from their employer on these grounds. A similar out-of-court settlement was also reached in the Brent case where 53 workers lost their jobs after restructuring using aptitude tests. The particular tests used were found to be in error because they did not effectively take into account cultural differences.

A number of further concerns arise from the use of psychometric tests, which have been designed for other purposes, in downsizing decisions. Not least is the issue that effective testing relies on candidates behaving openly and honestly, and when some of the consequences of the test are redundancy and downgrading this is very difficult to achieve. Despite these problems, the use of tests for redundancy purposes is growing. It seems that managers like the idea of laying the blame for unpopular redundancy decisions on 'science' and the individual employee rather than accepting responsibility themselves.

Sources: Rich and Donkin, 1994; *Financial Times* 16 December, 1995: 13; Smith, 1996

Employee support

A wide variety of post-redundancy assistance can be offered to dismissed workers. There is considerable evidence to suggest that such help can have a very positive impact on the management of redundancy at a relatively low cost (e.g. Guest and Peccei, 1992). The forms of support include redeployment centres, business start-up advice, training and loans, retraining, outplacement support, pre-retirement education, financial advice, job search help, counselling, etc (IDS, 1999).

Redundancy counselling and stress management are emphasised to help employees overcome and come to terms with some of the intense damage to self-esteem, failure, loss of confidence, decreased morale, anxiety, bitter feelings of betrayal, debilitating shock and sense of loss that accompany downsizing. Real personal, social and financial problems also stem from redundancy situations.

Studies of redundancy counselling and assistance programmes report it as being valued by the recipients but somewhat unproven in its actual benefits (see Valencia, 1985).

The availability of support is usually much greater the more senior the redundant employee is. Thus outplacement support is more often reserved for more senior grades and, where it is provided for all employees, senior managers usually receive external specialist services whilst lower-grade employees have in-house services (IRS, 1995a). Surveys of outplacement report its considerable growth in the UK since its import from the USA in the mid-1970s. While most firms would claim expertise in wider career management advice, its main use is in downsizing situations. Its key aim is to help the redundant employee with the job search process by providing practical services such as office support and specific counselling and advice. At more senior levels this is often provided on a one-to-one basis involving psychometric tests and career counselling, while for other levels of employee group programmes of CV construction and job search strategies are provided. Thus, despite its grand title, outplacement for lower-level employees can often mean little more than having a job centre on the premises.

The benefits of using external consultants for outplacement are the specialist skills they provide and the fact that they are also seen as being more credible, professional, objective and, importantly, independent of the employer (Doherty *et al.*, 1993). They can also provide the time and resources that managers in the wake of downsizing are often unable to commit. A further key benefit is the public relations effect of appearing as a caring and concerned employer. However, external outplacement consultants have been criticised as being a 'global panacea' for redundancy management (Doherty, 1998). Outplacement is also expensive, typically costing up to 15 per cent of the total cost of redundancy, and its success rate, in terms of placing redundant workers, is difficult to assess.

The most common support for operatives is the statutory-supported one of time off to look for work. Some employers have even advertised the availability of redundant employees in the national newspapers to facilitate their re-employment. The need for support in finding alternative work is a very real one. Redundant workers suffer particularly in their search for a new job, the so called 'lemon effect' (Turnbull and Wass, 1997; Gibbons and Katz, 1991). Here recruiters become concerned about hiring an employee who has been discarded by another employer. Employers assume that a redundant worker must be of poor quality and potential. The labelling of redundant employees as inferior may well increase in the future as employers move to more performance-oriented selection criteria and away from seniority. Thus, those most likely to be made redundant are least likely to follow a smooth path to re-employment.

Severance pay

Arguably, the acid test of support for redundant employees is the level of compensatory financial support or severance pay. Some companies provide little else in the way of support for redundant workers. For example, the financially orientated Hanson Trust do not use outplacement but are said to 'use pound notes to staunch the blood', with generous severance packages (*The Guardian*, 30 July 1989: 21). Most employers offer better severance terms than the base line required by statute, with the main exception being public sector employers, except in the case of senior managers – sec below (Woodger, 1992). In part this reflects the paternalistic nature of British employers but also the pragmatic need for a form of inducement to encourage employees to volunteer. Severance is usually paid in the form of a lump sum, rather than staged payments, to facilitate a 'clean break'.

It is difficult to find accurate details of severance policies because there appears to be considerable secrecy surrounding the precise nature of the arrangements, often so as to preserve 'flexibility' in individual cases. Managers generally, especially senior managers, are treated more favourably. The public sector, it seems, is no different from the private sector in this respect. For example, following the adverse publicity of an extremely generous severance package for the vice chancellor of Huddersfield University, a National Audit Office report called in its wake found severance payments of £6 million made to some 86 public sector staff, with an average settlement cost of £70,000 (NAO, 1995). Over half of all these payments were approved solely by a group of senior governors and senior staff. Unsurprisingly, this situation is resulting in more legal challenges by redundant workers over severance arrangements. Given the litigation culture of the USA, legal challenge is much more prevalent and employers are now commonly inserting waiver clauses in severance terms to limit such actions (Flynn, 1995).

Survivors

The needs of those who remain post-downsizing often appear to be overlooked. For example, a survey of financial services found 79 per cent of firms provided outplacement services for those employees who left but less than half gave support to the 'lucky' ones who remained (Doherty and Horsted, 1995). Yet we have increasing evidence that such forgotten employees are often in need of support and counselling. For example, there is considerable evidence that remaining employees feel shocked, embittered towards management, fearful about their future and guilty about still having a job whilst colleagues have been laid off (see, for example, Brockner *et al.*, 1985). The effects of such feelings are not difficult to predict. Such employees are more likely to have lower morale and increased stress levels, be less productive, and less loyal, with increased quit levels. Sennett describes survivors as behaving as though 'they lived on borrowed time, feeling they had survived for no good reason' (1998: 125). Indeed, the threat of further downsizing may create difficulties in that the most able seek alternative employment. Moreover, employees may be asked to do jobs they are untrained or ill-qualified to do. Kettley (1995) suggests that there are a number of risk factors which indicate when downsizing is most likely to hit survivor morale, including the failure to convince the workforce that job reductions are necessary, the perceived unfairness in deciding on individual redundancy, lack of alternative career options, unclear expectations for survivors and managers not providing individual support.

A number of downsized companies have recognised such problems, have set up training courses for managers in how to deal with downsizing effects, and have provided counselling programmes and helplines. One study found that the response of survivors is closely linked to the treatment received by those laid off (Brockner *et al.*, 1987). Survivors react most negatively when they perceive their colleagues to have been badly treated and poorly recompensed. The implications are clear here for managers; humane treatment of redundant employees has a double payoff.

Conclusions: downsizing or dumbsizing?

The last decade or so has witnessed unmatched levels of workforce reduction in many industrialised countries. Few organisations have not undergone some form of downsizing. For example, even trade unions have been affected, with the UK's largest union, Unison, experiencing delayering and job reduction during 1999 (Lamb, 1999). A number of key questions remain about downsizing. These are not so much about its nature or the effects on the redundant or surviving employees, rather they are centred on whether organisations, and, in turn, whole economies, are now in better shape post-downsizing. Are such organisations leaner and fitter or understaffed and anorexic? Has downsizing resulted in increased competitive advantage for those companies who have undergone it? What are the drivers of continuing downsizing?

An increasingly popular view is that the effects of downsizing are the equivalent of an industrial nuclear war:

> Below the chief executive and his cheer-leading human resources department, a number of companies resemble nothing so much as buildings blasted by a neutron bomb. The processes and structures are all there, but no human life to make them productive.
>
> (Caulkin, 1995: 19)

> Far from bounty, corporate America these last few years has created an employment Armageddon, a nuclear death zone of disenfranchised workers.
>
> (Touby, 1993: 21)

In the UK, a survey of BT managers found surviving managers with low morale (Newell and Dopson, 1996) and it appears that the Japanese management systems seem now to be following American 'best practice' in downsizing (Mrockzowski and Kanaoka, 1997).

There is thus mounting evidence that all is not well in the downsized organisational form. As Pfeffer puts it: 'downsizing may cut labour costs in the short run, but it can erode both employee and eventually customer loyalty in the long run' (1990: 192). An increasing number of case studies report that downsizing has failed to prevent declining performance (Labib and Appelbaum, 1994) and may even have exacerbated problems by getting rid of employees with key expertise, denuding firms of 'organisational memory' and resulting in much unnecessary wheel reinventing (Tomasko, 1992), as well as the lowering of the loyalty, productivity and commitment of those who remain (Greengard and Filipowski, 1993). After Eastman Kodak announced a lay-off of 4,500 employees in 1989, reported employee satisfaction dropped from 75 per cent to 35 per cent (De Meuse *et al.*, 1997: 170). As Sennett notes, the reasons for this failure were in part self-evident: the morale and motivation of workers dropped sharply in the various squeeze stages of downsizing. Surviving workers waited for the next blow of the axe rather than exulting in competitive victory over those who were fired (1997: 50).

Employment security is often seen as a precondition for the practice of HRM (Pfeffer, 1998) yet, as we discuss above, the trend has been away from secure tenured employment in the slimmed-down anorexic organisation form of the 1990s. Cappelli *et al.* note that for new work arrangements to pay off, employment needs to be reasonably stable:

> The investment in learning required to make employees completely content in new works systems is costly for employers, who recoup the investment only when the systems settle down and start performing well. If employees are continuously moving in and out of these systems, the cost of the investments in learning goes through the roof and cannot be recouped. Having a constant stream of new workers coming in, being trained, and then leaving means that the investment in learning is simply wasted. Furthermore, the work systems in which these employees sit while they are learning are constantly disrupted and never perform well. Downsizings and other restructuring that move employees around inside organizations also disrupt these work systems and seem incompatible with them.
>
> (Cappelli *et al.*, 1997: 210–11)

In some cases headcount may have gone down but labour costs have increased as companies were forced to rehire, often ex-employees, as consultants, temps and interims. A survey of downsizing in the USA reported that less than half of firms which had downsized as part of a cost reduction strategy actually achieved their targets (Bennet, 1991). Cameron *et al.*'s study of the US motor industry's downsizing programmes found few firms improving productivity relative to pre-downsizing levels. Cascio's (1993) study of downsizing finds a considerable discrepancy between the anticipated and actual economic benefits. Corporate goals of downsizing are rarely achieved, with share prices of downsized firms tending to decline over time. There is thus little evidence that downsizing improves long-run profitability and financial performance (see also De Meuse *et al.*, 1997).

A possible explanation for this increasingly reported negative relationship between downsizing and economic performance can be found in Hamel and Prahalad's (1993) analysis of competitive advantage via resource productivity, both capital and human. They suggest that there are two ways to achieve this. Firstly, via downsizing and secondly by the strategic discipline of stretch and leverage. This latter approach seeks to get the most from existing resources. Their view is that leveraging is mostly energising, while downsizing is essentially the reverse, resulting in demoralised managers and workforces. In the jargon, it appears that to achieve economic effectiveness downsizing is far from always 'rightsizing'. Strategic decision-makers seem to have forgotten the benefits of growth strategies. Stephen Roach (Chief Economist, Morgan Stanley), the guru of downsizing business, has now disowned the practice of 'slash and burn' restructuring (Carlin, 1996). According to Roach, 'if you compete by building you have a future . . . if you compete by cutting you don't'.

Given such a grim picture of the effects of organisational downsizing, why then do managers continue with it? A number of explanations have been put forward. Firstly, it is increasingly argued that managers have simply become addicted to downsizing because being lean and mean is now fashionable in itself. Downsizing, according to Brunning (1996), has become a corporate addiction and the 'cocaine of the boardroom'. For McKinley et al. (1995) the fashion leaders, and culprits, behind this trend are the very visible downsizings of prestigious firms, the teachings of business school academics, and popular managerial texts (such as the excellence movement). To this we would add the profit improvement strategies promoted by the large management consultancy groups. The use of management consultants by an organisation leads employees to associate them with imminent job losses (Preedy, 1987). De Meuse et al. argue that downsizing is not a quick, one-off fix, and compare it to cheating on one's spouse: 'most likely, the first time one does it, it is a very painful, gut-wrenching decision. However, once a spouse cheats, it becomes progressively easier and easier' (1997: 172). As Lowe remarks, 'nobody believes the Great War syndrome – the downsizing to end all downsizing – any more' (Kennedy, 1996: 62).

Secondly, rather than a more 'acceptable' and appropriate use of downsizing because firms are now more productive or better organised or too bureaucratic and overstaffed, managers are often forced to resort to it by the market's demands for short-term boosts in profits. Even if downsizing does not deliver on profitability over the long term, it seems that the very fact of announcing it can give short-term stock gains as investors and market makers respond favourably to such announcements (Worrell et al., 1991). Depressingly, it seems that downsizing acts as a reassuring signal to markets that managers are 'in control' and acting to put things right. Thirdly, Hitt et al. (1994) suggest that the current rage for 'mindless' downsizing is linked to the merger and acquisitions mania of the last decade as managers attempt to solve the problems associated with acquisitive rather than organic growth. Acquisition strategies are argued to promote conservative short-term perspectives amongst managers – hence downsizing as a solution rather than investing in human capital. Indeed, there is a case that with greater internal flexibility (e.g. wider jobs), there may be less necessity for external flexibility (e.g. via downsizing) as workers can cope more ably with adjustments and change. It is important to see security in the context of other policies. Workers are more likely to contribute ideas if they do not feel they are endangering their own colleagues' jobs, and both employer and employee are more likely to see investments in training as worthwhile.

Thus, despite the real sufferings of many workers in an era of redundancy there have been precious few long-term benefits to justify its level and severity, nor an overwhelming economic justification for its continuing blanket use. The redundant find meaningful, well-paid and stable work difficult to come by, whilst those who remain in employment are stretched thin, worried about their security and subject to considerable work stress in anorexic organisations. Questions may well be asked of MDs and CEOs who are still rewarded with high and increasing salaries and perks. As De Meuse points out, the complaint is that if we need to cut costs and save money as a company why is Mr CEO making £2 million? Lastly, it seems that the claim of HRM that people are an organisation's most valuable resource is difficult to sustain in the light of how such resources are so wantonly discarded and underutilised. As Pfeffer argues, what we have seen in the era of widespread downsizing is simply an 'unplanned, haphazard management of the employment relationship' (1998: 164).

Managing downsizing and change through involvement at Scotchem

Adrian Wilkinson and Tom Redman

Introduction

Winning the support of managers and employees alike is central to successful downsizing and change programmes. This may involve negotiating the terms of consent, from the traditional 'arm's length' control philosophy of British manufacturing to a greater emphasis on achieving active employee commitment. The trade unions may feel threatened by any such new approach, particularly where it threatens their positions as a conduit between management and the shopfloor. While involvement is important to the success of downsizing, a key problem is that often managers simply see it as a time wasting exercise (Fowler, 1993).

Scotchem is a large multinational with deeply rooted traditions for managing labour, many of which it is trying to modify in a human resource management direction. In such a context, 'strategy' emerges through the interplay between various management and employee stakeholders, any of whom can threaten the smooth implementation of downsizing. In particular, strong trade unions can pose a formidable obstacle to any radical change in management style. The change process described below utilised new direct methods of communicating with and involving employees. As Chapter 10 shows, increased involvement of employees is seen in the literature to reduce potential conflict during actual downsizing and in its aftermath, to produce greater effort and, in turn, improvements in organisational performance from those who remain (see Cameron, 1994).

Greater product market pressures and management's growing awareness of the need to harness employee commitment to gain competitive advantage, were the external pressures which led to a management review of its approach to employee relations. This phenomenon can be seen in two 'waves'. Firstly, in the early 1980s when the continued operation of the plant was in serious jeopardy. Here developments were regarded as a 'temporary truce' between management and workers, with the acceptance of critical changes held together by the immediate and crucial aim of organisational survival. There was greater readiness by managers to 'involve' employees, at least via downward communications exercises, confronted as the company was by severe market contraction (Cressey *et al.*, 1985). In essence, this concerns a temporary but urgent alignment of complementary goals, namely those of survival and job maintenance. This is what Cameron (1994) would term a workforce reduction strategy.

In the late 1980s, the proposed changes formed part of a much broader and longer-term cultural change initiative. This was the 'last piece in the jigsaw', aimed at putting the employment relationships on a new and different long-term footing. Cameron's model would characterise this development as a systemic strategy aimed at more than simply reducing workforce size.

This two-stage pattern of experience can be broadly seen as reflecting a development from what Cressey *et al.* (1985) term 'lifeboat democracy', where the emphasis was on compliance with short-term 'imperatives', to an attempt to develop a more fully co-operative relationship where 'empowerment' and commitment were seen as central to the new way of working.

The Scotchem case study

The structure of the case study is as follows. First we examine the background to both phases of development, describing the company and existing work organisation. We then discuss the experience of the early 1980s and how this evolved into a more fundamental attempt to refashion the employment relationship. Next we examine the thinking behind this, the processes involved and how the actors perceived the changes. Finally, we discuss the future of these initiatives and assess the experience.

The Scotchem site

The site is located in Scotland and produces pigments on a bulk commodity basis. The site employed approximately 700 staff in the mid-1990s – a little more than half the number which worked at the site at the end of the 1970s, although production has more than doubled over the period. Almost all the manual workforce is made up of men. Labour turnover there is low, partly because of high unemployment in the area. Many blue-collar workers have built up considerable service at the firm, a large number having started there in the mid-1960s. Indeed, the long service profile is one of the problems management faces in attempting to alter the deep-rooted workplace culture.

There are several plants on the Scotchem site. It is particularly notable that plants producing an identical product vary widely in the demands placed upon the workforce because of different technologies. The old units are essentially manually controlled, with men charging the machines, manhandling drums, and standing at the filling points. In contrast, the new dry grinding unit, for example, is a computer-driven plant with a built-in system for dealing with dust explosions, which provides a cleaner environment for operators through the use of new material handling techniques which entail no contact with the product. The unit is controlled by operators inputting information to the computer from a terminal within the control room or via local operator panels within the plant. There is some manual work (e.g. forklift trucks and bag handling) although the latter process is to be automated.

Technology is not, however, the only reason for differences in work organisation. For example, in the newer plants, operators are encouraged to rotate tasks amongst themselves and complete their own worksheets, rather than having work allocated. This dichotomy between old and new is replicated through the other units. However, despite the broad differences outlined, there are also similarities. In most units there is a wide range of tasks and even the most automated of these require some manual labour. Equally, the wide range of tasks has facilitated job rotation. The new units require fewer staff, and include less manual work, but at the same time they require greater knowledge of processes and greater teamwork, thus creating opportunities for employee involvement.

With regard to union organisation, there are three bargaining units at the site. The first comprises the management committee and those reporting to them, a group of staff which is largely non-union. The second unit comprises clerical, technical and supervisory staff, and belongs to MSF, which also has representation rights for the first group. The third unit is the blue-collar group, covering both process and craft employees represented by the TGWU, and the AEEU. Membership is 100 per cent in the last group and high in the second group. The unions are well organised and there are three convenors and over 20 shop stewards who meet as a group on a quarterly basis. Hence, the unions form an important interest group regarding any new developments.

The first wave of change – crisis and downsizing in the early 1980s

Until the early 1980s the site was essentially a production manufacturing facility for the company. There was little contact with external customers. These characteristics were regarded as a prominent cause of the plight of the site in the early 1980s, which had become simply too isolated from business requirements. After steady business growth in the 1960s and 1970s, it was now felt to be grossly overmanned. With considerable losses accumulating, corporate management perceived three options:

1. To close down the site.
2. To rationalise production, maintaining no more than 200 staff in key plants. However, this was regarded as being no more than a short-term palliative as it was felt unlikely that customers would remain if only a small product range was offered.
3. To restructure the business. This was the strategy eventually chosen by senior management at the site, and subsequently approved by the UK head office.

As we can see, whatever overall strategy was chosen, downsizing was part of the final organisational outcome. Although the need to maintain a full portfolio of products restricted rationalisation, Scotchem's downsizing process stripped out all non-essential operations; some buildings were closed down and blocked up (to avoid paying rates), some were bulldozed and a number of plants 'mothballed' i.e. put on a care and maintenance only basis. The number of employees was reduced

from over 1,200 to around 700 over an 18-month period, principally via voluntary severance – although there were some compulsory redundancies for
white-collar staff. The relationship with Head Office was restructured, with
Scotchem becoming more consumer-oriented and given international marketing
responsibilities for its principal products. Consequently, this downsizing phase was
characterised by a 'hard times' approach to human resources management.

The company began the downsizing process by providing detailed financial
commentaries to all employees – information which had not been previously available even to some managerial staff. Trade unions co-operated in changes to
working practices. However, this involvement did not extend to participation in
the key decision-making process, and the authoritarian nature of change in this
period is readily acknowledged by senior managers. Workforce–management co-
operation was attributed to what the managing director referred to as the 'green
monster' effect: employees were simply fearful for their jobs and involvement was
a tool to facilitate employee understanding of changes taking place. As one manager said, 'We've moved away from "You'll do this" to "This is why you'll do
this"'. The Turnaround Project was seen as a great success, with profits returning
in the mid-1980s. Following a return to profits there was substantial investment of
£40 million over two years in new technology, including the introduction of new
units and more sophisticated computer control operations.

While the Scotchem plant had never been strike-prone, it is evident from recent
developments and observations from all sides that the 'fear factor' and changes in
relative power did affect the way relationships developed. Unions were described
by management as more 'stubborn' than 'aggressive' and there was general recognition from trade unions that Scotchem is a good employer. One union
representative referred to a 'carefully cultivated paternalistic management
approach' and pointed out that even in the bleakest days of the early 1980s,
Scotchem had never forced the pace even when they were 99 per cent certain of
achieving it. During these days many workers were sent home on full pay and a
road-building programme was undertaken on the site so as to avoid redundancy.
Employees were well aware of the fate of their colleagues who went to work for
more money at a nearby car plant but were soon laid off.

Nevertheless, despite these feelings, the refashioned relationship of the period
owed more to fear and a realistic appraisal by shop stewards of their relative
weakness, rather than a greater degree of trust. However, the number of minor
disputes and grievances has dropped dramatically from the 1970s and unions no
longer used these as a lever to negotiate over wider issues. 'New realism' appeared
to have taken root in the wake of the company's experience of downsizing.
However, as we shall see below, weakened trade unions in no way guaranteed
greater employee commitment on management terms. Job insecurity is not a good
platform on which to build long-term employee commitment to the organisation.

The second wave of change – refashioning the employment relationship through the Way Ahead programme

Origins

The origins of the programme to initiate cultural change can be found in the Turnaround Project, during which much greater information was disseminated to the workforce. This was 'lifeboat' communication in its simplest form. But as senior managers pointed out, 'it was not easy to get off the tiger' once clearer waters had been reached. Hence the ideas of full information and more open management could not immediately be abandoned, nor did management regard it as desirable to do so. The Turnaround Project had achieved its aims in substantially reducing headcount costs, building new units, revamping the organisational structure and attaining production targets. However, the people element was seen as the 'final piece in the jigsaw'. Furthermore, it was felt that recent investment demanded new approaches to work, as did the mature nature of the market. Thus, it was argued that differentiation and competitive advantage was to be achieved by people, rather than technology and capital investment, which were easily replicated. There was much talk of changing culture, so as to create a self-motivated, better-educated workforce, with operators no longer regarded as a 'pair of hands'. Management felt that this could not be achieved by a single step forward but through a long-term evolutionary approach.

Beginnings

The managing director was the key actor in terms of the development of this programme and was very critical of Anglo-American approaches in treating staff purely as a variable cost. He was both the architect of and the stimulus behind the Way Ahead initiative, which was introduced via the MD's annual presentation on business performance to all staff. He talked of the need for a vehicle to achieve change.

Steering group

The first reaction of the union to a new way forward was one of apprehension and reluctance to change. In part this stemmed from the worry that this was simply downsizing disguised in the form of 'culture change'. Union representatives attended an off-site meeting with senior management to discuss the key issue of low trust. A central theme of the Way Ahead was therefore greater openness between management, unions and employees and it was in this spirit that managers gave the union a folder containing 'the business plan'. This was received initially with some apprehension by the union representatives, who were surprised to find it was only a blank sheet of paper. It was a way of saying 'we want your input' said the personnel manager. The most important issues which were raised included status differences, staff fears and inter-union rivalry. A steering group consisting of senior management and union representatives was established to discuss (not negotiate) the Way Ahead, and this met monthly. However, in the process of winning union 'hearts and minds', middle management felt 'short-circuited' and the unions were uncomfortable in discussing matters which did not result in immediate action.

Six working parties were set up in order to cater for the need for action, the involvement of middle management and the necessity of getting 'champions'. These discussed shifts, flexibility, multiskilling, single status and other key issues. As one manager put it, this was a method of throwing 'big stones in the pond to see what ripples would come back'. However, because the working parties were made up of representatives from each union group in addition to managers, the different aspirations of the unions and an unwillingness to compromise meant progress was slow.

Mission statement and cascades

A mission statement was distributed to all employees, explaining the Scotchem vision. However, it became apparent that this was a premature move as employees had yet to understand the message, and the consultants who had been brought in argued that the programme had simply put 'the cart before the horse' in that working parties had examined areas for change but not *why* changes were being made. Consequently, acceptance was not easily achieved. Furthermore, the shopfloor employees who were expected to change had been entirely left out of the process. The absence of 'crisis' also meant a less receptive workforce.

This led to the 'cascade', which started with the management committee and went down through the organisation. Each session took several hours and attempted to explain management thinking, the Way Ahead and the mission statement as tools to achieve company goals. This was the first time ordinary employees had been informed about and involved in any real sense in management thinking. These sessions emphasised quality, customer satisfaction, cost control and new products. The overall package was designed to 'create pride in what we do' and to demonstrate that 'people are the most important factor'. It was emphasised that people should be treated as a resource, with managers occupying a supportive rather than directive role, summed up in the term 'moving from cops to being coaches'. Hence training, teamwork, communication and involvement were highlighted. Employees generally regarded the cascade as positive although supervisors were concerned about their future. Furthermore, the shift from the steering group and the working parties to the cascade led to some union fears that managers had simply taken over the process.

The early optimism of the programme diminished when it ran into a number of difficulties with the second cascade and its aftermath. Firstly, due to production pressures and vacation problems the gap between the two cascades, in some cases seven to eight months, meant the early impetus was lost. However, expectations had been built up and there was growing scepticism about management's commitment to change. The second cascade was designed to produce action plans for each department in an attempt to achieve there what had been achieved in the division as a whole, namely, responsibility for managing their own affairs. This too ran into difficulties when there was no flood of response to the second cascade and managers were therefore left with the choice of either doing nothing or throwing 'logs on the fire' themselves. This led to union concern that the cascade was not consultation but manipulation. Nevertheless, despite numerous gripes, the *process* of involvement was regarded as very useful in that work groups met with their supervisors and better communication resulted.

The test beds

The philosophy of the Way Ahead was first to be applied in two new production units, which would, in effect, provide a testing ground for these ideas. In this light a totally new approach to setting up the new units was taken; whereas previously Scotchem had simply transferred people and given them new job titles, a vigorous selection procedure now took place (with the emphasis on interpersonal skills rather than just technical ability) along with substantial training, which included a six-week full-time programme dealing with problem-solving skills, product knowledge and teamworking. This was designed to encourage operators not to see their job in narrow terms, but to take on and solve problems themselves rather than immediately passing responsibility to their supervisor. The emphasis on the 'team' was reflected in supervisors being renamed as team-leaders (i.e. from cops to coaches) and given more responsibility in hiring, firing, training and discipline. Team spirit was reinforced outside work by social functions and within the workplace by changing the shift pattern of the workers to that of their team leaders.

The application of these ideas in the new units was designed to promote the change management desired, and it was hoped that a successful operation would produce a groundswell in favour of applying such ideas elsewhere. In practice, however, the plan ran into a number of problems. First, the training finished four months before the new plant was ready. This meant frustrated expectations amongst employees. Secondly, there was enormous production pressure on the new units and output was therefore the driving force. Thirdly, this combined with start-up difficulties, especially with software problems and the plants not running according to design. Finally, the 'blaze of glory' became something of a damp squib. Some felt the training programme was too good – 'it got them going so they felt ten feet high but they came down to earth with a bump'. In one unit operators expected a 'wonderful new plant' but instead ended up using 'a big hose and a shovel'. In another, promoted as a clean plant, dust problems arose. Senior management felt those on the line had been incapable of handling these morale problems. Regular meetings planned as part of the new concept were abandoned because of lack of time and analytical problem-solving was replaced by 'Fire fighting'. There was also some tension between the workers in the new units (mostly young and with craft skills), and those in the older units. The result of all this was that some of the workers from the new units even began to apply for jobs in the older units, and the 'flagships' appeared to be in serious trouble.

Impact of the Way Ahead

We now examine the project's impact on the attitudes of middle management and supervisors, unions and workers.

Middle management and supervisors

The key issues in relation to this group were the perceived impact on their jobs and their doubts concerning both the philosophy and operation of the new approach. Thus, it was quite clear that many felt threatened by the changes in role and style which were being introduced. The well-established view was that 'bosses are bosses and kick ass'. There was also concern about job prospects if the traditional charge-hand role was eroded. In broad terms, there was objection both to the actual implementation of the programme and, more significantly, its underlying philosophy. In regard to the first, supervisors felt that the delay between the two cascades, the length of the programme (almost two years) and the lack of specific changes had undermined its credibility and reduced trust, with the result that 'people think it's a cosmetic exercise'. More fundamentally, they had doubts about the philosophy of the programme.

Thus there was considerable hostility to the senior management's vision of the Way Ahead, in particular, the manner with which they saw senior managers 'eulogizing' the workforce. As a personnel manager acknowledged, supervisors are a good deal less idealistic – 'they feel a branding iron is a more suitable instrument to work with than any concept of employee involvement'. This was a view strongly held by supervisors pointing to the 'hairy-arsed culture' (anecdotes of workers urinating in each other's tea mugs). Supervisors themselves were seen as the 'muscular type not necessarily with fine feelings' and managers acknowledged that they operated in a 'pretty basic and brutal context'. Supervisors were not happy at having to devote time pandering to a 'long-haired idealistic view of workers'. Given their perception that workers only wanted to 'take, take, take', their apprehension that the Way Ahead was likely to be construed as 'soft management' is understandable. This was evident in their opposition to the removal of the double clocking system (i.e. clocks at both site and plant). Given this context, supervisors were keen for a 'hard' element to be in the message: 'We're going softly, softly, but we need the big sticks to come out as well.' Others claimed that meticulous checking and attention to detail was 'a foreign trait which won't operate here – it's not British'.

Union view

There was considerable ambiguity in union ranks regarding the Way Ahead programme. On the one hand, the union representatives were anxious that the programme might weaken employee attachment to their unions. However, they were also aware that if workers were happy with developments, this left the unions in a strange position. The union dilemma was that they found it difficult to challenge the logic of management's programme, and indeed saw many developments as benefiting individuals in the long run, but at the same time they saw the possibility of a clear diminution in the unions' role in the company.

Management believed there was now greater trust, which could be clearly illustrated through an examination of the formal management–union monthly meetings, which comprised both negotiation and consultation. They were described by managers as being characterised by a high degree of trust, this itself being reflected by less frequent and shorter meetings. This was attributed by managers to there being less contentious business to be discussed – unions no longer seeing agenda issues as a sign of strength and hence not feeling a sense of failure if there were few items to discuss. It was also because other mechanisms/channels, especially the 'Way Ahead', but also a monthly *aide-mémoire* slide package, were attracting material previously the preserve of these meetings. Managers agreed that the volume of material had diminished over the years and, while this could be attributed to political and economic changes, it was also due to the drawing together of management and unions at the behest of management. Second, managers pointed to changes in behaviour over the annual pay negotiations as evidence of higher trust in management – union relations. In the mid-1980s the structure of negotiations changed, with one set of negotiations covering clerical, process and craft workers rather than, as hitherto, three sets of negotiations. Moreover, due to the Way Ahead programme and the creation of more open relations, negotiations in the late 1980s were over in less than a day, settlement being facilitated by the range of information provided on competition, exchange rates, comparative pay settlements and other financial data.

However, that is not to say that the transition had been easy or that the unions were comfortable with the changes. In fact complaints regularly surfaced concerning the non-attendance of senior managers at these committees.

> Their absence creates a sense of loss of esteem within the committee. Whilst recently we have no earth-shaking matters to discuss, the lack of a senior management presence gives our members the feeling that the monthly meetings are only concerned with small talk. This, allied to the fact that managers appear to want to talk directly to members rather than through the stewards, tends to demean the role of the stewards' committee.
>
> (Convenor, minutes)

This picture of a move towards relations of greater trust needs to be qualified. Thus, in relation to pay negotiations one reason for the much less protracted negotiations related to the introduction of a bonus scheme, which provided a local payment based on site contribution to divisional performance. The calculation is a complex one (needing a Philadelphia lawyer to understand it, according to the unions) but in practice it reduced the union role in pay negotiations to discussing inflation plus the going rate. Thus, as one steward complained, 'there is nothing left to negotiate about'. Second, there was considerable concern over the bypassing of the unions, via the communications sponsored by the Way Ahead and the more proactive role taken by supervisors. Furthermore, the nature of consultation was also questioned. One convenor complained that:

> We have comments from managers about feedback on the Way Ahead which look and sound as though they had come from members. This is not the case. They have sometimes come from supervisors and other points are from the manager himself. We then find that managers are implementing the changes on our people.

Employee view – Overall, while the unions appeared to recognise the need for change and the positive aspects of management strategy, the stewards' concern over their future role was further complicated by the attitudes of their constituents. One steward argued that while the unions were well aware of the 'big picture', workers in the region were 'isolationists', suspicious of anyone who appeared to get on with management, suspecting collaboration. This fundamental distrust was based on 'people being divided into bears [workers] and gaffers [management], and the bears don't trust the gaffers'.

Nevertheless, when asked to compare employee involvement and communications with the situation in 1985, over 80 per cent claimed it had improved, including over a third who said it was much better. In contrast, the Way Ahead with its ambitious agenda of transforming the employment relationship met with considerable scepticism among the workforce. According to stewards, the Way Ahead 'had not yet converted anybody'.

Only a minority of staff felt it offered more opportunity for individual advancement and many saw it as too vague. Clearly, the programme had fallen short of expectations. The shop-floor view was that all the benefits – for example, the tapping of shop-floor expertise – went to management. Thus 'What's in it for me?' was a central concern and the lack of specific benefits for shop-floor staff meant a degree of indifference as to the ongoing discussions. As one steward put it, the workers were 'all fired up with the concept of getting not giving', and if there was no money to be had 'people like to be left alone'. Thus, workers were dubious about the reciprocity and mutual benefits which were claimed for the Way Ahead. Given the history of the plant and the widespread downsizings generally in manufacturing in the UK, the 'benefits' of job security via an individual's enhanced employability and collectively from increased organizational performance, lacked the power to convince many workers that they were getting a fair return.

Future developments

The view from the top management was that 'trust' was the key to the future. To reinforce this there was an undertaking from the managing director that jobs would not be lost as a result of the Way Ahead. A very long-term view was being taken, illustrated by statements such as: 'We're looking 20 years on and not next month or next year' and 'We don't need to maximise profits in the short run'. Moreover, it was a strongly held view of senior management that Scotchem did not want to 'impose a solution but to redefine a relationship'. Thus, it was vital to achieve consensus and common ground so people could feel they owned the process and 'they would all pull together on the same line'. Given this long-term approach, slow progress was not necessarily a failure, although one manager complained that: 'The only horizon they know is the one on the holiday brochure.'

However, senior management felt there was thus no point being 'starry-eyed' about events. Staff acceptance of change would clearly temper management actions. Nevertheless, they appreciated to some extent the views of middle management that to keep momentum going 'something must happen'. So, while senior

330 Chapter 10 / Downsizing: the dark side of HRM

management did not want simply to 'throw them goodies' – an approach which was attributed to other chemical companies – an 'act of faith' had to be shown. It was acknowledged that workers needed something tangible 'to feel, to see, to touch', relating the broad process of change to a reference point at the workplace. Thus, some short-term gains needed to be seen by the workforce.

Consequently, the focus turned to 'looking for something viable to do' and 'creating the right splash' in terms of affordability and impact. Management did not want the Way Ahead to be seen as a 'block of things' to be attained but to be understood more broadly as being about new approaches and attitudes. However, there were some areas where changes could be made. The feedback or the cascade would facilitate change in that it was possible to pick out what managers wanted and claim support of the workforce. Under consideration was the introduction of single status (in particular abolishing clocking practices), changing shift patterns to align operator and team-leader working hours (and hence emphasise teamwork), the development of personal assessment (a form of appraisal without pay attached) and multiskilling (workers to have a prime trade and an additional skill). All of these had industrial relations implications. Changing shift patterns and working hours raised pay, clocking was supported by one union on safety grounds, multiskilling involved craft issues, and personal assessment had to be sold as developmental rather than control- or pay-related.

Achieving change through downsizing and change management

In relation to the workforce generally there appeared little evidence of any fundamental change of attitude. Yet, the conditions appeared potentially fruitful. The role of the managing director in the transformation of Scotchem was a crucial one but his very centrality – the only person you can trust, according to the unions – also points to the fragility of change and the development of high-trust relations, with both managers and unions apprehensive of what his departure would do to the programme. Moreover, unlike other cases, where a single employee involvement technique has been used, which seemed unlikely by itself to transform industrial relations, here we have a wide-ranging programme of change. As the world's leading pigments producer, Scotchem had the luxury of time in refashioning relationships and making changes; senior managers appear relatively unconcerned about the slow progress of the Way Ahead (although middle management have a rather different view) and have been happy to employ a long-term strategy of setting up 'test beds' and filtering the feedback from the cascade to build up an apparent or real groundswell for change which does not appear to be directed from the top. Clearly, the programme rests on the assumption that this will be forthcoming. If this is not the case, management may feel they need to proceed with the programme without the consensus upon which Way Ahead philosophy is based.

Questions

1. According to Cameron (1994), organisations which conduct systematic analysis involving staff and increase communication have more chance of success. How far is this the case at Scotchem?

2. Pablo Picasso is credited with saying, 'Every act of creation is first of all an act of destruction.' To what extent is this statement true of Scotchem's organisational strategy in that 'destructive' downsizing had to precede the 'creative' cultural change programme?

3. Kettley (1995) identifies a number of risk factors indicating when downsizing is most likely to hit morale. These include the failure to convince the workforce that job reductions are necessary, perceived unfairness in deciding on individual redundancies, lack of alternative career options, unclear expectations for survivors, and managers not providing individual support. To what extent are these present in the Scotchem case in both phases?

4. Explain the union role in the programme.

5. To what extent do HR professionals have a role to play in downsizing?

References

Cameron, K. (1994) 'Strategies for successful organization downsizing', *Human Resource Management*, 33(2): 189–211.

Cressey, P., Eldridge, J. and MacInnes, J. (1985) *Just Managing: Authority and Democracy in Industry*, Milton Keynes: Open University Press.

Fowler, A. (1993) 'A more humane approach to redundancy', *Personnel Management*, January: 6.

Kettley, P. (1995) 'Employee morale during downsizing', *Institution of Employment Studies Report*, No. 291.

Marchington, M., Goodman, J., Wilkinson, A. and Ackers, P. (1992) *New Developments in Employee Involvement*, Employment Department Research Paper Series No 2, London: HMSO.

References to Chapter 10

Adams, S. (1996) *The Dilbert Principle*, London: Boxtree Press.

Anfuso, D. (1996) 'Strategies to stop the layoffs', *Personnel Journal*, June: 66–99.

Armstong, M. (1997) *A Handbook of Personnel Management Practice*, London: Kogan Page.

Bamber, G., Review of C. Berggren and M. Nomula, *The Resilience of Corporate Japan, British Journal of Industrial Relations* (forthcoming).

Barbee, G. (1986) 'Downsizing with dignity', *Retirement Planning*, Fall: 6–7.

Barrar, P. and Sullivan, T. (1988) 'Employment adjustments in recession: a wire industry study', *Employee Relations*, 10(1): 22–31.

Bennet, A. (1991) 'Downsizing doesn't necessarily bring an upswing in corporate profitability', *The Wall Street Journal*, 6 June: 1.

Brockner, J. (1992) 'Managing the effects of lay-offs on survivors', *California Management Review*, 34(2): 9–28.

Brockner, J., Davy, J. and Carter, C. (1985) 'Lay-offs, self-esteem and survivor guilt: motivational, affective and attitudinal consequences', *Organizational Behavior and Human Decision Processes*, 36(2): 229–44.

Brockner, J., Grover, S., Reed, T., DeWitt, R. and O'Malley, M. (1987) 'Survivors' reactions to lay-offs: We get by with a little help from our friends', *Administrative Science Quarterly*, 32: 526–41

Brunning, F. (1996) 'Working at the office on borrowed time', *Macleans*, February: 8–9.

Bulmer, M. (1971) 'Mining redundancy: a case study of the workings of the Redundancy Payments Act in the Durham coalfields', *Industrial Relations Journal*, 26(15): 227–44.

Cameron, K. S. (1994) 'Strategies for successful organizational downsizing', *Human Resource Management*, 33(2): 189–211.

Cameron, K. S. (1998) 'Downsizing', in Poole, M. and Warner, M. (eds) *International Encyclopaedia of Business and Management: Handbook of Human Resource Management*, London: ITB Press, 55–61.

Cameron, K. S., Freeman, S. J., and Mishra, A. K. (1991) 'Best practices in white collar downsizing: managing contradictions', *Academy of Management Executive*, 5(3): 57–73.

Cappelli, P., Bassi, L., Katz, H., Knoke, D., Osterman, P. and Useem, M. (1997) *Change at Work*, Oxford: Oxford University Press.

Carlin, J. (1996) 'Guru of "downsizing" admits he got it all wrong', *The Independent on Sunday*, 12 May.

Casey, B. (1992) 'Redundancy and early retirement: the interaction of public and private policy in Britain, Germany and the USA', *British Journal of Industrial Relations*, 30(3): 425–43.

Cascio, W. F. (1993) 'Downsizing: What do we know, what have we learned?', *Academy of Management Executive*, 7(1): 95–104.

Caulkin, S. (1995) 'Take your partners', *Management Today*, February: 26–30

Clabaugh, A. (1997) 'Downsizing: implications of older employees', Working Paper, Edith Cowan University.

Cole, R. (1993) 'Learning from learning theory', *Quality Management Journal*, 1(1): 9–25.

Cressey, P., Eldridge, J. and MacInnes, J. (1985) *Just Managing: Authority and Democracy in Industry*, Milton Keynes: Open University Press

Cully, M., Woodland, S., O'Reilly, A. and Dix, G. (1999) *Britain at Work*, London: Routledge.

Deakin, S. and Wilkinson, F.(1999) 'The case of Great Britain', *Labour*, 13(1): 41–90.

De Meuse, K.P., Bergmann, T.J. and Vanderheiden, P.A. (1997) 'Corporate downsizing. Separating myth from fact', *Journal of Management Inquiry*, 6(2): 168–76.

De Meuse, K., Vanderheiden, P. and Bergmann, T. (1994) 'Announce layoffs: their effects on corporate financial performance', *Human Resource Management*, 33(4): 509–30.

Dickson, T. and Judge, D., (1987) *The Politics of Industrial Closure*, London: Macmillan.

Doherty, N. (1998) 'The role of outplacement in redundancy management', *Personnel Review*, 27(4): 343–51.

Doherty, N. and Horsted, J., (1995) 'Helping survivors to stay on board', *People Management*, 12 January: 26–31.

Doherty, N., Tyson, S. and Viney, C. (1993) 'A positive policy? Corporate perspectives on redundancy and outplacement', *Personnel Review*, 22(7): 45–53.

Donnelly, M. and Scholarios, D. (1998) 'Workers' experiences of redundancy: evidence from Scottish defence-dependent companies', *Personnel Review*, 27(4): 325–42.

Dougherty, D. and Bowman, E. (1995) 'The effects of organizational downsizing on product innovation', California Management Review, 37(4): 28–44.

Edwards, P. and Hall, M. (1999) 'Remission: possible', *People Management*, 15 July: 44–46.

Flynn, G. (1995) 'Does your severance plan make the cut?', *Personnel Journal*, August: 32–40.

Fombrun, C. (1992) *Leading Corporate Change*, New York: McGraw Hill.

Fowler, A. (1993) 'A more humane approach to redundancy', *Personnel Management*, January: 6.

Francis, G. J., Mohr, J. and Andersen, K. (1992) 'HR balancing: alternative downsizing', *Personnel Journal*, 71 (1): 71–76.

Garfield, A. (1999) 'Barclays shares soar as city welcomes job cuts', *The Independent*, 21 May.

Gibbons, R. and Katz, L.F. (1991) 'Layoffs and lemons', *Journal of Labor Economics*, 9(4): 351–80.

Greengard, S. and Filipowski, D. (1993) 'Don't rush downsizing: plan, plan, plan', *Personnel Journal*, 72(11): 64–73.

Guest, D. and Peccei, R. (1992) 'Employee involvement: redundancy as a critical case', *Human Resource Management Journal*, 2(3): 34–59.

Hamel, G. and Prahalad, C.K. (1993) 'Strategy as stretch and leverage', *Harvard Business Review*, March–April: 75–84.

Hardy, C. (1987) 'Investing in retrenchment: avoiding the hidden costs', *California Management Review*, 29(4): 111–25.

Heckscher, C. (1995) *White-Collar Blues*, New York: Basic Books.

Hendry, C. (1994) *Human Resource Management. A Strategic Approach to Employment*, London: Butterworth.

Hill, S. (1989) *Competition and Control at Work*, London: Heinemann Books.

Hitt, M.A., Hoskisson, R.E., Harrison, J.S. and Summers, T.P. (1994) 'Human capital and strategic competitiveness in the 1990s', *Journal of Management Development*, 13(1): 35–46.

Hunt, J. (1984) 'The shifting focus of the personnel function', *Personnel Management*, February: 14–18.

Hutton, W. (1997) *The State to Come*, London: Vintage.

IDS (1986) 'Redundancy terms', IDS Study No. 369: 1–6.

IDS (1999) *Managing Redundancy: IDS Studies*, London: IDS.

IRS (1994) 'Security of employment deal facilitates change at Tate & Lyle Sugars', *Employment Trends*, No. 572: 6–10.

IRS (1995a) 'Managing redundancy', *Employment Trends*, No. 580: 5–16.

IRS (1995b) 'Dealing with redundancy and job loss: a union response', *Employment Trends*, No. 588: 5–12.

IRS (1995c) 'Early retirement survey 1: Ill-health retirement', *Employment Trends*, No. 581: 5–12.

IRS (1995d) 'Early retirement survey 2: Redundancy and employee's request', *Employment Trends*, No. 581: 5–12.

IRS (1995e) '"No Secrets" deal wins over gas showroom staff', *Pay and Benefits Bulletin*, No. 379: 4–5.

IRS (1998a) 'The 1998 IRS redundancy survey Part 1', *Employment Trends*, No. 658: 5–11.

IRS (1998b) 'The 1998 IRS redundancy survey Part 2', *Employment Trends*, No. 659: 9–16.

Kemske, F. (1996) *Human Resources: A Business Novel*, London: Nicholas Brearley.

Kennedy, C. (1996) 'The incredible shrinking company', *Director*, April: 62–68.

Kettley, P. (1995) *Employee Morale During Downsizing*, Brighton Institute of Employment Studies, Report No. 291.

LRD (1997) 'UK workers – the simplest to sack', *Labour Research*, 86(3): 25–26.

Labib, N. and Appelbaum, S.H. (1994) 'The impact of downsizing practices on corporate success', *Journal of Management Development*, 13(7): 59–84.

Lamb, J. (1999) 'UK's largest union resorts to delayering programme', *People Management*, 28 October: 19.

Lane, D.A. (1988) 'Redundancy counseling for those still in employment', *Journal of Managerial Psychology*, 3: 17–22.

Lewis, P. (1993) *The Successful Management of Redundancy*, Oxford: Blackwell.

Mallier, T. and Shafto, T.A.C. (1994) 'Flexible retirement and the Third Age', *International Journal of Manpower*, 15(1): 38–54.

Manpower Argus (1995) 'Fewer older men in Europe's work force', *Manpower Argus*: 11.

Marchington, M., Goodman, J., Wilkinson, A. and Ackers, P. (1992) *'New Developments in Employee Involvement'*, Employment Department Research Paper Series No. 2, London: HMSO.

Mason, E.S. (1997) 'Political language: the case of corporate anorexia', *Journal of Applied Management Studies*, 6(1): 93–102.

McGoldrick, A. and Cooper, C.L. (1989) *Early Retirement*, Aldershot: Gower.

McKinley, W., Sanchez, C.M. and Scheck, A. (1995) 'Organizational downsizing: constraining, cloning, learning', *Academy of Management Review*, 9(3): 32–41.

Millward, N., Stevens, M., Smart, D. and Hawes, W. (1992) *Workplace Industrial Relations in Transition*, Aldershot: Dartmouth.

Mitchell, Lee Marks (1993) 'Restructuring and downsizing', in Mirvis, Philip H. (ed) *Building the Competitive Workforce*, New York: John Wiley.

Morris, T., Storey, J., Wilkinson, A. and Cressey, P. (2000) *Industry Change and Union Organization in Retail Banking*, Working Paper.

Morton, C. (1994) *Beyond World Class*, London: Macmillan.

Mrockzowski, T. and Kanaoka, M. (1997) 'Effective downsizing strategies in Japan and America – Is there a convergence of employment practices?', *Academy of Management Review*, 22(1): 226–56.

National Audit Office (1995) *Severance Payments to Senior Staff in the Publicly Funded Education Sector*, London: HMSO.

Newell, S. and Dopson, S. (1996) 'Muddle in the middle: organizational restructuring and middle management careers', *Personnel Review*, 25(4): 4–20.

Papalexandris, N. (1996) 'Downsizing and outplacement: the role of human resource management', *International Journal of Human Resource Management*, 7(3): 605–17.

Peters, T. (1992) *Liberation Management*, London: Macmillan.

Pfeffer, J. (1998) *The Human Equation*, Boston, Mass: Harvard Business School Press.

Preedy, J. (1987) 'What you should expect from consultants', *Personnel Management*, January: 20–25.

Purcell, J. and Hutchinson, S.(1996) 'Lean and Mean?', *People Management*, 10 October: 27–33.

Rich, M. and Donkin, R. (1994) 'A testing time in the job market', *The Financial Times*, 19 December: 10.

Rowlinson, S. (1996) 'Low inflation is bringing out ageism in employers', *People Management*, 7 March: 19.

Savery, L. K., Travaglione, A. and Firns, I.G.J. (1998) 'The links between absenteeism and commitment during downsizing', *Personnel Review*, 27(4): 312–24.

Sennett, R. (1997) *The Corrosion of Character*, New York: W.W. Norton & Co.

Sinclair, J., Seifert, R. and Ironside, M. (1995) 'Performance-related redundancy: schoolteacher lay-offs as management control strategy', paper presented at British Universities Industrial Relations Association Conference, Durham, July.

Smith, S. (1996) 'A fair test?', *Personnel Today*, 16 January: 26–30.

Stebbins, M.W. (1989) 'Downsizing with "mafia model" consultants', *Business Forum*, Winter: 45–47.

Storey, J., Wilkinson, A., Cressey, P. and Morris, T. (1999) 'Employment relations in banking', in Regini, M., Kitay, J. and Baethije, M. (eds) *From Tellers to Sellers: Changing Employment Relations in the World-wide Banking Industry*, Cambridge, Mass: MIT Press, 129–58.

Stuller, J. (1993) 'Why Not "inplacement"?', *Training*, 30(6): 37–41.

Sullivan, T. and Hogge, B. (1987) 'Instruments of adjustment in recession', *R&D Management*, 17(4).

Thatcher, M. (1993) 'Is change as good as a pay-off?', *Personnel Management Plus*, 4(10): 24–25.

Tomasko, R.M. (1992) 'Restructuring: getting it right', *Management Review*, 81(4): 10–15.

Torrington, D. and Hall, L. (1998) *Human Resource Management*, London: Prentice-Hall.

Touby, J. (1993) 'The business of America is jobs', *Journal of Business Strategy*, 14(6): 21–28.

Turnbull, P. and Wass, V. (1997) 'Job insecurity and labour market lemons: the (mis)management of redundancy in steel making, coal mining, and port transport', *Journal of Management Studies*, 34(1): 27–51.

Turnbull, P. (1988) 'Leaner and possibly fitter: the management of redundancy in Britain', *Industrial Relations Journal*, 19(3): 201–13.

Turner, K. (1988) 'Natural attrition: the preferred option?', *Journal of Industrial Relations*, 30(3): 363–80.

Valencia, M. (1985) 'Redundancy counselling for manual workers', *Employee Relations*, 7(2): 12–16.

Vanderheiden, P.A., De Meuse, K.P. and Bergmann, T.J. (1999) 'Responding to Haar's comment – and the beat goes on: corporate downsizing in the twenty-first century', *Human Resource Management*, 38(3): 261–8.

Wass, V. (1996) 'Who controls selection under voluntary redundancy?', *British Journal of Industrial Relations*, 34(2): 249–65.

Wedderburn, D. (1965) *Redundancy and the Railwaymen*, Cambridge: Cambridge University Press.

Westergaard, J., Noble, I. and Walker, A. (eds) (1998) *After Redundancy – The Experience of Economic Insecurity*, Cambridge: Polity.

Weyer, M.V. (1994) 'The old men on the board', *Management Today*, October: 64–67.

Wickens, P . (1995) *The Ascendant Organization*, London: Macmillan.

Wood, J. (1995) 'How organizations can survive redundancy', *Personnel Management*, December: 38–41.

Woodger, J. (1992) 'The final pay-off: severance practice in the UK, US and Canada', *Personnel Management*, October: 30–32.

Worrell, D.L., Davidson, W.N. and Sharma, V.M. (1991) 'Lay-off announcements and stock-holder wealth', *Academy of Management Journal*, 34: 662–78.

Wright, M. (1994) 'A comparative study of the contents of personnel and human resource management textbooks', *International Journal of Human Resource Management*, 5(1): 225–47.

Chapter 11

Empowerment

Adrian Wilkinson

Introduction

> Widespread realisation that the systems-driven model had suppressed individual initiative explains why managers flocked to implement one of the most influential management fads of the late 1980s and early 1990s – employee empowerment. Promoted by management gurus and packaged by consultants, empowerment came to encompass anything from the introduction of an employee suggestion scheme to the restructuring of the organisation around self-managed teams. Although some of these initiatives bore fruit, many more paid mere lip service to this deceptively simple and appealing notion. To countless overloaded top executives struggling with issues and challenges they did not fully grasp, the idea of pushing their backlog of problems back down into the organisation had great appeal. Under the sanctioned umbrella of 'empowerment', many handed off responsibilities and delegated decisions so broadly, so quickly, and with so little support that the process could better be described as 'abandonment'.
>
> (Ghosal and Bartlett, 1998: 312)

In recent years, the term 'empowerment' has become part of everyday management language (Foy, 1984; Collins, 1994; Cunningham *et al.*, 1996; Lashley, 1997; Hennestad, 1998; Wilkinson, 1998). It has also been associated with popular ideas and movements such as Total Quality Management (TQM), Business Process Re-engineering (BPR), Teamworking and the Learning Organisation. In many ways empowerment might be regarded as providing a solution to the age-old problem of bureaucratic workplaces where initiative is stifled and workers become alienated. It is part of a much wider management initiative of employee participation, although empowerment has a distinct and recent literature largely consisting of prescription and exhortation (see, for example, Block, 1986; Clutterbuck and Kernaghan, 1994) and is very much associated with the last twenty years. It has been described as 'the managerial equivalent of Viagra' (Collins, 1998: 596).

An examination of the empowerment literature reveals a number of problems. Firstly, the term 'empowerment' is elastic and hence it is not always clear that when we discuss empowerment, even within the same organisation, we are comparing like with like. Second, the study of empowerment is rarely located in an historical context: empowerment is seen as an entirely new phenomenon. Thirdly, there is little detailed discussion of the difficulties likely to arise when implementing empowerment or the conditions which are necessary for such an approach to be successful. It is assumed that employees will simply welcome its introduction, regarding it as beneficial to them and the organisation. The literature also takes a universalistic approach, regarding empowerment as appropriate to all organisations in all circumstances. Fourthly, the literature trivialises the conflict that exists within organisations and ignores the context within which empowerment takes place (Marchington, 1995). In this chapter we examine the roots of empowerment, examine why it came into prominence in recent years, suggest a classification of empowerment, and discuss the evidence as to its impact.

'Empowerment' is generally used to refer to a form of initiative which was widespread from the 1980s and focused on task-based involvement and attitudinal change. As Cunningham *et al.* note: 'employee empowerment represents the most recent manifestation of involvement practice' (1996: 143). Unlike other initiatives designed to restructure decision-making at work, such as industrial democracy, there is no notion of workers having a right to a say: it is employers who decide whether and how to empower employees. While there are a wide range of programmes and initiatives which are titled 'empowerment', and while empowerment initiatives vary as to the extent of power which employees actually exercise, most schemes are purposely designed not to give workers a very significant role in decision-making but rather to secure an enhanced employee contribution to the organisation. The aims of empowerment, therefore, are not primarily democratic. They are, instead, economic and are focused upon the attempt to improve economic performance in terms of both productivity and quality. 'Empowerment' therefore takes place within the context of a strict management agenda. Empowerment schemes tend to offer direct forms of involvement in decision-making, based on individuals or small groups, in clear contrast with industrial democracy and other participative schemes such as consultative committees, which are collectivist and representative in nature. (See Chapter 7.)

Empowerment in context: the latest wave of participation?

It is easy to assume empowerment is simply a new phenomenon in that standard texts on involvement and participation make scant reference to the term (see, for example, Brannen, 1983; Poole, 1986; Marchington, 1992; Hyman and Mason, 1995). Thus, many accounts present empowerment as if it were entirely a product of the times, and so fail to see it in an historical context. However, one could argue that, although empowerment in its current form reflects recent developments, the ideas underlying it go much deeper. Empowerment can be seen in many respects as a rejection of the traditional classical model of management associated with F.W. Taylor and Henry Ford. Fordist production methods were designed to manufacture standardised products, and production techniques allowed economies of scale to be realised since they rested upon a complex division of labour, where workers carried out fragmented and repetitive jobs. Economic man was seen as accepting a trade-off of relatively high wages for poor quality of working life. Under this regime, workers had little discretion, with conception separate from execution, and brainpower centred with management. The system was based on worker compliance. While scientific management was very successful in terms of boosting productivity, there was concern over the alienation of workers reflected in high labour turnover, absenteeism and conflict. The Human Relations School criticised Taylorism and suggested that involving and integrating workers had strong business as well as moral benefits. Workers could be self-motivated and carry out good work without close supervision. However, fundamental structural job redesign was not envisaged (Rose, 1978).

In the 1960s work enrichment was established as an alternative work paradigm (based upon the motivation-hygiene theory of Herzberg), the aim being to provide meaningful work for employees, with some degree of control and feedback on performance (Buchanan, 1979). Job enlargement was a horizontal process, adding new tasks but not increasing staff responsibility, while job enrichment was a vertical process, raising autonomy and skills. The main aim was to enrich jobs by reintegrating maintenance tasks and providing some decision-making opportunities. The best example of this in the UK was the ICI experiment in the late 1960s (Roeber, 1975).

The Tavistock Institute developed the socio-technical systems theory and the notion of a semi-autonomous work group whereby work groups were given responsibility for a whole task. The socio-technical systems school stressed the need to design technical and social components alongside each other to optimise the two. Their influential study of coal mining in Britain showed how work could be redesigned within the existing technical basis so as to retain traditional features such as skill variety and a degree of autonomy (Trist *et al.*, 1963). In the 1970s and 1980s the 'Quality of Working Life' initiative consolidated these ideas. In the 1970s there was greater interest in industrial democracy, which emphasised workers' rights to participate. This model of participation reached its high point in the UK with the 1977 Bullock Report on 'Industrial Democracy' which addressed the question of how workers might be represented at board level. This report emerged in a period of strong union bargaining power and the Labour government's 'Social Contract', an atmosphere which provided the Bullock approach to industrial participation with several distinctive features. The Bullock report was partly union-initiated, through the Labour Party, and based on collectivist principles which saw trade unions playing a key role, although it was not without controversy within the movement (Brannen, 1983). In addition, it was wedded to the general principle of employee rights established on a statutory basis (Ackers *et al.*,

1992: 272). Experiments were initiated at the Post Office and the British Steel Corporation, but both had been discontinued by the early 1980s.

In the 1980s, there was a quite different agenda for participation, retitled Employee Involvement (EI). The context was reduced union power and an anti-corporatist Conservative government, which resisted statutory blueprints (excepting some tax breaks for profit sharing) and encouraged firms to evolve the arrangements which 'best suited them'. The requirement in the 1982 Employment Act that companies employing more than 250 staff must include a statement in their Annual Report, indicating what they had done in relation to information, consultation and involvement, had little impact – perhaps not surprising, given that there were no sanctions. This agenda differs from that of the 1970s in several ways. First, it was management-initiated, often from outside the industrial relations sphere, and with scant reference to trade unions. Second, the new EI was individualist and stressed direct communications with the individual employee. Third, it was seen as being driven by business criteria concerning economic performance and the 'bottom line', stressing the impact upon employee motivation and commitment (Ackers *et al.*, 1992: 272). Unlike notions of industrial democracy, EI stems from an economic efficiency argument. It is seen to make business sense to involve employees, as a committed workforce is likely to understand better what the organisation is trying to do and be more prepared to contribute to its efficient operation. But it is management who decide whether or not employees are to be involved. The key point about these schemes is that they did not challenge management prerogative (Marchington *et al.*, 1992).

There was a sizeable growth in direct EI and communications during the 1980s as management stepped up their communication with employees as a whole. The implementation of 'new' EI initiatives speeded up during the latter part of the 1980s and the 'systematic use of the management chain' was described by respondents as the most frequently employed method of communication (Millward *et al.*, 1992: 166). Regular meetings between managers and employees also grew, as did suggestions schemes and newsletters (Millward *et al.*, 1992: 167).

In the 1998 *Workplace Employee Relations Survey* (Cully *et al.*), direct participation was evident in teamworking (65 per cent of all workplaces employing 25 or more people); team briefing (61 per cent); staff attitude surveys in the last five years (45 per cent) and problem solving groups such as quality circles (43 per cent). There were also regular meetings of the entire workforce (37 per cent), a practice which was rather more extensive than the existence of a workplace-level joint consultative committee, employee share ownership schemes for non-managerial employees, guaranteed training for staff, and individual performance-related pay schemes. However, there are issues of definition and width. In the case of teamworking, for example, it was reported in 65 per cent of workplaces, but in only 5 per cent did it take the form of autonomous work groups (i.e. those in which team members were given responsibility for their task, jointly decided how work was to be done or appointed their own leader) (Marchington and Wilkinson, 1999).

Why empowerment?

The case for empowerment in management is essentially seen in pragmatic terms. It is assumed firstly that workers have the opportunity to contribute to organisational success and that, as they are closer to the work situation, they may be able to suggest improvements which management would be unable to do by virtue of their position in the hierarchy. Involving staff would also increase job satisfaction and reduce turnover as workers would feel more committed to organisational goals. In addition, empowerment reduces the need for complex and indeed dysfunctional systems of control, hence increasing efficiency. There is an assumption that workers are an untapped resource with knowledge, experience and an interest in becoming involved, which can be appropriated by employers if they will provide opportunities and structures for worker involvement. It is also assumed that participative decision-making is likely to lead to job satisfaction and better-quality decisions. Thus empowerment is a win-win scenario with gains available both to employers (increased efficiency) and workers (job satisfaction).

According to Foy (1994: xvii), '"empowering" people is as important as involving them was in the 1980s, or getting them to participate in the 1970s'. While earlier involvement initiatives may have been empowering, empowerment as we came to understand it in the 1990s needs to be seen in a particular business and political context. The rhetoric of enterprise which reflected the shift to the political right in Western Europe and the USA, underpinned the new management approach (Legge, 1995). Peters and Waterman's best-selling but much-criticised book *In Search of Excellence* (ISOE), published in 1982, was influential in helping the modern empowerment movement to create a suitable climate and language and the perceived wisdom and buzzwords became quickly and widely disseminated within the business community. The crusading message was the need to move away from the hard rationalist models driven by accountants and engineers to a more simple intuitive style of management summed up by such catchphrases as: 'Productivity Through People'. Successful organisations focused on managing culture. Implicit in this analysis was the view that managers could unleash the talents of individuals by dismantling organisational bureaucracy. Managers were exhorted to trust and involve employees, to treat people like adults. 'Every man becomes a pioneer, an entrepreneur, a leader' (Peters and Waterman 1989: 323). While much of the ISOE tract was discarded with subsequent volumes, the message of moving beyond hierarchy (Peters, 1992) and trusting people to make decisions: ('involve everyone in everything; leading by empowering people') remained a central theme of this work. The discourse of empowerment fitted with notions of enterprise culture, with individuals seen as entrepreneurs taking destiny into their own hands. Schonberger (1990) exhorted organisations to empower staff ('we want take charge employees') to 'add value'. Empowerment was associated with a host of buzzwords – liberation management (Peters, 1992); world-class management (Morton, 1994) and new logic management (Lawler, 1996). A flood of books advocating empowerment began to appear (Byman,

1991; Foy, 1994). It was seen as the 'latest offering with magical properties to secure the missing links between employee commitment and bottom-line organizational performance' (Cunningham *et al.*, 1996: 143).

There was a strong unitarist tone, assuming mutuality of interest. According to Marchington, many of the accounts of empowerment tend to be one-dimensional, written from a managerial and anecdotal perspective.

> The stories have a simple purpose, a unified thread running through them, and a relatively unproblematic outcome in which unchallenged corporate goals are willingly embraced by an empowered workforce. Unfortunately, a few minor characters are 'lost' along the way, sacrificed in the interests of the plot, but even so most of those who are made redundant or 'rationalised' find salvation via sophisticated outplacement practices and caring redeployment professionals.
>
> (Marchington, 1995)

The promotion of empowerment as a solution to the problems of managing should also be viewed as taking place against a backcloth of changing market conditions. It was argued that markets were now more competitive (indeed, turbulent and chaotic) partly due to the globalisation of competition and liberalisation by governments, and customers were becoming more demanding in terms of choice, quality, design and service. The move to customised products with flexible specialisation (Piore and Sabel, 1983) and flatter and leaner structures was seen as the new route to competitive advantage and this meant increasing focus on labour as a resource. Furthermore, jobs were seen as far more complex than in the days of scientific management, with change taking place at a much quicker rate. It was seen as vital to achieve greater flexibility through the use of people and reduce 'organisational constipation'. Rather than trying to control employees, they should be given discretion to provide better and speedier service and achieve a higher standard of work. Nor was the public sector immune from such pressures as privatisation, and commercialisation increased pressure on them to meet various performance criteria. The new management paradigm emphasised by writers such as Drucker (1988) and Kanter (1989) includes debureaucratisation (end of hierarchy and prescriptive rules), and delayering, decentralisation and the utilisation of project-based teams as part of a movement towards a new knowledge-based organisation.

As Walton (1985: 76) put it, managers have now 'begun to see that workers respond best – and most creatively – not when they are tightly controlled by management, placed in narrowly defined jobs, and treated like an unwelcome necessity, but, instead when they are given broader responsibilities, encouraged to contribute, and helped to take satisfaction from their work'. However, whilst traditional external controls such as supervisory attention may have been eroded, sophisticated measurement systems (technical control) monitor the performance of individuals and teams and peer pressure (social control) also serves management's objectives (Delbridge *et al.*, 1992; Sewell and Wilkinson, 1992). (See Chapter 3.) With the issue of control in mind it is worth noting that sectoral and labour market changes shifted the balance of power to employers so as to facilitate the introduction of empowerment and other employee involvement mechanisms, which changed work relationships on employers' terms. In addition, the 1980s and 1990s saw rationalisation and downsizing as very much the order of the day (see Chapter 10). In this context empowerment became a business necessity as the destaffed and delayered organisation could no longer function as before. Empowerment was inevitable as tasks had to be allocated to the survivors in the new organisation. Thus, talk of enrichment and job satisfaction were very much secondary to simply getting the job done.

Making sense of empowerment

A central problem confronts those who would attempt to analyse empowerment at work: the term 'empowerment' has been used very loosely by practitioners and the literature itself is hazy (Cunningham *et al.*, 1996: 144). At its simplest, empowerment would commonsensically be associated with the redistribution of power, but in practice empowerment is usually seen as an initiative designed by management, intended to generate commitment and enhance employee contributions to the organisation. While some empowerment initiatives may provide employees with new channels through which their influence is enhanced, empowerment does not involve any *de jure* sharing of authority or power. The onus is on employers to involve employees or give employees the opportunity to be involved. It is individualist rather than collectivist in its orientation, i.e. empowerment is based on individual workers or work groups but not on larger groups such as trade unions. It encompasses direct rather than indirect involvement in work practices. Thus a distinction could be made between empowerment initiatives and initiatives which may empower (the latter including industrial democracy).

The new language deployed in the study of decision-making at work is significant, suggesting an upbeat view of management with the positive and vague association making the appeal immediate (Collins, 1999). The empowerment movement has appropriated language from wider political movements – feminism and the ecology movement, where empowerment is also seen as a positive force, but a key difference is that these movements are rooted in the oppressed, i.e. helping people to help themselves, whereas the empowerment movement is driven by those in power, i.e. it helps managers to manage the organisation (Hennestad, 1998). Thus, one needs to question who is empowering whom and why, as well as examining to whom the benefits (if any) belong. For some, empowerment could be seen as letting someone else take the risk and responsibility (Sisson, 1994).

Empowerment can be seen as a flexible and even elastic term (Cunningham *et al.*, 1996; Lashley, 1997). It clearly fits within the 'voluntarist' tradition which left managers and workers (in practice reflecting power structures, usually the former) to decide on a suitable approach for the organisation. Empowerment can also be seen as being similar to the 1970s QWL movement in that it is a management-led approach yet it is different in so far as the QWL movement emphasised labour issues such as job satisfaction, absenteeism and labour turnover, whereas empowerment emphasises more direct business considerations, such as quality, flexibility and productivity (Buchanan, 1994). There is a greater emphasis, as with HRM, on 'attitudinal and behavioural characteristics of employees rather than on procedures for policy or a formal set of work rules' (Cunningham *et al.*, 1996: 145). It is management who empower employees and the initiatives have tended to cover direct workforce involvement over a relatively small number of issues, usually connected with the production process or service delivery, with the rationale that highly committed and empowered staff were more likely to engage in a 'beyond contract' effort. There has tended to be little union negotiation concerning the principle of the initiative, with design and planning excluding union involvement. In practice, however, issues arising out of the implementation of empowerment often become industrial relations matters. For example, job enlargement can threaten traditional demarcation lines as well as raise remuneration issues.

In spite of the fact that, as we have observed, the term is quite elastic, there is a tendency in the existing literature to lump together all the various forms of empowerment (Lashley, 1997). Of course, attempts to separate or to distinguish forms of empowerment are problematic. All categorisation schemes for empowerment are unsatisfactory in the sense that the boundaries between different types are not distinct and range from the mechanistic (i.e. structural change) to the more organic (concerned with attitudes/culture). However, taking account of these notes of caution we can identify five main types, namely information sharing, upward problem-solving, task autonomy, attitudinal shaping and self-management.

Information sharing

For employees to be empowered, information is a central component. There has been a great deal of interest in recent years in management increasing downward communication to employees, typically via newsletters, the management chain or team briefing, which communicates organisational goals and the business position of the organisation to 'win hearts and minds'. The logic here is that employees will be more understanding of the reasons for business decisions and, as a result, more committed to the organisation's action. Moreover, communication is direct to the workforce rather than being mediated by employee representation or trade unions. Thus, as Beale puts it, 'employee involvement programmes provide an alternative source of information, of ideas and interpretation of workplace experiences, an alternative to those provided by the union' (Beale, 1994: 120). The aim is to have employees identifying more with the employer: 'them' becomes the competition and 'us' the company. Critics have argued that such schemes 'incorporate' workers and/or bypass trade unions and are designed not to provide 'better' information to empower workers but to convince them of the logic of management action and hence reduce the scope for genuine empowerment, i.e. the opportunity to influence or change decisions. In short, it may be a form of pseudo participation (Pateman,

1970) with a move away from 'You will do this' to 'This is why you will do this' (Wilkinson *et al.*, 1993: 28).

Another aspect of information sharing is that employees should have the opportunity to express their views and grievances openly and independently through a form of upward communication, rather than being able to raise only task-related problems. Of course 'voice' could be achieved through trade union organisation and collective bargaining, or through formally established grievance and disputes procedures, but empowerment tends to favour individual action through speak-up schemes which offer employees protection if their complaints are not heard sympathetically.

Upward problem solving

Again there are various dimensions to this form of empowerment. Within the existing job this may involve informing management of problems and letting them deal with it. A typical example in manufacturing would be workers having the ability to halt the line because of production problems or defective material. Even in taylorised action plans such as that at the New United Motor Manufacturing Inc (NUMMI) – GM – Toyota Venture, identifying and solving problems was evident. In services, employees may be able to make customer-related decisions (e.g. replacing defective products). In short, there may be greater autonomy and responsibility at the point of production or service delivery. Outside the basic work process itself are suggestion involvement (Bowen and Lawler, 1992), where workers make suggestions but management decide whether to act upon these, or more significantly, where workers have some autonomy through quality circles/groups/teams, addressing problems and in some cases implementing improvements themselves. However, it needs to be part of a 'no blame culture' so risks can be taken. For clearly where there are flexibly specialised processes, which rely on employee skill, discretion and organisational capabilities, employees are more likely to have more influence over decisions than in organisations where there are scrutinised and standardised processes that are capable of being tightly controlled from above and where there is a tradition of such control.

Task autonomy

Task flexibility has been a key theme of much restructuring in British manufacturing. At its most basic level this may mean removing inspectors from the production line as workers take on wider responsibility, or it may involve the more significant restructuring of work units into cells (often around product flows) or teams, or the creation of semi-autonomous work groups now commonly referred to as teamworking or self-managing teams. This differs from job rotation, enlargement and enrichment in that the work group itself decides details of production and work group norms to a much larger extent than the former job restructuring schemes. Such teams can have autonomy concerning task allocation and scheduling, monitoring of attendance, health and safety issues, the flow and pace of production and can also be responsible for setting improvement targets (Wall and Martin, 1987). Teams can also have responsibility for the recruitment and training of temporary staff as well as controlling overtime levels. Developing a cell-base team structure is seen as helping communication, acceptance of change, and, through peer pressure, reduces the need for tight supervision and other forms of external control. This then facilitates delayering. Such groups can have what psychologists term 'skill discretion' (solving problems with the knowledge of the group) and 'means discretion' (choice in organising the means and tools of work) (Cooper, 1973), but are still working within a structure determined by senior management and remain focused on operational rather than strategic issues.

Attitudinal shaping

This views empowerment as a psychological process and is often seen in the service industry (Jones et al., 1997), where the objective of training is to inculcate service quality values among staff (Rosenthal et al., 1997). There may be no change in work or organisational structure but employees are trained/educated to 'feel' empowered (a state of mind) (Berry, 1995: 208) and to play a more confident role in their interaction with the customer. Internalisation of the new values is seen as the key to new behaviour. Taylor (1998: 98) notes, as competition increases, 'service sector employers are increasingly demanding that employees deep act – actively work on and change their inner feelings to match the display required by the labour process in order to meet the perceived expectations of internal customers'. Working on feelings and building a rapport, treating customers like guests in their homes is seen as central to this although there is a difference between deep acting (i.e. a genuine response) and feigned surface acting (Taylor, 1998: 87).

Self-management

This is the most far-reaching form of empowerment but tends to be rare in any real sense. Clearly, self-managing work groups are a limited form of this approach, but are constrained by working within certain limits set by senior management (e.g. self-managing in relation to a set of work tasks). One member of a self-directed team reported: 'I like the small group . . . people give you a sense of community. The disadvantage is that you feel more responsible for the job. The advantage is that we have more freedom, no supervisor standing over our shoulder. There's the satisfaction in handling problems, on our own. For example, sales dropped once and then we figured out how to correct it' (Batt and Applebaum, 1995). Ideally self-management should involve divisions between managers and workers being eroded and decisions, rules and executive authority no longer being set by the few for the many (Semler, 1989). Others have referred to high involvement (Bowen and Lawler, 1992), where business information is shared and employees have participation in wider business decisions. In Semler's account of his family's manufacturing company, the workforce had voting rights on all issues affecting the firm and involving salary. But as Hilmer and Donaldson argue, someone still has to control the agenda and present the issues for voting, leading to their conclusion that it is a safety valve or 'a supplement not a substitute for hierarchy' (1996: 48).

Clearly, these types may overlap as many initiatives incorporate several of these dimensions. For example, information is important to empowerment in general and not just as a separate form. Similarly, a change in attitude and self-efficacy is seen by some writers as being at the core of any form of empowerment (Conger and Kanungo, 1988).

Issues

Effectiveness

Business effectiveness, and attempts to enhance the effectiveness of business, lie at the heart of the current interest in empowerment. However, effectiveness can be examined from a number of perspectives, and much depends on how one sees management motivation for the introduction of such initiatives. While there has been much discussion of empowerment from a humanist perspective there is no doubt that in the 1980s and 1990s, management have regarded business considerations as the primary force behind empowerment. The degree of formal participation offered by empowerment does not extend to significant power-sharing or participation in higher-level strategic decisions such as product and investment plans. While there have been business benefits arising from empowerment, it is often difficult to disentangle the contribution of empowerment given that it is typically part of wider organisational change process (TQM, BPR, etc), with other changes such as new payment systems, training and new technology often part of the package. Respondents to Cunningham et al. (1996) reported improvements in cost savings, quality and employee commitment. Similarly, direct participation in the EPOC survey was found to have a strong impact on economic performance and workplaces with a strong participative culture (either direct or representative) outperformed those which had no such culture (EPOC, 1998). In terms of whether it leads to greater worker influence the answer appears to be yes but within heavily constrained terms (Cunningham et al., 1996; Rees, 1996; Edwards et al., 1997; Wilkinson et al., 1997). Batt and Applebaum's research suggests both employees and the firm benefit from self-managed teams with enhanced jobs and greater responsibility for work quality, with team-based participation having a bigger impact on attitudes than what they term 'off line' (i.e. indirect) participation (1995). Rosenthal et al. (1997: 486) conclude from their case in retailing that '... the enlargement of discretion cannot be disputed. There has been an advance over the virtual absence of discretion under the old regime and this is not trivial in the eyes of store staff. On the other hand, we would assess this empowerment as being fairly limited.'

One model of empowerment?

While the names given to empowerment initiatives may sound superficially similar, it is not possible to compare organisations on this basis. We need to move away from any simplistic or unilinear conceptions of empowerment (Lashley, 1997). Not only is it the case that varying types of empowerment carry different meanings, but also techniques with the same name, structure and processes may be experienced in very different fashions by different workforces. As a result, empowerment initiatives cannot be analysed in isolation from the wider contextual matters that impact on the employment relationship (Collins, 1998). Whilst the catalyst for the introduction of empowerment initiatives may have been the same at the most general level, i.e. intensifying competitive pressure, the extent of these pressures may differ. In one organisation empowerment may be part of a wider move to a more progressive and open style of management, while, in another, management may be forced towards changes in work organisation and 'empowerment' as part of an immediate and desperate struggle to survive, with increased intensification and 'management by stress' (Parker and Slaughter, 1993) the outcome, and workers putting up with the new regime because of a fear of dismissal. In short, one needs to analyse the real terrain upon which the empowerment initiative is operationalised (Roberts and Wilkinson, 1991).

Empowerment and HRM

A central problem for management and workers concerns situations where empowerment and downsizing are linked. In such circumstances, it is all too easy for empowerment to become abandonment (Adler, 1993). Thus there is too often a contradiction between the rhetoric of empowerment and reality. As Warhurst and Thompson (1998: 9) note: 'the hollow laugh heard when mentioning the word "empowerment" in most organisations is the true test that employees at many levels experience the "great innovation" less as the opportunity to exercise discretion and more as necessity to undertake more tasks'. The notion of empowerment as the 're-enhanchantment' of work seems a little far-fetched. However, the credibility and acceptance of any initiative is partly governed by the management's treatment of the workforce. Studies point to the importance of supporting changes in human resource policy, such as moves towards single status, in producing a conception amongst the workforce of an 'open management style' and helping to produce a more positive evaluation of management (Rosenthal et al., 1997). Research on high-performance work teams which encompass empowerment identifies the context within which the teams operated as critical to their success. Management had a clear vision of how the teams fitted in with the broader business strategy and this was shared with all employees. Moreover, the teams were supported by a whole raft of other initiatives, such as an open management style, open-plan layout, flexitime and the removal of clocking, and a payment system based on skills acquisition (Buchanan, 1994). Thus empowerment needs to be nurtured by the whole work environment within which it operates. Schneider and

Bowen argue that, for empowerment to work, it requires the redistribution of four ingredients: power (to make decisions that influence organisational direction and performance); information (about the performance of the organisation); rewards (that are based on organisation performance); and knowledge (that enables employers to understand and contribute to performance) (1995: 250). Schneider and Bowen argue that employees are truly empowered to the extent that they share in all four of these pieces. Together, these pieces give employees a reason to really care about the success of the business because they now feel more control over what happens on their jobs, more *aware* of what's going on around them in the business, and more *accountable* for what happens in the form of their rewards changing as performance changes (Schneider and Bowen, 1995: 251).

Control and empowerment

A common problem with empowerment in practice is that the decision-making process is not clear so that workers suggest ideas but management are unable to respond adequately to these. These problems are partly the result of the need to adapt to new production techniques and downsizing rather than enhancing empowerment per se. In other words, empowerment is not without costs both in terms of establishing a new approach to management (involving training costs, costs of new reward and information systems) and in its operation (involving issues of integration, consistency and unintended consequence) (Lawler, 1996). From a business perspective a concern in recent years is the implication of a loss of management control. In one piece of research a manager pointed out: 'the teams are self directed but not really empowered as they have to check first to make sure it is okay and managers still make the final decision'. In others, supervisors sat in on the quality circle to make sure the time was spent sensibly! (see Wilkinson, Marchington, Dale and Godfrey, 1997c). However, an individual acting alone brought down Barings Bank, and in other organisations, such as Sears Roebuck, embarrassing headlines resulted from employees using their initiative and subverting control mechanisms (Simons, 1995). As some commentators have pointed out, Oliver North is also part of the roll-call of empowered employees (Micklethwait and Woodridge, 1996: 333). Hamel and Prahalad note, 'Empowerment without a shared sense of direction can lead to anarchy. While bureaucracy can strangle initiative and progress, so too can a large number of empowered but unaligned individuals who are working at cross-purposes. Of course, every employee should be empowered, but empowered to do what? Empowerment implies an obligation and an opportunity to contribute to a specific end. The notion of a shared direction, what we call a "strategic intent", reconciles the needs of individual freedom and concerted, coordinated effort' (Hamel and Prahalad, 1996: 319).

Employee responses

It is becoming clear that, despite the explosion of new managerial initiatives designed to elicit greater effort and commitment either through new methods of control or the attempt to manipulate meaning, these cannot be assumed to have happened. Much of the critical literature can be seen as a mirror image of the applied management work in that critical scholars share with management's gurus a vision of workers as the passive recipients of whatever management desire. In other words, both these schools have been too eager to accept the rhetoric of empowerment at face value. Thoughtful scholarship on empowerment, however, demonstrates that workers are seldom dupes of management rhetoric (Collins, 1999).

Research on empowerment is often polarised into those who report greater work effort and more demanding jobs and those who report more job satisfaction, but there is some evidence of both occurring simultaneously. Thus, research suggests that work can be more satisfying with increased discretion over the work process (Purcell and Hutchinson, 1996), while making more explicit and rigorous demands of employees (Collinson *et al.*, 1998). According to an employee:

> I'm forty-six and I've been doing this new job for nearly two years and I've been completely turned around. It has given me a new lease of life. I'd rather work this way. It's hard work with more responsibility and more worry, but there is a lot more job satisfaction.

> (McArdle *et al.*, 1995: 164)

There is also clearly a paradox in the empowerment process in that while workers may be empowered to improve a process, once that change has been made it is standardised and hence constraining.

It is taken for granted in much of the prescriptive literature that employees will welcome and be committed to the new approach. Indeed, there is evidence that workers welcome the removal of irritants (e.g. close supervision) and the opportunity to address problems at source as well as the ability to decide work allocation. However, there is also evidence that employees are often not sufficiently trained for empowerment in the West, especially where empowerment is a result of downsizing. When it is introduced less as a strategic new way of managing and more as a means of dealing with financially driven shake-out empowerment becomes abandonment (Adler, 1993). In contrast, in Japan the success of job enrichment has been attributed to newly hired workers being trained to do all the jobs on the line (a process taking six to twelve months), so they understand the entire process and are better able to identify problems (Garvin, 1988). Some commentators have suggested that employees' empowerment is simply a smokescreen:

> Far from heralding a radical shift towards a world in which there is more room for 'creativity and worker autonomy', BPR contrives to make work even more tightly prescribed by urging, or requiring, employees to dedicate their hearts and minds, and not just their bodies, to tasks that have been designed by others. These tasks may be performed by teams in which members are required to self-organise their activities, exercise

their discretion and monitor their own performance. But, crucially, they are tasks that have been (re)engineered by others and which in principle require employees to be more self-disciplined as they monitor each other, as team members, to ensure that processes are effectively managed.

(Willmott, 1995: 96).

However, to what extent are the aims of management met? Ackroyd and Thompson (1999: 161) point out, 'What is problematic about many current accounts of corporate culture, and teamworking and TQM is not the argument concerning what those who design the system want, but the bizarre belief that they have almost no difficulty getting it'. The evidence indicates that employees are not 'cultural dopes' (Hill, 1995: 50) and do not simply buy into rhetoric in an unconditional way. Their support is dependent upon trust in management and the perceived benefits to themselves. There is evidence of a failure to win hearts and minds (Watson, 1994) and indeed of a tendency to be highly critical of management rhetoric (Collinson, 1994) and 'Yankee bullshit'. Employees interpret, evaluate and (re)act towards managerial initiatives, and in their own way serve to 'audit' the viability of managerial initiatives. Thus it could be argued that although management try to limit 'empowerment', employees themselves may see the discourse as a resource in their struggles with management to bring managers into line with workforce expectations (Rosenthal et al., 1997). Indeed, they may question how they are treated and rewarded in the organisation as a whole, and the extent to which they participate in key business decisions and hence construct their own agenda (Wilkinson et al., 1997a). While unions do not present an obstacle to the introduction of empowerment (Cunningham et al., 1996), by restructuring work responsibilities and making the team central to the workplace, as well as encouraging employees to identify with managerial objectives, empowerment can marginalise unions and in some cases is clearly intended to do so (Beale, 1994).

Cops to coaches?

The prescriptive empowerment literature suggests that the role of middle managers and supervisors changes from that of holders of expert power to that of facilitators (or coaches). However, many middle managers perceive the removal of expert power as a significant threat and participative management as a burden and it is not surprising that they do not universally welcome it (Marchington et al., 1992; Denham Lincoln et al., 1997). Their sense of anxiety is exacerbated by fears of job loss as levels in the hierarchy may be reduced as part of wider changes, as well as possible reduction in status and increasing workload (Klein, 1984). Hence, there is a danger that they 'act' their compliance to empowerment, affecting the ultimate success of the initiative (Denham et al., 1997). Delayering and empowerment have an association with downsizing and job loss. As Heckscher says, 'empowerment is fine as long as it means allowing each person a clear domain of responsibility; they are quite happy to have their superiors stop "micro-managing" them, and they generally believe they should allow their subordinates the same autonomy. Where they grow deeply uncomfortable is when empowerment means the blurring of individual responsibilities and roles, or the loss of clarity in the decision-making process. They want to know what they will be held accountable for, and where to go to resolve a dispute' (Heckscher, 1995: 110.) Moreover, some see moves towards employee empowerment as 'soft' management or 'loose discipline', removing their authority over subordinates, and a recipe for chaos. However, research suggests that opposition may owe more to the fact that they were not provided with the resources required, were not sufficiently trained or were not evaluated on this in terms of performance appraisal and therefore did not see it as of much importance (Marchington *et al.*, 1992) and that the problem relates to systems and structures rather than the personnel of middle management (Edwards *et al.*, 1997). In other cases middle managers may feel that they themselves gain influence over decisions taken elsewhere in the organisation that affect their work. Some may also feel that it gives them a chance to show their initiative and so increase their career prospects despite losing a degree of functional expert power.

Conclusion

Empowerment has arisen from the employee involvement initiatives of the 1980s, and has largely been aimed at shopfloor workers, with the goals of increasing productivity and commitment to employers' goals. While a variety of forms of empowerment have developed, they share a common basis in being managerially driven and hence within an agenda which allows for largely task-based empowerment. However, it needs to be recognised that empowerment has different forms and should be analysed in the context of broader organisational practice. The importance of these initiatives is in the context of the translation of their supposedly formal properties within the real terrain of the workplace. Empowerment may not in practice dilute overall management control: rather it can reconstitute the nature of such control, with a recomposition rather than a reassertion of managerial authority (Edwards, 1995). This does not mean that empowerment is without benefits to employees. Nor, while these benefits may be limited, should they be dismissed as simply small beer. A pragmatic approach should be taken. As Pfeffer (1994: 206) suggests, one should 'compare programmes not to some ideal but to the situation that would exist in their absence. In other words, just because a programme does not solve every problem or move the organisation all the way, particularly initially, to where it wants and needs to be does not mean that it is a failure. A programme fails when it produces either no sustained change or else change that is dysfunctional and ineffective. Some remediation of problems in managing the employment relation is certainly better than nothing at all.'

Central to our understanding of worker responses is the issue of trust. A paradox of much of new management techniques is that techniques which require, indeed demand, commitment and high-trust relations simultaneously erode any basis for such relations. This takes us back to the critical issue of context. Individuals empowered to make decisions are rightly sceptical and also may be unwilling to use their discretion if they feel continually under the watchful eye of Big Brother. This is perhaps most obvious in the public sector as 'technologies of distrust' (Miller, 1997) and the audit society (Power, 1997) undermine professional judgement or at least place such judgement under the gaze of rational – often accounting – expertise. Not only might such approaches not work, but they may lead to dysfunctional and unintended consequences as employees subvert the system. Much of the evidence indicates that most British firms have proceeded in a half-hearted and partial way with empowerment adopted in an *ad hoc* and piecemeal manner rather than taking the holistic, integrated approach which is required to make it work effectively, and a new paradigm of work remaining an ideal. Given this, it would be possible to argue that we have not seen a good test of the potential benefits of empowerment.

Note: My thanks to David Collins for his helpful comments.

Developing empowerment at PackageCo

Adrian Wilkinson and Kevin Morrell

PackageCo is a transit heavy-duty packaging company with a main plant in the UK (PackageCo UK) and a number of satellite plants elsewhere in the UK and Europe. The current market is stagnant, although the trend is for smaller orders and quicker lead times. There are 1,700 workers employed in PackageCo as a whole, with nearly 200 at the UK site. The density of unionisation for shopfloor employees is close to 100 per cent, but other staff are non-union.

A quality initiative began with the appointment of the current MD, who had experienced TQM in his previous job in a European plant. This initiative led to a number of improvement projects and a push for ISO 9002 registration, which was achieved two years ago. More recently, the MD became committed to Total Quality Performance (TQP) and this was followed by corporate initiatives, e.g. vision and mission statements, the appointment of a European quality director and the development of a quality improvement framework.

PackageCo UK is viewed as the leading company in PackageCo, which means that it is allowed considerable autonomy for its own operations. There is a Quality Council with directors and departmental heads to oversee the process and a number of cross functional quality improvement teams; these teams are currently helping to put into place the internal customer/supplier concept. There are also some quality circles (shopfloor based) which have been running for two years. These team activities are facilitated by a total quality co-ordinator.

The TQP initiative is seen to have had a significant impact on bottom line performance, with delivery performance having been improved and a reduction in the cost of complaints over a twelve-month period. A major benefit is seen to be greater teamwork across PackageCo UK. One of the aims of TQP has been to improve the quality of the company's direct contact with its employees (as opposed to relying solely on the more traditional methods of consultation via trade unions) and this has been achieved. TQP had to overcome a number of problems early on, relating to inconsistent objectives and lack of data, as well as scepticism from trade unions and employees that TQP was 'nothing new'. Prior to implementing TQP, a conscious decision was made to involve middle managers from the very start. There was also a perceived hiccup less than a year ago as it was felt senior management had taken their 'eye off the ball', and the drive towards total quality seemed to lose momentum, but the appointment of a full-time facilitator has helped to overcome problems relating to sustainability. There is now a much greater awareness of HR issues as a result of TQP. For example, bonus schemes and induction are being examined in the light of TQP, with output-related bonuses in particular being critically reviewed. Teamworking is being developed, with managers taking on a training role and emphasising people managing themselves and taking decisions.

However, staff complain that they have little guidance and get a 'bollocking' if they make the wrong decisions. A number of employees say it is not their job. The suggestion scheme output has dried up. Management style is also being examined following an attitude survey of employees which reported that style was friendly, but not very responsive. The unions have complained that the company has a very narrow view of EI, largely restricted to upward problem-solving and downward communication, with little opportunity for other contributions. Many are also concerned with potential job losses as a major contract has been lost.

Until now the only HR presence has been a personnel assistant, whose role is one of general administrative duties and the routine collection of statistics, recruitment and development of trainees. She is involved in the Quality Council, but has little influence on the strategic direction of TQP. There is no training function, with training being carried out in-house by appropriate managers and also by consultants. The critical HR influences at the site are through the MD and the *ad hoc* intervention of the group personnel director. It has now been decided that there needs to be a professional personnel presence to review HR practices in the light of the company's strategy.

Assignment

You have been appointed as personnel manager at PackageCo UK as the group personnel director has found it increasingly difficult to cope with all the issues on a part-time basis and with little day-to-day involvement. Your first task is to review HR practices in the light of developments in the last few years. The MD, who recently attended a conference on world-class manufacturing, is interested in the idea of empowering staff.

Empowerment at Hotelco

Adrian Wilkinson and Kevin Morrell

Hotelco is part of a large UK-based chain of hotels with a national coverage. The industry is highly competitive and the company is trying to improve its cost structure without damaging quality. It has grown from one site to 20 in the last 20 years, with an *ad hoc* HR approach, largely concerned with recruitment and dismissal. Although there is a corporate personnel philosophy, this was drawn up by the first personnel manager who left two years ago and has never been replaced. This philosophy has tended to be ignored by the various hotel managers and the hotels are managed rather differently when it comes to HR practice. Some hotels recruit largely on word of mouth and new colleagues are often friends and relatives. Although staff are paid on an hourly rate, the way tips are distributed is also *ad hoc*.

There are increasing HR problems in the company, particularly high turnover, despite Hotelco's paying wages which are above the industry average. In addition, feedback from customers suggests they are not happy with the quality of service. At the same time, staff complain that they never know what is going on. Communication is supposed to be done through line managers, but these managers say they do not have time to do it and tell staff what they need to know. Staff also complain that they are powerless when customers complain and they do not have the authority to deal with refunds/compensation. In 1998 an empowerment programme was launched, entitled 'Putting Customers First', and staff were authorised to make refunds up to £50 without prior authorisation. However, management are concerned that refunds are now given for the most trivial complaints and there is a problem of consistency. Furthermore, while the permission of line managers is not required, they make their views clear on what they regard as appropriate, and different shifts and departments have quite different approaches. Staff have complained that the programme should be called 'Putting employees last!'

Assignment

As someone studying HRM you have been asked by one of the partners to produce a report to the company on the following issues:

1. Should the company now have a full time personnel manager?

2. What changes are required to policies for:

    a. recruitment and selection
    b. training and development
    c. employee reward
    d. employee involvement and communications

You have been asked to justify your recommendations and provide some broad costings.

Introducing empowerment in PublicOrg

Nicola Denham Lincoln, Cheryl Travers and Peter Ackers

You have been called in as a group of consultants to PublicOrg and told that there is a lot of distrust and resistance to their empowerment policy. As a result, you have collected the following information and interviewed some of the employees and managers, who tell you how they feel.

PublicOrg is a public sector organisation, providing a service to 22 million customers which, since its development as an executive agency, has attempted to remove itself from the traditional hierarchical tradition which for so long characterised the civil service. The organisation employs approximately 72,000 staff, about a sixth of whom work part-time. The services are provided by the agency through a network of local offices arranged into districts throughout the United Kingdom. Each district is now organised as a separate cost centre after a fundamental restructuring of the civil service that emphasises the importance of value for money and customer service. Empowerment has been introduced to develop a workforce who are able to take on more responsibility and who are more multi-skilled so that customers are able to get their queries answered and dealt with quickly and easily by one person.

The changes required in PublicOrg to make it more customer-focused and competitive meant that managerial practices needed to alter accordingly and that staff were expected to take on more responsibility for the day-to-day running of the business. The managing director stated that:

> Empowerment is about enabling our staff to influence the way things happen; it is about giving our front-line staff the power to pull the levers that count as we strive to deliver a quality service and good value for money; it is about providing greater job satisfaction for staff and it is about ensuring that all of our staff have an equal opportunity to contribute to the success of the Agency.

The organisation has never given a single definition of empowerment as they believe that it is more beneficial to have a debate over what it means and explore what actions, behaviours and beliefs are needed for empowerment to flourish. One manager suggests to you that he thinks this is one of the main barriers to empowerment but doesn't tell you why.

The actual empowerment programme was initiated at head office by a team responsible for quality within the organisation and has the absolute backing of the Managing Director. Documents have been distributed to senior managers outlining which duties each grade can do and which can be devolved to lower levels. They call these their listings of requirements and freedoms. Since the implementation of empowerment, the appraisal system has been geared at rewarding people for their achievements rather than their tenure. The appraisal system on which pay is based now requires employees to provide evidence that they are taking part in empowering activities (suggestion schemes; quality improvement teams, etc) if they are to get anything but the minimum pay band. Many employees mention to you that they haven't got the time to do extra activities because of all the work that has been devolved to them via the listings of requirements and freedoms.

Empowerment training differed according to grade, with senior managers having a week away in a hotel and some non-managerial employees claiming they have had no training whatsoever. Those lower grades who *were* allowed on an empowerment training course, had a one-day session in the office where they were asked to discuss the issues of empowerment. Many came back enthused from this training, you are told, but one manager quietly whispers to you that the employees had come back thinking they could do anything and that he had had to reinforce his control.

Your interviews

The middle managers you interview in PublicOrg are at the line or department management level within two districts. They are generally people who, like other supervisors, have worked their way up from the lowest levels and who are unlikely to be promoted further. Most managers tell you that they think empowerment is a good thing and that it is the only way forward, but some feel that employees are still not able to take on many of the responsibilities and admit having difficulty 'letting go' of their authority. The employees tell you that when they had had the training they were enthusiastic about the thought of empowerment:

> the problem was either the departmental or middle managers didn't get that message, or didn't agree, and we came out with all this 'Oh empowerment is going to be great, we can, like, make our own decisions' and they said 'No, you're not'.

It is clear that the employees feel that management have not understood what empowerment is all about: 'They've got the wrong end of the stick haven't they?' asks one.

They agree that nothing changed after this training and that the managers took charge again as soon as they returned to work. They talk to you about a suggestion scheme which had been introduced but express their irritation that, whilst they get a pat on the back and £10, none of their ideas are ever implemented. The problems associated with the grade structure are highlighted when you talk to employees and management about the issue of being able to let go of some of the responsibility to lower levels. They tell you that whilst managers use the rhetoric of empowerment (said all the right things), they do not act in an empowering way.

They also imply that they don't think the departmental managers really believe in empowerment:

> The District Manager's all for Quality like, you know, empowerment and everything and the (departmental managers) are like 'Yes Joe' but then they get back to their department and it's like 'That Joe talks a load of rubbish'.

> As you leave, you hear some employees complaining that they feel their managers don't trust them and are always double-checking any work they have been delegated to do.

Your brief

The organisation wants you to assess the success of their empowerment programme and asks you to suggest any ways in which it might be improved. In so doing, you have to address the following questions:

1. What does empowerment *mean* in this organisation?
2. Who is benefiting from empowerment and why?
3. Why has there been resistance to empowerment by
   a. middle management?
   b. employees?
4. What recommendations would you make to overcome the difficulties this programme is experiencing?

Case study 11.4

Empowerment at Aerospace Co

Paul J.T. Biddis

Aerospace Co is concerned with the final stage of production in the manufacturing of military aircraft. In recent years the company has seen an industry-wide fall in demand for defence products plus a strengthening of the US defence industry and an emergence of new competitors. With high costs and poor sales the company was becoming increasingly uncompetitive and had to consolidate many of its business interests. Since the beginning of this decade it has reduced its workforce by nearly half. As a result, Aerospace Co focused on new ways of tackling the problems it was facing. This was first marked by a move into one purpose-built hangar, and there has also been heavy investment in updating plant and equipment together with a new logistics system to oversee the planning of the build process. The company has also focused on 'softer' issues such as increased flexibility, training and involvement. Whilst change was urgently needed Aerospace Co did not rush into adopting initiatives. They made sure that the initiatives were relevant to the needs of the company and given the necessary support, e.g. management commitment.

The product (a military aircraft) is hand-built. Due to its age, the product was not designed with the aid of computers. Specification did not have the precision more modern aircraft have. Production is separated into four stages with each stage having a team responsible for all work within that stage. Assembly is long-cycle: over a two-week period, workers would undertake a range of activities. Once the team had completed all the build requirements for its stage of production the product would be moved by hand to the next stage. Workers had significant control over their work and production as a whole. They also had the opportunity to move between teams vis-à-vis stages.

Employees supported the introduction of new work practices (NWPs) in the mid-1990s and were aware of the reasons for change: to improve efficiency, reduce costs and improve customer service. Few felt that they were introduced purely for employee benefit, nor were they promoted as such. Support was built upon a realisation of the company's situation – an awareness helped by a management change programme. Employees were also personally aware of the volatile environment because of recent job losses. To survive, Aerospace Co could no longer continue to work in the 'very inefficient' and 'expensive' way it was. Changes were needed to allow it to respond to the demands placed upon it. While change could be a threat to their jobs, many regarded NWPs as a means to ensuring continued employment, any fear being outweighed by the wider issues of long-term survival.

Five years on, support has not only remained but increased, the main explanation for this being that NWPs have brought about expected benefits. Production is more efficient and better planned, costs have been reduced and customer service has improved. The business has become more competitive and consequently employees feel more secure in their jobs. There have also been other unexpected benefits. Communication has increased, which has brought about a more open and co-operative environment. There has been a distinct improvement in employee–management relations – prior to change employees considered relations to be 'poor'. The move into a new and modern hangar has made way for better work conditions and safety. In addition, employees felt that NWPs have helped further their own potential and increased job enrichment.

There was a general consensus that work has become harder and that employees were under more pressure to get work completed, yet this was considered acceptable. Employees were working harder for various reasons. There has been a strong focus upon reducing time wasted through practices that incurred a lot of idle time/non-value activity. Improving the layout of the storage room has made it easier and less time-consuming to find the necessary equipment. Old equipment has been replaced with new (such as power tools and cranes) making work quicker and physically easier to undertake. While the logistics system required each job to have a specific time frame, few saw this development as a means to make them work harder; times were calculated by the workers themselves and estimations based upon previous experience. None considered 'new' technology, targets/reports and appraisals, fellow colleagues and the demands of customers to have had a bearing on work effort. Working harder was not an unwanted development and most considered it a source of a better work experience. It made work more 'enjoyable' and 'interesting', helped establish a 'sense of pride and purpose' and 'relieved boredom'.

Increased flexibility has meant that employees now undertake a range of jobs. While before they had a certain degree of flexibility (the limits determined by their trade), they now had the opportunity to work on areas that were not part of their trade. The 'type-cast "one job for life" doesn't exist anymore'. The logistics system has meant that all work activity is laid out in detailed procedures. There has not, however, been a standardisation of work and a resulting diminishment in skill. While work is now more uniform and consistent, it remains highly skilled. The product is still hand-built and the actual work itself has not altered in any way. Workers made similar comments that 'there is no way' work could be standardised or deskilled – neither production nor the product allowed for it. Employees were still expected to have a trade even in the wake of flexibility and new forms of training. But they are now also qualified in other, specialist, aspects of the build programme, in addition to the skills of aircraft production they learnt when they first joined. There are certain aspects of production that require specific training, e.g. weapons guidance and engine running. Whereas before these were left to the expertise of the test pilot or component manufacturer, workers were now able to gain qualifications in these areas and undertake the jobs themselves.

There was now greater involvement. Employees noted a marked increase in both downward (information sharing) and upward (problem-solving) communication. They had a better awareness and understanding of management decisions, management were now keener to include employees in work matters and their suggestions were now taken more seriously. Workers felt they now had greater influence in designing new work practice(s) – a point that was lacking in previous attempts by management and consequently led to worker apprehension. A key feature of this has been the setting up of an improvement team, comprising key workers and headed by the project (senior) manager. Its role is to analyse work processes and identify areas that could be improved. Many of the changes in operation have come directly from its recommendations.

With a move away from direct inspection, workers must now check and clear their own work. This has been achieved by the use of stamping; each worker has their own stamp number and once a job is finished they stamp it off as fit for flight. Faults can therefore be traced back to the individual responsible. Employees are also required to identify the mistakes of others:

> If you make a mistake and someone else picks it up you are more likely to get a warning. That's the regime they're running now. We have been instructed by senior management that where we normally put an X against a fault (don't know who's done it) now it's, if you know who's to blame then blame them. Fail it and quote who did it!

Failure to rectify mistakes or clear bad work could lead to penalties – especially if they threatened the safety of the aircraft. However, these developments did not appear to have created any mistrust amongst workers. In any case, many took pride in their workmanship and wanted to provide high-quality work, so this was not a regular issue. Even when a fault was identified and logged this did not necessarily mean action would be taken against the individual concerned, unless it became a regular occurrence. Employees did not regard this as an attempt by management to extend control or consider that fellow workers were a form of surveillance. The nature of the product made workers a lot more willing to accept criticism:

> It's important for people to own up to their mistakes. People are a lot more open to criticism because of the product. Mistakes can be drastic so you don't mind if someone found any that you had made. You shouldn't take it as a sign that you're incompetent. You're trained at the very beginning to be open and honest and by-and-by it works.

Workers also had the discretion to make alterations. It must not be forgotten that the nature of production/aircraft required workers to make decisions daily without having to continually seek management's approval. Consultation and the ability to make alterations did not extend to all areas of work. While workers had a relatively free hand in certain areas this did not extend to aspects that concerned the functioning/handling (flight-critical) elements. The product was a complex piece of machinery and mistakes could be fatal. Indeed, workers were neither willing nor prepared to take complete responsibility in view of the risks involved. These limitations were therefore accepted and not minded.

A lot of enjoyment stemmed from working on military aircraft. This brought a high sense of personal gratification – 'Going into the hangar where there are live aeroplanes gives you one hell of a buzz ... I really enjoy working on aircraft.' Watching the finished product in operation also furthered feelings of satisfaction. This interest also made workers put up with aspects that were not enjoyable. Because the aircraft were hand-built, employees took exceptional pride in their work – it was a 'craft' that required skill and expertise.

Favourable experiences of NWPs were strongly influenced by the attitude(s) and approach of local management towards workers and the initiatives. Improved communication and greater involvement were only possible because their product manager was committed to encouraging this. He openly communicated with employees, sought their advice and gave them the support they needed. This influence was reinforced by comparisons employees made with the approaches of previous managers or managers elsewhere in the company who were not as enthusiastic and consequently less rewarding to work for. The present manager is a lot more open and honest, easily approachable and 'not in an ivory tower ... like it used to be'. Even those more critical of the changes admitted that the product manager had a positive impact.

Questions

1. What factors have led to employee support and how might these shape their views and the way findings are interpreted?

2. Do you think the way NWPs were implemented may influence employee opinion?

3. To what degree are employees involved at work and what factors defined the limits of their involvement?

4. Where would you position the findings using the ideas offered by contemporary debate?

5. 'NWPs are nothing more than a means to intensify work, deskill and exploit employees and increase management control.' Using the case study above discuss this statement.

Changing patterns of participation: boilermakers to bankers

Ian Roberts and Adrian Wilkinson

Introduction

In this comparative case study we examine the changing nature of participation through two organisations drawn from widely different sectors, contrasting them not only in terms of types of participation, and in terms of context and workforce, but also in the attitude of the managers at the time of the research. In contrasting the experiences of participation, the case studies seek to question the characterisation of employee participation as either a neutral but progressive 'tool' of management or a strategy for total control through diminution of trade union power at work. Rather, the meaning of participation at work varies with the context, both in terms of the objective form of the labour process, e.g. manual, non-manual, etc., and of wider social structures.

Bankco

Background

The bank, located in the North of England, was established in the nineteenth century. It established a reputation for innovation in the 1980s, most notably with the introduction of 'free banking', and its customer base increased fourfold. However, its competitive position changed as the financial services sector underwent rapid change. Deregulation removed barriers to entry, and new technology altered the basis of competition. Furthermore, growing consumer sophistication increased competition between banks and within the financial sector as a whole. Bad debt abroad had led to a refocus on the domestic market by the major banks. This, together with the entry of building societies into the personal lending and transmission area, the interest shown by stores and foreign banks in retail banking and the flotation of the TSB and Abbey National, brought a new competitive environment.

The bank struggled to adjust to these changing conditions. Growth in market share was falling in a number of areas by the mid-1980s. The bank's market position had become indistinguishable from that of other major banks, having lost its main source of differentiation. This placed it at a competitive disadvantage because of the high awareness the other banks enjoyed with respect to size, high street presence and advertising expenditure. The bank experienced a period of stagnant profits and low return on assets.

Human resource management

The bank employed 4,000 staff in the mid-1980s, in 80 branches, a clearing centre and a customer services bureau responsible for processing paper. The bank had awarded negotiation rights to BIFU for all staff, and operated a closed shop for a number of years. The bank has gradually moved over the years to traditional IR banking practices, away from a mix of banking and co-operative culture.

Banking policy towards staff has been characterised by high levels of paternalism, and an internal labour market encouraging an ethos of teamwork, shared interest and loyalty. The small size of branches (many with no more than 20 staff) facilitates informal communication and reduces 'them and us' attitudes.

Banks remain highly centralised bureaucratic organisations with a high degree of managerial prerogative. In the Bank, 25 volumes of practice and procedure lay out in detail the work activity of the branch. Personnel policies are highly centralised in terms of pay negotiations and working practices. Each branch has an office (union) representative, who mostly deals with minor issues.

Banking culture is conservative, with banks historically not regarding themselves as simply in business for profit, but with wider community responsibilities. This and what one manager referred to as an 'ingrained civil service attitude' needed changing. The bank had to become market-driven and develop a sales culture; tellers became sellers promoting products and creating profit, rather than merely handling paper.

A human resources manager from outside the bank was appointed to update employee relations practice and move the bank towards human resource management (HRM). The bank attempted to integrate the human resource function into business planning. This was seen as providing the missing link between business planning and management processes. Widespread changes followed; the line manager's role was enhanced, a remuneration review took place, performance-related pay was introduced, and training programmes were revised. The people element was emphasised: 'Banking is about people, and people make you unique,' said one senior manager. Participative mechanisms were introduced as part of this reconstruction of personnel practices.

Participation – origins and structures

The main formal participative structure was the staffing review committee (SRC) which meets quarterly to discuss:

> The implications for employees which may arise from the adoption or development of new or revised business practices and/or procedures and changes in trading or other circumstances.

The representatives on the committee were senior officials of the bank and union. In practice, the SRC never attained much status and did not become a central feature of industrial relations. The SRC was not seen as making significant contributions to decision-making processes and was regarded as irrelevant by the majority of staff. The bank decided to pursue an additional path to participation, designed to be of greater relevance to staff and to enhance employee commitment to company goals.

There were three major components of the bank's new approach to employee involvement (EI). Firstly, management style was emphasised; secondly, profit sharing was introduced; thirdly, there was team briefing. These measures were designed to create identification with and commitment to the bank, and greater commercial awareness.

Open management style

The human resource manager emphasised that:

> Effective communication and culture change can be achieved if the bank operates an open management style. Such an approach would in no way diminish management's ability to operate. It merely reinforces management's authority in a different manner.

Managers were encouraged not to exhort, but involve staff more in setting objectives. Other initiatives encouraged 'open door policies' and 'walking the job'.

Profit sharing

By the mid-1980s a group of senior managers felt that profit sharing was essential to the success of the organisation, it would be a vital component in the bank's drive to change culture and to get staff to appreciate the importance of profit. One senior manager said: 'Unless we got their minds linked with profit, we weren't going to get anywhere on the Corporate Plan.' Another senior manager welcomed its acceptance by the board: 'If this doesn't crystallise their minds and make things easier for them to see how to help customers, I don't know what will.'

Profit sharing was introduced almost simultaneously with a new pensions scheme, similar to those in major banks. These produced a positive framework for other changes taking place in the organisation.

Team briefing

One problem with many of the EI initiatives was the uncertain context of their introduction: initiatives to increase commitment and identification with corporate objectives, and to develop staff as a resource were being introduced at a time of prospective redundancy and relocation and there was considerable uncertainty amongst staff as to their prospects.

The bank regarded its actions as both 'logical and sensible' and fair, given market conditions. It admitted that many moves would be unpopular and did not want to be seen as forcing change as this could endanger other initiatives. It was felt that a more open management style and better communication could dispel the apprehension of staff.

Team briefing was introduced partly to facilitate change and it fitted with long-term objectives of increasing commitment to business goals. There were multiple objectives. An industrial relations audit raised questions over staff's commercial awareness. A proper communications structure was needed as the organisation underwent major change, with possible negative consequences for bank employees. The briefing process emphasised the role of the line manager, a major aim of the bank's HRM policy, providing an alternative channel of communication to that provided by the union. Briefing would also defeat the grapevine and clarify management responsibility for communication.

Briefing was based upon principles advanced by the Industrial Society and its introduction was facilitated by consultants, who provided training. Briefing was conducted by immediate line managers, and lasted between 15 and 25 minutes, although there were occasional one-off briefs, mixing central and local information. Briefing took place after the core brief was received from head office (after the senior managers' meeting), the process was usually completed within 48 hours.

Participation in practice – an assessment

An initial assessment can be given of what was essentially a long-term strategy to change culture. Some line managers doubted the motivational value of profit sharing, saying that for a real impact, group or individual allocation was required. Many said that it was impossible for an individual to relate their performance to the profit of the bank as a whole. Some optimistic managers said profit sharing was another benefit, helping staff to view the bank as a 'good employer', and in this indirect way attitudinal change would come. Staff wholeheartedly supported the scheme, but in an instrumental manner, most seeing it as 'extra dosh'; some were cynical, saying that the other banks had had such schemes for years; others did see an importance in terms of motivation, because 'we're all part of it now'. One manager saw the effect as positive but small, but felt that one should not expect too much: 'People weren't sticks of Brighton rock with Bankco through the middle.'

Profit sharing, however, was certainly welcomed by the union and staff as a whole, although for the first year it was worth no more than 3 per cent of pay. The union had been fighting for such a scheme for a number of years on grounds of comparability and greeted the scheme as a vindication of their stance. There were a number of teething problems in relation to communication policy, many of the early briefs' contents were revised because of irrelevance and too much 'party line' promotion. Style and lack of feedback were criticised; organisation and timing were a problem, especially in branches where a customer interface had to be maintained. Often briefs were 'token' efforts because of work pressure; the grapevine was still doing its job. Briefing in general was welcomed, both by managers and staff as part of a shift from a 'need to know' to 'nice to know' approach, despite criticisms of the actual operation of the scheme. Senior managers expressed satisfaction with the scheme and felt it had contributed to successful pay negotiations with messages of 'ability to pay', 'not pricing the bank out of the market', and greater staff awareness of commercial considerations.

The central concern with briefing was the difficulty of communicating change positively, if there was uncertainty as to what the change would be. There was a paradox here: if staff were not told of prospective changes, they became suspicious and apprehensive; if they were told, on many occasions plans were vague and inadequate in addressing their fears. Reinforcing the position of the line manager proved difficult in this context. Managers set themselves up as the person to see, no longer 'headmasters' but 'team leaders'. While the union did not perceive that briefing was designed to undermine their positions, some office representatives were worried about their role. However, in practice, as one remarked, 'it goes the other way'. Managers were not always able to answer or deal with the issues or queries raised by staff, either because of disagreement with staff, or because they themselves did not have the answers. The office representatives pointed out that 'the union came back into it again'.

Many managers at the workplace did not see briefing in terms of ensuring that the union would not be the main vehicle of communication or even take the view that '[the one] who communicates leads'. Thus, the bank felt it important that benefits accruing to staff as a result of negotiation with the unions should be announced by management. However, in a number of cases managers let the office representative handle it – perhaps itself a reflection of branch managers' unitary perception of employment and/or lack of awareness of HRM considerations. Such concerns did not loom so large as to obviate the overall positive response of the staff to briefing. It would be wrong to assume an identity of views between staff and the union and staff did not expect briefing to produce all the answers. Most welcomed it as a step in the right direction. One said: 'It's not perfect by any means, but we are learning more about what's going on in the bank. There are a lot of things we never knew before.' Another drew attention to feedback: 'The manager seems to listen much more now. He may not do much, but we are working on that too.'

One must see the introduction of participatory mechanisms as part of a wider process of change, and one cannot understand staff perception of such initiatives without taking this into account. It was true that such initiatives were designed to engineer consent to change and create identification with corporate goals. The need for change was presented in terms of market logic, hence it is endorsement of management policies which is sought, not some form of co-determination.

However, staff regarded employee involvement initiatives as part of a broader package of HRM, which for them offered direct material incentives in terms of an improved pension scheme and the introduction of profit sharing, and the promise of a resource-based employee relations approach with more attention to individual development and training. Had issues of redundancy come much more to the fore, this positive perception of initiatives might well have been threatened, and as the bank and the financial sector continue to experience changes in branch structure and organisation and the prospect of rationalisation and redundancy, it is an open question as to how such participatory mechanisms will adapt to this new context.

Sunderland Shipbuilders Limited

Background

The British shipbuilding industry since the early years of the twentieth century has been in a period of sustained relative decline. A concern shared by the state and management throughout the postwar period was the relatively poor level of productivity within the British industry. Two reports were commissioned, firstly the Shipbuilding Enquiry Committee of 1965–66 (Geddes Report) and then the Commission on Industrial Relations (CIR) Report of 1971. The most notable conclusion of the Geddes Report was that units of capital were too small in the British industry and it recommended amalgamation. The CIR Report noted the distinctiveness of the labour process in the shipbuilding industry.

> Many of the tasks performed in the construction of a ship give the work group a high degree of discretion over the manner in which they are carried out. Because the work lends itself to self-supervision the traditions of the industry protect the autonomy of the work group. It is a common feature of the industry that this often extends to some control over the times when work actually starts and finishes.
>
> (CIR, 1971: 103).

Participation – the first phase: industrial democracy?

Sunderland Shipbuilders were taken into public ownership in 1974 following the collapse of the parent company. The nationalisation was undertaken purely on pragmatic grounds, with no other offers forthcoming. Initially, at least, the change in ownership was to have little effect upon the shopfloor: 'There was no line drawn and said "This is before and this is after", you know. The same workforce and the same management.'

Between 1974 and the nationalisation of the whole industry in 1977, there was little coherent managerial strategy in Sunderland Shipbuilders. This was to change when the Labour government's nationalisation plans for the industry were brought to fruition on 1 July 1977. The approach to industrial relations was to be a consensual one, which included as one of the five main duties of the corporation:

> The obligation to promote industrial democracy ... the main objective of industrial democracy is to create a climate which will enable the performance of the industry to be raised.
>
> (British Shipbuilders Corporate Plan, 1978, 27/4).

In a policy document the boilermakers saw the creation of the corporation positively as resulting from: 'The constant pressure exerted by workers for some meaningful control over the conditions which affect their security of employment.' According to the document, the method of achieving such control was through greater participation, extending the scope of existing provision rather than imposing 'alien' structures.

Several new initiatives were introduced, including board-level participation for the representative of the Confederation of Shipbuilding and Engineering

Unions (CSEU) and joint consultative committees. These initiatives were synonymous with other areas of trade union activity and they had a minimal impact upon the mass of workers. The promotion of 'industrial democracy in a strong and organic form' (BS Annual Report 1978/79: 6) amounted to an institutional accommodation, management and unions, in an atmosphere of consensus. These participatory structures existed more as an expression of consensus than as a tool of its creation.

By the time of nationalisation in July 1977 the market had taken a nosedive. The corporate plan of 1978 proposed the option for the following five years of maintaining the market share of British Shipbuilders through an initial decline in capacity followed by a 25 per cent rise in productivity with constant manpower levels. Subsequent developments, the slump in demand, and policies of the new Conservative government ensured that the plan was hopelessly optimistic. The workforce was slashed and the profit centres were sold off, leaving the remaining yards trying to recover in enhanced productivity what had been lost in other spheres. This was the context of declining labour input and yet the search for higher productivity in which the second phase of 'participation' was located.

Participation on Wearside – the second phase: employee involvement

The situation that British shipbuilders were faced with throughout the 1980s was an impossible one. The government had decided that the nationalised industries should be subject to the same market criterion as the private sector, i.e. profitability. At the same time they persisted in privatising any parts of the corporation which were making a profit.

At yard level management attempted to attain a reduction in losses through enhanced productivity. Changes in working practices represented a radical interpretation of the scope for local agreements on working practices under a nationally negotiated package, the Wages and Salaries Restructuring, Harmonisation and Productivity (WSRHP) agreement.

A change of management attitude began to manifest itself in the form of a tightening of control over work allocation and time. These processes occurred unevenly between locations and shifts. The traditionally looser form of direct control on night shift remained. Similarly, control in 'shops' tightened up more appreciably than on the ship. This meant that different forms of the effort bargain existed simultaneously at different locations within the same yard.

A feature of this period was the lack of resistance offered by the workforce. Whilst these moves were not particularly welcomed, they were seen to some extent as legitimate. As time passed the managerial offensive continued, it started to encroach on areas clearly deemed illegitimate by the workforce. Even on night shift the foreman announced that men would not be allowed out 20 minutes before finishing to turn their cars around as had traditionally been the practice. During this period discussions commented upon the extent to which foremen appeared to be 'living in fear'; however, sympathy began to wane, as frustrations built.

Such frustrations were fuelled by changes in practices agreed to by the unions as phase four of the WSRHP both nationally and locally. The main points in the national agreement included moves towards interchangeability and flexibility; the local agreement went further. Area supervision and integrated work groups were labelled 'composite groups' and signalled the end of the single trade work group. Workers received £7 a week for accepting the deal, on union advice. The changes were felt very quickly, as a painter complained: 'It's ridiculous. I've been working in the joiners' shop today, sweeping up – me, a skilled painter!' It was explained that training would be given:

> Each person will be expected to carry out whatever work is necessary to complete the job, including work that has been thought of as 'belonging' to only one group. Retraining will be organised.

> (Sunderland Shipbuilders, *op cit*, : 2).

According to the personnel director, such training amounted to 'multi-skilling', and the management welcomed the rising skill level in shipbuilding. He claimed that while the changes in working practices had been 'driven through in the face of an adverse economic climate', workers were happier and more involved in their work because they could follow through the processes on the yard floor.

The reality was rather different, retraining was seen as a mockery. A shipwright lamented: 'I served a five-year apprenticeship to become a shipwright but now after three days hanging about with the welders, I'm a welder, three days I'm a rigger, two days I'm a burner, and two days and I'm a plater!' The claim that the workforce were happy with the changes was made only one month after Sunderland Shipbuilders had commissioned research looking at attitudes in the firm. Dissatisfaction with the situation was clear, only 18 per cent agreed with the statement that 'Sunderland Shipbuilders is a pretty good place to work – I would recommend a friend or member of my family to work here', while 70 per cent disagreed with this statement. This provides a clear indication that the vast majority of employees feel that this is not a good place to work. In other surveys we have carried out, it is possible to observe that, despite many complaints and grumbles about one's workplace, it is still possible to feel that overall it is a fairly good place in which to work. The answer to this question reveals that the concerns that the workforce had have gone particularly deep. Throughout the period of these changes elements of EI were introduced. The composite work teams have already been mentioned in this respect, such moves being generally presented positively under the heading of 'job redesign' or task participation. The workforce did not experience such job redesign in positive terms. Rather it was experienced as an insult to their skilled status.

Other techniques were also evaluated in negative terms. The management made a video which workers were shown. The subject was the amount of working time lost by late starting and early finishing. The video began by noting the different levels of productivity of British and Japanese shipbuilding workers, and went on to show scenes of the Wear yards with men standing talking, repeatedly returning to a shot of a clock with a voice asking: 'Why are these men still here? Work should have begun 20 minutes ago.'

The response of the workers was one of outrage and, far from increasing commitment to work, the video had the opposite effect. Questions were asked as to what management spent their time doing, and why they started at 9.00 am when everyone else started at 7.30 am? A feeling was rising that management were 'acting daft' and that the only response for workers was to act twice as daft. The position of the shop stewards become impossible, with workers continually raising grievances and management becoming less responsive. Many stewards gave up their posts or volunteered for redundancy, the work having become 'just too much hassle'.

Another technique introduced was that of abolishing the practice of clocking in, replacing it with face-to-face timekeeping and a morning team briefing led by individual foremen. Such initiatives are supposedly consistent with an approach stressing management by consent but they were experienced by workers in exactly opposite terms. Face-to-face timekeeping was seen as direct control, an attempt to re-establish the power of the foreman. Team briefing was resented particularly by members of the composite work teams who were not of the same trade as the foremen. In such situations individual craftsmen withdrew goodwill and protested ignorance in order to test the knowledge of the foreman.

Participation in practice – an assessment

There were two distinct waves of participation in Wearside shipyards. The first owed much to the conception of participation understood as industrial democracy. The idea of promoting industrial democracy in a 'strong and organic' form was an ideal concretised in negotiations between the shipbuilding unions and the Labour opposition in the early 1970s. By the time these plans were operationalised the context had changed, an immediate cut in capacity was called for. Moreover, the election in 1979 of a Conservative government, which was unsympathetic to this conception of participation, ensured that such ideals would not be pursued by a corporation dependent on government support for its very survival. The impact of this form of participation at yard level had been minimal. Its very existence was an expression of a consensual accommodation between capital and labour rather than a device to create it.

The second wave of participation was characteristic of a type of EI which has expanded over the past 20 years. Such EI is often task-related and characteristically introduced unilaterally by management. In this case the involvement techniques cannot be separated from the wider changes in working practices, the division of labour and the status of skilled workers.

If the objective of such techniques was the production of consent or the raising of employee morale and integration they must be deemed to have failed miserably. The individual and collective effect of these techniques as experienced by the workforce was an increase in direct control and decrease in 'responsible autonomy'. The total effect of the changes in working practices allied to these techniques of 'involvement' was to radically restructure the frontier of control and push it away from the workforce and towards the management. One objective of management that was realised during this period was the securing of enough 'voluntary' redundancies in order to avoid the issue of 'forced' layoffs; the changes outlined were seen as instrumental in producing enough 'volunteers'.

Questions

1. Why was participation introduced at the two organisations?
2. What was the experience of workers at the bank and the shipyards and what accounts for the differences in their experience?
3. What was the union perspective on EP?
4. What were the main problems in introducing EP at these workplaces and what solutions would you offer to deal with these problems?`

References to Chapter 11

Ackers, P., Marchington, M., Wilkinson, A. and Goodman, J. (1992) 'The use of cycles? Explaining employee involvement in the 1990s', *Industrial Relations Journal*, 23(4): 268–83.

Ackroyd, S. and Thompson, P. (1998) *Organisational Misbehaviour*, London: Sage.

Adler, P. (1993) 'Time and motion regained', *Harvard Business Review*, January–February: 97–108.

Batt, R. and Applebaum, E. (1995) 'Worker participation in diverse settings: Does the form affect the outcome and, if so, who benefits?', *British Journal of Industrial Relations*, 33(3): 353–70.

Beale, D. (1994) *Driven by Nissan? A Critical Guide to New Management Initiatives*, London: Lawrence and Wishart.

Berry, L. (1995) *On Great Service*, New York: Free Press.

Block, P. (1986) *The Empowered Manager*, San Francisco: Jossey Bass.

Bowen, D. and Lawler, E.E. (1992) 'The empowerment of service workers: Why, how and when?', *Sloan Management Review*, Spring, 33(3).

Brannen, P. (1983) *Authority and Participation in Industry*, London: Batsford.

Buchanan, D. (1979) *The Development of Job Design Theories and Techniques*, Aldershot: Saxon House.

Buchanan, D. (1994) 'Principles and practices in work design', in Sisson, K. (ed) *Personnel Management*, Oxford: Blackwell.

Byman, W. (1991) *Zapp! The Lightning of Empowerment*, London: Century Business.

Clutterbuck, D. and Kernaghan, S. (1994) *The Power of Empowerment*, London: Book Club Associates.

Collins, D. (1994) 'The disempowering logic of empowerment', *Empowerment in Organisations*, 2(2): 14–21.

Collins, D. (1998) 'Il a commencé à penser avant d'avoir rien appris: a processual view of the construction of empowerment', *Employee Relations*, 20(6): 594–609.

Collins, D. (1999) 'Born to fail? Empowerment, ambiguity and set overlap', *Personnel Review*, 28(3): 208–21.

Collinson, D. (1994) 'Strategies of resistance', in Jermier J.J., Knights, D. and Nord, W. (eds) *Resistance and Power in Organizations*, London: Routledge.

Collinson, M., Rees, C, Edwards, P. and Innes, L. (1998), *Involving Employees in Total Quality Management*, London: DTI.

Conger, J. and Kanungo, R. (1988) 'The empowerment process: integrating theory and practice', *Academy of Management Review*, 13(3): 471–82.

Cooper, R. (1973) 'Task characteristics and intrinsic motivation', *Human Relations*, Vol. 26, August: 387–408.

Cotton, J. (1993) *Employee Involvement*, Newbury Park, Ca: Sage.

Cully, M., O'Reilly, A., Millward, N., Forth, J., Woodland, S., Dix, G. and Bryson, A. (1998) *The 1998 Workplace Employee Relations Survey: First Findings, Department of Trade and Industry*, London: HMSO.

Cunningham, I., Hyman, J. and Baldry, C. (1996) 'Empowerment: the power to do what?', *Industrial Relations Journal*, 27(2): 143–54.

Delbridge, R., Turnbull, P. & William, B. (1992) 'Pushing back the frontiers', *New Technology, Work and Employment*, 17(2): 97–106.

Denham Lincoln, N., Ackers, P. and Travers, C. (1997) 'Doing yourself out of a job? How middle managers cope with empowerment', *Employee Relations*, 19(2): 147–59.

Drucker, P. (1988) 'The coming of the new organisation', *Harvard Business Review*, January–February: 45–53.

Edwards, P. (1995) *Industrial Relations*, Oxford: Blackwell.

Edwards, P., Collinson, M. and Rees, C. (1997) 'The determinants of employee responses to Total Quality Management', *Organisation Studies*, 19(3): 449–475.

EPOC (1998) *New Forms of Work Organisation. Can Europe Realize its Potential?*, European Foundation for the Improvement of Living and Working Conditions.

Foy, N. (1994) *Empowering People at Work*, London: Gower.

Garvin, D. (1988) *Managing Quality*, New York: Free Press.

Ghosal, S. and Bartlett, C. (1998) *The Individualized Corporation*, London: Heinemann.

Hamel, G. and Prahalad, C. (1994) *Competing for the Future*, Boston, Mass: Harvard Business School Press.

Harley, B. (1998) The Myth of Empowerment, *Work, Employment and Society*, March.

Heckscher, C. (1995) *White Collar Blues*, New York: Basic Books.

Hennestad, B. (1998) 'Empowering by de-powering: towards an HR strategy for realizing the power of empowerment', *International Journal of Human Resource Management*, 9(5): 934–53.

Hill, S. (1991) 'Why quality circles failed but Total Quality might succeed', *British Journal of Industrial Relations*, 29 December: 541–68.

Hill, S, (1995) 'From quality circles to Total Quality Management', in Wilkinson, A. and Willmott, H. (eds) *Making Quality Critical*, London: Routledge.

Hilmer, F. and Donaldson, L. (1996) *Management Redeemed*, New York: Free Press.

Hyman, J. and Mason, B. (1995) *Managing Employee Involvement and Participation*, London: Sage.

Jones, C., Taylor, G. and Nickson, D. (1997) 'Whatever it takes? Managing "empowered" employees and the service encounter in an international hotel chain', *Work, Employment and Society*, 11(3): 541–54.

Kanter, R.M. (1989) 'The new managerial work', *Harvard Business Review*, November–December: 85–92.

Klein, J. (1984) 'Why supervisors resist employee involvement', *Harvard Business Review*, 84(5): 87–95.

Lashley, C. (1997) *Empowering Service Excellence: Beyond the Quick Fix*, London: Cassell.

Lawler, E. E. (1996) *From the Ground Up*, San Francisco: Jossey-Bass.

Legge, K. (1995) *Human Resource Management: Rhetorics and Realities*, London: Macmillan.

Marchington, M. (1992) *Managing the Team*, Oxford: Blackwell.

Marchington, M. (1995) 'Fairy tales and magic wands: new employment practices in perspective', *Employee Relations*, 17(1): 51–66.

Marchington, M., Goodman, J., Wilkinson, A. and Ackers, P. (1992) *New Developments in Employee Involvement*, Employment Department Research Paper, No. 2.

Marchington, M. and Wilkinson, A. (1999) 'Direct participation', in Sisson, K. and Bach, S. (eds) *Personnel Management in Britain*, Oxford: Blackwell.

McArdle, L., Rowlinson, M., Proctor, S., Hassard, J. and Forrester, P. (1995) 'Total Quality Management and participation' in Wilkinson, A. and Willmott H. (eds) *Making Quality Critical*, London: Routledge, 156–72.

Micklethwait, J. and Woodridge, A. (1996) *The Witch Doctors*, London: Heinemann.

Miller, P. (1997) 'Dilemmas of accountability' in Hirst, P. and Khilnani, S. (eds) *Reinventing Democracy*, Oxford: Blackwell.

Millward, N. and Stevens, M. (1986) *British Workplace Industrial Relations 1980–1984*, Aldershot: Gower.

Millward, N., Stevens, M., Smart, D. and Hawes, W. (1992) *Workplace Industrial Relations in Transition*, Aldershot: Dartmouth.

Morton, C. (1994) *Becoming World Class*, London: Macmillan.

Parker, M. and Slaughter, J. (1993) 'Should the Labour movement buy TQM?', *Journal of Organisational Change Management*, 6(4): 43–56.

Pateman, C. (1970) *Participation and Democratic Theory*, Cambridge: Cambridge University Press.

Peters, T. (1989) *Thriving on Chaos*, London: Pan.

Peters, T. (1992) *Liberation Management*, London: Macmillan.

Peters, T. and Waterman, R. (1982) *In Search of Excellence*, New York: Harper Row.

Piore, M. and Sabel, C. (1983) *The Second Industrial Divide*, New York: Basic Books.

Pfeffer, J. (1994) *Competitive Advantage Through People*, Boston, Mass: Harvard Business School Press.

Poole, M. (1986) *Towards a New Industrial Democracy: Workers' Participation in Industry*, London: Routledge.

Power, M. (1997) *The Audit Society*, Oxford: Oxford University Press.

Purcell, J. and Hutchinson, S. (1996) 'Lean and mean', *People Management*, October: 27–33.

Rees, C. (1996) 'Empowerment through quality management: rhetoric or reality?', paper presented at Open University Business School Conference on 'HRM – the inside story', Milton Keynes, April.

Roberts, I. and Wilkinson, A. (1991), 'Participation and purpose: boilermakers to bankers', *Critical Perspectives on Accounting*, 2: 385–413.

Roeber, J. (1975) *Social Change at Work*, London: Heinemann.

Rose, M. (1978) *Industrial Behaviour*, Harmondsworth: Penguin.

Rosenthal, P., Hill, S. and Peccei, R. (1997) 'Checking out service: Evaluating excellence, HRM and TQM in retailing', *Work, Employment and Society*, 11(3): 481–503.

Schneider, B. and Bowen, D. (1995) *Winning the Service Game*, Boston, Mass: Harvard Business School Press.

Schonberger, R. (1990) *Building a Chain of Customers*, London: Hutchinson Business Books.

Semler, R. (1989) 'Managing without managers', *Harvard Business Review*, September–October: 76–84.

Sewell, G. and Wilkinson, B. (1992) 'Empowerment or emasculation? Shopfloor surveillance in a Total Quality organisation', in Blyton, P. and Turnbull, P. (eds) *Reassessing Human Resource Management*, London: Sage.

Simons, R. (1995) 'Control in an age of empowerment', *Harvard Business Review*, March–April: 80–88.

Sisson, K. (1994) *Personnel Management*, 2nd edition, Oxford: Blackwell.

Taylor, S. (1998) 'Emotional labour and the new workplace', in Thompson, P. and Warhurst, C., *Workplaces of the Future*, Basingstoke: Macmillan.

Trist, E., Higgin, G., Murray, H. and Pollock, A. (1963) *Organisational Choice: Capabilities of Groups at the Coalface Under Changing Technologies*, London: Tavistock.

Wall, T. and Martin, R. (1987) 'Job and work design', in Cooper, C.L. and Robertson, I.T. (eds) *International Review of Industrial and Organisational Psychology*, Chichester: John Wiley.

Walton, R. (1985) 'From control to commitment in the workplace', *Harvard Business Review*, March–April: 77–84.

Warhurst, C. and Thompson, P. (1998) 'Hands, hearts and minds: changing work and workers at the end of the century', in Warhurst, C. and Thomson, P, (eds) *Workplaces of the Future*, Basingstoke: Macmillan: 1–28.

Watson, T. (1994) *In Search of Management*, London: Routledge.

Watson, T. (1995) *Sociology, Work and Industry*, 3rd edition, London: Routledge.

Wilkinson, A. (1998) 'Empowerment', in Poole, M. and Warner, M. (eds) *International Encyclopaedia of Business and Management Handbook of Human Resource Management*, London: ITB Press.

Wilkinson, A., Marchington, M., Ackers, P. and Goodman, J. (1993) 'Refashioning the employment relationship: the experience of a chemical company over the last decade', *Personnel Review*, 22(3): 22–38.

Wilkinson, A., Godfrey, G. and Marchington, M. (1997a) 'Bouquets, brickbats and blinkers: TQM and employee involvement in context', *Organisation Studies*, 18(5): 799–820.

Wilkinson, A., Marchington, M., Dale, B. and Godfrey, G. (1997b) *Quality and the human resource dimension*, EPSRC final report.

Wilkinson, A., Redman, T., Snape, E. and Marchington, M. (1998) *Managing with Total Quality Management: Theory and Practice*, London: Macmillan.

Willmott, H. (1995) 'The odd couple? Re-engineering business processes, managing human resources', *New Technology, Work and Employment*, 10(2): 89–98.

Chapter 12

Employment ethics

Peter Ackers

Ethics: The philosophical study of the moral value of human conduct and the rules and principles that *ought* to govern it (*Collins Dictionary*, my emphasis).

Introduction

Employment ethics, as a subdivision of business ethics, involves the application of general moral principles to the management of employees' wages and conditions. In the same way as, say, sports or medical ethics, it begins with a concern about human relationships and how we treat other people. There are two dimensions to this: personal ethical issues at work; and broader questions of business social responsibility. The first addresses the way you or I *should* behave, as responsible individuals, towards other employees and our employer. This might include questions like personal honesty in completing expenses forms, using the work telephone or internet facilities (see Mars, 1973), resisting the temptation of bribes, or simply kindness and consideration towards our workmates. Without a culture of personal ethics, high standards of business ethics are inconceivable. For this reason, many organisations now have an *ethical code of practice* to guide employee behaviour. The focus of this chapter, however, is on the second category, where you act as a management agent for the business organisation. In this case, while there is still scope for personal discretion, your approach to other employees will be heavily circumscribed by business policy. For instance, if 'the company' decides to close a factory – as Ford has done at Dagenham – you will be left, as an individual manager, to implement a decision whether or not you agree with it.

In this light, the chapter aims to guide the student through employment ethics as it applies to *real business management practice* in the United Kingdom, past and present. Following some discussion of the complexities of applying ethics to business, various *ethical theories* are introduced by applying them to a real-life ethical problem. An *employment ethics agenda* is then established, contrasting a right-wing emphasis on the free market with left-wing social regulation. These are then linked to two competing unitarist and pluralist conceptions of *management* as an ethical agent in employment relations. The next section sketches the *history of ethical employment management*, followed by an assessment of a critical development of recent decades, *the advent of HRM* as a new way of talking about labour management. The chapter closes by advocating a Left-wing, stakeholder view of employment ethics as an antidote to *three fallacies* of recent HRM theory and practice.

To begin with, however, the process of translating ethics from personal behaviour to business practice is not straightforward. As we have seen, one initial complication to business ethics is that decisions about right and wrong are made by an impersonal organisation, rather than a single identifiable individual, as in some other spheres of moral decision-making. A further apparent difficulty, compared this time to other fields of management activity, is that ethics is about what *ought* to be, rather than what is. In short, it involves value judgements and differences of opinion rather than just technical decisions. In truth, the same is true of almost all organisational policy affecting human beings; only elsewhere these value-judgements are hidden behind technical sounding words like 'efficiency'. As Fox (1966) has argued, employment relations are always viewed through competing *frames of reference* leading to different interpretations of the situation. In this sense, 'ethics' should be seen as part and parcel of everyday personnel policy, not some entirely different realm of activity.

Employment ethics is still a highly problematic issue for two further reasons. While modern business seeks the moral high ground, often for public relations purposes, sceptics retort that business ethics in general is an oxymoron, a contradiction in terms. Is not the main goal of business, after all, to maximise profits, with all other considerations, such as the treatment of employees, coming a poor second? On the other hand, the *employment relationship*, between employer and employee, can become an especially deep-rooted and durable bond, evoking ethical notions of trust and loyalty. Paid work occupies many of our working hours and shapes our life chances, while HRM theory suggests that employees are a crucial resource to be nurtured, developed and retained by the business organisation (see Legge, 1995). Some argue that good ethics is, in fact, good business and, therefore, that no serious conflict exists between doing the right thing towards employees and improving business performance. This may be true for some businesses, some of the time. But more often 'being ethical' involves making difficult choices between expedience and principle.

While all ethics starts with common-sense claims about what is 'right' and 'fair', we soon find there are very different views about what these words mean. For this reason, we cannot say whether some employment policy is ethical or unethical, without referring back to which *ethical theory* we are applying. One central employment issue is how much we pay people. Let me imagine for a moment that I am the main shareholder and senior manager of a business organisation. A group of manual workers have asked for a 20 per cent wages increase, to provide 'a fair day's pay for a fair day's work'. Their language asserts an ethical claim. I want to act 'ethically', but how can I decide whether their claim is a just one? To take the matter further, we must enter what is popularly known as a 'moral maze'. While the detailed facts of the case are always important, the way we interpret them will be shaped by which ethical theory we choose to follow as the road to truth (see Chryssides and Kaler, 1993: 79–107; Winstanley and Woodall, 1999).

Ethical theories: enter the moral maze

One common-sense starting point is to look to the costs and benefits of awarding a pay rise and to enter the passage to the maze marked *Consequentialism*. Almost immediately, I begin to wonder how to weigh and measure these consequences. For instance, a pay increase will benefit these workers, but it will cut into my income as owner, perhaps reducing the amount I invest in new plant and machinery, spend on myself, or give to charity. How do I know *which* consequence is more beneficial? By now, however, my path has branched into another fairly wide thoroughfare entitled *Utilitarianism*, which claims to answer this question. Accordingly, whichever action gives the greatest happiness or utility is to be preferred. Since my employees are more numerous than me and on lower incomes, it may seem that a wage increase would be the most ethical course. But what of the broader consequences for happiness in society, if higher labour costs raise the cost of living for customers, or cut the incentive of entrepreneurs, like me, to establish business and create jobs? Another problem is that I do not know what the *actual* consequences will be, and can only guess. For instance, higher wages may benefit the business in the long run by improving employee performance and reducing labour turnover. Alternatively, higher labour costs may reduce competitiveness and lead to job loss. Thus, utilitarianism can nearly always provide good ammunition for both sides in an employment argument. More worrying, perhaps, it seems to provide a ready rationale for any employer seeking to wriggle out of any social responsibility – which of course, I am not.

A little discouraged, I retrace my steps to another, narrower passage, with the strange off-putting title of *Deontology*. On closer inspection, however, we discover that this merely means that I should act out of duty and choose to 'do the right thing' irrespective of consequences. Indeed, this way purports to lead to a 'kingdom of ends' with two cardinal principles to guide my sense of duty. One is that I should be prepared to generalise or *universalise* my decision. So that if I give these manual employees an increase, we will also have to consider the situation of office workers and whether they are being treated consistently. The second principle is that we must show a *respect for persons*, by treating them as an end in themselves and not a means to an end. In practical terms, this could mean that I should not sacrifice my present duty towards these employees – by rejecting their wage claim – in order to pursue the long-term best interests of my business and society. Indeed, one path branches off, called *Human Rights*, announcing that all employees have a 'right' to a decent living wage and so on. In this way, Kant's ethic of duty can appear so high-minded that it prevents business management from even considering economic factors, which may affect the long-term viability of the firm. Moreover, the assumption that we must act out of a sense of duty to be genuinely ethical appears to outlaw any considerations of economic self-interest. What happens, for instance, if my motive is disinterested, but I am also aware that granting an increase will solve the firm's labour turnover problems? Am I still acting ethically?

Table 12.1　Fitting the ethical theories together

Consequentialist	Non-consequentialist
Utilitarianism	Kantianism
Happiness of the greatest number	Human dignity an end in itself
The end justifies the means	Universal moral rules
Language of economic utility	Language of human rights

But how do I know that my primary duty lies towards these employees? Suddenly I notice two less obvious paths leading in diametrically opposite directions, each also departing from the deontological mainstream. The first states boldly, 'Your primary duty is to the *shareholders* who own and invest in the company.' Indeed, it turns out that their property rights can only be protected by keeping costs to a minimum, maximising profits and returning the best possible dividend. It is hard to see how a pay increase for employees can match these goals, unless it has a sound economic basis such as labour shortages or increased productivity. In this view, business efficiency must serve the shareholder, first and foremost. An alternative way, termed *Stakeholding*, argues that shareholders or investors are just one of several interest groups represented in the business corporation, including employees, customers, suppliers and the wider community. Accordingly, my ethical duty is to balance the needs of these different groups. Hence, if the pay and conditions of employees have been neglected in recent years, a pay award may be a justifiable piece of 'rebalancing'. On the other hand, if pay is already very high compared to elsewhere, and has been passed on in high prices to customers – as in Premier League football – it will not be the right thing to do. The general problem remains of how to adjudicate ethically between the claims of the competing stakeholders. By this point, many passages have begun to merge and overlap, as stakeholding and shareholding each blur into utilitarianism on the one side, and human rights on the other, at some point on the way.

At a clearing in the maze, however, a broad new passage begins, called 'Theories of Justice'. Yet within a few feet, this has divided in two completely different directions. The first route, *Justice as Entitlement*, eventually runs into the shareholder path on which we travelled earlier (see Nozick, 1993). This argues that human beings have a right to acquire and transfer property freely, providing they follow due process and avoid fraud and theft. Neither the government, nor any other organised pressure group, has a right to interfere in this free, and therefore fair, exchange. Seen in this light, my employees should conclude individual deals with me over wages and conditions, and accept whatever is the commercial going rate. Although I may pay them more, through kindness and charity, this is an 'imperfect duty' or an act of gratuitous generosity and it remains quite just to pay them the bare market rate. If, by banding together in a trade union, my employees are trying to 'force' me to pay a higher rate than I would from free choice, this is unjust and I would be right to resist their efforts. This view of justice places little social responsibility on the business to protect the wages and conditions of employees and can lead to great economic inequality. It also demonstrates how far some ethical theories can depart from common-sense notions of fair treatment.

The other path, *Justice as Fairness* leads to a table and chairs, where we all sit down, don blindfolds and think about what sort of society we would like to live in, without knowing what position we would occupy in it (see Rawls, 1993). The conclusion drawn is that we would choose equal treatment except where differences work to the benefit of the worst off. We would not choose 'justice as entitlement' for fear that we might be born without talent or resources, and end up penniless and sleeping in the streets. Applied to my situation, this suggests that if the claimants are substantially poorer than I, or other shareholders and white-collar employees, I must either demonstrate that they benefit from these inequalities, or allow the pay claim. In defence, my unique skill and responsibility may be an adequate justification. Maybe to stay within the spirit of this *social contract*, I should give employees some say in the running of the business. This might involve establishing a consultation committee, including union representatives, having 'workers' directors' or even turning the business into some sort of co-operative owned by the entire workforce, similar to the John Lewis Partnership. These options, if taken, lead into a common passage, shared with *Stakeholding*. One linking way is *Communitarianism* (see Etzioni, 1995), whereby we ponder not just the distribution of economic resources in terms of poverty and inequality; but also the impact on social cohesion. In short, will high manual pay contribute to a more tightly knit workforce and community?

After all this wandering in the moral maze, it is easy to become confused and disheartened. And there are three wide avenues radiating from a clearing, each promising a quick route to a satisfactory ethical conclusion. One termed *Divine Judgement* invites us to abandon all this confusion and buy a tried-and-tested set of moral rules off the religious shelf. My problem is that rules like the Ten Commandments were devised long before the genesis of modern business, and are too general to tell me what to do in this precise situation. In addition, many of my employees already have alternative sets of rules – which will make them hard to convince. Another path, *Ethical Relativism*, runs in precisely the opposite direction, reassuring me that such diversity of opinion is unavoidable in our post-modern society, and recommending that I avoid the sort of universal claims made by the deontologists earlier (see Smith and Johnson, 1996). Far better, this approach suggests, to follow the shared opinion of my particular subculture. I belong, however, to many social circles each with different ethical views, while my business friends simply press a shareholder view that is quite unacceptable to my employees. Finally, I encounter *Enlightened Self-Interest*, a way that reassures me that I worry too much (see Pearson, 1995). In the long term, good wages and conditions create loyal, productive, well-trained trustworthy employees, who, in turn, produce great rewards for all the stakeholders at the same time. This is the familiar human resource management (HRM) theory to which we return below. Yet still I wonder, how does this pay award help or hinder and what about the short-term?

An employment ethics agenda

While the various ethical theories offer plenty of clues for what an ethical employment policy might look like, there are no straightforward and easy solutions that can be drawn from them. Moreover, most general ethical theories can be interpreted in very divergent ways. This said, the big debate in employment ethics concerns how far the state and social agencies, like trade unions, should be allowed to regulate the free market in order to protect workers' wages and conditions. And we can quickly see two main sides lining up and drawing together different elements from the above ethical theories. In general terms, this division bears an uncanny resemblance to the Right – Left political divide in Britain and America, between conservatives on one side and liberals or social democrats on the other. The *Right wing* stresses the utilitarian benefits of free-market capitalism, duty to the shareholder, justice as the entitlement to own and freely dispose of property, and a paternalist version of enlightened self-interest which renders state intervention unnecessary. The *Left wing* emphasises the disutilities of short-term, free-market capitalism for society, employee rights, stakeholding, justice as fairness and a sceptical view of enlightened self-interest which presupposes the need for substantial state regulation to ensure good employment practices. In these terms, the question of what is ethical employment practice transmutes into the question: how should employment be regulated and to what ends? But first, what sort of employment issues are we talking about?

Business ethics in general is already a major preoccupation of most large companies. Many corporate mission statements and ethical codes pay lip service to

Table 12.2 Capitalism and theories of justice – an interpretation

	Theory of justice	Corporate responsibliity	Employment policies
Right-wing	Nozick (entitlement)	Shareholder (unitarist)	Free market
Left-wing	Rawls (fairness)	Stakeholder (pluralist)	Regulated market

virtues such as integrity, fairness and loyalty and envision a variety of stakeholders, including employees. In some cases, this enthusiasm for ethics has been prompted by a scandal, which damaged a company's or industry's reputation, as with criticism of the banks for misselling pensions in the 1990s or Shell's bad publicity over human rights in Nigeria. In other cases, ethics has been used as a marketing tool in a more proactive way. Hence, the Body Shop launched itself around a strong opposition to testing on animals for cosmetic purposes and has campaigned for fair trade with the Third World; while the Co-operative Bank has responded to customer objections to fur farming and investment in oppressive regimes (see Burchill, 1994). By and large, these companies have concentrated their attention on external public relations and the customer as a stakeholder, with the often undeclared assumption that stakeholding will work directly to improve the position of the shareholder. In all this, employees often appear as a poor relation in the family of stakeholders, such that banks, for instance, can flaunt their ethics to customers while making thousands of workers redundant. Any distinctively employment ethics agenda will revolve around the damage caused to workers' wages and conditions by unregulated, flexible, free-market capitalism. In so far as customers and shareholders benefit from this regime – high dividends and low prices at the expense of low wages, for instance – it may reflect a clash of stakeholder interests. As a consequence, employment ethics tends to deploy Left-wing ethical arguments against free-market capitalism. Let us briefly rehearse four of these.

One points to *just pay* and the enormous gap that has opened up between executive pay and perks, on the one hand, and those of people in low-paid, temporary jobs on the other. In deciding whether these are 'just' rewards we can apply Rawl's test – for example, senior management rewards are much lower in the powerful Japanese economy than in Britain and the USA – and explore issues of 'merit' and 'need'. The *national minimum wage* is prompted by an ethical assessment that the 'market rate' is not always a fair rate and that the state has to intervene to regulate bad employers. Another issue related to the flexible labour market concerns individual and family welfare associated with *working time*. Some workers today are trapped in such sporadic, part-time and temporary work that they find it hard to support themselves, let alone a family. Other, better-paid salaried workers find it hard to draw boundaries between their work and home lives, such that they suffer stress and their relationships and children suffer neglect. In all these cases, as communitarians argue, the price for society may be family and community breakdown (see Ackers, 1999). Once more, the European Union (EU) *Working Time Directive*, laying down a maximum 48-hour working week and minimum holiday provisions, rests on the assumption that in certain circumstances the free market can fail employees and society.

Two other issues are less directly economic in character. The first regards the right to *employee participation*, or the entitlement of workers (and the local community in cases of major plant closure) to have some say in the running of their business organisation. This relates to broader issues of corporate governance, and whose interests the business organisation should serve. Full-blown stakeholding or pluralism demands some sort of representative structure by which workers can influence company decision-making. In the past, trade unions played this role, and in many cases they still do. Legislation on *statutory trade union recognition* offers to bolster this union role. But this still begs the question of what happens across a good half of the economy where trade unions are completely absent. The *European Social Chapter* includes a right to worker participation and *European works councils* already provide for this in large companies. In addition to such positive rights, there is the issue of negative rights or *civil liberties*. If Left-wing thinking has often underestimated the threat of the state to individual freedom, Right-wing thinkers are equally blind to the threat posed by the large business. *Equal opportunities* issues around race, gender and sexuality are already established in law and public policy. But can an employer dismiss someone because they are fat, smoke, wear an earring or tattoo, or have eccentric religious or political views? In short, how far can a business, seeking to mould corporate culture, invade the private self of the individual employee or potential employee? This conundrum links to the question of *whistleblowers* or workers who expose unethical practices in their company. Does the business own their conscience because it pays the wages, or do they have a higher obligation to society?

Here again, a pluralist or stakeholding view of the corporation begs forms of external regulations to underpin these rights. Enlightened companies may address these issues of their own accord, through voluntary agreements, procedures and codes of practice. But, from this perspective, business as a whole cannot be trusted to do so. And firms with bad employment practices may gain short-term cost advantages and undermine the high standards elsewhere. In several of the above examples, recent British government or EU regulation has been prompted by the decline of trade unions and collective bargaining, leaving many employees exposed to the full power of the employer. Moreover, as we shall see below, employers in general have failed to fill this 'ethical gap' by voluntary action. This said, the state can only secure minimum standards, leaving great scope for companies and managers to establish exemplary wages and conditions. Today, these may also include well-resourced efforts to train and involve workers, as well as 'family-friendly' policies such as extended maternity and paternity provision, flexitime or nursery facilities.

Shaping an ethical workplace

If employment ethics is to mean anything in practice, we need to identify institutions or *agencies* capable of implementing it. Individual virtue is necessary, but not sufficient. Rarely does one person have the capacity to resolve a moral dilemma, as in the wages scenario earlier. Economic life is highly complex and beyond the scope of personal acts of goodwill. Only the state or substantial social institutions can impress some ethical pattern on the relationships that ensue. As Clegg's (1979) rule-making framework for employment relations suggests, three agencies can help to build an ethical approach into the very structure and process of economic life: from above, companies and their managers; from below, workers' own self-help organisations, most notably trade unions; and, finally, from without, the state as an expression of society's collective moral conscience.

Let us turn now to the most pervasive rule-making agent in most contemporary employment relationships: employers and the professional managers who act on their behalf. Even where the state and trade unions play a central part in framing the employment relationship, the style of employers and managers is crucial in defining the experience of work. While some good practices can be imposed from outside – as with racial and sexual discrimination or minimum wages – the devil is in the detail, and management culture may become a major obstacle to the full realisation of an ethical workplace. In order to understand what role management can play, I will sketch the historical evolution of management practice, particularly in relation to the personnel function, and then look more closely at the experience of HRM since 1979. First, though, we need to understand what management is and how this shapes the ethical tone of the enterprise.

Today, employer regulation is only rarely exercised by the single owner in person, except in the small business. Management is the collective name for those specialist, technical workers who act as the employer's agents in day-to-day dealings with the workforce. As businesses grow in size, and as the personality of the individual owner fragments into the thousands of anonymous individual and institutional shareholders of the modern public limited company, managers become the visible hands and face of employer power. In line with modern rational-legal authority and scientific management, the extensive and ill-defined prerogatives of the individual master are broken down into a specialist management hierarchy. In large, complex organisations, this managerial division of labour is characterised by horizontal layers according to seniority, and vertical lines of function. At the apex, there are senior managers, headed by the managing director, who concentrate on business strategy; while, at the base, are line managers or supervisors who deal directly and regularly with ordinary workers. In between, lie various strata of middle managers who connect the two types of activity. Those at the two opposite ends of the management ladder tend to be general managers, but most of the intermediaries are allocated some specialist function, such as marketing, production, or personnel. This Management specialism is reinforced by some professional organisation and identity as is the case with groups like accountants, or more pertinently for us, HRM or personnel managers.

While few would dispute this general description of management, there is far greater controversy over who exactly managers are answerable to, and what their social responsibilities are. What we expect of managers in the business organisation depends largely on our chosen frame of reference and this is likely to dovetail with one of the competing ethical theories, discussed above. For the *unitarist*, differences of management function and level are a purely technical issue, subordinate to his single purpose as the unquestioning agent of the shareholder owners. This 'stockholder' conception is enshrined in Anglo-American company law, though not in continental European 'stakeholder' traditions. As the Right-wing economist, Milton Friedman (1993) argues, once managers or companies take on goals and responsibilities which do not serve their ultimate aim of higher profits, they betray their ultimate employers and endanger the whole future of the enterprise, indeed of capitalism itself. In short, absolute adherence to market principles outside the business, and to the single line of authoritarian command within it, are but two sides of the same unitarist coin.

By contrast, *pluralists* are likely to perceive and welcome much greater diversity of allegiance and objectives amongst modern managers for two main reasons. First, from a purely sociological point of view, this conforms to their image of the business as fractured by competing interest groups, including various management levels and functions. Thus, senior company directors often belong to the Institute of Directors, while line managers join supervisory trade unions, like Manufacturing, Science and Finance (MSF). Personnel specialists seek professional status and accreditation through the Chartered Institute of Personnel and Development (CIPD) courses and exams – modelled on other professional bodies such as the British Medical Association and the Law Society. Second, from a more normative perspective, this view of managers also provides them with some scope to exercise independent ethical action, as is implied in the ethical codes of bodies like the CIPD. They are no longer just servants of the shareholders, at their every beck and call. Rather, they hold responsibilities to all the *stakeholders* in the organisation, including workers, customers and the local community, and to society as a whole. As always, observed fact and value judgement become intertwined. Postwar pluralist industrial relations thinkers like Flanders (1974) found hope in the growing separation between the ownership and control of large public limited companies, precisely because it created new scope for professional managers to exercise a more spacious and socially responsible role. For them formal ownership no longer mattered, since *de facto* pluralism reigned even where, as in Britain, company law did not provide for this. In this they have been proved mistaken, for under Mrs Thatcher a free-market government rolled back the blanket of state protection and trade union influence to reveal the short-term shareholder model beneath. For these reasons, the role of management must be closely related to the responsibilities of business and the way in which society defines these.

The greatest burden of pluralist hope lay upon the shoulders of personnel, the company function and department which specialises in dealing with employees and their representatives. This aspiring management profession seemed to personify the broader social concerns of management, as in the conception of personnel managers as enlightened umpires, bringing management and workers together, and creating industrial relations concord. As we shall see, the history of personnel management has parallels with the growth of social work, beginning as a predominately female caring profession concerned with people. Below, I ponder whether the new title of HRM marks a rediscovery of this ethical mission, as some suggest, or an irrevocable break from any emphasis on workers as social beings, towards a calculating image of them as mere economic counters. But the management of people has never been the exclusive mandate of personnel. So it is important to set personnel's fluctuating role in the broader context of the overall management style adopted by the business towards employees, from the senior managers who attempt to shape the culture of the organisation, down to the line managers who actually conduct most relations between management and ordinary workers (see Fox, 1974).

The history of ethical employment management

In *History and Heritage* (1985: 1–30), Alan Fox identifies two competing systems of labour control as, from the eighteenth century onwards, British society adjusted to the modern, capitalist employment relationship. Each operated at the level of state policy and law and through the strategies of individual business units. In this, there is much that is familiar today. The first strategy, *paternalism*, was carried over from the pre-industrial past, and combined notions of worker deference and a rigid social hierarchy with a sense of ruling class social responsibility. Hence, for many years, wage levels and customary rights were underwritten by law, partly for fear that a desperate and dispossessed poor would prove dangerous to the rich and powerful. The second strategy, *market individualism*, was informed by the new capitalist economic order that was breaking free of these semi-feudal bonds. This challenged the notion of a fixed social order and focused on the rights of individuals in politics, while reinterpreting the employment relationship as a private economic contract. Either approach was a mixed blessing for ordinary working people. While paternalism locked workers into a position of permanent subordination, as a price for some moral concern and social protection, market individualism threatened to cast them adrift with no reliable source of income or living, in exchange for the opportunity to freely sell their labour at the best price and better themselves.

Today, the balance between these two strategies has been largely reversed, at least at the level of the firm, with market individualism being regarded as the normal economic relationship and paternalism a noteworthy and deviant one (see Ackers, 1998). Nonetheless, the same tension in management strategy continues and connects with that central Right-wing – Left-wing ethical divide, outlined above. Should the business manage labour as an economic commodity, to be bought on the market at the cheapest possible price; or seek a long-term social relationship with their employees that transcends instant economic calculation? In most cases, the solution is a compromise between market and managerial relations, for, while labour may be hired in an outside marketplace, it can only be put to work in the social context of the workplace. For these reasons, though market individualism may be in the driving seat, it can rarely control the vehicle without some element of paternalism seated alongside. The development of management in general, and personnel management in particular, reflects this need to control and motivate the workforce as a social group, and passed through two main stages prior to 1979.

Stage one, roughly from 1850 to 1945 in most large companies, saw a new social hybrid, *paternalist capitalism*, emerge from the anti-social anarchy of early capitalism (see Joyce, 1980; Ackers and Black, 1991). It is not surprising, therefore, that the birth of personnel management, as a distinctive profession, with its own authoritative body, code of practice and range of qualifications, coincided with the late Victorian movement towards a more socially conscious, if paternalist, employer style of management. As Britain settled down into more stable work communities, some large employers, influenced by Christian ideas about social responsibility, sought to shape a stronger social dimension to their businesses and the communities in which they operated. Many work towns of the early industrial revolution were merely factories surrounded by cheap housing for their workers. They lacked the most basic facilities, such as schools and sewage systems. To a large extent, the new working classes began to create their own civilisation through self-help bodies like trade unions, local religious congregations and co-operative societies. However, enlightened employers also played an important part, for a mixture of motives including disinterested public service, personal self-aggrandisement, and a concern for work discipline and social cohesion. Through involvement in local government or by personal direct donations, they sponsored the creation of social and cultural amenities like parks, chapels, and libraries. At the turn of the century, the Quaker, George Cadbury, built the chocolate factory and garden city of Bournville, Birmingham for his workers and the local community, and it remains an impressive spectacle today. In the midst of acres of pleasant houses with large gardens, stood the model factory, with its exemplary working conditions, splendid playing fields and welfare facilities.

Personnel management emerged from large-scale Victorian paternalist capitalism, as direct personal contact between master and servant declined, and the employer families sought more institutional expressions of their ethical calling. According to Torrington and Hall's (1991) rather idealised seven-stage taxonomy, *social reformers* were the first on the scene, notably the Quaker chocolate manufacturer's wife, Elizabeth Fry, who conducted social work outside the factory and campaigned for legislation to protect health and safety. Next, during the full flowering of Christian paternalism, on the Bournville scale, came the *welfare officer*, again usually a woman, who conducted industrial social work within the workplace. This brought social concern in line with the modern management division of labour then emerging in large factories. Thus, in 1913, the Institute of Welfare Officers was formed at Rowntree's chocolate factory. In this respect, personnel began with the same high ideals of caring for employees as the best representatives of paternalist capitalism, and travelled with them from a personal to a professional and institutional expression of these values.

However, a number of factors began to unpick the fabric of paternalist capitalism, so that from the 1930s onwards a new *modern bureaucratic* company emerged associated with a more scientific and less moralistic personnel outlook. By 1945 the sense of religious mission had entered into decline, as part of the general secularisation of mid-twentieth-century Britain. Trade unions had advanced during 'the people's war', which itself had eroded the spirit of worker deference. A comprehensive welfare state, meanwhile, had superseded many company provisions. Otherwise, the main reason for the retreat of religious paternalism was the demise of the owner-manager and the private family company. This presents something of a paradox for pluralist advocates of social responsibility, since the growing separation of ownership and control destroyed the personal moral responsibility of individual or family ownership. Business owners moved away from the dirty towns they had created to live as country gentlemen, passed the running of the business completely to professional managers, and, ultimately, sold their shares to the highest bidder. Their children were educated at exclusive schools, and most preferred a genteel lifestyle to managing an ugly factory. As ownership of the new joint stock companies devolved to a multitude of passive shareholders and pension funds, only interested in a return on their investment, the guiding hand of employer paternalism slipped from view. To many employees this was welcome, since company beneficence had often gone with a desire to interfere in and shape their private lives outside work.

In this new era of rational-legal authority, when professional, career managers ran business and trade unions represented workers' interests, the religious language of calling and service appeared condescending and redundant. The emerging professions of teaching, social work and personnel reflected a new spirit of value-free social engineering. At work, social science theories of behaviour, such as scientific management and human relations, supplanted ethical idealism. During this phase, most employers withdrew from an active ethical role in both their business and the local community, as the welfare state and local government supplanted many of their earlier roles. Workers became more independent of their employers, preferring higher pay to cricket pitches, sermons and company picnics, and trade unions to consultative arrangements. In the long run, however, there would be a price to pay for this, as the business corporation was able to divest itself of any social responsibility beyond the efficient pursuit of profit.

Torrington and Hall (1991) identify four new and overlapping personnel roles which arose in this period. The *humane bureaucrat*, a management specialist with skills in selection and training, first appeared during the interwar years at public limited companies like the chemical giant, ICI. Later, after the Second World War, a company-level industrial relations role gained increasing importance. From the 1950s onwards, collective bargaining with trade unions was pulled down to the workplace, calling for negotiating expertise at that level. This saw the arrival of the *consensus negotiator*, or contracts manager, a tough masculine part, involving new skills of conflict resolution. At the same time, the *organisation person* was concerned with the effectiveness of the whole organisation, and not just employee welfare, linking together other management activities through their role in management development. Meanwhile, the *manpower analyst* set about quantifying human resources, for instance, by measuring the cost of labour turnover and planning the labour supply. A concern for workers still lingered on in these roles, though not as an end in itself, even in theory. Even the consensus negotiator restricted his relations with employees to the arm's length, institutionalised relationship with trade union representatives. If the soul had gone out of personnel management, it seemed that at least a disinterested profession had been created with an apparently social scientific knowledge base linked to practical skills.

Before turning to contemporary developments associated with HRM, it is important to qualify this generalised image of British business. *Sophisticated modern* companies, such as Cadbury's, were far from the norm in the history of British industrial relations. What we have seen so far is the best parts of British business putting their best face forward. For, as Fox (1985) argues, market individualism remained the dominant preference of British employers, tempered only by the often uninvited presence of trade unions that forced businesses to confront the collective nature of the employment through detailed personnel policies. These *standard modern* employers embraced trade unions as a short-term and pragmatic response to organised labour, rather than as a principled, long-term social vision of the employment relationship (Fox, 1974). Most industrial relations commentators see this dual view of labour – as a commodity in the external market and a cost within the firm – as conducive to a relatively low-skilled, low-waged and poorly trained labour force – in contrast to the best continental practice in economies like Germany. Arguably, too, this mentality has denied personnel its proper status in the business organisation, creating a ragbag of low-status administrators and industrial relations firefighters, rather than a cohesive profession of influential employment architects (see Sisson, 1994). This, in turn, has stymied the development of distinctively ethical employment policies.

The advent of HRM

The period from 1979 to 1997 presented a remarkable opportunity for business to demonstrate its concern for employees, unhindered by state or trade union regulation. For two decades, the Right-wing ethical perspective reigned supreme. During these years, management was cast as the principal agent of social change, and the rhetoric of the *enterprise culture* spoke eloquently of employee involvement and commitment, while remaining strangely silent about justice and rights at work (see Ackers, 1994). For personnel, HRM was the big new theme in management thinking that tied together these various initiatives, and promised a new constructive role for people management in the workplace. It is to this that we now turn. Hitherto, the academic debate over HRM has revolved around the poles of 'rhetoric' and 'reality' (Legge, 1995). In other words, has business lived up to the promises it has made? We begin, therefore, with the claims of HRM *in theory* and then turn to what this has meant for the employment relationship *in practice*.

The ethical rhetoric of HRM is everywhere in contemporary business and society. Some variation on the phrase – 'this business regards employees as its number one resource' – has become part of the ritual of company reports and briefings, tripping easily from the lips of chief executives. The CIPD's magazine, *People*

Management, is now subtitled 'the magazine for human resources professionals'. The sleek new HRM model is boldly contrasted with the 'bad old days' of personnel past, much as a born-again Christian celebrates his new creation by darkening his own past (see Clark, 1993; Ackers and Preston, 1997). Before, labour was a cost to be controlled; now, a resource to be nurtured. Before, personnel was a routine administrative activity; now, a strategic champion of people management for heightened business performance. Before, industrial relations was adversarial and arm's length; now, founded on consensus and employee consent. Before, personnel coveted people management; now, a human relations gospel for all. Rather than chase all these hares, as so many others have already, let us concentrate first, on HRM's central claim – to have made human resources more central to today's businesses than they were a generation ago. This, after all, is one key test of the ethical employment credentials of contemporary business.

Sisson's (1994: 42) authoritative summary of the survey and case-study evidence on the free-market experiment in Britain, concludes that 'personnel management in many organisations in Britain is locked into a vicious circle of low pay, low skill, and low productivity'. This is surprising, as he recognises, since HRM had promised exactly the opposite, arguing that people are the key to competitive advantage for Western economies where Third World low-cost labour is not an option. Old, rigid and authoritarian forms of management control were supposed to yield to 'the development of a highly committed and adaptable workforce willing and able to learn new skills and take on new tasks'. At face value, British business appeared to be placing a new stress on human resources, and this is the conventional wisdom taught in many business schools. However, the research paints a much more depressing picture. Following Fox (1985) and MacInnes (1987), this suggests that the enterprise culture has exacerbated the laissez-faire, short-term, cost-reduction employer attitudes to labour, endemic in the British employment relations tradition. Moreover, the definitive Workplace Industrial Relations surveys, suggest that HRM in practice has been largely a chimera (Millward *et al.*, 1992; Cully *et al.*, 1999). Yes, some HRM techniques, like employee involvement, are widespread in mainstream companies where trade unions remain a factor; no doubt partly as a means of countering their influence. Yet, where management has a free hand, in the now majority non-union sector, there is little evidence of a new 'ethical' HRM approach to managing labour.

The obvious conclusion is that union representation and effective joint consultation have been replaced, not by a new enlightened HRM, but by a tough 'Bleak House' hire-and-fire employment policy. Overall, the evidence supports the view of labour as a disposable commodity, a cost to be controlled rather than a resource to be developed. At this level, employment ethics is mainly about good public relations towards customers and staying on the right side of the law. Accordingly, this Anglo-American share or 'stockholder' model concentrates on short-term costs, profits and dividends, dictated by city and financial markets. As in the past, British capital is short-term and cost-minimising in outlook, and has failed to invest in labour as a resource, while management remains attached to crude, cost-effective payment-by-results systems. Within this framework, there is very little space for active employment ethics. For this to change, Sisson (1994: 42–4) argues,

> There would have to be a fundamental reappraisal of the way in which British companies are run . . . A policy of *laissez-faire* not only sends the wrong signals, above all to small and medium-sized businesses, it also fails to take into account that, left to their own devices, many UK companies will find the 'high pay, high skill, high productivity' route quite simply beyond them.

Writing before the 1997 general election, when the prospects were 'extremely remote', Sisson (1994) proposed the following stakeholding initiatives:

> overhauling the regulatory framework of companies and their relationships with the city; developing an appropriate training system; and introducing a legal framework of rights and obligations that would help to raise standards. . .the kind of framework that our partners in Europe are anxious to introduce in the form of the Social Charter.

Since then, some modest moves have been made in this direction. Overall, though, HRM rhetoric has failed to translate into a management approach that values people, even in its own economic terms, as a resource. If the reality of HRM was a disappointment, maybe the idea at least was worthwhile. It is to this that we now turn.

Conclusion: three fallacies of HRM ethics

Much of this analysis presupposes that HRM has failed because British institutions have frustrated the managerial reforms that could have made it a reality, not that HRM itself presents a positive barrier to any progress towards a more 'ethical' workplace. Only rarely has anyone asked whether the rhetoric, let alone the practice, offers an attractive and credible vision of the world of work and management's place in this (see Hart, 1993; Torrington, 1993). We might, for instance, regard HRM as some do organised religion, and conclude that, despite all the bad things done in its name, there remains a valuable ethical essence that is worth retaining. Some academics and trade unionists have approached HRM in this spirit, arguing that we can 'play back' promises about 'people being our number one resource' and ask management to live up to these. In purely pragmatic terms, there is much to be said for this approach in a business environment where HRM is unlikely to go away, as I have argued elsewhere (see Ackers and Payne, 1998). On the other hand, if we do not go beyond such necessary opportunism, there is a danger of becoming ensnared within the HRM worldview. For once we peel away the layers of HRM hyperbole, we reach a hollow core: an impoverished ethical vision of the employment relationship. This rests upon three ethical fallacies, which I will term 'golden calf', 'enlightened self-interest' and 'happy family'.

The *golden calf* fallacy assumes that all human values should be subordinated to business considerations and calculations. At the heart of the HRM worldview stands the claim that the human resource is a business's most valued asset. This appears, at first glance, a noble belief, even if it flies in the face of the manner in which many employers actually treat their workers. In particular, it suggests a culture in which companies invest in workers' long-term development, instead of regarding them as merely costs, to be cut and controlled. Yet, there is a dangerous flaw in this ethical vision, and this relates to the broader stream of Right-wing ethical thinking, which redefines human beings with their complex social, spiritual and material needs, as mere rational economic categories, be these consumers or human resources. Such language assumes that business and its economic terminology should shape human aspirations, and not the other way round. From a practical management point of view, enlightened employment policies will always require a business rationale. Ethics should not be a recipe for economic suicide or ridicule. But to have a long-term competitive advantage at the back of your mind is not to subordinate every decision to short-term economic calculus, as HRM implies. For workers, the choice is between being a most valued economic asset, and being a rounded human being whose dignity should be respected by all – in Kant's terms, a subject that should never become an object. This has grave implications for the role of managers, since they are asked to lead the worship at the altar of false values. They too are required to treat their subordinates as merely a means to economic ends, to count the cost of every act of kindness. To personnel management in particular, HRM offers a Faustian pact within the enterprise culture. The prize advertised is an ever-growing personnel influence inside the business organisation; the price is personnel's professional soul and its total commitment to goals defined by senior executives and large shareholders, over and above all other stakeholders.

The *enlightened self-interest* fallacy takes the heresy a stage further, by pretending that business considerations alone are sufficient for companies to look after their employees, without outside regulation from the state or trade unions. As Pearson (1995) argues, a business needs to build long-term trust relationships with employees, customers and other companies in order to thrive, and therefore it needs to behave with integrity towards all these groups. Thus HRM theory fosters the seductive idea that it is in the self-interest of business to treat workers well, and that, for this reason, they no longer need to fear for their own protection. Yet numerous businesses, large and small, thrive on short-term, one-sided relationships, as the evidence for the failure of HRM shows. Perhaps, as Sisson suggests, this is against the long-term interests of Great Britain PLC, but there is little reason why that thought should detain for long the mobile, well-rewarded, modern business executive. The significance for workers' pay and conditions is that their entitlements are entirely contingent upon what makes business successful. If profitability demands investment in the human resource, employers will undertake this; if it entails exploiting cheap disposable labour, and breaking trade unions to this end, they will do the same. Once more, an economic theory that makes human rights entirely conditional on business convenience, and puts a price on human dignity, lies at the heartless centre of HRM's view of the world.

The *happy family* fallacy assumes that the state and trade unions are unwelcome intrusions into a fundamentally harmonious, unitarist employment relationship. Most HRM theory is unitarist in outlook and either silent about or actively hostile to trade unions as representative bodies (Guest, 1989). HRM claims to place this happy paternalist conjunction of self-interest and employee wellbeing on a new, harder, more calculative footing. However, it does so against all the evidence that the tradition went into decline long ago, and has collapsed in the postwar period. The way we live now, in postmodern Britain, talk of company loyalty is as specious and insincere as easy appeals to 'community' and calls for street parties to mark national anniversaries. The break-up of occupational communities, founded on steel, coal, cotton, tin, fishing or carpets, where large extended families all worked for the same firm, has created a much greater occupational and social fragmentation and a far more mobile workforce. When the HRM 'good news' hit British business in the early 1980s, most large companies had already shed their family benefactors, faded out the welfare provisions, sold off their leafy garden villages to middle-class professionals, turned their consultative committees into a branch line on which hardly anyone travelled, and begun building on their playing fields. Like the Cheshire Cat, too often all that remains of paternalism is the smile. Management can still make a central contribution in the creation of a more co-operative and cohesive employment system. However, it will not do so by pretending that one exists already, if only we could see it.

The sheer ambiguity of HRM may pose the biggest ethical problem, leading to charges of misrepresentation and bad faith. What so often sounds like a species of Left-wing ethical thinking, promising something extra for employees, turns out on closer examination to be a sugar-coated edition of Right-wing moral and economic philosophy. Milton Friedman (1993), from the latter perspective, suggests that such spurious claims to added 'social responsibility' are better left unsaid and merely detract from the strong, unvarnished case for capitalism. And it is true that Right-wing ethical thinking has a firm grounding in certain business, economic and social realities. Most of us recognise, *to some degree*, the utilitarian benefits of a capitalist economic system, wherein countless selfish, individual market transactions produce unprecedented living standards for most people. In our personal lives, we expect this 'hidden hand' (Smith, 1993) to be allowed *considerable freedom*, in order to ensure that our pensions keep pace with inflation and our supermarket groceries are as cheap as possible. We also want to be free to use our own money and property as freely as possible *without undue interference from the state*. We probably regard this economic freedom from state control (including the freedom to change job when we wish) as *one essential freedom* in a liberal democratic society. For all these reasons, any framework of employment ethics which, like socialism in the past, threatened to 'kill the goose that laid the golden egg' is likely to be unacceptable to us. The problem with Right-wing ethical thinking is that it forces these genuine concerns to an extreme (neglecting the qualifications in italics), so that only the most *minimal, individual ethics*, such as honesty and trust in contracts, is deemed either necessary or possible. By denying the reality of a long-term employment relationship and presenting the labour contract as a spot-market transaction, like buying a bag of apples, Right-wing ethics sends HRM managers into the workplace naked. They either have to imagine new clothes, like the Emperor, and hope their employees will believe them. Or else they have to look somewhere else.

Perhaps the crucial distinction here then is between employment ethics as a public relations façade and rationalisation for what business already does out of short-term economic self-interest; and employment ethics as an active commitment to employees above and beyond this. For managers can and should play a crucial role in constructing socially responsible, business organisations at the heart of a decent society. This would require, however, a *pluralist institutional framework* which placed the long-term employment relationship and the wages and conditions of employees, alongside other stakeholders, at the heart of the business organisation. In these circumstances, we could speak meaningfully of *social partnership*, loyalty and commitment. Within a framework of *relationship capitalism*, managers could regain their professional autonomy and integrity, as public servants with a stakeholder ethos, rather than the handmaidens of private capital (see Hutton, 1995). In communitarian language, the workplace would become a genuine 'moral community' responsive to society as a whole. HRM presents us with a paradox, because it talks of developing *people*, while considering its subjects as *human resources*. The reversion to economic language, and the lack of evidence for modern welfare capitalism (see Jacoby, 1997), leads to the suspicion that when push comes to shove, the calculator will always take priority over the human being. Although the rhetoric of HRM contains elements that appeal to ethical employment principles, it fails to meet its promises on two counts. First, it bears little relation to the main developments in British employment relations, and thus presents itself as a mystifying ideology, a false promise of a better life in another world which will never arrive. Second, it abdicates any autonomous, ethical role for management, beyond doing whatever makes large shareholders and senior executives richer.

Employment ethics at A&B Stores

Peter Ackers

Introduction

A&B is a chain of department stores, selling clothes, food and hardware. It employs 10,000 UK workers in retail, distribution and office positions, mostly on permanent, full-time contracts. In addition, around 1,000 manufacturing workers, employed by its main subcontractor, are highly dependent on A&B's success and employment policy. The case study presents an opportunity to assess the ethics of the business at all stages in its development (was it doing the 'right thing' towards employees?), and to address a major contemporary dilemma between remaining competitive as a business and retaining a reputation as an ethical employer. It allows you to explore various ethical theories and to consider this business dilemma as a choice between different ethical frames of reference.

In the beginning

A&B was founded in 1900 as a small store in a medium-sized Scottish town by an austere, very religious Presbyterian (with his elder brother as a 'sleeping partner'). In the early days, the founder knew all his employees by their first name and exercised a strong 'fatherly' influence over their lives in and out of work. This had both benign and harsh aspects. The company was generous at times of family sickness, with the founder often visiting in person, though sometimes employees wondered if he was really checking up on them. And any employees who were caught with the smell of alcohol on their breath at work, or even drunk outside work, were summarily dismissed. The founder also promoted a strong sense of family values, organising (alcohol-free) works picnics and providing a free hamper every Christmas and at the birth of any child (up to three in number) and 200 cigarettes to the 'employee of the month'. Christian prayers were compulsory before each morning's work began. He also initiated and contributed towards various 'self-help' savings and mortgage schemes. Wages were generally slightly above the industry norm, according to the discretion of the founder, who liked to quote the parable of 'The Workers in the Vineyard' and reward those who he thought deserved and needed most. Women employees who married were required to leave, in order to fulfil their family duties, and all managerial positions were reserved for men with families. The firm promised lifetime job security for male employees and encouraged children to follow their parents into the trade. For many years, jobs were only rarely advertised externally.

Growth

The founder died in 1940 and ownership and control passed completely into the hands of his two sons. The boys had been educated at an English public school and lived in the Home Counties. But the founder's personal control had declined long before, as the company grew first into a Scottish chain in the 1920s, and then a nationwide chain during the Second World War. He had always strongly opposed trade unions as inimical to the family atmosphere of the firm, and in 1923 the firm fought off an organising campaign by the shop workers' union which was already well-established in the stores of the strong Scottish co-operative movement. As a result, 20 'ringleaders' were dismissed. During the 'hungry thirties' A&B gained a good reputation for maintaining employment when other businesses were laying off people. This was partly due to good business performance, but it was also widely believed that the owning family accepted lower profits in order to continue both to keep the loyal workforce and invest in the expansion of the firm.

The workforce was now counted in thousands rather than tens, so it was impossible for senior managers to retain personal, face-to-face contact – though local store managers were encouraged to do so. In response, the company developed a professional personnel department to create a more systematic set of provisions and policies. These included a non-union, representative company council that operated monthly at store level, and biannually across the whole company. Representatives were elected from every work group, and both negotiated with management over wages and consulted over any issues affecting the welfare of the workforce. There was also a welfare and sports society, which was heavily subsidised by the company, and provided local A&B social clubs – initially on a strict temperance basis. These organised competitions for football, cricket, ballroom dancing and so on. Company developments and these social activities were reported in *Voice of A&B*, a monthly company newspaper produced by the personnel department. The firm also pioneered a number of other welfare benefits, including a contributory pension scheme for all employees, and a seniority and promotion system called Growing Our Own, which meant that nearly all middle and senior managers were recruited from the shopfloor. Following one year's service, all employees joined the company profit sharing scheme, which, in most years, added a further 10 per cent to their income.

PLC

In 1965, A&B became a public limited company (PLC), and within a few years family shareholdings had been dwarfed by those of pension funds and other outside investors. No senior managers now belonged to the original family, and many were being recruited from outside the business, rather than rising through its lower ranks as they had in the past. A new graduate recruitment programme had short-circuited the old seniority systems, though most middle managers had still risen from below. The business had also had to adapt to outside social trends, such as legislation for sexual and racial equality, and relaxed social mores – leading, among other things, to the serving of alcohol in A&B Clubs. A&B was still perceived by workers, customers and the general public as a family-run business with a strong ethical commitment to fair play. This was reflected in the trust and loyalty of long-service employees (and very low labour turnover), as of customers who repeatedly told surveys that they would not buy their clothes anywhere else. A&B continued to play a high-profile public charitable role, both in the town of its origin, where the head office remains, and in the wider community. In the latter case, the company sponsored a City Technology College in inner-city Glasgow during the 1980s and actively supported 'Business in the Community'. It also funded the first professorship in Business Ethics at a leading British business school.

The company had developed another long-term business relationship since its first major expansion in 1920, with a large clothing manufacturing firm situated in the town where the founder was born and A&B originated. Although Smiths & Co is an independent firm, 70 per cent of its output is contracted to A&B – whose letters also prefix the name of the local football team. Company head office and the local store employ between them 750 people, while the founder had presented to the town a park and art gallery, as well as a row of cottages for long-service company pensioners. The founder's wife had played a prominent charitable role in the interwar town, including organising youth clubs and holidays for children of the local poor and unemployed.

Today

A&B's personnel policy has remained fairly stable since the main structures were set in place in the 1930s. In line with 1960s and 1970s labour law and 'best practice', however, the company council system had been supplemented by a more formal (but still non-union) grievance and disciplinary procedure. Employees have shown no further interest in union membership, partly because wages and conditions are as good as those of most comparable unionised firms, and partly because they know A&B senior management are strongly anti-union and fear they might lose existing benefits if they push the issue. A new company interest in equal opportunities for women was partly inspired by the national policy mood, but also by labour shortages and recruitment difficulties in the postwar retail labour market. As a result, there has been a small influx of women graduates into managerial and supervisory roles, and the old distinction between 'men's' and 'women's' jobs has been replaced by a formally nondiscriminatory, A–G grading system. Equally, criticism that internal recruitment reproduced an 'all white' workforce, even in cities with large ethnic minorities, has led the company to advertise all vacancies in job centres and local newspapers, followed by a formal interview.

Once again, outside policy influences have dovetailed with business concerns that its workforce should reflect the stores' potential customer base. Notwithstanding these developments, personnel policy still cultivates a long-term relationship with both the directly employed workforce and the manufacturing subcontractor. In the latter case, A&B has insisted on exercising substantial 'quality control' over the subcontractor's production process, while offering Smith & Co employees access to its social clubs and welfare provisions (though wages and conditions are handled separately). The company's commitment to high-quality, British-made products was a major attraction for its traditional customer base.

Until recently, A&B has interpreted the new wave of HRM thinking as largely an extension of its existing personnel practices. For instance, it has added team briefing, quality circles and a modest element of performance related pay to its existing communications, consultation and reward structures. In some respects, like profit sharing, the firm was already a pioneer. Today, however, major changes in the retail market are forcing the company to reassess all elements of its activities. After years as a market leader, with steadily rising profits, A&B is now in some commercial difficulty. In particular, it faces competition from a new generation of fashion shops, which threaten its core clothing market. These firms source their products from low-cost Third World suppliers and are happy to switch these where and when the market justifies. They also employ a raw, if enthusiastic UK workforce of students and young people, almost entirely on short-term and temporary contracts. Their wages are close to the national minimum, often about 25 per cent less than A&B, and they spend far less on training and welfare. A&B has already responded to this threat by shedding 10 per cent of its workforce through natural wastage, early retirement and voluntary redundancy, while terminating one major contract with Smith & Co.

The ethical and business dilemma

A new managing director has been appointed to 'turn around' A&B. He has asked all the main functional directors to present a root and branch analysis of how the business can regain its market position and restore stock market confidence. These papers will be presented to and discussed at a 'Retail 2050: Future Directions' seminar, the outcome of which will determine the new business strategy to be presented to the next company Annual General Meeting.

The recently appointed head of marketing has already stolen a march on the others by circulating radical plans for a new marketing-led, customer-focused, flexible firm that breaks almost completely with the traditional shape of the business, including its much-vaunted ethical employment policies. She proposes a new 'culture of entrepreneurship' which will withdraw the 'comfort zone' and 'time-serving' of current employment practices. Using a cricket metaphor, she argues that the point is 'not to occupy the crease but to score runs'. This will include establishing specialist boutiques and other facilities (including restaurants) within the stores, run on a franchise basis, using external subcontractors wherever possible, transferring all remaining direct employees to part-time contracts, except for a core of 'enterprise managers and supervisors' who, in future, will be paid largely according to performance. In addition, she moots the closure of the Scottish company headquarters and complete withdrawal from the town to smaller, more convenient facilities in an English new town; and the ending of the contract with Smith & Co to enable A&B to buy on the open market and benefit from low labour costs in South-East Asia. In the marketing director's view, the traditional paternalist approach is now completely archaic and untenable in the fast-moving retail market.

To further complicate matters, a whistleblower, within either senior management or the marketing department, has leaked these plans to the media. Rumours are circulating that A&B has been negotiating with a military dictatorship in the Far East for access to its labour force. Concerns about the abandonment of existing employees and the exploitation of Third World 'cheap labour' have been tabled by the founder's family for the company AGM. There have been demonstrations by employees in the original 'company town', addressed by outside trade union leaders, who called for union recognition for A&B employees under the new legislation and an effective European works council. A petition has been presented to the Scottish Assembly by local MPs and church leaders, describing A&B as 'the unacceptable face of capitalism' and urging a consumer boycott of stores nationwide.

Historically, the personnel function, now renamed HRM, has been seen as the custodian of the company's ethical employment policies. As we have seen, these centre on a long-term relationship with a stable workforce. Concerned at the bad publicity the business is attracting, the managing director has asked you, as personnel director, to frame an explicitly ethical employment policy which overcomes the difficulties you are facing and draws on some of the business's existing strengths. There are signs that the adverse publicity is affecting customers and undermining their trust and loyalty towards the company. No options are barred, but the managing director has asked you to specifically consider the following questions:

Questions

1. How far was A&B's original employment policy 'ethical' in modern terms? What sort of ethical principles did it draw upon? Which elements would be acceptable today, and which would not?

2. How justified was the decision to prevent trade union organisation and is it still appropriate today? Consider the arguments *for* and *against* and the principles involved.

3. Construct an ethical case in favour of the flexible firm solution proposed by the director of marketing, explaining which principles you draw on.

4. Devise an alternative, HRM-driven business and ethical case for maintaining the existing long-term relationship with employees, customers and subcontractors.

5. Which stakeholder groups should take priority when push comes to shove? What duty, if any, does the company owe to its employees and shareholders in a modern free-market society?

Exercise

Design an up-to-date and realistic, *ethical employment code of practice*, consistent with your answers to the above questions, which can be issued by the personnel department to all employees and used for external public relations purposes. Begin with some general principles and then identify key areas of business and employee rights and responsibilities.

Further Discussion Questions

1. How far is an ethical employment policy consistent with a successful business strategy, in this case? Is good ethics, good business? Are there any examples of this in the case study?

2. To what extent can the modern business organisation get away with faking good ethics to stakeholders?

3. Which ethical theory is most useful in unscrambling this sort of problem and why? Choose only one.

4. In what ways does the public limited status of the modern company either *increase* or *decrease* its opportunities to behave as an ethical employer?

5. How far was the whistleblower who leaked the proposed changes acting ethically?

6. When, if ever, should a business organisation interfere in employees' private lives outside work?

7. What part, if any, can state regulation play in guiding companies like this towards ethical employment policies?

Exercise

In the spirit of Rawl's 'veil of ignorance', imagine how it would feel to occupy someone else's role in society. Consider the following roles:
a. Rover carworker
b. Black civil servant
c. Hospital cleaner
d. Female junior doctor
e. Supermarket manager
f. Social worker

What workplace issues might concern you? What would justice mean to you? Think of both issues specific to your new situation and more general issues affecting workers and employees.

Note: While A&B is a fictional ideal-type company, it incorporates many real-life elements from a number of leading British manufacturing and retail organisations. These all began as paternalist family firms with their own ethical ideas about how employment should be managed and adapted and developed these as they grew into large, modern businesses.

References to Chapter 12

Ackers, P. (1994) 'Back to basics: industrial relations and the enterprise culture', *Employee Relations*, 16(8): 32–47.

Ackers, P. (1998) 'On paternalism: seven observations on the uses and abuses of the concept in industrial relations, past and present', *Historical Studies in Industrial Relations*, 6, Spring: 173–93.

Ackers, P. (1999) 'Industrial relations and the spirit of community', Loughborough University Business School Working Paper, 1999: 15.

Ackers, P. and Black, J. (1991) 'Paternalist capitalism: an organisation culture in transition', in Cross, M. and Payne, G. (eds) *Work and the Enterprise Culture*, London: Falmer.

Ackers, P. and Payne, J. (1998) 'British trade unions and social partnership: rhetoric, reality and strategy', *The International Journal of Human Resource Management*, 9(3), June: 529–50.

Ackers, P. and Preston, D. (1997) 'Born again? The ethics and efficacy of the conversion experience in contemporary management development', *Journal of Management Studies*, 34(5), September: 677–701.

Ackers, P., Smith, C. and Smith, P. (eds) (1996) *The New Workplace and Trade Unionism*, London: Routledge.

Armstrong, P. (1989) 'Limits and possibilities for HRM in an age of management accountancy', in Storey, J. (ed) *New Perspectives on Human Resource Management*, London: Routledge, 154–66.

Burchill, J. (1994) *Co-op: The People's Business*, Manchester: Manchester University Press (reviewed by this author in *Review of Employment Topics*, 5 (1), September 1997: 206–209).

Carroll, S.J. and Gannon, M.J. (1997) *Ethical Dimensions of International Management*, London: Sage (reviewed by this author in *Human Resource Management Journal*, 9(1), 1999: 89–91).

Chryssides, G.D. and Kaler, J.H. (eds) (1993) *An Introduction to Business Ethics*, London: Chapman and Hall (reviewed by this author in *Human Resource Management Journal*, 5(1): 103–105).

Clark, J. (1993) 'Procedures and consistency versus flexibility and commitment in employee relations: a comment on Storey', *Human Resource Management Journal*, 3(4).

Clegg, H.A. (1979) *The Changing System of Industrial Relations in Great Britain*, Oxford: Blackwell.

Cully, M., Woodland, S., O'Reilly, A. and Dix, G., (1999) *Britain at Work, as depicted by the 1998 Workplace Employee Relations Survey*, London: Routledge.

Etzioni, A. (1995) *The Spirit of Community: Rights, Responsibilities and the Communitarian Agenda*, London: Fontana.

Flanders, A. (1974) *Management and Unions: The Theory and Reform of Industrial Relations*, London: Faber.

Fox, A. (1966) 'Industrial sociology and industrial relations', *Royal Commission on Trade Unions and Employers' Associations*, Research Paper 3, London: HMSO.

Fox, A. (1974) *Beyond Contract: Work, Power and Trust Relations*, London: Faber.

Fox, A. (1985) *History and Heritage: the Social Origins of the British Industrial Relations System*, London: Allen and Unwin.

Friedman, M. (1993) 'The social responsibility of business is to increase its profits', reprint of 1973 article in Chryssides, G.D. and Kaler, J.H. *An Introduction to Business Ethics*, London: Chapman and Hall, 249–54.

Guest, D. (1989) 'HRM: its implications for industrial relations and trade unions', in Storey, J. (ed) *New Perspectives on Human Resource Management*, London: Routledge.

Guest, D. (1999) 'Human resource management – the workers' verdict', *Human Resource Management Journal*, 9(3).

Hart, T.J. (1993) 'Human resource management – time to exorcise the militant tendency', *Employee Relations*, 15(3): 29–36.

Hutton, W. (1995) *The State We're In*, London: Cape.

Jacoby, S.M. (1997) *Modern Manors: Welfare Capitalism since the New Deal*, Princeton, NJ: Princeton University Press (reviewed by this author in *Historical Studies in Industrial Relations*, 8: 188–194).

Joyce, P. (1980) *Work, Society and Politics: the Culture of the Factory in Later Victorian England*, Brighton: Harvester.

Legge, K. (1995) *Human Resource Management: Rhetorics and Reality*, London: Macmillan.

Legge, K. (1996) 'Morality bound', *People Management*, 19 December: 34–36.

Marchington, M. and Wilkinson, A. (1996) *Core Personnel and Development*, London: Institute of Personnel and Development.

Mars, G. (1973) 'Hotel pilferage: a case study in occupational theft', in Warner, M., *The Sociology of the Workplace: An Interdisciplinary Approach*, London: Allen and Unwin.

MacInnes, J. (1987) *Thatcherism at Work: Industrial Relations and Economic Change*, Milton Keynes: Open University Press.

Millward, N., Stevens, M., Smart, D., Hawes, W.R. (1992) *Workplace Industrial Relations in Transition: The ED/ESRC/PSI/ACAS Surveys*, Aldershot: Dartmouth.

Nozick, R. (1993) 'Anarchy, state and utopia' (extract) in Chryssides, G.D. and Kaler, J.H. (eds) *An Introduction to Business Ethics*, London: Chapman and Hall, 209–13.

Pearson, G. (1995) *Integrity in Organisations: An Alternative Business Ethic*, London: McGraw-Hill (reviewed by author in *Employee Relations*, 18(6) 1996: 97–98).

Priestley, J.B. (1934, 1977 edition) *English Journey*, London: Penguin.

Rawls, J. (1993) 'A theory of justice' (extract) in Chryssides, G.D. and Kaler, J.H. (eds) *An Introduction to Business Ethics*, London: Chapman and Hall, 213–21.

Sisson, K. (1989) (ed.) *Personnel Management*, Oxford: Blackwell.

Sisson, K. (1994) (ed.) *Personnel Management*, 2nd edition, Oxford: Blackwell.

Smith, A. (1993) 'The wealth of nations' (extract) in Chryssides, G.D. and Kaler, J.H. (eds) *An Introduction to Business Ethics*, London: Chapman and Hall, 63–66.

Smith, K. and Johnson, P. (1996) (eds) *Business Ethics and Business Behaviour* London: International Thomson (ITP) (reviewed by this author in *Human Resource Management Journal*, 8(2): 97–98).

Storey, J. (1989) (ed.) *New Perspectives on Human Resource Management*, London: Routledge.

Storey, J. and Sisson, K. (1993) *Managing Human Resources and Industrial Relations*, Milton Keynes: Open University Press.

Torrington, D. and Hall, L. (1991) *Personnel Management: A New Approach*, Hemel Hempstead: Prentice Hall.

Torrington, D. (1993) 'How dangerous is human resource management?: A reply to Tim Hart', *Employee Relations*, 15(5): 40–53.

Warren, R.C. (1999) 'Against paternalism in human resource management', *Business Ethics*, 8(1), January: 50–60.

Winstanley, D. and Woodall, J. (1999) (eds) *Ethical issues in Contemporary Human Resource Management*, London: Macmillan.

Chapter 13

Managing diversity

Catherine Cassell

Introduction

Within the management and organisation literature there has been an increased interest in managing diversity as a way of addressing equal opportunity issues. A broad term that encompasses a number of concepts, 'managing diversity' refers to the systematic and planned commitment on the part of organisations to recruit and retain employees from diverse demographic backgrounds (Thomas, 1992). Building on the notion that all differences between groups and individuals within an organisation should be recognised and valued, managing diversity essentially presents a business case for equal opportunities. In linking equal opportunities initiatives directly in with business strategy, the concept has similarities to the notion of strategic HRM.

The aim of this chapter is to outline the principles behind the managing diversity approach and to examine some of the key issues and tensions around diversity debates. The chapter begins by outlining the context in which managing diversity has arisen. The principles of managing diversity strategies are then discussed, together with some of the techniques and tools that managers can use to this end. A series of key issues and debates are then outlined. These include a consideration of the research evidence upon which managing diversity initiatives are based; the integration of managing diversity initiatives with HR policies and practices; and a critique of the business case upon which managing diversity initiatives are based.

The managing diversity context

To understand why managing diversity has become a pertinent issue now, rather than having a history in HRM and personnel generally, one needs to understand the context in which it has arisen. Two particular factors are important here: changing demographic trends, and the state of equal opportunities.

Demographic trends

The development of managing diversity strategies is clearly located within the context of shifting demographic trends. It is now almost a cliché within HRM that the composition of the workforce in many countries is changing, with an increased number of women and members of ethnic minority groups entering those workforces. Additionally, the age profile of the working population is changing, with an increase in the average age of employees. Prasad and Mills (1997) point out the impact that these shifts have had within North America:

> Few trends have received as much publicity or gained as much attention in management circles as the recent interest in managing diversity. It can be argued that much of this interest can be traced back to Johnston and Parker's (1987) influential report, *Workforce 2000*, which alerted organizations to the dramatic demographic changes that were in the process of transforming the North American workforce. . . Confronted with the prospect of these major imminent changes, management practitioners, business educators, and organizational consultants quickly began preparing to meet the challenges of a new and diverse workforce in a number of ways
>
> (Prasad and Mills, 1997: 4)

Kandola (1995: 138) in summarising changes in the UK and Europe suggests that similar demographic changes to those that have occurred in North America are anticipated. In his view the changes that specifically relate to the nature of the workforce are:

1. *Sex* – increasing numbers of women entering the labour market
2. *Ethnic minorities* – they will be forming an increasing part of the workforce
3. *Age* – the ageing of the working population.

Therefore demographic trends have created the necessity to expand the labour pool to include those groups traditionally disadvantaged in the employment market. This, together with the increasing internationalisation of markets, means that, as Kandola points out, organisations will have to deal with managing diversity not just in their own countries, but also in other countries.

The state of equal opportunities

A further contextual issue is important here. Within the field of equal opportunities (EO) there has been an increasing disillusionment amongst activists, practitioners and employers alike about the effectiveness of equal opportunities policies and practices. Despite the existence of equal opportunities legislation, Wilson (1995) suggests that the notion that equal opportunity now exists is a myth. Indeed, there seems considerable disappointment and disillusionment about the current state of equal opportunities for disadvantaged groups, given

25 years of British EO legislation. Despite the initial high expectations of such legislation, in comparison to other equality legislation in Europe and the United States, it has been found to be lacking. Moreover, such legislation does little to rectify the more indirect forms of discrimination since, by their very nature, they do not appear discriminatory, but rather a part of normal everyday working patterns (Townley, 1994).

Another concern about developments in equal opportunities surrounds the language within which such policies are framed and their appropriateness or attractiveness to employers. Ross and Schneider (1992) suggest that employers have resisted EO legislation precisely because it has been imposed upon them. They suggest that the law has enshrined the moral case for equal opportunities and has therefore given employers the responsibility to create a fair and equal society. Indeed, if they do not do this then they end up facing legal action. They argue that we all know that imposed change is likely to be resisted and causes a 'backlash' (1992: 50), therefore as equal opportunity policies rely on the law and ethics, and are externally driven and imposed, it is inevitable that employees will respond unfavourably towards them. As they suggest:

> So long as equal opportunities was equated simply with complying with legislation, then it's always going to be about group parity, and getting the numbers 'right'. This was a recipe for inertia over the last fifteen years, this is pretty much what we experienced.
>
> (Ross and Schneider, 1992: 36)

They recommend that EO needs to be seen as business-driven in order to be attractive to employers – clearly a different case from that of fairness, justice or group parity.

Kandola and Fullerton (1998) suggest that the body of ideas seen to represent conventional wisdom in equal opportunities has changed very little during the last 15 years. They argue that, despite this, the face of equal opportunities is changing as a result of a number of factors. These factors include a more overt emphasis on the business case; an increased amount of research and recognition that a wide range of groups within the workplace face discrimination and harassment (for example on the basis of age, sexuality or disability); and an increasing concern about ethics and ethical behaviour in the workplace, a key element of which is equal opportunities (Kandola and Fullerton, 1998: 13). They suggest that the implication of this changing face is a recognition that the time is right for a reconsideration of conventional approaches to EO. They propose a focus on managing diversity as an alternative approach which is more appropriate to the current challenges facing organisations.

An alternative approach to equal opportunities: the business case

Given the problems with the equal opportunities approach outlined above, it is not surprising that an alternative approach has emerged. Managing diversity is based very clearly on a business case. The business case focuses on the business benefits that employers accrue through making the most of the skills and potential of all employees. The argument is that the loss or lack of recognition of these skills and potential, usually as a result of everyday discriminatory practices, is very costly. Consequently, the business case is fundamentally linked to the principles of strategic HRM, where the human resource and its full utilisation is seen to give a company the competitive edge (Storey, 1995). Additionally, it is crucial that equal opportunities initiatives are seen to tie in with the overall strategic direction of a company. A business case sees achieving equality as essential to achieving organisational goals. Again, in the same way that HRM is linked into the general strategy of a firm, so equal opportunities pervades every aspect of business policy, rather than being an add-on.

In 1995 the Equal Opportunities Commission launched a campaign to highlight the business case for equal opportunities. The aim was to demonstrate that in economic terms, equality made good business sense. A leaflet produced at the time outlines the benefits of equality and costs of inequality. The benefits of equality include:

- best use of human resources
- flexible workforce to aid restructuring
- workforce representative of the local community
- improved corporate image with potential employees and customers
- attracting ethical investors
- managers can integrate equality into corporate objectives
- new business ideas from a diverse workforce.

The costs of inequality include:

- inefficiency in use of human resources (high staff turnover; low productivity; and restricted pool of talent)
- inflexible workforce limiting organisational change
- poor corporate image with prospective employees and customers
- management time spent on grievances
- losing an industrial tribunal case.

These costs and benefits are linked in to the demographic trends outlined earlier.

To summarise, it is worth examining the differences between the diversity model based on the business case and traditional models of equal opportunity. Kandola and Fullerton propose, that whereas EO is externally initiated, legally driven, and focuses on numbers and problems, diversity is internally initiated, business needs-driven and focuses on qualitative and opportunity outcomes. EO approaches tend to assume assimilation and are reactive, whereas diversity approaches assume pluralism and are proactive. Finally, EO approaches focus on a particular set of differences, usually race, gender and disability, whereas diversity approaches focus on all differences. Therefore diversity approaches based on a business case represent a different way of looking at equal opportunities.

Ross and Schneider (1992) sum up the advantages of the business case with the following list:

> Equal Opportunities makes business sense. It enables organizations to: manage change by attracting people with new and different ways of thinking; create a working environment where total quality can take root; anticipate and meet the changing needs of customers; recruit and promote the best people by widening the traditional sources of candidates; retain the best people by ensuring that their needs are fully taken into account; increase productivity by raising motivation and commitment; increase profitability by reducing attrition and recruitment costs.
>
> (Ross and Schneider, 1992: 109)

Managing diversity

The management of diversity presents a business case for moving towards a diverse workforce where the skills of all groups are recognised. The application of the business case through the management of diversity will now be explored in more detail.

General principles

The general argument behind managing diversity initiatives is that, given the current shortage of skilled labour, the effective use of diverse skills within an organisation makes good business sense. Diversity management is particularly popular in the United States, where the skill shortages are more pronounced than in Britain. Management of diversity is based on the notion of difference and the effective management of difference. Valuing difference is seen as an important concept because it is specifically linked to an organisation's culture and values. A key element is to move towards 'cultures of inclusion' (Thornberg, 1994), recognising that various organizational practices often lead to certain groups feeling left out or unwelcome. Exponents of the management of diversity perspective (Thomas, 1990; Cox, 1992; Jackson and Associates, 1992; Kandola and Fullerton, 1998) argue that all differences must be valued, including those of white males. Kandola and Fullerton provide a useful working definition of managing diversity:

> The basic concept of managing diversity accepts that the workforce consists of a diverse population of people. The diversity consists of visible and non-visible differences which will include factors such as sex, age, background, race disability, personality and workstyle. It is founded on the premiss that harnessing these differences will create a productive environment in which everybody feels valued, where their talents are being fully utilised and in which organizational goals are met.
>
> (Kandola and Fullerton, 1998: 8)

The concept of managing diversity has become very popular, particularly in North America. The language surrounding diversity initiatives focuses on the notion of celebrating differences, as Prasad and Mills (1997) suggest:

> Diversity is celebrated with the help of evocative metaphors such as the melting pot, the patchwork quilt, the multicolored or cultural mosaic, and the rainbow. All of these metaphors evoke enormously affirmative connotations of diversity, associating it with images of cultural hybridity, harmonious coexistence, and colorful heterogeneity.
>
> (Prasad and Mills, 1997: 4)

Robinson and Dechant (1997: 21) suggest that developing a business case for diversity is more difficult than for other business issues, mainly because 'evidence of diversity's impact on the bottom line has not been systematically measured and documented for easy retrieval and use'. They suggest that in putting the case, a number of business reasons can be suggested. These include cost savings such as decreased turnover and absenteeism and the avoidance of lawsuits. More positively, they outline a range of ways in which diversity can drive business growth. These include improving marketplace understanding; increasing creativity and innovation; producing higher-quality problem-solving; enhancing leadership effectiveness; and building effective global relationships. The authors report a survey where human resource executives from 15 Fortune 100 companies were asked to identify the main business reasons for engaging in diversity management. The top reasons given were better utilisation of talent (93 per cent); increased marketplace understanding (80 per cent); enhanced breadth of understanding in leadership positions (60 per cent); enhanced creativity (53 per cent); and increased quality of team problem-solving (40 per cent). As Robinson and Dechant suggest, the executives focus more on the added value that emerges from diversity initiatives rather than the more negative penalties of mismanagement, such as the avoidance of lawsuits, for example.

Kandola and Fullerton (1998) suggest that managing diversity must pervade the entire organisation, if it is to be successful. They propose a MOSAIC vision, which summarises the key characteristics of the diversity-oriented organisation. MOSAIC is used here as an acronym for **M**ission and values, **O**bjective and fair processes, **S**killed workforce: aware and fair, **A**ctive flexibility, **I**ndividual focus, and **C**ulture that empowers. In highlighting these key characteristics it is clear that the managing diversity approach is considerably different from previous conventional approaches to equal opportunities. The focus becomes that of ensuring that all individuals within an organisation can maximise their potential, regardless of any groups to which they may belong. It is an all-embracing concept where the focus is cultural change and learning, rather than promoting fairness and avoiding discrimination. Crucially, managing diversity is seen as a key element of overall business policy, linked into an organisation's strategy, rather than a personnel or HR policy. Given that, the emphasis is clearly on the business benefits that the successful management of diversity can accrue for a company.

Techniques and examples

A whole range of initiatives can be subsumed under the heading of diversity initiatives. Arnold (1997: 179) lists some of the interventions that characterise diversity initiatives. They include:

- multicultural workshops designed to improve understanding and communication between cultural groups
- multicultural 'core groups' which meet regularly to confront stereotypes and personal biases
- support groups, mentoring and relationships and networks for women and cultural minorities
- advisory councils reporting to top management
- rewarding managers on the basis of their record on developing members of targeted groups
- fast-track development programmes and special training opportunities for targeted groups.

To take a case example, Walker and Hanson (1992) describe some of the components of the 'Valuing Differences' philosophy that has been introduced and implemented at DEC (Digital Equipment Corporation), a company with 120,000 employees in 64 countries throughout the world. The philosophy:

> focuses employees on their differences. Employees are encouraged to pay attention to their differences as unique individuals and as members of groups, to raise their level of comfort with differences, and to capitalize on differences as a major asset to the company's productivity
>
> (Walter and Hanson, 1992: 120)

The 'Valuing Differences' work is done in a variety of ways, including awareness and skills training; celebrating differences events (e.g. Gay and Lesbian Pride week, Hispanic Heritage month); and leadership groups and support groups. A particularly radical intervention is that of the establishment of an informal network of small ongoing discussion groups, known as core groups and described as 'groups of 7–9 employees who commit to coming together on a monthly basis to examine their stereotypes, test the differences in their assumptions, and build significant relationships with people they regard as different' (1992: 121). The authors conclude that 'capitalizing on diversity means helping employees become their very best by learning to accept, trust and invest in others' (1992: 136). They propose that Digital have yet to learn how to quantify the impact of the 'Valuing Differences' programme on profitability but evidence would suggest that the company has some specific concrete advantages from the programme so far. The authors outline these as:

- a solid reputation as one of the best places to work – not just for women and minorities, but for everyone
- empowered managers and leaders who empower others

- greater innovation
- higher employee productivity
- effective global competition.

Clearly the authors see the programme as being highly beneficial to the organisation on a number of criteria.

Another example which is perhaps more typical is outlined by Ellis and Sonnenfeld (1994) in their review of corporate diversity programmes. They describe how National Transportation Systems (NTS) run a one day 'Diversity' workshop which is mandatory for all full-time managers and supervisors. The aim of the workshop is:

> to increase managers' awareness of the growing diversity of the workforce, to teach them the necessity of learning how to manage that diversity, and to help them identify personal biases that may interfere with their ability to manage cultural diversity.
>
> (Ellis and Sonnenfeld, 1994: 85)

The workshop begins with an introductory video which features the CEO explaining the importance of diversity and its link with the bottom line. A discussion then takes place about each participant's race and gender biases. As Ellis and Sonnenfeld suggest, for the workshop to be successful, individuals have to feel safe enough to reveal sensitive information about themselves. They suggest that the two key criteria that impact upon this are the quality of the facilitator and the cultural mix of participants. The authors summarise the overall impact of this diversity initiative:

> NTS is making great strides in enhancing its ability to manage diversity and promulgating the message that the firm values cultural differences, but its biggest hurdle in this area may be the cultural homogeneity of top level management, virtually all of the corporate leaders are white males. This homogeneity leaves subordinates from diverse backgrounds with few top level role models and inadvertently sends out the message that to make it to the top of the firm, one needs to be a white male.
>
> (Ellis and Sonnenfeld, 1994: 88)

This highlights that diversity initiatives in themselves may be limited in the extent to which they can convey positive messages regarding differences and how difference is valued.

Despite some of the problems with implementing such initiatives, the benefits of the successful management of diversity are seen to be very rich. Cox (1992: 34), for example, describes them as 'better decision-making, greater creativity and innovation, and more successful marketing to different types of customers'. Thornberg (1994) outlines three phases which represent a company's evolution towards a more diverse, heterogeneous culture. The first is to bring in more women and minorities, the second is to emphasise working on problems of individual and group behaviour associated with race and gender, that is, to begin to understand how people are different and why; and the third is a focus on company culture which involves evaluating all of the organisation's policies and procedures. Diversity interventions are therefore characterised as comprehensive and inclusive.

Although most case studies of diversity initiatives are North American-based, British-based research is beginning to emerge. Rather than assessing the success of comprehensive diversity initiatives, a couple of studies have looked at comparisons between firms that have elements of a diversity policy and those that do not. Shapiro (2000) describes research designed to explore the link between organisational approaches to employee involvement and managing diversity. Using eight case studies from five European countries, she argues that employee diversity can be seen as the missing link that can encourage the success of innovations such as TQM and employee involvement. Indeed, Shapiro suggests that unless organisations explicitly consider the differences that exist between employees then they will have difficulty in meeting their key corporate improvement objectives. Research conducted in Britain (Hicks-Clarke and Iles, 1999) has also demonstrated that positive employment attitudes (e.g. job satisfaction and employee commitment) are related to a company having a positive climate for diversity (as indicated by perceptions of policy support; organisational justice; support for diversity and recognition of the need for diversity).

Key issues and tensions

The account above has outlined the key principles in managing diversity and described some typical examples of diversity interventions. Although diversity initiatives are sometimes presented in an unproblematic way in the literature, in practice there are a number of key issues in this area that need to be addressed. These are explored in the next section.

The research evidence

A key question about managing diversity initiatives is the extent to which they actually work. The search for empirical evidence to validate the success of managing diversity programmes can be a fairly frustrating exercise. One of the problems is that many of the case studies of diversity programmes that are reported in the literature do not contain any evaluative element. Indeed, sometimes these case study reports focus more on promoting a particular company approach with evangelical zeal, rather than assessing and evaluating the success of a given programme. An additional source of concern is that most of the studies that do look at diversity interventions are American-based. This in itself is not a problem, but there is the issue of how transferable the context is, given that the demographic trends experienced in the USA are a considerably exaggerated version of what is currently happening in the UK labour market. Jones, Pringle and Shepherd (2000) point out the paradox that as managing diversity develops as a worldwide vocabulary for examining or celebrating difference, US cultural dominance may be reinforced by a US model of difference being applied globally.

As was suggested earlier, the impact of diversity on the business bottom line is difficult to assess. Studies are starting to emerge, however, that consider the financial benefits of diversity programmes. One such analysis is provided by Wright, Ferris, Hiller and Kroll (1995). Using data from 1986 to 1992, they examined the impact that announcements of US Department of Labor awards for exemplary affirmative action had upon the stock returns of winning corporations, together with the effects that announcements of damage awards from the settlement of discrimination lawsuits had on the stock returns of guilty corporations. Their results indicated that announcements of equality affirmative action programmes were associated with an increase in stock prices, and conversely, announcements of discrimination settlements were associated with significant negative stock price changes. The authors conclude from this study that:

> the prevalent organizational ethnic and gender bias (Hitt and Barr, 1989) should be eradicated not only because such bias is not ethical or moral, but also because it does not make economic sense. As the climate of competition becomes more intense, no enterprise can afford the senseless practice of discrimination. In fact, America's cultural diversity may provide a competitive advantage for unbiased US corporations over both domestic rivals that discriminate and European and Japanese companies in the world marketplace.
>
> (Wright *et al.*, 1995: 284)

Other discussions of diversity programmes focus on particular companies. Totta and Burke (1995) outline the processes by which the Bank of Montreal became committed to workforce diversity. The aim was to integrate issues of diversity and equality into the day-to-day working life of the bank, so that each and every business decision was influenced by diversity issues. The leaders of the organisation recognised that this would require a cultural transformation, at the centre of which would be a climate of workplace equality where individuals felt welcomed. A series of interventions was created to further these aims, including changes in a wide range of procedures and practices, and 26 action plans: 'initiatives that would dramatically transform every aspect of the way business was conducted at the bank, from hiring practices to performance review criteria, from approaches to learning to the definition of corporate values' (Totta and Burke, 1995: 35). Totta and Burke's account is that of work in progress, rather than a systematic evaluation of the programme, but it provides an example of many of the cases that are published about the introduction of diversity programmes. Other examples include: American Express (Wolfe Morrison and Mardenfeld Herlihy, 1992); Pepsi-Cola (Fulkerson and Schuler, 1992); DEC (Walker and Hanson, 1992); and International Distillers and Vintners (Kandola and Fullerton, 1998).

A different approach is taken by Kandola and Fullerton (1998). After reviewing a range of managing diversity models from the literature they produced their own strategic implementation model that focuses on eight processes (the clarity of the organisation vision; the extent of top management commitment; the auditing and assessing of needs; the setting of clear objectives; the degree of accountability; the degree of communication within the organisation; the extent of co-ordination; the degree to which the strategy and actions are evaluated). The authors then conducted two surveys. The first was a study of 285 organisations, examining the initiatives that each had put in place to manage diversity, and how successful they were perceived to be. The second survey was conducted with 49 organisations to test out the model proposed. The results from the surveys validated the model proposed, which, as the authors suggest, make it the 'first ever to have been empirically tested and validated' (Kandola and Fullerton, 1998: 97).

Results from their survey demonstrate that the initiatives perceived to be the most successful by HR managers were those that were related to equalising treatment between staff, or actions for universal benefit, as Kandola and Fullerton describe them. This is important given the focus of the managing diversity philosophy on all individuals rather than specific groups. Such initiatives include eliminating age criteria from selection procedures and introducing the same benefits for part-time workers as full-time workers. The initiatives perceived to be the least successful were those focused on specific groups in the workforce. Such measures included setting targets for the composition of the workforce and using positive action in recruitment training. Additionally, including equal opportunities as part of business plans was also seen as unsuccessful by 53 per cent of the organisations who had sought to implement it. The authors point out that this result could be an indication that the importance of diversity as a central business issue has not yet been recognised by many UK organisations.

The Kandola and Fullerton work is an asset to the literature in that it does have an empirical base. The limitations of the study are that its focus is the views of one senior manager within each of the companies studied, rather than the impact of diversity initiatives on the ground. It is, however, a useful starting point for those keen to evaluate the success or otherwise of diversity initiatives.

A number of authors have pointed to some of the problems that emerge when trying to implement diversity initiatives in organisations. Ellis and Sonnenfeld (1994) review three pioneering diversity programmes currently operating in USA companies. They conclude that although it makes sense that the benefits of such programmes may translate into higher productivity and lower turnover, few organisations actually measure the transfer of the educational interventions into actual changes in human resource practices such as recruiting, management development and promotion. Their article highlights some of the emerging pitfalls with new corporate diversity programmes. They suggest that the programmes:

> are positive in tone, yet often lack systematic firm-wide integration into other human resource policies and do not tap the passionate disagreement that often rages beneath a platitudinous facade.
>
> (Ellis and Sonnenfeld, 1994: 80)

One of the problems they highlight is the lack of time actually spent on training in some diversity initiatives:

> These programes seem to be based on the premise that contact with members of different ethnic groups – if only for a few hours – or propaganda announcing the benefits of diversity, will clear up any misperceptions or ill will that some employees feel towards certain ethnic groups. Evidence often shows the contrary; simply pointing out differences among various groups, if not handled sensitively, can increase hostility and misunderstanding.
>
> (Ellis and Sonnenfeld, 1994: 83)

Of significance here is the danger that diversity training may actually reinforce old stereotypes, or create new tensions. Ellis and Sonnenfeld point out that, when evaluating a 'Valuing Diversity' seminar, they found that a minority of respondents disliked it. In particular, white males complained that they were 'vilified' in the training materials, which depicted bias and miscommunication in their interactions with women and minorities. The authors suggest that leaders need to continuously monitor the messages that are being put across through diversity initiatives. They also conclude that studies of the effects of managing diversity programmes are rarely conducted. So although an individual may be asked to evaluate the training they've received through an evaluation questionnaire, the impact is rarely measured at the level of the firm, for example, through the business benefits accrued.

Kossek and Zonia (1992) describe the importance of the diversity climate in an organisation, suggesting that climate and context, not numbers, are the real issues pertaining to the implementation of diversity policies. They conducted a study based on intergroup theory to examine relationships between perceptions of diversity climate and group and organisational characteristics. Their results suggest that diversity initiatives were more embraced by white women and ethnic minorities, most of whom were not high up enough in the company hierarchy to effect any change. Their results also point to:

> the need to better understand issues of backlash and perceptions of equity regarding employer activities to promote a diverse workforce. In an era of shrinking resources and downsizing, the competition between groups for scarce organizational resources will intensify... Our results suggest that conducting cosmetic diversity activities in an organization that is still overwhelmingly dominated by white males may, in fact, exacerbate negative intergroup processes such as hostility and splitting.
>
> (Kossek and Zonia, 1992: 77)

There is evidence within the literature that a more critical approach to managing diversity is emerging. Cassell and Biswas (2000) suggest that much of the literature that exists on the subject is largely atheoretical. Prasad and Mills (1997) suggest that management academics have adopted an approach which they describe as 'distant cheerleading' (1997: 5) where, although they endorse the importance of managing diversity, it isn't treated as a serious research area. Their own book: *Managing the Organizational Melting Pot: Dilemmas of Workplace*

Diversity (Prasad, Mills, Elmes and Prasad, 1997) represents a refreshing attempt to address some of the more difficult issues surrounding diversity. As they suggest:

> Metaphorically speaking, the melting pot may well have become a cauldron (Nash, 1989), the quilt may have been torn, cracks may have begun to appear in the mosaic, and the rainbow may have become twisted out of shape. Yet, much of the management literature on workplace diversity (with few exceptions) tends to ignore or gloss over these dilemmas while continuing to stress the potency of workshops and training to accomplish the goals of workplace diversity.

In conclusion, it would seem that the jury is still out on whether or not diversity initiatives meet their long-term goals. To be fair, compared to other forms of organisational intervention, diversity initiatives are relatively new, which may account for the current lack of long-term studies evaluating their impact.

Integrating diversity management with HRM policies and practices

Given the nature of managing diversity initiatives, and their historical context, one would expect that they would be clearly integrated into HRM policies and practices in organisations. One of the prime aims of managing diversity is to ensure that all the talent within a company's workforce is appropriately harnessed towards the company's objectives. Therefore the HR professional should, in theory, have a key role in the implementation of such initiatives. Jackson and Associates (1992) suggest that making the most of workforce diversity is a key challenge for HR professionals. She suggests that it is those professionals who are 'best able to educate business leaders about the strategic importance of working through diversity to mobilise them to take immediate actions' (1992: 27). She also suggests that HR professionals have a wide range of tools available to them for changing the attitudes and behaviours of their organisation's employees. Such tools include recruitment and selection systems, performance evaluation and appraisal, compensation and reward, training and development. Celebrating diversity could, therefore, be reinforced through the use of these tools. This approach sees diversity as a strategic imperative and therefore clearly linked into HRM.

However, there is little evidence yet that managing diversity practices and policies are integrated into HRM. Current textbooks on HRM for the UK market contain few references, if any, to managing diversity. Even discussion texts about HRM seem to neglect the diversity theme (e.g. Mabey, Salaman and Storey, 1998). This leads us into the thorny question of whether the effective management of diversity is really an HRM issue. As Kandola (1995) suggests, whereas equal opportunities is often seen as an issue for personnel and HR practitioners, managing diversity is seen as a central concern for all managers.

In considering the role of the manager, a key question here is the extent to which managing diversity is really anything new. Is it not just the appropriate use of general management skills? The role of the manager is clearly significant within the diversity process. In particular there has been an emphasis on the role of the individual leader. Managing diversity initiatives, like other change initiatives, will inevitably fail without top management commitment. Joplin and Daus (1997) suggest that, because diversity is a relatively new phenomenon in the workplace, it is not a self-managing process. Given this, it is important that leaders take a dynamic stance. They suggest that there are six particular challenges that need to be managed. These are:

■ changed power dynamics
■ diversity of opinions
■ perceived lack of empathy
■ tokenism, real and perceived
■ participation
■ overcoming inertia.

This seems like a daunting list and it is seen to be the role of the line manager rather than the HR team to translate managing diversity into everyday practice.

Arnold (1997) points out that there is a significant difference between learning to like diversity and learning to manage it. He suggests that much social psychological research has shown us that the former is difficult enough and that most of us tend to equate difference from ourselves as being worse or wrong. He proposes that, even when we learn to appreciate difference, it doesn't mean that we necessarily know how to manage it. McEnrue (1993) has argued that the successful management of diversity at the interpersonal level requires the acceptance of the relativity of one's own knowledge and perceptions together with a tolerance for ambiguity and the ability to demonstrate empathy and respect whilst being willing to change one's own beliefs. This could, of course, be a list of skills required to be a good manager, rather than those explicitly linked with managing diversity.

Given the chequered history of the link between HRM and equal opportunities, perhaps it is not surprising that there is little evidence of integration between HR practices and policies and managing diversity initiatives. Taking gender as an example, Biswas and Cassell (1996) argue that in some cases there is a conflict of interest between strategic HRM and the implementation of equal opportunities policies. Others have argued that the gender equality assumption within HRM is more rhetoric than reality. Dickens (1994) argues that in a number of ways HRM has different implications for men and women at work and demonstrates how the implementation of apparently gender-neutral HRM concepts and policies perpetuates rather than challenges gender inequalities. HRM concepts and practices are, of course, gendered, as Townley (1994) has highlighted.

So the extent of integration between HR policies and the management of diversity interventions, where they exist, is somewhat uncertain. Indeed, one could argue that the two are somewhat contradictory. Johnson and Gill (1993) point out that most HRM literature focuses on cultural homogenisation. This form of cultural management is seen as a way of securing employees' identification with, and sense of commitment to, the firm. Homogenisation, in any format, seems a major contradiction to notions of celebrating cultural diversity.

Critiquing the business case

A final important issue to consider is the extent to which the business case on which managing diversity is based holds any weight in relation to equal opportunities. Prasad and Mills (1997) suggest that the economic showcasing of diversity is both credible and persuasive to the public. However, the underlying economic assumptions of that case are drawn from human capital theories where people are treated explicitly as economic resources with their skills, qualifications and characteristics having potential value for the firms that employ them. But this ignores alternative economic approaches. If we take women as a group, for example, it could be argued that opportunities for women employees in the labour force are enhanced when the perceived economic climate necessitates it. Where historians have conducted studies on the changes in women's participation in the labour force, interesting information has emerged about the conditions under which women have been encouraged to leave their homes and work (Alpern, 1994; Farley, 1994). A key theme in many such accounts is the role of war. During the Second World War the employment of women from a variety of social, economic and racial backgrounds was legitimised (Chafe, 1977). Campbell (1984) outlines how in the United States, women entered managerial positions in droves, yet once the war ended, an intense reaction towards working women created 'a devastating impediment to women's entrance into management' (Alpern, 1994: 39). The changes in the postwar period in the ideology around women and work have been well documented. In this context, in evaluating the business case, the key question must be: what happens when demographic trends alter and skill shortages disappear? In other words, one can envisage a time when there is no business case for employing or promoting women and their diverse skills.

Examples of a sudden restriction in equal opportunities developments can be found as a response to the economic recession in Britain in the early 1990s. Donaldson (1993) documents how positive initiatives for women staff were cut when cost-cutting became the key business imperative. She describes how, for example, childcare has fallen down the agenda for some of the Opportunity 2000 companies. Perhaps the most high-profile casualty was the Midland Bank's famous programme of 200 crèches which was halted halfway at 115. As she suggests:

> Cost factors have influenced these decisions, but the recession, high unemployment, and consequently the diminution of concern about the demographic timebomb have also played a part in reducing the attraction of childcare support as a recruitment initiative. In contrast, flexible, part-time working arrangements have grown in attractiveness to employers. Such arrangements are seen both as an effective retention measure and as a way of reducing business costs by matching staff more closely to demand peaks.
>
> (Donaldson, 1993: 11)

The problem with an economic case is that it is only persuasive within a given economic climate. Consequently, its impact in facilitating long-term change must be seriously questioned.

Within the literature on the business case and the management of diversity, the links between valuing diverse skills and business success tend to be discussed in a way that renders them unproblematic. However, there are some examples that complicate the notion that equal opportunities makes business sense. Adkins (1995) in her analysis of gender relations in the tourist industry outlines how women workers were recruited to a variety of jobs at the Funland theme park on the basis of their physical appearance. The reason given for using such selection criteria was: 'because of the customers'. Consequently, women deemed as sexually attractive were employed in order to please the clients, 'sexual servicing' as Adkins calls it. Similarly, Biswas and Cassell (1996) outline a case study of a hotel where the work was clearly divided on gender lines. It was argued that it was crucial that receptionists were physically attractive, as they were the first point of contact for the customer, and they would have an impact on whether that customer used the hotel again. In this context, it was argued that accentuating the sexuality of women employees through styles of dress, etc, made business sense – that is, it was perceived that there was a business case for women doing typically female jobs and men doing specifically male jobs, because the customers liked it.

Such examples render the perceived clear link between equal opportunities and business benefits problematic. Dickens (1994), for example, suggests that some organisations will benefit from the absence of equal opportunities in that discriminatory practices can contribute to the bottom line. As she puts it:

> Organizations can, and do, obtain cost benefits from the non-recognition (but utilization) of women's skills, the undervaluing of women's labour, and from the exploitation of women as a cheap, numerically flexible (easily disposed of) workforce.
>
> (Dickens, 1994: 13)

Indeed, a business benefits argument could, in this context, be used to legitimise a gendered status quo.

A final point is that the business case may not apply equally to all diverse groups. Woodhams and Danieli (2000) suggest that there is very little written within the diversity literature about the business case for employing disabled people. They suggest that the rationality underlying the diversity approach falters in relation to the employment of disabled people in a number of ways. As they are a considerably heterogeneous group who are not segregated within the labour market, a managing diversity approach based on the identification of group-based characteristics has little to offer. This leads us to the view that some diverse groups may be more suitable to the business case than others. Arnold (1997) points out that the prevailing use of the business case could be more appropriate to workers at different levels of organisations. So although there may be a need to value diversity amongst middle and senior management where there is a need for innovative, skilled staff, the impetus may not be the same with casual or unskilled staff who may be easily replaceable.

This leaves us with the question of whether there is actually a business case for equal opportunities at all. Dickens (1994) is suspicious about this. She suggests:

> In practice in the UK, there is not a business case for EO, but rather a number of business arguments which have greater or lesser attraction for particular employers in particular circumstances. The business-case arguments, although valid, are contingent on, and made within, variable decision-making contexts. Receptiveness to them, therefore, is likely to be uneven and they will not guarantee action on the part of all employers, at all times.
>
> (Dickens, 1994: 5)

This discussion highlights the complicated nature of the processes through which issues of power, fairness and equality are reformulated into issues of competitive advantage. The potential for fundamental change within such an approach becomes questionable.

Conclusions

To conclude, four key issues emerge from this analysis of the managing diversity literature. The first is the extent to which there is evidence that organisations that manage diversity are more successful than organisations that do not. As suggested earlier, there is clearly a need for more research in this area. Ideally, research needs to focus on longitudinal assessment of diversity programmes, using a range of criteria from impact on economic performance to the attitudes of those groups that the interventions have been designed to address. Only then can the claims made for the success of managing diversity be properly evaluated.

Secondly, there is the question of the extent to which a movement that originated in North America translates easily into the British and European context. It would seem that the business case for managing diversity is more partial in other economic contexts. Sparrow, Schuler and Jackson (1994) address the issue of the extent to which HRM practices are seen to be linked to an organisation's attempts to gain competitive advantage. They performed secondary data analysis on survey data from 2,961 senior HRM managers in organisations from 12 different countries collected by IBM and Towers/Perrin. As part of the analysis the authors looked at the importance placed on promoting a diversity and equality culture. The US organisations scored higher than any of the European countries, with 53 per cent reporting that a diversity and equality culture was important for attaining competitive advantage. This was compared with 41 per cent in Germany, 40 per cent in the UK and 37 per cent in France. Therefore, it would seem there is either less awareness of managing diversity initiatives in Europe, or less of a commitment to them than exists in North America.

A further issue in this context is the problematic nature of universalistic notions of managing diversity. In practice, the term does not have a unitary meaning; it means different things to different people, and can mean different things in different cultures or organisations. Jones, Shepherd and Pringle (2000) argue that the discourse of managing diversity emerging from the US management literature cannot simply be mapped on to organisations in other cultural contexts. Using Aotearoa/New Zealand as an example they highlight how notions of diversity based on US demographics and culture may obscure key local diversity issues. They argue for: 'a genuinely multi-voiced "diversity" discourse that would focus attention on the local demographics, cultural and political differences that make the difference for specific organisations' (2000: 364).

A third issue that is rarely addressed is resistance to change. As with any change initiative, we would expect some resistance to managing diversity programmes. Yet this resistance is rarely addressed within the literature, as managing diversity is promoted as being in the interest of all groups, regardless of their differences. Arnold (1997) suggests that one of the risks with diversity initiatives is the white male backlash. Indeed, Prasad and Mills (1997) suggest that the literature on managing diversity has paid little attention to a growing hostility towards policies that promote workplace diversity (for example affirmative action and employment equity) within North America. They refer to a growing 'white rage' which is fuelled by

> harsh economic conditions, increased immigration of non-European people, the polar-
> ization of cultural differences within Canada and the United States
> (Prasad and Mills, 1997: 14)

Therefore the issue of resistance, why it occurs, and how it can be effectively managed, needs to be addressed, together with the consequences of that resistance for those traditionally disadvantaged groups who may be seen to gain from diversity initiatives.

A final, but significant issue, is the extent to which managing diversity is really new. Kandola (1995) suggests that much that has been written under the heading of managing diversity is striving to make it appear to be a new area. He suggests that at best this is naive, and at worst somewhat dishonest. He outlines how, for example, there have been generations of work looking at the impact of heterogeneity and homogeneity on the performance of groups in the workplace. Additionally, the work on diversity-focused organisations has produced very similar sets of characteristics to those identified elsewhere in the literature as the characteristics associated with learning organisations.

Having said that, perhaps the extent to which the debate is new is of little significance, if, as an area of discourse and intervention, managing diversity can offer new hope for furthering equal opportunities. More impetus is clearly needed to further moves for equality for those groups within the labour force who are traditionally discriminated against. What managing diversity approaches highlight is the economic costs to organisations of losing talented staff through discriminatory practices – surely a crucial issue for HRM policy and practice.

Managing diversity at Hinchcliffe Cards, Atherton Education Publishers and Cosmic Cosmetics

Catherine Cassell

Below are three different cases that draw on a range of diversity issues.[1] Case study questions are given at the end of the case descriptions.

Hinchcliffe Cards

Hinchcliffe Cards was started by William Hinchcliffe in 1874. Hinchcliffe had an artistic talent which he used for drawing individual greetings cards for his family and friends. As demand for the products he made increased, members of William's family joined him in creating the more intricately decorated cards. As the products of the firm grew in popularity, Hinchcliffe cards began to expand, investing in its first printing press in the early 1900s. The business continued to grow and moved into the mass production of greetings cards for the family market. William, who by then was managing director of the firm, was keen that some element of the origins of the company remained, and, despite the focus on mass production, a small sideline in the design and production of handmade cards remained.

After William Hinchcliffe died in 1934 the firm remained in the family and is now managed by chief executive James Hinchcliffe, who is William's great-grandson. The company headquarters, warehouse and packaging plant are housed in the same Lancashire town where William originally started the business in his own home. Indeed, the firm prides itself on being a family firm and having a paternalistic culture. James Hinchcliffe is often heard to say: 'Now, what would great-grandfather do in this situation?' when discussing any key strategic or problem issues. Despite the paternalistic culture, James is keen that the company moves with the times. Having recently completed an MBA at a local business school, he is keen to hear about new ideas and new methods of working that he can introduce into the company.

The company employs about 250 people. Seventy per cent of the workforce are women who work mainly on the production line and 10 per cent are from ethnic minority backgrounds. All the managers and senior management team, except the human resource manager (a white woman) are white males. Turnover in the company is generally low, though James Hinchcliffe suspects that there is a growing unease amongst the workforce about a number of issues.

The cards produced by Hinchcliffe's feed into two main markets. Firstly, there is the mass production of greetings cards. In particular, the firm recently won a couple of key contracts to produce Christmas cards for two of the larger chain stores. This has caused some problems in terms of work scheduling as production needs to be far higher in the spring months to meet the Christmas demand. In particular some of the more sophisticated machines that are used occasionally – for foiling, for example – are in 100 per cent use at this particular time. Putting coloured or silver foil on a card is an expensive process and the two men who work that machine are highly skilled. There is currently a shortage of such skills within the printing industry. To deal with the increase in output required at this time of year, the firm has tended to employ around 20 casual workers for the spring period when these cards are produced. There is evidence, however, that the permanent production workers display animosity towards the temporary workers. As one suggested: 'They're just here to make a quick buck, they don't seem bothered about the quality of what they do, their mistakes affect all of our bonuses.'

The production workers have also recently been complaining about some other issues to do with their opportunities in the workplace. Some of the female workers have been asking why they have not been trained on the more complex machines, which seem to be used exclusively by the male workers. Indeed, it is the production jobs based on those machines that carry the highest remuneration. Additionally, there are concerns amongst the female workers that they are expected to work very long hours at short notice during peak production periods. This is seen to interfere with their family lives. As one woman commented:

> They expect us to work into the evening at the drop of a hat but we don't get that flexibility in return. Cheryl who recently left to have a baby wanted to come back and work here part-time, but they said they couldn't slot her in. It would be too difficult to have one person working different hours from everyone else.

Apart from these issues, the production workers are generally happy about their work. Hinchcliffe's has a good name in the local area for being a decent employer who pays the going rate for the job. It is almost an institution in the Lancashire mill town in which it is based.

The other market that Hinchcliffe's serves is the demand for handmade products. Orders for these cards come from all over the world. To tap these markets the firm has recently started a mail order business. In order to meet the increasing demand for handmade products, production has largely moved out of the factory. The cards are now made by 50 workers in their own homes. These homeworkers are mainly women from ethnic minority groups. One issue that concerns the firm is the high rate of turnover amongst the homeworkers. They are generally perceived as having little loyalty to the firm and are unreliable in meeting agreed dates for production. There has been some talk within the firm of investing in a team of designers employed officially by the firm who can be based in the firm's headquarters. The plan is that some of the current homeworkers would be employed on this basis. Early evidence suggests that they may not be particularly interested in this option. Indeed, the majority of these workers are women who fit in their drawing work around looking after small children. Additionally, their view is that the company often treats them with little respect. An example of this is the common complaint that the materials needed to make the cards are often dropped off at their homes later than promised, sometimes with incorrect specifications. One homeworker has hinted that there may be some covert racism in the way some of the homeworkers are treated.

There is a recognition within the senior management team that the company is in a position to expand. A couple of the directors believe that there would be a considerable market for Hinchcliffe products in the European Union. This diversification of markets would, however, require a more diverse set of skills from the sales and marketing staff. In particular, there would be a requirement for sales staff to speak at least one other European language and be comfortable dealing with a set of managers from a range of European cultures. The mail order catalogues have generated a lot of interest in the handmade products that needs to be followed up by the small team of sales staff that Hinchcliffe's employs. The current sales director is concerned that his sales team are lacking in these skills.

The prospect of diversification into Europe raises a number of issues for James Hinchcliffe. He is desperately keen to investigate the available avenues, but is also keen that the firm retains its Lancashire roots. He believes that the handmade products are just as good and as popular as the product his great-grandfather produced years ago. As he suggests:

> I think we have to diversify into European markets. One of our greatest challenges in doing that is to get those homeworkers on board. We could no longer deal with them dropping the cards off here at the factory a day late because the baby threw up or whatever. In fact, we may have to abandon them altogether and go for an in-house design team. I know Great-grandfather was always keen to support the local community but maybe things have to change at some point.

At a recent board meeting the HR director suggested that some of the issues the firm was facing were actually management of diversity issues. James Hinchcliffe is keen to get any advice he can. Though the other senior managers are uncertain, they have agreed to invite in a team of consultants to progress the issues further.

Atherton Educational Publishers

Atherton Educational Publishers was initially established in 1902 as a publisher of educational textbooks. Starting off with a small printing press in a London backstreet, by the 1920s the firm employed 20 people in the selling and production of high-quality educational texts. After the 1944 Education Act the demand for educational texts increased and Atherton became one of the leaders in the market, with a name for commissioning and publishing language texts. Initially focusing on English, the senior management team realised after the Second World War that there would be an increased demand for tuition in European languages. Their proactivity in addressing this new market led to the firm successfully developing a reputation as the leading publisher of foreign language texts. During the 1960s the senior management team, led by Dan Walker, predicted a growth in multicultural texts aimed at schools. In advancing in this direction Atherton took a large share of what was to be an increasingly important market. At the same time Atherton was taken over by a large multinational media corporation. Dan Walker and his senior management team felt they had done quite well out of the deal, retaining the major decision-making power as to the strategic direction of Atherton, whilst benefiting from the networks carried by the corporation.

The economics of the publishing environment changed considerably during the twentieth century, and particularly during the last ten years. A move has clearly occurred towards a more business-oriented and market-focused culture, with a reorientation in values away from an editorial focus towards marketing and sales. As one of the employees at Atherton said:

> Publishing is about making sound commercial decisions about what people need and want. It used to be a gentleman's profession, but now we have had to tighten up our act – we need to publish things cheaply and quickly.

Currently, Dan Walker still chairs the board of 18 directors at Atherton. He is a powerful, charismatic figure who is said to inspire his colleagues and staff. Atherton currently has 870 employees. Although 53 per cent of the managers in the company are women, only three women sit on the board. Recently, there has been considerable dissatisfaction amongst the female staff, who perceive that there is a glass ceiling at senior management and board level. There is a clear consensus amongst the female staff that sexual discrimination at work is covert rather than overt:

> I've not directly experienced any prejudice, but I've seen evidence of it around. It's not easy to move higher in the organisation. If you're exceptional then you rise, but then women have to be a bit better than men in order to do that. It's still grey suits at the top.

Having children is one of the pertinent issues that is seen to influence the promotion prospects of women. Although the women managers recognised that Atherton had good maternity policies, they feel that covert messages are given about having children and its impact on a woman's career. Most of the female managerial staff don't have children. Combining a successful career with motherhood is seen to be a difficult option, given the long hours and travel often associated with the work. Recent company evidence from the HR department suggests that talented female managers are leaving the company to work freelance, an option seen to tie in more favourably with raising a family. One of the female managers summed up this issue in the following way:

> Women are not promoted to senior editor positions and it's clear that women have often left due to frustration about this. It's difficult to see obvious cases of discrimination. My predecessor went on maternity leave: why didn't she come back? Women just become frustrated.

By far the majority of employees at Atherton are white. This creates issues with regard to selling multicultural texts. In the last couple of years Atherton has tried to recruit a number of ethnic minority publishers and sales people. Dan Walker's view is that they will serve to keep the company on top of the growing multicultural educational market, so employing a more diverse workforce would make business sense. Indeed, a number of clients purchasing multicultural texts have commented on the lack of ethnic diversity amongst Atherton selling staff. This is particularly apparent in the schools market, where Atherton's sales staff go out to meet multicultural education co-ordinators in schools. Despite actively trying to recruit from the ethnic minority labour market, Atherton has not had much success in both recruiting and retaining ethnic minority employees. Where ethnic minority workers have been employed, they have rarely stayed at Atherton long, commonly complaining about the lack of access to 'real' opportunities. One particular salesman expressed his feelings of tokenism in the following way:

> I'm sick of being the black face of Atherton's, the guy who goes out just to get orders from the black customers. There doesn't seem to be any other role for me here other than that.

Dan Walker is concerned that some of the smaller, newer publishing firms are making inroads into the multicultural market, and are enticing away those customers who were previously loyal to Atherton. He knows that the firm needs to do something soon to retain, if not expand, its position in this market, a key market for the future. He wonders whether the firm actually has a problem with its image as an employer of the white, well-spoken middle classes. He is also concerned that some of the older members of the workforce who have been around for a long time are reinforcing this traditional image of the firm by their very presence. In such a competitive market, where sales is a primary driver, Dan is beginning to think that he needs some external business advice. Given these issues, he has decided to invite a team of consultants into the organisation to assess whether there are 'any real diversity issues to worry about' or whether 'we're just like any other company'.

Cosmic Cosmetics

Cosmic Cosmetics design and distribute cosmetics and toiletries derived from vegetable and fruit ingredients. The company was founded in the 1960s at Glastonbury by two hippies dedicated to animal rights and environmentalism. They recognised that many of the visitors to Glastonbury at the time could benefit from the use of such products, but were concerned not to partake, or invest in what were seen to be environmentally damaging products. With the benefits of a keen family investor, Sara Newsome and Thom Nolan toured the wilds of Europe and South America finding appropriate ingredients for their products. On return they set up Cosmic Cosmetics. At first, they were keen to maintain a collective spirit within the company and the organisation ran efficiently as a collective of 15 people for the first five years. Demand for Cosmic products was increasing rapidly, and its base in Glastonbury was seen as a prime site for tourist visitors. In

1971 Sara Newsome married and her new husband, Will Sonner, became heavily involved in the company. Over the next couple of years the company went through a period of turmoil as Will built up a power base around his own concerns about expanding the company within a more commercial framework, including the development of a mail order business. In 1973, a key turning point emerged with a number of the initial members of the collective leaving, suggesting that they were unhappy that the collective spirit of the firm had somehow been lost. The next few years were times of considerable growth for the company. Moving to a larger shop in Glastonbury, they also opened outlets on Carnaby Street in London and in Brighton and Edinburgh.

Currently, Sarah Newsome still has a major role in the company, responsible for marketing and HR issues. Thom Nolan is now in charge of research and development of new products and spends much of his time searching the globe for exotic ingredients on which to develop new products with his partner, David. Meanwhile Will Sonner is MD of the ever-expanding firm. Those three key individuals still maintain much of the idealism of the 1960s and company policies are seen to be quite liberal. Recently, however, there have been a number of instances where staff have been complaining about their treatment. The company currently employs over 900 people at mail order distribution sites and shops all over Britain. Each of these sites is headed by a 'co-ordinator' whose job is to oversee the operation of the company in that outlet. Twice a year the trio meet regularly with the co-ordinators, but will also make site visits as necessary. In practice the top trio rely heavily on the co-ordinators to run their own outlets in line with the company's guiding philosophies. Consequently, HR policies in each of the outlets may be considerably different. The head office is still in Glastonbury, seen as the 'spiritual home' of the firm. About 20 per cent of the workforce are gay. As a result of the company image and philosophy, and the open homosexuality of one of the founders, Cosmic was always seen as a relatively safe place to work, free from discrimination. However, some members of this group are now asserting that they are treated less favourably than the heterosexuals when it comes to management opportunities. In particular, there have been suggestions that outside of the Glastonbury headquarters there is considerable intolerance towards gay staff.

These allegations have been taken seriously by the senior management team. Sara Newsome is extremely concerned about this situation. Being deeply committed to equal opportunities, she is considerably distressed that such discrimination may be happening within her firm. Additionally, this kind of allegation could threaten the good reputation of Cosmic, which is renowned not just for its products, but also its radical philosophy. She has therefore, in conjunction with Thom Nolan and Will Sonner, decided to approach a group of consultants to see if they can provide some advice on the way forward to address some of these issues. Specifically, she wants advice on developing an overall strategy on managing diversity for the company as a whole. She is keen that all employees feel that their talents are recognised and rewarded, regardless of any differences that may exist between them.

Tasks

Stage 1 – Intervention

You are a member of a team of consultants who has been called in by the firms outlined above to give advice on diversity issues. Specifically, your task is to design a diversity intervention that will meet the diversity issues that are outlined in each of the cases. In designing the interventions you will find it useful to refer to the 'Diversity Interventions Checklist' in Box 13.1. This will give you some pointers and issues to think through about the design, process, and content of the intervention.

BOX 13.1

Diversity interventions checklist

1. Research
- What research do you need to conduct to design the intervention?
- What information do you need?
- How will you access that information?
- Who do you need to talk to?
- What do you need to ask them?
- What other research is necessary (e.g. audit of company culture)?

2. The context of the intervention
- What is the motivation behind the intervention?
- Is there a vision?
- What is the scope of the intervention (e.g. all diverse groups)?

3. Designing the intervention
- What are the objectives of the intervention?
- What will it consist of?
- Who will be involved?
- How will assumptions be addressed?
- How will systems or structures be addressed?
- How will the intervention be communicated?

4. Implementing the intervention
- How will the intervention be implemented?
- Who will be responsible for implementation?
- What will be the timescale?

5. Evaluating the intervention
- How will the intervention be evaluated?
- What criteria will be used for the evaluation?

6. Issues in the long term
- Who will be accountable for diversity issues in the future?
- How will they be accountable?
- What will be the role of the consultants in this process?

Source: Cassell, 1999

Stage 2 – Questions

Now you have designed your intervention consider the following questions:

1. What response do you think the plan will receive from the diverse groups in each of the organisations?

2. What response do you anticipate from the senior management teams in each of the organisations?

3. Are there any particular problems you would anticipate in the implementation of the plan/s?

4. How do the plan/s link in with the overall business strategy of the organisations?

5. What are the similarities and differences between the organisational situations?

6. What are the similarities and differences between the diversity plans?

7. What were the key difficulties you experienced in devising the diversity plans?

8. Can the demands of managing diversity interventions be effectively linked in with overall business strategy?

Note

1 Earlier versions of these case studies can be found in Cassell, C.M. (1999) 'Managing diversity', in Clegg, C., Legge, K. and Walsh, S. (eds) *The Experience of Managing: a Skills Guide*, Basingstoke: Macmillan.

References to Chapter 13

Adkins, L. (1995) *Gendered work: Sexuality, Family and the Labour Market*, Buckingham: Open University Press.

Alpern, S. (1994) 'In the beginning: a history of women in management', in Fagenson, E.A. (ed) *Women in Management: Trends, Issues and Challenges in Managerial Diversity*, Newbury Park, Ca: Sage.

Arnold, J. (1997) *Managing careers into the 21st century*, London: Paul Chapman Publishing.

Biswas, R. and Cassell, C.M. (1996) 'The sexual division of labour in the hotel industry: implications for strategic HRM', *Personnel Review*, 25(5): 51–66.

Campbell, D. (1984) *Women at War with America: Private Lives in a Patriotic Era*, Cambridge Mass: Harvard University Press.

Cassell, C.M. (1999) 'Managing diversity', in Clegg, C., Legge, K. and Walsh, S. (eds) *The Experience of Managing: a Skills Guide*, Basingstoke: Macmillan.

Cassell, C.M. and Biswas, R. (2000) 'Managing diversity in the new millennium', *Personnel Review*, 29(3): 268–73.

Chafe, W.H. (1977) *Women and Equality*, New York: Oxford University Press.

Cox, T. (Jnr.) (1992) 'The multi-cultural organization', *Academy of Management Executive*, 5(5): 34–47.

Dickens, L. (1994) 'What HRM means for gender equality', *Human Resource Management Journal*, 8(1): 23–40.

Dickens, L. (1994) 'The business case for women's equality. Is the carrot better than the stick?', *Employee Relations*, 16(8): 5–18.

Donaldson, L. (1993) 'The recession: a barrier to equal opportunities?', *Equal Opportunities Review*, 50, July–August.

Ellis, C. and Sonnenfeld, J.A. (1994) 'Diverse approaches to managing diversity', *Human Resource Management*, 33(1): 79–109.

Equal Opportunities Commission (1995) *The Economics of Equal Opportunities*, Manchester: EOC.

Farley, J. (1994) 'Commentary', in Fagenson, E.A. (ed) *Women in Management: Trends, Issues and Challenges in Managerial Diversity*, Newbury Park, Ca: Sage.

Fulkerson, J.R. and Schuler, R.S. (1992) 'Managing worldwide diversity at Pepsi-Cola International', in Jackson, S.E. and Associates (eds) *Diversity in the Workplace: Human Resource Initiatives*, New York: Guilford Press.

Hall, D.T. and Parker, V.A. (1993) 'The role of workplace flexibility in managing diversity', *Organizational Dynamics*, 22(1): 5–18.

Hicks-Clarke, D. and Iles, P. (1999) 'The effects of positive climate for diversity on organisational and career perceptions and attitudes', *Proceedings of the 1999 British Academy of Management Conference, Manchester 1–3 September*, Volume 1.

Hitt, M.A. and Barr, S.H. (1989) 'Managerial selection decision models: Examination of configural cue processing', *Journal of Applied Psychology*, 59: 705–11.

Jackson, S.E. and Associates (1992) *Diversity in the Workplace: Human Resource Initiatives*, New York: Guilford Press.

Johnson, P. and Gill, J. (1993) *Management Control and Organizational Behaviour*, London: Paul Chapman Publishing.

Johnston, W.B. and Packard, A.H. (1987) *Workforce 2000: Work and Workers for the 21st century*, Indianapolis: Hudson.

Jones, D., Pringle, J. and Shephard, D. (2000) '"Managing diversity" meers Aotearoa/New Zealand', *Personnel Review*, 29(3): 364–80.

Joplin, J.R.W. and Daus, C.S. (1997) 'Challenges of leading a diverse workforce', *Academy of Management Executive*, XI(3): 32–47.

Kandola, R. and Fullerton, J. (1998) *Managing the Mosaic: Diversity in Action*, London: Institute of Personnel and Development.

Kandola, R. (1995) 'Managing diversity: new broom or old hat?', in Cooper, C.L. and Robertson, I.T. (eds) *International Review of Industrial and Organizational Psychology*, Vol. 10, Chichester: John Wiley and Sons.

Kossek, E.E. and Zonia, S.C. (1992) 'A field study of reactions to employer efforts to promote diversity', *Journal of Organisational Behaviour*, 14: 61–81.

Mabey, C., Salaman, G. and Storey, J. (1998) *Strategic Human Resource Management: A Reader*, London: Sage.

McEnrue, M.P. (1993) 'Managing Diversity: Los Angeles before and after the riots', *Organizational Dynamics*, 21(3).

Nash, M. (1989) *The Cauldron of Ethnicity in the Modern World*, Chicago: University of Chicago Press.

Prasad, P. and Mills, A.J. (1997) 'From showcase to shadow, understanding the dilemmas of managing workplace diversity', in Prasad, P., Mills, A.J., Elmes, M. and Prasad, A. (eds) *Managing the Organizational Melting Pot: Dilemmas of Workplace Diversity*, Thousand Oaks, Ca: Sage.

Prasad, P., Mills, A.J., Elmes, M. and Prasad, A. (1997) *Managing the Organizational Melting Pot: Dilemmas of Workplace Diversity*, Thousand Oaks, Ca: Sage.

Robinson, G. and Dechant, K. (1997) 'Building a business case for diversity', *Academy of Management Executive*, XI(3): 21–31.

Ross, R. and Schneider, R. (1992) *From Equality to Diversity: a Business Case for Equal Opportunities*, London: Pitman.

Shapiro, G. (2000) 'Employee involvement: Opening the diversity Pandora's box?' *Personnel Review* (in press).

Sparrow, P.R., Schuler, R.S. and Jackson, S.E. (1994) 'Convergence or divergence: human resource practices and policies for competitive advantage worldwide', *International Journal of Human Resource Management*, 5(2): 267–99.

Storey, J. (1995) *Human Resource Management: a Critical Text*, London: Routledge.

Thomas, R.R. (Jnr) (1990) 'From affirmative action to affirming diversity', *Harvard Business Review*, 68(2): 107–17.

Thomas, R.R. (1992) 'Managing diversity: a conceptual framework', in Jackson, S.E. (ed) *Diversity in the Workplace: Human Resource Initiatives*, New York: Guilford Press.

Thornberg, L. (1994) 'Journey towards a more inclusive culture', *HRMagazine*, February.

Totta, J.M. and Burke, R.J. (1995) 'Integrating diversity and equality into the fabric of the organization', *Women in Management Review*, 10(7): 32–39.

Townley, B. (1994) *Reframing Human Resource Management, Power, Ethics and the Subject*, London: Sage.

Walker, B.A. and Hanson, W.C. (1992) 'Valuing differences at Digital Equipment Corporation', in Jackson, S.E. and Associates (eds) *Diversity in the Workplace: Human Resource Initiatives*, New York: Guilford Press.

Wilson, F.M. (1995) *Organizational Behaviour and Gender*, London: McGraw-Hill Book Company.

Woodhams, C. and Danieli, A. (2000) 'Disability and diversity: a difference too far?', *Personnel Review* (in press)

Wright, P., Ferris, S.P., Hiller, J.S. and Kroll, M. (1995) 'Competitiveness through management of diversity: effects on stock price valuation', *Academy of Management Journal*, 38(1): 272–87.

Woolfe Morrison, E. and Mardenfeld Herlihy, J. (1992) 'Becoming the best place to work: Managing diversity at American Express Travel related services', in Jackson, S.E. and Associates (eds) *Diversity in the Workplace: Human Resource Initiatives*, New York: Guilford Press.

Chapter 14

New management techniques in small and medium-sized enterprises

Tony Dundon, Irena Grugulis and Adrian Wilkinson

Introduction

This chapter is concerned with New Management Techniques (NMTs) in small and medium-sized enterprises (SMEs). Structurally, this chapter differs from others in the book. This is partly because of the need to understand the employment relationship in the context of a small social setting and partly because of the differences in managerial strategies between small and large firms. Most HRM textbooks have relatively little to say about smaller companies, despite the importance of this sector in many industrialised economies (Lane, 1995). This importance is evident both by their centrality to the economy and by the statements of policy makers and mainstream politicians, who argue that it is the growth and prosperity of smaller firms that will stimulate growth in the economy as a whole (Department of Employment, 1992). In Britain, SMEs account for 99 per cent of all companies and 57 per cent of non-government employment (DTI, 1998). However, there are dangers in using these figures in a homogeneous and deterministic way. One SME may not resemble another and lessons obtained in one sector may not necessarily be generalisable elsewhere. It is for these reasons that this chapter presents four brief case studies since these can help to explore the significance of both organisational context and management practice in smaller firms.

The key theme of the chapter is the uses (and abuses) of 'soft HRM and NMTs' in SMEs. Techniques such as cultural change programmes, employee involvement schemes, teamworking and devolved control systems are evident among SMEs (Duberley and Walley, 1995; Bacon et al., 1996; Wilkinson et al., 1998; Downing-Burn and Cox, 1999; Cully et al., 1998) but, as in larger firms, this development is not necessarily positive. Many HRM practices implicitly and explicitly rely on the existence of such managerial techniques to justify 'harder' employment outcomes

(Keenoy, 1997). Moreover, as noted above, SMEs are heterogeneous. In such diverse organisational contexts the use of NMTs needs to be assessed against a variety of influences: product and labour market factors, their dependency on larger firms, as well as the internal dynamics of a small social setting.

Despite the general consensus that employment relations in this sector are worthy of study (Westhead and Storey, 1997), there is a tendency in the existing literature to oversimplify the practices found among SMEs into one of two divergent perspectives (see Table 14.1). The first is the view of the Bolton Commission (Bolton, 1971) that 'small is beautiful'. Here, a low incidence of strikes among SMEs is used to argue that the close proximity of owner-managers to employees ensures informal and harmonious relations, good communications and greater flexibility. This is problematic since, as Edwards (1995) argues, strikes are only one (particularly dramatic) form of industrial discontent and, while the absence of strikes may demonstrate high or increasing levels of trust, communication and commitment between employer and employee, it may also show a fear of management and an abuse of the managerial prerogative. In practice, there is rather more evidence to suggest that discontent is taking forms other than the withdrawal of labour, than there is to suggest that high levels of trust have replaced industrial unrest (Kelly, 1998).

In contrast is Sisson's (1993) 'Bleak House' perspective which indicates that the small firm may manage its labour in ways that are authoritarian, dictatorial and exploitative (see also Goss, 1988; Rainnie, 1989, 1991; Ram, 1991; Ram and Holliday, 1993). Indeed, as Philpott (1996) notes, the majority of employees who earn less than £3.50 per hour can be found within the SME sector. Conflict is not lacking but rather expressed through high levels of absenteeism and labour turnover, as well as a greater propensity for problematic 'interpersonal' relations to develop and ferment over time. In practice, owner-managers tend to take a unitarist view of the enterprise that aspires to a 'happy ship', assuming 'what is good for their business is good for employees' (Goodman *et al.*, 1998).

Table 14.1 From small is beautiful to Bleak House

Positive HR	Negative HR
Harmonious	Hidden conflict
Good HR	Bleak House
Little bureaucracy	More instability
Family style	Authoritarian

Source: Wilkinson, 1999: 207

Interesting as these two divergent perspectives are, theorising about human resource management techniques for such a large proportion of Britain's working population in such extreme 'either-or' terms tends to oversimplify and polarise practices that are, in fact, remarkably diverse and complex. Nor in this sector have the empirical studies or core textbooks on HRM helped to counter such simplifications, since the bulk of evidence and theoretical models presented in these is drawn from large organisations (see, for example, Storey, 1992, 1995; Guest and Hoque, 1993; Beardwell and Holden, 1997; Gratton *et al.*, 1999; Bach and Sisson, 2000). These issues and debates are explained later in the chapter, after the significance of the SME sector in Britain is briefly outlined.

The SME sector

There is no single or acceptable definition of a small firm (Storey, 1994: 8). In Britain, firms that employ fewer than 200 workers are defined as small, while in France, Germany and America the figure is 500 (Odaka and Sawai, 1999). One difficulty is that size can be defined by a combination of indicators, including profitability, rate of tax returns (pre-and post-tax), sales, annual turnover, or the number of employees and there is no clear agreement about which are the most acceptable. Of equal significance here is the issue of organisational context. For example, a hairdressing salon with 20 staff would be small in relation to a chemical plant with 100 workers. However, in the *context of their respective industries*, the hairdressing establishment would be large (possibly with a working owner on site) and the chemical plant small (but subject to greater technological control and possibly collective bargaining). These contextual issues suggest that a range of other factors need to be examined when exploring management strategy in smaller firms, such as the relationships that exist between small and big business, the role of product and labour markets along with the ideologies of owner-managers.

The Bolton Report (1971) defined a small firm as one with fewer than 200 employees and a medium-sized company as one which employed up to 500 workers. For particular sectors a combination of other measures have been used: in road transport the size of a firm was related to both the number of employees and vehicles owned by the organisation; in the retail sector, financial turnover was the main criterion. More recently, the Department of Trade and Industry (DTI, 1998) have adopted a (non-binding) European recommendation that defines smaller firms either as a *micro, small* or *medium*-sized enterprise (see Table 14.2). This appears to fit with recent evidence confirming that organisations are now generally smaller. According to the latest research (Cully *et al.*, 1999: 18; Millward *et al.*, 2000: 29) the typical workplace size is just over 100 employees, with SMEs accounting for 99 per cent of all businesses in Britain (DTI, 1998).

However, such strict statistical definitions can be misleading when used to inform assumptions about employment practices, as SMEs are characterised by high heterogeneity (Curran and Stanworth, 1979; Goss, 1988; Rainnie, 1991). Research suggests that labour–management relations in a small social setting can be complex, diverse, and above all, informal (Scott *et al.*, 1989; Roberts *et al.*, 1992; Ram, 1994). Take the hairdressing salon and chemical plant mentioned earlier. Each would be subject to quite specific internal and external factors that could influence managerial strategies. Managing people at a small chemical plant may be influenced by the dependency of a few (even single) large customers,

Table 14.2 European Commission SME definitions

Criterion	EC SME Definitions		
	Micro	Small	Medium
Max. number of employees	10	50	250
Max. annual turnover	–	7 m–ecu	40 m–ecu
Max. annual balance sheet total	–	5 m–ecu	27 m–ecu
Max. % owned by one, or jointly by several, enterprise(s) not satisfying the same criterion.	–	25%	25%

Note: To qualify as an SME, both the employees and the independence criteria must be satisfied and either the turnover or the balance sheet total criteria.

Source: DTI, 1998

capital-intensive process technologies and possibly collective negotiation with trade unions. By contrast, the hairdresser's may be dependent on a large number of individual customers and rely on part-time and casual non-union employees who are subject to managerial autocracy (paternalism), with the owner-manager actually working alongside other employees. It is these contextual variations which suggest that deterministic definitions of the small firm sector ought to be treated with caution. One major problem is the assumption that HRM in larger organisations can be easily transposed to SMEs without an appreciation of the contextual diversity of smaller firms.

Diversity of NMT in SMEs

There is a growing debate about the use of managerial techniques in smaller firms (Duberley and Whalley, 1995; Bacon et al., 1996; Kinnie et al., 1999) that mirrors 'best practice HRM' (Pfeffer, 1998; Wood, 1995). Examples include devolved managerial responsibilities, cultural change programmes, teamworking and a range of employee involvement (EI) initiatives (Wilkinson et al., 1999). The WERS survey found that in firms employing fewer than 100 people, 28 per cent had introduced 'five or more' NMTs (see Table 14.3). Further evidence suggests that, when it comes to the introduction of these initiatives, SMEs may not be too far behind their larger counterparts. In a study among small engineering firms it was shown that managerial techniques such as teamworking and quality audits are on the increase (Downing-Burn and Cox, 1999). According to Bacon et al. (1996), the use of such management techniques among many SMEs may not even be 'new'. In a survey of over 200 SMEs they discovered that management change programmes were introduced in less formal ways than those found among many larger firms. They conclude that smaller businesses offer a better setting for the implementation of HRM initiatives, given their existing flat hierarchy and the organic nature of communication flows between employee and employer.

It is also possible that in smaller firms the 'type' of manager is changing, many of whom can more easily adopt the role of 'champion' for certain HRM practices

Table 14.3 Examples of new management initiatives in smaller firms*

	% of workplaces
No 'new' management practices or employee involvement schemes	8
Five or more of these practices and schemes	28
Joint consultative committee at workplace	17
One or more equal treatment practices	24
Union presence	22
Union recognition	12
Worker representative at workplace	10
Employees with one or more flexible/family-friendly working arrangements	48
Employees with high or very high job satisfaction	61
Low-paying workplaces (quarter or more earn below £3.50 per hour)	21
High productivity growth	33
Industrial tribunal complaints (rate per employee)	2.4

Note: Stand-alone private sector workplaces with 10–99 employees.
Figures are weighted and based on responses from 250 managers and 2,957 employees.

Source: Cully *et al.*, 1998:26

(Marchington, 1992). For instance Bacon *et al.* (1996: 90) report that several SMEs were run by owner-managers who had been made redundant from larger firms and used that experience to introduce sophisticated HR practices into their smaller business. They show that a new managerial agenda was not intended to replace informal practices with formal systems, it was to maintain the informality associated with a small social setting while at the same time promoting professional managerial techniques.

Reports from workers employed in SMEs have also been surprisingly positive. Guest and Conway (1999: 397) comment that there are discernible 'shades of grey and occasional shafts of light' emerging from the 'black hole' of SMEs. In their survey 29 per cent of employees said they were 'very satisfied' with their job and 31 per cent displayed 'a lot of loyalty' to their firm. Similarly, the WERS data show that workers in both big and small firms display broadly similar (positive) patterns of workplace 'wellbeing' (Cully *et al.*, 1999: 179, 271). In explaining these results Guest and Conway (1999) suggest that employees in smaller firms appear to experience several features related to the psychological contract, such as perceptions of fairness and trust, that may be characteristic of social harmony.

Yet the interpretation of these survey results can be problematic. In the WERS survey, for example, while 65 per cent of all managers reported that most employees work in designated teams, only 3 per cent confirmed that such teams were fully autonomous in deciding how the work will be performed with self-appointed team leaders (Cully *et al.*, 1999:43). Other evidence suggests that broader 'soft' HRM practices can actually translate to 'hard' employment outcomes (Keenoy, 1997; Bacon, 1999). Research suggests that the majority of smaller firms tend to recruit workers through word-of-mouth, and few SMEs provide any formal training for employees (Holliday, 1995; Carroll *et al.*, 1999; Westhead and Storey, 1997). Moreover, industrial relations tends to be based on systems of 'unbridled individualism', with informality the central *modus operandi* in the day-to-day management of people (Scott *et al.*, 1989; Lucas, 1996). Many of those employed in smaller firms experience work-related illness, face dismissal and have less access to union representation than their counterparts in larger organisations (Millward *et al.*, 1992; IRS, 1998; Cully *et al.*, 1999: 272).

Explaining management diversity among SMEs

The risk of oversimplification notwithstanding, two broad approaches can be identified within the existing literature to account for the diversity of managerial techniques in SMEs.

The political economy of small business

The first approach focuses on the political economy of small business. This seeks to assess the pattern of management action against four types of relationship: *dependent, dominated, isolated* or *innovative* links between big and small firms (Rainnie, 1989, 1991). *Dependent* SMEs rely on large firms for their survival. Blyton and Turnbull (1998) show the implications of such a *dependency* relationship for a small clothing firm that manufactures garments for Marks & Spencer (M&S). In this case authoritarian management, strict supervision and piece rate wages reflect the relationship between the small firm and M&S rather than the unique features of the clothing industry. In other organisations a similar relationship led workers to view 'the customer as being in charge', rather than the company management (Delbridge, 1998). However, these dependency relationships can also influence HR practices among the smaller partners in less direct ways. MacMahon (1996) found that outsourcing was little more than a shift in 'risk' from larger firms to the workers of many smaller enterprises. In this way small subcontracting firms became vulnerable as they were dependent on supplying the products and services deemed non-essential by large corporations. These included catering, cleaning, security, construction, food and drink and transport, where a significant number of employees work part-time on low-paid casual and temporary contracts (Dale and Kerr, 1995; Guest and Conway, 1999).

Dominated SMEs exist in (very) competitive markets. Many offer lower rates of pay and fewer employee benefits in order to compete with larger firms. Examples include corner shops that have to compete with new (and large) out-of-town supermarkets. Employees tend to be those with weak bargaining power – women, family members, the young and ethnic minorities – and are often employed on a short-term and casual basis. Barrett and Rainnie (1999) challenge current government thinking by arguing that these working conditions are closer to those of a flea market than a sector which is viewed as the engine of economic recovery.

The third relationship, *isolation*, is slightly more cumbersome to define. Isolated enterprises either specialise in discrete geographical markets and/or operate in sectors with potentially low profit margins. Larger firms avoid these markets because they promise only low rates of return or because specialised services and products offer few economies of scale. Examples of isolated firms are diverse, and range from small professional service enterprises such as accountancy and law, to networks of small firms that are embedded in local community traditions. One example of the latter is the brewing industry in Bavaria. Here there is a highly fragmented group of small breweries which cater largely to local consumer taste. The opportunities for growth and large-scale returns are therefore limited (Hilbert *et al.*, 1994). Such SMEs often rely on extended social networks in attracting and retaining employees, as many owe their survival to low labour costs (an effective provision of subsidy from employees to employer).

The final category is that of *innovative* SMEs. Examples of such organisations can be found in emerging high-tech markets. Here larger organisations may 'wait on the sidelines' until risk-takers have finished the pioneering work and the market starts to offer the potential for both stable and profitable returns. It is at that point that the larger organisation may provide capital investment, franchise arrangements or distribution and production facilities for the smaller firm. It is often difficult for owner-managers to recruit and retain qualified employees given the (individualised) bargaining position of highly skilled workers in these innovative enterprises (Scase, 1995).

While not all SMEs may fit into these categories in ways that are simple and clear cut, this framework, by focusing on the relationships between 'small' and 'large' capital, provides interesting insights into both corporate context and organisational bargaining power. As a result, both explicitly and implicitly, it regards particular managerial techniques as highly unstable. Blyton and Turnbull (1998: 257) comment that:

> the field of play is determined by the customer, and while the *precise* rules of the game may be subject to interpretation (negotiation), the larger firm can always move the goalposts or take the ball elsewhere to play.

Small firms and workplace dynamics

A second school of thought is concerned with the social dynamics in the small workplace (Scase and Goffee, 1987; Goss, 1988, 1991; Scase, 1995; Ram, 1994; Ram and Holliday, 1993; Ram, 1999). Goss (1988, 1991) maintains that management style in the smaller firm fuels an illusion of social harmony. In these establishments even the more pleasant forms of management – such as fraternal and paternalistic strategies – inevitably lead to greater exploitation of labour in order to retain a competitive edge. Here managerial techniques ultimately seek to foster *identification* between employees and owner-managers, highlighting the interdependency of both parties since owner-managers often rely upon employees for business survival, but at the same time the worker is also dependent upon the firm for employment (Goss, 1991; Scase, 1995). As a result, managerial initiatives can vary between brutal autocracy and paternalistic involvement where personal and friendly ties between employer and employee extend beyond the work environment (see Figure 14.1). In other words, the contrasting images of sweatshop exploitation and family harmony are used, albeit in different ways, to reinforce the managerial prerogative.

A variant of this school of thought is offered by Ram (1994) and Ram and Holliday (1993) in which the complicated nature of family and personal ties, ethnicity and gender focus managerial techniques around an informal yet conflictual bargain at the workplace. Here the interrelationships between managerial ideology, employee skill, market conditions and a 'familial culture' that promote a degree of trust toward managerial and organisational goals are of particular significance. This is characterised as 'negotiated paternalism' as owner-managers are often dependent on employees, demonstrating an important and contested 'frontier of control' through forms of direct and individual bargaining. More recently, Ram (1999) has shown that these informal processes are as relevant in small professional (i.e. associate) firms as they are among small exploitative (i.e. clothing sector) enterprises. Essentially, informality is the key to understanding the co-existence of high trust and struggle as a central component of managerial action in SMEs:

> Despite the many references by owners to being 'like a family', neither autocracy nor harmony were the concrete outcomes. The struggles around day-to-day activities on the shopfloor were illustrative of the complex, contested and contradictory nature of social relations at work.
>
> (Ram and Holliday, 1993: 645–46)

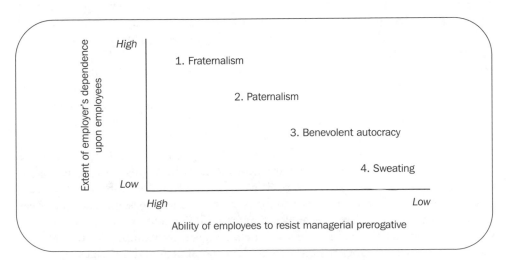

Figure 14.1 Types of small firm management control strategies
Source: Goss, 1991: 73

The practice of NMT in SMES

Clearly, such diversity has implications for management practice. Given the discussion above, it is difficult to argue that our understanding of a *dependent* SME, employing poorly skilled workers on low wages, can necessarily be enhanced by an explanation of an *innovative* organisation employing highly skilled people. Accordingly, and in an attempt to consider the ways in which this diversity may impact on the way people experience work, this chapter continues with a series of brief case studies, each of which explores a different aspect of Rainnie's (1989, 1991) typologies. In each of these the emphasis is on the uses (and abuses) of NMTs. Table 14.4 presents a summary of the management techniques reported in these firms, with all four adopting 50 per cent or more of the practices named. The most frequently cited interventions include teamworking and job flexibility, closely followed by systems of devolved management and performance appraisals (reported for some if not all the workers employed by each company). Broadly speaking, these findings are comparable with other studies on NMTs in SMEs (e.g. Duberley and Walley, 1995; Bacon *et al.*, 1996; Cully *et al.*, 1999; Guest and Conway, 1999). However, rather than relying on the self-reporting of NMTs by owner-managers, the impact, meaning and interpretation of this new managerial agenda was explored in a little more detail.

Compu Co: Coping with customer dependency

Compu Co is a small high-tech firm that employs 26 people. It was founded in 1980 by three colleagues, who had previously worked together in a large multinational organisation. The company manufactures 'real time' mainframe computer systems used for robotic assembly by large organisations. Given that around 95 per cent of its business is with one major customer, Zeneca, Compu Co can be characterised as a *dependent* SME. The remaining 5 per cent is accounted for by occasional one-off contracts with companies in the motor trade. The Zeneca contract was obtained in 1989, after which company size more than doubled. Because of the relationship with Zeneca, Compu Co has largely been cushioned from the turbulence that has been a feature of much of the market for advanced technology. Typically, commercial contracts last for between 5 and 10 years for each mainframe computer manufactured for Zeneca by Compu Co.

The workforce consists mainly of professional and technical employees. There are 11 engineers who are based off-site at various Zeneca locations. While there is no formal grading system, there is a general rule of thumb that the more senior or technically competent team member is also the project manager. These off-site employees are assisted by four grades of technician (junior, graduate and analyst programmers) who make and test the mainframe computers designed by Compu Co. In addition, there are four clerical support staff, two modern apprentices and two sales reps.

Management at Compu Co is a combination of informal practice and formalised quality initiatives. Responsibility for personnel was described as an 'add-on function' for one of the three founding directors, with informality seen as

Table 14.4 The range of New Management Techniques in the four case studies

Managerial techniques	Compu Co	Care Co	Consultancy Co	Motor Co
		Large–small firm relationship typology (Rainnie, 1991)		
	Dependent	Isolated/Dominated	Innovative	Dominated
Cultural change	X	✓	✓	X
Devolved management	✓	%	%	✓
Teamworking	✓	✓	✓	✓
Performance appraisals	✓	X	✓	%
Mission statement	X	X	✓	✓
Team briefings	%	✓	✓	✓
Customer quality schemes (i.e. ISO/BS)	✓	✓	X	✓
Harmonised terms and conditions	X	X	X	X
Psychometric tests	X	X	%	X
Delayering/restructuring	X	✓	X	✓
Job flexibility	✓	✓	✓	✓
Training programme for all employees	✓	✓	✓	X
Performance pay/bonus	X	%	✓	X
Staff suggestion schemes	%	%	✓	X
Company-wide meetings	X	✓	✓	X
Staff attitude surveys	X	X	✓	X
NMTs present or present in part	8	11	14	8

Note: ✓ = Technique present
       X = Not present
       % = Technique present in part

a pragmatic response to the skill and expertise of key workers. Owners had little choice but to rely on employees to manage themselves, given the time they spent away from the office. Indeed, the two team leaders in the research did not regard themselves as 'managers', and none could recall having to deal with any 'people matters'. This emphasis on informality was explained by one engineer:

> It smacked me straight away, that you can just go in and ask the Director something. At BA there was an open-door policy, but you wouldn't ever get past so and so's secretary.

Even where formal procedures are adopted by the director responsible for personnel, informality and individualism tend to prevail. A self-completed performance appraisal for each employee is officially intended to form the basis of pay discussions. However, one of the directors reported that the appraisal system had not actually been used for the past couple of years, mainly because of a 'lack of time, and when objectives are set, these are never realistic anyway'. Instead, there is reliance on individual bargaining between engineers and directors. Pay is set either on the basis of personal relationships that exist between employee and owner-manager, or on market conditions that determine how important a particular employee's skill is to the organisation at that moment in time. For other workers, such as programmers and clerical staff, pay is determined unilaterally by directors without consultation.

Recruitment was also informal, with prospective employees selected through informal networks. The director explained the most recent methods:

> One manager we've brought in lived next door to my bank manager. He's a technical engineer made redundant . . . and had additional quality control stuff we thought looked good. The second was an engineering student serving behind the bar in the local pub . . . Another bloke met a director by accident when sharing a taxi home from a night out in Manchester, who happened to comment he was an engineering student. He was invited for a chat and has worked here ever since . . . and also got his mate a start here, who was another engineering student

However, the company's relationship with Zeneca mediated against such informal and *ad hoc* practices. One of Zeneca's requirements was that Compu Co adopt and conform to ISO9001 quality procedures. This had a significant impact on the company's work processes. In one instance a Zeneca employee made 400 modifications to the design of a piece of equipment. In itself this is not too unusual when building one-off high-tech computers from scratch. The problem was that each modification, no matter how minor, had to be completed on a special ISO9001 form, in duplicate. The time constraints and effect of training Compu Co employees to these new methods of work design were onerous. Work intensified as employees grappled with an alien quality system and increasing levels of paperwork, as one technician commented:

> What's definitely clear to me is that having a quality procedure isn't the same as getting a quality system or quality product. Even the managers who are all for the system eventually circumvent it because it gets in the way of some basic tasks, especially when you're on a time-sensitive project

More cynically, another engineer replied: 'It's easier to check ISO standards by *weighing* them than *reading* them.'

Care Co: Responding to competitive pressures through people

Care Co is a private residential nursing home for the elderly. There are 45 employees who all work various shift patterns to provide round-the-clock cover every day of the year. The home was opened in 1991 and is owned by a single owner-manager, although most day-to-day HR issues are devolved to a head matron. The majority of employees are women (care assistants, nurses, cooks and ancillary staff) who work part-time. At the time when this research was conducted, in 1998, many earned less than the national minimum wage of £3.60 per hour (hourly rates varied between £2.80 and £3.80). The home is situated in a semi-rural village and is the major employer in the local area. Approximately 80 per cent of residents are fee-paying while the remaining 20 per cent are funded by the local authority. Care Co does not easily fit any of the four typologies outlined by Rainnie (1991). The competitive nature of private nursing and use of low wages could imply that Care Co is a *dominated* SME. Alternatively, the geographical position of the home would suggest that Care Co conforms to some extent to the *isolated* model.

While seeking to attract new fee-paying residents and retain labour in the home, the owner-manager sought to engineer a new quality-conscious approach among care assistants. Work schedules were redesigned and care assistants encouraged to work closely with a particular group of residents rather than provide general assistance across the home. This approach sprang from an earlier desire to reduce labour turnover. The job of care assistant can be both physically and emotionally demanding and many staff leave within a few weeks of appointment. Given that local authority regulations stipulate a strict ratio for the number of employees to residents, vacancies had to be filled within a relatively short period. At Care Co labour turnover increased when the village shop began trading as a mini-supermarket. With longer opening hours and Sunday trading, the local grocers became a major source of competition for labour in the village. Within one week of this shop opening, around 30 per cent of staff left the residential home to work in the supermarket, most employees being attracted by the prospect of a less demanding job and marginally better pay.

In response to this Care Co embarked on a variety of NMTs that sought to lower staff turnover and enhance the quality of residential care. These focused mainly on the bottom end of the Marchington *et al.* (1992) escalator of employee involvement, and included top-down communication methods, shift changeover meetings, weekly briefings by the head matron, a monthly meeting organised by the owner, a staff suggestion scheme, bi-monthly appraisals and separate quality audits for housekeeping, care assistants, nurses and kitchen staff (see also Wilkinson *et al.*, 1999). A company-wide NVQ training scheme was launched with the assistance of the local TEC to broaden the customer skills of all employees and a bonus was linked to each level of the NVQ qualification. Previously, there had been no formal training. Some employees had worked in other nursing homes and were assumed to be already trained, while others learned 'on the job'. Essentially, the NMTs introduced at Care Co sought to encourage employees to take on greater responsibility for their own development plans and to link these to resident (customer) care.

However, these NMTs did not resolve the tensions between employer and employees and on occasions they even exacerbated them. Both the scope and form of employee involvement techniques led to disillusionment among many workers as staff meetings and briefings were held out of working (e.g. paid) time, and the NVQ scheme had to be paid for by individual employees (at a cost of £400). Care assistants were cautious of new initiatives and more concerned with 'bottom-line' bread-and-butter issues, as one worker commented:

> What communications? There's a big lack of that here. We don't get paid for meetings which are outside the shift, so I go home . . . I've no time for that NVQ lark . . . It's all in the girls' own time, and bloody expensive, I'm not going for that.

Given this response, it is difficult to argue (as some surveys do) that the existence of NMTs invariably translates into improved levels of employee motivation and performance, or that they can be used as a substitute for employers' willingness to develop 'resourceful humans'. Here, NMTs were seen as little more than 'out-of-hours' meetings and 'pay-for-your own NVQ'. Many workers commented that the training scheme, staff meetings and appraisals ran counter to the informal relations they associated with a small residential home. Nor would it be fair to categorise these employees as typical of the 'Bleak House' perspective of small firms. The attitudes that many of the workers displayed toward employment, residents and the owner-manger were complex. Care assistants demonstrated a strong attachment to their work and a compassion for residents. In an attitude survey almost 90 per cent of employees said that they enjoyed the job and found co-workers and residents supportive. Yet this did not resolve the underlying tension between employee and employer. One worker commented that NMTs meant little when the owner was 'coming up' with ways to circumvent the national minimum wage:

> [The owner] isn't going to part with money . . . I can't see her paying the minimum wage . . . She'll go for more and more part-timers; girls on less hours . . . She doesn't see what we have to do; it's bloody hard work. Don't get me wrong, we love the residents, but we want rewarding for it . . . They've come up with this thing called 'Carer of the Month' and we all get points . . . A pound or two on the rate would be more beneficial.

Consultancy Co: Managing HR through fun and culture

Consultancy Co was founded in 1992 by one owner and operates in what may be described as an *innovative* niche market. The company specialises in providing consultancy, technology software, radio communications and security systems to a wide range of blue chip companies, local authorities and national governments. In a little over five years Consultancy Co had achieved impressive results. Turnover increased by 30 per cent each year, the company won several small business and quality excellence awards and the staff grew to 150 (of whom 70 per cent were consultants and engineers). Consultancy Co's main office is based in the North of England, with satellite offices in Edinburgh, Dublin and Dallas (USA). It was set up by an owner-manager and 11 colleagues who had all worked together. All were friends who not only worked together but also socialised with one another. This combination formed the basis of a distinctive 'work hard and play hard' culture at Consultancy Co (see also Grugulis *et al.*, 2000). In an attempt to preserve this distinctive culture, when the number of employees grew beyond the limits of a single social circle, the owner-manager appointed a full-time 'culture manager' and allocated 2 per cent of company turnover (about £250,000) to the business of culture management.

The preservation of this cultural identity took several forms. The culture manager paid particular attention to recruitment, targeting young graduates who displayed a friendly and extrovert personality. Technical and job competency was often secondary to behavioural attributes, with potential recruits selected through a combination of formal and informal techniques including psychometric testing, multiple interviewing and presentations to the founding members of Consultancy Co. High-calibre graduates in science and technology disciplines from top universities were contacted and invited to open days. These were carefully planned to coincide with a fancy-dress day at the office in support of 'Red Nose Day.' The reactions of potential recruits, attending for perhaps their first-ever job interview, were assessed and used for short-listing purposes. If they were anything but enthusiastic about the notion of dressing-up and generally being seen to 'have a laugh', their application went no further.

BOX 14.1

Consultancy Co culture mission statement

Consultancy Co. culture is one where individuals are encouraged to:

- Have fun and enjoy work

- Always put the client first

- Make quality a part of everything we do

- Share knowledge with others

- Work as a team

- Develop your full potential

- Make decisions

- Take ownership and resolve problems

- Learn from mistakes without fear or recrimination

Once workers had been recruited, management techniques sought to develop them in line with the company's 'culture statement' (see Box 14.1). Top of the list was 'having fun at work', which was actively encouraged by the owner-manager through an open and friendly style. There was a strong emphasis on mutual trust and respect both inside and outside the workplace, with employees at all levels on first name terms.

These interventions were underpinned by social activities funded from the 'culture budget'. They included weekend trips to Dublin, white-water canoeing in Wales and a river cruise-cum-office party. There were regular inter-company football tournaments among staff when the men played and the women dressed as American-style cheerleaders as well as fancy dress and dress down days in the office. More serious matters were also mixed with humour to engender an informal atmosphere. Individual appraisal interviews and group induction events for new staff were regularly held as a social event at the company's expense.

These social events were time-consuming and attendance was only notionally voluntary yet workplace controls, by contrast, were much more relaxed. Consultants were free to determine their own work schedules: they could base themselves at home, in the office or spend weeks at client sites across the globe.

Considerable emphasis was also placed on personal and professional development. All 12 directors were studying for the Institute of Directors professional examination, another 30 staff had attained the Institute of Electronic Engineers membership, four had doctorates and several were working toward MBAs. In addition, two separate company-wide training days were held each year when the whole workforce would be taken to a hotel to discuss new projects and receive company information.

Many employees were enthusiastic advocates of these NMTs. Most valued their in-house friendships and many enjoyed the social events. But tensions and problems still existed. Pay was set by the owner and no formal criteria were published on how individual performance was evaluated. This research was conducted when the company was performing well and the majority of employees were extremely well satisfied with the pay awards. However, one clerical worker complained about the lack of overtime pay, and other employees lower down the hierarchy were critical of both the long hours and difficulties in achieving a performance pay award as few worked exclusively on client (fee-earning) projects. Consultants were engaged in interesting and responsible work, but taking ownership for decisions, actively negotiating contracts with clients and participating in social activities often demanded long hours at work. During the research at Consultancy Co, a group of consultants worked through the night to complete a client project on time.

Motor Co: Management style and exploitation in the Bleak House

Motor Co is a family-run enterprise that displayed many of the hallmarks of a *dominated* SME. Established in 1987, Motor Co is the largest of three separate dealerships owned by the same family in the North-west of England. The company employs 65 workers, including motor mechanics in a garage workshop, clerical support staff, warehouse stores and forecourt sales. The company's main business is the sale and leasing of trucks and coaches to local bus companies and HGV hauliers. These on-going commercial arrangements account for approximately 80 per cent of all business, which includes the regular servicing and replacement of vehicles. Individual customers account for the remaining 20 per cent of business, usually in the form of one-off sales or vehicle repairs. In the past, the reputation of high-quality vehicles has ensured a relatively stable market position for Motor Co.

However, by the late 1990s the company faced a sharp rise in local market competition. A number of other garages had opened up in the region as direct competitors, and the vehicle manufacturer was in the process of reviewing all existing franchise dealers. In response to this commercial uncertainty, the family-owners introduced several NMTs to formalise and restructure employment arrangements (see also Dundon *et al.*, 1999). A new general manager was appointed in the hope of reassuring the vehicle manufacturer as to the company's management structure during the franchise review. Younger and increasingly assertive line managers were hired to take on greater departmental responsibilities and the daughter of the founding-owner was appointed as the personnel manager. Formal procedures were introduced and policies such as recruitment changed, with a combination of formal applications and interview selection replacing more *ad hoc* means of seeking potential employees from friends and acquaintances in the motor trade. Individual appraisals, regular communications and employee involvement techniques were also introduced in an attempt to formalise employee relations.

Yet while the managers emphasised the use and utility of these NMTs, no workers did. Among the eight employees interviewed, none could recall staff appraisals being conducted and in a survey of the whole workforce (n=45) only 11 per cent spoke favourably of management communications. Most respondents referred to what was perhaps a well-intentioned but nonetheless insensitive pay review policy. One garage mechanic commented that:

> I know when we get a rise. It's each Christmas. It's not automatic though, you only get a rise if they think you should have a pay rise [and] . . . that's based on not dropping a bollock in the year . . . It's a letter in the Christmas card saying we're getting a rise . . . it really pisses the lads off. I mean a little card, 'all the best and all that', but naught about your money and so and so next to you gets something.

Against the rhetoric of so-called enlightened NMT, the family-owners maintained a 'no work – no pay' policy at all levels of the organisation. This even applied to employees who had sustained injuries at work. When a garage mechanic lost two fingers in an industrial accident not only did he have his wages stopped, but Motor Co also began dismissal procedures because of his prolonged absence from work. The personnel manager had little sympathy for him:

> Two people have been off for a long time this year. The first person had a bad workplace accident here – both people were blue-collar. The first guy was suing for loss of earnings – but that case might have been dropped, he's gone to work for another company so he's not too badly damaged. Though he has lost his (two) fingers.

A more common effect of this policy was that employees were required to use holiday leave to cover periods in which they were ill. As one clerical employee said:

> A sick pay scheme should be introduced. Either lose a day's pay or take holidays – which they don't let you take now at short notice. It reminds me of a Victorian mill-owner, and make sure [the personnel manager] doesn't hear that.

The new management techniques and new managerial structure at Motor Co were intended to mark a departure from earlier informal relations in which 'walking the shopfloor' was the main way owner-managers engaged with employees. But their introduction was not accompanied by a shift in power relations nor (despite the customary association of employee commitment with 'soft' HR practices) did it involve any increase in trust. As one employee concluded: 'The firm is run by "family-men". What they say goes. It's as simple as that.'

Conclusion and discussion

This chapter has been concerned with the impact of NMTs in four case studies broadly based on Rainnie's (1991) SME typologies. However, none of the explanations reviewed in this chapter can fully account for the diversity in employment relations at these organisations. The NMTs introduced at Motor Co had little substantive impact on employment relations in the firm, employees at Care Co gained satisfaction from their relationship with residents but this did little to lessen the tensions between workers and the owner-manager, consultants at Consultancy Co were trusted and well rewarded but only as long as they conformed, and NMTs in Compu Co meant additional administrative burdens and work intensification for staff. Given this, it is difficult to argue that NMTs are all necessarily 'good' or 'bad' in themselves or that their presence in an organisation signifies a certain managerial strategy.

Throughout this chapter relationships between small and large firms have been emphasised. This has the advantage of locating analysis in relation to wider macro factors that may shape managerial action in a micro context. In each of the four case studies the categories suggested by Rainnie (1991) help understand the patterns of NMT found in these firms. For example, the *dependency* experiences reported at Compu Co and the *dominated* market of Motor Co were a function of their relations with large firms.

The framework does, however, have a significant disadvantage: its comparative neglect of factors internal to each SME. Yet, as seen here, management style had a significant influence on the pattern of employment relations. While Consultancy Co would appear to be an *innovative* SME, its distinctive features of freedom at work and constraint over social life are equally (if not more) important than the organisation's place in Rainnie's typology in understanding both managerial and worker behaviour. In these four case studies the uses (and abuses) of new managerial techniques translate into both the exploitative use of labour through low wages and casualisation, and also the intensification of highly paid professional work.

By reporting direct research evidence this chapter has been able both to illuminate the dynamic nature of NMTs in smaller organisations and to subject existing frameworks to critical analysis. It is the complex interplay of external and internal factors, relationships with large firms, management style and the nature of the employees' work, which supports the view that theorising about human resource management in polarised perspectives (small is beautiful or Bleak House) simplifies complicated processes. Further, reliance on self-reported surveys is problematic because this form of evidence does not necessarily demonstrate that employees are being treated as an asset. Yet until the processes of change management in small firms are explored more fully and the complexity used to inform and shape current debates about HRM, then theoretical models can only ever be partial. Above all, there is a need for more study into the management of people employed in SMEs, both to construct a more grounded and complex picture of activity and to influence the way HRM is currently defined and taught.

Case study 14.1

Cultural management in Consultancy Co

Tony Dundon, Irena Grugulis & Adrian Wilkinson

Introduction

Managing culture is often portrayed as a key lever to win employees' 'hearts and minds', that will secure competitive advantage (Deal and Kennedy, 1982; Schein, 1985). By targeting employees' attitudes and norms, companies can eliminate the need for irksome systems of control and effectively substitute 'active employee commitment' for 'resigned compliance' (Ogbonna, 1992/93).

In this particular case study the management of 'corporate culture' was not intended to change the organisation's values or atmosphere, but actively preserve them during a period of growth. The key objective at Consultancy Co was cultural *continuity* rather than culture change (Grugulis *et al.*, 2000).

The company

Consultancy Co specialises in computer software and security technologies. The company was founded in 1992 by one owner, 'Ian Reese', and is based in the North of England with subsidiary offices in Edinburgh, Dublin and Dallas (USA). Ian started the company with 11 colleagues, all of whom previously worked together for the same large organisation. In commercial terms Consultancy Co's results are impressive. It has maintained an annual 30 per cent increase in turnover for the past 5 years, has grown from 12 to 150 people and has won several small business and quality excellence awards.

It is important to note that the founding members were all friends as well as co-workers. Not only did they work together on a daily basis, but they also socialised together. This helped create a bond of interpersonal loyalty as well as a strong sense of identification with 'their' organisation. Quite often they raised money for charity, participated in local sports activities and enjoyed weekends away together. It was this friendly relationship between Ian Reese and his colleagues that helped shape Consultancy Co's approach to managing culture.

The culture: work hard and play hard

As the company grew, the links between work and socialising became a central feature of management activity. In 1997 Ian appointed 'Anna Culbertson' as culture and training manager. Anna had been one of the company's first employees.

She was allocated 2 per cent of company turnover (£250,000) to manage and preserve a culture defined as 'work hard and play hard'.

One area to which Anna paid particular attention was the recruitment of people. Here technical and job competency was viewed as secondary to the behavioural attributes and attitudes of prospective employees. Most recruits were carefully selected through a combination of formal and informal techniques. Each year Anna organised a graduate recruitment event to coincide with 'Red-Nose Day', when most of the employees arrived in fancy dress. Applicants' reactions were assessed and used as criteria for short-listing. If they displayed any sign of criticism, their application went no further. Once these 'suitable souls' had been recruited, Anna's role focused on supporting employees in line with the company's culture statement.

Consultancy Co. culture is one where individuals are encouraged to:
- Have fun and enjoy work
- Always put the client first
- Make quality a part of everything we do
- Share knowledge with others
- Work as a team
- Develop your full potential
- Make decisions
- Take ownership and resolve problems
- Learn from mistakes without fear or recrimination

'Having fun and enjoying work' was actively promoted by Ian Reese through an open and friendly style of *paternalistic* management. Informal social relations were encouraged among staff both inside and outside the workplace. The emphasis was on mutual trust and respect with employees and managers on first name terms. Sean, an office junior, remarked:

> It's a happy office, everyone's approachable, you're never left on your own and being a good team member is regarded as an important thing. I mean, there's no problem having a laugh with anyone. [Ian] is as approachable as anyone.

A range of social activities were financed by the company. These included weekend trips to Dublin, regular office parties and an internal company football tournament. Other formal work processes were mixed with fun and humour to engender an informal and relaxed atmosphere. Individual appraisals were held as coffee afternoons and staff induction events were regularly undertaken during a 'night out' financed by the company. Anna explained:

> It's important to involve new starters in our extra curricular activities. . . I'm thinking of a few things at the moment, which has been prompted by new people coming in. I don't know whether to have a night out bowling or just pick up the bar bill in a pub. I quite fancy a Chinese meal night – I just don't know yet. We like new people to feel part of the culture right from the start and get involved with everyone socially – this is work hard, and then we all play hard.

In practice, there was a great deal of freedom for employees at Consultancy Co. Consultants were free to determine their own work schedules as long they satisfied client demands. They could work at home, in the office or spend weeks at client sites. It was common practice for staff to work and mix with colleagues in other sections of the firm and learn different aspects of the business, which helped develop cross-functional team working.

In supporting this distinctive culture company training was high on the agenda, as Ian Reese commented: 'Our people are a key asset and we regard their training and development as vital to the business.' The most extensive of these training initiatives were two company-wide training days held each year. During these events two telephonists were left to staff the office while all other employees would spend the day at a local hotel developing team skills, playing games and receiving presentations from Ian Reese about the future plans of the company.

Between these training events Consultancy Co supported other activities to help develop staff. The company subscribed to a number of professional journals that were scattered around the office, was willing to invest in the latest software and allowed consultants to 'play around' with the technology in designing new client products. There was also 'Consultancy Co University'. Here consultants presented seminar papers to other staff members about client projects, outlined new technological developments or talked about the fun in their work. Senior consultants were also expected to give formal papers at international business and technology management conferences. This supported both their own personal development and helped to market Consultancy Co to prospective clients. Finally, consultants were encouraged to obtain professional qualifications at the company's expense. All 12 directors were studying to become members of the Institute of Directors, another 30 staff attained graduate membership of the Institute of Electronic Engineers and several consultants were studying for MBAs.

Attitude survey at Consultancy Co

Table 14.5 is a summary of results from an attitude survey conducted by the authors at Consultancy Co. Overall, this shows that high numbers of employees trusted management, felt they were part of a family and were generally supportive of the values espoused by firm.

Culture and (mis)behaviour

Yet, despite such high levels of satisfaction, it is difficult to argue that all employees' 'hearts and minds' were entirely given over to the company.

Many employees were dissatisfied with communications. In the above survey the negative results all relate to a lack of information between employee and employer. Indeed, over half the sample (59 per cent) disagreed with the statement that management involved them in decisions. At one staff briefing the communication was all one way. Ian Reese and other directors made very quick statements to

Table 14.5 Percentage of respondents agreeing / disagreeing with question items

Question item	Agree	Not sure	Disagree
On the whole, I feel I can trust the information provided by management at Consultancy Co.	85	11	4
People are treated fairly by the management of Consultancy Co.	83	12	5
Working here is like being part of a team and family.	79	10	11
The values and beliefs of Consultancy Co. are very similar to my own personal beliefs.	74	18	8
Communications here are very informal and relaxed.	28	34	38
Employees are kept fully informed of changes within Consultancy Co.	26	32	42
Management involve employees in decisions at Consultancy Co.	18	23	59
I regularly have the chance to discuss my pay with management	14	20	66

Note: $N = 82$

the workforce and questions or comments from staff were actively discouraged. The meeting started at 8 am (with breakfast provided) and employees returned to their desks ready for work by 8.30 am.

In addition, pay and hours were at times problematic at Consultancy Co. While consultants were relatively well paid (earnings varied between £28,000 and £45,000, plus benefits such as a car and health insurance), they were also expected to work extremely long hours in return. Most seemed to accept this, something that was not necessarily true of their less well-rewarded colleagues. One clerical employee was critical of the lack of overtime pay and the long hours.

The voluntary nature of participation in social events was only notional. While this research was being conducted the HR manager, 'Helen', was sacked, not because of poor work or lack of competence but because, as Anna argued, 'she did not fit in with the "people" way of doing things' at Consultancy Co. Helen's participation in company socials was seen as reluctant and both Anna and Ian wanted enthusiasm. The dismissal was acrimonious and a settlement was only agreed after Ian Reese was advised that an employment tribunal was unlikely to rule in the company's favour. The repercussions of this on other employees and company culture were predictable. The same week that Helen was dismissed, other employees received their individual appraisal reports in envelopes marked 'Confidential'. Several workers feared that they were also being dismissed. Anna's attempt to reassure them was not successful:

> When I said (rhetorically), 'Do you really think we'd ever do anything like that?', they said 'Yes, isn't that how it happened to Helen?'

Conclusion

Events in Consultancy Co are very different from those reported elsewhere in the 'culture' literature. Here the key objective was cultural *continuity* rather than culture change. The process of management was generally pleasant, most employees spoke highly of both it and the organisation, and most participated with the required level of enthusiasm. However, the significance of these events extends beyond 'innocent' play. These were more than simple, informal friendly gatherings. Here, attending weekend trips to Dublin or meals out at a restaurant became part of the employees' normal work, and the boundaries between work and family life were blurred. For employees at Consultancy Co, the price of enjoying freedom in the workplace and subsidised socials was the intensification of work and the sacrifice of personal time to the company.

Questions

1. Is having 'fun' at work an effective way of managing staff?

2. What problems might be encountered if such schemes were introduced in your company (or another company with which you are familiar)?

3. From the events described here, discuss whether culture can be managed. Why? /Why not?

4. What does culture management tell us about power in the employment relationship?

5. To what extent is the small size of Consultancy Co. an important factor in culture management?

6. Why do you think culture is such a popular feature of the management literature?

References

Deal, T. and Kennedy, A. (1982) *Corporate Culture: The Rites and Rituals of Corporate Life*, Reading, Mass: Addison-Wesley.

Grugulis, I., Dundon, T., and Wilkinson, A. (2000) 'Cultural control and the "culture manager": employment practices in a consultancy', *Work, Employment & Society*, 14(1): 97–116.

Ogbonna, E. (1992/93) 'Managing organisational culture: fantasy or reality?', *Human Resource Management Journal*, 3(2): 42–54.

Schein, E. (1985) *Organisational Culture and Leadership*, New York: Jossey-Bass.

Employee involvement at Beverage Co

Tony Dundon, Irena Grugulis and Adrian Wilkinson

Introduction

Employee involvement (EI) has retained a central role in HRM over the last two decades (Marchington *et al.*, 1992; Marchington and Wilkinson, 2000). It can be seen as a key component of best practice HRM or high-commitment management (Wood, 1995; Pfeffer, 1998). It is often regarded as a form of employee participation (EP), but unlike the theory of industrial democracy there is no 'right' for workers to be involved in organisational decisions. In practice, employers decide whether to have EI and what form it should take. The main reason for management interest in EI has been the claim that it may increase employee commitment, improve product quality and enhance customer satisfaction (Schuler and Jackson, 1987).

Much of the existing research on EI has focused on 'large' or 'mainstream' organisations where a combination of techniques have been introduced (Marchington *et al.*, 1992). (see Chapter 11). Here we report on EI in a small organisation. Because of the apparent absence of formalised relations within many SMEs, the role of EI may be qualitatively different from that in larger firms (Wilkinson *et al.*, 1999). It can be less formal given the nature of communication flows, together with the flexibility that is often associated with a small social setting (Scott *et al.*, 1989; Roberts *et al.*, 1992). While such informality has been a long-standing feature in the following case study, the range of EI techniques introduced were also limited and at times problematic. In particular, the managerial motives for EI were not always understood among employees and the objective of greater employee commitment and loyalty was not achieved. The use of employee involvement techniques tended to work against rather than with the informal relations that had existed earlier.

The company

Beverage Co manufactures intermediary products for the food and drink industry. It employs 150 workers, split between its head office in Manchester and a manufacturing site in Cheshire. There is union recognition for around 65 process operatives based at the manufacturing plant. Here, the nature of work is organised around distinct production cells. Each production cell comprises approximately ten employees who all work on different production lines, which make food and drink flavourings, including vanilla, coke, soup, and meat additives. A similar team structure exists at the head office. Here, the majority of employees are clerical workers involved in administration, sales and marketing. There is no union recognition for these employees and, despite several requests from the GMB union, management has decided to keep this side of the business non-unionised.

In the late 1990s Beverage Co experienced a period of commercial uncertainty. It faced increasing UK competition for food and drink flavourings, lost a few important export contracts and, in 1997, made ten workers redundant. This was the first time that Beverage Co had ever experienced any form of job losses. The company had been owned by members of the same family for more than a century and their management style was characterised by benevolent paternalism. However, with increased market competition, declining profits and redundancy, the company's owners decided to distance Beverage Co from its informal industrial relations history. In its place they introduced a more strategic form of human resource management, much of which included several employee involvement schemes.

EI techniques and management style at Beverage Co

This new HR strategy had a profound impact on organisational culture and management style. In the past family-owners were highly paternalist and the industrial relations procedures were informal. Indeed, the previous chairman and managing director, descendants of the founding owner, were known for stopping production quite regularly and asking manual employees to help repair the family Bentley, Jaguar and collection of classic sports cars. This all changed when non-family members were appointed to senior management and board-level positions. A personnel department was established with the aim of formalising HR policies and practices across the two sites. Key performance targets for profits, quality and customer satisfaction were linked to staff appraisals and merit pay was introduced, based on individual targets. In addition, production supervisors and team leaders were given responsibility for staff appraisals and team meetings. In describing this approach the new MD regarded the strategy as 'a route to building a world-class organisation'. The range of EI techniques that helped support this objective are summarised in Table 14.6.

'Downward communication' was the most extensive of all forms of EI at Beverage Co. These included a quarterly staff newsletter, monthly team briefings, formal presentations by the MD to the whole workforce (held twice a year in the staff canteen), a staff suggestion scheme, e-mail communications and electronic message boards. The latter included e-mails for clerical staff in the head office and electronic display screens for manual workers, which were located at various points across the manufacturing plant. The underlying objective was to inform employees about new products, encourage quality and share financial information. For example, the company-wide presentations by the MD explained company objectives, profit details and more general HR developments to staff,

Table 14.6 EI techniques introduced at Beverage Co

EI category	EI technique introduced
Downward communications	Staff newsletter
	Notice boards
	Electronic message boards (manual staff only)
	E-mail communications (clerical staff only)
	Site-wide meetings led by MD
	Team/cell briefings by team leaders
	Personnel management surgeries
	Individual performance reviews/appraisals
Upward problem solving	Staff suggestion scheme
	Staff attitude surveys
Task participation	None
Financial involvement	Merit pay
Representative participation	Company joint consultative committee

including the merit pay scheme or Beverage Co's attempt to achieve Investors in People (IiP) accreditation.

However, the introduction of these communication techniques was met with some suspicion among employees. Team leaders who held monthly briefings were regarded as 'supervisors on the cheap' by many staff. In effect, team leaders were the same grade as other workers but were also required to carry out briefing sessions without extra pay. The personnel manager compiled the information and team leaders then cascaded this down to shopfloor level. The site-wide meetings introduced by the new MD were also questioned. Several workers suggested that the information presented was often partial, with management controlling the agenda for discussion or questioning. A middle manager explained:

> There's a reluctance to show the whole picture. We have canteen meetings but they're controlled, the information is very selective. That's a general feeling that not all the info is given out.

Across the manufacturing plant, electronic notice boards would regularly 'flash' with messages from the personnel department. Typical examples included the latest figures for customer complaints, current absenteeism rates or the volume of products made hour by hour and compared against (management's) expected target. As one process operator commented during his lunch in the canteen: 'There's no getting away from them [i.e. management messages] here.'

Other EI mechanisms included a 'weekly surgery' held by the personnel manager. The aim was to allow employees to discuss issues of concern in private without appointment. In addition, a staff suggestion scheme was introduced to encourage workers to make improvements to product quality. A financial payment ranging from £10 to £1,000 was given for adopted suggestions. Individual staff appraisals were also introduced where supervisor and worker could discuss objectives for the coming months.

In practice, these EI techniques fell short of their intended objective. Few employees would attend the surgery. Indeed, according to the personnel manager, this time was often used to meet with the shop steward or to inform team leaders about the next briefing. Several clerical employees were also critical of the staff suggestion scheme, especially the lack of any formal criteria for determining the amount of financial award. In response, the MD explained that any individual award depended on the 'quality of the idea' as well as the 'cost savings' for the company. Further, employees at both sites commented that any 'discussion' about appraisal plans was a myth, as supervisors tended to 'inform' workers about new targets without any agreement or discussion.

The range of EI at Beverage Co can be seen to fit broadly those categories where management maintains greatest control, namely downward communications. Moreover, the use of communications tended to bureaucratise and formalise management style, as one production supervisor commented:

> Too much communications in one sense – we've forgotten to use general conversation. They try and make things too formal, thinking it's a better way, which isn't always the case.

Indirect forms of EI were reduced at Beverage Co in favour of the more direct techniques described above. Representative participation remained with the GMB union for manufacturing employees, although a former bi-monthly joint consultative committee (JCC) met on a quarterly basis, and its remit was restricted to heath and safety matters, whereas it had formerly dealt with all employment terms and conditions. Similarly, collective bargaining became the responsibility of two local shop stewards, the MD and personnel manager. Previously, a full-time regional official had negotiated pay with family-owners. The pay rise for non-union clerical employees was reviewed by the personnel manager, and usually set in accordance with the negotiated settlement for manual workers. In addition, merit pay accounted for up to 10 per cent of the gross salary for most staff. This was determined on the basis of set targets from the performance appraisal, which was assessed by line managers.

Table 14.7 provides a summary of employee responses to a survey conducted at Beverage Co by the authors. While workers confirmed that management pass on information (52 per cent) and encouraged staff to make suggestions (82 per cent), only 15 per cent of respondents said that management acted on such suggestions. Overall, there were few positive responses to the range of EI techniques introduced. One-quarter of employees suggested that management sought their views while over 80 per cent disagreed with the statement that management involved them in decisions.

Workplace sabotage at Beverage Co

Shortly after these EI techniques were introduced a series of sabotage attacks was carried out at the manufacturing plant. The production unit in question manufactured food flavourings for a Far East contract, which Beverage Co eventually lost.

Table 14.7 Employee responses (%) to EI at Beverage Co

EI Indicator	Agree	Not sure	Disagree
At Beverage Co management regularly seek the views of employees	25	21	54
Employees are kept informed about changes at Beverage Co	36	7	57
Management pass on information regularly	52	12	36
Management involve employees in decisions at Beverage Co	9	10	81
Management encourage staff to make suggestions	82	13	5
Management at Beverage Co act on staff suggestions	15	25	60

Note: N = 67

The sabotage took a variety of forms. Flavouring products were labelled incorrectly, such that beef stocks were marked as vegetable soup ingredients and garlic batches packaged as cola additives. Other acts included racial and sexual graffiti written inside cartons. The commercial impact of these events was highly significant. Beverage Co flavourings form essential ingredients for food and drinks made by other organisations. Not only did this sabotage damage Beverage Co's reputation it also, owing to the intermediary character of the products, resulted in lost production of thousands of tonnes of food and drinks products. When incorrectly labelled food flavourings were used to produce final goods manufactured by Beverage Co's customers, these subsequently had to be destroyed.

Management were anxious to attribute these problems to the youth and immaturity of workers involved. One production supervisor attributed the sabotage to the use of agency staff brought in to help meet sudden demand. For the shop steward, however, the sabotage was a form of resistance to increased supervisory powers and poor working conditions. The nature of work was explained as dirty, dusty and intense. Interestingly, the system of cell working meant that management failed to identify the culprits. It was common for employees to work on several flavouring production lines simultaneously and switch to packaging duties during the same shift. As a result, management could not identify the employees who had been working on specific duties at the time of the sabotage.

Questions

1. What are the likely benefits for workers of employee involvement as practised at Beverage Co? Are these likely to differ in each of the union and non-union parts of the company? Why?/Why not?

2. The family owners of Beverage Co have asked you to produce a report (or a short presentation) on the efficacy of EI in the company. Using the information in the case study, identify the main barriers to EI and make recommendations to help the new management team gain the commitment of staff to these (or other) techniques.

3. What influence has the small firm context had on EI at Beverage Co?

4. Should trade unions be worried about the introduction of EI techniques? Why?/Why not?

5. To what extent has the change in management style and HR strategy exacerbated the tensions and contradictions in the employment relationship at Beverage Co?

References

Marchington, M., Goodman, J., Wilkinson, A. and Ackers, P. (1992) *New Developments in Employee Involvement*, Employment Department Research Paper, Series No. 2.

Marchington, M. and Wilkinson, A. (2000) 'Direct participation', in Sisson, K. and Bach, S. *Personnel Management in Britain*, 3rd edition, Oxford: Blackwell.

Pfeffer, J. (1998) *The Human Equation: Building Profits by Putting People First*, Boston, Mass: Harvard Business School Press.

Roberts, I., Sawbridge, D. and Bamber, G. (1992) 'Employee relations in smaller enterprises', in Towers, B. (ed) *Handbook of Industrial Relations Practice*, London: Kogan Press.

Scott, M., Roberts, I., Holroyd, G. and Sawbridge, D. (1989) *Management and Industrial Relations in Small Firms*, London: Department of Employment Research Paper, No. 70.

Schuler, R. and Jackson, S. (1987), 'Linking competitive strategies with human resource management', *Academy of Management Executives*, 1(3): 206–19.

Wilkinson, A., Dundon, T. and Grugulis, I. (1999) 'Exploring employee involvement in SMEs', Paper delivered at the British Universities Industrial Relations Association, HRM Conference, Cardiff University, January.

Wood, S. (1995) 'The four pillars of HRM: are they connected?', *Human Resource Management Journal*, 5(5): 49–59.

References to Chapter 14

Atkinson, J. B. and Storey, D. (1994), 'Small firms and employment', in Atkinson, J.B. and Storey, D. (eds) *Employment, the Small Firm and the Labour Market*, London: Routledge.

Bach, S. and Sisson K. (2000) (eds) *Personnel Management*, 3rd edition, Oxford: Blackwell.

Bacon, N. (1999) 'Union de-recognition and the new human relations: a steel industry case study', *Work, Employment & Society*, 13(1): 1–17.

Bacon, N., Ackers, P., Storey, J. and Coates, D. (1996) 'It's a small world: managing human resources in small businesses', *International Journal of Human Resource Management*, 7(1): 82–100.

Barrett, R. and Rainnie, A. (1999) 'We've gotta get out of this place! Assessing the state of industrial relations theory and research in small firms', *Employment Studies Working Paper 31* (UHBS 1999: 24), University of Hertfordshire Business School.

Beardwell, I. and Holden, L. (1997) (eds) *Human Resource Management: A Contemporary Perspective*, 2nd edition, London: Pitman Publishing.

Blyton, P. and Turnbull, P. (1998) *The Dynamics of Employee Relations*, 2nd edition, London: Macmillan.

Bolton, J.E. (Chair) (1971) *Report of the Commission of Inquiry on Small Firms*, Cmnd 4811, London: HMSO.

Carrol, M., Marchington, M., Earnshaw, J. and Taylor, S. (1999) 'Recruitment in small firms: processes, methods, and problems', *Employee Relations*, 21(3): 236–50.

Cully, M., O'Reilly, A., Millward, N., Forth, J., Woodland, S., Dix, G. and Bryson, A. (1998) *Workplace Employee Relations Survey: First Findings*, London: Routledge.

Cully, M., Woodland, S., O'Reilly, A. and Dix, G. (1999), *Britain at Work: As depicted by the 1998 Workplace Employee Relations Survey*, London: Routledge.

Curran, J. and Stanworth, J. (1979) 'Worker involvement and social relations in the small firm', *Sociological Review*, 13(3): 317–42.

Dale, I. and Kerr, J. (1995) 'Small and medium-sized enterprises: their numbers and importance to employment', *Labour Market Trends*, December: 461–66.

Delbridge, R. (1998) *Life on the Line in Contemporary Manufacturing*, Oxford: Oxford University Press.

Department of Employment (1992) *People, Jobs and Opportunities*, London: Department of Employment/HMSO.

Department of Trade and Industry (1998) *Small and Medium Sized Enterprise Statistics for the UK*, Ref: P/98/597, London: Department of Trade and Industry/HMSO.

Downing-Burn, V. and Cox, A. (1999) 'Does size make a difference?', *People Management*, 5(2): 50–3.

Duberley, J. and Walley, P. (1995) 'Assessing the adoption of HRM by small and medium-sized manufacturing organizations', *International Journal of Human Resource Management*, 6(4): 891–909.

Dundon, T., Grugulis, I. and Wilkinson, A. (1999), 'Looking out of the black hole: non-union relations in an SME', *Employee Relations*, 21(3): 251–66.

Edwards, P. (1995) 'Strikes and industrial conflict', in Edwards, P. (ed) *Industrial Relations: Theory and Practice in Britain*, Oxford: Blackwell.

Goodman, J., Earnshaw, J., Marchington, M. and Harrison, R. (1998) 'Unfair dismissal cases, disciplinary procedures, recruitment methods and management style', *Employee Relations*, 20 (6): 536–50.

Goss, D. (1988) 'Social harmony and the small firm: a reappraisal', *Sociological Review*, 36(1): 114–32.

Goss, D. (1991) *Small Business and Society*, London: Routledge.

Gratton, L., Hope Hailey, V., Stiles, P. and Truss, C. (1999) *Strategic Human Resource Management*, Oxford: Oxford University Press.

Grugulis, I., Dundon, T., and Wilkinson, A. (2000) 'Cultural control and the "culture manager": employment practices in a consultancy', *Work, Employment & Society*, 14(1): 97–116.

Guest, D. and Conway, N. (1999) 'Peering into the black hole: the downside of the new employment relations in the UK', *British Journal of Industrial Relations*, 37(3): 367–89.

Guest, D. and Hoque, K. (1993) 'The good, the bad and the ugly: employment relations in new non-union workplaces', *Human Resource Management Journal*, 5(1): 1–14.

Hilbert, J., Sperling, H.J. and Rainnie, A. (1994) *SMEs at the Crossroads?: Scenarios on the Future of SMEs in Europe*, FAST – Future of Industry in Europe, Vol. 9, Brussels: European Commission.

Holliday, R. (1995) *Investigating Small Firms: Nice Work?*, London: Routledge.

IRS (1998) 'Predicting union membership', *Employment Trends*, No 669, Industrial Relations Service, December.

Keenoy, T. (1997) 'Review article: HRMism and the language of re-presentation', *Journal of Management Studies*, 34(5): 825–41

Kelly, J. (1998), *Rethinking Industrial Relations: Mobilization, Collectivism and Long Waves*, London: Routledge.

Kinnie, N., Purcell, J., Hutchinson, S., Terry, M., Collinson, M. and Scarbrough, H. (1999) 'Employment relations in SMEs: market-driven or customer shaped?', *Employee Relations*, 21(3): 218–35.

Lane, C. (1995) 'The small-business sector: source of economic regeneration or victim of economic transformation?', in Lane, C. *Industry and Society in Europe*, Aldershot: Edward Elger.

Lucas, R. (1996) 'Industrial relations in hotels and catering: neglect and paradox?', *British Journal of Industrial Relations*, 34(2): 267–86.

MacMahon, J. (1996) 'Employee relations in small firms in Ireland: an exploratory study of small manufacturing firms', *Employee Relations*, 18(5): 66–80.

Marchington, M. (1992) *Managing the Team: A Guide to Successful Employee Involvement*, Oxford: Blackwell.

Marchington, M., Goodman, J., Wilkinson, A. and Ackers, P. (1992) *New Developments in Employee Involvement*, London: Department of Employment Research Series No. 2 (May).

Millward, N., Stevens, M., Smart, D. and Hawes, W.R. (1992) *Workplace Industrial Relations in Transition. The ED/ESRC/PSI/ACAS Surveys*, Aldershot: Dartmouth.

Millward, N., Bryson, A. and Forth, J. (2000) *All Change at Work? British Employment Relations 1980–1998, as portrayed by the Workplace Industrial Relations Survey series*, London: Routledge.

Philpott, J. (1996) *A National Minimum Wage: Economic Effects and Practical Considerations*. Issues in People Management No. 13, London: Institute of Personnel and Development.

Odaka, K. and Sawai, M. (1999) *Small Firms, Large Concerns: The Development of Small Business in Comparative Perspective*, Oxford: Oxford University Press.

Pfeffer, J. (1998) *The Human Equation*, Boston, Mass: Harvard Business School Press.

Rainnie, A. (1985), 'Small firms, big problems: the political economy of small businesses', *Capital & Class*, 25, Spring: 140–68.

Rainnie, A. (1989) *Industrial Relations in Small Firms: Small Isn't Beautiful*, London: Routledge.

Rainnie, A. (1991) 'Small firms: between the enterprise culture and new times', in Burrows, E. (ed) *Deciphering the Enterprise Culture*, London: Routledge.

Ram, M. (1991) 'Control and autonomy in small firms: the case of the West Midlands clothing industry', *Work, Employment & Society*, 5(4): 601–19.

Ram, M. (1994) *Managing to Survive: Working Lives in Small Firms*, Oxford: Blackwell.

Ram, M. (1999) 'Management by association: interpreting small firm–associate links in the business service sector', *Employee Relations*, 21(3): 267–84.

Ram, M. and Holliday, R. (1993) 'Relative merits: family culture and kinship in small firms', *Sociology*, 27(4): 629–48.

Roberts, I., Sawbridge, D. and Bamber, G. (1992) 'Employee relations in smaller enterprises', in Towers, B. (ed) *Handbook of Industrial Relations Practice*, London: Kogan Press.

Scase, R. (1995) 'Employment relations in small firms', in Edwards, P.K. (ed) *Industrial Relations in Britain: Theory and Practice,* Oxford: Blackwell.

Scase, R. and Goffee, R. (1987) *The Real World of the Small Business Owner*, 2nd edition, London: Croom Helm.

Scott, M., Roberts, I., Holroyd, G. and Sawbridge, D. (1989) *Management and Industrial Relations in Small Firms*, London: Department of Employment Research Paper, No. 70.

Sisson, K. (1993) 'In search of HRM', *British Journal of Industrial Relations*, 31(2): 201–10.

Storey, D. (1994) *Understanding the Small Business Sector*, London: Routledge.

Storey, J. (1992) *Developments in the Management of Human Resources*, Oxford: Blackwell.

Storey, J. (1995) (ed) *Human Resource Management: A Critical Text*, London: Routledge.

Westhead, P. and Storey, D. (1997), *Training Provision and the Development of Small and Medium Sized Enterprises*, London: Department for Education and Employment, Research Report No. 65.

Wilkinson, A. (1999) 'Employment relations in SMEs', *Employee Relations* (Special Issue), 22(3): 206–17.

Wilkinson, A., Redman, T., Snape, E. and Marchington, M. (1998) *Managing with Total Quality Management: Theory and Practice*, London: Macmillan.

Wilkinson, A., Dundon, T. and Grugulis, I. (1999) 'Exploring Employee Involvement in SMEs', Paper delivered at the British Universities Industrial Relations Association, HRM Conference, Cardiff University, January.

Wood, S. (1995) 'The four pillars of HRM: are they connected?', *Human Resource Management Journal*, 5(5): 49–59.

Index

Note: all references are to United Kingdom, except where otherwise indicated. Page references in **bold** indicate chapters

Contemporary Human Resource Management